CONTRACT LAW

CONTRACT LAW

Akhileshwar Pathak
IIM, Ahmedabad

OXFORD
UNIVERSITY PRESS

OXFORD
UNIVERSITY PRESS

Oxford University Press is a department of the University of Oxford.
It furthers the University's objective of excellence in research, scholarship,
and education by publishing worldwide. Oxford is a registered trade mark of
Oxford University Press in the UK and in certain other countries

Published in India by
Oxford University Press
YMCA Library Building, 1 Jai Singh Road, New Delhi 110001, India

ISBN 13: 978-019-807222-5
ISBN 10: 0-19-807222-8

Typeset in 10.5/13.1 Minion Pro by Excellent Laser Typesetter, New Delhi

To my son, Ishaan and friend, Bhushan Oza,
for encouraging me to write this book

Contents

Preface

Law is about ideas, concepts, and principles. A study of law is in developing a thorough grasp of the ideas and principles. We understand the best when we discover concepts and principles ourselves through exploration and engagement rather than being a passive recipient of information. This book is driven by these interests.

The principles of contract law are not random, arbitrary creation of the common law judges. There was a basis for them. This was in the prevailing notions of reason and justice in everyday practices. Similarly, the constituents of contract law—agreement, consideration, termination, performance, breaches, and damages—are not unrelated to each other. As they all are about the same phenomenon, these can never be disparate. The principles and themes are conceptually tied together to constitute they field of contract law. There is a rich corpus of court cases for us to forge these linkages, and explore the field in its interrelatedness.

Contract law is an old field comprising thousands of cases from the British and the Indian courts. Some cases, at length, explore and puzzle with the principles and concepts. We will engage with these cases for developing our understanding of the subject. Yet, there are other cases that apply the principles in newer or different contexts. These cases not only further our understanding of the principles, but also equip us with their application. An example of this is the application of the principles of formation of contracts to transactions on the internet. These cases add significantly to our understanding of the subject. Other cases do not explore or elaborate the principles but only apply the principles to the facts before them. There is always something to be learnt from every case. However, a random study of the cases does not significantly advance our understanding of the principles. To the contrary, referring to cases indiscriminately takes away the space to engage with the landmark cases, clutters up the text, and becomes a hindrance in understanding the subject. Thus, the book takes up the significant cases, and creates the space for the reader to engage with it.

I thank the editorial team at the Oxford University Press India, with whom I interacted at different stages, for their commitment to the project, support, and guidance.

Introduction

Most of us know a fair amount about contract law. We enter into contracts everyday without even being conscious of it. Everyday facilities, like taking a bus, buying a newspaper, and using a mobile phone, come to us through contracts. The college we study in, the refreshments we buy from cafés, and the movies we go to are the outcome of contracts. The apartments we rent, the electricity that is supplied, the television cable services we use, all are provided through contractual relationships. Taking a job is a contract, and so is representing a client as a lawyer. Big commercial projects, such as those for building airports, metro rails and exploration of natural gases, are created through contracts. Companies are entities created through contracts. The contract is essential to our society, which is based on transactions of goods and services. Contract law governs the formation and performance of contracts.

Contract law is commonsense and universal. It is universal because the contemporary human society is based on exchange of goods and services. Under feudalism, a peasant cultivated the land to provide for his necessities, and he subsisted on what he produced. The ruler appropriated the surplus from the peasants. The peasant did not voluntarily part with his resources, but was required to do so, if need be, by force. This practice led to the notion that the ruler had a right to tax the peasant and the peasant was duty-bound to pay the tax. This concept became the foundation for the law dealing with taxation. In addition to imposing taxes, the rulers imposed on the subjects in other aspects of their conduct. The peasant subjects had to follow the directions of the rulers and kings. This became the basis for the state and law. The state, the ruling mechanism of the society, made the law and the subjects were required to follow it under the threat of coercion. The subjects, of course, related with one another, within their family and community, to help each other with resources and support.

As surpluses from agriculture grew, traders emerged who bought and sold goods to the peasants and other traders. This was a voluntary relation between subjects. It was different from mutual help and support in the community; two people got together and agreed to exchange goods and services. The state stepped in to ensure that the parties did what they had undertaken to do, if not, nobody could exchange and trade their goods and services. This unified set of concepts was called a contract.

As surpluses were generated from agriculture within a feudal context, trading made a humble beginning. As we know, trading developed vastly over centuries, leading to the industrial revolution. Further consolidation resulted in a global industrial capitalism, leading to restructuring of society based on contractual transactions. A salaried person, a professional, or a trader in India today produces nothing for self-consumption. He earns money instead, with which he or she buys goods and services. Even a tribal peasant in a remote village produces only some basic food for self-consumption. All his other necessities—food, clothes, utensils, foowear and health care—are acquired through contracts. Even to support his subsistence agriculture, he has to buy agricultural implements, fertilizers, and pesticides from the market. Thus, in the present day society most exchanges are contractual in nature. Contract is the foundation on which the present day society rests.

Contract law was founded on the principle that individuals were the bearers of rights. Individuals bargain with each other to get into agreements to exchange goods and services. If abiding these agreements became a matter of individual discretion, the entire social and economic order founded on contracts would collapse. Thus, the state entered in, recognized the agreements, and enforces it or gives remedy to an aggrieved party. Contracts in all systems of law are founded on this principle.

OVERVIEW OF THE STATE, LAW AND CONTRACT

Human society has always had laws. Earlier, the directives of the rulers and kings were the law. This included, among others, imposition of taxes and obeisance to the ruler. Different parts of the world, including India, had their own peculiar kinds of law. The divergences, however, came to acquire a degree of uniformity with British colonial expansion. The British colonized the world, moving to America, Canada, Australia, New Zealand, India and other parts of Asia and Africa. Wherever they went, there had to be law, order and a system for adjudication of disputes. In short, a legal system had to be set up. For this they brought in features of their own legal system. Thus, India has come to share features of the British system, like many other countries.

In England, law making came to be entrusted to the Parliament. The law made by the Parliament was called an act, also called a statute; and the law was called statutory law. The Parliament would make law to regulate the social, economic and business life of the society. The provisions of the act were executed by the officers of the state. The courts settled the disputes in relation to the execution of the law. As the British consolidated their control and rule over India, by the late 1700s they created legislative bodies, like Governor-General's Council, comprising British officers, to make laws for ruling India. The laws made by these legislative bodies were also called acts. Examples of this are the Permanent Land Settlement Act, 1792; Ryotwari Act, 1807; and Forest Act, 1865.

Beyond the prohibitions of the law, individuals were free to do what they liked. In exercising their volition, individuals interacted with others, forming familial and social relationships. At other times, they would get into relationships to exchange goods and services with each other. These relationships for exchange of goods and services were contracts. Merchants had traded goods in India and other parts of the world much before the

British came to India. However, the colonial experience shaped the law on contracts not only in India but worldwide.

Merchants and traders had travelled within England and Europe and later overseas, trading goods. When disputes arose in England, these were taken to the courts. The merchants, traders and other property owners raised several questions, have the parties got into a voluntary agreement? Can a person pull out after getting into an agreement? If a person does not perform his part, what benefit should be given to the aggrieved? What if agreement is formed through lies and deception? What if an agreement is formed which is opposed to the state's law? These were only some of the questions which arose.

Judges decided cases on the basis of reason, commonsense and the prevailing notions of justice. They relied on prior judgments. Following similar judgments on similar cases, general reasoning and principles came to be formulated. The courts, thereafter, followed these principles as the law. Through this process of precedence, a body of judge-made law came to develop. The judiciary-made law, as it was derived from the experiences and practices of the common people, was called common law. This was in contrast to the acts made by the Parliament, which was an intervention imposed by the legislature. This was called statutory law.

At the same time, the form in which we know contract law emerged in the nineteenth century with the Industrial Revolution. The Industrial Revolution transformed England from an agrarian society to a commercial, industrial society. It brought about a fundamental change: mines, mills and factories sprang up for the manufacture and sale of goods. The agrarian order was to be replaced with a world order based on exchange. The courts were also called upon to decide a much larger number of cases. The courts revised some of the older ways of looking at contracts and founded the field of contract law as a well-integrated, coherent body of principles.

The first common law to develop in the field of trade and commerce was the contract law. This was to be the foundation of business law. As trade and commerce developed, business practices became specialized. Corresponding to this, the principles formulated by the courts could also be clustered into different areas. For example, the sale of goods was a specific form of contract. It raised a specific set of issues in relation to the quality of goods, transfer of ownership, and payment of price. Carriage, finance, banking, and insurance were the other business relations to emerge. The courts developed the law on these fields on the foundation of contract law. Thus, contract law became the foundation for all business law.

As trade and commerce flourished, common law developed. And with the growth of trade and commerce, a newer context arose for the legislature to restrict, regulate, or foster trade. Thus, alongside common law, statutory law was being enacted for the regulation of trade and commerce. By the late 1800s, the decisions of the courts were vastly expanded and became unwieldy. At times, this led to uncertainty as to what the law on a given point was. It was decided that the principles formulated by the courts be written down as the law, to be enacted by the Parliament. This writing down of the common law came to be called 'codification'. The written down law was to be enacted by the Parliament. The attempt to codify the common law was successful in leading to the enactments in several fields. However, contract law was too foundational to be codified. Despite attempts at it, it was considered best to not disturb the status quo. Thus, contract law was never codified in England.

As mentioned earlier, the 'law' formulated by the courts was adopted the world over through colonialism. Other countries were not constrained by the weight of tradition in codifying contract law. Australia and some states of America borrowed the common law from England and codified it. India had the advantage of having the two countries as precedents for its contract law, the Indian Contract Act, 1872. The countries under England came to share contract law with England. This included Ireland, Australia, New Zealand, Canada, Singapore, and British India, which then comprised India, Pakistan, and Bangladesh.

Other countries that did not follow the common law were called civil law systems. Examples of these are Germany, France, Japan, and China. In the civil law system, the law is made by the legislature, which the courts apply in resolving disputes. As contract law has been foundational, it is similar in all the countries. Of course, for specific details, there would be difference between contract law based on common law when compared with contract law in different civil law countries. Our interest is in the Indian Contract Act, 1872.

The first part of the Indian Contract Act, 1872, contained the general principles for governing all contractual relationships. The subsequent parts contained specific forms of contract, including sale of goods, bailment, indemnity, pledge, guarantee, principle-agent relationship, and partnership. The provisions on the sale of goods was expanded and enacted as separate legislation, the Sale of Goods Act, 1930. The last part, on partnership, has also been taken from the Contract Act and made into separate legislation, the Partnership Act, 1932.

Indian industrialization started between the two world wars. Since then, industrialization, which requires great exchange of goods and services, has come to be the backbone of the economy and the foundation of social relationship. In other words, there has been proliferation of contractual relationships in society. This has been in accordance with the principles codified in the Indian Contract Act, 1872. After Independence and the adoption of the Constitution in 1950, law-making came to be invested in the Parliament and the state legislatures. As trade, industry, and commerce in the post–World War II years became the motors of the economy and society, understandably, the legislatures enacted laws to foster and regulate business. For example, manufacturing and selling of food products is regulated by the Prevention of Food Adulteration Act, 1954. The Drugs and Cosmetics Act, 1940 restricts manufacturing and selling of pharmaceutical products. As acts regulating business were restricting formation of contracts, these used the conceptual categories and terms from contract law.

Approach of the Book

Contract law derives from principles that are commonsensical. There are reasons for this bold claim. As we have noted, the Indian Contract Act is a dossier of common law prevailing prior to 1872. By this time, the Industrial Revolution had taken place in England, and India had been a British colony for over more than hundred years. Through the colonial connection, trade and commerce had become global. The telegraph and railway were well established. Despite these advances, compared to our contemporary context, trade, commerce and specialization in society can only be described as basic. As contract law was the reason and common sense of this period as formulated by the judges, it should be highly accessible to us.

That the society then was not as specialized compared to our contemporary society does not mean that the entire intellectual resources of the society were trivial and would be readily accessible. The foundations of Western philosophy and political economy had already been laid down with the works of thinkers like Kant, Hegel, Marx, and Adam Smith. The courts, however, by their role, were there to solve problems and disputes. Their job was not to write philosophical treatises on all the dimensions of the disputes that were brought to them. Instead, in delivering justice, their role was to formulate principles that would be reasonable, sensible and accessible to the common person. The judges thus produced clear, cogent principles for solving disputes before them. Further, we live in an order based on exchange of goods and services, that is, contracts. As we are socialized in its context, we have already received its principles as common sense.

If the contract law is only common sense, what is there to study in it? Common sense is accessible, but not trivial. It is also profound, leading to contesting interpretations. Further, with changes in business practices, newer contexts arise, and the principles have to be applied to the new relationship. For example, as the principles formulated in the nineteenth century were applied to examining the formation of contracts in self-service stores in 1950, the same principles are being applied to sale through the internet now. The application of the principle to different situations over a period of time has sharpened its scope and application. However, in addition to understanding the principle, one has to explore the application of the principles by the courts.

There has been tremendous development of trade and commerce in the twentieth century. The contract law and principles remained the same. However, as trade and commerce developed, several principles have been used together by contracting parties to set up their rights and obligations. To give an example, party A, based in one city, contracts with party B, based in another city. The parties wanted to go to a court for resolution of a dispute in relation to the contract. The question arose whether it should be the court in A's city or B's. From such cases, the business world learnt to stipulate the court to which a dispute should be taken to in the contract itself. Similarly, in the case of a breach of a contract, the courts attempted to understand the intention of the parties in order to settle on compensation. This would often prove unsatisfactory to the parties. The business world realized that there is no harm done in contemplating that the contract may not be performed and decided to specify the damages itself as a part of the contract. As a result of this accumulation, contracts increasingly came to be in writing and included terms on the respective interests of the parties, including damages, the jurisdiction of the court, impossibility of performance, and arbitration. Following this accumulation, all businesses deal with their customers through standard pre-printed contract documents running into several pages.

In fact, even business-to-business contracts have come to be in standard forms. A business entity could be buying several items from different parties. The transaction cost involved in negotiating with each party would be huge. Thus, corporations have come up with standard terms and insist that they will do business only on those terms. These are called general conditions of contract (GCC). There are general conditions of contract for different sectors and activities, like banking, insurance, telecommunication, transportation, and telecasting. Thus, modern contracts weave together several of the principles to create rights and obligations. To understand the import of the contract, one has to understand the principles and the effect of combining them together.

Contract law is based on the principle that parties bargain to form agreements to exchange goods and services and, in the case of a dispute, the courts have to give effect to it. As we learn the best when we discover ideas and concepts ourselves, we will follow the case method of deriving law. In the early parts of the book, we will take up simple situations and disputes from our everyday experience and settle them by applying our commonsense ideas of justice and fairness. In deciding the disputes, we will formulate principles, and thus recreate the law for ourselves. Following such a case method, we would not only find out what the book, *The Indian Contract Act, 1872* contains, but also why it says what it says. Having discovered the principles, we may apply ourselves to a case or a situation that helps us develop alternate and conflicting approaches to the problem. This will be followed by a review of landmark cases on the theme to confirm what we have learnt. Instead of giving a brief review of every case related to the principle, the book takes up landmark cases and quotes extensively so that the reader will appreciate the point in its fullness as formulated by the judges.

The key thrust is the development of concepts and ideas. Thus, the cases that critically discuss, contest, and debate a theme are taken up. Most of the cases happen to be from the British courts. Wherever there is a case from the Indian Supreme Court that adopts or applies the principles, it is reviewed. In India, should we not study only cases coming from the Indian Supreme Court? After all, only the cases coming from the Supreme Court are binding on the courts in India. The cases from the British courts, at the most, can only be suggestive recommendations. However, in the past 10 years, there is a basic shift in what a law student studies contract law for. To get equipped to appear before a court in a case involving contract law is only one of the interests of a law student in contract law.

Contract law came to be the conceptual and legal foundation of business law. Common law courts took the principles of contract law as given to develop specialized forms of contracts, for example, sale of goods, bailment, guarantee, indemnity, negotiable instruments, and carriage. We cannot understand these laws unless we have a thorough conceptual understanding of contract law. Further, these laws in turn are structures on which the contemporary acts, dealing with or regulating business in different sectors of the economy, are founded. We will be floundering with the entire field of business law without a conceptual understanding of contract law.

Second, most commercial contracts have arbitration clauses. Thus, the disputes between parties go to an arbitrator; and law persons represent the parties before an arbitrator. The arbitrators follow the law of the country governing the contract. In a contract governed by the Indian law, the parties would bring the cases from the Indian court to resolve the dispute. However, in the absence of it, a directly relevant case from a British court would have persuasive value. There are not many cases coming from the Indian Supreme Court on the subject of contract law. One of the reasons, perhaps, is that commercial disputes are being arbitrated and getting resolved before an arbitrator. Thus, an important role of a law person in the field of contracts is to draft contract documents, advise on the working of the contracts, and appear before arbitrators. In this context, focusing attention exclusively on the cases coming from the Indian courts would be inadequate.

Third, as contract law has come from common law, courts the world over continue to refer to the old as well as new court judgments coming from the British courts as a guiding direction. As we would study the Indian courts are guided by the British courts if it is not in conflict with the express statutory provisions. The reason why the British courts have continued to be a guiding force in the field of contract law is that England has long been a free-trade country and an important industrial, commercial and financial centre. Thus, over time, a corpus of cases was developed on every possible theme. Further, in a context where India has been integrated with the global economy, Indian businesses are getting into contracts whose jurisdictions are outside India. Law persons in India would increasingly be required to have an understanding of the laws in other jurisdictions.

This book has seven parts, covering the formation of contracts; consideration; setting aside of contracts; void contracts; discharge of contracts; quasi-contracts; and breach, termination as well as damages. Let us begin our journey with the formation of agreements.

Part 1

FORMATION OF AGREEMENT

The essence of contract law is that the state supports and enforces contracts made by individuals. Contracts are voluntary agreements reached between individuals which have benefits for both the parties. Two individuals are in agreement when their minds meet. This happens through a communicative process between the individuals. In almost all cases, an agreement is formed when one person makes an offer, and the other accepts it. All contracts, big or small, are formed on one party making an offer to the other, and the other party accepting the offer. The simple formulation unfolds in several interesting dimensions on formation of contracts. This includes different modalities by which people can communicate offer, acceptance, and rejection. The parties can communicate not only in words but also by action, omission, and conduct. Not all communication between the parties is a term of the contract. What has been offered and accepted decides what the terms of the contract are. Place where the offer and acceptance are made can decide the place where the contract is formed. This can decide the court where a dispute on the contract would be taken to. In this part, we will explore formation of agreement through acceptance of offer, and several concepts which derive from this.

2

Offer, Acceptance, and Agreement

We live in a market-based economic system. Individuals are bearers of property rights. The essence of a market-based system is that the individuals voluntarily exchange their property rights. The system presupposes a state that invests individuals with the legal rights and guarantees the exchange. Contract law is made up of the rules of this exchange. Individuals were not always the bearers of legal rights. They became the bearers of legal rights as trading emerged over the centuries within the feudal order and transformed society. The market-based system was consolidated, became global through the Industrial Revolution during the nineteenth century, and created an economic order based on market transactions. Legal ideas on contracts had accumulated over the centuries. With the Industrial Revolution, legal ideas were revised and integrated, giving birth to modern contract law.

AGREEMENT: MEETING OF MINDS

The essence of contract law is that the state guarantees the voluntary arrangement reached by individuals for the exchange of their rights. How do individuals get into an arrangement with each other? This happens when they reach an agreement through a communicative process. When two individuals come to hold the same opinion, understanding or belief, their minds have met and they are in agreement. Processes of formation of agreement are central to contract law. As communication is a part of our everyday lived experience; its principles are commonsense to us, which, as we noted in Chapter 1, make up contract law. However, what is commonsense can also be profound, and simple principles can have a complex application. A study of contract law will present us with this wide and exciting terrain. We shall have to move from the simple to complex. Let us begin with some preliminary observations.

Consider the case of a grocer who had supplied goods worth Rs 6,000 on credit to A. In addition, the grocer solicited a donation of Rs 2,000 for his son's education, to which A consented. Later, A refused to pay both sums as he lost money on stock transactions. There are two different agreements between the parties, one for paying to the grocer Rs 6,000, and the other, a gift of Rs 2,000. As we have noted, an agreement between individuals has to be enforced. It would be unfair if the grocer were not paid Rs 6,000. The customer has already availed itself of the benefit in terms of goods supplied. However, the agreement to give the grocer Rs 2,000 is a gift. The customer does not benefit from it. And as he does not benefit, he never intended to be bound by the agreement.

The benefits that the two sides promise each other are called considerations. Only an agreement with consideration for both the parties is enforceable. These agreements are called contracts. One can insist that even in the case of a gift, the donor derives emotional satisfaction, and thus benefits from it. However, contract law has been developed to deal with such disputes arising among traders; and as traders came together to exchange goods and services, material exchange became an essential component of a contract. In contrast to this were exchanges that were social and familial in nature. A business relationship was about parties exchanging goods and services, while a social relationship was about co-operation and mutual help. Social relationships were for the society to shape, while only business relationships were to be mediated by the law. Thus, the presence of consideration came to decide whether the relationship was a business relationship or not.

Let us consider a case where Vijay says to Paul, 'I can sell this book to you now for Rs 300. Will you buy it?' Paul responds, 'Yes. Give me the book. Here is the money.' Vijay initiated the communicative process by making an offer to Paul. When Paul responded in the affirmative to the offer, the two minds agreed on the immediate sale of the book for Rs 300. Paul acquired the right to be given the book, and Vijay, the money. But seconds later, Paul says, 'Sorry, I made a mistake. I already have a copy of this book. I will not buy it.' Vijay insists that an agreement had been formed between the parties and that Paul was

breaching the contract. An agreement was indeed formed between the parties, creating rights and obligations for the two parties. Let us contrast it with the following variation.

Paul says to Vijay, 'Where did you find this book? I have been looking for it for months but cannot find it in any store.' Vijay replies, 'I got it from Delhi for Rs 600 a copy. I have an extra copy and I have been looking for weeks for anyone to sell it to for that price.' The two exclaim together, 'We have a deal!' Seconds later, Paul says, 'Actually, I cannot buy it from you because I would need a receipt from a bookstore to claim a reimbursement from my office.' Vijay insists that an agreement has been formed between the parties. Paul contests it.

The two minds were in agreement on the sale when they exclaimed in unison. But we would hesitate to bind them to rights and obligations. The difference between the two cases is that in the second case, the consensus is spontaneous and not deliberate. This is how social groups come to have a shared view. The formation of business agreements involved specific parties who communicated with each other about, among other things, the specific goods to be traded, their price, delivery schedule, and carriage. The communication and reaching of consensus happened through a process of dialogue and was not spontaneous. For this reason, the formation of agreement has been described as a bargain, where each party works out its consideration.

Offer, Acceptance, and Meeting of Minds

A meeting of minds is secured through dialogue and communication. One person initiates, the other responds, and a communicative process is set into motion. We will explore it further with the following case.

Case: Offer and Acceptance

Explore the following three different possible communications between a taxi driver and an intending passenger.

Situation 1: The intending passenger says to the taxi driver, 'Take me to Church Gate. I will give you Rs 50. That is what I give everyday.' Taxi driver replies, 'Fine.'

Situation 2: The intending passenger says to the taxi driver, 'Take me to Church Gate. I will give you Rs 40. That is what I give everyday.' Taxi driver replies, 'Sorry, Sir. Petrol prices have gone up. It will cost you Rs 50.' The intending passenger replies, 'All right.'

Situation 3: The intending passenger says to the taxi driver, 'Church Gate. I will give you Rs 40. That is what I give everyday.' Taxi driver replies, 'Sorry Sir. Petrol prices have gone up. It will cost you Rs 60.' The intending passenger replies, 'Petrol prices have gone up but not to the extent that you can charge another twenty rupees. I will pay you Rs 50.' The taxi driver replies, 'Fine.'

In situations 1, 2, and 3, an agreement was formed between the parties. The substance of the agreement was the same in all the three cases, that is, the passenger will pay Rs 50 for his passage to Church Gate. The process of communication in the three cases, however, was different. In all the three cases, the last bit of communication between the parties is decisive. The very last communication is affirmation or acceptance of the offer or proposal put up by the other party. For the formation of an agreement, one party puts up an offer or proposal to another, and the other person accepts it. An offer is the penultimate act leading to the agreement. Once accepted, both parties are bound by the agreement. Thus, in situations 1 and 3, the intending passenger offered and the taxi driver accepted.

In situation 2, the taxi driver offered and the intending passenger accepted.

Making an offer leads to serious implications. Once made, the other person has to just say 'yes' to bind both the parties in an agreement. Having made an offer, the person loses all control and is bound by the volition of the other party. As the principles of contracts derive from the yester centuries, an offer was described in the metaphor of gun powder. It only needed light (acceptance) to explode it. One cannot be casual in making an offer, but it must also be confirmed that a communication made by a person is indeed an offer. Agreement is about the meeting of minds. For this to be secured, the offer must be clear, definite and unambiguous, indicating the person's intention to be bound to it. The followings are examples of communication that cannot be taken to be offers: A person says to another, 'I may consider selling my house to you for Rs 15 lakhs.' A vendor says to an intending customer, 'Usually, the price of a 1.5 ton AC is about Rs. 20,000.' A wholesaler to a retail dealer, 'The price of the goods you are interested in can be anything upwards of Rs. 20,000.' The statements do not indicate the intention to be bound to them on the part of the person making them.

Principle: An agreement is the meeting of two minds. This can be formed when one party makes an offer and the other person accepts it.

Case: Rejection of Offer

Consider further variations of the preceding case, where an intending passenger is considering whether to take a taxi.

Situation 1: The intending passenger says to the taxi driver, 'Take me to Church Gate. I will give you Rs 50. That is what I give everyday.' Taxi driver replies, 'No'.

Situation 2: The intending passenger says to the taxi driver, 'Take me to Church Gate. I will give you Rs 40. That is what I give everyday.' Taxi driver replies, 'Sorry Sir. Petrol prices have gone up. It will cost you Rs 60.' The intending passenger replies, 'Agreed, but not to the extent that you can charge another twenty rupees. I will pay you Rs 50.' The taxi driver replies, 'No sir. Look for another taxi.'

Situation 3: A taxi driver announces, 'Church Gate, Church Gate. Come, Sir, only fifty rupees.' The intending passenger, 'No thank you. I have a fixed taxi driver to take me every evening.'

In Situation 2, the intending passenger offered, but the taxi driver rejected the offer. In situation 3, the taxi driver offered, but the intending passenger rejected the offer. No person is under an obligation to make an offer to another. And the person to whom an offer is made is under no obligation to accept it. He is free to accept or reject the offer. However, if an offer is made and accepted, an agreement is formed and the parties are bound by rights and obligations to each other. Thus, contract formation is a voluntary activity among the parties.

Principle: An offer or proposal can be accepted or rejected. An agreement is formed on the acceptance of the offer. No agreement is formed if the offer is rejected.

Case: Implied Offer and Acceptance

A person enters a shop selling newspapers and magazines and approaches the counter. He points his finger at a stack of newspapers next to the shopkeeper. The shopkeeper gives him a copy of the newspaper. The person gives the shopkeeper Rs 10, and the latter returns a five rupee coin. Within half a minute, the customer has left the store.

Not a single word was exchanged between the customer and the shopkeeper. There certainly was an agreement between the parties to sell a newspaper for Rs 5. If there was an agreement, there must have been an offer and an acceptance. Who made the offer? What was the modality followed for communicating the offer and acceptance?

The shopkeeper offered by giving the newspaper to the customer and the customer accepted by giving him money in exchange. Human beings communicate with their facial expressions, gestures and body language. It is a part of the everyday communicative practices. Thus, offer and acceptance can be expressed in written or spoken words, or can be implied through gestures, actions, commissions, and omissions.

Principle: Offers and acceptance can be expressed (spoken or written in words) or implied through gestures, body language, actions, commissions, and omissions.

Identify the modalities of offer and acceptance in the following situations.

Situation 1: A customer says to an attendant in a shop, 'I cannot buy this shirt for Rs 700. Will you sell it to me for Rs 600?' The attendant does not say anything but puts the shirt in a bag and gives it to customer.

Situation 2: In a self-service restaurant, food items are kept on a table. The price of each item is also written. A person picks up a sandwich, sits at a table, and eats it. An attendant brings him a bill, which he pays.

Situation 3: A person, seeing an approaching taxi, raises his hand. The taxi stops. The person gets into the taxi. The taxi drives off.

In Situation 1, the customer makes an express offer and the shopkeeper accepts it implicitly by putting it in a bag and giving it to him. In Situation 2, the restaurant makes an implied offer by putting food items on a table. The acceptance of the customer is implied in his act of eating it. In Situation 3, the offer for carriage is implied in the taxi stopping next to him and the acceptance in the customer getting inside the taxi.

Some might argue that only written contracts are enforceable. However, contracts formed through oral or implied offers and acceptances are as valid as written contracts. The working of the state, law enforcement agencies and courts is done through documentation in written form. Governance is done through written records. In the context of the domination of written records, one assumes that, as contracts are about law, only written agreements would be legitimate and be enforced. However, the proliferation of written records is a recent phenomenon, and trade and commerce has existed for centuries. Traders, like everyone else, communicated through spoken words, facial expressions, gestures, body movements, and actions and omissions. The courts developed contract law around trading practices. Seen in this chronology, it is the written means of forming agreements that is exception, and the rule was non-written contracts. Thus, contracts formed orally or implicitly were always valid and enforceable. The state has had no reason to make these contracts invalid by its lawmaking. On the contrary, requiring every contract to be in writing would increase the transaction cost and would make everyday life very inconvenient.

Principle: Contracts formed through spoken or implied offers and/or acceptance, are as valid as contracts formed through a written offer and acceptance.

Offer and acceptance are only the means by which we discern the formation of an agreement. The founding principle is the meeting of minds through a dialogue. If a person coerces another to accept an offer, technically, there is an agreement, but no meeting of minds. On the other hand, in some cases, there may be a meeting of minds, but no discernable offer and its acceptance. Thus, meeting of minds is the basis for the formation of agreements. We will explore this aspect in detail in subsequent chapters. The Latin expression for the meeting of minds, *consensus ad idem*, is frequently used.

Invitation to Offer

Case: Advertisement by Airlines

An advertisement of an airline on the bill boards says, 'Fly from Mumbai to Delhi for Rs 3,200. Call our airline at number...' A potential customer calls the airline and asked for a ticket for a flight departing the next week. The airline refuses to give a ticket for that fare. The customer insists that the airline had made an offer to sell the ticket, and he has accepted by calling the airline and asking for a ticket. The airline disagrees.

For an agreement to be formed, there must be an offer followed by an acceptance. The customer claims to have accepted an offer from the airline. Was the communication from the airline an offer? The airline has a limited number of flights and seats. If its advertisement were to be an offer, the airline could be bound to a large number of interested passengers. The airline does not intend this. For this reason, the advertisement requires the persons interested to call the airline. The advertisement could not be accepted on its own. Thus, the advertisement was not an offer. It is the customer who offers to buy the ticket. Following this, the airline can accept or reject the offer. If the intending passengers make the offer, what was the role of the advertisement? It was soliciting or inviting persons to make an offer. Thus, communications preceding the making of an offer, or those that solicit an offer, are called an 'invitation to offer'.

Subjective and Objective Agreements

Let us explore the relevance of what a person intends and expresses to the invitation to offer, the offer, and the acceptance.

Case: Interpreting Communication

A seller signs an offer document and faxes it to a customer. The offer document reads:

I offer to sell you 50 Remington pendrives (capacity 1 Gb each) for a price of Rs 20,000. The price is inclusive of all taxes. We will have the goods delivered to your premises free of charge. The goods will be delivered to you within a week. Kindly send your acceptance by signing a copy of the fax and returning it to us by fax.

As the fax was just about to get transmitted, the seller noticed that he had made a mistake in writing the price; he had intended to write Rs 22,000. He tried to contact the customer on the phone but the phone was busy. A minute after the fax was sent, the seller received a signed copy of the fax from the customer accepting the offer. Has there been a meeting of minds? Is an agreement formed between the parties?

The seller never intended to sell the goods for Rs 20, 000. Thus, there was no meeting of minds. Is there a subsisting contract between the parties? A contract is formed by two specific individuals as a result of their intentions and understanding. Thus, the contract is what the two minds intended. The deciding factor in ascertaining a meeting of minds should be the subjective positions of the parties. If one were to go by the subjective intentions, however, several difficulties would arise. The subjective intention is not directly accessible to others, even to the other party. A person manifests his intention through utterances and actions. Only this is accessible to others. From this, we infer the intentions of the person. In other words, one only has access to objective manifestations. How does one

interpret these? One way could be to bring out the entire fact of the incidence and establish that the seller inadvertently sent a wrong price. However, if this recourse were to be followed, there would be no end to contextualizing the communication to reach the subjective intention of the party.

Further, if subjective intentions were the basis for a contract, anyone not interested in meeting the obligations under a contract would assert that in his mind he never intended to get into the contract. This will make contracts meaningless. Business transactions would become uncertain. Thus, the courts do not go by the subjective and specific intentions of the parties. Working with the objective manifestations, one asks not what the specific person intended, but, ordinarily, what a normal person in those circumstances would have intended. In other words, one takes the objective manifestation and asks what most people would understand from it. For example, on reading the fax from the seller, nobody would doubt it to be an offer to sell pendrives for Rs 20,000. Law only explores what an ordinary and reasonable person would understand from a communication, whether it is an invitation to offer, an offer or an acceptance. Lord Denning has expressed this position thus:

In contracts you do not look into the actual intent in a man's mind. You look at what he said and did. A contract is formed when there is, to all outward appearances, a contract. A man cannot get out of a contract by saying: 'I did not intend to contract', if by his words he has done so. His intention is to be found only in the outward expression ... If they show a concluded contract that is enough.[1]

Invitations to offer, offers, and acceptance are communicated by the parties. In understand-

---

[1] *Storer* v. *Manchester City Council*, (1974) 3 All ER 824.

ing the communication of a party, we ignore what the person actually meant (subjective intention), and instead take the objective viewpoint as to what it would mean to an external 'ordinary and reasonable' person.

INDIAN CONTRACT ACT, 1872

An agreement is formed through a communicative process. Chapter 1 of the Indian Contract Act, 1872, which is titled, 'Of the Communication, Acceptance and Revocation of Proposals' details this aspect. Section 2(a) and (b) define what we have been calling offer, acceptance, and agreement.

Section 2(a): When one person signifies to another his willingness to do or to abstain from doing anything, with a view to obtaining the assent of that other to such act or abstinence, he is said to make a proposal;

(b) When the person to whom the proposal is made signifies his assent thereto, the proposal is said to be accepted. A proposal, when accepted, becomes a promise;

(c) Every promise and every set of promises, forming the consideration for each other, is an agreement.

The common law courts have used the words 'offer' and 'proposal' interchangeably. Similarly, 'acceptance' and 'assent' have been used interchangeably. Thus, the above section states the basic principle of formation of agreement through the communicative process of offer and acceptance. The use of the term 'promise' and 'reciprocal promise' has lingered from a feudal context, preceding the market-based system. We will work with the key words 'offer', 'acceptance', and 'agreement', but let us become more familiar with the term 'promise'.

Example 1: A says to B, 'I can sell you this coat for Rs 2,000'. B says, 'Accepted.' An agreement is formed between the parties. The terms of the agreement are that A will give the coat to B and B will pay Rs 2000. In the language of Section 2(a), A signifies to B his willingness to hand over the ownership of the coat to B, with the intention of getting B's consent. This is an offer, or a proposal. B replies, 'Yes'. Following Section 2(b), B has accepted the proposal. Following Section 2(e), an agreement has been formed. Further, the respective obligations to each other are the promises of the parties. Thus, A has promised to give the ownership of the coat to B; and B has promised to give Rs 2,000 to A.

Example 2: X says to Y, 'I will let you keep my book for three more days, for a price of Rs 50'. Y says, 'All right.' The terms of the agreement are that Y can keep the book for three more days and X would receive Rs 50 from him. In the language of Section 2(a), X is offering or proposing to abstain from taking his book back from Y. X has promised not to take the book back from Y; while Y has promised to give X Rs 50.

In a feudal social setting, as there was no exchange, there were only promises. In this social context, the undertaking of a person was associated with his class and status. Men of honour lived up to their word and promise. Thus, when a lord told a starving peasant, 'Come to my palace tomorrow, I will give you 10 kg of wheat', he must keep his promise. Trade and commerce emerged from within this social setting. Traders were involved in equal exchanges. A trader could have said, 'I will give you 10 kg of wheat for 2 kg of your cotton'. However, the only way of expressing this emergent transaction was in the language of 'promise'. Thus, the transaction was expressed: (1) A has promised to give 10 kg of rice to B, and (2) B has promised to give 2 kg of cotton to A. For a long time, each promise was seen in isolation from each other, to be fulfilled on its own. Only with practice did it come to be emphasized that the two promises were related to each other, and these came to be called reciprocal promises. However, for a long time, contractual relationships had not been about promises but about bargains, where parties got into an exchange by offering and accepting. Thus, the terms 'promise' and 'reciprocal promise', conceptually, are archaic terms and should not be used at all. Instead, the terms 'offer' and 'acceptance' should be used. Promises are the terms of the contracts, creating rights and obligations for the parties.

Section 9 of the Indian Contract Act, 1872, expresses the idea we had formulated earlier that offer and acceptance can be express or implied. It provides:

Section 9. Promises, express and implied. In so far as the proposal or acceptance of any promise is made in words, the promise is said to be express. In so far as such proposal or acceptance is made otherwise than in words, the promise is said to be implied.

Cases for Analysis

Let us apply the principles learnt so far to the following cases and disputes. As preparation for this, let us note that formation of an agreement is a voluntary act undertaken by individuals capable of intention and communication. As expected, it is only real and biological individuals who can offer, accept and get into agreements. Later, law, through the device of registration, invested companies and other forms of organizations with the rights of a legal person. Through this mechanism, companies and other bodies also get into agreements. A corporate body, of course, is not a natural person; on its own, it is not capable of intention and action. People must act as the instruments of the corporate body to make and accept offers to get the corporate body into agreements.

Apply the principles learnt to identify in each of the following cases whether the communication is express or implied, and identify the invitation to offer, the offer and the acceptance.

1. **Price List:** Restaurants and cafés put up a price list. This is displayed on a board and also presented as a card. Catalogues are also of the same nature, describing the good and its price. It is certainly a communication from the seller. Is the communication an offer or invitation to offer? Let us explore with the following cases:

a. A group of 200 students from a college was visiting another college. The canteen of the college had displayed the food items it served along with the price for each of the items. The instructor organizing the group visit demands 200 bottles of soft drinks. The canteen was not expecting the visit. If they meet the order, they will not have sufficient stock for the next three days for the students of their college. The canteen declines to serve soft drinks to the visiting students. The instructor insists that he has a right to be served the 200 bottles.

b. A student asks for a fixed meal at the college café. The café had put up a price list declaring the price to be Rs 30. The café informs the student that they have run out of the food item. The student insists that he has a right to be served the fixed meal.

c. A student asks for a cheese sandwich at the college café. The café had put up a price list declaring the price of cheese sandwich to be Rs 20. The café tells the student that they will provide him a sandwich, but the price of cheese sandwich has been increased to Rs 25 since that morning. The student insists that he has a right to be given the cheese sandwich for Rs 20.

2. Pamphlets: Putting up advertisements in newspapers and distributing pamphlets informing customers of special prices, discounts and schemes is a common business practice. Is the communication an offer or invitation to offer? Let us explore with the following case. A home delivery pizza store has a pamphlet distributed in all the residential areas in the city. It reads, 'The New Year's Eve family-size pizza for just Rs 100.' In response to calls to the pizza store on New Year's Eve, the store apologizes to the customers and says that they had made a mistake in printing the prices; the intended price had been Rs 200. The store is willing to sell a family-size pizza for Rs 200. A customer insists that the store is under an agreement to sell for Rs 200.

3. Showcase and Shop Window: Shops display wares in shop windows. The displayed goods also have a label declaring the price. Is the display an offer to sell the very good put in the showcase? Is it an offer to sell goods of the description put in the showcase? Is the display not an offer but only invitation to offer? Let us consider this with the following cases:

a.   A person sees a cricket bat in the showcase of a shop. A sticker on the bat declares the price to be Rs 3000. He goes inside the store to the sales counter and says, 'Give me ten cricket bats.' The store attendant responds, 'Sorry, we only have three pieces. You could come after a week.' The customer said, 'I live in another city and will be flying there in the evening.' The customer claims that a contract was formed when he placed his order for ten bats. Is this true?

b.   A person walks into a sports store and asks for the cricket bat displayed in the shop window. The shop window declared the price to be Rs 4,000. The

attendant brings out five bats of the same make and description. However, the customer insists on being given the bat in the display, as a famous cricketer had inaugurated the store two days before and had held the bat in his hand. The customer claims that the display in the window with a price tag is an offer to sell that very piece, and the store is bound to give it to him. The store refuses to oblige. What could be the reasons for the store's unwillingness to sell the displayed piece?

4. Self-service store: The following situations are with reference to self-service stores. In a self-service store, goods are put on shelves and their prices are declared. A customer browses through the store with a trolley or a basket and picks up the items he is interested in. The customer then comes to the cash counter and gives the items to an attendant, who does the billing for the goods. The customer pays the money, collects the goods and leaves the shop. In a store, thousands of contracts are made everyday. The stores, however, do not specify the terms and conditions of the formation of a contract between the store and the customer, as they do not want to put off the customers with legal terms. Instead, the stores put up advertisements for discounts and schemes for promoting purchase. In this context, let us explore the following different situations:

a.   A cricket match is to start at 2.30 PM in the afternoon. A t-shirt bearing the logo of the team and the name of the city is being promoted for the spectators to wear for the game. A customer picks up all 15 t-shirts remaining on the shelf. He shops some more and settles down to have a cup of coffee and a sandwich. While going to the cash counter with the trolley, he receives a phone call on his mobile phone telling him not to buy the t-shirts. The customer gives all the items he took off the shelves to the attendant besides the t-shirts. However, since the customer picked up the t-shirts, more than 50 customers went away disappointed at not getting a shirt. The attendant insists that as the customer had put it in his trolley, he has to pay for it and take it. Who is in the right here?

b. This is a variation of the above case, where the self-service store has put up bold declarations everywhere in the shop that read, 'Goods once selected and put in the basket or trolley cannot be put back on the shelf. The customer has to pay for it.' The store insists that the customer has to pay for the t-shirts he took off the shelves. Is the store correct?

c. In a self-service store, a customer found chocolate bars of a reputed brand that were being sold at a very cheap price. The customer puts the entire stock on the shelf in his trolley. At the cash counter, the attendant tells the customer that he can take only ten bars. The store had advertised the special price of the chocolate in the newspapers and through pamphlets. If a single customer took away all the stock, the other customers would be disappointed. The customer claims that, having picked up the stock from the shelf, he has a right to all the goods in his trolley. Is he correct?

d. A customer picks up a box of washing powder. A sticker on the powder box states the price to be Rs 150. At the cash counter, the attendant discovered that the store staff had put the wrong sticker on the box. The price of the box was Rs 200. The customer insists that he has a right to take the box for Rs 150.

5. **Written Communication:** Consider the following communication between the parties.

a. A seller sends the following signed letter to a customer: 'We offer to sell you 20 pieces of Remington pendrive (capacity 1 Gb) for a price of Rs 10,000 on the following terms. The price is inclusive of all taxes. We will deliver the goods to you within a week at your premises free of charge. The price will be paid by you within a week of delivery of the goods. Kindly communicate your decision at the earliest.'

The customer replies through a letter, 'We accept your offer dated...'

Is the offer and acceptance express or implied? Who has made the offer? What are the terms of the offer?

b. A customer approached a courier company to send a book. The attendant noted the address the book was being sent to and the value of the book on a pre-printed form. The customer had brought the invoice for the book to authenticate the price. The attendant asked the person to sign the form. Thereafter, the attendant signed a counterfoil and gave it to the customer and collected Rs 30, the courier charges.

The courier company lost the book. The customer now demands a refund of the courier charges in addition to Rs 2,000, the value of the book. He is glad to have carried the invoice for the attendant to write down the value of the book. The courier company is willing to give him a refund of Rs 30 and only Rs 100 for the lost book. The courier company brings to his notice the terms mentioned on the form he had signed. The counterfoil had the same terms. It reads:

Terms and Conditions

1. The courier company will not provide any insurance coverage for any consignments sent, even if the value of the consignment is declared by the sender or required to be declared by the courier company.

2. No compensation or refund will be paid for late delivery of consignment.

3. The liability of the courier company for loss or damage to the shipment is limited to Rs 100 for each consignment.

4. The courier company will not be responsible for any consequential losses.

5. Queries on consignment should be raised within 30 days from the date of dispatch of the consignment.

6. Octroi, or any other tax or duty levied on the consignment shall be borne by the consignor/consignee. The amount would be required to be paid by the consignor/consignee immediately on demand.

7. Any dispute, controversy, or claim arising out of or relating to the contract shall be subject to the jurisdiction of the courts of Mumbai.

Who has set the terms of offer? Who makes the offer? Who accepts it? What are the liabilities of the courier company for the lost packet? What would have been the liabilities of the courier company if it had omitted the third term? The sender had not read the terms at the time of sending the courier. Was a meeting of minds between the parties secured? Is the term binding on the sender?

6. Auction: Auction is a mechanism for finding a party to make a contract with. It can take different forms. Let us explore the formation of agreement in the following situations.

a. A popular singer, at the end of a show, announces an auction of the jacket he is wearing during the performance. The proceeds from the sale are to go to a charity. Several bids are made, the last one for Rs 50,000. As no further

bids are made, the singer says to the last bidder, 'It is yours.'

b. Sigma Limited advertised in the newspapers with the heading 'Auction Notice'. The company was auctioning 50 used computers on an as-is where-is basis. The money was to be paid immediately and the computers were to be taken by the evening. Several persons made bids. The last bid was for Rs 1.8 lakh. When no further bids were coming, the manager of the company, who was conducting the auction, struck a hammer, announcing the closure of bid.

c. Zed Limited is selling several items through an auction. The terms of the auction stated, 'The goods put to auction will be sold to the highest bidder.' A car was one of the items put to auction. There are only two bids for the car. The highest bid is Rs 20,000. This is a throwaway price for a car that had just done 20,000 km, and the company refuses to sell the car. The highest bidder claims that an agreement has been formed for the sale of the car and the company cannot refuse it.

7. Tender: Tender is another means for finding a party to make a contract with. Unlike an auction, parties do not have to be present face-to-face. Let us explore the formation of a contract through a tender.

a. Omega Limited has advertised in the newspaper with the heading 'Tender Notice', inviting tenders for installing a specified antivirus software in the 200 computers owned by the company. Semantics Computers Private Limited is the lowest bidder. All the bid values are tabulated and communicated to all the seven parties who had put their tender. A week later, the company makes an arrangement directly with another software manufacturing company and buys its antvirus software. Semantics Computers Private Limited claims that as the lowest bidder, it has the right to be given the contract for installing the antivirus software.

b. Summit Hospitalities Limited has advertised in the newspapers, soliciting tenders for the purchase of 500 television sets of a particular model for installation in the rooms of its hotel. The tender document can be bought from the company for Rs 5,000. The tender document provides the details of the television set and the time and place of delivery. The tender documents are to be sealed and delivered by the 15th of the month. The tender documents were opened on 16th of the month. The lowest quoted price is from Shanti Entertainment Private Limited. The second-lowest price is from Vinay Electronics Limited. The company awards the contract to Vinay Electronics Limited as they had a business relationship with them for over a decade. Identify the offeror and the acceptor. Who has set the details of the offer? Can the company award the contract to Vinay Electronics Ltd?

c. A computer manufacturing company is looking to set up its showroom in a city in India and has put up the following advertisement:

The company requires suitable premises, carpet area 2500 to 3000 sq. ft., ground/first floor, on lease basis. Kindly send technical and financial offers in two separate sealed envelops marked 'Technical Bid' and 'Financial Bid'. The technical bid should contain technical specifications like the size and location of the premises. The financial bid should contain the financial aspects of the lease of premises, including the expected rent and other terms and conditions of the lease.

The company reserves the right to accept or reject any or all offers without assigning any reasons.

Identify the invitation to offer, the offeror and the acceptor. What is the significance/meaning of the technical and financial bids? Contrast this case with the previous one. Why was a technical bid not asked for in the previous case? The advertisement declares, 'The company reserves the right to accept or reject any or all offers without assigning any reasons.' What is the significance of this statement? Would it make any difference if this declaration were not made?

d. A food manufacturing company invites tenders for the supply of raw material including sugar. Sagar Limited submits the following tender: 'We tender to supply sugar at the rate of Rs 25/Kg with such quantities as is ordered from time to time between 1 January 2010 and 31 December 2010.' The food manufacturing company responds, 'We are pleased to inform you that your tender for the supply of sugar has been accepted. We will be in communication with you.'

The food manufacturing company had a similar tender from another company for supplying at the rate of Rs 23 per kilogram. The company took its entire requirement from this company. As a result, Sagar Limited did not receive any order from the food manufacturing company. Sagar Limited claims that the food company has breached the contract.

e. Semantics Private Limited has three main shareholders, X, Y and Z, holding 20 per cent, 40 per cent, and 40 per cent shares respectively. X wants to sell his shares and both Y and Z are interested in buying them as the purchase would give them controlling rights on the company. X sends an email to both Y and Z, saying, 'Kindly communicate your price for my entire holding in the company by email by 5.00 PM tomorrow evening. The shares will be sold to the person quoting the higher price.' Y quotes the higher price. After the deadline of 5.00 PM, X enters into communication with Z, who matches the price offered by Y. X sells the shares to Z. Y contends that an agreement was already formed with him. Is he correct?

8. Advertisement: Think about the following advertisements.

a. A manufacturer of laptops published an advertisement saying, 'We now offer a new laptop model for less than Rs 30,000 … Contact nearest dealer.' Is the statement an offer?

b. The newspaper *Times of India* puts up an advertisement titled 'Reader's Offer'. The advertisement prints a photo of the product, describes its features and quotes a price. A person can order the product by calling a phone number. The payment can be made by a credit card or cheque. In this arrangement, who makes the offer? Who accepts it? At the bottom of the advertisement, the following is stated: 'By choosing to buy this product you agree to our terms and conditions mentioned at http://www.shopping.indiatimes.com.' The terms and conditions mentioned at this site included the following: 'All products/

services and information displayed on Indiatimes.com shopping constitute an 'invitation to offer'. Your order for purchase constitutes your 'offer', which shall be subject to the terms and conditions as listed below. Indiatimes.com reserves the right to accept or reject your offer.'

Discuss the implications of the above term.

c. The following advertisement was put up in the newspapers by a self-service store:

Sunday, 10 a.m. Sharp

3, Allure, Perfume for Women worth Rs 1,000 each

For only Rs 50 each. First Come First Served.

A man reaches the store before it has opened. As soon as it does, he goes to the shelf and picks up the three bottles of perfume. At the sales counter, the attendant, who is still switching on the computer, does not dispute that the customer was the first to reach the counter. However, he refuses to sell the perfume, stating that according to the store rule, the advertised goods are to be sold only to women. The customer claims that a contract has been made between the parties and the store has to execute the sale. Is he correct?

These analyses should help us understand the process of formation of agreement in most of the everyday practices and business relations through invitation to offer, offer and acceptance. In the next chapter, we will match our analysis with the application of the principles by the courts.

3

Business Practices and Formation of Agreements

As we have already discussed, an agreement is formed when minds have met. Often, this is secured by one person making an offer and another person accepting it. The communication of offer and acceptance can be express or implied. The meaning of the communication is to be judged objectively, as it would be understood by a reasonable person. In this chapter, we will explore how courts have applied these principles to explain the formation of agreements in different contents. Section 1 explores everyday practices including price lists, catalogues, displays in shop windows, advertisements, and self-service stores. The courts have given a special meaning to signed documents. In section 2, we examine agreements formed through signed documents. Tender and auction are some of the means employed by business organizations for entering into contracts. Section 3 reviews the judgments of the courts on auction and tender. Section 3 also reviews the formation of agreement on the internet.

Agreement is about two minds becoming one, not each pursuing his own goal in isolation from the other. The meeting of minds has to be inferred from the communication between the parties. Advertisements often use the word 'offer', for example in the following: 'We now offer the latest model of laptops...Contact nearest dealer.' The statement is only an invitation to offer, even if it describes itself as an 'offer'. Consider the statement: 'We agree to sell the house for Rs 20 lakh. Kindly communicate your decision within two weeks.' This is only an offer even if the word 'agreement' is used. The use of word 'offer' is not necessary for making an offer and the use of the word does not make the communication an offer. The intent of the parties is to be inferred from the communication between them.

EVERYDAY PRACTICES

Price List, Catalogue, and Menu Card

In this context, in a business sense, a price list, menu card or catalogue communicates the price of the goods. Is the communication an offer from the seller? The communication is express; however, it does not put itself as an offer. An offer has to be clear and definite, expressing the willingness of the offeror to be bound by it. The second problem is that if it were an offer, the seller would be contractually bound to supply an unlimited quantity of goods to a large number of persons. The person putting up the price list or catalogue does not intend this. Thus, price lists and catalogues are not offers but only invitations to offers. The founding case on this is *Grainer* v. *Gough*. The court noted:

The transmission of such a price list does not amount to an offer to supply an unlimited quantity... described at the price named, so that as soon as an order is given, there is a binding contract to supply that quantity. If it were so, the merchant might find himself involved in any number of contractual obligations to supply... which he would be quite unable to carry out, his stock... of that description being necessarily limited.[1]

In the UK, under the Protection of Birds Act, 1954, it was an offence to 'offer to sell or sell' wild birds. When a journal, *Cage and Aviary Birds*, carried an advertisement for sale of birds, the court noted: 'When one is dealing with advertisements and circulars, unless they indeed come from manufacturers, there is business sense in their being construed as invitations to treat and not offers for sale.'[2] Thus, a mere indication of price does not make a communication to be an offer. A communication becomes an offer only if it explicitly and definitely puts itself to be an offer.

Showcase and Shop Window

A display in a shop window can be with a label indicating the price or without it. If the price is indicated, two possibilities arise. Like a price list, it could be an offer to sell the goods of that description at the mentioned price. The shop owner would not intend this as he would then be bound to supply an unlimited

quantity to a large number of people. It could also be an offer to sell the very piece put in the showcase. This is a less plausible contention. Construed from the perspective of an 'ordinary and reasonable' person, the shop owner would not open the shop window and remove the specific piece on display. The inventories of the shop are inside the store, from which the shop owner would get an item to make the sale. The piece in the shop window may only be the cover or exterior of the good. Further, the display piece may have been specifically prepared for display and the items are aesthetically arranged. Thus, objectively construed, a display of goods in a shop window is not an offer but only an invitation to offer. A landmark judgment on the theme is *Fisher* v. *Bell*.[3]

The Restriction of Offensive Weapons Act, 1959, of the United Kingdom made it an offence if anyone 'manufactures, sells... or offers for sale' flick knives. The police found a flick knife in the showcase of a shop run by a Mr Bell. On query by the police office, Bell passed the onus onto the manufacturers, saying, 'Why do manufacturers still bring them round for us to sell?' Bell was prosecuted for offering a flick knife for sale. Lord Parker, CJ noted:

The sole question is whether the exhibition of that knife in the window with the ticket constituted an offer for sale within the statute. I confess that I think most lay people and, indeed, myself when I first read the papers, would be inclined to the view that to say that if a knife was displayed in a window like that with a price attached to it was not offering it for sale was just nonsense. In ordinary language it is there inviting people to buy it, and it is for sale; but any statute must of course be looked at in the light of the general law of the country. Parliament in its wisdom in passing an Act must be taken to know the general law. It is perfectly clear that according to the

---

[1] *Grainer* v. *Gough*, (1896) AC 325.
[2] *Partridge* v. *Crittenden*, (1968) 1 WLR 1204.

[3] *Fisher* v. *Bell*, (1961) 1 QB 394.

ordinary law of contract the display of an article with a price on it in a shop window is merely an invitation to treat. It is in no sense an offer for sale the acceptance of which constitutes a contract. That is clearly the general law of the country. Not only is that so, but it is to be observed that in many statutes and orders which prohibit selling and offering for sale of goods it is very common when it is so desired to insert the words 'offering or exposing for sale,' 'exposing for sale' being clearly words which would cover the display of goods in a shop window. Not only that, but it appears that under several statutes—we have been referred in particular to the Prices of Goods Act, 1939, and the Goods and Services (Price Control) Act, 1941—Parliament, when it desires to enlarge the ordinary meaning of those words, includes a definition section enlarging the ordinary meaning of 'offer for sale' to cover other matters including, be it observed, exposure of goods for sale with the price attached.

In those circumstances I am driven to the conclusion, though I confess reluctantly, that no offence was here committed. At first sight it sounds absurd that knives of this sort cannot be manufactured, sold, hired, lent, or given, but apparently they can be displayed in shop windows; but even if this—and I am by no means saying it is—is a *casus omissus* it is not for this court to supply the omission.

In the second paragraph, *casus omissus* is a Latin expression meaning a case or a point that has been overlooked. The court inferred that the Parliament intended to penalize invitations to offer; however, the text of the law omitted it by mistake. However, the court stated that its role was to interpret the express text of the law and not insert clauses. It was for the Parliament to amend the law and add the missing terms. What should the arresting officer have done instead? He should have collected documentation for sale of flick knife by the store and prosecuted it for the sale. Alternately, he could have bought one and then prosecuted for the sale of a prohibited article. For all we know, following this, the police might have launched another prosecution for just that, but as the decision would have been a straightforward one and not reported in a law journal, we do not know.

Self-service Stores

Self-service is the means by which retail business is commonly done in Western countries. It saves labour cost for the store and gives freedom to the customer to select his purchases. This form of retail has also emerged in the cities in India. The nature of legal transaction is important as it affects a large number of people. The stores do not put up terms and conditions for sale. It is unlikely, as the stores are run by large corporations, that they do not anticipate that disputes could arise with the customers. The stores want to be inviting to the customers. Putting up terms and conditions at the entrance would take away from the ambiance and make the customer wary. Thus, in displaying goods on the shelves, an implied communication has to be construed. We will explore this idea with the cases posed in the previous chapter.

A store was unusual as it had presented the terms and conditions for sale. One of the terms read, 'Goods once selected and put in the basket or trolley cannot be put back on the shelf. The customer has to pay and take it.' In express terms, the store has made the display in the store an offer. The acceptance comes from the customer in putting it in the trolley. In the absence of the term, as was the case where a person had put all the T-shirts in the trolley, the customer would be justified in putting things back on the shelf or abandon an item he picked up. If a survey were conducted among a large number of shoppers, few would agree a customer is bound to buy an item he has picked up. If the display on the shelf were an offer, putting an item in the trolley would be taken to mean the customer's acceptance. Thus, the display is not an offer but only an invitation to offer. The next communication between the store and the customer takes place at the cash counter. The customer gives the selected item for billing. The customer makes an offer to buy the goods and the store accepts it. A landmark case on the topic is the *Pharmaceutical Society of Great Britain* v. *Boots Cash Chemists (Southern) Limited.*[4]

In the UK, it was an offence to sell specified pharmaceutical products without the approval and supervision of a pharmacist.[5] Boots, a retail store, introduced the self-service system for its customers. The pharmacist was seated next to the cashier to superintend the sale. The pharmacist, if he thought fit, could prevent any customer from removing any drugs from the premises. The store was prosecuted by the Pharmaceutical Society of Great Britain, the body entrusted with the enforcement of the law, for violating the law in selling the specified drugs without the supervision of a pharmacist. The contention was that the drug was already sold by the time the customer came to the counter, where the pharmacist was seated. The issue was to understand when, where and by whom was an offer made in a self-service store. Lord Goddard, CJ for the Queen's Court, noted:

… what was done here came to no more than that the customer was informed that he could pick up an article and bring it to the shop-keeper, the contract for sale being completed if the shop-keeper accepted the customer's offer to buy.… If one were to hold that in the case of self-service shops the contract was complete directly the purchaser picked up the article, serious consequences might result. The property would pass to him at once and he would be able to insist on the shop-keeper allowing him to take it

away, even where the shop-keeper might think it very undesirable. On the other hand, once a person had picked up an article, he would never be able to put it back and say that he had changed his mind. The shop-keeper could say that the property had passed and he must buy.… Therefore, in my opinion, the mere fact that a customer picks up a bottle of medicine from a shelf does not amount to an acceptance of an offer to sell, but is an offer by the customer to buy. I feel bound also to say that the sale here was made under the supervision of a pharmacist. There was no sale until the buyer's offer to buy was accepted by the acceptance of the purchase price, and that took place under the supervision of a pharmacist. Therefore, judgment is for the defendants [Boots].

The case went in appeal to the Court of Appeal, the second highest court of the UK. Somervell, LJ, approving the judgment of the Queen's Court noted:

… one of the most formidable difficulties in the way of the plaintiffs' case [Pharmaceutical Society]… if they were right, once an article has been placed in the receptacle the customer himself is bound and he would have no right, without paying for the first article, to substitute an article which he saw later of the same kind and which he preferred. I can see no reason for implying from this arrangement any position other than that… it is a convenient method of enabling customers to see what there is for sale, to choose, and, possibly, to put back and substitute, articles which they wish to have, and then go to the cashier and offer to buy what they have chosen. On that conclusion the case fails, because it is admitted that in those circumstances there was supervision in the sense required by the Act and at the appropriate moment of time.

If the offer could be made by the customer only on reaching the cashier's point, how do we understand the display of products in the store? The display was not an offer; it was only an invitation to the potential customer to select goods and take them to the cashier to make an offer. In other words, the display is an invitation to offer. Thus, a self-service store is justified in refusing to sell goods selected by a customer. This could be for several reasons.

[4] *Pharmaceutical Society of Great Britain* v. *Boots Cash Chemists (Southern) Limited*, (1953) 1 All ER 482.
[5] Ibid.

First, the store may have wrongly priced the goods. In this case, the store can refuse to sell at the mentioned price and agree to sell to the customer only at the revised price. Second, the store could have put up the goods for sale by mistake. In this case, the store can refuse to sell the goods altogether. Third, a customer could be taking away a large inventory of the goods to the disadvantage of the store. The store can prevent this by refusing to sell to the customer.

The position of the law is at variance with the common-sense understanding of the customer. The customer, conscious of his consumer rights, feels that when he selects the goods, the store should be made to sell them to him. Irrespective of this, the position that a customer has a right to the selected goods would be beneficial to the consumers. Thus several writers have attempted to critique the position of the law. The most promising direction is to claim that the shop makes an offer by displaying goods on the shelves and the customer accepts it by taking it to the cash counter. In effect, at the cashier's counter the customer says, 'I have accepted your offer to buy these things.' In this interpretation, the customer is left with the freedom to put items back on the shelf after having picked it up.

If both parties, that is, the customer and the store, work towards an interpretation beneficial to the customer, the above position can be reached. If this were the case, no dispute would ever rise between the parties. The stores would always accommodate the customers. In fact, a good deal of this has been happening in the West in a market that is highly competitive. A store is much better off earning the goodwill of the customer than getting involved in the legality of the respective rights. Despite this, however, disputes do arise between parties, and the law has to settle the point.

The response of the store is simple. Let us go with the argument that the display of goods on the shelves by the store is an offer to the customer. The offer can either be accepted or rejected. The offer is a continuing one. Only when the customer goes out of the shop can we can say that the customer rejected the offer for all the things he did not buy. When the customer picks up an item from the shelf, he is responding to the offer. If the customer examines the product and puts it back on the shelf, he has shown his disinterest. However, when he puts it in the trolley, he has responded to the offer. The store understands it to be acceptance of the offer. If the customer were free to contend that his act is not acceptance, the store should also be free to contend that its act of displaying goods on shelves was not an offer but only an invitation to offer. Formation of agreement, we must remember, is about the meeting of minds, not divergence of minds.

It has been suggested that the Boots case was about a statutory law and punishment for an offender. It was not about contractual rights and obligations between the store and the buyers. The suggestion is that the court would have taken a different position if it were a case between the store and the buyers. Ewan McKendrick comments:[6]

In terms of the outcome of the case, the important factor was the place at which the contract was concluded, rather than the precise way in which the contract was concluded. It sufficed for the court to decide that the contract was concluded at the cash-desk and thus under the supervision of the pharmacist. The court could have concluded that the offer was made by the shop in displaying the goods for sale at fixed prices, but that the offer was not accepted by the customer until the goods were taken

[6] Ewan Mckendrick (2008), *Contract Law: Text Cases and Material*, 3rd edition (Oxford: Oxford University Press), p. 67.

to the cash-desk. In such a case the contract would still have been concluded under the supervision of the pharmacist. But this was not the reasoning that the court chose to employ. It treated the display as an invitation to negotiate and stated that the offer was made by the customer which the defendants could then decide whether to accept or reject.

This reasoning is not adequate. The manner in which a contract is formed will settle the question of the place where the contract is made. The court was rightly addressing the question of the way in which an agreement was formed in a self-service store. Further, if the customer were to accept the goods at the cash-desk, the agreement would have been without pharmacist supervision. The moment the customer gave his basket to the cashier, even before the cashier or the pharmacist could examine the contents, an agreement would have been made. Thus, in a self-service store, the customer offers at the cashier's desk and the store accepts. However, this may change if the store puts up terms and conditions or makes further communications. We would have to examine this additional communication. An interesting case is *Lefkowitz* v. *Great Minneapolis Surplus Store, Inc.*,[7] a decision of the Supreme Court of Minnesota, USA.

Court Case: Lefkowitz v. Great Minneapolis Surplus Store, Inc

Lefkowitz responded to the following advertisement published by Great Minneapolis Surplus Store, Inc. in a Minneapolis newspaper:

Saturday 9 A.M. Sharp
3 Brand New Fur Coats Worth to $100.00
First Come First Served $1 Each

[7] *Lefkowitz* v. *Great Minneapolis Surplus Store, Inc,* 86 N.W.2d 689, (Minn. 1957).

He was the first one at the counter to buy the advertised goods. The store refused to sell him the goods. They claimed that according to the 'house rule' of the store, the offer was intended for women only. Lefkowitz claimed that an agreement was formed between the parties. Excerpts from the judgment of the Supreme Court of Minnesota are as follows:

… where the offer is clear, definite, and explicit, and leaves nothing open for negotiation, it constitutes an offer, acceptance of which will complete the contract.… Whether in any individual instance a newspaper advertisement is an offer rather than an invitation to make an offer depends on the legal intention of the parties and the surrounding circumstances. We are of the view on the facts before us that the offer by the defendant (store) … was clear, definite, and explicit, and left nothing open for negotiation. The plaintiff having successful managed to be the first one to appear at the seller's place of business to be served, as requested by the advertisement, and having offered the stated purchase price of the article, he was entitled to performance on the part of the defendant (store).… The defendant contends that the offer was modified by a 'house rule' to the effect that only women were qualified to receive the bargains advertised. The advertisement contained no such restriction. This objection may be disposed of briefly by stating that, while an advertiser has the right at any time before acceptance to modify his offer, he does not have the right, after acceptance, to impose new or arbitrary conditions not contained in the published offer.

Since the *Pharmaceutical Society of Great Britain* v. *Boots Cash Chemists (Southern) Limited* case in 1953, there has been tremendous expansion of the economy, competition and the rise of consumerism, particularly in developed countries. The expectations of a consumer are different from what the law provides. Atiya comments: '… law is today out of touch with modern social conditions … Most people would probably be surprised to discover that a shopkeeper is not obliged to sell an article at the price indicated if a customer offers to pay for it ...'[8]

Contract law is foundational and commonsensical. It asks basic questions on the processes of human communication. It would be arbitrary to change the answer because customers have come to have different expectations. The elegance of contract law is in its simplicity. In addressing complex contemporary questions, the courts base their responses on the simple foundational principles. It is for the legislature to build on the foundation of contract law by making acts to address emerging expectations of the consumers and to regulate business practices and contracts. A trader not selling goods at the advertised or marked price could constitute a false bargain and an unfair trade practice under the Consumer Protection Act. The consumer courts can direct the trader to stop the practice. However, a mere display in the show window or shelves does not create a contractual relationship.

Advertisements

An advertisement is only a communication. The content of the communication decides whether it is an offer or not. We have already reviewed the *Lefkowitz* v. *Great Minneapolis Surplus Store, Inc.* case, which relates to advertisement. A classic case on advertisement is the Carbolic Smoke Ball[9] case.

Court Case: Carbolic Smoke Ball

Carbolic Smoke Ball Limited. manufactured a device for dispensing medicine for the prevention of cold and influenza called a Carbolic Smoke Ball.[10] It was a hollow rubber ball with a nozzle at the top. Medicinal powder, also manufactured by the company, was to be put inside the ball. On compressing the ball, the powder was expelled, forming a cloud of infinitesimally small particles resembling smoke. Accordingly, the company had called the device a Smoke Ball. The company published the following advertisement on 13 November 1891 in London newspapers.

A £100 reward will be paid by the Carbolic Smoke Ball Company to any person who contracts the increasing epidemic influenza, colds, or any disease caused by taking cold, after having used the ball three times daily for two weeks, according to the printed directions supplied with each ball. £1000 has been deposited with the Alliance Bank, Regent Street, shewing our sincerity in the matter.

During the last epidemic of influenza, many thousands of carbolic smoke balls had been sold as preventives against this disease, and in no ascertained case was the disease contracted by those using the carbolic smoke ball.

One carbolic smoke ball will last a family several months, making it the cheapest remedy in the world at the price, 10s, post free. The ball can be refilled at a cost of 5s. Address, Carbolic Smoke Ball Company, 27, Princes Street, Hanover Square, London.

During 1890 to 1892, there was an epidemic of influenza in London. It was not necessarily life-threatening, but it was debilitating. A lady named Edina Carlill bought a smoke ball from a chemist. She had never had influenza before, but she was anxious to prevent its occurrence. She used it as directed, three times a day for two months. Despite the proper use of the smoke ball, not just for two weeks, but for two months, she contracted influenza. She claimed from the Carbolic Smoke Ball Limited 'the 100 pounds promised in your advertisement and in accordance with the contract between us.' The company

---

[8] Stephen A. Smith (2006), *Atiyah's Introduction to the Law of Contract*, 6th edition (New Delhi: Oxford University Press), p. 42.

[9] *Carlill* v. *Carbolic Smoke Ball Company*, (1983) 1 QB 256.

[10] Ibid.

refused to pay and Ms Carlill took the matter to court. The company contended that the advertisement was vague and uncertain and, hence, not an offer capable of being accepted. The court ruled:

Read the advertisement how you will, and twist it about as you will, here is a distinct promise expressed in language which is perfectly unmistakable—'£100 reward will be paid by the Carbolic Smoke Ball Company to any person who contracts the influenza after having used the ball three times daily for two weeks according to the printed directions supplied with each ball. ... The deposit is called in aid by the advertiser as proof of his sincerity in the matter—that is, the sincerity of his promise to pay this £100 in the event which he has specified.

The essence of the judgment is that an advertisement is only a communication. We need to explore what is being communicated to decide whether it is an offer or not. The case is also a founding one on the subject of unilateral contract and consideration. We will return to the case in subsequent chapters.

Signed Documents

Increasingly, business contracts have come to be in writing. A common business practice is for the trader or service provider to prepare a standard pre-printed form and for the customer to sign it. Businesses in all fields, including banking, insurance, carriage, electricity, telecommunications, and travel, have come to require the customer to sign a pre-printed standard form. This becomes the offer document, which the trader or service provider accepts. The trader, as he prepares the terms of the contract, casts everything in its favour. It excludes itself from liability for breach of contract or other losses suffered by the customer. For this reason, a term of this nature is called an 'exclusion clause'. The customer has no opportunity for negotiating the terms. It is a 'take it or leave it' decision for the customer. Even if the consumer goes to another service provider or seller, he will encounter another standard form. The terms are often set out in several pages. Even if the consumer labours to read through them, he has no option of negotiating them. Thus, most people do not even care to read the terms. They sign where it is required. Lord Diplock in *Schroeder Music Publishing Co Limited* v. *Macaulay* noted:

This [standard form of contract] is of comparatively modern origin. It is the result of the concentration of particular kinds of business in comparatively few hands. The terms ... have not been the subject of negotiation between the parties to it, or approved by any organisation representing the interests of the weaker party. They have been dictated by that party whose bargaining power, either exercised alone or in conjunction with others providing similar goods or services, enables him to say: 'If you want these goods or services at all, these are the only terms on which they are obtainable. Take it or leave it'.[11]

Denning in *Levison and Another* v. *Patent Steam Carpet Cleaning Co Limited*, took it further:

... the weaker party is not even told: 'Take it or leave it.' He is simply presented with a form to sign, and told: 'Sign here'; and so he does. Then later on, when the goods are lost or damaged, the form is produced, and the stronger party says: 'You have no claim. Look at the conditions on the form. You signed it and are bound by those conditions.[12]

The reason for the propagation of the standardization has been that it has greatly reduced the transaction cost. If a corporation were to negotiate and settle terms of contract with each customer, both the parties would have to spend great amount of time, energy

[11] *Schroeder Music Publishing Co Limited* v. *Macaulay*, (1974) 3 All ER 616.
[12] *Levison* v. *Patent Steam Carpet Cleaning Co. Limited*, Court of Appeal, Civil Division, (1977) 3 All ER 498.

and resources in doing it. Thus, standardization has led to efficiency and passing of the benefits to the customers. Are the terms set out in the standard forms binding? Are these terms binding even if the customer has not read the terms? Can the customer claim that the exclusion clauses do not apply as he was not aware of them? Can he claim that there was no meeting of minds as he did not know the contents of the documents? *L'Estrange* v. *F Graucob, Limited* is a leading case emphasizing that parties are bound to their signature, whether they have read the document or not.

Court Case: L'Estrange v. F Graucob, Limited

F Graucob, Limited manufactured cigarette vending machines.[13] L'Estrange, a café owner, was visited by a representative of the company, and she decided to buy a machine. The representative entered the relevant details of the purchase in a pre-printed form addressed to the manufacturer, gave it to her to sign it. The document read, 'Please forward me as soon as possible: One Six Column Junior IIam Automatic Machine…which I agree to purchase from you on the terms stated below…and to pay for the same in the following manner: ….'

Two days later, she received a document from F Graucob, Limited titled 'Order Confirmation'. Thus, the offer to buy the machine was made by L'Estrange through the signed form and accepted by the manufacturer through this written communication. The machine was delivered six weeks later. In a few days, the machine got jammed and became unworkable. The buyer demanded that the machine be taken back and the advance be returned. The document L'Estrange had

[13] *L'Estrange* v. *F Graucob, Limited*, (1934) 2 KB 394.

signed contained several clauses in small print. One of the clauses was to the effect that she would have no remedy even if the machine were defective and unworkable. Scrutton LJ for the Court of Appeal noted:

The main question raised is whether that clause formed part of the contract. If it did, it clearly excluded any condition or warranty.… In *Parker* v. *South Eastern Rail Co. Mellish*, LJ, laid down in a few sentences the law which is applicable to this case. He there said:

> 'In an ordinary case, where an action is brought on a written agreement which is signed by the defendant, the agreement is proved by proving his signature, and, in the absence of fraud, it is wholly immaterial that he has not read the agreement and does not know its contents.'

> …When a document containing contractual terms is signed, then, in the absence of fraud, or, I will add, misrepresentation, the party signing it is bound, and it is wholly immaterial whether he has read the document or not.…

> In this case the plaintiff has signed a document headed 'sales agreement,' which she admits had to do with an intended purchase and contained a clause excluding all conditions and warranties. That being so, the plaintiff (L'Estrange), having put her signature to the document and not having been induced to do so by any fraud or misrepresentation, cannot be heard to say that she is not bound by the terms of the document because she has not read them.

Maugham LJ delivered a concurring judgment, and expressed the following sentiment: 'I regret the decision to which I have come, but I am bound by legal rules and cannot decide the case on other considerations.' The documents signed by L'Estrange contained clauses in small print. Maugham noted that clauses were in 'regrettably small print, but quite legible'. A signed standard form, usually, is the offer. An offer can be invalid only if it uncertain, indefinite or ambiguous. A small but legible print does not make it any of this. However, a font so small that it cannot be read would make the offer uncertain.

Thus, having signed contract documents, parties are bound by it whether they have read the terms or not, or were aware of the terms or not. However, a contract secured through misrepresentation or fraud can be set aside by the innocent party. This is irrespective of the means—written, oral, or implied—by which a contract is formed. Scrutton LJ was referring to this as the only possible escape for L'Estrange from her signature. In a later case, Lord Denning has expressed the principle pithily:[14]

The present case is of importance because of the many instances nowadays when people sign printed forms without reading them, only to find afterwards that they contain stringent clauses exempting the other side from their common law liabilities. ... If the party affected signs a written document, knowing it to be a contract which governs the relations between him and the other party, his signature is irrefragable evidence of his assent to the whole contract, including the exempting clauses, unless the signature is shown to be obtained by fraud or misrepresentation.

Maugham expressed his helplessness in protecting the buyer from the excessive exclusion clause. In subsequent decades, the courts found other grounds for holding excessive exclusion clauses to be inoperative. We will take them up in a subsequent chapter. The Supreme Court of India has reiterated the law that the parties are bound by signed contracts in the *Bharati Knitting Company* v. *DHL Worldwide Express Courier* case.[15]

Court Case: Bharati Knitting Company v. DHL Worldwide Express Courier

Bharati Knitting Company, a manufacturer of apparel, exported a consignment of summer clothes to Germany.[16] Several documents are generated when goods are exported. These include the invoice, packaging list, original export certificate, certificate of origin, and bill of lading. The importer has to produce the documents to be entitled to receive the consignment. Bharati Knitting Company sent the documents to the German importer through DHL Worldwide Express Courier. The packet, containing the original documents, got lost in transit. The exporter, on learning of the non-delivery of the documents, sent a copy of the original documents to the importer. This time, the importer received the courier. The importer, using the copy of the original documents, could secure release of the consignment. By this time, however, summer was over. As the consignment was delayed, in damages, the German buyer paid only DM 35,000, instead of the invoice value of DM 56,469.[17] Bharati Knitting Company approached a consumer court to claim damages for deficient service provided by the courier company.[18]

DHL had a printed form that contained several terms and conditions. The DHL filled up the form with the details of the courier and required the sender to sign it. The terms and conditions, printed on the consignment note limited the liability of the courier company to a maximum of $ 100. The National Consumer Forum, in appraising the case, ruled:

It is manifest that the appellant (DHL) was negligent in not delivering the consignment to the consignee (German buyer) and due to the deficiency in service the consignment was lost ... thus ... there is deficiency in service and because of the negligence, loss has

[16] Ibid.

[17] DM, or deutschmark, was the German currency.

[18] Till the amendment of the Consumer Protection Act in 2002, companies could also approach a consumer forum for relief against deficient service.

[14] *Curtis* v. *Chemical Cleaning and Dyeing Co., Limited*, (1951) 1 All ER 631.

[15] *Bharati Knitting Company* v. *DHL Worldwide Express Courier*, AIR 1996 SC 2508.

occurred to the complainant (Bharati). However, we are of the view that the loss has to be restricted as per the terms of the contract … the liability of the appellant for any loss or damage to the shipment is limited to the lesser of US $ 100 or the amount of loss actually sustained or the actual value of the shipment without regard to the commercial utility or special value to the consignment. In this case, therefore, the loss has to be restricted to the sum of US $ 100.

The Supreme Court approved the judgment of the consumer court by reiterating the established law on contract: 'A person who has signed a document containing contract and terms is normally bound by them even though he has not read them, and even though he is ignorant of their precise legal effect.'

As noted earlier, the exception to the principle is in the cases where the signature is obtained through coercion, fraud, or misrepresentation. The courts are aware that customers are effectively made to sign documents without reading or knowing what the document contains. Where is the meeting of minds when a person does not know what he is signing? The courts do not take up this argument for obvious reasons. Signing of documents is not only for forming contracts. Public administration is based on signing of permissions, licenses, and orders. Signing a document has come to mean consent, authority, permission and approval. The economic and administrative order is based on written and signed records. Questioning the sanctity of signature would lead to a collapse of the system. For example, having signed a cheque, a person could raise the claim that he never intended to sign it or signed it without paying attention. Thus, the courts go by the objective criterion that a person who signs a document ought to have read and understood the document.

BUSINESS CONTRACTS

The Standard Contract Document was first developed by companies to do business with their customers. With the development of trade and commerce, its use was extended to business-to-business contracts. For example, even a medium-size manufacturing company buys thousands of items from hundreds of vendors. The items could range from computers for office use to furnace oil for boilers. Negotiating with each vendor for each order was time-consuming and expensive. Putting up standard terms on which an organization would buy from any person reduced the transaction costs significantly. The standard document would contain all the relevant details that could possibly arise in any contract of sale of goods, for example, the quality of goods, modalities of payment, transportation, insurance, delivery and dispute resolution. Such a document came to be called the General Conditions of Contract (GCC). An associated document, in contrast to GCC, is the Special Conditions of Contract (SCC). SCC contains terms specific to a particular contract, for example, the name of the seller, quantity of the goods ordered and the time and place of delivery. The SCC has also become standardized with minimal details to be entered in pre-printed forms.

The standardization has progressed even further. Every organization has to buy goods for similar uses. Thus, a new organization need not reinvent the wheel by writing its own GCC. It can borrow from one of the existing ones. From here, it was only a short step for standard industry-wide GCCs to emerge. For example, the World Bank has come up with a GCC on buying of goods, which is very popular. This is adopted by organizations worldwide. A professional body, the International Federation of Consulting

Engineers (FIDDIC), has come up with GCC for several business activities. A company can buy a licence to use the document. The shipping industry has its own standard contract documents. There is a similar mushrooming of standard documents for different sectors and activities. Law persons, increasingly, have come to work with a GCC rather than negotiate and design terms of a contract.

Auction

Auction is a means to find a party to contract with. Its advantage is in making all the interested parties compete with each other. Conventionally, an auction is concluded when the auctioneer strikes a hammer. Thus, striking of the hammer implies acceptance by the auctioneer of the offer put up by the last bidder. In an auction, the bidders make offers and auctioneer accepts it. As the highest bid is also only an offer, the auctioneer is free to accept or reject it. Following this, announcement of an auction is only an invitation to offer. *Harris* v. *Nickerson* has established this.[19] An auction was advertised in the newspapers, but the advertised goods were not put to auction. Mr Harris, who had come from another city to participate in the auction, claimed train fare and money for loss of two days. The court noted on the contention put by Harris:

… the advertisement amounted to a contract by the defendant with anybody that should act upon it, that all the things advertised would be actually put up for sale, and that he would have an opportunity of bidding for them and buying. This is certainly a startling proposition, and would be excessively inconvenient if carried out. It amounts to saying that any one who advertises a sale by publishing an advertisement becomes responsible to everybody who attends the sale for his cab hire or travelling expenses.

[19] *Harris* v. *Nickerson* (L R) 8 QB 286.

Thus, an invitation to attend an auction is a pre-contract activity. No contractual obligations arise till a contract is formed. In addition, however, if the invitation to attend the auction and its cancellation were done as a mischief or to commit fraud, it would attract criminal charges. The advertiser could be prosecuted and even punished. Further, it may become a case of a false bargain, and thus an unfair trade practice, under the Consumer Protection Act, 1986. The act has provisions to direct the person to stop the practice of false bargain. However, there would still be no contractual obligations for the parties. Thus, an advertisement for an auction is only an invitation to offer. A later case, *British Car Auctions Limited* v. Wright, emphasized the same point.[20]

British Car Auctions Limited was engaged in the auction of cars. In everyday language, it was common to describe an auctioneer as a person who 'offers to sell.' In fact, some of the documents of the company, for example, the printed form of the company, to be completed and signed by the owner of the car, read: 'I/We hereby authorise British Car Auctions Limited., to offer the said vehicle for sale in accordance with the said conditions.' The company, however, was conducting an ordinary auction. Some of its terms read: 'The auctioneer may without giving any reason therefore refuse to accept the bidding of any person or persons ... On the fall of the hammer a contract of sale is completed between the person or persons signing the Entry Form in respect of the vehicle concerned and the purchaser.'

A car put to auction by the company was not road-worthy due to defects in the steering

[20] *British Car Auctions Limited* v. *Wright*, (1972) 3 All ER 462.

gear and a tyre. Under the Road Traffic Act, 1960, it was an offence to sell or offer to sell a car that was not road-worthy. The car was, however, sold by the owner. The question was whether the auctioneer had made an 'offer to sell' to be prosecuted under the law. Lord Widgery, CJ noted:

I confess that, free of authority, I should have thought that the colloquial acceptance of an auctioneer as a person who offers the goods for sale is so strong that the use of a phrase such as 'offer for sale' in a statute of this kind might readily be construed as including the function of the auctioneer when he carries out an auction in the ordinary way. But, of course, as a matter of strict law of contract, forgetting for the moment the colloquial meaning of the phrase 'offer for sale', the auctioneer when he stands in his rostrum does not make an offer to sell the goods on behalf of the vendor; he stands there making an invitation to those present at the auction themselves to make offers to buy. In the strict law of contract there is no doubt whatever that has always been the law, that when an auction sale takes place, the offer comes from the bidder in the body of the hall and the acceptance is communicated by the fall of the auctioneer's hammer. It is technically incorrect to describe an auctioneer as offering the goods for sale for that reason.

The auctioneer, of course, is free to introduce terms of auction and provide otherwise. For example, as most government auctions do, the terms mention that contract would be formed only after the selected person deposits the security money and signs the contract. In this case, a contract is not concluded on the striking of the hammer. The auction was only a means to identify a person with whom contract could be made later. The legal position, that in an auction the highest bid is only an offer that the auctioneer can accept or reject, weakened the economic advantages of an auction. If the bidder had a good deal, the auctioneer could simply reject the offer and not strike the hammer. As a result, the participation in an auction could be indifferent.

To regain the advantages of auction, traders modified the position of the law by announcing that the auctioneer was bound to accept the highest bid. This came to be called auction 'without reserve'. 'Without reserve' meant that the auctioneer did not reserve the right to turn down the highest offer. In contrast, auctions that did not announce that they were 'without reserve' came to be called auction 'with reserve'. The main reason for an auctioneer to turn down the highest bid was the price. Thus, auctions indicated a minimum price called the 'reserve price'. The auctioneer bound himself to sell if the highest bid was higher than the reserve price. If an auction does not mention it otherwise, it is an auction 'with reserve'. A landmark case on auction 'without reserve' is *Warlow* v. *Harrison*. Harrison put up the following advertisement for 'without reserve' auction for the sale of a race mare: 'The property of a gentleman, without reserve, Tenet Pride, a brown mare without white, five years old, by Jago out of Stormy Petrel. For performances see "Racing Calendar."'

Warlow made a bid for £60. Thereafter, another person, Henderson made a bid for £61. Warlow, to his dismay, was informed that Henderson was the owner of the horse. As a result, he made no further bids. Henderson had bid as he was not happy with the price he was getting. The auctioneer knocked down the mare to him and entered his name as the purchaser in the sale book. Warlow went at once into the auctioneer's office and claimed he was the last bona fide bidder and, thus, the rightful buyer in an auction without reserve. The auctioneer maintained that the mare was knocked down in favour of the highest bidder, Mr Henderson. The court ruled that the owner could not also be the buyer, and thus, the bid by Henderson was not valid. The auctioneer should not have accepted it. Alternately, a bid from the owner can be constructed to communicate that the authority to sell on behalf of the owner was withdrawn. In this situation, the court noted:

We entertain no doubt that the owner may, at any time before the contract is legally complete, interfere and revoke the auctioneer's authority, but he does so at his peril, and if the auctioneer has contracted any liability in consequence of his employment and the subsequent revocation or conduct of the owner, he is entitled to be indemnified.

...

In a sale by auction there are three parties, namely, the owner of the property to be sold, the auctioneer, and the portion of the public who attend to bid, which includes the highest bidder. In this, as in most cases of sale by auction, the owner's name was not disclosed; he was a concealed principal. The names of the auctioneers ... alone were published, and the sale was announced by them to be 'without reserve.' This, according to all the cases, both at law and in equity, means that neither the vendor nor any person on his behalf may bid at the auction, and that the property shall be sold to the highest bidder whether the sum bid be equivalent to the real value or not.

Thus, as the bid of the owner was not valid, the last valid bid was by Warlow. In an auction 'without reserve', the auctioneer has to contract with the highest bidder. Thus, the court directed the sale in favour of Warlow. In an auction, ordinarily, bidders offer and the auctioneer accepts. An auction 'without reserve' does not fit into the formula of offer and acceptance. If the bidders were the offerors, the auctioneer would have the freedom to reject even the highest bid. If the auctioneer was the offeror, the very first bid would be the acceptance leading to a contract. However, when a bid is made, it is not known whether it will be the highest bid. Only subsequent events would decide this. Formation of agreement is about meeting of minds, its expression

in the language of offer and its acceptance is only procedural. The courts have held that the auctioneer is bound to the highest offer, even if it is not possible to identify the offer and acceptance. The decision of the Court of Appeal in *Barry* v. *Heathcote Ball & Co (Commercial Auctions) Limited*[21] is the latest attempt to think through this puzzle. The Court of Appeal, approving the reasoning of the lower court, noted:

... it would be the general and reasonable expectation of persons attending at an auction sale without reserve that the highest bidder would and should be entitled to the lot for which he bids. Such an outcome was in his view fair and logical. As a matter of law he held that there was a collateral contract between the auctioneer and the highest bidder constituted by an offer by the auctioneer to sell to the highest bidder which was accepted when the bid was made.

In other words, effectively, the auctioneer has put up an offer to everyone that if the person emerges as the highest bidder, the contract would be made with him. The bid, irrespective of its final outcome, depending on whether it eventually turned out to be the highest bid or not, was acceptance of the offer to create an agreement associated with or supportive of the main offer. Thus, it was called a collateral contract between the auctioneer and every bidder.

Tender

As trade and commerce expanded, parties came to be increasingly distant from each other. Tender became an effective means of selling goods or getting a service contract performed. Persons could be requested to express their interest in writing. The person inviting tender could select the best party to contract with. To tender is only to com-

---

[21] *Barry* v. *Heathcote Ball & Co (Commercial Auctions) Limited*, (2001) 1 All ER 944.

municate. We need to explore the import of the communication. In most tenders, the communication is so structured that the tender is an offer and the party inviting the tender accepts or rejects it. The 'notice inviting tender' is an invitation to offer. Often, the tendering party has a tender form. This is the offer document. The bidder procures it from the party inviting tender and submits its 'bid' or 'offer' in this form. In some situations, the party inviting tender knows exactly what it wants; for example, a particular make and model of machinery. The tender document mentions the details and the parties are only to mention the price, that is, the financial bid. In other situations, the party inviting the tender may not have the details of the subject matter of the contract. An example of this is building available for hire. In such cases, the two-bid system, a technical bid and a financial bid, is followed. The bidder is required to furnish the technical details, for example, the features of the premises, and the financial bid. The technical bid is not actually a bid. It only provides information. The party inviting tender appraises the bids to select a party to contract with. A tender is only a means to identify parties to contract with, and the parties must settle on the terms of contracts. The party inviting tender would have a GCC, and the notice to tender and tender document would mention it.

In some cases, a tender may be so worded for it to be an offer. In the cases posed under the heading tender in the previous chapter, the tender for supply of sugar by the sugar manufacturing company was only a perpetual offer, a 'standing offer'. Each order from the food processing company is an acceptance of the offer. The initial acceptance of the tender is only a concurrence to the standing offer. If the hotel had rejected it, the offer would have been extinguished and the hotel would have

lost the right to place orders on the manufacturer. The initial acceptance only keeps the offer alive. Till an order is placed, there is no binding agreement between the parties for the supply of the goods.

A case relating to this is the *Great Northern Railway Company* v. *Witham*.[22] Following an invitation to tender, Witham submitted the following communication: 'I hereby undertake to supply the Great Northern Railway Company, for twelve months, from … with such quantities of each or any of the several articles named in the attached specifications as the company's store-keeper may order from time to time, at the price set opposite each article respectively.' The company's officer wrote in reply: 'I am instructed to inform you that my directors have accepted your tender … to supply this company at Doncaster station any quantity they may order during the period ending 31st of October, 1872, of the descriptions of iron mentioned on the enclosed list, at the prices specified therein.' The court held that the tender from Witham was a standing offer that the company could accept at any point of time during the year. A case on tender from the Supreme Court of India is the *Union of India* v. *Maddala Thanthaiah*.[23]

Court Case: Union of India v. Maddala Thanthaiah

General Manager of the Madras and Southern Mahratta Railway invited tenders for the supply of jaggery.[24] The quantity and schedule of supply was as follows: '3,500 *maunds* on 1 March 1948; 3,500 *maunds* on 22 March

[22] *The Great Northern Railway Company* v. *Witham*, (L R) 9 CP 16.
[23] *Union of India* v. *Maddala Thanthaiah*, AIR 1966 SC 1724.
[24] Ibid.

1948; 3,500 *maunds* on 5 April 1948; and 3,500 *maunds* on 21 April 1948.' *Maund* was a measure of weight. Clause 2 of the tender provided: 'This Administration reserves the right to cancel the contract at any stage during the tenure of the contract without calling up the outstandings on the unexpired portion of the contract.'

The tender submitted by Maddala Thanthaiah was accepted by the Railways. However, after he supplied the first instalment, by a letter dated 8 March 1948, he was informed that the balance quantity of jaggery outstanding be treated as cancelled and the contract closed. Maddala Thanthaiah protested, but the railway administration took the stand that the right to cancel the contract at any stage was reserved to it. In deciding the tender to be only a standing offer, the Supreme Court noted:

Reference may also be made to what is said in 'Law of Contract', by Cheshire and Fiftoot (5th Edition) at p. 36.

'There is no doubt, of course, that the tender is an offer. The question, however, is whether its "acceptance" by the corporation is an acceptance in the legal sense so as to produce a binding contract. This can be answered only by examining the language of the original invitation to tender. There are at least two possible cases. First, the corporation may have stated that it will definitely require a specified quantity of goods, no more and no less as for instance, where it advertises for 1,000 tons of coal to be supplied during the period January 1st to December 31st. Here the "acceptance" of the tender is an acceptance in the legal sense, and it creates an obligation. The trader is bound to deliver, the corporation is bound to accept, 1,000 tons and the fact that delivery is to be by installments as and when demanded does not disturb the existence of the obligation'

On the basis of this note, the acceptance of the respondent's tender by the Deputy General Manager may even amount to a contract in the strict sense of the term, but we do not consider it in that sense in view of the provisions of Paras 8 and 9 of the tender requiring a deposit of security and the placing of the formal order.

The other case illustrated by Cheshire and Fiftoot is:

'Secondly, the corporation advertises that it may require articles of a specified description up to a maximum amount, as, for instance, where it invites tenders for the supply during the coming year of coal not exceeding, 1,000 tons altogether, deliveries to be made if and when demanded, the effect of the so-called 'acceptance' of the tender is very different. The trader has made what is called a standing offer. Until revocation he stands ready and willing to deliver coal up to 1,000 tons at the agreed price when the corporation from time to time demands a precise quantity. The 'acceptance' of the tender, however, does not convert the offer into a binding contract, for a contract of sale implies that the buyer has agreed to accept the goods. In the present case the corporation has not agreed to take 1,000 tons, or indeed any quantity of coal. It has merely stated that it may require supplies up to a maximum limit.'

'In this latter case the standing offer may be revoked at any time provided that it has not been accepted in the legal sense; and acceptance in the legal sense is complete as soon as a requisition for a definite quantity of goods is made. Each requisition by the offeree is an individual act of acceptance which creates a separate contract.'

The Supreme Court concluded: 'We construe the contract between the parties in the instant case to be of the second type.' In all cases of formation of contracts, one has to go by the substance of the communication than its nomenclature. Just by the name, a tender is neither an offer nor an acceptance of offer. It depends on the substance of the communication between the parties. In this case, the terms on which tender was invited made it clear that it was only a standing offer. Thus, each order formed an agreement for the supply of the quantity mentioned in the order.

The wording of a tender can as well make the solicitation of tender an offer and the tender acceptance. The case on this is *Harvela Investments Limited* v. *Royal Trust*

Company of Canada Limited.[25] A shareholder of a company was looking to sell his shares to the two other shareholders. He made them compete through a tender to get a good price. The terms of soliciting tender stated: 'We confirm that if any offer made by you is the highest offer received by us we bind ourselves to accept such offer.' A dispute arose on the formation of agreement. The Court of Appeal noted: '... the clause confirming ... to accept the highest offer received by them made it clear that it was not a mere invitation to treat. ... It was either an offer which when the highest bid was received completed a contract of sale or at least completed a contract to enter into a contract of sale.'[26]

Like the case of auction 'without reserve', the court was clear that a contract had been formed with the higher bidder. The challenge was to cast it in the language of offer and acceptance. The invitation of tender was definitive enough to be actually an offer. The offer got completed by the act of putting in the higher bid.

Internet

The internet is a new medium by which people have come to communicate. Is communication through the internet an offer or invitation to offer? The internet is only a medium; it depends on what is put up on the internet. A lot of material on the internet are advertisements, quite like advertisement in the newspapers. Web pages display goods along with prices. These are like displays on shop windows and thus, invitations to offer. Several web pages, however, also sell goods and services online or through e-shopping. Thus, a web page is everything at the same time, a newspaper advertisement, a display on the shelf, and a shop window, as well as a shop.

In the case of online shopping, invariably, the offer would come from the customer, along with payment through a credit card and acceptance from the seller. The acceptance can be the printing of the ticket in the case of railways or airlines or confirmation of sale order in the case of goods. Once the payment is received, the servers are programmed to generate the auto-acceptance. There is no gain in manually processing offers submitted by the customers. It will take away the advantages of automation. Thus, on most web pages, a response to an offer from the customer, which can potentially be an acceptance, is auto-generated. If the web page makes a mistake in putting up the items and their prices, it may end up in an agreement with the customers to supply goods at the mentioned price. Many contracts may get concluded before the merchant realizes the mistake and corrects it. A case illustrating the point is the decision of the Singapore High Court in *Chwee Kin Keong and Others v. Digilandmall.com Private Limited.*[27] The court put the matter succinctly:

There is no real conundrum as to whether contractual principles apply to Internet contracts. Basic principles of contract law continue to prevail in contracts made on the Internet. However, not all principles will or can apply in the same manner that they apply to traditional paper-based and oral contracts. It is important not to force into a Procrustean bed principles that have to be modified or discarded when considering novel aspects of the Internet.

Website advertisement is in principle no different from a billboard outside a shop or an advertisement in a newspaper or periodical. The reach of and

---

[25] *Harvela Investments Limited v. Royal Trust Company of Canada (Ci) Limited*, Court of Appeal, (1984) 2 All ER 65.

[26] Ibid.

[27] *Chwee Kin Keong and Others v. Digilandmall. com Private Limited.*, (2004) 2 SLR 594.

potential response(s) to such an advertisement are however radically different. Placing an advertisement on the Internet is essentially advertising or holding out to the world at large. A viewer from any part of the world may want to enter into a contract to purchase a product as advertised. Websites often provide a service where online purchases may be made. In effect the Internet conveniently integrates into a single screen traditional advertising, catalogues, shop displays/windows and physical shopping.

...

Historically, the common law has recognised an anomaly in the contractual features pertaining to a display of goods for sale. The goods are not on offer but are said to be an invitation to treat. The prospective buyer has to make an offer to purchase which is then accepted by the merchant. While this is the general principle for shop displays, it is open to a merchant to offer by way of an advertisement the mechanics of a unilateral or bilateral contract. This is essentially a matter of language and intention, objectively ascertained. As with any normal contract, Internet merchants have to be cautious how they present an advertisement, since this determines whether the advertisement will be construed as an invitation to treat or a unilateral contract. Loose language may result in inadvertently establishing contractual liability to a much wider range of purchasers than resources permit.

The known availability of stock could be an important distinguishing factor between a physical sale and an Internet transaction. In a physical sale, the merchant can immediately turn down an offer to purchase a product that has been advertised; otherwise he may be inundated with offers he cannot justify. ...

In an Internet sale, a prospective purchaser is not able to view the physical stock available. The web merchant, unless he qualifies his offer appropriately, by making it subject to the availability of stock or some other condition precedent, could be seen as making an offer to sell an infinite supply of goods. A prospective purchaser is entitled to rely on the terms of the web advertisement. The law may not imply a condition precedent as to the availability of stock simply to bail out an Internet merchant from a bad bargain, *a fortiori* in the sale of information and probably services, as the same constraints as to availability and supply may not usually apply to such

sales. Theoretically the supply of information is limitless. It would be illogical to have different approaches for different product sales over the Internet. It is therefore incumbent on the web merchant to protect himself, as he has both the means to do so and knowledge relating to the availability of any product that is being marketed. As most web merchants have automated software responses, they need to ensure that such automated responses correctly reflect their intentions from an objective perspective. Errors may incur wholly unexpected, and sometimes untoward, consequences as these proceedings so amply demonstrate.

The judgment establishes that the internet constitutes everything: advertisement, display window and shop. As we saw in the Carbolic Smoke Ball case, the wording of an advertisement can make it into an offer. Thus, the advertiser has to be clear on the language used and the intention conveyed. The problem of an advertiser inadvertently communicating an offer gets magnified in the case of the internet. In the ordinary case, the merchant will notice the mistake with the first response. In the case of the internet, as the responses are automated by software, the merchant may be bound by numerous contractual obligations before discovering the error.

To conclude, an agreement is formed on meeting of the minds. This is often assessed in identifying acceptance of an offer. An offer is distinguished from the communication preceding it, the invitation to offer. In this chapter, we reviewed the application of these principles by the courts to everyday practices and business relations. The principles have remained invariant; however, these have had to be applied to newer situations. In the 1950s, it was the self-service stores and in the 2000s, the internet. In the next chapter, we will explore different dimensions and means of the communication of acceptance and rejection of offer.

Acceptance and Rejection of Offer

Agreement is secured through a communicative process where one person offers and the other accepts the offer. In this chapter, we will explore different aspects, processes and details associated with the simple formulation that an agreement is formed on acceptance of an offer. An offer leads to an agreement on acceptance. However, an offer can also be extinguished for it to be capable of being accepted. Section 1 of the chapter explores how offers get extinguished. An offer can be extinguished when the offeror withdraws it or the other person rejects it. An offer also lapses on the expiry of the prescribed time of its validity. Section 2 explores the means to be followed for communicating acceptance. As agreement is about the meeting of minds, the acceptance should be directed to the person making the offer. An offer can prescribe the means for communicating acceptance, for example, requiring the acceptance to be in writing or performing certain actions. Section 2 explores compliance with it for securing a meeting of minds. We further develop our understanding of the principles on formation of agreements by applying these in deciding the unanswered cases in Section 3.

LAPSE OF OFFER, REVOCATION, AND REJECTION

Lapse of Offer

Zed Limited made an offer to sell 1,000 copies of a book for a total price of Rs 3 lakhs. The last line mentioned: 'The offer is open till 5.00 PM coming Friday'. The party to whom the offer was made communicated his acceptance on Saturday. Is an agreement formed between the parties? Agreements are about meeting of minds to reach a consensus. Zed Limited was available only till Friday for a meeting of minds to be secured. The offer expired at 5.00 PM, Friday. Thus, an offer gets extinguished on expiry of the specified time. It is standard business practice to mention a validity period for an offer.

Vijay offered to sell his second-hand car to Deep for Rs 3 lakhs. Deep communicated his acceptance after six months. In the meantime, Vijay had already sold the car to another person. Deep is claiming damages for breach of contract. Is an agreement formed between the parties? Do we take the long silence of Deep as an interest or disinterest in the offer? Silence implies disinterest. From the long silence, Vijay understood that Deep was not interested in the offer. A long silence impliedly communicates rejection of an offer. A case related to this is *Ramsgate Victoria Hotel Company Limited* v. *Montefiore*.[1] Montefiore applied for allotment of shares, with a deposit of £50, to Ramsgate Victoria Hotel Company. The company allotted him shares after six months. He contended that a long silence from the company amounted to rejection of the offer. The court held that as the shares were not allotted within a reasonable time, he was not bound to accept the shares. The principle has been thus explained in another case:

It has long been recognised as being the law that, where an offer is made in terms which fix no time limit for acceptance, the offer must be accepted within a reasonable time to make a contract. ... if the offeree does not accept the offer within a reasonable time, he must be treated as having refused it ... having failed to accept the offer within a reasonable time, he has manifested an intention to refuse it.[2]

What is a reasonable period of time would depend on the facts and circumstances of the case. On the stock market, even hours can be a reasonable period. In other situations, months can be a reasonable period for the person to communicate his decision. The *Ramsgate case* was decided in 1864. Since then, company law has significantly expanded and come to regulate application for allotment of shares, allotment and refund of money. The theme of long silence was explored in *Manchester Diocesan Council for Education* v. *Commercial and General Investments, Limited*.[3] The court attempted to work out the foundation for the principle:

It has long been recognised as being the law that, where an offer is made in terms which fix no time limit for acceptance, the offer must be accepted within a reasonable time to make a contract. There seems, however, to be no reported case in which the reason for this is explained.

There appear to me two possible views on methods of approaching the problem. First, it may be said that by implication the offer is made on terms that, if it is not accepted within a reasonable time, it must be treated as withdrawn. Alternatively, it may be said that, if the offeree does not accept the offer within a reasonable time, he must be treated as having refused it. On either view the offer would cease to be a live one on the expiration of what in the circumstances of the particular case should be regarded as a reasonable time for acceptance.

It does not seem to me that either party is in greater need of protection by the law in this respect than the other. Until his offer has been accepted it is open to the offeror at any time to withdraw it or to put a limit on the time for acceptance. On the other hand, the offeree can at any time refuse the offer...

The problem, however, would arise if the offer were accepted and the question of reasonable time were raised. The court would need to decide whether the offer was accepted within a reasonable time or not.

X made an offer to Y for the sale of computer accessories. Y could accept the offer by depositing a security amount of Rs 2 lakh in X's account by Friday, followed by acceptance of the offer. Y did not deposit the amount of money on Friday but communicated his acceptance. No agreement is formed between the parties as Y has not done what was required of him to accept the offer. Y is free not to accept the offer. However, acceptance would happen only when Y follows the conditions set by X.

X makes an offer to Y. X dies the next day but Y does not know of the death. Y sends a communication to the address of X accepting the offer. Is an agreement formed between the parties? Before examining the case, we will

[1] *Ramsgate Victoria Hotel Company Limited* v. *Montefiore*, (1866) LR 1 Ex 109.
[2] *Manchester Diocesan Council for Education* v. *Commercial and General Investments Limited*, Chancery Division (1969) 3 All ER 1593.
[3] Ibid.

need to become familiar with the implication of death on the property of the person. A person dies leaving behind a house in Delhi, some shares in a company and Rs two lakh in his bank account. The bank cannot appropriate the money; the tenant, the house; or company, the shares. The personal law governing the person decides how the property devolves on heirs. The property of the person is called his estate. By the same reasoning, the liability the person has incurred, for example, a loan, would also attach to his estate. In this case, the requirements of offer followed by acceptance are met. Thus, a binding contract is formed even if the offeror is dead. What if the person knew of the death of the offeror? In this case, there is no meeting of minds as X is not there. Thus, no agreement is formed between the parties. Thus, an offer lapses if the other party knows of the death of the offeror.

Revocation

Revocation is one of the means by which an offer is extinguished. X made an offer to Y and before Y could accept it, he communicated to Y the withdrawal of the offer. Y accepted the offer and claimed that an agreement was formed, as according to him, an offer once made could not be withdrawn. Till an offer is accepted, neither of the parties have obligations to each other. The person to whom the offer is made is free to reject the offer. Consistent with this, the person making the offer should also be free to withdraw the offer. Formation of agreement is a voluntary activity and a meeting of minds would be secured only when both the parties are willing. Withdrawal of offer is also called 'revocation of offer'. The founding landmark case on revocation of offer is *Pane* v. *Cave*.[4]

In an auction for a tub, the auctioneer, Pane, dithered on the last bid of Cave for £40. Pane was trying to get further bids. An impatient Cave said, 'Why do you dwell? You will not get more.' Pane replied that the tub was a very heavy one and was worth more than £40. Cave challenged him to have the tub weighed. The auctioneer ignored the suggestion. Following this, Cave declared that he would not buy the tub. The auctioneer had not struck the hammer as yet. The tub was sold the next day for £30. Pane claimed the balance of £10 as compensation for the breach of contract. The court ruled that no agreement was formed between the parties. It formulated: 'Every bidding is nothing more than an offer on one side which is not binding on either side till it is assented to. But according to what is now contended for, one party would be bound by the offer and the other not, which can never be allowed.' Thus, an offer can be withdrawn before it is accepted. The Indian Contract Act expresses the principle on revocation in Section 5:

Section 5. Revocation of proposals and acceptances—A proposal may be revoked at any time before the communication of its acceptance is complete as against the proposer, but not afterwards.

Let us consider a modified version where X makes an offer to Y that is open for ten days. X withdraws the offer on the third day. Is the withdrawal valid? The argument of *Pane* v. *Cave* case also applies to this withdrawal. The offeror cannot be bound to the offer if the other person is free to reject the offer. Thus, an offer can be revoked even if the offer has mentioned the period for which it is open. An alternate construction is that irrespective of the decision of Y, the parties have made a collateral agreement that the offeror would not withdraw the offer. However, the agreement is not binding and enforceable as

---

[4] *Pane* v. *Cave*, (1775–1802) All ER Rep 492.

it is not supported by consideration for both the parties. A landmark case on the theme is *Dickinson* v. *Dodds*.[5]

Court Case: Dickinson v. Dodds

John Dodds signed and delivered to George Dickinson an offer to sell a house that ended: 'P.S.—This offer to be left over until Friday, 9 o'clock, A.M. …12th June, 1874.'[6] Dickinson had made up his mind to accept the offer but did not communicate his decision as he thought he had time until Friday 9 a.m. to decide. As the court concluded, impliedly, the offer was revoked before the stipulated time. The court ruled that the postscript did not create an enforceable contract:

There was no consideration given for the undertaking or promise, to whatever extent it may be considered binding, to keep the property unsold until 9 o'clock on Friday morning … it is clear settled law, on one of the clearest principles of law, that this promise, being a mere nudum pactum, was not binding, and that at any moment before a complete acceptance by Dickinson of the offer, Dodds was as free as Dickinson himself.

A *nudum pactum* is a Latin expression that literally means 'bare promise', a promise not supported by a consideration from the other person. As the agreement lacked consideration, it was not enforceable. Section 6 of the Indian Contract Act expresses other means by which an offer can come to an end:

6. Revocation how made—A proposal is revoked

(1) by the communication of notice of revocation by the proposer to the other party;

(2) by the lapse of the time prescribed in such proposal for its acceptance, or, if no time is so prescribed, by the lapse of a reasonable time, without communication of the acceptance;

(3) by the failure of the acceptor to fulfil a condition precedent to acceptance; or

[5] *Dickinson* v. *Dodds*, (1876) 2 ChD 463.
[6] Ibid.

(4) by the death or insanity of the proposer, if the fact of his death or insanity comes to the knowledge of the acceptor before acceptance.

Rejection

In this section, we will explore different ways in which an offer can be rejected. X makes an offer to sell his car to Y, which Y rejects. The next day Y accepts the offer, but X has sold the car to another person in the meantime. Y claims that an agreement was formed when he accepted the offer. By rejecting the offer, Y extinguishes the offer and frees X of all future obligations. In metaphorical terms, if acceptance is fire to the gunpowder, rejection is water which dampens the gunpowder. Would it make any difference if Y rejected the offer by shaking his head rather than saying 'no' in words? The shaking of the head also communicates rejection to the offeror. The communication between the parties can be in express or implied terms. Implied communication is as effective as express communication. Thus, an offer can get extinguished by express or implied rejection.

Let us apply the principle to bargaining between two parties over the sale of a good. X says, 'Rs 30,000'. Y in reply says, '25,000'. X responds, '28,000'. Y says, 'Accepted.' The communication between the parties began with an offer from X. Y responded by another offer. The import of the communication was, 'I am not willing to buy for Rs 30,000. Would you sell it for Rs 25,000?' In other words, Y impliedly rejected the offer. Putting up another offer or changing the terms of an offer becomes an implied rejection of the offer, and thus a counter-offer. Finally, the offer from X for Rs 28,000 was accepted by Y to form a contract. In this case, the counter-offer changed the price. The change of term can be on schedule of delivery, quantity to be supplied or manner of performing the contract. As changing the terms of an offer amounts to impliedly rejecting the offer, it frees the offeror from the obligations of the offer. A judgment on the above themes is *Hyde* v. *Wrench*.[7]

Wrench offered to sell his farm to Hyde for £1,000. Hyde wrote back, offering to buy the house for £ 950 pounds. Wrench responded that he could not accept that offer. Hyde responded by communicating acceptance of the original offer for £1,000. Wrench received the communication, but was no longer interested. A dispute arose whether an agreement had been formed by Hyde letter's accepting the offer. The court ruled:

The defendant (Wrench) offered to sell it for £1,000, and if that had been at once unconditionally accepted, there would undoubtedly have been a perfect binding contract; instead of that, the plaintiff (Hyde) made an offer of his own, to purchase the property for £950, and he thereby rejected the offer previously made by the defendant (Wrench). I think that it was not afterwards competent for him to revive the proposal of the defendant, by tendering an acceptance of it; and that, therefore, there existed no obligation of any sort between the parties...

At times, a communication, while intending or purporting to accept an offer, changes the terms of the offer. This makes it an implied rejection and a counter-offer. As a result, the original offer is extinguished. The acceptance should be exactly of what is offered. For this reason, the principle is called the 'mirror image rule'. The acceptor only mirrors the offer. As the implications of the rule are serious, it is important to look at the correspondence between the parties carefully to distinguish between seeking clarifications or additional information from putting up another offer. A landmark case on the point is *Stevenson*

v. *McLean*.[8] To an offer from McLean to sell iron, Stevenson sent the following telegram: 'Please wire whether you would accept forty for delivery over two months, or if not, longest limit you would give.' McLean took this to be a counter-offer and sold the iron to another buyer. In the meanwhile, Stevenson communicated acceptance of the offer. The parties disputed whether a contract was formed between them or not. The court ruled:

... the form of the telegram is want of inquiry. It is not 'I offer forty for delivery over two months' which would have likened the case to Hyde v. Wrench ... Here there is no counter-proposal. The words are 'Please wire whether you would accept forty for delivery over two months, or if not, longest limit you would give.' There is nothing specific by way of offer or rejection but a mere inquiry which should have been answered and not treated as a rejection of the offer. This ground of rejection therefore fails.

Thus, it need be judged whether a communication is a counter-offer or only seeking information and clarifications about the offer. There is nothing that prohibits the parties from making communication other than provisional acceptance and counter-offer. One only has to ascertain that the communication is not a counter-offer.

COMMUNICATION OF ACCEPTANCE

To an offer, X responded, 'I accept the offer but I will confirm it tomorrow.' Thereafter, X did not get back to the offeror. The offeror claims that a contract is formed between the parties as X had indicated his acceptance. But X did not definitively accept the offer. His subsequent communication the next day could have been an acceptance or rejection. There was no meeting of minds as yet on the sale. A provisional or qualified acceptance is not an acceptance. An acceptance must be

---

[7] *Hyde* v. *Wrench*, (1840) 49 ER 132.

[8] *Stevenson* v. *McLean*, (1880) 5 QBD 346.

clear and definite. The Indian Contract Act states this principle in Section 7(1):

7. Acceptance must be absolute—In order to convert a proposal into a promise, the acceptance must—(i) be absolute and unqualified; …

Agreement is formed through a process of communication between two persons. Let us examine the relevance of modalities of communication. Suppose that X makes an offer to Y. Y tells Z that he has decided to accept the offer. Z informs X that Y has decided to go along with the offer. In the meantime, Y changes his mind and communicates his rejection of the offer to X. X claims that as both the parties were agreeable at one point of time, an agreement had been formed. Is this claim valid? A meeting of minds between two persons is secured when they direct communication at each other. Thus, acceptance must be directed and communicated to the person making the offer.

Let us consider another case. An application form for a college states that the names of the candidates selected for admission will be put up on the webpage of the college on 25 June. X saw his name on the list and saved the file. Later, he received a rejection letter from the college. X claims that his application (offer) was accepted when his name was put up in the list of the selected candidates. As contracts are voluntarily formed, the parties are free to set the terms of the contract. The parties are also free to decide the means or procedure of communication between them. As the acceptance must be the 'mirror image' of the offer, the initiative for specifying the means would be in the offer. Thus, an offer can specify the means by which communication of acceptance should be done. The other person is free to reject the offer. However, if he wishes to accept, a meeting of minds would happen only when the mode prescribed in the offer is followed. Thus, ordinarily, communication of acceptance should be directed to the offeror. However, as the offer itself stated that the acceptance should be done by placing it on the webpage, a contract for admission was formed the moment the list was put by the college on the webpage. A subsequent rejection is irrelevant as a contract has already been formed. Thus, an offer can specify the means of communication of acceptance. This should be followed. If the offer does not mention on the means of acceptance, it should be communicated to the person making the offer.

Let us consider the following scenario: A written offer mentions that acceptance should be done by returning a signed copy of the offer. The person to whom the offer was sent calls up the offeror on the phone and accepts the offer. The offeror points out that acceptance has to be sent as specified in the offer. It follows from our earlier examination that if the procedure mentioned in the offer is not followed, no agreement is reached between the parties. Consider the variation where the offeror, on receiving acceptance on the phone, does not insist on the procedure in the offer to be followed. It would be unfair if later he claimed that no agreement was formed as that procedure had not been followed. In this case, the parties have impliedly modified the procedure of communication mentioned in the offer. Thus, acceptance must be by the means of communication indicated in the offer. However, the offeror can waive the prescribed mode of communication.

Not all offers would specify the procedure of communication of acceptance. What would be an appropriate means of communication in the following situations? (1) An order placed for home delivery of pizza on the phone. (2) An offer for selling a shirt sent through email. (3) An offer from a roadside vendor for sale of a handkerchief. (4) A signed letter offering a person the assignment of conducting a training programme for school teachers. It is reasonable that a written offer should be accepted in writing and an oral offer is capable of being accepted orally. An offer on the phone could be accepted through the phone and offer through email by email.

Consider the following case: An offer states, 'If we do not hear from you within 15 days, we will understand that you have accepted our offer.' The person to whom the offer was sent did not send a rejection of the offer. The offeror claims that a contract is formed between the parties. Agreement is formed with communication. Silence is the opposite of communication and signifies disinterest and rejection. The offer, by turning silence into acceptance, has violated a basic principle of communication. The implication of allowing this would be grave. The easiest way of forcing a person into an agreement would be to swamp him with offers. Everyone would end up getting into agreements they never intended to get into. Thus, silence can only imply rejection, not acceptance. A case relevant to this is *Felthouse* v. *Bindley*.

Felthouse was negotiating with his nephew, John, for the sale of a horse.[9] He wrote to John, 'If I hear no more about him, I consider the horse is mine at £ 30 15s.' John did not send any reply. Six weeks later, John instructed an auctioneer, Bindley, to sell his farming stock. The horse was also catalogued as a farming stock. John told the auctioneer that the horse was already sold and not to be included in the property to be auctioned. The auctioneer inadvertently sold the horse, and later acknowledged his mistake in doing so. Felthouse claimed that Bindley should restore

[9] *Felthouse* v. *Bindley*, (1862) 142 ER 1037.

the horse back to him as it was already sold to him and was his property. The court ruled:

It is clear, therefore, that the nephew in his own mind intended his uncle to have the horse at…£30 15s.: but he had not communicated such his intention to his uncle, or done anything to bind himself. Nothing, therefore, had been done to vest the property in the horse in the plaintiff… when the horse was sold by the defendant. It appears to me that…there had been no bargain to pass the property in the horse to the plaintiff, and therefore that he had no right to complain of the sale.

Thus, silence does not amount to acceptance. Silence includes both express and implied communication. A person nodding his head may not have spoken, but is not 'silent', as he has communicated through other means. Let us become familiar with the expression of the principles on communication we have discussed in the India Contract Act. Section 2 establishes that a communicative process is secured by the parties directing communication to one another. It reads:

Section 2 (a) When one person signifies to another his willingness to do or to abstain from doing anything, with a view to obtaining the assent of that other to such act or abstinence, he is said to make a proposal:

(b) When the person to whom the proposal is made signifies his assent thereto, the proposal is said to be accepted. A proposal, when accepted, becomes a promise:

Section 3. Communication, acceptance and revocation of proposals—The communication of proposals, the acceptance of proposals, and the revocation of proposals and acceptances, respectively, are deemed to be made by any act or omission of the party proposing, accepting or revoking by which he intends to communicate such proposal, acceptance or revocation, or which has the effect of communicating it.

Section 7 provides on the procedure for acceptance of the offer. It reads:

Section 7. Acceptance must be absolute—In order to convert a proposal into a promise, the acceptance must—

(1) be absolute and unqualified;

(2) be expressed in some usual and reasonable manner, unless the proposal prescribes the manner in which it is to be accepted. If the proposal prescribes a manner in which it is to be accepted, and the acceptance is not made in such manner, the proposer may, within a reasonable time after the acceptance is communicated to him, insist that his proposal shall be accepted in the prescribed manner, and not otherwise; but if he fails to do so, he accepts the acceptance.

It need be noted that the person to whom the offer is made is free to deviate from the prescribed procedure. The onus of objecting to the deviation and insisting on the procedure in the offer being followed is left with the offeror. Silence of the offeror would amount to acceptance of the deviation from the prescribed procedure.

CASES FOR ANALYSIS

Apply the principles learnt on acceptance, provisional acceptance, rejection, and modalities of communication to the following cases.

Court Case: Compassionate Appointment

Food Corporation of India (FCI) introduced a voluntary retirement scheme on medical grounds. The inducement was to provide appointment to dependants of the employees. The terms of the scheme included the followings:

(a) The worker should seek voluntary retirement on medical grounds before completing the age of 55 years.

(b) Such request should be accompanied by a medical certificate issued by an Authorised Medical Officer, subject to verification by FCI.

(c) The benefit of compassionate appointment shall be given only to a male dependant, (of the age group between 18 years and 30 years), that too in the handling labour category, subject to an Authorised Medical Officer confirming the medical fitness of such dependant to handle/carry bags of big size.

(d) The application for compassionate appointment shall be made in the prescribed form, within three months from the date of retirement.

(e) Compassionate appointment will be given only in deserving cases, that is, where there is no earning member in the family of the retired worker, or where it is found that the financial benefits which are available to the worker on retirement will not be sufficient to meet the needs for running the family.'

The senior regional manager/regional manager was designated the competent authority under the scheme. The scheme provided the appointment was discretionary and not a matter of right. It stated:

Notwithstanding anything contained in the above, the compassionate ground appointment is not as a matter of right but purely at the discretion of the competent authority taking into the account the circumstances and conditions of the family of the medically retired workers and also subject to availability of the vacancy.

Mr Yadav, an employee in the Azamgarh Food Storage Depot of the FCI, made the following application, dated 26 April 1999, seeking voluntary retirement:

Sub: Appointment of my son Sri Ram Kesh in consideration of my retirement on medical ground…

… as I am unable to do handling work of loading due to inability of carrying bags, I desire to go on retirement on medical ground, if my above-named son would be provided with an employment in my place as handling labour. Further I am the only earning member of my family and on my retirement if none of my family is employed, the entire family would be put to suffer hardship. Kindly allow me to go on retirement on medical ground and provide employment to my above-named son in my place as handling labour…

Acting on the application, the competent authority, through a letter dated 29 July 2000, retired him from the service with effect from 31 July 2000. The Azamgarh Branch of FCI forwarded a proposal to its Lucknow Regional Office for the appointment of Ram Kesh Yadav on compassionate grounds. The Regional Office noted from the proposal and records that the date of birth of Mr Yadav was 6 February 1944. In the usual course, he would have attained the age of superannuation on 6 February 2004. Thus, he was not eligible under the scheme, and the Lucknow office rejected the proposal. Mr. Yadav had understood all along that his retirement and compassionate appointment went together. The son approached the court for appointment. Was the Lucknow office correct in rejecting the proposal?

Case: Voluntary Retirement

The Punjab National Bank came up with a voluntary retirement scheme for certain grades and class of employees who had completed 15 years of service or 40 years of age. The scheme gave several benefits, like gratuity, commuted pension, leave encashment and ex-gratia to make it attractive for the employees. Eligible employees, seeking voluntary retirement, were to submit the following signed application to the Zonal Manager through the Branch Manager.

1. I hereby offer to seek voluntary retirement from the services of the Bank in accordance with the terms and conditions stipulated in the PNB Employees' Voluntary Retirement Scheme, 2000 circulated vide Personnel Division Circular No. 1755 dated 29-9-2000, which I have carefully read and understood the contents of the same.

2. I accept the terms and conditions stipulated in PNB Employees' Voluntary Retirement Scheme 2000 unconditionally and irrevocably.

3. I furnished the required particulars in the APPENDIX enclosed for consideration of my offer to seek voluntary retirement from the service of the bank under the above scheme.
Yours faithfully,
(Name and signature)

The employee was also required to send a copy of the application directly to the Personnel Department, Head Office, in Delhi. The Branch Manager and Zonal Manager were to appraise the applications and also send their recommendations to the Head Office, who would take the final decision. The following were the general conditions of the scheme:

10.4. A mere request of an employee seeking voluntary retirement under the scheme will not take effect until and unless it is accepted in writing by the competent authority.

10.5. It will not be open for an employee to withdraw the request made for voluntary retirement under the scheme after having exercised such option.

10.6. The competent authority shall have absolute discretion either to accept or reject the request of an employee seeking voluntary retirement under the scheme depending upon the requirement of the bank. The reasons for rejection of request of an employee seeking voluntary retirement shall be recorded in writing by the competent authority. Acceptance or otherwise of the request of an employee seeking voluntary retirement will be communicated to him in writing.

The scheme attracted a large number of applications. Later, several employees sent letters to the employer withdrawing their application. The bank did not recognize the withdrawal of the application and proceeded to retire the employees. This led to disputes on the nature of the scheme and the right of the employees to withdraw their applications. Is voluntary retirement a contractual relationship? Identify the parties making the invitation to offer, offer, and acceptance. What are the different agreements one can delineate in the case? Could the employees have validly withdrawn their applications?

Court Case: National Highway Authority of India v. M/s Ganga Enterprises

The National Highway Authority of India invited tenders for collection of tolls on a portion of a highway running through Rajasthan.[10] The terms of tender required a bid security of Rs 50 lakhs to be submitted with the tender. The last date of submission of bids was 31 July 1997. Clauses 7.1 to 8 detailed the requirement of the bid security. It provided as follows:

7. Bid Security

7.1. The bidder shall furnish, as a part of his bid, a Bid Security in an amount of Rs. 50 lakhs (Rupees Fifty Lakhs only), or an equivalent amount in a freely convertible currency. The Bid Security shall, at the bidder's opinion, be in the form of a Bank Draft, or Guarantee from a Bank located in India. The Bank Guarantee shall be in the form of Bank Guarantee for Bid Security included herein, valid for 150 days after the last date of submission of the bid.

7.2. A bid not accompanied by an acceptable bid security shall be rejected by National Highway Authority of India as non-responsive.

7.3. The Bid Security of unsuccessful bidders will be returned by National Highways Authority of India as promptly as possible but not later than 30 days after the expiration of the period of bid validity.

7.4. The Bid Security of the successful bidders will be returned by National Highways Authority of India soon after the bidder has furnished the required Performance Security.

7.5 The Bid Security may be forfeited:

(a) if the bidder withdraws his bid during the period of bid validity...

8. Bid Validity

Bid shall remain valid for a period of 120 days after the last date of bid submission.

M/s Ganga Enterprises submitted a tender and furnished a bank guarantee of Rs 50 lakhs as bid security. In August, the technical bids were opened. In September, the financial bids were opened and M/s Ganga Enterprises was found to be the highest bidder. The National Highway Authority of India had not yet communicated its acceptance of the bid to Ganga Enterprises. M/s Ganga Enterprises withdrew its bid on 21 November 1997. The bids were valid for a period of 120 days, which would end on 28 November 1997. The Highway Authority accepted the withdrawal and forfeited the earnest money of Rs 50 lakhs. M/s Ganga Enterprises contested the forfeiture before the Delhi High Court. Was the forfeiture valid?

Court Case: Winn v. Bull

Bull, the owner of a house, made a written agreement with Winn to lease him the house for seven years for a stipulated rental.[11] The agreement had the following as the last line: 'This agreement is made subject to the preparation and approval of a formal contract.' The parties later contested whether the written agreement was binding. Is this true?

Case: Union of India v. M/s. Bhimsen Walaiti Ram

The Excise Department conducted an auction to award licenses to run liquor shops in Delhi.[12] The excise rules provided detailed rules and procedures for conducting the auction. Clauses 31 and 33 of the conditions of auction provided as follows:

31. The Chief Commissioner is under no obligation to grant any license until he is assured of financial status of the bidder. At the conclusion of the auction an enquiry will be made into the financial position of any bidder not known to the excise staff and any such bidder shall if necessary be called upon to furnish security for the observance of the terms of his licence as required by sub-section (2) of Section 34 of

[10] *National Highway Authority of India* v. *M/s Ganga Enterprises*, AIR 2003 SC 3823.

[11] *Winn* v. *Bull*, (1877) 7 ChD 29.

[12] *Union of India* v. *M/s. Bhimsen Walaiti Ram*, AIR 1971 SC 2295.

the Punjab Excise Act I of 1914, as extended to Delhi Province.

33. All final bids will be made subject to the confirmation by the Chief Commissioner who may reject any bid without assigning any reasons. If no bid is accepted for any shop, the Chief Commissioner reserves the right to dispose it of by tender or otherwise as he thinks fit…

Further, clause 21 of Rule 5.34 of the Excise Rules provided:

A person to whom a shop has been sold shall pay one-sixth of the annual fee within seven days of the auction…By the 7th of the month in which he begins his business under his license and by the 7th of every subsequent month the licensee shall pay one-twelfth of the annual fee till the whole fee is paid. But he may at any time pay the whole amount due if he wishes….

Bhimsen Walaiti Ram was the highest bidder in the auction. At the conclusion of the auction, he was required to pay one-sixth of the bid value, Rs 4,01,000, within seven days. The papers were sent for the approval of the Chief Commissioner. Bhimsen did not make the deposit. As a result, the Chief Commissioner did not confirm the bid of Bhimsen. The Excise Department organized another auction and awarded the license to the highest bidder. The highest bidder deposited the requisite amount and the bid was confirmed by the Chief Commissioner. The new bid was Rs 2,20,000, that is, Rs 1,81,000 less than Bhimsen's bid. Under Clause 22 of Rule 5.34, the Excise Department proceeded to recover the deficit from Bhimsen. Clause 22 provided:

When a license has been cancelled, the Collector may resell it by public auction or by private contract and any deficiency in price and all expenses of such resale or attempted resale shall be recoverable from the defaulting licensee in the manner laid down in Section 60 of the Excise Act as applied to the Delhi Province.

Bhimsen contested the recovery. Examine this case.

Court Case: Dresser Rand S.A. v. M/s. Bindal Agro Chem Limited

BINDAL Agro Chem Limited was setting up a fertilizer plant.[13] For this, it needed to procure equipment and materials domestically and from international suppliers. To this end, it prepared a standard set of documents. This included 'Instructions to Bidders' and 'General Conditions of Purchase' for buying plant and machinery. BINDAL got in touch with an international company, Dresser Rand S.A. (DR), for the supply of compressors for the plant. The representatives of the organizations met in Delhi to discuss the technical performance of the compressors manufactured by DR. DR proposed several modifications to the BINDAL's 'General Conditions of Purchase'. As the parties settled on a revised version after four revisions, the final version was called 'General Conditions of Purchase, Revision 4'. This document was signed by both the parties on 10 June 1991. The 'General Conditions of Purchase' of BINDAL contained 27 clauses. The following clauses in the fourth revision of the 'General Conditions of Purchase' are relevant to the case. The clauses are presented along with the revision by DR.

1. DEFINITIONS
In this General Conditions of Purchase the following terms shall be interpreted as indicated.
1.1 The PURCHASE ORDER means the agreement entered into between OWNER or by CONTRACTOR on behalf of OWNER and the SUPPLIER as recorded in the PURCHASE ORDER Form, signed by the parties, including all attachments and annexures thereto and all documents incorporated

[13] *Dresser Rand S.A.* v. *M/s Bindal Agro Chem Limited*, AIR 2006 SC 871.

by reference therein together with any subsequent modifications thereof in writing. [No change]

1.5 OWNER shall mean BINDAL AGRO CHEM LIMITED having their Registered office at Gopala Tower, 12th Floor, Rajindra Place, New Delhi 110 008, India, and shall include all their legal representatives, successors and assignees. [No change]

1.7 SUPPLIER or VENDOR shall mean the individual or firm supplying the GOODS and SERVICES under this PURCHASE ORDER. [No change]

27.3 Legal Construction

Subject to the provision of Article 27.4 the PURCHASE ORDER shall be, in all respects, construed and operated as an Indian Contract and in accordance with Indian Laws as in force for the time being and is subject to the jurisdiction of the Courts in Delhi. [Deleted]

27.4 Arbitration

27.4.1 In case of indigenous PURCHASE ORDERS all disputes which cannot be settled by mutual negotiations, the matter shall be referred for arbitration in accordance with Indian Arbitration Act,1940 of any statutory modification of enactment thereof for the time being in force. [Deleted]

27.4.2 In case of foreign SUPPLIER all disputes which cannot be settled by mutual negotiations shall be settled under the Rules of Conciliation and Arbitration of International Chamber of Commerce, Paris by one or more arbitrators appointed in accordance with rules. [No change]

27.4.4 The venue of Arbitration in all cases shall be Delhi and shall be conducted in English language only. (Deleted)'

On the conclusion of the negotiations between the representative of DR and BINDAL, the representative of BINDAL sprung a surprise on DR. They issued the 'Letters of Intent' not on their letterhead but of another company, K.G. Khosla Compressors Limited. (KGK). Two identical letters of intent, dated 12 June 1991 were issued, stating the intention to place an order for the following two compressors:

(a) One Dresser Rand Model 463 B.5/5 and one Model 373 BR8/1 vertically split compressor for Synthesis Gas Service and Steam turbine driver model SBQ at a price of FF 49,300,000 [French Francs].

(b) Two Dresser Rand Model 3M9.8 and Two Model 260-8B5/4 Centrifugal compressors for CO2 service and steam turbine driver Model QUBVT at a price of FF 52,625,000.

Except for the descriptions of the machinery and the price, the letters of intent were identical in their terms. Some of the relevant terms were as follows:

I. PURCHASE ORDER

This Letter of Intent will be followed by a regular and detailed Purchase Order to be issued by KGK simultaneous with the establishment of the Letter of Credit mentioned at para B of this letter.

C. TERMS AND CONDITIONS

The Purchase Order shall be subject to the 'General Conditions of Purchase' included in inquiry and as amended by DR's comments thereto, Revision 4 dated June 10, 1991, initialled by DR and KGK separately.

M. GOVERNMENT OF INDIA APPROVALS

This Letter of Intent is being issued subject to the necessary approvals to be given by Indian Government Authorities.

B. PRICE AND TERMS OF PAYMENT

1. ...

2. Payment shall be made through an irrevocable and confirmed Letter of Credit (Confirmation charges being to DR's account) allowing partial payments releasable in one or several drafts, and according to the terms and conditions of this Letter of Intent, to be opened by 31st August, 1991 by Bank of America, Barakhamba Road, New Delhi, or any other Bank acceptable to DR., notified and payable to DR by Bank of America, Paris. The said Letter of Credit will be construed in accordance with the Uniform Customs and Practices for Documentary Credits of the International Chamber of Commerce. Draft of such Letter of Credit is provided for in Attachment II of this Letter of Intent and is subject to changes proposed by KGK or its bankers and prior written agreement by DR or its bankers. The said Letter of Credit shall be valid for a period of 15 months from its notification to DR and shall be extendable by two (2) months period at DR's request in order to allow complete drawings of the said Letter of Credit.'

D. DELIVERY DATE

The delivery date (last shipment) shall be 15-1/2 (Fifteen and One Half Months) after DR's receipt of this Letter of Intent. For the purpose of assessing liquidated damages for delivery, delivery time shall be calculated on the basis of issuance of DR's Certificate of readiness to ship, after inspection by KGK or its authorized agents and in the event of their failure to do so, a declaration by DR that one month's notification of readiness to ship and invitation to inspect was given. The time lag between the first and the last shipment will not exceed 12 weeks.

G. OPTIONAL PERFORMANCE TEST

KGK has an option of asking DR to carry out shop performance test (PTC-10 class III) for the equipment described in this LOI for an extra price of FF. 875,020. The said option shall be exercised by 19th June, 1991 in writing by KGK. It is agreed that the delivery period described in para D of this letter shall be extended by three weeks in case performance test is desired to be carried out.

F. AUTHORIZATION TO PROCEED

This Letter of Intent shall serve as DR's authorization to proceed with this order.

L. ENTRY INTO FORCE

This contract will come into force upon receipt of this Letter of Intent by supplier.

If by August 31, 1991 KGK is unable to fulfil the obligations described in this LOI, the contract performance schedule and prices may be revised.

The representative of Bindal asked the representatives of DR to counter-sign a copy of the letter of intent and return it to them. DR obliged. The parties remained in communication for the remaining of 1991 and 1992. Bindal did not proceed any further. It sent the following communication to DR: 'Indian Government had pressurized BINDAL to buy Indian equipment and, therefore, BINDAL proposed to purchase the equipment from BHEL and not from DR.' This perhaps was only an excuse. BINDAL realized that DR was not a specialist in making the kind of compressors it needed. Following the arbitration clause in the 'General Conditions of Purchase, Revision 4', the parties had signed,

DR took the dispute in arbitration to ICC, Paris. In response, BINDAL and KGK filed an application in the Delhi High Court, for a declaration that there was no arbitration agreement between BINDAL and DR and for an injunction to be granted restraining DR from proceeding with the arbitration. The case came in appeal before the Supreme Court. The issues to be decided were: (i) Was there an arbitration agreement between DR and BINDAL; and (ii) Was there an arbitration agreement between DR and KGK?

Case: Life Insurance

The process followed by insurance companies to issue life insurance policies is as follows. The company has a standard pre-printed 'proposal' that the applicant has to fill in. The insurance companies have a panel of doctors. The applicant gets examined by a doctor and the doctor sends the report directly to the company. The premium amount to be paid as the first instalment is written on the form itself. A cheque for the premium amount has to be attached along with the form and submitted to the insurance company. Insurance companies have agents to get business and help customers.

Rohan, with the help of an agent, was examined by a doctor and submitted the proposal along with a cheque for the first premium. Three weeks later, Rohan noted that the insurance company had encashed the cheque. He felt relieved that his medical tests must have been positive, otherwise, the insurance company would not have taken the step of encashing his cheque. Unfortunately, a week later, Rohan died in an accident. Rohan's wife claimed the insurance money. The insurance company declined, claiming that there was no insurance contract between Rohan and the company. Is this claim correct?

Court Case: Forest Tender

The following case relates to the auction of forest rights to a 'coupe' by the Forest Department of the Government of Bihar.[14] The Forest Department auctions the right to harvest the standing forest on a patch of forest. A patch earmarked for harvesting is called a 'coupe'. A standard condition of the auction by the Forest Department was that a bid higher than Rs 5,000 could only be provisionally accepted by the Divisional Forest Office, subject to a confirmation by the chief conservator of forests and the Forest Department of the Bihar Government. Further, if the accepted bid was lower than the reserve price, the approval of the Finance Department would have to be taken.

The Forest Department advertised the auction of a coupe of Bamboo forests in the Hazaribagh district, which is now in Jharkhand. The Divisional Forest Officer conducted the auction on 7 August 1970. The reserve price for the auction was Rs 95,000. The highest bid, accepted by the Divisional Forest Office, was for Rs 92,001 by Haridwar Singh. According to the terms of auction, Haridwar Singh deposited a security amount of Rs 23,000 and signed the agreement. As the bid was higher than Rs 5,000, the acceptance had to be approved by the superior officers. Further, as the auction had been concluded for a price lower than the reserve price, the approval of the Finance Department had to be sought.

The Finance Department asked the Divisional Forest Office why the highest bid was short of the reserve price. Through a letter dated 30 October 1970, the Divisional Forest Officer submitted his explanation to the Finance Department. Haridwar Singh, who

[14] *Haridwar Singh* v. *Bagun Sumbrui*, AIR 1972 SC 1242.

realized that the auction has been caught in the bureaucratic web, wrote a letter dated 26 October 1970 and 3 November 1970, on the basis of being the highest bidder, expressing his willingness to take the settlement at the reserve price of Rs 95,000. The papers were put up to the Forest Minister. The Forest Minister, by his proceedings dated 27 November 1970, directed that the coupe be awarded to Haridwar Singh at the reserve price.

Thereafter, one Mr Md Yadub proposed to the Government of Bihar that he would take the settlement of the coupe for Rs 1,01,125. The Forest Minister directed that the coupe instead be awarded to Yadub. The earlier order was still in the administrative channel and no communication had reached the Divisional Forest Office, who instead received the communication to award the forest right to Yadub. The Divisional Forest Officer, by letter dated 23 December 1970, directed Yadub to pay the first instalment and execute the agreement. Yadub deposited the money and executed an agreement. Haridwar Singh moved the court claiming that a contract had already been formed with him. Who should the contract have been awarded to?

Case: Lost Consignment

Pratap sent a consignment through a transport company, but it was lost in transit. He made a claim of Rs 30,000 from the transport company. The transport company sent a reply in a standard form:

Dear Sir,
    We regret the loss of consignment of the following details. …
    We offer you Rs. 12,000 as full and final settlement of the claim for the lost consignment. Kindly find a cheque for the amount enclosed.
    In case the above offer is not acceptable to you, the cheque should be returned forthwith to this office. The retention or encashment of the cheque will amount to acceptance in full and final satisfaction of

the claim for the lost consignment. Thereafter, you would be barred from claiming further relief on the subject.

Pratap encashed the cheque and sent the following letter:

I deeply regret that my genuine claim for Rs 30,000 has been settled for a paltry Rs 12,000, despite the negligence on your part in losing the consignment. I reject your offer of full and final settlement of the claim for Rs 12,000. Kindly, therefore, remit the balance amount of Rs 18,000 within a period of 15 days from the date of receipt of this letter, failing which I will be compelled to go to a consumer court for the recovery of the balance amount. Please treat this as most urgent.

The transport company did not pay the balance amount claimed by Pratap. Pratap's contention before the court was that he had rejected the offer through his letter, while the company claimed that their offer was accepted by the encashment of the cheque. Who is correct?

5

Formation of Agreement: Review of Judgments

In the previous chapter, we discovered the principles of a lapse of offer, rejection of offer, provisional acceptance, and procedures of communication. We applied the principles to the unanswered cases. In this chapter, we will explore the court judgments related to these topics. Section 1 of the chapter explores the courts judgments on the general theme of formation of agreement through acceptance of offer. Section 2 is on provisional acceptance. Any qualification in the acceptance of an offer makes it a provisional acceptance. A provisional acceptance does not secure a contract and the parties do not develop any rights and obligations to each other. Section 3 is a review of the court judgments on the modalities to be followed for accepting an offer.

Offer and Acceptance

Acceptance of an offer leads to formation of a contract. We have reviewed several cases on the principle. The case of *Food Corporation of India* v. *Ram Kesh Yadav* shows the rigorous application of the simple principle, no matter how startling the outcome.

Court Case: Food Corporation of India v. Ram Kesh Yadav

The detailed facts of the case were presented in the previous chapter.[1] The application of Mr Yadav was irrespective of the scheme. The offer had two terms, (a) retirement of Mr Yadav, and (b) appointment of the son. The FCI accepted the offer by retiring Mr Yadav. FCI is a legal person but not a natural person. It is not capable of action on its own. Human instrumentalities, the officers of the Corporation, make the FCI do things. Officers are authorized to perform different functions for the Corporation. The application was made to the Azamgarh Office and the competent person had the power to accept resignation of the employees. Thus, the FCI did accept the offer of Mr Yadav, which included providing employment to the son. The Supreme Court ruled:

The second respondent's [father's] application dated 26.4.1999 was a composite application for conditional voluntary retirement on medical grounds, subject to

[1] *Food Corporation of India* v. *Ram Kesh Yadav*, AIR 2007 SC 1421.

appointment of his son in his place. The application specifically stated that he desired to go on retirement on medical grounds if his son was provided with employment in his place. The second Respondent [father] had thus clearly indicated that if employment on compassionate ground was not provided to his son, he was not interested in pursuing his request for retirement on medical grounds. FCI ought to have informed the employee that he could not make such a conditional offer of retirement contrary to the scheme. But for reasons best known to itself, FCI did not choose to reject the conditional offer, but unconditionally accepted the conditional offer. There lies the catch. … When FCI accepted the offer unconditionally and retired the second respondent from service by office order dated 29.7.2000, it was implied that it accepted the conditional offer in entirety. …

The limited question is whether FCI, having accepted the offer and accepted performance of the offer by the second Respondent [father], can refuse to perform or comply with the condition subject to which such offer was made. The answer is obviously in the negative. Having accepted the offer, FCI cannot avoid performance of the condition subject to which the offer was made. As noticed earlier, nothing prevented FCI from rejecting the application of the employee outright, or inform the employee before accepting the offer of voluntary retirement that it could not accept the condition, so that the employee would have had the option to withdraw the offer itself.

The court phrased the term 'conditional offer', to indicate that the terms of the offer where related and contingent. That is, give employment to the son if the father is retired. Similarly, a contract for fire safety could have terms requiring the service provider to extinguish fire if there is a fire. This should be distinguished from an offer itself being conditional; for example, the statement: 'I will offer to sell an umbrella to you if it rains today.' An acceptance can be conditional and a conditional acceptance is no acceptance. However, a 'conditional offer' makes the offer indefinite, uncertain and thus, not capable of acceptance. Thus, a 'conditional offer' is

a nullity. We should refer to the details of a valid offer, even if these are contingent and inter-related, simply as terms of the offer.

Court Case: UP Rajkiya Nirman Nigam Limited v. Indure Private Limited

The Uttar Pradesh Rajkiya Nirman Nigam Limited (Nigam) and Indure Private Limited intended to put a joint bid to a tender floated by the Uttar Pradesh State Electricity Board (Electricity Board) for supply and setting up of mechanical equipment and construction work.[2] Towards this, Nigam and Indure were working towards getting into an agreement settling the procedures of their join bid. The Nigam sent an agreement document to Indure for their signature. Indure signed the agreement; however, it deleted Clause (10) of the agreement and significantly altered Clause (12). The two clauses pertained to liabilities, providing for joint liabilities. Indure changed it so as to make the Nigam individually liable. The Nigam unilaterally submitted a tender that indicated that the work was to be done jointly by the Nigam and Indure. However, it subsequently withdrew the tender. Indure claimed damages from the Nigam on the grounds that there was a concluded contract between the parties.

The Supreme Court noted that unless there is an acceptance of the proposal, a contract is not made. As Indure had deleted Clause 10 and modified Clause 12, it was not an acceptance of the proposal by the Nigam but a counter-offer. It was argued by Indure that the tender submitted by the Nigam indicating that the work would be done jointly was implied acceptance of the counter-offer. The Court, illustrating the principle that an offer can be accepted by conduct, noted:

---

[2] *U.P. Rajkiya Nirman Nigam Limited* v. *Indure Private Limited*, AIR 1996 SC 1373.

... an offer to buy goods can be accepted by supplying them; and an offer to sell goods, made by sending them to the offeree, can be accepted by using them. ... There is no dispute to the proposition of law but two factors have to be kept in mind. viz. when the counter-offer was made by the respondent (Indure) and whether the unilateral offer amounts to acceptance by submitting the tenders by the appellant (Nigam) to the Board. We find that it does not amount to acceptance of counter proposal. It is seen that admittedly, Clause (10) which thrusts responsibility on the first respondent was deleted in the counter-proposal. In Clause 12, for joint responsibility unilateral liability was incorporated. In other words the respondent disowned its material responsibilities. Unless there is acceptance by the appellant to those conditions no concluded contract can be said to have emerged.

Case: Bank of India v. O.P. Swaranakar

The facts of the case were stated in the previous chapter. Nationalized banks came up with schemes for voluntary retirement.[3] A large number of employees applied for it. However, several of them withdrew their application. The banks proceeded to retire them on the grounds that according to the terms of the scheme, an application once made could not be withdrawn. Employment is a contractual relationship. In this case, the scheme was a voluntary scheme for the employer and employee to reach an agreement. The question then arose whether an offer could be revoked before it was accepted.

The Supreme Court emphasized the point that the use of the term 'offer' or 'proposal' was not decisive. In a given situation, one would need to discern offer and acceptance. The Court identified the scheme to be invitation of offer and the application from the employees offer. The court concluded:

[3] *Bank of India* v. *O. P. Swaranakar*, AIR 2003 SC 858.

The request of employees seeking voluntary retirement was not to take effect until and unless it was accepted in writing by the competent authority. The competent authority had the absolute discretion whether to accept or reject the request of the employee seeking voluntary retirement under the scheme. ... The procedure laid down therefore suggests that the applications of the employee would be an offer which could be considered by the bank in terms of the procedure laid down therefore. There is no assurance that such an application would be accepted without any consideration. ... Acceptance or otherwise of the request of an employee seeking voluntary retirement is required to be communicated to him in writing.

The court ruled that since the scheme was contractual in nature, provision contained in the Indian Contract Act, 1872, would apply. Now, the application of employees could be an acceptance only if the scheme was an offer. Section 2(a) of the Act defines a proposal (offer) as follows:

(a) When one person signifies to another his willingness to do or to abstain from doing anything, with a view to obtaining the assent of that other to such act or abstinence, he is said to make a proposal.

The court noted that the banks had not expressed their willingness to do or abstain from doing anything with a view to obtaining assent of the employees to such act. To the contrary, the banks had absolute discretion in accepting or rejecting applications. It is the bank which was accepting the offer. On the revocation offer, the court reasoned that there was an agreement between the bank and an applicant that the application for voluntary retirement would not be withdrawn. The agreement is made the moment the application is submitted. However, for the agreement to be binding on the parties, it must have consideration for both the parties. On the face of it, in the agreement not to withdraw the offer, the employee gets no benefit. We would further examine the issue in the chapters on consideration

PROVISIONAL ACCEPTANCE

In this section, we will review the principle that acceptance must be absolute and unqualified and not provisional. Section 7 provides the principle:

7. **Acceptance must be absolute**—In order to convert a proposal into a promise, the acceptance must—

(1) be absolute and unqualified;

There are several contexts where the acceptance may be provisional. A provisional acceptance does not create a contract. Let us consider the case where the auctioneer puts up the following terms for auction: (1) The selected bidder will deposit one-third the amount and sign a contract. (2) The contract will be formed only on the signing of the contract. Hence, the striking of the hammer by the auctioneer is only a provisional acceptance of the offer. This leaves it open for the bidder to revoke the offer as well as for the auctioneer to reject the bid. Neither party has to assign any reasons or justify its action. An offeror has a right to withdraw an offer till its final acceptance and conversely, an offer can be rejected by the person.

A misimpression persists that signing a document is a firm conclusion of a contract. This, no doubt, comes from a context in the past, where most people were illiterate and written records and signature were being introduced. Signing amounts to concurrence with the written document. The point, however, is what does the document say? A contract would be formed only if the document unconditionally creates a contract. In the *Winn* v. *Bull* case,[4] on leasing of a property, the last line of the signed agreement

---

[4] *Winn* v. *Bull*, (1877) 7 ChD 29.

---

mentioned: 'This agreement is made subject to the preparation and approval of a formal contract.' A dispute arose between the parties whether the agreement was binding on them or not. The court noted:

It comes, therefore, to this, that where you have a proposal or agreement made in writing expressed to be subject to a formal contract being prepared, it means what it says; it is subject to and is dependent upon a formal contract being prepared. ... The result is, that I must hold that there is no binding contract...

Letter of Intent, work order and purchase order are some of the names of the documents used in response to offers received through tenders or negotiated contracts. 'Letter of Intent', literally, is a letter indicating only one's 'intent' and not a firm commitment. The word 'order' in work order and purchase order connotes definitiveness and finality. The importance, however, is not of the name given to the document but its content. The question to be asked is 'What does the document say?' If a work order or purchase order has conditions or qualifications, it is only a provisional acceptance. And if a 'letter of intent' accepts an offer without reservations, it is an acceptance creating binding rights and obligations for the parties.

Signing of Contract

It is in the parties' interests to create documentary evidence of the contract. The best means of achieving this is to have a written contract signed by both parties. This, however, is not as simple and straightforward as it appears. Before putting the contract down on paper, parties would already be communicating with each other. It may be clear to both parties that the contract has to be in writing and signed. However, a dispute may arise on the nature of the communication preceding the signing of the document. There can be two different communications between the parties. One, the parties agree subject to the writing and signing of the document. The agreement in this case is only provisional. The agreement will be formed only when the parties sign the document. Second, the parties have already gotten into an oral agreement. A part of the performance of the contract is to sign a document listing the terms the parties have orally agreed to. In this case, signing the document becomes a duty of the contracting parties. The following cases will explore the theme.

Court Case: Kollipara Sriramulu v. T. Aswatha Narayana

T. Aswatha Narayana was a partner in a firm consisting of about thirty partners that was running a mill named Vasavamba Oil and Rice Mill at Vijayawada.[5] The partnership also owned other properties, including a cinema theatre. There was an oral agreement between T. Aswatha Narayana and all other partners, other than one, for the sale of their shares in a property. The rate for the shares was fixed at Rs 422. A written agreement was to be drawn in two or three days. It was further agreed that the sale deeds were to be executed in three months. In pursuance of the agreement, several co-sharers executed sale deeds and T. Aswatha Narayana became the owner of 98 shares. A dispute arose on the validity of the oral agreement. It was contended that as the parties had contemplated execution of a formal document, the oral agreement could not conclude a contract. The Supreme Court noted:

We proceed to consider … whether the oral agreement was ineffective because the parties contemplated the execution of a formal document… It was submitted on behalf of the appellant that there was

no contract because the sale was conditional upon a regular agreement being executed and no such agreement was executed. We do not accept this argument as correct. It is well established that a mere reference to a future formal contract will not prevent a binding bargain between the parties. The fact that the parties refer to the preparation of an agreement by which the terms agreed upon are to be put in a more formal shape does not prevent the existence of a binding contract. There are, however, cases where the reference to a future contract is made in such terms as to show that the parties did not intend to be bound until a formal contract is signed. The question depends upon the intention of the parties and the special circumstances of each particular case.

The court cited the following famous passage on the theme from *Von Hatzfeldt-Wildenburg v. Alexander*:[6]

It appears to be well settled by the authorities that if the documents or letters relied on as constituting a contract contemplate the execution of a further contact between the parties, it is a question of construction whether the execution of the further contract is a condition or term of the bargain or whether it is a mere expression of the desire of the parties as to the manner in which the transaction already agreed to will in fact go through. In the former case there is no enforceable contract either because the condition is unfulfilled or because the law does not recognise a contract to enter into a contract. In the latter case there is a binding contract and the reference to the more formal document may be ignored.

A leading case of the Supreme Court on provisional acceptance is the *Union of India* v. *M/s. Bhimsen Walaiti Ram*.

Court Case: Union of India v. M/s. Bhimsen Walaiti Ram

The case was mentioned in the previous chapter. Walaiti Ram, the highest bidder, did not pay the deposit of one-sixth of the contract value to the Excise Department, as

---

[5] *Kollipara Sriramulu* v. *T. Aswatha Narayana*, AIR 1968 SC 1028.

[6] Judgment by Parker, J in *Von Hatzfeldt-Wildenburg* v. *Alexander*, (1912) 1 Ch 284.

a result, the Commissioner did not confirm the bid. The Excise Department auctioned the license to another person and claimed the deficit from Walaiti Ram as loss due to 'resale'. The Supreme Court ruled:

… the contract of sale was not complete till the bid was confirmed by the Chief Commissioner and till such confirmation the person whose bid has been provisionally accepted is entitled to withdraw his bid. When the bid is so withdrawn before the confirmation of the Chief Commissioner the bidder will not be liable for damages on account of any breach of contract or for the shortfall on the resale. An acceptance of an offer may be either absolute or conditional. If the acceptance is conditional the offer can be withdrawn at any moment until absolute acceptance has taken place.

… the Chief Commissioner has disapproved the bid … If the Chief Commissioner had granted sanction … the auction sale in favour of the respondent would have been a completed transaction and he would have been liable for any shortfall on the resale. As the essential pre-requisites of a completed sale are missing in this case there is no liability imposed on the respondent for payment of the deficiency in the price.

Within the contract law, the best course for the Chief Commissioner was to grant sanction to Bhimsen and communicate the firm acceptance of the offer. This would have bound Bhimsen to the contract. Failure to pay the due money would have given remedy to the Excise Department. However, the Chief Commissioner may not have had the freedom within the rules to grant sanction to an erring bidder.

Case: Dresser Rand S. A. v. M/s. Bindal Agro Chem Limited

The facts of the case were presented in the previous chapter. The case involves three companies, Dresser Rand S.A. (DR), BINDAL Agro Chem. Limited (BINDAL) and K.G.

Khosla Compressors Limited (KGK).[7] The dispute was whether there was an arbitration agreement between DR and KGK, and DR and Bindal. The first contention was that DR and Bindal had agreed on 'General Conditions of Purchase' (revision 4). The document had the following arbitration clause. 'In cases of foreign supplier, all disputes which cannot be settled by mutual negotiations shall be settled under the Rules of Conciliation and Arbitration of ICC.' Thus, there was a binding arbitration agreement between the parties. The Supreme Court disagreed. It noted:

The tender document or the invitation to bid of BINDAL (containing the 'instructions to bidders' and the 'general conditions of purchase'), by itself, is neither an agreement nor a contract. The instructions to bidders informed the intending bidders how the bid should be made and laid down the procedure for consideration and acceptance of the bid. The process of bidding or submission of tenders would result in a contract when a bid or offer is made by a prospective supplier and such bid or offer is accepted by BINDAL. The second part of the Invitation to Bid consists of the 'General Conditions of Purchase', that is, the conditions subject to which the purchase order will be placed or offer will be accepted. The 'General Conditions of Purchase' were made available as a part of the Invitation to Bid, so as to enable the prospective suppliers to ascertain their obligations and formulate their offers suitably.

Where a tenderer is not willing to make his offer subject to the 'General Conditions of Purchase' prescribed and stipulated by the purchaser, he would either suggest his own terms and conditions or suggest modifications to the 'General Conditions of Purchase' prescribed by the intending purchaser (person inviting the offers). Many 'Invitations to Bid' contain a condition that the tenderers will not be entitled to make any changes in the 'General Conditions of Purchase', in which event he is required to mould his offer strictly in accordance with the 'General Conditions of Purchase' stipulated by the

---

[7] *Dresser Rand S.A.* v. *M/s. Bindal Agro Chem Limited*, AIR 2006 SC 871.

purchaser. The reason for insisting upon adherence to Purchaser's 'General Conditions of Purchase' is not far to seek. If several persons submit their offers subjecting them to different terms and conditions of supply, it will be difficult or virtually impossible to evaluate them with reference to a common denominator. The general conditions of purchase act as a common denominator for all tenderers to base their offers and for evaluation of such offers. Further, the said General Conditions stipulated by the purchaser enable the tenderer to assess his obligations and calculate the offer price accordingly. For example, there will be a marked difference in the responsibility of a supplier and the pricing, if the purchaser seeks a three year warranty instead of one year warranty, or seeks delivery of machinery at site instead of at supplier's factory, or seeks delivery to be expedited instead of the normal period. Many a time the supplier is able to persuade the purchaser to agree for modification of the 'conditions of purchase' stipulated by the purchaser, particularly where a supplier is in a position of strength and the purchaser is keen to purchase a particular product of that supplier. There are also several suppliers who stipulate their own 'conditions of sale' and refuse to go by the conditions of purchase stipulated by the purchaser. The intending purchaser and the intending supplier are at liberty to negotiate and agree upon the terms subject to which offers will be made and accepted. As contrasted from sale of ready goods sold off the shelf across the counter, sale/purchase of complex machinery/equipment made to order, to suit particular requirements of the purchaser, have several facets relating to pricing, period of delivery, mode of delivery, period and nature of warranty, suitability for the intended purpose, patent rights, packing, insurance, incidental services, consequences of delay and breach, rejection/replacement force mejeure etc. Agreeing upon the terms subject to which offer is to be made and accepted, is itself a complicated and time consuming process. But, reaching an agreement as to the terms subject to which a purchase will be made, is not entering into an agreement to purchase.

Therefore, when DR suggested modifications to the general conditions of purchase, and when BINDAL agreed to them, and both parties initialled Revision No. 4 containing the modifications to the General Conditions of Purchase, on 10-6-1991, no contract or agreement came into existence as it did not involve either an offer or acceptance or performance of any promise. 'Revision No.4' dated 10-6-1991 only consisted of the modifications to the General Conditions of Purchase, subject to which it was willing to enter into a contract with BINDAL for sale of machinery.

The second contention of DR was that BINDAL, represented by its agent KGK, placed a purchase order on it through the letters of intent. The letters of intent were accepted by DR by counter-signing it. The letters of intent contained the clause: 'The Purchase Order shall be subject to the 'General Conditions of Purchase' included in inquiry and as amended by DR's comments thereto, Revision 4 dated 10 June 1991, initialled by DR and KGK separately.' Thus, the arbitration clause contained in the 'General Conditions of Purchase (revision 4) created a binding arbitration agreement. The court recognized that KGK was an agent for BINDAL. However, the court ruled that the letter of intent issued by BINDAL/KGK was only a provisional acceptance, and thus there was no binding contract between the parties. The court ruled:

The Preamble to the Letters of Intent states that KGK 'hereby confirms its intention to place an order on Dresser Rand'. This is further made clear from Clause (I) of each letter of intent which provides that 'this letter of intent' will be followed by a regular and detailed purchase order to be issued by KGK simultaneous with the establishment of the Letter of Credit mentioned in Para B of letter of intent. This makes it clear that the letter of intent is only a prelude to the purchase order and not itself the purchase order. The last para of Letters of Intent requires DR to sign and return the duplicate copy of the letter as token acceptance of DR having agreed to the Letters of Intent. This would mean that the person issuing the Letters of Intent wanted concurrence of DR to the terms contained in the Letter of Intent so that it can place an order in terms of the conditions mentioned in the Letters of Intent. The concurrence sought was to the contents of Letters of Intent and not acceptance of any order for supply.

Clause 'C' of Letters of Intent provides that the purchase order shall be subject to the 'General Conditions of Purchase' included in the inquiry, as amended by DR's comments thereto, Revision 4 dated 10-6-1991'. Therefore, the General Conditions of Purchase which contains the arbitration clause, is not made a part of the Letters of Intent nor are the Letters of Intent made subject to the General Conditions of Purchase. The Letters of Intent merely provide that if and when the purchase order is placed, the purchase order will be subject to the General Conditions of Purchase, as modified by Revision No. 4. Therefore, the point of time at which the General Conditions of Purchase will become applicable, is the point when the purchase order is placed and not earlier. Consequently, Clause 27.4.2 of the General Conditions of Purchase containing the arbitration clause would become applicable and available to the parties only when the purchase order was placed and not earlier.

The term 'purchase order' has a specific meaning and connotation. The purchase order is the 'agreement entered into between BINDAL and the prospective supplier as recorded in the purchase order form (prepared in the form of Attachment-VII to the General Conditions of Purchase) signed by the parties, including all Attachments and annexures thereto and all documents incorporated by reference therein together with any subsequent modifications thereof in writing.' Admittedly, no such purchase order was placed by either BINDAL or any one authorized by BINDAL. It is also evident from Clause (I) of the Letters of Intent that the purchase order was to be issued simultaneously with the Letter of Credit. Clause (M) made it clear that the Letters of Intent were being issued subject to necessary approvals being given by the authorities of the Indian Government. These provisions clearly indicate that the Letters of Intent were only a step leading to purchase orders and were not, by themselves, purchase orders. Therefore, issue the Letters of Intent by KGK, assuming that it was done on behalf of BINDAL, did not mean that the General Conditions of Purchase which contains the provision for arbitration became a part of the Letters of Intent or became enforceable.

It is now well-settled that a Letter of Intent merely indicates a party's intention to enter into a contract with the other party in future. A Letter of Intent is not intended to bind either party ultimately to enter into any contract.... It is no doubt true that a Letter of Intent may be construed as a letter of acceptance if such intention is evident from its terms. It is not uncommon in contracts involving detailed procedure, in order to save time, to issue a letter of intent communicating the acceptance of the offer and asking the contractor to start the work with a stipulation that the detailed contract would be drawn up later. If such a letter is issued to the contractor, though it may be termed as a Letter of Intent, it may amount to acceptance of the offer resulting in a concluded contract between the parties. But the question whether the letter of intent is merely an expression of an intention to place an order in future or whether is a final acceptance of the offer thereby leading to a contract, is a matter that has to be decided with reference to the terms of the letter. Chitty on Contracts (Para 2.115 in Volume 1- 28th Edition) observes that where parties to a transaction exchanged letters of intent, the terms of such letters may, of course, negative contractual intention; but, on the other hand, where the language does not negative contractual intention, it is open to the courts to hold the parties are bound by the document; and the courts will, in particular, be inclined to do so where the parties have acted on the document for a long period of time or have expended considerable sums of money in reliance on it. Be that as it may.

35. Learned counsel for DR referred to Clauses (B), (D), (F), and (L) of the Letters of Intent to contend that they were the purchase orders. Clause (B) mentioned the total price exclusive of taxes and duties payable and provided that the Letter of Credit should be opened by 31-8-1991 by a bank acceptable to DR. Clause (D) provided that delivery date shall be 15½ months from the date of receipt of the Letter of Intent by DR. Clause (F) stated that 'this Letter of Intent shall serve as DR's authorization to proceed with this order'. Clause (L) stated that 'This contract will come into force upon receipt of this letter of intent by supplier'. DR contends that as the Letters of Intent were referred to as 'this order' and 'this contract' in clauses (F) and (L), and as clause (F) authorized DR to proceed with the order, the Letters of Intent were, in fact, purchase orders.

When all the terms of the Letter of Intent are harmoniously read, what is clear is that Letters of Intent merely required the supplier to keep the offer open till 31-8-1991 with reference to the price and delivery schedule. They also made it clear that if the purchase orders were not placed and Letter of Credit was not opened by 31-8-1991, DR was at liberty to alter the price and the delivery schedule. In other words, the effect of Letters of Intent was that if the purchase orders were placed and LCs were opened by 31-8-1991, DR would be bound to effect supply within 15½ months, at the prices stated in the Letter of Intent. Therefore, it may not be possible to treat the Letters of Intent as Purchase Orders.

Even if we assume that the Letters of Intent were intended to contracts for supply of machinery in accordance with the terms contained therein, it may only enable DR to sue for damages or sue for the expenses incurred in anticipation of the order and opening of LC. But that will not be of any assistance to contend that there was an arbitration agreement between the parties.

We have already noticed that the letters of intent dated 12-6-1991, do not contain any arbitration clause. The contention of DR is that arbitration clause in the General Conditions of Purchase is incorporated by reference, having regard to clause (C) of Letters of Intent. But clause (C) specifically provided that 'the purchase order' shall be subject to General Conditions of Purchase as amended by Revision No. 4. Clause (C) did not say that 'this Letter of Intent is subject to the general conditions of purchase as amended in Revision No. 4'. One other aspect may be noticed. Clause (C) refers to Revision No. 4 initialled by DR and KGK. It is now admitted by DR that there is no document (Revision No. 4 or otherwise) modifying the general conditions of purchase, which is initialled by DR and KGK. The Revision No. 4 was initialled only by DR and BINDAL. Therefore, the general conditions of purchase containing the arbitration clause, never became a term of the Letters of Intent dated 12-6-1991. Clause (C) of the Letters of Intent made it clear that it is only the purchase orders which were to be placed in future on or before 31-8-1991 (along with opening of LC) that was to be subject to the General Conditions of Purchase. Therefore, we hold that the Letters of Intent, even if assumed to result in any binding contract, did not provide for arbitration. ...

In this case, the principle that provision acceptance is no acceptance was applied. Some terms of the Letter of Intent purported to be acceptance of the offer while others made the acceptance tentative. The terms qualifying the acceptance made the acceptance provisional. Take the case where an acceptance letter is absolutely clear in all its clauses other than the statement: 'The acceptance is subject to obtaining permission from the government which is almost certain to come.' We only have to assess the document to judge where it is an acceptance or provisional acceptance. Any qualification would tend to make the communication provisional acceptance. It is not open for the offeror to examine whether the permission from the government has indeed been obtained. Further, the communication will not become a firm acceptance if the permission is indeed obtained. Further, the offeror cannot allege that the person did not make an effort to obtain permission from the government. All these considerations are extraneous. The only thing to be done is to assess the communication when it is made and decide whether it has qualified the acceptance in any manner. A provision acceptance leaves the offer open and has to be followed up with an acceptance to create a contract. The difference between provisional acceptance, rejection, and counter-offer is that a rejection or counter-offer extinguishes the offer. A provisional acceptance neither accepts the offer nor extinguishes it. Effectively, it amounts to making no communication. Only a subsequent acceptance or rejection would be decisive.

MODALITIES OF COMMUNICATION

An offer can prescribe how the offer would be accepted. The means of acceptance can take many forms. It could specify whether the acceptance should be oral or in writing. It can include the procedure of delivery of acceptance, for example, by post, courier, fax, e-mail, or telex. The offer can specify the address to which the acceptance should be sent. The offer can also specify the acceptance to be by conduct. For example, the prescribed acceptance for selling the goods could be by delivering them. Further, the offeror is at liberty to waive the prescribed mode of communication and accept an alternate one. After all, the parties are free to set the terms of the contract and modalities of getting into an agreement with each other. Once the offeror accepts a modality of communication other than the prescribed one, he has impliedly waived the requirement of the prescribed mode. An interesting case on the working of this is the Manchester Diocesan case.[8]

Case: Manchester Diocesan Council for Education v. Commercial and General Investments, Limited

Manchester Diocesan Council for Education invited tender to sell a school premises. Clause 4 of the conditions of the tender provided: 'The person whose tender is accepted shall be the purchaser and shall be informed of the acceptance of his tender by letter sent to him by post addressed to the address given in the tender.' Commercial and General Investments, Limited was a property developing company. It bid for the tender and mentioned the address in the tender document to be: No. 15, Berkeley Street. Both the parties were represented by solicitors. The acceptance of the tender was sent not to the mentioned address but to the solicitor representing the party. As the offer document had specified that it was to be sent to a different address, a dispute arose about whether an agreement was formed by sending

the letter to the solicitor's address. The court ruled:

There can be no doubt that in the present case, if the plaintiff or its authorized agent had posted a letter addressed to the defendant company at no. 15, Berkeley Street, on or about 15th September informing the defendant company of the acceptance of its tender, the contract would have been complete at the moment when such letter was posted, but that of course was not taken. Condition 4, however, does not say that that shall be the sole permitted method of communicating an acceptance. It may be that an offeror, who by the terms of his offer insists on acceptance in a particular manner, is entitled to insist that he is not bound unless acceptance is effected or communicated in that precise way, although it seems probable that, even so, if the other party communicates his acceptance in some other way, the offeror may by conduct or otherwise waive his right to insist on the prescribed method of acceptance. Where, however, the offeror has prescribed a particular method of acceptance, but not in terms insisting that only acceptance in that mode shall be binding, I am of opinion that acceptance communicated to the offeror by any other mode which is no less advantageous to him will conclude the contract.

If an offeror intends that he shall be bound only if his offer is accepted in some particular manner, it must be for him to make this clear. Condition 4 in the present case had not, in my judgment, this effect.

The law is settled that the prescribed mode of communication mentioned in the offer must be followed. The case, however, raises the question as to what actually is the prescribed mode of communication(s) in a given offer. For example, the prescribed mode of sending acceptance by fax is usually intended to communicate in writing and to expedite matters. Sending a scanned copy of the document as an e-mail attachment or expeditiously delivering the original document serves the purpose equally well. If the offeror insisted that only fax and no other means would be acceptable, the offer should mention this explicitly. On the other hand, the requirement that

---

[8] *Manchester Diocesan Council for Education* v. *Commercial and General Investments, Limited,* (1969) 3 All ER 1593.

acceptance should be in writing is intended to generate a record of the acceptance. A fax and e-mail is as good as in writing and could suffice. If the offeror wants a hard copy, he must specify that the acceptance should only be through a hardcopy.

In the case, the court also noted that while the Commercial and General Investments, Limited was the offeror, the terms of the offer were settled by the Manchester Diocesan Council for Education. The Council had done this for its own protection. It is not that it was the offeror's insistence that the tender must be accepted at the address mentioned in the tender document. Further, Clause 4 does not state that communication must be done only at the mentioned address or communication at any other address would not be accepted. In this context, the judgment held the communication of acceptance at the address of the Solicitor of Commercial and General Investments, Limited adequate.

Let us review *Life Insurance Corporation of India* v. *Raja Vasireddy Komallavalli Kamba*, which was decided by the Supreme Court, to further our understanding of communication between contracting parties.

Court Case: Life Insurance Corporation of India v. Raja Vasireddy Komallavalli Kamba

The case was presented earlier in the chapter as the life insurance case. Increasingly, corporations have come to do business in writing through pre-printed forms. The corporations set the terms of the contract, print them and make the customer, the offeror. Thus, they retain the commanding position of accepting or rejecting the offer. The terms set by the LIC had not mentioned when a contract would be formed. Mr Vasireddy had enclosed the requisite cheque—the premium for the policy—along with the application. The LIC encashed the cheques. Mr. Vasireddy learnt of

this when he updated his passbook. The contention of his widow was that a contract got formed when the LIC encashed the cheque.

We should be clear that the passing of the consideration does not necessarily mean the formation of an agreement, and for the formation of an agreement, no consideration need pass. Take the following cases: A motor car company has a long waiting list for its car. It requires the applicants to pay the full amount for the car. A lottery is conducted for selecting people for the allotment of the cars. The money of those who are not chosen is returned. In this arrangement, the would-be consideration, price of the car, has passed but no agreement is formed. The other cases of the consideration passing without the formation of an agreement are by the urban development authorities for allotment of houses, and giving of goods on sale or return basis.

No consideration need be transacted for the formation of an agreement. The passing of the consideration can be in the future, subsequent to the agreement. For example, A agrees to do catering for a marriage party, two months hence, for party B. The money is to be paid after the catering is done. A and B are bound by the agreement, but the consideration has to pass later in the future. Thus, in examining whether a contract has been formed between the parties, we should examine whether an offer has been made and accepted or not. From this perspective, the fact that the LIC took and appropriated the money has no significance in itself. Money can be returned. The claim was that the appropriation of the money amounts to the acceptance of the offer. The LIC differed. The Supreme Court noted in its judgment: 'The mere receipt and retention of premium until after the death of the applicant or the mere preparation of the policy document is not acceptance. Acceptance must be signified by some act or acts agreed on by the parties or from which the law raises a presumption of acceptance.'

In support it, the Supreme Court quoted from Corpus Juris Secundum:

The mere receipt and retention of premiums until after the death of applicant does not give rise to a contract, although the circumstances may be such that approval could be inferred from retention of the premium. The mere execution of the policy is not an acceptance; an acceptance, to be complete, must be communicated to the offerer, either directly, or by some definite act, such as placing the contract in the mail. The test is not intention alone. When the application so requires, the acceptance must be evidenced by the signature of one of the company's executive officers.

We know that silence cannot be inferred to be acceptance. The Supreme Court noted on this aspect:

Though in certain human relationships silence to a proposal might convey acceptance but in the case of insurance proposal, silence does not denote consent and no binding contract arises until the person to whom an offer is made says or does something to signify his acceptance. Mere delay in giving an answer cannot be construed as an acceptance, as, prima facie, acceptance must be communicated to the offeror. The general rule is that the contract of insurance will be concluded only when the party to whom an offer has been made accepts it unconditionally and communicates his acceptance to the person making the offer. Whether the final acceptance is that of the assured or insurers, however, depends simply on the way in which negotiations for an insurance have progressed.

Applying the principles to the case, the Supreme Court concluded that there was no concluded insurance contract between the parties.

Case: Haridwar Singh v. Bagun Sumbrui

The facts of the case were presented in the previous chapter. Let us summarize the case by listing the significant developments in a chronological order:

- 22 July 1970: Advertisement for auction.
- 7 August 1970: Auction is held in the DFO's office and Haridwar Singh's bid is provisionally accepted. Mr Singh deposits Rs 23,000.
- 30 October 1970: DFO explains to the Finance Department why the auction amount is lower that the reserve price.
- 3 November 1970: Hardwar Singh writes to the DFO expressing to take up the coupe for Rs 95,000.
- 27 November 1970: Minister directs the officers to settle with Hardwar Singh at the reserve price of Rs 95,000.
- Before 23 December 1970: Minister directed the officers to give the coupe to Md Yadub for Rs 1,01,125.
- 23 December 1970: DFO directs Yadub to deposit the security amount and execute an agreement.

Mr Singh contended that there was a conditional acceptance of the offer by the divisional forest officer. Once the government confirmed the action of the divisional forest officer, the acceptance became unconditional. Thus, there was a concluded contract once the government confirmed the acceptance, even though the confirmation was not communicated to him. The Supreme Court considered the situation where a provisional acceptance has to be confirmed. It summarized previous court judgment:

… to have an enforceable contract, there must be an offer and an unconditional acceptance and that a person who makes an offer has the right to withdraw it before acceptance, in the absence of a condition to the contrary supported by consideration. He further said the fact that there has been a provisional or conditional acceptance would not make any difference as a provisional or conditional acceptance cannot in itself make a binding contract.[9]

The Supreme Court judged that there was never any confirmation of the provisional acceptance of the divisional forest officer. The Minister did not confirm the acceptance made by the divisional forest officer. He accepted the offer made by Mr Singh that he would take the coup for the reserved price of Rs 95,000. There was, therefore, no confirmation of the acceptance of the bid to take the coup in settlement for the amount of Rs 92,001. There was no communication of the offer to Mr Singh. The Supreme Court noted:

... we do not think that there was any communication of the acceptance of that offer to the appellant. .... The acceptance of the offer was not even put in the course of transmission to the appellant; and so even assuming that an acceptance need not come to the knowledge of the offer, the appellant cannot contend that there was a concluded contract on the basis of his offer contained in his communication dated October 26, 1970, as the acceptance of that offer was not put in the course of transmission. Quite apart from that, the appellant himself revoked the offer made by him on October 26, 1970, by his letter dated November 3, 1970, in which he stated that the coup may be settled upon him at the highest bid made by him in the auction. We are, therefore, of the opinion that there was no concluded contract between the appellant and the government.

Interestingly, an offer changing the terms of an existing offer by the offeror is also a counter-offer. Impliedly, it revokes the previous offer. Thus, the previous offer is extinguished and cannot be accepted. By revising his auction bid, Haridwar Singh extinguished it.

Case: M/s Bhagwati Prasad Pawan Kumar v. Union of India
M/s Bhagwati Prasad Pawan Kumar booked two consignments of iodised salt with the

Indian Railways.[10] The first consignment consisted of 767 bags and the second, 744 bags. The consignments were not delivered. The firm lodged two claims for the value of the lost goods, for Rs 53,264 and Rs 51,686. Through two identical standard letters dated 7 April 1993 (despatched in August, 1993), the Railways admitted the claims only to an extent of Rs 9,111 and Rs 9,032 and enclosed two cheques in favour of the firm for the sum of Rs 9,111 and Rs 9,032. Both the cheques were dated July 27, 1993. The letters mentioned:

In case the above offer is not acceptable to you, the cheque should be returned forthwith to this office: failing which it will be deemed that you have accepted the offer in full and final satisfaction of your claim. The retention of this cheque and/or encashment thereof will automatically amount to acceptance in full and final satisfaction of your above claim without reason and you will be estopped from claiming any further relief on the subject.

On receipt of two letters along with the two cheques, the firm wrote two identical letters dated 20 August 1993 to the Railways. The first letter read:

We regret to inform you that our above noted claim has been settled for Rs. 9111/- instead of Rs. 53284/- the claimed amount. The same is therefore placed under : PROTEST : and cannot be accepted. Please therefore remit the balance amount to us within a period of 15 days from the date of receipt of this letter, failing which, we shall be compelled to lodge a civil suit against the Railways for recovery of the balance amount. Please treat this as most urgent.

The Railways did not pay the balance amount claimed by the firm. Following this, the firm filed a claim application before the Railway Claims Tribunal. The contention of Railways was that the encashment of the cheque was

[9] *Somasundaram Pillai* v. *Provincial Government of Madras*, AIR 1947 Mad 366.

[10] *M/s Bhagwati Prasad Pawan Kumar* v. *Union of India*, (2006) (5) SCC 311.

acceptance of their offer of final settlement. And the contention of the firm was that they had explicitly rejected the offer by their letter. Encashment of the cheque was only a part payment of the total claim. The case came in appeal before the Supreme Court. The Supreme Court noted:

Section 8 of the Contract Act reads as under:

'8. Acceptance by performing conditions, or receiving consideration—Performance of the conditions of a proposal, or the acceptance of any consideration for a reciprocal promise which may be offered with a proposal, is an acceptance of the proposal'.

Section 8 of the Contract Act provides for acceptance by performing conditions of a proposal. In the instant case, the Railways made an offer to the appellant [Bhagwati Prasad] laying down the condition that if the offer was not acceptable the cheque should be returned forthwith, failing which it would be deemed that the appellant (Bhagwati Prasad) accepted the offer in full and final satisfaction of its claim. This was further clarified by providing that the retention of the cheque and/or encashment thereof will automatically amount to satisfaction in full and final settlement of the claim. Thus, if the appellant (Bhagwati Prasad) accepted the cheques and encashed them without anything more, it would amount to an acceptance of the offer made in the letters of the Railways dated April 7,. 1993. The offer prescribed the mode of acceptance, and by conduct the appellant (Bhagwati Prasad) must be held to have accepted the offer and therefore, could not make a claim later. However, if the appellant (Bhagwati Prasad) had not encashed the cheques and protested to the Railways calling upon them to pay the balance amount, and expressed its inability to accept the cheques remitted to it, the controversy would have acquired a different complexion. In that event, in view of the express non acceptance of the offer, the appellant (Bhagwati Prasad) could not be presumed to have accepted the offer. What, however, is significant is that the protest and non acceptance must be conveyed before the cheques are encashed. If the cheques are encashed without protest, then it must be held that the offer stood unequivocally accepted. An 'offeree' cannot be permitted to change his mind after the unequivocal acceptance of the offer.

It is well settled that an offer may be accepted by conduct. But conduct would only amount to acceptance if it is clear that the offeree did the act with the intention (actual or apparent) of accepting the offer. … Each case must rest on its own facts. The courts must examine the evidence to find out whether in the facts and circumstances of the case the conduct of the 'offeree' was such as amounted to an unequivocal acceptance of the offer made. If the facts of the case disclose that there was no reservation in signifying acceptance by conduct, it must follow that the offer has been accepted by conduct. On the other hand if the evidence discloses that the 'offeree' had reservation in accepting the offer, his conduct may not amount to acceptance of the offer in terms of Section 8 of the Contract Act.

Coming to the facts of this case if the appellant (Bhagwati Prasad), before encashing the cheques, had sent the communication dated August 20, 1993, it could perhaps be argued that by retaining but not encashing the cheques, it did not intend to accept the offer made in the letter of the Railways dated April 7, 1993. At the same time if the evidence disclosed that it encashed the cheques and later sent a protest, it must be held that it had accepted the offer unconditionally by conveying its acceptance by the mode prescribed, namely by retaining and encashing the cheques, without reservation. Its subsequent change of mind and consequent protest did not matter.

In the instant case there is neither pleadings nor evidence on record as to the date on which the cheques were received and the date on which the same were sent for encashment. … It was for the appellant (Bhagwati Prasad) to plead and prove that it had not accepted the offer and had called upon the Railways to pay the balance amount. … In the absence of such evidence it must be held that by encashing the cheques received from the Railways, the appellant (Bhagwati Prasad) accepted the offer by adopting the mode of acceptance prescribed in the offer of the Railways.

The communication from the Railways was an offer. It was for the firm to accept or reject the offer. Let us examine several variations of the case to develop an understanding of the principles. If the firm sent a letter accepting the offer, an agreement would have got formed. The offer did not say that only by encashing the cheque could the offer be accepted. Encashment of the cheque, as it is a prescribed modality of acceptance in the offer document, leads to formation of an agreement.Suppose a firm neither encashed the check nor made any communication, in other words, it retained the cheque. The Railways could claim that retention amounted to acceptance of the offer. However, the stipulation in the offer makes silence (inactivity) into acceptance. The principle is that silence signifies disinterests and thus, rejection, and not acceptance. Thus, no contract would be formed by mere retention of the cheque.

To conclude, use of the words 'offer' or 'proposal' does not make it an offer. One has to infer from the context whether it is indeed an offer or not. A provisional acceptance does not create a contract. Changing the terms of an offer is a counter-offer as it extinguishes the original offer and puts up a new offer. The difference is that a provisional acceptance keeps the original offer open for its subsequent acceptance. Thus, the parties have to be careful in making communications in response to an offer. The acceptance should follow the procedure provided for it in the offer. The offeror, however, can waive the procedure specified and consent to an alternate one. If the offer is silent on the procedure of communication, a reasonable means of communication should be followed.

6

Place of Formation of Contract

A meeting of minds takes place only when the offeror receives the acceptance. Thus, the agreement is made where the offeror receives the acceptance. The place where the contract is made is relevant in deciding which court the parties could take the dispute to. It could also be important in deciding the law that would apply to the contract. The rule that the agreement is made when and where the offeror receives the communication of acceptance was not followed when the parties were communicating by post; the agreement was taken to be formed where the acceptor posted the letter. This variation came to be known as the postal rule. Section 1 introduces the general principle and its variation in the postal rule. The section also introduces the provisions in the Civil Procedure Code, and its linkage with the contract law, in the deciding jurisdiction of the court. Section 2 presents cases to develop an understanding of the principles on the means of communication and jurisdiction of the courts. Section 3 reviews how the common law courts and the Indian courts have extended the rules to the newer means of communication, like telephone and telex. The parties can keep out the application of the rules by settling on the court that would have jurisdiction on the contract. Section 4 explores the effect of such stipulations in contracts.

COMMUNICATION AND THE TIME AND PLACE OF CONTRACT

Let us take up the case where X and Y are across a stream, in the balcony of their houses. The stream is also the boundary of the states Gujarat and Maharashtra. X is in Gujarat and Y in Maharashtra. X shouts out an offer to Y. Just then, a speed boat roars along the stream, drowning X's voice. Has an offer been made? X has spoken but Y has not heard. X is interested in securing an agreement with Y. This is possible only when Y gets to hear his offer. X must speak again. The principle is, thus, expressed in Section 4 of the Indian Contract Act:

Section 4: The communication of a proposal is complete when it comes to the knowledge of the person to whom it is made.

In response, Y speaks out, 'I accept your offer.' Just then, another speed boat drowns Y's voice. The purpose of Y speaking is to secure the communication of acceptance to X. Only when X hears Y that is the communication of acceptance complete. X hearing Y's acceptance makes the two minds one. Till X hears, no contract is concluded. Thus, a contract is made the moment the offeror hears the acceptance. Consistent with this, the contract is made where the offeror is located. In our case, the contract is made in the State of Gujarat.

Let us extend the principle to the case where the parties are at a distance and communicating through post. X, based in Delhi, posts an offer to Y, based in Mumbai. Y, in response, posts the acceptance to X. By the same reasoning, the contract would be made in Delhi when X receives the acceptance letter. Curiously, the law on formation of contract by post is contrary to our reasoning.

Communication by Post

With the term 'post', we now associate post office and courier companies. The early form of postal service, however, was that a person would collect the letter and employ horses and carriages to take letters from one town to another. As the sender had to pay, the carrier maintained an account of letters sent. At the other end, the letter merely had to be delivered to the receiver. Post offices, stamps, registered letters and acknowledgement forms, which generated records of letters delivered, came later. In this arrangement, logically, the contract was made at the offeror's location when the offeror received the acceptance. The courts, however, were confronted with the problem that an offeror no longer keen to go ahead with a contract could simply insist that he never received the acceptance letter. The acceptor could prove that he posted the acceptance but not that the offeror received it. As trade and commerce expanded, communication through post became the backbone of the economy. The law that the contract is made when the offeror receives the acceptance neither did justice to the parties, nor was conducive to trade and commerce. The courts had to find a way out. The only available option was to rely on the evidence of the acceptor.

The courts, thus, took the position that the agreement is formed as soon as the acceptance letter is posted. In this arrangement, the claim of the acceptor that he never accepted the offer could be readily countered by the offeror producing the acceptance letter. This position would, however, be unjust to the offeror in the case where the letter was actually lost. An agreement would be formed without the offeror getting to know about it. There was injustice involved no matter which position was taken. From the point of view of the courts, the injustice in this case was far less, as it would be confined to the genuine cases of letters getting lost. The principle was first formulated in 1813 in *Adams* v. *Lindsell* case.[1] Consolidation of the principle came in the House of Lords case *Dunlop* v. *Higgins*.[2] The decision was best summarized in a later case: '... as a rule, a contract formed by correspondence through the post is complete as soon as the letter accepting an offer is put into the post, and is not put an end to in the event of the letter never being delivered.'[3]

The courts have to work by reason. They cannot put up anything to somehow produce a desired result. Yet, the courts function in a social and economic context. Reason is not embedded in the nature, which we can discover. Reason is produced by the society, in its practices and attempts to solve its problems. Thus, the courts could not throw reason to

[1] *Adams* v. *Lindsell*, (1818) 106 ER 250.
[2] *Dunlop* v. *Higgins*, (1848) 9 ER 805.
[3] *Household Fire and Carriage Accident Insurance Co.* v. *Grant*, Court of Appeal, (1874–1880) All ER Rep 919.

the winds, and yet there had to be continuous attempts to re-work logic and reason to find solutions. We should understand contract law, as we have been doing, from the perspective of commonsense and reason. At the same time, commonsense and reason are invented by human beings. Commonsense and reason would change with the changing contexts and needs of the society. In this sense, law would admit of peculiarities arising from its historical development. The courts worked out their legal reasoning for this practical expediency. The post office was treated as an agent of the offeror, who took the letter of offer to the offeree and brought back the acceptance. This arrangement was explained as follows: '... as soon as the letter of acceptance is delivered to the Post Office, the contract is made as complete and final and absolutely binding as if the acceptor had put his letter into the hands of a messenger, sent by the offeror himself as his agent, to deliver the offer and receive the acceptance.'[4] The position had its detractors even at that time. But the exception of the postal rule prevailed.

Thus, the master principle that a contract is made when the offeror receives the acceptance, was not breached. It was only juggled around by treating the post office as a messenger of the offeror, receiving the acceptance for the offeror. The courts, in thus formulating the law in relation to post, no doubt, were at their ingenious best. Facilitation of business with the development of post must have appeared to be a spectacular achievement. The judges could not have known that in the decades ahead, the telephone, telex, fax, email, internet, and video-conference would be invented, making their theory obsolete.

[4] Ibid.

Contracts and Jurisdiction of Courts

The contract law only settles the time and place of formation of contracts. The jurisdiction of courts is a much wider issue, which is settled by the procedural law. There are two broad kinds of law, civil law and criminal law. The procedure to be followed in settling a civil matter in India is provided in the Civil Procedure Code and for criminal matters in the Criminal Procedure Code. Contract matters are civil in nature and thus, the Civil Procedure Code is relevant. Section 20 of the Code provides:

20. Other suits to be instituted where defendants reside or cause of action arises—Subject to the limitations aforesaid, every suit shall be instituted in a court within the local limits of whose jurisdiction—

(a) the defendant, or each of the defendants ... actually and voluntarily resides, or carries on business, or personally works for gain, or

(b) ... the defendants ... acquiesce in such institution, or

(c) the cause of action, wholly or in part, arises.

To illustrate Section 20, if A, based in Mumbai, has to file a suit against B in Bangalore, it has to be filed in a court in Bangalore, and not at his own location, Mumbai. However, if A files a suit in Mumbai and B proceeds with it, Mumbai would become a valid court for the suit. Section 20(c) provides that a suit can also be instituted in a court in whose jurisdiction 'the cause of action, wholly or in part, arises'. A dispute on a contract is only a kind of civil dispute and subject to Section 20 for the jurisdiction of the courts. As the 'cause of action' arises due to the contract, the court of the place where the contract is formed acquires jurisdiction under Section 20(c). The other places where a cause of action arises in a contract are the place where the contract was to be performed and the place from where the money for the performance was to be paid. It is in this context that the place of formation of a contract becomes relevant for the jurisdiction of the court. Let us now appraise the following cases in relation to formation of contracts.

CASES FOR ANALYSIS

Case: Telephone
X, based in Ahmedabad, made an offer from Ahmedabad via telephone to Y in Delhi. Y, while on the line, accepted the offer. Later, a dispute arose over the performance of the contract. Which court would have the jurisdiction over the case, Ahmedabad or Delhi?

Case: Email
Yogesh, based in Chennai, sent an email to Rajesh, a trader in Bangalore: 'We offer to sell 1,000 hand towels of dimension 25 cm × 25 cm for Rs 30 a piece. The consignment will be sent by road. The price includes the transportation charges. Kindly send acceptance by email.' Rajesh replied from Bangalore: 'I accept your offer.' Which court will have jurisdiction over the contract?

Case: International Contract
Paperline Inc. is a tissue-paper manufacturing company based in New York. It had a standard form in which it required the buyer to make an offer to the company to sell its goods. Koel Limited, a company based in Delhi, made an offer in the standard document. Paperline Inc. accepted the offer. The parties were soon in dispute over the contract. The offer document had a clause saying that the parties would submit every dispute to arbitration. Would the arbitration be taken up in Delhi or New York?

Case: Oil and Natural Gas Commission, Dehradun v. Modern Construction and Company, Mansa
Modern Construction, Mansa is a registered partnership firm engaged in the construction work, with its office at Mansa in Mehsana District.[5] The Surat office of the Oil and Natural Gas Commission (ONGC) invited offers by tender notice for construction work. Three of the tenders of Modern Construction were accepted. Modern Construction had sent the tender from its office in Mansa. The ONGC accepted the tenders of Modern Construction by sending telegrams from Surat. The work was to be executed in Surat and money paid from the Zonal office of the ONGC in Mumbai. Parties were in dispute over payment of money. Modern Construction approached the court in Mehsana. The contention of the ONGC was that the Mehsana court did not have jurisdiction over the court. Were they right? Where else could Modern Constructions have filed its suit?

Case: Courier Company
The general conditions of contract of an apparel manufacturing company mentioned that all disputes would be subject to the jurisdiction of the courts in Ahmedabad. The seller had made an offer to sell apparel by post from its marketing office in Surat. The buyer had accepted the offer from Chennai. The parties then had a dispute. Which court should the buyer go to? Is the term on jurisdiction of court in the general conditions of contract relevant?

---

[5] *Oil and Natural Gas Commission, Dehradun and Others* v. *Modern Construction and Company, Mansa*, AIR 1998 Gujarat 46.

PLACE OF CONTRACT AND JURISDICTION OF COURT

Common law has formulated the principle that when an acceptance is sent by post, the agreement is formed the moment the letter is posted. The Indian Contract Act has adopted the common law position in a peculiar manner. Section 4 declares:

4. **Communication when complete**—The communication of a proposal is complete when it comes to the knowledge of the person to whom it is made.

To illustrate, X offers, by letter, to sell a house to Y at a certain price. The communication of the offer is complete when Y receives the letter. On this we never had any doubt. This is the same as the common law position. In relation to communication of acceptance, Section 4 provides as follows:

The communication of an acceptance is complete—as against the proposer, when it is put in a course of transmission to him, so as to be out of the power of the acceptor; as against the acceptor, when it comes to the knowledge of the proposer.

This is a variation of the common law rule. In common law, the contract is made for both the parties when the letter of acceptance is posted. In the Indian law, when Y posts the letter of acceptance, X is bound by it. X cannot revoke the offer once the letter is posted by Y. Even if the letter never reaches him, the contract is concluded. However, Y is not bound by it. Y will become bound when the letter reaches X. This position is peculiar but consistent with the practicality of adducing evidence. X cannot escape the contract if Y produces any evidence of posting the letter. And Y cannot get away when X can show his letter of acceptance. Thus, the Indian law creates two different times for the formation of contract for the parties.

It is also interesting that common law developed the rule with reference to 'posting' of the acceptance. The Indian Contract Act, however, uses the term 'put in a course of transmission'. It may have to do with the fact that by that time, that is 1872, the telegraph had come to be in use. The term could be to include the new mode of communication. Since then, several other modes of communication, including the telex, fax, phone, email, and video conferencing have come into use. These modes of communication have to be accommodated in the principles that had been formed earlier. Let us examine the extension of the principles to the new modes of communication with the following cases.

Court Case: Entores Limited v. Miles Far East Corporation

Entores Limited was a company registered in England, with its registered office in London.[6] Miles Far East Corporation was a company registered in the USA, with its headquarters in New York, in the State of New York. The Miles Corporation had agents all over the world. A principal–agent relationship is one of the special forms of contracts. In this, the principal allows the agent to represent the principal and bind them into contractual relations with other party.

In September, 1954, a series of communications passed over telex between Entores Limited in London and an agent of Miles Corporation based in Amsterdam. Email and fax have now displaced telex as a means of communication. In 1954, it was a new means of communication. In a telex, the parties connect to each other by dialling the telex number. The message typed at one end

---

[6] *Entores Limited* v. *Miles Far East Corporation*, (1955) 2 All ER 493.

is instantaneously printed on paper at the other end. Thus, the parties can interact with each other and, at the same time, generate a record of the communication. On the telex machine, Entores Limited made an offer to buy 100 tons of cathodes at a price of £239 per ton to the agent from Miles Corporation in Amsterdam. The agent from Amsterdam accepted the offer by telex. The parties later had a dispute on the contract. The question arose whether the case should be taken up in the courts in London or Amsterdam. This question depended on resolving the place of formation of the contract. Lord Denning delivered the following judgment for the Court of Appeal:

When a contract is made by post it is clear law throughout the common law countries that the acceptance is complete as soon as the letter of acceptance is put into the post box, and that is the place where the contract is made. But there is no clear rule about contracts made by telephone or by telex. Communications by these means are virtually instantaneous and stand on a different footing.

The problem can only be solved by going in stages. Let me first consider a case where two people make a contract by word of mouth in the presence of one another. Suppose, for instance, that I shout an offer to a man across a river or a courtyard but I do not hear his reply because it is drowned by an aircraft flying overhead. There is no contract at that moment. If he wishes to make a contract, he must wait till the aircraft is gone and then shout back his acceptance so that I can hear what he says. Not until I have his answer am I bound. ...

Now take a case where two people make a contract by telephone. Suppose, for instance, that I make an offer to a man by telephone and, in the middle of his reply, the line goes dead so that I do not hear his words of acceptance. There is no contract at that moment. The other man may not know the precise moment when the line failed. But he will know that the telephone conversation was abruptly broken off, because people usually say something to signify the end of the conversation. If he wishes to make a

contract, he must therefore get through again so as to make sure that I heard. Suppose next that the line does not go dead, but it is nevertheless so indistinct that I do not catch what he says and I ask him to repeat it. He then repeats it and I hear his acceptance. The contract is made, not on the first time when I do not hear, but only the second time when I do hear. If he does not repeat it, there is no contract. The contract is only complete when I have his answer accepting the offer.

Lastly take the Telex. Suppose a clerk in a London office taps out on the teleprinter an offer which is immediately recorded on a teleprinter in a Manchester office, and a clerk at that end taps out an acceptance. If the line goes dead in the middle of the sentence of acceptance, the teleprinter motor will stop. There is then obviously no contract. The clerk at Manchester must get through again and send his complete sentence. But it may happen that the line does not go dead, yet the message does not get through to London. Thus the clerk at Manchester may tap out his message of acceptance and it will not be recorded in London because the ink at the London end fails or something of that kind. In that case the Manchester clerk will not know of the failure but the London clerk will know of it and will immediately send back a message not receiving. Then, when the fault is rectified, the Manchester clerk will repeat his message. Only then is there a contract. If he does not repeat it, there is no contract. It is not until his message is received that the contract is complete.

In all the instances I have taken so far, the man who sends the message of acceptance knows that it has not been received or he has reason to know it. So he must repeat it. But suppose that he does not know that his message did not get home. He thinks it has. This may happen if the listener on the telephone does not catch the words of acceptance, but nevertheless does not trouble to ask for them to be repeated: or if the ink on the teleprinter fails at the receiving end, but the clerk does not ask for the message to be repeated: so that the man who sends an acceptance reasonably believes that his message has been received. The offeror in such circumstances is clearly bound, because he will be estopped from saying that he did not receive the message of acceptance. It is his own fault that he did not get it. But if there should be a case where the offeror without any fault on his part does not receive the message of acceptance yet the sender of it reasonably believes it has got home when it has not then I think there is no contract.

My conclusion is that the rule about instantaneous communications between the parties is different from the rule about the post. The contract is only complete when the acceptance is received by the offeror: and the contract is made at the place where the acceptance is received. ... Applying the principles which I have stated, I think that the contract in this case was made in London where the acceptance was received. It was therefore a proper case for service out of the jurisdiction.

The ratio, that is the binding principle, of the Entores case is that where the communication is interactive and spontaneous, whether face-to-face or through telephone or telex, the ordinary rule that the offeror must receive the acceptance would apply. The postal rule would apply only in the cases where post is used. Email is like a letter delivered to the other party. It is not an interactive means of communication. Thus, the postal rule would apply to communication by email. The House of Lords approved the position of Entores case decades later in *Brinkibon Limited* v. *Stahag Stahl und Stahlwarenhandelsgesellschaft mbH*.[7] *Bhagwandas Goverdhandas Kedia* v. *M/s. Girdharlal Parshottamadas and Co.* case came before the Supreme Court of India to decide the place of formation of contract when the parties communicate on the phone.

Court Case: Bhagwandas Goverdhandas Kedia v. M/s. Girdharlal Parshottamadas and Co.

The buyer, based in Ahmedabad, offered to buy from the seller in Khamgaon on the phone, and the seller accepted the offer in the same phone communication.[8] The seller failed to supply the goods and the buyer claimed damages. The dispute was whether the case should be taken up by the courts in Ahmedabad or Khamgaon. The trial court ruled that the contract was made in Ahmedabad. The case came before the Supreme Court in appeal. The contention of the seller was that under Section 4, irrespective of the mode of communication, the contract is made where the acceptance is put into 'a course of transmission'. Thus, the contract was made in Khamgaon when the seller uttered his acceptance of the offer in the phone. The buyer contended that receiving the intimation of acceptance of the offer was essential to the formation of a contract. Thus, the contract was made in Ahmedabad when the buyer heard the acceptance of the seller on the phone. The bench comprising of three judges was divided in its judgment. We will first explore the majority view:

The principal contention raised by the defendants [Kedia] raises a problem of some complexity which must be approached in the light of the relevant principles of the common law and statutory provisions contained in the Contract Act. A contract unlike a tort is not unilateral. If there be no 'meeting of minds' no contract may result. There should, therefore, be an offer by one party, express or implied, and acceptance of that offer by the other in the same sense in which it was made by the other.

...

The Contract Act does not expressly deal with the place where a contract is made. Sections 3 and 4 of the Contract Act deal with the communication, acceptance and revocation of proposals. By S. 3 the communication of a proposal, acceptance of a proposal, and revocation of a proposal and acceptance, respectively, are deemed to be made by any act or omission of the party proposing, accepting or revoking, by which he intends to communicate such

---

[7] *Brinkibon Limited* v. *Stahag Stahl und Stahlwarenhandelsgesellschaft mbH*, (1982) 1 All ER 293.

[8] *Bhagwandas Goverdhandas Kedia* v. *M/s Girdharlal Purshottamdas and Co.*, AIR 1966 SC 543.

proposal, acceptance or revocation, or which has the effect of communicating it. ... S. 4 deals not with the place, but with the completion of communication.

The challenge before the court then was to explore when the communication of acceptance is to be taken to be complete. This would fix the time and place of formation of the contract. The court summarized the evolution of the ordinary rule for completion of communication of acceptance and its exception in the postal rule:

When parties are in the presence of each other the method of communication will depend upon the nature of the offer and the circumstances in which it is made. When an offer is orally made, acceptance maybe expected to be made by an oral reply, but even a nod, or other act which indubitably intimates, even if the offeree has resolved to accept the offer a contract may not result. But on this rule is engrafted an exception based on grounds of convenience which has the merit not of logic or principle in support, but of long acceptance by judicial decisions. If the parties are not in the presence of each other, and the offeror has not prescribed a mode of communication of acceptance, insistence upon communication of acceptance of the offer by the offeree would be found to be inconvenient, when the contract is made by letters sent by post. In *Adams* v. *Lindsell*, (1818) I B ... it was ruled as early as in 1818 by the Court of King's bench in England that the contract was complete as soon as it was put into transmission. ... The rule in Adams' case was approved by the House of Lords in *Dunlop* v. *Vincent Higgins* (1848) 1 HLC 381. The rule was based on commercial expediency, or what Cheshire calls 'empirical grounds'. It makes a large inroad upon the concept of consensus, 'a meeting of minds' which is the basis of formation of a contract. It would be futile, however, to enter upon an academic discussion, whether the acceptation is justifiable in strict theory, and acceptable in principle. The exception has long been recognised in the United Kingdom and in other countries where the law of contracts is based on the common law of England. Authorities in India also exhibit a fairly uniform trend that in case of negotiations by post the contract is complete when acceptance of the offer put into a course of transmission to the offeror: see

Baroda Oil Cakes Traders case, AIR 1954 Bom 451, and cases cited therein.

...

The defendants (Kedia) contend that the same rule applies in the case of contracts made by the conversation on telephone. The plaintiffs (Girdharlal) contend that the rule which applies to those contracts is the ordinary rule which regards a contract as complete only when acceptance is intimated to the proposer. In the case of a telephonic conversation, in a sense the parties are in the presence of each other; each party is able to hear the voice of the other. There is instantaneous communication of speech intimating offer and acceptance, rejection or counter-offer. Intervention of an electrical impulse which results in the instantaneous communication of messages from a distance does not alter the nature of the conversation so as to make it analogous to that of an offer and acceptance through post or by telegraph.

...

In the administration of the law of contracts, the courts in India have generally been guided by the rules of the English common law applicable to contracts where no statutory provision to the contrary is in force. ... In England the Court of Appeal has decided in *Entores Ltd.* v. *Miles Far East Corporation* (1955) 2 QB 327, that:

'... where a contract is made by instantaneous communication, e.g., by telephone, the contract is complete only when the acceptance is received by the offeror, since generally an acceptance must be notified to the offeror to make a binding contract;'

The judgment summarized the Entores case, relied on it, and continued:

Obviously the draftsman of the Indian Contract Act did not envisage use of the telephone as a means of personal conversation between parties separated in space, and could not have intended to make any rule in that behalf. The question then is whether the ordinary rule which regards a contract as completed only when acceptance is intimated should apply, or whether the exception engrafted upon the rule in respect of offers and acceptances by post and by telegrams is to be accepted. If regard be had to the essential nature of conversation by telephone, it would be reasonable to hold that the parties being in a sense in the presence of each other, and negotiations are concluded by instantaneous communication of speech, communication of acceptance is a necessary part of the formation of contract, and the exception to the rule imposed on grounds of commercial expediency is inapplicable.

The Trial Court was, therefore, right in the view which it has taken that a part of the cause of action arose within the jurisdiction of the City Civil Court, Ahmedabad, where acceptance was communicated by telephone to the plaintiffs.

Hidayatullah, J gave a dissenting judgment. Let us briefly note some passages from the lengthy dissenting judgment:

The rules to apply in our country are statutory but the Contract Act was drafted in England and the English Common law permeates it; however, it is obvious that every new development of the Common law in England may not necessarily fit into the scheme and the words of our statute. If the language of our enactment … cannot be made to yield to any new theories held in foreign courts our clear duty will be to read the statute naturally and to follow it.

The judge followed the above principle and assessed that the Entores case was not in conformity with the Indian Contract Act:

On reading the reasons given in support of the decision and comparing them with the language of the Indian Contract Act I am convinced that the Indian Contract Act does not admit our accepting the view of the Court of Appeal.

…

The rule about acceptance by post or telegram is adopted in all countries in which the English Common law influence is felt and in many others and … the Indian Contract Act gives statutory approval to it. That rule is that a contract is complete when a letter of acceptance, properly addressed and stamped is posted, even if the letter does not reach the destination or having reached it is not read by the proposer. The same principle applies to telegrams. The first question is whether the general rule or the special rule applies to contracts made on the telephone and the second what is the position under the Indian Contract Act. The answer to the first question is that there is difference of opinion in the countries

of the world on that point and to the second that the Indian Contract Act does not warrant the acceptance of the decision in the Entores case.

The basis for the conclusion that the Entores case was contrary to the provisions in the Indian Contract Act was that the common law postal rule has been put in general and broad terms in Section 4. Under the section, communication of acceptance is complete against the proposer when the acceptance is 'put in the course of transmission'. Not only letters, but in all modes, including telegram and telephone, communication is put in the course of transmission. The judge continued:

What may be said in the English Common law, (which is capable of being moulded by judicial dicta), we cannot always say under our statutory law because we have to guide ourselves by the language of the statute. … It is plain that the law was framed at a time when telephones, wireless, tester and early bird were not contemplated. If time has marched inventions have made it easy to communicate instantaneously over long distance and the language of our law does not fit the new conditions it can be modified to reject the old principles. But we cannot go against the language by accepting an interpretation given without considering the language of our Act.

In my opinion, the language of S. 4 of the Indian Contract Act covers the case of communication over the telephone. Our Act does not provide separately for post, telegraph, telephone or wireless. Some of these were unknown in 1872 and no attempt has been made to modify the law. It may be presumed that the language has been considered adequate to cover cases of these new inventions.

…

Regard being had to the words of our statute I am compelled to hold that the contract was complete at Khamgaon.

Thus, in deciding the case, the court raised the important and interesting point of the relevance of the judgments of the British courts to the Indian courts. As we have seen, the provisions of the Indian Contract Act,

1872, came from the principles formulated by the common law courts. However, once the principles have been written down as an act, should we strictly interpret the provisions—text of the law—or go back to the sources, the cases from which these principles have come?

India borrowed from common law and wrote the Indian Contract Act. Despite several attempts; the United Kingdom, however, has not managed to codify its contract law. Thus, the common law tradition of deciding the cases on the basis of precedence set in the earlier cases still continues in the UK. A further point the case raised, in this context, was whether the cases of the British courts, after the enactment of the Indian Contract Act, 1872, should be of relevance to the Indian courts.

What difference did this make to the views of the majority and dissenting judgment? Surprisingly, the difference was not in the principle but on emphasis. In the majority view, the rules of English common law were welcome as a guide, so long as there was 'no statutory provision to the contrary'. The dissenting view was to go by the text of the act and rely on the common law only if it is fully in conformity with the act. The first view is liberal in setting a discourse between the act and the common law. It lets common law act as a guide in nebulous and ambiguous areas. The second makes the common law only confirm and support interpretation of the act. This reflected in the approach to the case. The dissenting view went strictly by the phrase 'put in the course of transmission' and refused to accommodate the Entores case. The majority view recognized the expression to be a codification of the common law postal rule and was willing to put the text in the context of the prior common law rules it was attempting to codify.

The British courts went through a similar debate over the codification of the common law. Despite several attempts, the contract law could not be codified. However, other common law fields, including the sale of goods, were codified. The law on sale of goods was codified as the Sale of Goods, 1893. In interpreting the provisions of the act in the early years, some judges took the position that as the act was a statutory enactment, they should start afresh and interpret the text of the law as it was without reference to the prior judgments. While others maintained that as the act was a codification of the prior rules, the text should be interpreted in the context of the prior court judgments. The second view came to prevail. However, the first held the rider that if the provision of the act was clearly contrary to the common law rule, it could not be assimilated.

The courts in the common law jurisdictions have taken this position in relation to the statutes codifying common law. This has led to referring to judgments from the other courts, particularly, of the contemporary and past British court judgments by the other courts.

Court Case: Oil and Natural Gas Commission, Dehradun v. Modern Construction and Company, Mansa

The ONGC accepted the tenders from Modern Construction by sending telegrams from Surat. The work was to be executed in Surat and money paid from the zonal office of ONGC in Mumbai. Parties were in dispute over payment of money. Modern Construction approached the court in Mehsana. The ONGC's contention was that the Mehsana court did not have jurisdiction over the court. The High Court examined Section 20 of the Civil Procedure Code, which deals with the jurisdiction the courts:

The principle underlying Section 20(a) and Section 20(b) is that suit has to be filed at a place where defendant can defend the suit without undue trouble. Section 20(c) provides that suit can be instituted in a civil court within the local limits of whose jurisdiction the cause of action, wholly or in part, arises. Needless to state that suit is always based on cause of action. CAUSE OF ACTION means every fact, which, if traversed, it would be necessary for the plaintiff to prove in order to support his right to a judgment of the court. It is time and again held in number of cases that it is bundle of facts which taken with the law applicable to them, gives, the plaintiff a right to relief against the defendant. It is, therefore, incumbent upon the plaintiff to prove that cause of action has arisen in part or wholly within the jurisdiction of the civil court where the suit is instituted. Obviously, cause of action must be antecedent to the institution of the suit.

We are vitally concerned with the cause of action founded upon the contracts. In suits arising out of contract, the cause of action arises within the meaning of Section 20 (c) of the C.P.C.

The cause of action under Section 20 (c) could arise where the contract was made, the contract was to be executed, and the place from where the money was to be paid. Following the postal rule, as the telegram was posted from Surat, the contract was made in Surat. Thus, the suit could be filed in Surat. Further, as the work was to be executed in Surat and money paid from Mumbai, the suit could have been filed from Surat or Mumbai. In this arrangement, Mehsana court did not have the jurisdiction over the contract. The court noted:

In suit for damages for breach of contract, cause of action consists of making of contract and of its breach so that suit may be filed either at the place where contract was made or at the place where it could have been performed or where breach of contract occurred.
...
Making of contract is part of cause of action and suit on contract, therefore, can also be filed at a place where contract was concluded or made. Determina-

tion of the place where it came to be made is part of the law of contract. ... In the present case ... the contract became concluded qua proposer... contractor not upon receipt of intimation of telegram at Mansa sent from Surat by ONGC. ... In the circumstances, considering the provisions of Section 20(c) of the CPC and provisions of Section 4 of the Contract Act, part of cause of action arose at Surat or Bombay and not at Mansa.

TERMS OF CONTRACT AND MEANS OF COMMUNICATION

Contracts are voluntarily formed. It is for the contracting parties to decide all aspects of the contract, including the mode of communication and formation of agreement. If the contract stipulates the time of formation of the contract, the place of formation of the contract, or the jurisdiction of the court, the stipulated term would apply. The postal rule, like most other provisions in the Indian Contract Act, is only the default rule, where the parties do not provide on the theme. A case on this is *Holwell Securities Limited* v. *Hughes.*[9] The offer documents required that written acceptance must reach the offeror. The acceptance letter was lost, but the acceptor could establish the dispatch of the acceptance. The acceptor claimed that, following the postal rule, a contract was formed the moment the letter was posted. The court did not apply the postal rule as the parties had decided that the acceptance must reach the offeror.

Internet and Place of Contract

We need to judge every new means of communication to see whether it is dialogic and instantaneous, or discrete like the post. Following this, postal rule should apply to email. The other transactions on the internet,

[9] *Holwell Securities Limited* v. *Hughes*, (1974) 1 All ER 161.

for example transactions with an electronic store, can be a dialogic one. In the *Chwee Kin Keong and Others* v. *Digilandmall.com Private Limited*,[10] which we have already reviewed in an earlier chapter, the court explored the nature on communication on the internet:

Different rules may apply to e-mail transactions and worldwide web transactions. When considering the appropriate rule to apply, it stands to reason that as between sender and receiver, the party who selects the means of communication should bear the consequences of any unexpected events. An e-mail, while bearing some similarity to a postal communication, is in some aspects fundamentally different. Furthermore, unlike a fax or a telephone call, it is not instantaneous. E-mails are processed through servers, routers and Internet service providers. Different protocols may result in messages arriving in an incomprehensible form. Arrival can also be immaterial unless a recipient accesses the e-mail, but in this respect e-mail does not really differ from mail that has to be opened. Certain Internet service providers provide the technology to inform a sender that a message has not been properly routed. Others do not.

Once an offer is sent over the Internet, the sender loses control over the route and delivery time of the message. In that sense, it is akin to ordinary posting. Notwithstanding some real differences with posting, it could be argued cogently that the postal rule should apply to e-mail acceptances; in other words, that the acceptance is made the instant the offer is sent.... (The) acceptance would be effective the moment the offer enters that node of the network outside the control of the originator. There are, however, other sound reasons to argue against such a rule in favour of the recipient rule. It should be noted that while the common law jurisdictions continue to wrestle over this vexed issue, most civil law jurisdictions lean towards the recipient rule. In support of the latter it might be argued that unlike a posting, e-mail communication takes place in a relatively short time frame. The recipient rule is therefore more convenient and relevant in the context of both instantaneous or near

instantaneous communications. Notwithstanding occasional failure, most e-mails arrive sooner rather than later.
...
The applicable rules in relation to transactions over the worldwide web appear to be clearer and less controversial. Transactions over websites are almost invariably instantaneous and/or interactive. The sender will usually receive a prompt response. The recipient rule appears to be the logical default rule. Application of such a rule may however result in contracts being formed outside the jurisdiction if not properly drafted. Web merchants ought to ensure that they either contract out of the receipt rule or expressly insert salient terms within the contract to deal with issues such as a choice of law, jurisdiction and other essential terms relating to the passing of risk and payment. Failure to do so could also result in calamitous repercussions. Merchants may find their contracts formed in foreign jurisdictions and therefore subject to foreign laws.

Telecommunication and electronic medium present yet another possibility. With a mobile phone, a phone call can be made or an email sent from any location. An offer and acceptance could be sent by both the parties while in transit. Following the development of the law and proliferation of the means of communication, every written contract provides for the jurisdiction of the court. The term is usually worded as follows: 'Any dispute, controversy or claim arising out of or relating to the contract shall be subject to the jurisdiction of Courts of...' The Information Technology Act, 2000, provides the default option in the case of electronic communication. Section 13(3) reads:

(3) Save as otherwise agreed to between the originator and the addressee, an electronic record is deemed to be dispatched at the place where the originator has his place of business, and is deemed to be received at the place where the addressee has his place of business.

Thus, the contracting parties are free to stipulate the court that would have the jurisdiction

---

[10] *Chwee Kin Keong and Others* v. *Digilandmall. com Private Limited*, (2004) 2 SLR 594.

in the case of a dispute. In the absence of it, acceptance would be deemed to have been sent from the place of business of the acceptor and received by the offeror at his place of business.

To summarize, the place where a contract is formed is relevant in deciding the jurisdiction of the court over the contract. In face-to-face communication, an agreement is reached when the person making the offer hears the acceptance. The same rule is applied to all other modes of communication where communication is instantaneous and interactive, like telephone, fax and video conferencing. In the cases where the parties communicate by letter and do not specify further on the formation of agreement, the agreement is formed when the acceptance is handed over to the post or courier. This is called the postal rule. As email is like post, the postal rule applies to it. The contracting parties are free to stipulate a jurisdiction of the court to oust the application of the principles set by the contract law. This is the reason every written contract has a jurisdiction clause.

7

Unilateral and Bilateral Contracts

A contract can be either bilateral or unilateral. In a bilateral contract, both parties have obligations. Most of the examples so far have been of bilateral contracts. In a unilateral contract, only the party putting up the offer has obligations. We will explore the topic of unilateral contracts in this chapter.

X is a large corporation whose computers have got inflicted with a new virus called vermon. X wants antivirus software that will eliminate it. X offers Y Rs 20,000 to write software to eliminate vermon. Y accepts the offer. Consider an alternate offer from X to Y, 'If you deliver software that can eliminate vermon, I will give you Rs 30,000.' In the first case, a contract is formed between the parties. Both parties have rights and obligations. In the second case, Y cannot accept the offer by saying, 'I accept the offer.' Y can accept the offer only by actually delivering the software that can eliminate vermon. If Y delivers the software, X is bound to give the money. However, Y is under no obligation to deliver the software. Thus, only X has an obligation. This contract is called a unilateral contract ('uni' meaning single and 'lateral' meaning side). A unilateral contract is also called an 'if' contract, since the formation of the contract depends on whether the person to whom the offer is made executes his part. In contrast, in the first case, both the parties have obligations. This is a 'bilateral' contract ('bi' meaning two). Most contracts are bilateral.

Let us take up a variation of the above unilateral contract. X announces in the newspaper that he will give Rs 10,000 to anyone who provides him with software that can eliminate vermon. X is now bound to give Rs 10,000 to anyone who sends software that can eliminate vermon, but no one is bound to give him a software. The offer is made to the world at large. The announcement is a unilateral offer and can lead to formation of unilateral contracts. A bilateral offer can also be made to the world at large. For example, X announces in the newspapers, 'We offer to pay Rs 20,000 for delivery of software that will eliminate vermon. Kindly send acceptance of the offer at the following address…' Offers made to the world at large are usually, unilateral offers, promising a reward for performing a particular act, like finding a missing child, furnishing information on a criminal, or apprehending an offender. Advertisements, at times, can be unilateral offers.

The founding case on unilateral contract is the Carbolic Smoke Ball case, which he discussed in Chapter 3. The questions that arose were: Was the advertisement an offer? To whom was the offer made? Could the offer have been accepted so as to convert it into an agreement? Acceptance of an offer needs to be communicated to the person making the offer. Was the acceptance notified? The Carbolic Smoke Ball Company had put up the following contentions while claiming that it had no obligation towards Ms Carlill. First, the advertisement was not an offer as it was not made to any particular person. Second, even if it were an offer, Ms Carlill had not validly accepted the offer. Third, the advertisement was not meant to create any legal, binding relations. In response to the question that the offer had not been made to anybody in particular and, it was therefore could not be accepted by anybody, Justice Lindley noted:

Now that point is common to the words of this advertisement and to the words of all other advertisements offering rewards. They are offers to anybody who performs the conditions named in the advertisement, and anybody who does perform the condition accepts the offer. In point of law this advertisement is an offer to pay £100 to anybody who will perform these conditions, and the performance of the conditions is the acceptance of the offer.

Justice Bowen expressed the making of a unilateral offer, thus:

It was also said that the contract is made with all the world—that is, with everybody; and that you cannot contract with everybody. It is not a contract made with all the world. There is the fallacy of the argument. It is an offer made to all the world; and why should not an offer be made to all the world which is to ripen into a contract with anybody who comes forward and performs the condition? It is an offer to become liable to any one who, before it is retracted, performs the condition, and, although the offer is made to the world, the contract is made with that limited portion of the public who come forward and perform the condition on the faith of the advertisement.

The company was claiming that the advertisement was vague and uncertain and, hence, not an offer capable of being accepted. Justice Lindley noted:

Read the advertisement how you will, and twist it about as you will, here is a distinct promise expressed in language which is perfectly unmistakable—'£100 reward will be paid by the Carbolic Smoke Ball Company to any person who contracts the influenza after having used the ball three times daily for two weeks according to the printed directions supplied with each ball. ... The deposit is called in aid by the advertiser as proof of his sincerity in the matter—that is, the sincerity of his promise to pay this £100 in the event which he has specified.

There was another important and interesting point in the case. In a bilateral contract, the acceptance is communicated to the offeror. Till the communication of acceptance is secured, there is no meeting of minds. On this point, Justice Bowen noted: 'One cannot doubt that, as an ordinary rule of law, an acceptance of an offer made ought to be notified to the person who makes the offer, in order that the two minds may come together. Unless this is done the two minds may be apart, and there is not that consensus which is necessary.' The judge, however, noted that the requirement of notification could be dispensed by the person making the offer:

... as notification of acceptance is required for the benefit of the person who makes the offer, the person who makes the offer may dispense with notice to himself if he thinks it desirable to do so, and I suppose there can be no doubt that where a person in an offer made by him to another person, expressly or impliedly intimates a particular mode of acceptance as sufficient to make the bargain binding, it is only necessary for the other person to whom such offer is made to follow the indicated method of acceptance; and if the person making the offer, expressly or impliedly intimates in his offer that it will be sufficient to act

on the proposal without communicating acceptance of it to himself, performance of the condition is a sufficient acceptance without notification.
…

It follows from the nature of the thing that the performance of the condition is sufficient acceptance without the notification of it, and a person who makes an offer in an advertisement of that kind makes an offer which must be read by the light of that common sense reflection. He does, therefore, in his offer impliedly indicate that he does not require notification of the acceptance of the offer.

The contemporary advertisements are careful not to be taken as unilateral offer. Solicitations are so arranged that the advertisement remains only an invitation to offer. Further, by adding 'terms apply' or 'conditions apply' to the advertisement, the advertisement is made subject to detailed terms restricting formation of contracts. The application of unilateral cases is limited to the reward cases.

Court Case: Gauri Dutt's Missing Nephew

The nephew of one Gauri Dutt absconded from his home in Kanpur.[1] For several days, no trace of him could be found. Gauri Dutt gave money to his servants for railway fare and other expenses, and sent them to different places in search of the boy. One of the servants, Lalman Shukla, the *munim* in Gauri Dutt's firm, was sent to Haridwar. Later, after the servants had left, Gauri Dutt issued handbills offering a reward of Rs 501 to any one who might find the boy. He sent some handbills to Lalman Shukla also, in Haridwar. Lalman traced the boy to Rishikesh and brought him home. Gauri Dutt gave Lalman Rs 20 for having found the boy. Lalman must have been upset with the denial of the promised reward amount. Next, we learn that Lalman has ceased to be in the employment of Gauri

Dutt and has filed a suit for the recovery of Rs 501, the amount promised in the handbill. The court ruled:

In my opinion, a suit like the present can only be founded on a contract. In order to constitute a contract, there must be an acceptance of the offer and there can be no acceptance unless there is knowledge of the offer. Motive is not essential, but knowledge and intention are. In the case of a public advertisement offering a reward, the performance of the act raises an inference of acceptance. This is manifest from S. 8 of the Contract Act, which provides that 'Performance of the conditions of a proposal … is an acceptance of the proposal.'

The handbill was a unilateral offer made to the world at large. An offer can be accepted and a meeting of minds is reached only if the person has the knowledge of the offer. In this case, handbills were also sent to Lalman and thus, he had knowledge of it. Further, Section 8 provides: 'Performance of the conditions of a proposal … is an acceptance of the proposal.' Thus, finding the boy itself amounted to acceptance of the offer. As a result, a contract was formed between the parties. However, as we would learn in the part of consideration, the duty owed from a contract cannot be the consideration for another contract between the same parties. As Lalman was duty-bound to look for the boy in the course of his employment as *munim*, finding the boy could not be a valid consideration for the second agreement created through the offer put up in the handbill.

Court Case: Har Bhajan Lal v. Charan Lal

This is another reward case for finding a missing person.[2] A young boy aged 14 ran away from home. The father issued a pamphlet offer a reward for finding the boy. The court

---

[1] *Lalman Shukla* v. *Gauri Dutt*, (1913) 11 ALJ 489.

[2] *Har Bhajan Lal* v. *Charan Lal*, AIR 1925 All 539.

accepted the following English translation of the pamphlet. 'Anybody who finds trace of the boy and brings him home will get Rs 500.' The person who found the boy had seen the pamphlet and after overhearing a conversation realized that a boy at Bareilly railway station was the missing one. The court noted: 'The hand-bill was an offer open to the whole world and capable of acceptance by any person who fulfilled the conditions. The real condition of the promise in the hand-bill was, 'I will pay Rs. 500 to any one who finds my son and brings him home.' I am of the opinion that the plaintiff substantially performed the condition.'

Unilateral Contract and Consideration

In a unilateral contract, the action required to be performed is the consideration for the offeror. Let us examine this idea further with the following case.

Court Case: The Great Northern Railway Company v. Witham

The Great Northern Railway Company advertised for tenders for the supply of goods (iron, among other things) to be delivered at their station at Doncaster, according to a certain specification.[3] Samuel Witham sent in a tender as follows:

I, the undersigned, hereby undertake to supply the Great Northern Railway Company, for twelve months from the 1st of November, 1871, to 31st of October, 1872, with such quantities of each or any of the several articles named in the attached specification as the company's store-keeper may order from time to time, at the price set opposite each article respectively, and agree to abide by the conditions stated on the other side.

[3] *The Great Northern Railway Company v. Witham*, (LR) 9 CP 16.

The company accepted the tender and placed several orders for iron, and these were supplied by Witham. Ultimately, Witham refused to supply any more. A dispute arose on the contractual obligations of the parties. Witham claimed that while he had undertaken to supply, there was no obligation on the company to place the order. Thus, there was no consideration in the contract. As a result, Witham claimed, there was no enforceable agreement between the parties. Brett, J explored the contract as a unilateral contract. He noted:

If I say to another, 'If you will go to York, I will give you £100l.,' that is in a certain sense a unilateral contract. He has not promised to go to York. But, if he goes, it cannot be doubted that he will be entitled to receive the £100l. His going to York at my request is a sufficient consideration for my promise. So, if one says to another, 'If you will give me an order for iron, or other goods, I will supply it at a given price;' if the order is given, there is a complete contract which the seller is bound to perform. There is in such a case ample consideration for the promise. So, here, the company having given the defendant an order at his request, his acceptance of the order would bind them. … This is matter of every day's practice; and I think it would be wrong to countenance the notion that a man who tenders for the supply of goods in this way is not bound to deliver them when an order is given.

Revocation of Unilateral Offer

We have formulated that an offer can be revoked before it is accepted. In a bilateral contract, an agreement is formed when the notification of the acceptance reaches the offer. The offeror is free to revoke the offer till this specific incidence happens. The same applies to a unilateral offer made to a specific person. The revocation can be communicated to the person before he performs the act to bind the offeror. However, in the unilateral contracts where the offer is made to the world at large, how does one withdraw the offer?

The offeror has made the offer to the world at large. However, the communication of offer is complete to only those who have read the announcement. The communication of revocation, technically, must reach each of these people. The only case on this is from the American Supreme Court, *Shuey* v. *United States.*

Court Case: Shuey, Executor v. United States

The Secretary of War of the United States of America issued an announcement in the newspapers that a reward of $25,000 would be paid by the War Department for the apprehension of John H. Surratt, who was involved in the plot against the life of President Lincoln.[4] Seven months later, the reward was revoked through publication in the newspapers. Surratt was apprehended five months after the revocation. The person who secured the arrest did not know that the offer of reward was revoked. The court ruled:

The offer of a reward for the apprehension of Surratt was revoked on the twenty-fourth day of November, 1865; and notice of the revocation was published. It is not to be doubted that the offer was revocable at any time before it was accepted, and before any thing had been done in reliance upon it. There was no contract until its terms were complied with. Like any other offer of a contract, it might, therefore, be withdrawn before rights had accrued under it; and it was withdrawn through the same channel in which it was made. The same notoriety was given to the revocation that was given to the offer; and the findings of fact do not show that any information was given by the claimant, or that he did any thing to entitle him to the reward offered, until five months after the offer had been withdrawn. True, it is found that then, and at all times until the arrest was actually made, he was ignorant of the withdrawal; but that is an immaterial fact. The offer of the reward not having been made to him directly, but by means of

a published proclamation, he should have known that it could be revoked in the manner in which it was made.

Thus, the same mode and intensity of communication of revocation for making the offer would be adequate to revoke a unilateral offer made to the world at large. In a bilateral contract, the agreement is formed when the offer is accepted by saying 'yes', either expressly or impliedly. In a unilateral contract, however, the person to whom the offer is made can accept it, not by saying 'yes', but by performing the act required by the offer. The act could be providing a slogan or finding a missing boy or fugitive. A difficulty in revoking unilateral offer arises in relation to the aspect that an act has to be performed.

Case: Action and Revocation

Jeet tells Sham, 'If you run ten laps of this football field, I will give you Rs 5,000.' Let us look at the following responses to this unilateral offer.

Response 1: Sham says, 'I accept your offer.' However, he showed no signs of running laps of the football ground.

Response 2: The moment Sham heard Jeet, he started running. He completed 7 laps. However, he got tired and gave up.

Response 3: The moment Sham heard Jeet, he started running and completed 10 laps of the field.

Response 4: Immediately after making the offer, before Sham could start running, Jeet revoked the offer.

Response 5: Jeet revoked the offer when Sham was running the ninth lap.

Our analysis of the responses is as follows:

Response 1: A unilateral offer can only be accepted by doing the act required by the offer. It cannot be accepted by merely saying yes to it.

[4] *Shuey, Executor* v. *United States*, 92 US 73 (1875).

Response 2: Sham has taken up the act but not completed it. The contract will get formed only if the act is completed. Thus, there are no obligations for Jeet.

Response 3: Sham has completed the act and thus an agreement is formed between the parties.

Response 4: An offer can be revoked till it is accepted. Thus, Jeet can revoke the offer.

Response 5: An offer can be revoked till it is accepted. Sham is in the act towards accepting the offer, but he has not completed it as yet. It can be asserted that the offer can be revoked. However, it will be unfair to revoke the offer when the other person has set out to do the act. The common law courts, based on a sense of justice and fairness, have taken this position. Let us review the following case on the nature of unilateral offers and their revocation.

Court Case: Errington v. Errington

The case involved Mr Errington, his wife, son, and daughter-in-law.[5] Mr Errington bought a house for his son and daughter-in-law to live in. The total value of the house was £750. Mr Errington paid £250 in cash and borrowed £500 from a building society on the security of the house. Mr Errington was required to pay 15s to the building society every week as repayment of the loan amount and interest on it. He took the house in his own name. He told the daughter-in-law that the £250 was a present for them and they should pay the building society instalments of 15s a week themselves. He handed the building society book to her: 'Don't part with this book. The house will be your property when the mortgage is paid.' He promised that he would transfer it in their names when he retired. She

paid the building society instalments regularly and much of the mortgage was repaid.

Mr Errington passed away, leaving behind all his property by will, including the house which was in his name, to his wife. However, the daughter-in-law continued to pay the instalments to the building society. After the death of Mr Errington, the son went to live with her mother as she needed him, and asked his wife to join them. She refused to live with the mother, who filed a case to evict her daughter-in-law from her property. The case was on the nature of the contractual relationship among the parties and its implications. Denning in his judgment ruled:

It is to be noted that the couple never bound themselves to pay the instalments to the building society, and I see no reason why any such obligation should be implied. It is clear law that the court is not to imply a term unless it is necessary, and I do not see that it is necessary here. Ample content is given to the whole arrangement by holding that the father promised that the house should belong to the couple as soon as they had paid off the mortgage. The parties did not discuss what was to happen if the couple failed to pay the instalments to the building society, but I should have thought it clear that, if they did fail to pay the instalments, the father would not be bound to transfer the house to them. The father's promise was a unilateral contract —a promise of the house in return for their act of paying the instalments. It could not be revoked by him once the couple entered on performance of the act, but it would cease to bind him if they left it incomplete and unperformed, which they have not done. If that was the position during the father's lifetime, so it must be after his death. If the daughter-in-law continues to pay all the building society instalments, the couple will be entitled to have the property transferred to them as soon as the mortgage is paid off, but if she does not do so, then the building society will claim the instalments from the father's estate and the estate will have to pay them. I cannot think that in those circumstances the estate would be bound to transfer the house to them, any more than the father himself would have been.

[5] *Errington* v. *Errington*, (1952) 1 All ER 149.

As Lord Denning points out, the agreement would get formed only when all the instalments are paid. However, the offer cannot be withdrawn once the action towards formation of contract has commenced. The Court of Appeal in *Daulia Limited* v. *Four Millbank Nominees Limited* reached the same conclusion.[6] Goff, LJ noted:

The concept of a unilateral or 'if contract' is somewhat anomalous, because it is clear that, at all events until the offeree starts to perform the condition, there is no contract at all, but merely an offer which the offeror is free to revoke.

Doubts have been expressed whether the offeror becomes bound so soon as the offeree starts to perform or satisfy the condition, or only when he has fully done so.... Whilst I think the true view of a unilateral contract must in general be that the offeror is entitled to require full performance of the condition which he has imposed and short of that he is not bound, that must be subject to one important qualification, which stems from the fact that there must be an implied obligation on the part of the offeror not to prevent the condition becoming satisfied, which obligation it seems to me must arise as soon as the offeree starts to perform. Until then the offeror can revoke the whole thing, but once the offeree has embarked on performance it is too late for the offeror to revoke his offer.

Cases are settled on the rule; however, there are ambiguities in settling on a conceptual explanation. The general principle, coming from *Pane* v. *Cave*, is that an offer can be revoked till it is accepted. In a unilateral contract, the offeror should be able to revoke till the act of performance is completed. One argument is that it is implied in every unilateral contract that the offer will not be revoked once the performance has commenced.

[6] *Daulia Limited* v. *Four Millbank Nominees Limited*, (1978) Ch 231.

Communication of Acceptance

In a bilateral contract, the offeree can accept the offer only when he gets to know of it. Thus, the problem of the offeree and not knowing the offer does not arise. In a unilateral contract, however, as an action has to be performed, a person may perform the action without knowing of the offer. This may give rise to a dispute whether a contract is formed between the parties or not. For example, there is a reward for finding a missing child. A person finds a child unattended and takes him to his guardians. Later, he learns that there was a reward for finding the child. Should he be allowed to claim the reward? From one point of view, the offer has been accepted by doing the act. From another point of view, there is no meeting of minds, and thus no agreement between the parties.

A case on an associated theme is *R* v. *Clarke*. The Government of Western Australia had announced a reward of £1000 for 'such information as shall lead to the arrest and conviction of the person or persons who committed the murders' of two police officers. Clarke was himself arrested and accused of one of the murders. Clarke provided information that led to the conviction of those responsible for the murders. Clarke claimed the reward of £1,000. The court, however, found that he had acted 'exclusively in order to clear himself from a false charge of murder', not to claim the reward. According to the court, he did not have the reward offer in mind when he provided the information. Isaacs, one of the judges gave the following illustration:

An offer of £100 to any person who swims a hundred yards in the harbour on the first day of the year, would be met by voluntarily performing the feat with reference to the offer, but would not in my opinion be satisfied by a person who was accidentally or maliciously thrown overboard on that date and swam the distance simply to save his life, without any thought of the offer. The offeror might or might not feel morally impelled to give the sum in such a case, but would be under no contractual will obligation to do so.

Thus, according to the court that the act was not done towards accepting the offer, no agreement was formed between the parties.

Thus, contract law classifies contracts as unilateral and bilateral contracts. In a bilateral contract, both the parties are specific and have obligations towards each other. In a unilateral contract, only the offeror is under an obligation. However, if one were to successfully take up the task, the offeror would be bound to give the reward money. A unilateral offer cannot be revoked if a person has already set out to perform the act put up in the offer. Unilateral contracts are not a prevalent form of contract. Advertisements, by including conditions, make themselves invitation to offer. This has limited unilateral contracts to cases of rewards.

8

Battle of Forms

The founding principle is an agreement is about meeting of minds. A way of ascertaining formation of agreement is the acceptance of offer. In some situations, for example, an auction where the auctioneer promises to award the highest bidder, offer and acceptance are not discernible, yet the courts have maintained that an agreement is formed. As the contracts have become detailed, the founding principle—the meeting of minds— and the formula—acceptance of offer—have come into conflict. Most business contracts are detailed and have numerous terms. The parties often settle on some terms and negotiate on others. At the end of this process, the parties may conclude that they have reached an agreement. The rulings of the two common law cases, *Gibson* v. *Manchester City Council* and *Butler Machine Tool Company Limited* v. *Ex-Cell-O Corporation* have established that every contract must fit the formula of offer and acceptance. In this chapter, we will explore the different arguments through which the ideas were contested and resolved. Towards this, Section 1 of the chapter presents just the facts of the two cases and challenges the reader to develop arguments for resolving

the cases. Sections 2 and 3 review the court judgments.

CASES ANALYSIS

Court Case: *Gibson* v. *Manchester City Council*

The Manchester City Council is the elected body entrusted with the governance of the city of Manchester.[1] The city councils of the UK have developed housing, which they let out to persons needing accommodation. Manchester City Council also owned several houses it had let out. One of the tenants was Gibson. The City Council informed Gibson that it was going to repair the tarmac path of the house. The work had not been taken up as yet. The City Council took a decision to sell the houses owned by it to the tenants. It circulated brochures titled 'Full details of how you can buy your council house'. The brochure stated: 'The City Council are prepared to sell freehold … any Council house … to the tenant of that house, providing he has been in

---

[1] *Gibson* v. *Manchester City Council*, (1979) 1 All ER 972.

occupation of it for at least one year.' Towards fixing the price for a house, the Council took the market value and gave discounts on the basis of the length of the tenancy. Gibson received a letter from the city treasure, dated 10 February 1971, informing him that the council 'may be prepared to sell the house to you at the purchase price of £2,725 less 20% = £ 2,180 (freehold).' The letter further stated: 'This letter should not be regarded as a firm offer … If you would like to make formal application to buy your Council house, please complete the enclosed application form and return it to me as soon as possible.'

Gibson filled up the form titled 'Application to buy a Council house', which was a standard printed form. The price mentioned in the letter for the specific house was to be copied in the form. Gibson, however, had doubts about the price of the house. The Council had not repaired the tarmac, and Gibson did not know whether the price included or excluded the cost of repair. Thus, Gibson completed and signed the form but left the price blank. Gibson sent the form with a covering letter dated 5 March 1971. The covering letter, referring to the repair of the tarmac yet to be done by the Council, mentioned:

I would therefore like your assurance that Direct Works will not exclude these premises when re-surfacing or re-laying starts, or alternatively would you deduct an amount of money from the purchase price and I will undertake the repairs myself. Whichever decision you arrive at I would like to make an initial cash payment of £ 500—so I would be obliged if you will let me have the figures to allow for the deposit mentioned. I have left the purchase price blank on the application form until I hear from you.

The housing manager replied through a letter dated 12 March that the house was valued at £2,180 in its existing condition and the Council would not take up any repairs. Gibson replied through a letter dated 18

March replied: 'Reference your letter of March 12th … In view of your remarks I would be obliged if you will carry on with the purchase as per my application already in your possession.' Gibson did not get any reply from the Council. In May 1971, the political control of the Council changed hands. The Council was not in favour of the sale of the Council houses. It directed its officers not to go ahead with the sale of the Council houses where the contracts were not concluded. The Council informed Gibson, through a letter dated 27 July, that the Council would not proceed further with his application to purchase the house. Gibson claimed that an agreement had been formed between the parties. Let us explore the following issues:

1. An agreement is about a meeting of minds through a communicative process. Was the Council keen all along to the sell the house? Was Gibson communicating his commitment to buy the house all along? Did the parties have a meeting of minds on the sale of the house for £ 2,180? If yes, when?

2. A way for the parties to reach an agreement is the acceptance of an offer. Seen in this formulation, did the parties reach an agreement? When was a valid offer made? Who made the offer?

Court Case: Butler Machine Tool Company Limited v. Ex-Cell-O Corporation

Butler Machine Tool Co. Limited was a machine manufacturing company. Ex-Cell-O Corporation was in communication with the company to buy a miller machine.[2] Butler Machine Limited sent a quotation dated

[2] *Butler Machine Tool Company Limited* v. *Ex-Cell-O Corporation (England) Limited*, (1979) 1 All ER 965.

23 May 1969 to sell and deliver one 'Butler' double column plano-miller for the total price of £75,535. The quotation mentioned: 'DELIVERY: 10/11 months (Subject to confirmation at time of ordering). Other terms and conditions are on the reverse of this quotation.' On the back of the quotation, there were 16 conditions. A general condition was as follows: 'All orders are accepted only upon and subject to the terms set out in our quotation and the following conditions. These terms and conditions shall prevail over any terms and conditions in the Buyer's order.' Clause 3 mentioned:

Prices are based on present day costs of manufacture and design and having regard to the delivery quoted and uncertainty as to the cost of labour, materials etc. during the period of manufacture, we regret that we have no alternative but to make it a condition of acceptance of order that goods will be charged at prices ruling upon date of delivery.

Ex-Cell-O replied on its own standard printed order form, dated 27 May 1969. The order mentioned: 'Please supply on terms and conditions as below and overleaf.' Several of the terms in the order form of the buyer were different from the quotation sent by the seller, Butler Machine Limited. There was no separate and additional charge for the installation of the machine. According to the quotation of the seller, the buyer had to organize and pay for the transportation of the machine from the warehouse of the seller. The order of the buyer required the seller to deliver at the premises of the buyer at his own cost. Butler Machine Limited's terms had provided that the order could not be cancelled due to delay in delivery. Ex-Cell-O reserved the right to cancel the delivery if the order was not made in time.

The order of Ex-Cell-O had a tear-off slip, which read: 'ACKNOWLEDGEMENT: Please sign and return to EX-CELL-O CORP.

(England) LTD. We accept your order on the Terms and Conditions stated thereon-and undertake to deliver by … Date … Signed …' Butler Machine Limited was to put its signature and the date and return it to Ex-Cell-O. On 5 June 1969, Butler Machine Limited wrote the following letter to Ex-Cell-O:

We have pleasure in acknowledging receipt of your official order dated 27th May covering the supply of one 'Butler' Double Column Plano-Miller … This is being entered in accordance with our revised quotation of 23rd May for delivery in 10/11 months, i.e. March/April, 1970. We return herewith duly completed, your acknowledgment of order form.

Butler Machine Limited duly filled in the acknowledgment form and signed it. Let us consider the following hypothetical situations.

1. Ex-Cell-O received the letter sent by Butler Machine Limited on 5 June 1969. Thereafter, it bought the machine from another manufacturer and informed Butler Machine Limited that it would not buy their machine. Butler Machine Limited is claiming damages for breach of contract while Ex-Cell-O maintains that no agreement has been formed between the parties.

2. Ex-Cell-O received the letter sent by Butler Machine Limited on 5 June 1969. Thereafter, it bought the machine from another manufacturer but it did not make any further communication with Butler Machine Limited. Ten months later, Butler Machine Limited informed Ex-Cell-O that the machine was ready and they were going to deliver it. The parties dispute whether a contract had been formed between them.

What actually happened was this. At the time of delivery of the machine, Butler Machine

Limited claimed that there had been an increase in the cost of manufacturing. The seller, invoking Clause 3 of the quotation (price escalation clause), claimed an additional sum of £2,892. Ex-Cell-O Corporation claimed that the contract was made on terms sent in the order form of Ex-Cell-O. Thus, the price escalation had no application. Ex-Cell-O Corporation said, 'We did not accept the sellers' quotation as it was. We gave an order for the self-same machine at the self-same price, but on the back of our order we had our own terms and conditions. Our terms and conditions did not contain any price variation clause.'

Butler Machine Limited relied on their general conditions and on their last letter, which said, 'in accordance with our revised quotation of 23rd May' (which contained the price variation clause). Thus, the parties were settled that a contract was made between them, but disputed the terms on which the contract was made. Was a contract formed between the parties? If yes, on whose terms?

Offer and Acceptance v. Meeting of Minds

The origin of contract law dates back to a period when trade and commerce was simple, mainly related to farm produce and manufactures of craftsmen. The contracts were simple. It was easy for the parties to understand each other and determine whether they were going ahead with the contract or not. As trade and commerce has become increasingly more complex, the parties, even if they communicate in writing, may get into protracted negotiations, agreeing on some terms, disagreeing on others and keeping yet others undecided, to be settled at a future date. Invariably, this gives rise to doubts about when the parties actually had a meeting of minds and moved from being negotiating parties to contract-

ing parties. *Butler Machine Tool Company Limited* v. *Ex-Cell-O Corporation (England) Limited*[3] brings this out.

Let us analyse the case. Butler Machine Tool Company Limited sent a quotation dated 23 May 1969. This was an offer document containing the terms and conditions of the sale. Ex-Cell-O Corporation responded to the offer from the seller with its order form, dated 27 May 1969. The order form claimed to be an acceptance of the offer from the seller, but it changed the terms of the offer. The purported acceptance was a counter-offer. We know that a counter-offer is an implied rejection of the offer. Thus, the quotation of Butler Machine Tool Company Limited was rejected. The order of the Ex-Cell-O was standing for the seller to accept or reject. By signing the acknowledgement and returning it to the buyer, the seller purported to accept the order placed by the buyer. However, by adding further terms in the covering letter dated 5 June, insisting on the original terms of the seller, the seller put up a counter-offer. The parties next communicated at the time of the delivery of the machine, and when Butler Machine raised the demand for an additional payment under the price escalation clause, Ex-Cell-O insisted that the price escalation clause was not a part of the contract. We can understand the response of Ex-Cell-O in two ways. One approach could be to say that Ex-Cell-O had rejected the counter-offer of Butler Machine Limited. In that case, no agreement was formed between the parties and the parties have no rights and obligations towards one another. According to the second approach, by showing its willingness to take delivery of the machine, Ex-Cell-O has, expressly or impliedly, accepted the counter-offer of Butler Machine Limited. Thus, the

[3] Ibid.

price escalation clause would apply. Lord Denning commented on this, thus:

If those documents are analysed in our traditional method, the result would seem to me to be this: the quotation of 23 May 1969 was an offer by the sellers to the buyers containing the terms and conditions on the back. The order of 27 May 1969 purported to be an acceptance of that offer in that it was for the same machine at the same price, but it contained such additions as to cost of installation, date of delivery and so forth, that it was in law a rejection of the offer and constituted a counter-offer ... the counter-offer kills the original offer. The letter of the sellers of 5 June 1969 was an acceptance of that counter-offer, as is shown by the acknowledgment which the sellers signed and returned to the buyers.

To understand the concept of meeting of the minds, Lord Denning, in the changed context of business practices, found the 'traditional method' inadequate. He proposed that the processes by which business agreements were actually formed be examined more closely. He opined:

In many of these cases our traditional analysis of offer, counter-offer, rejection, acceptance and so forth is out-of-date. ... The better way is to look at all the documents passing between the parties and glean from them, or from the conduct of the parties, whether they have reached an agreement on all material points, even though there may be differences between the forms and conditions printed on the back of them.

Parties do not settle on all the terms of a contract at one time. Often, they negotiate and settle on some terms. They proceed with the confidence of convergence on some of the terms and settle over other terms. At one point of time, the negotiating parties become the contracting parties. Lord Denning was of the view that by following the communications between the parties, one would be able to ascertain the point of time at which the parties came to have a meeting of minds. He applied the principle later, in the *Gibson* v. *Manchester City Council* case.[4] In the case, the Manchester City Council was keen all along at selling the property for the £2,180. Gibson was also all along committed to buy the property, whether the price was with or without the discount for the repair of the tarmac. Certainly, by his covering letter dated 18 March 1971, he consented to the purchase: 'in view of your remarks I would be obliged if you will carry on with the purchase as per my application already in your possession'. Thus, there was a meeting of minds between the parties. Lord Denning took the view that one should explore the overall terms to determine whether there was a consensus. He noted:

It seems to me clear that, by writing that letter, Mr Gibson discarded the suggestion which he had made in the covering letter. He returned to the simple application which was already in their possession, of which they had intimated their acceptance. As I view this letter of 12 March 1971, they had intimated that they would accept his application if he did not press this point about repairs. We have had much discussion as to whether Mr Gibson's letter of 18 March 1971 was a new offer or whether it was an acceptance of the previous offer which had been made. I do not like detailed analysis on such a point. To my mind it is a mistake to think that all contracts can be analysed into the form of offer and acceptance. I know in some of the textbooks it has been the custom to do so; but, as I understand the law, there is no need to look for a strict offer and acceptance. You should look at the correspondence as a whole and at the conduct of the parties and see therefrom whether the parties have come to an agreement on everything that was material. If by their correspondence and their conduct you can see an agreement on all material terms, which was intended thenceforward to be binding, then there is a binding contract in law even though all the formalities have not been gone through.

...

[4] *Gibson* v. *Manchester City Council*, (1979) 1 All ER 972.

It seems to me that on the correspondence I have read ... the parties had come to an agreement in the matter which they intended to be binding.

The case went in appeal to the House of Lords. The House of Lords did not accept Lord Denning's reasoning. Lord Diplock noted:

Lord Denning MR rejected what I have described as the conventional approach of looking to see whether on the true construction of the documents relied on, there can be discerned an offer and acceptance ... there may be certain types of contract, though I think they are exceptional, which do not fit easily into the normal analysis of a contract as being constituted by offer and acceptance; but a contract alleged to have been made by an exchange of correspondence between the parties in which the successive communications other than the first are in reply to one another is not one of these. I can see no reason in the instant case for departing from the conventional approach of looking at the handful of documents relied on as constituting the contract sued on and seeing whether on their true construction, there is to be found in them a contractual offer by the council to sell the house to Mr Gibson and an acceptance of that offer by Mr Gibson. I venture to think that it was by departing from this conventional approach that the majority of the Court of Appeal was led into error.

In fact, at the Court of Appeal, one of the other two judges, Geoffrey Lane, LJ, had completely disagreed with Denning. In his judgment, he wrote: 'Unhappily, I find myself in embarrassing disagreement with the judgments which have been delivered in this case by Lord Denning MR and Ormrod, LJ.' Exploring the details of the communications between the two parties with the aim to try and find the offer and its acceptance, Lord Diplock noted that the communication from the Council had stated that the Council 'may be prepared to sell' the house and had imposed a requirement on the applicants, thus: 'If you would like to make formal application to buy your Council house, please complete the enclosed application form and return it to

me as soon as possible.' The conclusion, thus, was that the communication from the Council was only an invitation to offer and the application form submitted by Mr. Gibson was the offer, which the Council could accept or reject. Lord Russell put it thus:

My Lords, I cannot bring myself to accept that a letter which says that the possible vendor 'May be prepared to sell the house to you' can be regarded as an offer to sell capable of acceptance so as to constitute a contract. The language simply does not permit such a construction. Nor can the statement that the letter should not be regarded as a firm offer of a mortgage operate to turn into a firm offer to sell that which quite plainly it was not.

Thus, the House of Lords ruled that no agreement had been reached between Mr. Gibson and the Manchester City Council.

REVIEW OF BUTLER AND GIBSON CASES

In the *Butler case*, the other two judges had followed the conventional view of the contract law. However, all the three had reached the same decision, that is, the contract was made on the terms set by the buyer. Bridge, LJ held to the classical formulation: 'This is a case which on its facts, is plainly governed by what I may call the classical doctrine that a counter-offer amounts to a rejection of an offer and puts an end to the effect of the offer.' Lawson noted as follows:

The modern commercial practice of making quotations and placing orders with conditions attached, usually in small print, is indeed likely, as in this case, to produce a battle of forms. The problem is how should that battle be conducted? ... In my judgment, the battle has to be conducted in accordance with set rules. It is a battle more on classical 18th century lines when convention decided who had the right to open fire first rather than in accordance with the modern concept of attrition.

The rules relating to a battle of this kind have been known for the past 130-odd years. They were set out by the then Master of the Rolls, Lord Langdale, in

Hyde v. *Wrench*, and Lord Denning MR has already referred to them; and, if anyone should have thought they were obsolescent, Megaw J in *Trollope & Colls Ltd.* v. *Atomic Power Constructions Ltd.* called attention to the facts that those rules are still in force. When those rules are applied to this case, in my judgment, the answer is obvious.

It was Lord Denning who was making a departure in saying 'look at all the documents passing between the parties and glean from them … whether they have reached an agreement on all material points.' However, the Gibson case, which was also being contested around the same time, moved to the House of Lords, and the suggestions of Lord Denning were snubbed.

The initiative of Lord Denning to modernize the law had merit. The communication between contracting parties is not modular, where a singular offer is accepted. Law should have recognized this. Why was the House of Lords so averse to following the actual processes by which the parties reach a meeting of minds? From the point of view of the judges, the position required them to give a subjective judgment, based on all the correspondence, as to whether a meeting of minds has taken place or not, and if it did, when. An example of this can be found in the Butler case itself. Lord Denning, finding that the county judge took a position similar to his, said, 'I have much sympathy with the judge's approach to this case.' However, looking at the communication, the county judge was of the opinion that the agreement was made on seller's terms. Lord Denning did not agree with the county judge. His reasons were subjective: 'But I think that the documents have to be considered as a whole. And, as a matter of construction, I think the acknowledgment of 5 June 1969 is the decisive document.'

The institution of the judiciary is about applying settled principles of law. For the judges, their professional domain is in applying the principles, not delivering justice from their subjective viewpoint. When faced with an unstructured situation, judges try and come up with objective principles that can be applied to judge all similar situations. Despite their attempts at objectivity, there would still be some subjective elements present in all decisions. After all, judges are human beings. The general response of the judiciary to the intrusion of subjectivity, is to insist on even more rigorous scrutiny so as to become objective in their decision making, and not to celebrate and uphold subjectivity.

Thus, the courts were completely opposed to giving up the existing criterion of offer and acceptance in deciding on the formation of agreements for a subjective judgment of looking at the correspondence. Second, 'looking at the correspondence as a whole' makes the decision-making an onerous task. The contesting parties would bring out every bit of communication made between them before the courts. The courts would have to go through all the material. The load on the courts would be huge. Thus, the House of Lords emphatically asserted the formula that agreements are formed on the acceptance of an offer.

Reality, however, does not become simple merely by insisting on a simple formula of offer and acceptance. If the situation is complex, there would be much ambiguity involved while fitting the communication into the language of offer and acceptance. In a given situation, a clear offer and its acceptance might be missing. Technically, in such a situation, one would have to conclude that no agreement was formed. However, the parties could have gone ahead with the understanding that they have a contract and executed it. Later, a dispute could arise on the terms that they had agreed upon.

As contracts are about parties reaching a meeting of minds, it would be ironic if the parties thought they had a contract and went ahead with it, but the courts decided that there had been no meeting of minds, and therefore, no contract. Further, as the contract would already have been performed or partly performed, there would be far more hardship involved for both the parties if the court were to rule that no contract was formed. The courts are there to facilitate contracts, not strike them down at the first opportunity. Therefore, if the parties have gone ahead and executed a contract, the courts usually take the position that a contract was formed. The communication between the parties then has to be cast in the language of offer and acceptance. If the parties, however, get into a dispute before executing the contract, the court has the space to conclude that no agreement had been formed between the parties.

In the Butler case, the decision might have been different if the parties had disputed the formation of an agreement soon after the buyer sent the letter with the acknowledgement. The communication from Butler Limited could have been seen as a counter-offer as opposed to acceptance. As the parties did not contest that they had a contract, the judges were compelled to somehow cast it in the language of offer and acceptance.

The India Contract Act defines formation of agreement through acceptance of offer. Thus, technically, there should be no possibility for the debate started by Lord Denning. In every case, the court must insist of identifying an offer and its acceptance as opposed to looking for a meeting of minds through other means. However, as we noted earlier, the India courts recognize that the India Contract Act was only codification of the common law, and thus draws from the common law before and after the enactment of the Indian Contract Act. Thus, reference to *consensus ad idem* (meeting of minds) does come frequently. Like the common law courts, however, the Indian courts insist on offer and acceptance for concluding that a meeting of minds has taken place.

A case from the Indian courts on the parties negotiating different terms at different times and finding themselves in a dispute on the terms of their contract is *Gujarat State Fertilizers Co. Limited* v. *HJ Baker and Bros.*

Court Case: Gujarat State Fertilizers Co. Limited v. H.J. Baker and Bros

The Gujarat State Fertilizers Co. (GSFC) invited tenders for the import and supply of sulphur.[5] H.J. Baker and Bros submitted its offer. According to the GSFC, the offer was not strictly in accordance with the terms of invitation of tender. H.J. Baker had not followed the terms for shipping as prescribed in the tender. The GSFC took note of it in appraising the tender. It accepted the tender with the statement that other terms and conditions stipulated by H.J. Baker in relation to terms of shipping the goods would be confirmed separately.

As we know, tender is an offer made to the party inviting the tender. In this case, it is H.J. Baker who is making an offer to the GSFC. Whether the tender is made in the requisite form or not, it is still an offer. What did the GSFC do to the offer made by the H.J. Baker? It partly accepted it. All terms in conformity with the tender were accepted. The terms at variance, which were only on the terms of shipping the goods, were to be decided on later. Can some terms of an offer be accepted and others rejected or kept open? An offer

[5] *Gujarat State Fertilizers Co. Ltd.* v. *H.J. Baker and Bros*, AIR 1999 Gujarat 209.

stands as a single communication; it can only be accepted as a whole. The communication from the GSFC is not an absolute and unqualified acceptance.

Let us ask a hypothetical question: After receiving the letter of acceptance, can the H.J. Baker withdraw the offer? Clause 20 of the tender document provided that in case of a dispute, the parties would settle it through arbitration. Suppose that a few days after H.J. Baker received the acceptance letter from the GSFC, they had a dispute in relation to the tender and their negotiation. Is a contract formed between them to be bound by the arbitration clause?

In this case, however, further developments took place. The GSFC opened irrevocable letter of credit on 13 November 1992 in favour of H.J. Baker for making the supplies of Sulphur. Soon thereafter, GSFC claimed the Force Majeure clause of the tender document, claiming changed circumstances and severe constraint, requesting H.J. Baker to cancel the shipment. Subsequently, the GSFC repudiated the contract under the clause of the tender document. As mentioned earlier, Clause 20 in the tender document was on arbitration. The GSFC raised the contention that no agreement was formed between the parties as H.J. Baker had not followed the terms of the tender and GSFC had not accepted the offer. The high court noted:

… number of documents were referred to … A plain reading of these documents would definitely give an indication that there was prima facie concluded contract between the parties. There can be no dispute that for every contract there should not be written agreement. The contract can be entered into even by correspondence and also by telephonic talk. The only requirement is that there should be an offer by one party who is called the proposer and the offer should be accepted by the other party who is called the acceptor. Once there is acceptance of the offer the contract comes into existence. The contract can be

inferred even from the correspondence. In the case in hand the contract came into existence through tender notice. The tender is nothing, but invitation to offer. In response to such tender offer was made by the respondent No. 1. The offer was accepted with certain modifications by the revisionist. It is very difficult to accept at this stage that there was no concluded contract.

The GSFC argued that the tender submitted by the H.J. Baker was a 'counter-offer', in the sense that it was at variance with the prescribed terms and conditions of the tender. As it was at variance, it was completely independent of the tender process. Thus, the terms of tender cannot be inserted in the offer submitted by H.J. Baker. The high court differed: 'From the documents on record it transpires that there was no counter-offer, rather negotiations were going on between the parties regarding certain terms and those terms were essentially relating to shipping terms. Other terms and conditions were already accepted by the revisionist (GSFC).' The high court further relied on the conduct of the parties and noted: 'If there was no concluded contract, there was no occasion for the revisionist to repudiate the contract.' Thus, in this case, as the parties had already gone ahead with the execution of the contract, the court tended to see a contract and cast the communication in acceptance of an offer.

Uncertain Terms

In some situations, the parties may agree that they have an agreement, but the terms of the agreement may be vague, incomplete or uncertain. Let us take the following illustration.

A hotel reached an agreement with a supplier of mineral water. The agreement provided: 'The vendor shall sell to the hotel and the hotel will buy its required amount of bottled mineral water for running its hotel business for the next one year. The price will be agreed by the parties from time to time, depending on the retail sale price of the product in the market.'

The vendor supplied bottled water to the hotel for a month. However, the parties could not reach an agreement on the price. The case is brought before the court. Is there a problem with the agreement? How should the court approach it? If the parties had fixed the price at which they would sell, there would have been no dispute. The hotel could not have bought its required water from any other source. Here, a term of the agreement—the price—is not certain. The role of the court is to interpret the contract and enforce it. If the parties have made a contract whose terms are vague, incomplete, and uncertain, there is nothing specific and definite for the court to enforce. The parties should have taken care to have come up with definite terms. Further, it is not the role of the courts to insert terms into contracts. If the courts took that liberty, there would be no end to the court's interference. The court could, thus, take the position that as the terms of the contract are not certain, there is no enforceable contract between the parties.

Both parties, however, are clear that they have an agreement on all issues other than the price. The parties want to go ahead with the agreement. It is just that they cannot settle on the price. The nature of business does not often make it possible for the parties to decide each and every term in advance. Business requires flexibility. This gets into the contractual relationship between the parties. At other times, parties working on trust want to get on with the contract and not settle all the terms at one go in the confidence that the terms would be settled as and when these come up. It would be ironic if both parties insisted that they had an agreement while the court turned them away by judging that they did not have a contract. The role of the court is to give effect to the intent of the parties.

The courts are, thus, caught in a dilemma. The resolution of this is not easy. On the one hand, there is no gain in declaring an agreement as uncertain the moment an uncertainty is encountered in its terms. Effort should be made to make the uncertain certain by looking at the contract as a whole, extrapolating from other terms, inferring from the conduct of parties and even introducing reasonable terms. Beyond a point, however, the courts may not be able to salvage a contract and it may have to be declared as unenforceable due to uncertainty. Section 29 of the Indian Contract Act provides the simple principle:

29. **Agreements void for uncertainty**—Agreements, the meaning of which is not certain, or capable of being made certain, are void.

The Section includes the following illustrations:

(a) A agrees to sell to B 'a hundred tons of oil'. There is nothing whatever to show what kind of oil was intended. The agreement is void for uncertainty.

(b) A agrees to sell to B one hundred tons of oil of a specified description, known as an article of commerce. There is no uncertainty here to make the agreement void.

(c) A, who is a dealer in coconut oil only, agrees to sell to B 'one hundred tons of oil'. The nature of A's trade affords an indication of the meaning of the words, and A has entered into a contract for the sale of one hundred tons of coconut oil.

(d) A agrees to sell to B 'all the grain in my granary at Ramnagar'. There is no uncertainty here to make the agreement void.

(e) A agrees to sell to B 'one thousand maunds of rice at a price to be fixed by C'. As the price is capable of being made certain, there is no uncertainty here to make the agreement void.

(f) A agrees to sell to B 'my white horse for rupees five hundred or rupees one thousand'. There is nothing to show which of the two prices was to be given. The agreement is void.

A case from the Supreme Court of India on uncertain terms is *Keshavlal Lallubhai Patel v. Lalbhai Trikumlal Mills Limited.*[6]

Court Case: Keshavlal Lallubhai Patel v. Lalbhai Trikumlal Mills Limited

A fabric manufacturing company was under a contract to deliver a quantity of fabric to a buyer during the months of September and October 1942.[7] On 9 August 1942, the workers of the mills went on a strike in support of the Quit India Movement. The contracting parties, by mutual consent, renegotiated the delivery schedule on the terms of the following letter from the manufacturer:

Your goodselves are well aware of the present political situation on account of which entire working of our mills is closed.

At present, it is difficult to say as to how long this state of affairs will continue and as such we regret we cannot fulfil the orders placed by you with us in time. Under the circumstances please note that the delivery time of all your pending contracts with us shall be automatically understood as extended for the period the working is stopped and till the normal state of affairs recurs.

The strike came to an end and the mills resumed working on 22 November 1942. The parties were in dispute on the agreement to extend the delivery. The buyer claimed that the mill should supply as it has opened. The mill contended that there was no agreement for delivering the goods at any specific time. The Supreme Court ruled:

It would be noticed that the letter begins by making a reference to the current political situation which led to the closure of the mills and it adds that it was very difficult to anticipate how long the said state of affairs would continue. It is common knowledge that,

[6] *Keshavlal Lallubhai Patel v. Lalbhai Trikumlal Mills Ltd.*, AIR 1958 SC 512.
[7] Ibid.

at the material time, the whole country in general and the city of Ahmedabad in particular was in the grip of a very serious political agitation and nobody could anticipate how long the strike resulting from the said agitation would last. It is in that atmosphere of uncertainty that the respondent requested the appellants to note that the time for delivery would be automatically extended 'for the period the working is stopped and till the normal state of affairs recurs'. The first condition does not present any difficulty. As soon as the strike came to an end and the closure of the mills was terminated, the first condition would be satisfied. It is the second condition that creates the real difficulty. What exactly was meant by the introduction of the second condition is really difficult to determine. So many factors would contribute to the restoration of the normal state of affairs that the satisfaction of the second condition inevitably introduces an element of grave uncertainty and vagueness in the said proposal. If the normal state of affairs contemplated by the second condition refers to the normal state of affairs in the political situation in the country that would be absolutely and patently uncertain. Even if this normal state of affairs is construed favourably to the appellants and it is assumed that it has reference to the working of the mills, that again does not appreciably help to remove the elements of uncertainty and vagueness. When can normal working of the mills be deemed to recur? For the normal working of the mills several factors are essential. The full complement of workmen should be present. The requisite raw material should be available and coal in sufficient quantities must be in stock. Some other conditions also may be necessary to make the working of the mills fully normal. Now, unless all the constituent elements of the normal working of the mills are definitely specified and agreed upon, the general expression used in the letter in that behalf cannot be construed as showing anything definite or certain.

...

In this connection, we may usefully refer to the decision of the House of Lords in *G. Scammel and Nephew, Ltd.* v. *Ouston*, 1941 AC 251 (B). In this case, the respondent had agreed to purchase from the appellant a new motorvan but stipulated that this order was given on the understanding that the balance of purchase price can be had on the hire-purchase terms over a period of two years.

The House of Lords held that the clause as to hire-purchase terms was so vague that no precise meaning could be attributed to it and consequently there was no enforceable contract between the parties. In his speech, Lord Wright observed that

> 'the object of the court is to do justice between the parties, and the court will do its best, if satisfied that there was an ascertainable and determinate intention to contract, to give effect to that intention, looking at substance and not at mere form.... But the test of intention is to be found in the words used. If these words, considered however broadly and untechnically and with due regard to all the just implications, fall to evince any definite meaning on which the court can safely act, the court has no choice but to say that there is no contract.'

Then the learned Law Lord added that his reason for thinking that the clause was vague was not only based on the actual vagueness and unintelligibility of the words used but was confirmed by the startling diversity of the explanations tendered by those who think there was a bargain of what the bargain was. We would like to add that, when the appellants attempted to explain the true meaning of the second condition, it was discovered that the explanations given by the appellants' counsel were diverse and inconsistent. We must, therefore, hold that...the conditions mentioned by the respondent in its letter asking for extension of time were so vague and uncertain that it is not possible to ascertain definitely the period for which the time for the performance of the contract was really intended to be extended. In such a case, the agreement for extension must be held to be vague and uncertain and as such void under S. 29, Contract Act.

Thus, the courts do not declare a contract invalid the moment an uncertainty is encountered. The courts try to make uncertain certain by looking at the contract as a whole, extrapolating from other terms and inferring from the conduct of parties. However, a contract may have uncertain or vague terms beyond salvage. In this case, the courts declare the contract to be unenforceable.

In summary, a contract is formed on acceptance of an offer. However, in practice, one party does not come up with an offer document, containing all the details, and the other party accepts it to form an agreement. The communication between the parties can be protracted. The parties settle on some terms and proceed to negotiate further terms. Through this, at one stage, negotiating parties become contracting parties. The challenge before the law was whether it should follow the communicative processes to decide when and on what terms the contract was formed. The courts have ruled against this, requiring the contracting parties to cast their communication in a single offer that is accepted. At times, parties execute or partly execute on the mutual understanding that there is a contract between them. However, the courts may not discern a distinct offer and its acceptance. In such cases, the courts take a pragmatic position. The courts do the best that can be done to accommodate the communication in the formula of offer of acceptance.

9

Incorporation of Terms

The parties to a contract may have been in communication for a long time. At different times, different procedures of communication may be used. The parties may be in dispute as to which parts of the communication between them are the binding terms of the contract. Making terms binding on the parties is called 'incorporation'. Incorporation happens through different means. First, the parties could sign the document(s) containing the terms of the contract. This can happen if the parties sign the offer and acceptance documents. Alternately, or in addition, the parties may prepare a document containing all the terms and sign it. Second, the contract could be formed orally or impliedly, but the parties could exchange written terms associated with the contract. Terms printed on tickets and receipts are examples of this. Third, the parties to a contract may have had a long history of dealing with each other. Or, both the parties may be in a particular market or trade where the contracting practices are well established. A party may claim that the terms are well-known and understood by the parties, and thus implied in the contract. This is called incorporation by 'custom' or 'course of dealing'. In this chapter, we will explore each of the modalities of incorporation. Further, standard, pre-printed contract documents often exempt the party who has set the terms from liabilities. The courts have explored the validity of exemption clauses, which are dealt with in the last section of this chapter.

SIGNING OF DOCUMENTS

We discussed in an earlier chapter that signing a contract document, irrespective of whether that person had read the document or not, fully binds the person to the terms. Denning has expressed the principle pithily: 'If the party affected signs a written document, knowing it to be a contract which governs the relations between him and the other party, his signature is irrefragable evidence of his assent to the whole contract, including the exempting clauses, unless the signature is shown to be obtained by fraud or misrepresentation.'[1]

Signing of a document is the most effective way of incorporating terms to a contract. There are two exceptions to the rule that a signed document amounts to consent to the terms: first, if a person has entered in a contract due

---

[1] *Curtis* v. *Chemical Cleaning And Dyeing Co., Limited*, (1951) 1 All ER 631.

to coercion, fraud or misrepresentation (we will take up the theme in a subsequent part of the book), Second, a party to the contract claims that he failed to fully understand, without his fault, the document on which he was made to sign. This is called *non est factum*. The Latin expression means 'it is not my deed.' We would be tempted to say that even a person who has not read the document and signed can claim it. However, the exception is applied in narrow confines and only in cases of illiteracy or illness.

As India has high incidences of illiteracy, the exception is relevant. In *Ningawwa* v. *Byrappa Shiddappa Hireknrabar*,[2] the Supreme Court endorsed the principle. However, on the facts of the case, the illiterate women could not get the benefit of the exception. In *Dularia Devi* v. *Janardan Singh*,[3] the Supreme Court gave the benefit of the exception to an illiterate woman.

Court Case: Dularia Devi v. Janardan Singh

Dulari Devi is an illiterate person. Her daughter Rameshwari Devi is married to Yogendra Prasad Singh.[4] Arjun Singh and Janardan Singh, his brothers, gained Dulari Devi's confidence, and she confided to them her desire to make a gift of all her property in favour of her daughter. The two brothers readily agreed to make arrangements to execute and register the necessary deed. On 18 September 1971, they took her to the office of the sub-registrar. She paid the amount needed for the expenses. The brothers purchased stamp papers in the name of Dulari Devi. She put her thumb impression on two documents, having been told that, just as she wanted, she was executing a gift deed in favour of her daughter. She had in fact executed two deeds; one was a gift in favour of her daughter, and the other, a sale deed in favour of all the Singh brothers. The consideration for the sale shown in the document was Rs 14,000. This was secured by the connivance of the sub-registrar as well as the document-writer.

In June, 1974, Arjun Singh and Janardan Singh started interfering with her possession of the property. They told her that she had executed a sale deed in their favour. It was only on 2 July 1974 that she came to know of the full facts. She filed a suit for cancellation of the sale deed. The court had to consider the validity of the document. The court noted the established distinction between misrepresentation of the content of a document from misrepresentation as to its character. A common law case on this, as noted by the court, is *Foster* v. *Mackinnon*.[5] In the case, the innocent person claimed that he endorsed a bill on the fraudulent representation by the acceptor that he was signing a guarantee. The court ruled:

It [the signature] is invalid not merely on the ground of fraud, where fraud exists, but on the ground that the mind of the signer did not accompany the signature; in other words, that he never intended to sign, and therefore in contemplation of law never did sign, the contract to which his name is appended. ... The defendant never intended to sign that contract or any such contract. He never intended to put his name to any instrument that then was or thereafter might become negotiable. He was deceived, not merely as to the legal effect, but as to the 'actual contents' of the instrument.

The Supreme Court replying on the above judgment ruled:

From the facts ... there is no dispute, it is clear that this is a case where the plaintiff appellant [Dulari Devi] was totally ignorant of the mischief played

---

[2] *Ningawwa* v. *Byrappa Shiddappa Hireknrabar*, AIR 1968 SC 956.

[3] *Dularia Devi* v. *Janardan Singh*, AIR 1990 SC 1173.

[4] Ibid.

[5] *Foster* v. *Mackinnon*, (1869) LR 4 CP 704.

upon her. She honestly believed that the instrument which she executed and got registered was a gift deed in favour of her daughter. She believed that the thumb impressions taken from her were in respect of that single document. She did not know that she executed two documents, one of which alone was the gift deed, but the other was a sale of the property in favour of all the defendants. This was, therefore, a case of fraudulent misrepresentation as to the character of the document executed by her and not merely as to its contents or as to its legal effect. The plaintiff-appellant Dulari Devi never intended to sign what she did sign. She never intended to enter into the contract to which she unknowingly became a party. Her mind did not accompany her thumb impressions... and it was, therefore, a totally void transaction.

TERMS ON TICKETS AND RECEIPTS

It is a common practice of sellers or service providers to print conditions and exemptions on the back of the receipt. Familiar examples include drycleaners who provide on the back of their receipts that they are not responsible for the loss of goods. Shops repairing gadgets also have similar stipulations. These terms are called exclusion clauses. The customer may not read these stipulations or be aware of them. However, the parties could be clear that there is a contract between them. The dispute that could arise then is that whether the terms are a part of the contract or not. The problem first came before the courts in 1870s. It has received the attention of the courts since.

We will summarize the key concepts that were fused together to lead to the development of the law on the subject. This happened over several decades. One position was that the ticket came after the agreement was formed. Thus, the terms on the ticket were post-contract and, as a result, not binding on the parties. There were two problems in fully accepting this position. In maritime trade, it was a standard practice for the captain of the ship to issue the contract document 'bill

of lading' after the goods were loaded on the ship. The bill of lading contained all the terms of the contract. Similarly, in other cases, parties made oral agreements and recorded the terms later in writing. Accepting the position would have questioned the legitimacy of these well established contracts.

The second problem was that the argument that the ticket and the terms came after the contract was made could be readily dismissed by asserting that the person knew that there were terms associated with the ticket. As train and steamer services proliferated, a person could not claim that he did not know that their tickets came with terms. A particular service provider could claim that, having issued thousands of tickets, every customer impliedly knew of the terms.

Thus, the courts abandoned the reasoning that the terms were not binding as these came after the contract was formed. They developed the point that both the parties knew there were terms to the contract. The courts shifted their attention to the nature of the terms. What kinds of terms were impliedly shared between the parties? The answer of the court was the terms that a reasonable person would expect. Limiting the liability of a ticket issuer was certainly not a reasonable term. The courts insisted that unreasonable terms would not be binding unless notice was given of the terms to the customer—the more unreasonable the terms, the greater the effort to bring it to notice. We will explore how the amalgam of these ideas were applied and developed in subsequent cases.

In *Chapelton* v. *Barry Urban District Council*,[6] Mr Chapelton hired a beach chair by paying money and received a ticket. When he sat down, the canvas of one of the chairs

[6] *Chapelton* v. *Barry Urban District Council*, (1940) 1 All ER 356.

tore. Chapelton suffered an injury and had to see a doctor. He brought an action against Barry Urban District Council, the party hiring out the chairs. The Council claimed exemption on the basis of the following printed on the back of the ticket: 'The Council will not be liable for any accident or damage arising from hire of chair.' The court ruled:

… he merely pays money for something, and receives a receipt for it … he cannot be deemed to have entered into a contract in the terms of the words which his creditor has chosen to print on the back of the receipt … unless, of course, the creditor has taken reasonable steps to bring the terms of the proposed contract to the mind of the man.

In *Olley* v. *Marlborough Court Limited*, Violet Ellen Olley was a guest at the Marlborough Court Hotel.[7] Her jewellery and clothing were stolen from the hotel room. The hotel claimed exemption from liability as they had put the following sign on the inside of the room of Ms Olley: 'The proprietors will not hold themselves responsible for articles lost or stolen unless handed to the manageress for safe custody. Valuables should be deposited for safe custody in a sealed package and a receipt obtained.' The court ruled: 'As a rule, the guest does not see them until after he has been accepted as a guest. The hotel company, no doubt, hope that the guest will be held bound by them, but the hope is vain unless they clearly show that he agreed to be bound by them, which is rarely the case.' The only way the term could be made binding on the guests is 'by a written notice specifying certain terms and making it clear to him that the contract is in those terms' at the time of making of the contract.

[7] *Olley* v. *Marlborough Court Limited*, (1949) 1 KB 532.

Court Case: Thornton v. Shoe Lane Parking Limited

'Shoe Lane Parking' was an automatic parking area. At the entrance was a ticket machine. A motorist had to drive up to it and reach out to it through the car window. On pressing a button, the machine printed a ticket, the light turned green, and a bar blocking the lane opened up for the motorist to drive in and find a vacant space to park his car. The charges for parking on a per-hour basis were displayed at the entrance. The ticket mentioned that there were terms and conditions to the contract; however, these were displayed inside the garage. A customer, Mr Thorton was injured due to the negligence of the garage. The terms printed inside the garage exempted the garage from liability for negligence resulting in injury to the customers. Lord Denning for the Court of Appeal ruled:

The customer pays his money and gets a ticket. He cannot refuse it. He cannot get his money back. He may protest to the machine, even swear at it; but it will remain unmoved. He is committed beyond recall. He was committed at the very moment when he put his money into the machine. The contract was concluded at that time. It can be translated into offer and acceptance in this way. The offer is made when the proprietor of the machine holds it out as being ready to receive the money. The acceptance takes place when the customer puts his money into the slot. The terms of the offer are contained in the notice placed on or near the machine stating what is offered for the money. The customer is bound by those terms as long as they are sufficiently brought to his notice beforehand, but not otherwise. He is not bound by the terms printed on the ticket if they differ from the notice, because the ticket comes too late. The contract has already been made: see *Olley* v. *Marlborough Court Ltd.* The ticket is no more than a voucher or receipt for the money that has been paid (as in the deckchair case, *Chapelton* v. *Barry Urban District Council*), on terms which have been offered and accepted before the ticket is issued. In the present case the offer was contained in the notice at the entrance giving the charges for garaging and saying 'at owners risk', i.e. at the risk of the owner so far as damage to the car was concerned. The offer was accepted when the plaintiff drove up to the entrance and, by the movement of his car, turned the light from red to green, and the ticket was thrust at him. The contract was then concluded, and it could not be altered by any words printed on the ticket itself. In particular, it could not be altered so as to exempt the company from liability for personal injury due to their negligence.

…

…the customer is bound by the exempting condition if he knows that the ticket is issued subject to it; or, if the company did what was reasonably sufficient to give him notice of it. … All I say is that it is so wide and so destructive of rights that the court should not hold any man bound by it unless it is drawn to his attention in the most explicit way. … I do not think the defendants can escape liability by reason of the exempting condition.

The next landmark judgment taking the argument forward was *Interfoto Picture Library Limited* v. *Stiletto Visual Programmes Limited*.

Court Case: Interfoto Picture Library Limited v. Stiletto Visual Programmes Limited

Stiletto Visual Programmes Limited was an advertising agency.[8] It wanted to use some photographs from the 1950s for a presentation for a client. They telephoned Interfoto Picture Library Limited, who ran a library of photographic transparencies, inquiring if they had photographs from that period that might be suitable for the presentation. The two parties had not dealt with each other before. On the same day, Interfoto Picture Library Limited dispatched 47 transparencies packed in a bag with a delivery note. The delivery note clearly specified that the transparencies were to be returned by 19 March. On

[8] *Interfoto Picture Library Limited* v. *Stiletto Visual Programmes Limited*, (1988) 1 All ER 348.

the delivery note, the word 'CONDITIONS' was prominently printed in bold as a heading. It contained nine printed conditions. Condition 2 stated that all transparencies were to be returned within 14 days from the date of delivery and that 'A holding fee of £5 plus VAT per day will be charged for each transparency which is retained by you longer than the said period of 14 days.'

The Stiletto Visual Programmes Limited accepted the delivery of the transparencies but did not read any of the conditions. They did not use the transparencies for their presentation. Instead, they put them aside and forgot about them. The transparencies were not returned to Interfoto Picture Library Limited until 2 April. Interfoto Picture Library Limited sent Stiletto Visual Programmes Limited an invoice for £3,783, this being the holding charge calculated at £5 per transparency per day from 19 March to 2 April. The Stiletto Visual Programmes Limited refused to pay, leading to an action against them for the amount of the invoice. The case came before the Court of Appeal. The court constructed that the delivery note was a document coming to the customer after the making of the contract. Dillon, LJ ruled:

Condition 2 of these plaintiffs' conditions is in my judgment a very onerous clause. The defendants could not conceivably have known, if their attention was not drawn to the clause, that the plaintiffs were proposing to charge a 'holding fee' for the retention of the transparencies at such a very high and exorbitant rate.

At the time of the ticket cases in the last century it was notorious that people hardly ever troubled to read printed conditions on a ticket or delivery note or similar document. That remains the case now. In the intervening years the printed conditions have tended to become more and more complicated and more and more one-sided in favour of the party who is imposing them, but the other parties, if they notice that there are printed conditions at all, generally still tend to assume that such conditions are only concerned with ancillary matters of form and are not of importance. In the ticket cases the courts held that the common law required that reasonable steps be taken to draw the other parties' attention to the printed conditions or they would not be part of the contract. It is in my judgment a logical development of the common law into modern conditions that it should be held, as it was in *Thornton* v. *Shoe Lane Parking Ltd.*, that, if one condition in a set of printed conditions is particularly onerous or unusual, the party seeking to enforce it must show that that particular condition was fairly brought to the attention of the other party.

In the present case, nothing whatever was done by the plaintiffs to draw the defendants' attention particularly to condition 2 it was merely one of four columns' width of conditions printed across the foot of the delivery note. Consequently condition 2 never, in my judgment, became part of the contract between the parties.

Bingham, LJ gave a concurring judgment. He reviewed the 'ticket' cases, and noted 'very little to do with a conventional analysis of offer and acceptance' but has to do with 'fair dealing'. As a result, 'the more outlandish the clause the greater the notice which the other party' is required to give.

We have observed earlier that the evolution of law on terms in tickets and receipts was an amalgam of different conceptions of the formation of a contractual relationship. It could not be simply declared as inoperative, coming after the making of the contract. At the same time, the device of putting terms on receipts and tickets was unfair on the unsuspecting public. Thus, as the judgment in *Interphoto* v. *Stiletto* notes, the law has evolved to deal with unfairness. The law, as it stands, requires one to examine the terms on a ticket and receipt and grade them on their unfairness. Some terms may require no notice, even if these detract from the party, while the unusual terms would require active notice. Let us take the following terms on the back of the receipt of a drycleaner.

1. All claims of unsatisfactory service or damage to clothes should be raised within 30 days of the receipt of the clothes.

2. Clothes must be collected within 30 days of the delivery date. We will not be responsible for the clothes beyond 30 days.

3. The owner gives the clothes at his own risk. The dry cleaner would not be responsible for loss or damage to the clothes caused for any reason.

Term number 1 may not require any notice. Term 2 is moderate in severity and would need notice. Term 3 is unusually harsh and would need active notice.

The Indian courts have followed the position developed by the British Courts in *Lily White* v. *R. Munuswami*,[9] *M. Siddalingappa* v. *Nataraj*,[10] and *R.S. Deboo* v. *M.V. Hindlekar*.[11] These are the familiar cases of drycleaners where the receipt excludes liabilities. In *Prakash Road Lines (P) Limited, M/s.* v. *H.M.T. Bearing Limited*,[12] the court noted: '...the mere fact that a note is printed in the lorry receipt or consignment note, the same cannot be deemed to have been incorporated as one of the integral terms of the agreement.' In *Spl Secy, Govt of Rajasthan* v. *Venkataramana Seshaiyer*,[13] the winner of a lottery had lost the original ticket. The

[9] *Lily White* v. *R. Munuswami*, AIR 1966 Madras 13.

[10] *M. Siddalingappa* v. *Nataraj*, AIR 1970 Mysore 154.

[11] *R.S. Deboo* v. *M.V. Hindlekar*, AIR 1995 Bombay 68.

[12] *Prakash Road Lines (P) Limited, M/s.* v. *H.M.T. Bearing Limited*, AIR 1999 AP 106.

[13] *Spl. Secy, Govt. of Rajasthan* v. *Venkataramana Seshaiyer*, AIR 1984 AP 5.

ticket on its back had required the ticket to be surrendered to claim the prize money. The winner was denied the prize as he could only bring the original ticket. The Andhra Pradesh Court, quoted extensively from the British cases and applied the principle to the case before it:

> ... it is difficult to make any presumption ... that the plaintiff (buyer of ticket) perused the reverse side of the ticket before the plaintiff handed over the money ... and before he received the ticket, or that the defendants (seller of the ticket) did all that was necessary for them to draw the plaintiff's attention to it before the contract was entered into. ...
>
> There is no proof that the above clause which is contained on the reverse of the ticket ... is the result of a negotiated contract. The rulings both English and Indian are uniform and hold that if there is no such contract entered into by both parties, there must be proof that the terms which are printed on the reverse or otherwise notified elsewhere, have been brought to the notice of the customer or at least that all that could be reasonably done in that regard has been done by the defendants (seller of the ticket). The greater the rigour of the exclusion of liability, the more the need to bring such clauses to the plaintiff's knowledge, or to do all that could possibly be done in that direction. In any event, the said effort on the part of the defendant should have been made at or before the time the plaintiff entered into the contract.

INCORPORATION BY COURSE OF DEALING

Two parties could be dealing with each other frequently. Their dealings would have settled the terms on which they do business with each other. Importing the terms from the past is another means of incorporating terms. These are called terms arising from the course of dealing. Another means of incorporation is by custom. When parties to a transaction are in the same business and the business has well-settled terms on which business is conducted, it may be implied that both the parties had a shared understanding of the terms. The leading case on this is *British*

Crane Hire Corporation v. *Ipswich Plant Hire Limited.*[14]

The courts realized that the law and practices had put ordinary consumers at a disadvantage through the rule that signing amounted to irrefutable consent, and terms on tickets and receipts could be binding. The basis for the application of terms arising from course of dealing and custom is that they are implied terms. This gave a degree of freedom to the courts in interpreting them. The courts have limited the application of incorporation by course of dealing and custom. On one ground or the other, it is not available in cases involving ordinary consumers. In *Mccutcheon (A.P.)* v. *David Macbrayne Limited*, a steamer company ran the service of ferrying passengers and vehicles between an island and mainland. A passenger taking a vehicle on the steamer had to buy a ticket for himself and the vehicle. At the time of buying the ticket, the counter clerk would make the passenger sign a standard contract document. The contract document excluded the steamer company from liability for the lost or damage to the vehicles in the course of transit.

In business-to-business dealings too it is stringently applied. For terms arising out of 'course of dealings' to be considered as terms of the contract, there should be a well-established history of dealings and the terms should have been invariant. Incorporation by 'custom' refers to trade practices in a particular industry. This may apply only when both the parties are in the same trade. A prerequisite to its application is that the trade must have uniform practices. If the practices are evolving or there exist different practices, a particular practice would not be settled as 'custom'. As a result, incorporation by

---

[14] *British Crane Hire Corporation* v. *Ipswich Plant Hire Limited*, (1975) QB 303.

course of dealing and custom are the weakest means of incorporating terms in a contract. They are almost never recognized. In *British Crane Hire Corporation* v. *Ipswich Plant Hire Limited*,[15] a crane-hiring company urgently needed to hire a crane for deployment at a site. The companies reached an agreement on the phone. No terms for hiring were discussed. The crane sank in marshy land. The hirer claimed to annex its general conditions of contract. The Court of Appeal allowed this as the hiring of cranes was a specialized business and there was only one general condition of contract across the crane-hiring industry.

Parol Evidence Rule

In the case of written contracts, there is no difficulty in ascertaining the terms—the terms are those in the document. A party to the contract, however, can claim that in addition to the written contract, there were other orally agreed terms or other written terms. In *Henderson* v. *Arthur*, the court formulated the parol evidence rule that if a contract is in writing, then the writing is the whole contract.[16] The parties cannot bring additional evidence, particularly oral evidence, to 'add to vary or contradict that writing'. Clearly, the intention was to give certainty to written terms. Parties get into a written contract to have a record of their agreement and the terms. If the written document were to be qualified by other evidence, the very sanctity of written documents would be lost. The courts, thus, are reluctant to qualify written terms in written documents.

Contracting parties, however, can intend and form a contract partly orally and partly through written documents. In this case, the parol evidence rule would not apply as the contract is not exclusively written. The party claiming it to be part non-written will have to bring evidence to prove this and settle on the additional terms.

Following from this, in relation to every written contract, a party can always claim that the contract was intended to be partly oral and partly written. To ascertain this, in every contract that has written documents, oral evidence can be adduced to construct the terms of the contract. This makes the parol evidence rule a tautology. Thus, the courts are conservative in qualifying a written contract with oral evidence. However, this is not a firm rule. *J Evans and Son (Portsmouth) Limited* v. *Andrea Merzario Limited* and *Mendelssohn* v. *Normand Limited* are the two cases on this.[17]

Exemption Clauses

The courts have experienced the rise of the printed standard contract documents exempting the corporation of all liabilities. As the forms were required to be signed by the customer, the terms were incorporated and could not be challenged. Contracts are voluntarily formed. It is for the parties to settle on the terms of the contract. Thus, the courts took their role in not inserting or modifying the terms but only interpreting them. At the same time, the courts could not remain silent spectators to unjust contracts. In this contradiction, the courts have generally favoured the sanctity of contracts. Let us review the attempts of the British courts to address the concern. The courts have expressed their anguish on standard term contracts printed by the corporations; in the words of Lord Diplock:

---

[15] Ibid.

[16] *Henderson* v. *Arthur*, (1907) 1 KB 10.

[17] *J. Evans and Son (Portsmouth) Limited* v. *Andrea Merzario Limited*, (1976) 2 All ER 930; and *Mendelssohn* v. *Normand Limited*, (1969) 2 All ER 1215.

This [standard form of contract] is of comparatively modern origin. It is the result of the concentration of particular kinds of business in comparatively few hands. The terms…have not been the subject of negotiation between the parties to it, or approved by any organisation representing the interests of the weaker party. They have been dictated by that party whose bargaining power, either exercised alone or in conjunction with others providing similar goods or services, enables him to say: 'If you want these goods or services at all, these are the only terms on which they are obtainable. Take it or leave it'.[18]

Lord Denning added to the observations of Lord Diplock:[19]

I would only add that in this case—as in many others—the weaker party is not even told: 'Take it or leave it.' He is simply presented with a form to sign, and told: 'Sign here'; and so he does. Then later on, when the goods are lost or damaged, the form is produced, and the stronger party says: 'You have no claim. Look at the conditions on the form. You signed it and are bound by those conditions.'

Lord Denning was at the forefront in forging remedies against this. The courts came up with two principles for limiting the scope of the exemption clause. The first one was that the terms of contract should not be unreasonable. For example, a dry-cleaning company that had limited its liability to £40 without a word of warning for an expensive carpet was taken to be 'most unreasonable.'[20] The second principle was of 'fundamental breach'. Every contract has a basic fundamental purpose that brings the parties together. The contract would be meaningless if the performance of fundamental features were exempted. A warehouse exempting itself for the loss or destruction of the goods would be a funda-

mental breach.[21] A dry cleaner was meant to clean things and return them, not lose them. A dry cleaner that exempted itself from the liability of loss would thus be a fundamental breach.[22] An expression of the formulation was:

If a party uses his superior power to impose an exemption or limitation clause on the weaker party, he will not be allowed to rely on it if he has himself been guilty of a breach going to the root of the contract. In other cases, the court will, whenever it can, construe the contract so that an exemption or limitation clause only avails the party when he is carrying out the contract in substance, and not when he is breaking it in a manner which goes to the very root of the contract.[23]

Another procedure followed by the courts was to so interpret the exemption terms as to limit their scope application. In *Photo Production Limited* v. *Securicor Transport Limited*,[24] Securicor had a contract to provide security to the premises of Photo Production Limited. The contract was entered on Securicor's standard form. The printed terms had given complete exemption to the security company from liability. An employee of Securicor, while on duty, set a small fire on the premises which he could not prevent from turning into a conflagration. This ended in destroying the entire property. The employee was prosecuted and punished. Securicor claimed exemption from liability for the damage to the property under the terms of the contract. Lord Denning demonstrated the method of interpretation to limit the scope of the exemption clause:

---

[18] *Schroeder Music Publishing Co Limited* v. *Macaulay*, (1974) 1 All ER 174.

[19] *Levison and another* v. *Patent Steam Carpet Cleaning Co. Limited*, (1977) 3 All ER 498.

[20] Ibid.

[21] *J. Spurling, Limited* v. *Bradshaw*, (1956) 2 All ER 121.

[22] *Levison and another* v. *Patent Steam Carpet Cleaning Co. Limited*, (1977) 3 All ER 498.

[23] Ibid.

[24] *Photo Production Limited* v. *Securicor Transport Limited*, (1978) 3 All ER 146.

…in order to decide whether the exemption or limitation clause applied, you must construe the contract, not in the grammatical or literal sense, or even in the natural and ordinary meaning of the words, but in the wider context of the 'presumed intention' of the parties, so as to see whether or not, in the situation that has arisen, the parties can reasonably be supposed to have intended that the party in breach should be able to avail himself of the exemption or limitation clause.

As the 'presumed intent' could not be to exempt liability even if the fire was wilfully caused, the exemption clause should not apply. In the case, Lord Denning noted that all the principles for limiting the scope of exemption clauses had converged. He formulated the master principle:

It seems to me that the two ways can be seen to meet in practice so as to produce a result in principle which may be stated thus: Although the clause in its natural and ordinary meaning would seem to give exemption from or limitation of liability for a breach, nevertheless the court will not give the party that exemption or limitation if the court can say, 'The parties as reasonable men cannot have intended that there should be exemption or limitation in the case of such a breach as this'. In so stating the principle there arises in these cases the figure of the fair and reasonable man; and the spokesman of this fair and reasonable man … is and must be the court itself…

Thus we reach, after long years, the principle which lies behind all our striving: the court will not allow a party to rely on an exemption or limitation clause in circumstances in which it would not be fair or reasonable to allow reliance on it; and, in considering whether it is fair and reasonable, the court will consider whether it was in a standard form, whether there was equality of bargaining power, the nature of the breach, and so forth.

By the time the case came in appeal before the House of Lords, Parliament had enacted the Unfair Contract Terms Act, 1977. Lord Wilberforce for the House of Lords noted:

The doctrine of 'fundamental breach', in spite of its imperfections and doubtful parentage, has served

a useful purpose. There were a large number of problems, productive of injustice, in which it was worse than unsatisfactory to leave exception clauses to operate. … But since then, Parliament has taken a hand: it has passed the Unfair Contract Terms Act 1977. This Act applies to consumer contracts and those based on standard terms and enables exception clauses to be applied with regard to what is just and reasonable. It is significant that Parliament refrained from legislating over the whole field of contract. After this Act, in commercial matters generally, when the parties are not of unequal bargaining power, and when risks are normally borne by insurance, not only is the case for judicial intervention undemonstrated, but there is everything to be said, and this seems to have been Parliament's intention, for leaving the parties free to apportion the risks as they think fit and for respecting their decisions.

It was apparent to the House of Lords that the exemption clauses were causing injustice. However, it could not legitimate the attempts of the court of appeal to contort the language of the contract, and manipulate legal concepts to somehow produce a desired result. Most of these initiatives had been taken by Lord Denning while sitting in the court of appeal. The enactment of the Unfair Contract Terms Act, 1977, addressed the problem of exemption clauses in consumer contracts. The act had solved the problem of ordinary consumers. According to the House of Lords, the reason commercial contracts were not included in the ambit of the act was that in these contracts, generally, parties allocate risk. This is a part of business-to-business dealings. The House of Lords, thus, was undermining the legitimacy and significance of the doctrine of fundamental breach and principles of interpretation of exemption clauses, particularly in its application to business-to-business contracts. Lord Denning, in a later case, George *Mitchell (Chesterhall) Limited* v. *Finney Lock Seedy Limited*, commented on the initiatives of the court in interpreting the exemption clauses:

None of you nowadays, will remember the trouble we had, when I was called to the Bar, with exemption clauses. They were printed in small print on the back of tickets and order forms and invoices. They were contained in catalogues or timetables. They were held to be binding on any person who took them without objection. No one ever did object. He never read them or knew what was in them. No matter how unreasonable they were, he was bound. All this was done in the name of 'freedom of contract'. But the freedom was all on the side of the big concern which had the use of the printing press. No freedom for the little man who took the ticket or order form or invoice. The big concern said, 'Take it or leave it.' The little man had no option but to take it. The big concern could and did exempt itself from liability in its own interest, without regard to the little man. It got away with it time after time. When the courts said to the big concern, 'You must put it in clear words,' the big concern had no hesitation in doing so. It knew well that the little man would never read the exemption clauses or understand them.

...

Faced with this abuse of power, by the strong against the weak, by the use of the small print of the conditions, the judges did what they could to put a curb on it. They still had before them the idol, 'freedom of contract'. They still knelt down and worshipped it, but they concealed under their cloaks a secret weapon. They used it to stab the idol in the back. This weapon was called 'the true construction of the contract'. They used it with great skill and ingenuity. They used it so as to depart from the natural meaning of the words of the exemption clause and to put on them a strained and unnatural construction. In case after case, they said that the words were not strong enough to give the big concern exemption from liability, or that in the circumstances, the big concern was not entitled to rely on the exemption clause. If a ship deviated from the contractual voyage, the owner could not rely on the exemption clause. If a warehouseman stored the goods in the wrong warehouse, he could not pray in aid the limitation clause. If the seller supplied goods different in kind from those contracted for, he could not rely on any exemption from liability. If a shipowner delivered goods to a person without production of the bill of lading, he could not escape responsibility by reference to an exemption clause. In short, whenever the wide words, in their natural

meaning, would give rise to an unreasonable result, the judges either rejected them as repugnant to the main purpose of the contract or else cut them down to size in order to produce a reasonable result.[25]

Lord Denning, later in the judgment, said that the Unfair Contract Terms Act, 1977, had addressed the problem of the weaker party, and therefore, 'we should no longer have to go through all kinds of gymnastic contortions to get round them.' The legislature in India has not addressed the problem of exemption clauses and exclusion clauses, inserted by the stronger party. The Indian courts only have the precedence of the rise and fall of the doctrine of fundamental breach.

To conclude, all the communication between the parties does not constitute a term of the contract. Incorporation is the term used to describe the communication that has become a term of the contract. Signing the offer and acceptance is the most effecting means of incorporation. A signed contract document binds a party to its terms, even if the person has not read or is not aware of the terms. In some cases, a contract is formed first orally or by conduct and the terms of the contract come later. Examples of such contract documents are receipts, tickets, receipts, and vouchers. The terms in these documents exempting the issuer from liability or imposing onerous liability on the other party are not binding unless adequate notice of the terms is given to the party. Every contract is formed in a context. Both parties share the context. The context can be described as trade practices, the course of dealing, and customs. These are the least effective means of incorporations. Trade practices, the course of dealing, or customs are never implied in contracts dealing with ordinary consumers.

[25] *George Mitchell (Chesterhall) Limited* v. *Finney Lock Seedy Limited*, (1983) 1 All ER 108.

In a business-to-business contract, the courts permit its incorporation on very stringent test of uniformity of practice.

The stronger party to a contract came to include terms completely exempting them from any liability. 'Freedom of contract' made the courts duty-bound not to add or delete terms to a contract but only interpret it. The British courts gave relief to the weaker party by devising the doctrine of 'fundamental breach', according to which an exemption clause could not negate the very foundation of the contract. The British courts also so interpreted the exemption clauses as to limit their application. The enactment of the Unfair Contract Terms Act, 1977, by the British Parliament removed the need for judicial activism in limiting the scope of the exemption clauses in relation to consumer contracts. In India, however, there has been no legislation to limit the impact of exemption clauses in consumer contracts. Thus, the courts only have the rise and fall of the principle of fundamental breach as a possible guide.

10

Mistakes and Contracts

In this chapter, we will explore the topic of formation of contracts when one of the parties is mistaken about the identity of the person or the subject matter of the contract. On the face of it, there may be an offer and its acceptance, but no meeting of minds between the parties. We will explore different dimensions of the problem. Let us appraise the following three situations:

Situation 1: A person went into a shop, bought a gold ring, and left.

Situation 2: A person went into a shop and settled on a ring to buy. He offered a credit card to pay for it. The salesman told him that the machine for receiving credit card payment was out of order. The customer did not have enough cash to pay, but claimed that he owned a famous and well-known restaurant in the city. The shopkeeper had heard of the owner and gave the ring on credit. However, the customer was an impostor, and promptly disappears with the ring.

Situation 3: Mr Arvind Parikh wanted to buy a gold ring on credit. His friend negotiated it for him with a shopkeeper he knew well. Mr Parikh and the shopkeeper had a conversation over the telephone. The shopkeeper told Mr Parikh that he could give him

credit for a month for goods up to value of Rs 20,000. The shopkeeper suggested that he come at 11.00 a.m. and make his purchase. A swindler, X, overheard the telephone conversation. X went to the shop and introduced himself as Arvind Parikh. X took a gold ring worth Rs 18,000 and left.

With whom is a contract made in the three situations? In Situation 1, the contract is made with the customer in the shop. In Situation 2 too the meeting of minds takes place between the shopkeeper and the person in the shop. The shop was dealing with a customer who claimed to be a particular person. It is not that the shop specifically intended to deal with the owner of the restaurant. In Situation 3, however, the shopkeeper intended to deal specifically with Arvind Parikh. Thus, there was no meeting of minds between the shopkeeper and X.

Ownership and Mistaken Identity: Unilateral Mistake

Situation 3 is a case of mistake of identity in formation of a contract. As only one of the parties is under a misapprehension, it is called a unilateral mistake. All disputes in relation to mistake of identity arise in contract of sale of goods. The rogue makes the seller part with the goods on credit. The rogue immediately sells it further and disappears. The original owner and the buyer are left disputing as to who has the ownership over the goods. However, as in Situation 3, if there was no meeting of minds between the parties, there was no contract. Thus, the swindler and the buyer have illegal possession of the goods, and they must be restored to the owner. On the other hand, as in Situation 2, there is a contract between the owner and the person before him, the swindler. In this case, the ownership passes to the swindler, who in turn transfers the ownership to the buyer. The original buyer is an unpaid seller and he can only recover the price from the swindler. The swindler has certainly made a misrepresentation. As we will explore in a subsequent part, the seller can set aside the contract and claim his goods back. However, a transfer of ownership by the swindler in this while is a valid transfer. If the goods are already sold, the original owner can only claim damages from the swindler.

Thus, in all cases of mistaken identities, the fortunes of two innocent parties come to depend on the communication between the original owner and the swindler. Schematically expressed, A misrepresents to B that he is C towards a contract for sale of goods. B ends up giving the goods to A, and awaits his cash consideration. A is actually a swindler and sells the goods to X. X is a bona fide buyer. The fraud is discovered, and the goods are found in possession of X. A either cannot be found or has no money to pay. The only remedy for B is to have the goods recovered from X. X will be allowed to keep the goods if there was a meeting of minds between A and B. In other words, like the three situations we took up earlier, the fortunes of X will depend on the subtleties of the communication between A and B.

The topic has puzzled the British courts for more than a century. Business practices have changed over these years, but the problem of a wrongdoer making a misrepresentation manifests in the new situation. In fact, due to the internet and credit cards, the problem has become greater. For example, a person enters a store and uses a stolen credit card. The question is, did the store make a valid contract with the person before them? Let us examine the cases that have come before the British courts.

Court Case: Cundy v. Lindsay

A. Blenkarn, resident at 37, Wood Street, London, wrote to Lindsay & Co, linen manufacturers based in Belfast, ordering certain goods.[1] The letter mentioned the address as 37, Wood Street, and it was signed 'A. Blenkarn & Co.' in such a way as to look like 'A. Blenkiron & Co.' Blenkiron & Sons was a very reputed firm located at 123, Wood Street, London. Lindsay knew about the reputed firm and that it conducted its business from Wood Street, London, but they did not know the number of the premises. They entered into a correspondence with them and, ultimately, supplied the goods ordered, addressing them to 'A. Blenkiron & Co., 37, Wood Street.'

The fraud was discovered and Blenkarn was convicted of obtaining goods under false pretences. Before that, however, Blenkarn had sold the goods to Cundy in the ordinary course of business. Who should get to keep the goods?

Court Case: King's Norton Metal Company Limited v. Edridge, Merrett & Company Limited

A man named Wallis got notepaper printed in the name of Hallam & Co. and ordered a ton

[1] *Cundy* v. *Lindsay*, (1878) 3 App Cas 459.

of brass rivet wire from King's Norton Metal Company Limited.[2] The letter pad intimated that he was in business in a big way, running a large factory and having several depots and agencies. King's Norton delivered the wire on credit and Wallis promptly sold it to Edridge, Merrett & Company Limited. King's Norton Metal Company Limited remained unpaid and demand that the goods be restored to them.

Court Case: Phillips v. Brooks Limited

Phillips was a jeweller at Oxford Street, London. A customer entered the shop and asked to see some pearls and rings.[3] He selected some pearls for the price of £2550 and a ring for the price of £450. He took out a cheque book and wrote out a cheque for £3,000. While signing it, he said, 'You see who I am, I am Sir George Bullough.' He then proceeded to give an address in St James's Square. Phillips knew that there was a Sir George Bullough. He quickly checked in a directory and confirmed to his satisfaction that Sir George indeed lived at the mentioned address. Phillips said, 'Would you like to take the articles with you?' The customer replied, 'You had better have the cheque cleared first, but I should like to take the ring as it is my wife's birthday tomorrow.' Hearing this, Phillips let him have the ring. The cheque was dishonoured. The person was not Sir George Bullough, but someone named North. He was subsequently convicted of obtaining the ring under false pretences. The dispute again was between the jeweller and the person to whom the swindler had given the ring.

Court Case: Ingram and Others v. Little

Two sisters, Elsie and Hilda Ingram, and Mrs Mary Ann Maud Badger were the joint owners of a car.[4] They advertised for its sale in the newspapers. A swindler contacted Elsie Ingram, saying that he had seen the advertisement and would like to come and see the car. He gave the name of Hutchinson over the telephone, and said that he was staying for the weekend at the Savoy Hotel, Bournemouth. Later she telephoned the Savoy Hotel and talked to him to fix a time for him to come and see the car.

Hutchinson met the owners at their home. Upon his request, Elsie Ingram gave him a drive in the car, during which he proved to be very talkative. He spoke of his family and said that his home was at Caterham. After the drive they came back to the house, and Hutchinson expressed his desire to buy the car. The parties bargained and settled on £717. Hutchinson then pulled out a cheque book, but Elsie told him that she would not in any circumstances accept a cheque, and that she was only willing to sell the car for cash. She told him that the deal was over. She made as though to walk out of the room.

Hutchinson tried to convince her that he was a most reputable person, and then for the first time he gave his initials. He said that he was a P.G.M. Hutchinson, that he had business interests in Guildford, and lived at Stanstead House, Stanstead Road, Caterham. Hilda Ingram, who had been in the room, slipped out of the room and went to a nearby post office about two minutes away. In the telephone directory covering the district of Caterham she saw the entry 'Hutchinson, P.G.M., Stanstead House, Stanstead Road, Caterham 4665'. His story supposedly con-

---

[2] *King's Norton Metal Company Limited v. Edridge, Merrett & Company Limited*, (1897) 14 TLR 98.

[3] *Phillips v. Brooks Limited*, (1919) 2 KB 243.

[4] *Ingram and Others v. Little*, (1960) 3 All ER 332.

firmed, the owners decided that they would let him have the car in exchange for the cheque. The cheque, of course, bounced, and the swindler sold the car to another person. The owners approached the court to have the car restored to them.

Court Case: *Shogun Finance Limited* v. *Hudson*

This is the latest House of Lords judgment on the subject of mistaken identity.[5] In the UK, a customer can walk into a car showroom and walk out with his car. The showrooms have an arrangement with finance companies. Once the customer selects a car, the dealer gives the details of the driving licence that the customer produces as proof of his identity. The finance company verifies the licence-holder's name and address from the electoral register, and then checks whether there are any outstanding debts registered against him. If they approve the transaction, the dealer completes the forms; the man makes a down-payment and drives off with the car.

In this case, a person went into the showroom of Chris Varieva Limited in Leicester. He told the sales manager, Mr Bailey, that his name was Patel and that he wanted to buy a Mitsubishi Shogun, which was on display. They agreed on a price, subject to the obtaining of hire purchase finance. The seller had an arrangement with Shogun Finance Limited. Mr Bailey passed on the details given by the person as Durlabh Patel of 45, Mayflower Road, Leicester. The finance company checked the database and approved the sale. The person signed the contract form of Shogun Finance Limited. The form and the driving license were faxed to the finance company. The clerk at Shogun Finance Limited com-

pared the signatures on the faxed copies of the driving licence and the agreement form and had no reason to believe that they were different. They told the dealer that the proposal was accepted. The dealer accepted a 10 per cent deposit in cash and handed over the vehicle to the customer.

This customer was an imposter. He sold the car to Mr Hudson, who was a bona fide buyer. He then disappeared. Under the law in the UK, a sale made by a person of a vehicle in possession on hire-purchase is a valid transfer of ownership. Shogun Finance Limited maintains that there was no valid hire-purchase contract with the imposter and, therefore, they continue to be the owners of the car. Their claim, then, is to have the car restored to them from Mr Hudson. The House of Lords was divided in its judgment on the case. Two judges construed that there was a contract between the imposter and Shogun Finance Limited. The judges held that the contract for sale was made with the person in the shop much before the forms were signed. While the other three judges held that the contract was in writing and intended to be entered in only with Mr Patel and not the impostor. Each member had a different interpretation set out in a lengthy text of judgment.

MISTAKE OF SUBJECT MATTER

Another kind of mistake is about the subject matter of the contract. A party is, of course, not subjectively mistaken. If he were, he would have corrected the mistake. The party is unaware that he is mistaken. An objective person, looking at his communication, knows that he is mistaken. There can be two different situations. First, only one party is mistaken and the other knows of the mistake. This is called unilateral mistake. Second, both the parties are mistaken about the subject matter of the contract. This is a case of mutual

[5] *Shogun Finance Limited* v. *Hudson*, (2004) 1 AC 919.

mistake or common mistake. Let us examine unilateral mistake.

Court Case: Scriven Brothers & Co. v. Hindley & Co.

Scriven Brothers employed an auctioneer in London to sell a large quantity of Russian hemp and tow.[6] The goods were lying in the docks. The catalogue prepared by the auctioneer mentioned two lots: '63 to 67: 47 bales, 68 to 79: 176 bales.' Both were described with the shipping mark 'S.L.' The first lot was hemp, and second, tow. The two are very different commodities; tow is far inferior to hemp. The catalogue did not disclose this difference in the nature of the commodity. Samples of the goods were on display at a showroom for prospective buyers to examine. The samples from both the lots were marked as 'S.L.' Russian hemp and Russian tow were never unloaded from the same ship under the same shipping marks. The manager of Hindley was shown the sample of hemp as 'S.L. goods'. He did not intend to buy tow, thus, he did not inspect the samples of tow. Neither was his attention called to the fact that the tow was also marked 'S.L.'. There were reasons that the auctioneer had created this ambiguity. Some one had, in the words of the court: '…perpetrated a swindle upon the bank which made advances in respect of this shipment of goods it was peculiarly the duty of the auctioneer to make it clear to the bidder either upon the face of his catalogue or in some other way which lots were hemp and which lots were tow.'

When the second lot was put to auction, Handley made an extravagant bid and the auctioneer knocked it down to him. The court held that the parties were never *ad idem* as to the subject-matter of the proposed sale.

Thus, there was no contract of sale. The court ruled, 'Such a contract cannot arise when the person seeking to enforce it has by his own negligence or by that of those for whom he is responsible caused, or contributed to cause, the mistake.' In this case, the auctioneer had set it up to induce a mistake. When the bid was made, the auctioneer knew that the bidder was mistaken. Thus, no contract got made as the parties were not *ad idem*.

Court Case: Hartog v. Colin & Shields

Collins & Shield were negotiating to sell 30,000 Argentine hare skins to Hartog.[7] In the verbal and written communications between the parties, according to standard practice, the price was being negotiated on a per-piece basis. Finally, the offer which Hartog received from Collins & Shield mentioned the price on a per-pound basis. This made the price one-third of what was being negotiated between the parties. Hartog immediately accepted the offer and claimed the goods at the contracted price. The court ruled that there was an offer and acceptance, but there was no meeting of minds. Thus, no agreement had been formed between the parties. Such cases where a person realizes the other's mistake and gets into a contract to take advantage of it are known as 'snapping up'. Let us examine a contemporary case on 'snapping up', *Chwee Kin Keong and Others* v. *Digilandmall.com Limited*, from the Singapore High Court. What makes the case interesting is that it involves buying through the internet.

Court Case: Chwee Kin Keong and Others v. Digilandmall.com Limited

Digilandmall.com Limited is a company that sells information technology–related products

[6] *Scriven Brothers & Co.* v. *Hindley & Co.*, (1913) 3 KB 564.

[7] *Hartog* v. *Colin & Shields*, (1939) 3 All ER 566.

over the Internet.[8] As part of its business, it operates a website owned by Hewlett Packard (HP) at http://www.buyhp.com.sg, where only HP products are sold. The company also sells HP products on its own website at http://www.digiland.com. A related website for corporate clients and re-sellers is owned and operated by a related entity, Digiland International Limited (DIL).

DIL conducted a training session at the premises of Digilandmall.com Limited for its employees about the use of a new template for the web pages. The new template inter-linked all the three web pages and allowed price changes to be reflected in all of them simultaneously. For the purposes of training the employees, a real product number, 'HP 9660A', was inserted in the new template and fictitious prices were inserted for demonstration. The same evening, an employee inadvertently uploaded the training template. The price of the advanced and commercial purpose laser printers, which was $3,854 before the inadvertent uploading, became $66.

The general arrangement that was followed was that the customer made the offer and paid by credit card, following which the server generated an automated acceptance, leading to the formation of a contract between the parties. After the uploading, there were altogether 1,008 purchase orders for the laser printers placed by 784 individuals. There were 11 individuals who had ordered more than 50 laser printers. The company refused to supply the contracted goods. Six of the buyers who had ordered a large number of printers moved the court. The company claimed, among others things, that no contract had been formed as there was a mistake in relation to the subject matter of the contract. The court noted that

courts are generally hesitant in undermining contracts:

The very foundations of predictability, certainty and efficacy, underpinning contractual dealings, will be undermined if the law and/or equity expands the scope of the mistake exception with alacrity or uncertainty. The rigour in limiting this scope is also critical to protect innocent third party rights that may have been acquired directly or indirectly. Certainty in commercial transactions should not be trifled with, as this will inevitably affect how commercial and business exchanges are respected and effected. The quintessential approach of the law is to *preserve* rather than to undermine contracts.

In this overall context, the courts make an exception for the 'snapping up' case:

There is a distinct line of cases within the narrow confines of unilateral mistake where the common law has been resolutely disinclined to enforce apparent contracts. The case of *Hartog* v. *Colin & Shields* [1939] 3 All ER 566 is incontrovertibly the leading authority in this area.

…

The term 'snapping up' was aptly coined by James LJ in *Tamplin* v. *James* (1880) 15 Ch D 215 at 221. The essence of 'snapping up' lies in taking advantage of a known or perceived error in circumstances which ineluctably suggest knowledge of the error. A typical but not essential defining characteristic of conduct of this nature is the haste or urgency with which the non-mistaken party seeks to conclude a contract; the haste is induced by a latent anxiety that the mistaken party may learn of the error and as a result correct the error or change its mind about entering into the contract. Such conduct is akin to that of an unscrupulous commercial predator seeking to take advantage of an error by an unsuspecting prey by pouncing upon it before the latter has an opportunity to react or raise a shield of defence. Typical transactions are usually but not invariably characterised by (a) indecent alacrity; and (b) behaviour that any fair-minded commercial person similarly circumstanced would regard as a patent affront to commercial fairplay or morality.

In this case, the product was a commercial printer and the mistaken price ridiculously

---

[8] *Chwee Kin Keong and Others* v. *Digilandmall. com Private Limited*, (2004) 2 SLR 594.

low. An objective potential customer would have known that the price was a mistake. In addition, a large number of orders by non-commercial parties confirmed that this was a case of 'snapping up'. The court ruled in favour of Digilandmall.com.

Section 22 of the Indian Contract Act states the ordinary rule that a mistake by a party to the contract is no ground to invalidate it. It reads:

Contract caused by mistake of one party as to matter of fact—A contract is not voidable merely because it was caused by one of the parties to it being under a mistake as to a matter of fact.

Allowing a party to claim the benefit of his own mistake would erode the value of contracts and lead to uncertainty. It will also create a basis for a party unwilling to go through with a contract to claim to be under some kind of misapprehension or the other. However, we have explored two exceptions to this in this chapter: first, when a party by deception induces the other to make a mistake on identity, and second, in the case of snapping up, when a party well aware that the other person is mistaken rushes to form a contract to gain advantage of the mistake. In both the cases, the ends of justice are best served by protecting the mistaken party.

In this chapter, we have explored unilateral mistake, where one party is mistaken about the identity of the contracting party or the subject matter of the contract. When party A intends to form an agreement with B only, and C pretends to be B and gets into an agreement with A, no enforceable agreement is formed. When a party knows that the offeror is mistaken about a term of the offer, and rushes into a contract to take advantage of the mistake, it is called 'snapping up'. In such cases, no enforceable agreement is formed as there is no meeting of minds.

Part 2

CONSIDERATION

Contract law emerged to settle dispute among traders. Business relationships were about exchange of benefit and detriment, as opposed to social and familial relationships where a person benefited another. Social relationship was about co-operation and mutual help. Social relationships were for the society to shape, while business relations were for the law and courts to resolve. It was for the contracting parties to settle on the bargain. The benefit the parties exchanged was called the consideration. An agreement supported by consideration was a contract. Only agreements supported by consideration were enforceable. The simple concept of agreement has propagated the entire field of contract law. We will study different aspects of consideration in the following chapters.

11

Consideration: Introduction

Common law courts developed contract law to deal with disputes arising among traders. The exchanges in social relationship were distinctly different from business relationships. The courts took note of disputes among the traders; social relations were for the society to mediate. Thus, the presence of mutual exchange became essential for the court to enforce an agreement. The benefit for the parties was their respective consideration. The concept of consideration developed to permeate the entire field of contracts. In this chapter, we will look at the scope and significance of consideration. The consideration can be a benefit to a party or a detriment to the other. It can be tangible or intangible. In Section 2 of the chapter, we will explore the definition and scope of consideration in the Indian Contract Act. This is at variance with the common law. There must be consideration for both the parties, but the considerations need not be commensurate. We will explore this theme 'sufficiency of consideration' in Section 3.

CONSIDERATION: CONCEPTS

Identify the benefit for each of the parties in the following agreements: (1) A person buys a television set for Rs 20,000. (2) A person rents a house for Rs 2 lakh per year. (3) A customer gives his clothes for dry cleaning for a charge of Rs 20. (4) A person pays Rs 10,000 for displaying advertisements on the roadside. (5) The city administration awards a licence to a person to run a bus for Rs 1 lakh a year. Consideration for a party is the benefit flowing to him. In the first case, consideration for the seller is the price and for the buyer, transfer of ownership of goods. Both the parties must have a consideration for the agreement to be supported by consideration. As the illustrations show, consideration can be a good, service, cash, property, access, or right.

Consider the case where X agrees to pay Rs 5,000 to B if B swam across a river. In the agreement, the consideration for B is Rs 5,000. There is no benefit flowing from B to X. However, it would be unfair to B if X were not bound to the agreement. The courts reasoned that if a person takes up an activity, forbearance, suffering, or loss on the promise of another person, even if it gives no benefit to the other person, the action is a consideration for him. The idea was thus expressed in *Currie* v. *Misa*: 'A valuable consideration, in the sense of the law, may consist either in some right, interest, profit or benefit accruing to the one party, or some forbearance, detriment, loss or responsibility given, suffered or undertaken by the other.'[1]

Following the above principle, identify the consideration for the parties in the following agreements: (1) A landlord will not initiate eviction proceeding for three years for a charge of Rs 2 lakh. (2) An author agrees to get his book published by paying a publisher Rs 1 lakh. (3) A sportsperson gets in an agreement with a company that he will not endorse the products of a rival company for a charge of Rs 3 lakh. (4) Two shopkeepers get in an agreement that the first will not open his shop on Saturday and the second, on Sunday. (5) In a fair a stall was giving away a pen to any one who could drink a bottle of soft drink in less than 30 seconds.

In the first case, the undertaking of the landlord not to initiate eviction proceedings is the consideration for the tenant. In the second case, the undertaking of the publisher to publish is the consideration for the author. In the third case, the detriment to the sports person not to endorse products of the rival company is the consideration for the company. In the fourth case, the undertaking of one shopkeeper is the consideration for the other. In the fifth case, the suffering of the visitor is the consideration for the stall.

We need to distinguish consideration from its consequences. An advertising agency was commissioned to prepare a video clip for a food manufacturing company for a fee of Rs 30 lakhs. The clip submitted by the ad agency was satisfactory and met the requirements of the contract. Identify the consideration for the parties in the following three different situations. (1) The advertisement was a great success. As a result, the ad agency

got two more assignments from the company for a fee of Rs 50 lakh. (2) As a result of the advertisement, the company made an additional profit of Rs 50 lakh. (3) The advertisement was a failure. The profits of the company in the month fell by Rs 80 lakh. All the three cases are only the consequences of the agreement. The agreement and consideration remains the same, that is, Rs 30 lakh for the ad agency and a video clip for the company. In every agreement, we should discern the exact benefit or detriment as the consideration for the parties.

Time and Consideration

The time of passing of consideration and formation of agreements is an important concern. Let us explore the theme with the following possible agreements between a buyer who wants to buy a computer of a particular brand and specifications and the seller, a shop selling computers and accessories.

1. The buyer has to pay the entire price for the computer, Rs 40,000, to get into the contract. The seller will deliver the computer three days later.
2. The buyer is delivered a computer. He has the option of examining it and if satisfied with the product, of keeping it. The price for the computer has to be paid within the next five days.
3. The seller is to deliver the computer the next Monday and the buyer has to pay the price on delivery, after installation.

The consideration for the buyer is the computer and for the seller, Rs 40,000. In Situations 1 and 2, one party has received the consideration while the other is to receive it in the future. In fact, the contract gets formed only when a party receives the consideration. In Situation 3, however, the consideration for both the sides has to flow at a later point

---

[1] *Currie* v. *Misa*, (1875) LR 10 Ex 153.

in the future. This distinction, at times, is important. The contracts in which both the parties are yet to receive their considerations is called executory considerations and the contracts in which one person has received the consideration while the other is to receive one later are called executed contracts. The Supreme Court in *Union of India* v. *Chaman Lal*[2] explained the difference thus:

An executed consideration consists of an act for a promise. It is the act which forms the consideration ... No contract is formed unless and until the act is performed, e.g., the payment for a railway ticket ... In an executed consideration the liability is outstanding on one side only... In an executory consideration the liability is outstanding on both sides. ... The contract is concluded as soon as the promises are exchanged. In mercantile contracts this is by far the most common variety.

We need to distinguish executed consideration from past consideration. To do this, let us take the following illustration. Ajeet has lost his wallet. He announces that the person who finds and delivers it to him will be given Rs 500. Dev finds and returns it to Ajeet. This is the familiar case of a unilateral contract. To whom is the offer made? The world at large. Who accepts it? Dev, when he delivers the wallet to Ajeet. The contract is made the moment Dev gives the wallet to Ajeet. It is an executed contract, where Dev is to receive his consideration later. The later time may just be a minute. Contrast this with the following case. Ajeet lost his wallet. Dev found it and returned it to him. Ajeet profusely thanked Dev. In this case, Ajeet has got his wallet back but there is no agreement between the parties.

Let us extend the case further. Ajeet is very pleased and says, 'I will give you Rs 500 for

having recovered my wallet. Come to my office tomorrow and collect your money.' The next day, Ajeet refuses to give Dev Rs 500. He says Rs 100 is good enough, but Dev demands Rs 500. As we have noted, Dev did not get into a contract when he returned the wallet. Ajeet promised to give money to Dev for an act that Dev had already performed on his own, without reference to any offer. There was no agreement between the parties at any point of time that one would get the wallet while the other would give him Rs 500. Can the act of getting the wallet then be the consideration for the promise of Ajeet to pay Rs 500? The answer is no. Consideration is linked to bargain and exchange between the parties. In this case, there is no exchange or bargain. The two acts are unrelated. Thus, benefit or detriment in the past is not consideration. Let us review cases from the British courts on the subject.

Court Case: *Roscorla* v. *Thomas*

Roscorla bought a horse from Thomas for £30, which the latter had yet to deliver.[3] Later, Roscorla asked Thomas that he 'warrantied', that is, made it a part of the term and became responsible for it, that the horse was sound and free from vice. Thomas agreed. At a later stage, a dispute arose between the parties on the soundness of the horse and the liabilities of the seller. Lord Denman CJ noted:

It may be taken as a general rule ... that the promise must be co-extensive with the consideration. In the present case, the only promise that would result from the consideration ... and be co-extensive with it, would be to deliver the horse upon request. The precedent sale, without a warranty, though at the request of the defendant, imposes no other duty or obligation upon him. It is clear, therefore, that the consideration stated would not raise an implied

---

[2] *Union of India* v. *Chaman Lal*, AIR 1957 SC 652.

[3] *Roscorla* v. *Thomas*, (1842) 3 QB 234.

promise by the defendant that the horse was sound or free from vice,

Thus, the money paid by the buyer was the consideration for the horse on an 'as is' basis. It could not be consideration for the subsequent agreement between the parties as it was a past consideration. In the present context, in every sale of good it is implied that the good will be of merchantable quality (fit for its basic use). Thus, the soundness of the horse would be an implied term of the sale, irrespective of the subsequent warranty by the seller. The case, nevertheless, introduces the concept of past consideration. Another case on past consideration is *In Re McArdle*.

Court Case: In Re McArdle

In his will, William Edward McArdle had left his estate to be equally divided among his five children.[4] One of the children, Montague McArdle, and his wife, Marjorie McArdle, were living in a bungalow that formed a part of the father's estate. Mr and Mrs Montague McArdle made repairs and improvements in the bungalow. The latter paid a sum of £488 for the repairs. Subsequently, on the request of Montague McArdle, his three brothers and his sister signed the following document:

To Mrs. Marjorie McArdle

In consideration of your carrying out certain alterations and improvements to the property known as Gravel Hill Poultry Farm, Wimborne, at present occupied by you, we the beneficiaries under the will of William Edward McArdle hereby agree that the executors…shall repay to you from the said estate…the sum of £488 in settlement of the amount spent on such improvements.

A dispute developed with the executors of the property over the agreement between the family members. The court ruled:

[4] *In Re McArdle*, (1951) 1 All ER 905.

…as the work had all been done and nothing remained to be done by Mrs. McArdle at all, the consideration was wholly past, and, therefore, the beneficiaries' agreement for the repayment to her of the £488 out of the estate was…a promise with no consideration to support it. That being so, it is impossible for Mrs. McArdle to rely on this document as constituting an equitable assignment for valuable consideration.

What appears to be a past consideration at times can be a part of a valid contract. Let us explore it with the following illustrations.

Case: Car Mechanic

Chandra's car stopped in the middle of a highway. He knew how to drive but was unfamiliar with the mechanics of the car. Chandra opened the boot of the car but could not understand why the car would not start. A person passing by on a cycle stopped for him. He said, 'I am a car mechanic, let me see.' The mechanic examined the car and declared that the fuse of the electrical connection had melted. In the next ten minutes, he connected the power supply directly, bypassing the fuse box. He told Chandra that the car would work for now. Chandra was grateful and announced, 'I will give you Rs. 200.' The mechanic lived in a nearby town. He gave him his house address and asked him to visit the next day. The next day, Chandra was willing to spare only Rs 50. A dispute arose between them whether Chandra was obliged to pay Rs 200.

From one perspective, Chandra promised to pay the mechanic Rs 200 for a past consideration. Thus, there is no contract and the mechanic cannot demand Rs 200. He should be content with whatever Chandra gives him. There can, however, be another perspective of the event. The mechanic impliedly offered to fix the car and Chandra, by allowing him to do it impliedly accepted his offer. As the person had declared that he was a car mechanic, it was impliedly agreed between the parties that he would need to be paid for his services. Thus, fixing the car was a part of the agreement. The parties, subsequently, were only settling on a reasonable charge for the service. Constructing voluntary service as a 'to be paid for service' has long existed. The founding case dates to 1616, *Lampleigh* v. *Brathwait*.

Court Case: Lampleigh v. Brathwait

Brathwait had committed a murder. At his request, Lampleigh undertook a journey to go to the King to request a pardon. Subsequently, in consideration of this service, Brathwait promised to pay him £100. Brathwait, however, failed to pay the money. The court ruled, in the language of its times: '...a mere voluntary curtsey will not have a consideration...but if that curtsey were moved by a...request of the party...it will bind, for the promise, though it follows, yet it is not naked, but couples itself with the suit before.' Another landmark case is *In Re Casey's Patents, Stewart* v. *Casey*.

Court Case: In Re Casey's Patents, Stewart v. Casey

J. Stewart and T. Charlton were granted two patents[5] on 28 July 1887, one for 'Improvements and means and appliances for storing volatile or inflammable liquids', and the other for 'Improvements in and appliances or vessels for storing, or storing and transporting, volatile or inflammable liquids'. Subsequently, J. Stewart and T. Charlton signed the following document in favour of J. Casey.

Dear Sir,—We now have pleasure in stating that in consideration of your services as the practical

manager in working both our patents as above for transit by steamer or for any land purposes, we hereby agree to give you one third share of the patents above-mentioned, the same to take effect from this date. This is in addition to and in combination with our agreement of the 29th November last.

A dispute arose that the services of Casey were past consideration; thus, the promise to give Casey a one-third share was without consideration. The court examined the claim that past services are not a consideration:

Well, that raises the old question—or might raise it, if there was not an answer to it—of *Lampleigh* v. *Braithwait* a subject of great interest to every scientific lawyer, as to whether a past service will support a promise.... Even if it were true, as some scientific students of law believe, that a past service cannot support a future promise, you must look at the document and see if the promise cannot receive a proper effect in some other way. Now, the fact of a past service raises an implication that at the time it was rendered it was to be paid for, and, if it was a service which was to be paid for, when you get in the subsequent document a promise to pay, that promise may be treated either as an admission which evidences or as a positive bargain which fixes the amount of that reasonable remuneration on the faith of which the service was originally rendered. So that here for past services there is ample justification for the promise to give the third share.

The principle has been emphasized in a later case in these words[6]:

An act done before the giving of a promise to make a payment or to confer some other benefit can sometimes be consideration for the promise. The act must have been done at the promisor's request, the parties must have understood that the act was to be remunerated either by a payment or the conferment of some other benefit, and payment, or the conferment of a benefit, must have been legally enforceable had it been promised in advance.

[5] In *Re Casey's Patents, Stewart* v. *Casey*, (1892) 1 Ch 104.

[6] *Pao On* v. *Lau Yiu Long*, (1979) 3 All ER 65.

CONSIDERATION IN THE INDIAN CONTRACT ACT

Section 2(d) of the Indian Contract Act defines consideration as follows:

When, at the desire of the promisor, the promisee or any other person has done or abstained from doing, or does or abstains from doing, or promises to do or to abstain from doing, something, such act or abstinence or promise is called a consideration for the promise.

Apply Section 2(d) to the following situations:

Situation 1: Ajeet lost his key. He asked Dev to help him find it. Dev found the key and returned it to Ajeet. Ajeet profusely thanked Dev. Ajeet further promised to give him Rs. 50. Is there an enforceable agreement between the parties?

Situation 2: Manu asked Deep, 'Is this your wallet?' Deep replied, 'Yes, it is. As it is worn out, I have thrown it away.' Manu responded, 'It appears heavy to me. Kindly check if you have emptied it.' Deep had left his credit card in one of the inside pouches. He was very thankful to Manu. He promised to give him Rs 100. Is there an enforceable agreement between the parties?

We should note that Section 29(d), unlike common law, considers past action as a valid consideration if it has come 'at the desire' of the promisor. The section has also broadened the scope of the person from whom the consideration moves. Let us re-explore the following case. Deep wants to buy a laptop. He gets in an agreement with a retailer, R, where Deep will pay the money to the retailer, and the distributor D will supply the laptop to Deep.

In common law, the agreement between Deep and the retailer is not enforceable, as no consideration moves from the retailer. However, under Section 2 (d), the consideration can move from 'any person'. Thus, in the Indian law, the above is an enforceable agreement.

Agreements without consideration are not enforceable. Common law, however, made limited exceptions to this. Agreements recorded in writing and affixed with a seal were enforceable, even if they were without consideration. Affixing of a seal consisted in the government putting distinguishable marks on the document to preserve its authenticity. Later, this was substituted by registration of the document, where a copy was lodged and preserved by the government. The principle here was that if a person took the trouble of doing this, he must have intended to bind himself to the promise. Following this, The India Contract Act has made certain exceptions. The exceptions are in Section 25. It reads:

25. Agreement without consideration, void, unless it is in writing and registered, or is a promise to compensate for something done, or is a promise to pay a debt barred by limitation law—An agreement made without consideration is void, unless—

(1) it is expressed in writing and registered under the law for the time being in force for the registration of documents, and is made on account of natural love and affection between parties standing in a near relation to each other; or unless

(2) it is a promise to compensate, wholly or in part, a person who has already voluntarily done something for the promisor, or something which the promisor was legally compellable to do; or unless

(3)...

In any of these cases, such an agreement is a contract.

Explanation—Nothing in this section shall affect the validity, as between the donor and donee, of any gift actually made.

Section 25(3) and illustrations are not reproduced here. We will touch on them later. Let us first explore Section 25(2). The origin of the exception on past voluntary action is in the common law. *Lampleigh* v. *Brathwait* and *In Re Casey's Patents, Stewart* v. *Casey* were the two cases on the theme that we explored earlier. On the face of it, its inclusion under Section 25 may appear redundant as section 2(d) has already covered past actions as constitutive of consideration. However, there is a crucial difference. Under section 25, past voluntary action, even if it is not at the desire of the promisor, can be consideration. In fact, the two provisions occupy different spaces. If an action is at the desire of the promisor, it is solicited and thus cannot be voluntary. Let us review cases from the Indian courts.

Court Case: Kedar Nath Bhattacharji v. Gorie Mohamed

Howrah Town Hall Fund, a trust, was created to raise a subscription towards building a town hall in Howrah.[7] When the subscription list reached a point, the commissioners entered in a contract with a contractor for the construction. The contractor submitted a plan for the building and it was passed. As further subscriptions came, the budget for building the town hall also increased from Rs 26,000 to Rs 40,000. A person had put down his name in the subscription list to pay Rs 100. The question that arose was whether the money could be recovered from him. The court recognized that subscription to a charitable object would not have consideration. However, the arrangement in this case was different. The court ruled:

But in this particular case, the state of things is this: Persons were asked to subscribe knowing the purpose to which the money was to be applied, and they knew that on the faith of their subscription, an obligation was to be incurred to pay the contractor for the work. Under these circumstances, this kind of conduct

arises. The subscriber by subscribing his name, says, in effect, 'In consideration of your agreeing to enter into a contract to erect or yourselves erecting this building, I undertake to supply the money to pay for it up to the amount for which I subscribe my name.' That is a perfectly valid contract and for a good consideration; it contains all the essential elements of a contract, which can be enforced in law by the persons upon whom the liability is incurred.

The difference between this case and an ordinary case of donation is that the money was being raised for a specific purpose. The fund had taken an obligation to construct the town hall, which was the consideration for the subscriber. *Sindha Shri Ganpatsingji* v. *Abraham Alias Vajir Mahomed Akuji* is a case from the Bombay High Court on the subject of voluntary action.

Court Case: Sindha Shri Ganpatsingji v. Abraham Alias Vajir Mahomed Akuji

Sindha Shri Ganpatsingji litigated with his father over his right to succeed him. In British India, litigations on succession had been common.[8] During this period, Abraham 'rendered him great assistance and remained with him in times of distress.' After the litigation was over, Sindha promised him an allowance of Rs 125 a year. In English law, this would have been past consideration, unless it was taken as a voluntary act at the desire of Sindha Shri Ganpatsingji with the understanding that the services would be paid for. As the judgment brought out, the India Contract Act has dispensed with this requirement. The court ruled:

The Contract Act, though in the main founded on English case law, does not follow ... the present English law on the subject of consideration. We must turn to the Act itself. If the services of the plaintiff [Abraham] were rendered at the desire of the

[7] *Kedar Nath Bhattacharji* v. *Gorie Mohamed*, (1886) ILR 14 Calcutta 64.

[8] *Sindha Shri Ganpatsingji* v. *Abraham Alias Vajir Mahomed Akuji*, (1895) ILR 20 Bombay 755.

defendant … we do not doubt that they form a good consideration for the defendant's subsequent express promise to pay the annuity secured by the agreement. Services already rendered at the desire of the promisor and such services that are to be rendered, are placed in s 2(d) upon the same footing. Either will constitute a good consideration for a definite agreement. If the services were rendered without the desire of the defendant (and it is, we think difficult to conceive in the present case that they were rendered otherwise than at his express or implied request or desire), the case falls within S. 25 of the Act. The services will have been voluntarily rendered for the defendant. The section appears to cover cases where a person, without the knowledge of the promisor or otherwise than at his request, does the latter some service and the promisor undertakes to recompense him for it. In such cases, the promise does not need a consideration to support it.

The case distinguishes between Section 2(d) and 25 (2) in its application in relation to voluntary actions.

Court Case: Durga Prasad v. Baldeo

Durga Prasad, at the request of the Collector of the district, claimed to have developed a market place called Hume Ganj at his own expense.[9] The land must have belonged to the government. Close to a hundred people [occupied] the shops. Durga Prasad got a written agreement with the occupants of the shops to pay him a commission on the value of goods sold. The dispute in the case was whether the agreements between Durga Prasad and the shopkeepers were enforceable. The court ruled:

To render the agreement valid as a contract, it must be shown that there was consideration as defined in the Contract Act, or if not, that the agreement comes within the exceptions provided for in S. 25. Now the deed is silent as to the character of the consideration for the promise, and the only ground for making

the promise is the expense incurred by the plaintiff [Durga Prasad] in establishing the Ganj; but it is clear that anything done in that way was not 'at the desire' of the defendants [shop owners], so as to constitute a consideration, and … the circumstances do not bring the matter under cl 2, S. 25 … as has been contended. To bring it within the provisions of that clause, it must be shown that what was voluntarily done by the plaintiff [Durga Prasad], was done 'for the promisors' (shop occupiers) or 'something which the promisor was legally compellable to do,' … has not been shown … what he did was to please the Collector. In fact, when the plaintiff [Durga Prasad] established the Ganj, the defendants [shop occupiers] were not in his mind, and there was nothing done for them, for which compensation might be given.

Thus, there was no consideration between Durga Prasad and the shopkeepers. However, Durga Prasad may have had better rights over the collector and the government. However, the collector does not seem to have asked him in an official capacity to form a contract with the government.

Court Case: Raja of Venkatagiri v. Sri Krishnayya Rao Bahadur

The Raja of Venkatagiri made an undertaking to Ramakrishna for the advancement of money for him to pursue litigation.[10] After the Raja made several advances, Ramakrishna's grandson Krishnayya executed a promissory note, promising to pay the Raja a sum of Rs 1,50,000, with interest at 2 per cent per annum, 'in consideration of the amounts advanced from time to time for the Gollaprole litigation'. Later, Krishnayya refused to pay the money. His contention was that the promise to pay the money was not supported by consideration. The case was decided by the Privy Council. The case makes reference

[9] Durga Prasad v. Baldeo, (1880) ILR 3 All 221.

[10] Raja of Venkatagiri v. Sri Krishnayya Rao Bahadur, AIR 1948 PC 150.

to the courts in India through which the case had moved to the Privy Council. The Privy Council ruled:

When he denies liability under the note, he is not to be understood as saying there is no consideration; what he says being that there is consideration but he will show that it is past consideration which, not having moved at the 'desire' of the promisor, ie, himself, does not fall within S. 2, cl (d), Contract Act. He is not precluded from doing so by any provision or principle of law. As mentioned already, the courts in India have concurrently found that the advances of money for the litigation were made not as the result of the importunity of the respondent, but because of the undertaking given by the Maharaja of Venkatagiri to Ramakrishna, which their Lordships have now held to be binding on the appellant, and that the respondent had made no request which was not based on the Maharaja's undertaking to finance the litigation. No doubt the respondent pressed the appellant to furnish the necessary funds, but in doing so, he was only asking him to give effect to his grandfather's undertaking, contained in the letter of 29 January. Their Lordships accept these findings. The result is that it cannot be held that the advances of money were made at the 'desire' of the respondent, within the meaning of S. 2, cl (d), Contract Act.

It also follows from the findings, that S. 25, cl (2), Contract Act, cannot be relied upon in support of the appellant's case. To invoke the aid of that provision, it must be shown that there was a promise by the respondent to 'compensate' the appellant or his father for something which had been already done by them, 'voluntarily' for him. The findings of the courts, which their Lordships have accepted, show that the moneys which had been advanced were not advanced to the respondent 'voluntarily', but because of the undertaking given by the Maharaja of Venkatagiri at the time of the adoption. They also show that in executing the promissory note, the respondent was not promising to compensate the appellant for something which had been done for him voluntarily. It follows that the said promissory note is not supported by consideration; that being so, the other contentions raised by the respondent need not be considered by the Board.

In contrast to the above cases is the following case, where the court find not find any consideration in a donation.

Court Case: A. Lakshmanaswami Mudaliar v. *Life Insurance Corporation of India*

The Life Insurance Company sanctioned Rs 2 lakhs for the creation of a memorial trust that had been proposed to promote technical or business knowledge, including knowledge in insurance.[11] The company was later nationalized and taken over by the Life Insurance Corporation (LIC). The Life Insurance Corporation was not keen at the creation of the trust. A dispute was to arise on *bona fide* of the sanction and the obligations of the LIC to it. The case was mainly contested on the power of the board to have sanctioned the amount. A part of the dispute was whether the sanction created a binding contract for the company to pay the sum to the trustees. The Supreme Court ruled:

The contention ... that the resolution of the company and the acceptance thereof by the ... trustees of the trust constituted a contract is, in our judgment, futile. There was within the meaning of the India Contract Act no consideration moving from the trustees for accepting the amount, assuming that the resolution amounted to an offer. ... Mere willingness to utilise the monies for the purpose of the trust cannot be regarded as consideration, for consideration to support an agreement must be valuable. In the case before us even before the trust came into existence the Directors of the Company entertained a desire to make a donation in favour of the trust to be constituted, and a resolution of the company sanctioning the donation was passed. When the trust deed was executed the Directors paid over the amount pursuant to the resolution to the trust. By mere acceptance of the amount donated no consideration was rendered by the trust in favour of the company. Payment by

[11] A. Lakshmanaswami Mudaliar, Dr v. Life Insurance Corporation of India, AIR 1963 SC 1185.

the company of the amount resolved to be donated was therefore purely gratuitous: its acceptance made it a gift, and did not give rise to a contract.

Consideration: Written Registered Documents

Unlike the common law, the exception created by Section 25(1) is of a very specific nature. Section 25 mentions 'An agreement made without consideration is void, unless':

(1) it is expressed in writing and registered under the law for the time being in force for the registration of documents, and is made on account of natural love and affection between parties standing in a near relation to each other ...

To explore the provision, we first need to become familiar with the requirement of registration of documents. The Registration Act, 1908, is the general law on registration of documents. The thrust of the law is on the registration of documents dealing with transfer of interest in immovable property. The transfer of interest can be a sale, exchange, gift, lease, or mortgage. We need to locate the reasons for the emphasis on registration of documents creating rights in immovable property.

Earlier, revenue from agriculture was the main resource for the state. The state, thus, was interested in identifying the person from whom the revenue should be collected and the amount of revenue. Thus, the state started the measurement of land and maintaining records in relation to land. The records became elaborate, documenting crops, building, trees and water bodies. As market for land developed, the state required the parties to bring it to its notice so it would be informed of the person responsible for paying revenue. It developed a similar interest in tenancy, where the tenant became liable to pay tax rather than the owner. The transfer of interest in immovable property came to require execution in writing

and registration with the administration. The registration became the proof of ownership of land. Over a period of time, the records of the state became the only means to recognize ownership over immovable property. This became an important function of the state in maintaining order and administering justice.

The Registration Act, 1908, creates the office of registrars in districts. The act requires compulsory registration of documents that sell, lease, rent, mortgage, assign, gift or create any other interest on immovable property. The act makes it possible to register other documents. A document for which registration is compulsory, if not registered, is not admissible as evidence in a court of law. In other words, if the document is not registered, it is non-existent in the eyes of the law. An associated law is the Transfer of Property Act, 1882, dealing with the transfer of any interest in immovable property. We shall now study the consideration and registration of documents from the following cases.

Court Case: Lalit Mohun v. Basudeb

A father sold his business to his two sons.[12] It probably was an arrangement where an aging father was relinquishing his means of livelihood to his children and, wanted to be sure that he would not be helpless and at the mercy of his children. The sons entered into a written agreement to pay a monthly allowance to the father 'during his lifetime by way of pocket expenses a sum of Rs 50 in consideration of great regard they had for their father.' Things did not go smoothly for the family. Following a dispute over the sale of the business, the children did not pay the agreed allowance. The father approached the court to recover the amount due over a year.

[12] *Lalit Mohun* v. *Basudeb*, AIR 1976 Cal 430.

The contention of the sons was that there was no consideration for them in the agreement. Further, as the document was not registered, it did not meet the requirement for exception under Section 25(1). Section 25(1) requires the agreement to be 'registered under the law for the time being in force for registration of documents'. The Registration Act, 1908, requires contracts pertaining to immovable property to be compulsorily registered. A gift of immovable property must also be registered. The other documents can be registered but not compulsorily. The court explored this dimension of the requirement of registration. The court noted:

Under the Indian Registration Act, 1908 there is no provision for registration of an agreement simpliciter though there are various provisions for registration of other documents. Mr. Ghose [counsel for the sons] contended that if it was intended that the 'documents' in sub-section (1) of Section 25 of the Contract Act would include only agreement then the provision would be redundant, for if the agreements were to be registered under the Indian Registration Act this provision would be a superfluity.

It, however, appears to me that Indian Contract Act is a special enactment providing specifically for contracts and matters incidental thereto. In Section 10 of the said Act it is provided that all agreements would be contracts if they are made by free consent of parties competent to contract and made for lawful consideration and with a lawful object and are not expressly declared to be void. To this, there is a further provision which is to the following effect.

'Nothing herein contained shall affect any law in force in India and not hereby expressly repealed by which any contract is required to be made in writing or in the presence of witnesses or any law relating to the registration of documents'.

The word 'documents' obviously includes and is confined to agreements and any special provision in respect thereto by any other Act has been specifically preserved. In the same sense it has been used in section 25, so that, if under any law such a document is required to be registered its provision would not be affected by anything contained in Section 25. In this view of the matter, the agreements simpliciter in my opinion, are not required to be registered under the law for the time being in force for registration of such agreements but even so such documents are enforceable in law.

In other words, as the Contract Act is not to change provisions of other law in relation to registration of documents, the Registration Act, 1908, should be followed on its own. As it does not require registration of simple agreements, such agreements need not be registered. Section 18(f) of the Registration Act provides that any document 'may be registered'. Thus, it is not compulsory but possible to register simple agreements. According to the judgment, as the Registration Act does not require compulsory registration, the documents need not be registered.

Court Case: Provat Kumar Mitter v. Commissioner of Income Tax, West Bengal

Provat Kumar Mitter held 500 shares in a company called Calcutta Agency Limited.[13] With the intention to provide for his wife, he signed on a document which, after reciting that Mr Mitter was keen to provide for his wife, read: 'This deed witnesseth that for a effecting the said desire and in consideration of the natural love and affection of the settlor for the beneficiary, the settlor, as the beneficial owner, assigns unto the beneficiary the right, title and interest to every dividend and sum of money which may be declared … during the term of her natural life.'

The next year, as the dividend income, according to the document, had become the income of his wife, Mr Mitter did not include it in his annual income for computing and paying income tax. The income tax department contended that the dividend

[13] *Provat Kumar Mitter* v. *Commissioner of Income Tax*, West Bengal, (1959) 37 ITR 91.

income was his income. According to the department, the agreement was for love and affection, and there was no other consideration between the parties. The document, however, was not registered, and thus it could not avail the exception under Section 25. As a result, the document was of no relevance. The court ruled:

In holding that the deed was void because it was not registered, the Tribunal proceeded on the footing that section 25 of the Contract Act applied. In this, in my view, they were clearly wrong, because the deed is a unilateral document and does not contain any contract at all. In all material respects, it is similar to the deed on which the Judicial Committee pronounced in the case of *Gopal Saran Narain Singh* v. *Sita Devi*, (AIR 1932 PC 34). The only person who executed the deed was Sri Provat Kumar Mitter. His wife was not a party to it at all. The nature of the disposition again is the nature of a gift, although the settlor purports to bind himself to do certain things. Those, however, are in the nature of voluntary covenants of a unilateral character and cannot convert the transaction into a contract. It was said that there was a contract because the covenants were promises which, on being accepted, became agreements, but even then, the acceptance is not to be found in the deed and what the deed evidences are only the promises. Whether the deed was otherwise valid or not or whether the transfer sought to be made by it was effective or ineffective, it cannot, in my opinion, he said that it is bad for want of registration.

Thus, according to the high court, Section 25 applies only when there is an 'agreement', not a promise or a gift. For there to be an agreement, both the parties should have signed the document. However, the explanation to the section features the following illustration:

(b) A, for natural love and affection, promises to give his son, B, Rs. 1,000. A puts his promise to B into writing and registers it. This is a contract.

From the illustration it appears that only the father has signed the document. It also appears that the father has communicated it to the son orally. Thus, the two have reached an agreement. The father has then recorded the already formed agreement into writing and registered it.

Court Case: Smt. Rajlukhy Dabee v. Bhootnath Mookerjee

Bhootnath Mookerjee signed an *ekrarnama* (undertaking), promising to provide maintenance to his wife.[14] Mr Mookerjee later refused to honour the undertaking and the wife moved the court to claim the money. The court, thus, describes the content of the deed.

The plaintiff [wife] was not a party to the deed. The agreement refers to a mutual disagreement of minds 'between the husband and wife: to the probability of mutual quarrel,' and then proceeds: 'It having become inconvenient for you in many respects to live as aforesaid [and] finding it difficult to live in my family, you have claimed proper maintenance' and suitable habitation from me, I therefore make the following provision for your maintenance [and] habitation by this ekrarnama.' The recitals point merely to quarrels and disagreement not infrequent in married life: they do not indicate such a condition of affairs as would warrant the wife claiming a separate residence and separate maintenance from her husband.

The court ruled: '… the recitals do not show any consideration, moving from the wife, for the agreement. There is no promise on the part of the wife to do, or abstain from doing anything; she gives up no right.' As the deed was not motivated by love and affection, the court did not see it qualifying as an exception under Section 25, though the court below had done it. The court noted:

The learned judge in the court below, seems to have taken this view, for he finds the consideration in the natural love and affection between the parties. Though not expressed, he says that it must be

[14] *Smt Rajlukhy Dabee* v. *Bhootnath Mookerjee*, (1900) 4 CWN 488.

implied. He relies upon the proviso to s 25 of the Indian Contract Act.... I am quite unable to accept this view, which appears to me to be directly opposed to the recitals in the document.

In this case, the courts did not object to the *ekrarnama* signed only by the husband. It was struck on the ground that it did not flow from love and affection. In the present context, the courts would find consideration in an undertaking from a husband for the maintenance of the wife. The Supreme Court noted in *Ram Charan Das* v. *Girja Nandini Devi*:

Courts give effect to a family settlement upon the broad and general ground that its object is to settle existing or future disputes regarding property amongst members of a family. The word 'family' in this context is not to be understood in a narrow sense of being a group of persons, who are recognised in law as having a right of succession or having a claim to a share in the property in dispute ... The consideration for such a settlement, if one may put it that way, is the expectation that such a settlement will result in establishing or ensuring amity and goodwill amongst the persons bearing relationship with one another. That consideration having passed by each of the disputants, the settlement consisting of recognition of the right asserted by each other cannot be permitted to be impeached thereafter.[15]

Relying on the above, in *Manali Singhal* v. *Ravi Singhal*,[16] with reference to an agreement between a husband who was to pay monthly allowance for the maintenance of his wife, the Delhi High Court noted:

Parties more often than not settle their disputes amongst themselves without the assistance of the court in order to give quietus to their disputes once and for all. The underlying idea while doing so is to bring an era of peace and harmony into the family and to put an end to the discord, disharmony, acrimony and bickering. Thus the consideration in such type of settlements is love and affection, peace and harmony and satisfaction to flow therefrom.

There is no disagreement with the desired outcome of the case. The court, however, has listed the consequences of the consideration, not the consideration itself. A consideration could be the undertaking of the wife to use the money for her maintenance, not demand further resources and similar responsibilities.

Court Case: Ram Dass v. Kishan Dev

This was a case of family members contesting over property.[17] One member claimed inheritance by will. To keep peace and harmony in the family, the village elders negotiated a settlement by partitioning the property among the claimants. The agreement was recorded in writing and registered. The settlement was later disputed on the grounds that it lacked consideration. The court found consideration by noting 'that an arrangement for promoting peace and good-will between the members of a family is by itself good consideration for a family settlement.' In addition, the court ruled:

It is not disputed that the so-called settlement is in fact an agreement between the parties to resolve the dispute. The same is in writing and is registered and apparently made on account of natural love and affection between the parties standing in a near relation to each other. On this account alone, even if no material consideration was paid by the plaintiff, he is entitled to one-third share in the property as settled between the parties.

A promise motivated by 'love and affection' is contrary to a promise to avoid conflict and rancour. However, as the dispute was among family members, the court extended that the motivating factor is to restore love and affection.

---

[15] *Ram Charan Das* v. *Girja Nandini Devi*, AIR 1966 SC 323.

[16] *Manali Singhal* v. *Ravi Singhal*, AIR 1999 Delhi 156.

[17] *Ram Dass* v. *Kishan Dev*, AIR 1986 Himachal Pradesh 9.

Privity of Contract

Another aspect of consideration is the contracting parties and the parties from whom the consideration moves. Let us explore the relevance of this with the following illustrations.

Case 1: B and C get into an agreement whereby B will transfer the ownership of his laptop to C, and C will pay Rs 25,000 to B.

Case 2: B and C get into an agreement whereby B will transfer the ownership of his laptop to A and C will pay Rs 25,000 to B. B delivers the laptop to A but C refuses to pay B.

Case 3: B and C get into an agreement whereby A will transfer the ownership of his laptop to C and C will pay Rs 25,000 to B.

In Case 1, the consideration for B is Rs 25,000 and for C, the ownership of the laptop. There are only two parties to the contract. In Case 2, the consideration for B is Rs 25,000 and for C, the undertaking of B to give the laptop to A. Thus, both the parties have a consideration. It is incidental that a third party is benefiting from the contract.

In Case 3, the communication of offer and acceptance, and hence the agreement, is between B and C. The rights and obligations should be on B and C. In this arrangement, B has not taken any responsibility that can be enforced. For the agreement to be binding, B must undertake to transfer the ownership of the laptop to C. In other words, consideration must move from the contracting parties and not a third person. Under the common law, the agreement between B and C is not binding. The Indian Contract Act, however, has made such contracts valid. Under the definition of consideration, it can move from 'any person', so long as it is at the 'desire' of the promisor. Thus, the above is an enforceable contract in the Indian law. An example of such contracts in business practice is a contract where a buyer pays a retailer and the goods are delivered by the distributor. The retailer and the distributor, obviously, have some arrangement between themselves.

Benefit of Consideration to a Third Party

B and C get into an agreement whereby B will deliver certain goods to C, and C will pay Rs 1 lakh to A. B delivered the goods to C but C failed to give the money to A. A is claiming to recover Rs 1 lakh from C. A contract is a relationship between the contracting parties. Only the contracting parties acquire rights or liabilities towards each other. In the above case, A is not a contracting party, thus, he has no rights and obligations. The parties to a contract are in communication with each other, or 'privy' to each other. Thus, the concept that only the contracting parties can have rights and obligations to each other is referred to as 'privity of contract'. Other persons are third parties or strangers to the contract.

The founding case on privity of contract is *Tweddle* v. *Atkinson*.[18] William Tweddle agreed to marry Miss Guy. Their fathers entered into a contract under which each promised to pay William £100 after the wedding. William and Miss Guy got married, but Mr Guy died before paying the money. William claimed the money from the executors of Mr Guy's property. The court held that William could not claim the money since he was not a party to the contract. The court noted, '…it is now well established that at law, no stranger to the consideration can take advantage of the contract, though made for his benefit. If it were otherwise, a child might sue his own father in such a case as this.'

Let us look at a case where A, B, and C get into an agreement under which B will deliver certain goods to C, and C will pay Rs 1 lakh to

---

[18] *Tweddle* v. *Atkinson*, (1861) 1 B & S 393.

A. B delivered the goods to C, but C failed to give the money to A. A is claiming to recover Rs 1 lakh from C. In this case, A has privity of contract with C. However, no consideration has moved from A. Thus, A is a party to an agreement, but the part of the agreement relating to A is not enforceable as it is not supported by consideration. The common law courts did not enforce agreements where consideration did not move from the person claiming rights under the agreement. In the *Tweddle* v. *Atkinson* case, the court stated the principle 'the consideration must move from the party entitled to sue upon the contract. *Dunlop Pneumatic Tyre Co. Limited* v. *Selfridge & Co. Limited* is another landmark judgment on consideration.'

Court Case: Dunlop Pneumatic Tyre Co. Limited v. Selfridge & Co. Limited

The case involves three parties, Dunlop Pneumatic Tyre Co. Limited, Selfridge & Co. Limited, and Dew & Co.[19] We will refer to them as Dunlop, Selfridge and Dew. Dunlop was the manufacturer of motor tyres and Dew was a dealer in motor accessories. Dunlop had a scheduled price for its products. It sold tyres to Dew at a discount of 10 Per cent. Dew could sell the tyres to the end users as well as to other retailers. Dunlop wanted to ensure that the tyres were not sold to the consumer/last buyer at a price lower than the scheduled price. Towards this, Dunlop had a written agreement with Dew under which Dew could not sell the tyres to customers at less than the scheduled price. In the event of sale to a retailer or trade customer, Dew would take a written undertaking from that retailer or trade customer that the tyres would not be further re-sold for less than the scheduled

[19] *Dunlop Pneumatic Tyre Co. Limited* v. *Selfridge & Co. Limited*, (1914–1915) All ER Rep 333.

price. The text of the price maintenance agreement was provided by Dunlop. It stated: 'We agree to pay to the Dunlop Pneumatic Tyre Co. Limited the sum of £5 for each and every tyre, cover or tube sold or offered in breach of this agreement…'

Selfridge, a retailer of motor accessories, placed an order with Dew for Dunlop tyres. Dew obtained the tyres from Dunlop on the same day and delivered them with a price maintenance agreement to be signed. The agreement was signed by Selfridge. Selfridge, however, sold the tyres to its customers at less than the scheduled price. Dunlop moved the court to stop Selfridge from selling any more tyres at the lower price and claimed damages at the rate of £5 each for the tyres sold. The court ruled:

In the law of England certain principles are fundamental. One is that only a person who is a party to a contract can sue on it. Our law knows nothing of a…right…conferred on a stranger to a contract as a right to enforce the contract…A second principle is that if a person with whom a contract…has been made is to be able to enforce it, consideration must have been given by him to the promisor or to some other person at the promisor's request.

As neither of the above two requirements were fulfilled, Dunlop could not get relief from the court. The case brings out the following two principles of the common law:

1. Strangers to a contract have no rights, even if the contract is for their benefit.
2. Consideration must move from the person who is claiming rights in a contract. Consideration moving from another person is not adequate.

While the two concepts are logically consistent, at times they lead to unfair results. For instance, even contracts made for the benefit of a particular person give him no right to get it enforced. While framing the Indian

Contract Act, 1872, one part of this difficulty was removed. The rule of privity of contract does apply in India; however, the requirement that consideration must move from a party to a contract to enable him to claim benefit is dispensed with. Section 2(d) of the Act defines consideration as:

(d) When, at the desire of the promisor, the promisee or any other person has done or abstained from doing, or does or abstains from doing, or promises to do or to abstain from doing, something, such act or abstinence or promise is called a consideration for the promise.

Thus, under the definition of 'consideration' in the Indian Contract Act, the consideration can move from 'any person' so long as it is at the 'desire' of the promisor. Thus, the above is an enforceable contract in the Indian law. A case from the Indian court on this is *Chinnaya* v. *Venkataramaya*.

Court Case: Chinnaya v. Venkataramaya

On 9 April 1877, Raja Surranel Lakshmi Venkata Rau granted her share in the *zamindari* of Milavaram to her daughter, Chinnaya, through a registered deed of gift. Paragraph 12 of the deed provided: 'I have been till now, giving annually, Rs 653 to my brothers as I pleased, you also should therefore, until you give them a village which can yield the said income exclusive of *peshkash*, be paying them and their descendants.'[20] In other words, she was providing benefits to her brothers from the *zamindari*. As she was gifting the right to her daughter, she would have lost control to provide for her brothers. Thus, she made it a condition of the gift that the daughter would continue to provide the benefits to the brothers, that is, her uncles. On the same date, Chinnaya executed an agreement, a *kararnama*, in favour of her uncles covenanting to carry out the terms of Paragraph 12 of the deed of gift.

Chinnaya refused to fulfil her promise, and thus the brothers moved the court for claims in the agreement made by Chinnaya. Chinnaya pleaded that there was no consideration for the agreement and the brothers had no right to sue. The court ruled:

… As to the consideration, I should have had some doubt but for the very wide definition of the term 'consideration' in the Contract Act s 2 …

It appears to me that the deed of gift in favour of the defendant [daughter] and the contemporaneous agreement between the plaintiffs [brothers] and the defendant [daughter] may be regarded as one transaction, and that there was sufficient consideration for the defendant's [daughter] promise with the meaning of the Contract Act.

The doctrine of privity of contract is logical and consistent with the overall framework of agreements formed between parties. If it were otherwise, anyone could interfere in contracts between two parties, to their inconvenience and detriment. At the same time, it leaves genuine beneficiaries of contracts without recourse to claim the benefits. Some of its shortcomings have been remedied through enactments. The Consumer Protection Act, 1986, is one such attempt.

Trust and Privity of Contract

An exception to the doctrine of privity is the case of a beneficiary to a trust. We will explore the principle with the following case.

Court Case: Klaus Mittelbachert v. East India Hotels Limited

Klaus Mittelbachert, a co-pilot in Lufthansa, brought a plane into Delhi.[21] During the inter-

---

[20] *Chinnaya* v. *Venkataramaya*, (1881) ILR 4 Madras 137.

[21] *Klaus Mittelbachert* v. *East India Hotels Limited*, AIR 1997 Delhi 201.

vening period between his flights, he checked into the Hotel Oberoi Intercontinental and visited the swimming pool of the hotel. When he jumped from the diving board, he hit his head on the bottom of the swimming pool. He was pulled out, bleeding from the right ear and apparently paralysed in the arms and the legs. Klaus filed a case against the hotel, claiming damages for defective and negligent positioning of the diving board, which led to the accident. The hotel room was booked by Lufthansa, not Klaus. Thus, there was no privity of contract between Klaus and the hotel. The Delhi High Court noted:

The doctrine of privity of contract is subject to many exceptions, one of them being that a beneficiary can sue on a contract for enforcement of the benefit intended to confer on him by the contract.... The contract for stay in the Hotel was between Lufthansa and the Hotel, entitling the crew of Lufthansa to stay as guest in the hotel. The beneficiaries are those who would stay and hence, the contract was for their benefit. Consequent to the breach of the contract, those who stay in the Hotel would be entitled to sue. Any other view of the law would create an anomaly. Those who are staying in the Hotel would not be entitled to sue because they were not parties to the contract. Lufthansa would not be entitled to sue as it has not suffered any injury. A view of the law creating such an anomalous situation cannot be sustained.

A trust usually involves a transfer of property and the benefit flowing from that property. In this case, while Klaus was a beneficiary of the contract, there was no transfer of property from Lufthansa to the hotel, unless one constructs it broadly so as to infer that Lufthansa had a general arrangement to give money to the hotel for the benefit of its crew. The judgment brings out the inclination of the court to ignore the privity rule if the contract is specifically for the benefit of a person. The Supreme Court, in *M.C. Chacko* v. *State Bank of Travancore, Trivandrum*, summarized the position:

It is settled law that a person not a party to a contract cannot subject to certain well recognised exceptions, enforce the terms of the contract...Under the English Common Law only a person who is a party to a contract can sue on it and that the law knows nothing of a right gained by a third party arising out of a contract: *Dunlop Pneumatic Tyre Co.* v. *Seltridge and Co.*, 1915 AC 847. It has however been recognised that where a trust is created by a contract, a beneficiary may enforce the rights which the trust so created has given him. The basis of that rule is that though he is not a party to the contract his rights are equitable and not contractual. The Judicial Committee applied that rule to an Indian case *Khwaja Muhammad Khan* v. *Husaini Begam*, (1910) 37 Ind App 152. In a later case *Jamna Das* v. *Ram Autar*, (1911) 39 Ind App 7 the Judicial Committee pointed out that the purchaser's contract to pay off a mortgage debt could not be enforce by the mortgagee who was not a party to the contract. It must therefore be taken as well settled that except in the case of a beneficiary under a trust created by a contract or in the case of a family arrangement, no right may be enforced by a person who is not a party to the contract.[22]

SUFFICIENCY OF CONSIDERATION

An agreement is enforceable only if it has consideration for both the sides. However, must the consideration be commensurate? Let us explore the notion with the following case. A person received instructions from his employer to move with all haste to another location in another country. As time was short, he had to make a distress sell of his belongings. He did not mind it as his employer was giving him a generous dislocation allowance. He sold almost a new treadmill he had bought two months previously for Rs 1 lakh to an office colleague for Rs 10,000. Subsequently, the employer instructed him to remain in the same location. The person claimed that the contract was not binding as

[22] *M.C. Chacko* v. *State Bank of Travancore, Trivandrum*, AIR 1970 SC 504.

the price was not commensurate with value of the treadmill. Should the court enforce the agreement? Should the court make the buyer pay a higher, more commensurate price?

Parties get into contractual relationships voluntarily. The courts cannot set the terms for the parties. This would be interfering with the freedom of individuals and the sanctity of contracts. Thus, the courts have taken the position that the parties know the value of their transactions best. The courts must insist on finding a consideration, but not on examining whether it is commensurate or proportionate. Consistent with this, Section 25 of the Contract Act gives the following illustrations.

(a) A promises, for no consideration, to give to B Rs. 1,000. This is a void agreement.
(f) A agrees to sell a horse worth Rs. 1,000 for Rs. 10. A's consent to the agreement was freely given. The agreement is a contract notwithstanding the inadequacy of the consideration.
(g) A agrees to sell a horse worth Rs. 1,000 for Rs. 10. A denies that his consent to the agreement was freely given.

The inadequacy of the consideration is a fact which the court should take into account in considering whether or not A's consent was freely given.

We would explore in a later chapter that agreements formed through misrepresentation, fraud, or coercion can be set aside as the consent is not freely given. It stands to reason, as provided in Clause (g) above, that the court would examine the inadequacy of consideration in deciding the claim of a party that his consent was not freely given. Let us explore the theme of sufficiency of consideration further with the following landmark cases.

Court Case: Thomas v. Thomas

John Thomas had bequeathed his property to his relatives in his will. [23] On his death, his

house became their property. John Thomas had desired that his wife, Eleanor Thomas should have the use of their house if survived him. The relatives, to give effect to the wishes of John Thomas, had a written agreement with Eleanor Thomas. The agreement gave her full use of the house, furniture and the property. It mentioned that she would pay a sum of £1 for the ground rent and keep the 'premises in good and tenable repair'. After the agreement, the relatives refused to allow her the occupation of the premises. It was contended that there was no consideration in the agreement. The only consideration was the desire of John Thomas that his widow should be put in the possession of the premises. The court noted:

The cause for the gift was unquestionably respect for the memory of the testator. But we must not confound motive with consideration. A consideration, such as is recognised and known to our law, means a consideration of some value, moving from the plaintiff. Mere respect for the memory and wishes of a testator cannot be in any way construed as such. It is then argued, that, this being so, there is no consideration for the agreement at all, and that it is an agreement for a voluntary gift on certain conditions; but, looking at the agreement, we find, not a mere proviso, but an express agreement by the plaintiff to pay £1 towards a certain ground-rent, which apparently has been for the first time apportioned, and to pay it to the defendant, who is, I presume, liable to the whole ground-rent. It is not, therefore, a burden incident to the taking of the lease...

we find an express agreement by the person to whom the premises are to be conveyed, to pay £1 a year for a particular purpose, namely, towards the ground-rent, payable in respect of the premises, and others thereto adjoining; and she enters also into a distinct agreement, that, as long as she is in possession, she will do repairs. That is a sufficient consideration...

Let us explore the theme of consideration by examining the following cases.

[23] *Thomas* v. *Thomas* (1842) 2 QB 851.

Court Case: Carlill v. Carbolic Smoke Ball Company

We are familiar with the facts of this case, in which Edina Carlil, despite the use of the smoke ball, contracted influenza.[24] The company refused to pay the advertised sum of £100, claiming that there was no enforceable agreement as there was no consideration for the company. According to the company, that Ms Carlill contracted influenza could not be a consideration for the company. Justice Brown noted that consideration could be a benefit or detriment on the other party and reviewed the case:

Can it be said here that if the person who reads this advertisement applies thrice daily, for such time as may seem to him tolerable, the carbolic smoke ball to his nostrils for a whole fortnight, he is doing nothing at all—that it is a mere act which is not to count towards consideration to support a promise.... Inconvenience sustained by one party at the request of the other is enough to create a consideration. I think, therefore, that it is consideration enough that the plaintiff took the trouble of using the smoke ball.

Justice Lindley assessed the question of consideration as follows:

Does not the person who acted upon this advertisement and accepts the offer put himself to some inconvenience at the request of the defendants? Is it nothing to use this ball three times daily for two weeks according to the directions at the request of the advertiser? Is that to go for nothing? It appears to me that there is a distinct inconvenience, not to say a detriment to any person who so uses the smoke ball. I am of opinion, therefore, that there is ample consideration for the promise.

The court was applying the principle that 'some forbearance, detriment, loss or responsibility given, suffered or undertaken' by Carlill could be construed as consideration for the Carbolic Smoke Ball Company. The two judges also constructed that in the agreement, there was a 'benefit' involved, even if indirectly, for the company. Justice Brown reviewed the case as follows: 'But I think also that the defendants received a benefit from this user, for the use of the smoke ball was contemplated by the defendants as being indirectly a benefit to them, because the use of the smoke balls would promote their sale.'

Justice Lindley constructed the benefit as follows:

We must apply to that argument the usual legal tests. Let us see whether there is no advantage to the defendants. It is said that the use of the ball is no advantage to them, and that what benefits them is the sale; and the case is put that a lot of these balls might be stolen, and that it would be no advantage to the defendants if the thief or other people used them. The answer to that, I think, is as follows: It is quite obvious that in the view of the advertisers, a use by the public of their remedy, if they can only get the public to have confidence enough to use it, will react and produce a sale which is directly beneficial to them. Therefore, the advertisers get out of the use an advantage which is enough to constitute a consideration.

Thus, for consideration, the court mainly relied on the detriment faced by Ms. Carlill. The observation that the company would also benefit 'indirectly' supported and strengthened their decision.

Court Case: Chappell & Co. Limited v. The Nestle Co. Limited

The Nestle Co., Limited manufactures chocolate.[25] The company came up with an advertisement scheme where they offered to supply any one of six named gramophone records in return for a postal order for 1s. 6d. and three wrappers. The advertisement solicited: 'Save the wrappers from 6d. blocks.

[24] Carlill v. Carbolic Smoke Ball Company, (1983) 1 QB 256.

[25] Chappell & Co., Limited v. The Nestle Co., Limited, (1959) 2 All ER 701.

They will help you get smash hit recordings of skiffle calypso swing and ballad by Britain's newest stars all exclusive to Nestle's.' The manufacturers made the records and sold them to Nestle for 4d each. The record also featured an advertisement of the Nestle Company. Thus, while the objective was to advertise their products, Nestle ended up making a reasonable profit. The wrappers that were received had no value and were thrown away.

The copyright law of England provided for the reproduction of musical work without infringing copyrights. A person intending to make a reproduction of a musical work could give a notice of intention to make a reproduction for 'retail sale'. The person making the reproduction had to pay a royalty of 6.25 per cent of the 'ordinary retail selling price'. A notice was given to the copyright owner Chappell & Co., stating 1s. 6d. to be the ordinary retail selling price. Chappell & Co. refused to grant a license to reproduce the musical work. Their objection was that as wrappers were also demanded, it was not a retail sale. A sale is a special form of contract where the consideration for the seller is the price in cash. If the wrappers were a consideration, the company was not making 'retail sales'. The question, in others words, was whether something worthless like empty wrappers could be a consideration. The court held the wrappers were consideration for the contract. Lord Reid noted:

It is a perfectly good contract if a person accepts an offer to supply goods if he (a) does something of value to the supplier and (b) pays money; the consideration is both (a) and (b). There may have been cases where the acquisition of the wrappers conferred no direct benefit on the respondents Nestle but there must have been many cases where it did. I do not see why the possibility that, in some cases, the acquisition of the wrappers did not directly benefit the respondents Nestle should require us to exclude from considera-

tion the cases where it did; and even where there was no direct benefit from the acquisition of the wrappers there may have been an indirect benefit by way of advertisement.

...

The purchaser of records had to send three wrappers for each record, so he had first to acquire them. The acquisition of wrappers by him was, at least in many cases, of direct benefit to the respondents Nestle, and required expenditure by the acquirer which he might not otherwise have incurred. To my mind, the acquiring and delivering of the wrappers was certainly part of the consideration in these cases, and I see no good reason for drawing a distinction between these and other cases.

Lord Somervell of Harrow gave the following judgment:

The question, then, is whether the three wrappers were part of the consideration or, as ... I think that they are part of the consideration. ... It is said that, when received, the wrappers are of no value to the respondents The Nestle Co., Ltd. This I would have thought to be irrelevant. A contracting party can stipulate for what consideration he chooses. A peppercorn does not cease to be good consideration if it is established that the promisee does not like pepper and will throw away the corn. As the whole object of selling the record, if it was a sale, was to increase the sales of chocolate, it seems to me wrong not to treat the stipulated evidence of such sales as part of the consideration. For these reasons, I would allow the appeal.

The following is a case from the Calcutta High Court on sufficiency of consideration.

Court Case: Vijaya Minerals Private Limited v. Bikash Chandra Deb

Bikash Chandra Deb, a land owner in Keonjhar district, Orissa, reached an agreement with Vijaya Minerals Private Limited for the sale of manganese and iron ore.[26] The written agreement provided the price at which

[26] *Vijaya Minerals Private Limited* v. *Bikash Chandra Deb*, AIR 1996 Calcutta 67.

the ores were to be sold. It was a long term contract, but it did not provide for any price variation. Mr Deb provided the ores for a few years but later refused to comply with the contract. The company came before the court for the enforcement of the contract. Mr Deb contended that the price was grossly inadequate, barely 16 per cent of the market selling price. In fact, according to him, the price did not even meet the costs of extraction. Thus, it was pleaded that the contract should be set aside for violation of Section 25 of the Contract Act. The court ruled:

…an agreement between the parties cannot be rendered nugatory on the ground that the consideration is not adequate. The courts do not entertain the plea of inadequacy of consideration as a ground for refusal to perform the obligations under a contract.

Equity may give the relief of setting aside a transaction as it was 'improvidently obtained' when unfair advantage is taken of a person who is poor, ignorant or weakminded, or is for some other reason in need of special protection. … but mere inadequacy of consideration is not a ground for relief where the parties have bargained on equal terms.

Equity is a different branch of common law. The legal rights can arise from a contract or any other sources. In exceptional cases of hardship and injustice, however, the courts gave justice to the suffering party by suspending the legal right. As the principle of equity detracts from the legal rights of an individual, its application is cautious and conservative. We will explore the field of equity at appropriate places in the book. The high court did not give relief under equity.

Court Case: Desigowda v. Karnataka Industrial Area Development Board

The Karnataka Industrial Area Development Act, 1966, makes a provision for compulsory acquisition of land for industrial development.[27] It creates a body called the Karnataka Industrial Area Development Board for administering the act. It leaves two modes for the person whose land is being acquired under Section 29(2), the person can opt for an agreement with the board.' Alternately, under Section 29 (3), the case can be referred to the Deputy Commissioner for settlement of the compensation. Desigowda opted for an agreement under Section 29(2). The parties agreed for compensation at the rate of Rs 18,000. Subsequently, in relation to land in the same area, others followed Section 29(3) and were awarded compensation at the rate of Rs 28,500 per acre. Desigowda claimed that he should also be given compensation at the rate of Rs 28,500 per acre. An argument in the case before the Karnataka High Court was that the consideration was inadequate. The high court reiterated the law that a contract cannot be set aside on the grounds of inadequacy of consideration.

Thus, an agreement must have consideration for the parties to be enforceable. However, it does not have to be commensurate or adequate. This has reduced the concept of consideration to a technical requirement, that is, to whether any benefit or interest for one party, or inconvenience or detriment to the other party, can be found or not. This has been known as the 'peppercorn' rule in the common law. Even a peppercorn is an adequate consideration, but it must be there. The technical requirement has a significant role not only in agreements formed in practices but the unfolding of the contract law itself.

To summarize, an agreement is enforceable only if it is supported by consideration for both the parties. Consideration can be a 'right, interest, profit or benefit' for one party. It can

[27] *Desigowda* v. *Karnataka Industrial Area Development Board*, AIR 1996 Karnataka 197.

also be 'some forbearance, detriment, loss or responsibility given, suffered or undertaken by the other.' The definition of consideration in the Indian Contract Act is broader than the common law. Unlike the common law, past action is a valid consideration if it has come 'at the desire' of the contracting party. Further, under the act, the consideration can move from a third party. Agreements without consideration are unenforceable. However,

an exception has been made for registered written agreements 'on account of natural love and affection between parties standing in a near relation to each other.' Only the contracting parties have rights and obligations towards one another. All others are strangers and can claim no rights and have no obligations. This is called privity of contract. Consideration does not have to be commensurate or sufficient.

12

Consideration and Revocation of Offer

In some dealings between the parties, a collateral agreement providing that an offer cannot be withdrawn is formed. Let us examine whether the agreement not to withdraw an offer is binding in the following cases.

CASES FOR ANALYSIS

Case: Computer on Offer

X offered to sell a computer to Y for Rs 50,000. Y said, 'Let me mobilize resources and confirm in the next two days. But you cannot withdraw the offer during that time.' X said, 'All right. I will not withdraw the offer for the next two days.' X sold the computer the next day to another person and withdrew the offer. The parties are in dispute.

Case: Withdrawal of Offer

X offered to sell the shares of a company to Y for Rs 14 lakhs. X was not to withdraw the offer for ten days. For this, Y was to pay him Rs 10,000.

Mana offered to sell his house to Ajit for Rs 14 lakhs. Mana was not to withdraw the offer for ten days and Ajit was not to prospect to buy or receive any offer from others.

Are the agreements not to withdraw the offer enforceable?

Court Case: Bank of India v. O.P. Swaranakar

We took up this case in an earlier chapter. To summarize the facts, Indian nationalized banks sought applications from their employees for voluntary retirement.[1] A term of the scheme was that an application once made could not be withdrawn. Following this, the bank proceeded to retire even the employees who had written to the bank withdrawing their applications. The employees contested the decision of the bank before the courts and pleaded for their reinstatement. The scheme advertised by the State Bank of India and the State Bank of Patiala had additional clauses. In these schemes, Clause 5 provided fifteen days to the employees to withdraw their applications and Clause 8 provided two months to the bank to work out a management plan, including settling on the funds, depending on the number of retiring employees, to be committed. Are the differences

[1] *Bank of India* v. *O.P. Swaranakar*, AIR 2003 SC 858.

in the schemes of relevance? Is providing a window for withdrawing application consideration?

Court Case: National Highway Authority of India v. M/s Ganga Enterprises

We took up this case in an earlier chapter. The bidders were required to make an earnest deposit of Rs 50 lakhs along with their tender. The amount was to be forfeited if the bid was withdrawn before its acceptance. Following the withdrawal by M/s Ganga Enterprises, the Highway Authority forfeited the earnest deposit. M/s Ganga Enterprises moved the court to claim that the forfeiture of earnest deposit was without any foundation in law. Decide.

AGREEMENT AGAINST REVOCATION

There are several cases on the subject of agreement against revocation of offer from the Indian courts. We will examine this further with *Bank of India* v. *O.P. Swaranakar*.[2]

Court Case: Bank of India v. O.P. Swaranakar

Bank of India v. *O.P. Swaranakar*,[3] a case from the Supreme Court, relates to detriment as consideration. We have studied this case in an earlier chapter. The Supreme Court summarized the law on revocation: '(1) an offer may be revoked at any time before acceptance, and (2) an offer is made irrevocable by acceptance.' The Court applied the principles to the case. As there was no benefit to the employee or detriment or forbearance on the bank, the court ruled that the agreement not to withdraw the application was not enforceable. In this context, it is interesting to note that the Supreme Court took a different position

in relation to the schemes of the State Bank of India and State Bank of Patiala.[4] In these schemes, there was a window of fifteen days for the applicant to withdraw the application. Merely providing a window to withdraw an offer is no consideration. An offeror anyway has the right to withdraw an offer till its acceptance. The court examined the manner in which the schemes were to be administered, after the deadline for the withdrawal of the offer was over.

The court noted:

... the case of the State Bank of India stand slightly on a different footing. It ... permitted withdrawal of the applications.... The scheme floated by the State Bank of India contained a clause (Cl. 7) laying down the mode and manner in which the application for voluntary retirement shall be considered. The relevant clause as referred to herein before creates an enforceable right. In the event the State Bank failed to adhere to its preferred policy, the same could have been specifically enforced by a court of law. The same would, therefore, amount to some consideration.

As consideration does not need to be adequate, the court took features of the scheme that were only on a 'slightly ... different footing', creating entirely different results. The concept of consideration and adequacy of consideration has become a technical requirement, but it has significant implications.

Tender and Forfeiture of Earnest Money Deposit

Most tenders, particularly government tenders, require a deposit. The deposits go under different names, like earnest money deposit or bid deposit. The terms of tenders, generally, bar the bidder from withdrawing the tender. At other times, the bidder may be barred from withdrawing the tender after the

---

[2] Ibid.
[3] Ibid.

[4] *State Bank of Patiala* v. *Romesh Chander Kanoji*, AIR 2004 SC 2016.

bids have been opened. Whatever the terms may specify, there is an agreement between the parties not to withdraw the offer. However, such agreements are often one-sided. While the bidder is barred from withdrawing the tender, the party inviting the tenders makes no obligations or undertaking. To the contrary, the party inviting the tender casts things in its favour further by reserving the right to not award the tender to the highest bidder, or, for that matter, to any one. Thus, there is a collateral agreement between the parties that the bid would not be withdrawn. However, it may not be enforceable as it is not supported by consideration. There are several court judgments on the subject. We will look at a few leading cases on the subject.

Court Case: M/s Krishnaveni Constructions v. Executive Engineer, Panchayat Raj, Darsi

The executive engineer of the Darsi Panchayat Raj invited tenders for construction of a summer storage tank at Darsi.[5] The documents inviting tenders mentioned details of the work, including estimate of costs. M/s Krishnaveni Constructions submitted their tender along with an earnest deposit of Rs 1,12,800. The tender was opened in their presence on the due date. They were the lowest bidder. After opening of the tender they revoked the offer on the grounds that the schedule of rates mentioned in the tender document were not clear and they had been misled by this. A clause in the tender document was as follows:

…the tenders received will be decided within a period of three months of the last date prescribed for the receipt of tenders… In consideration of the Executive Engineer/Superintending Engineer, Chief Engineer undertaking to investigate and to take into

⁵ *Krishnaveni Constructions., M/s.* v. *Executive Er., Panchayat Raj, Darsi,* AIR 1995 Andhra Pradesh P 362.

account each tender and in consideration of the work thereby involved all earnest monies deposited by the tenderer will be forfeited to the Government in the event of such tenderer either modifying or withdrawing his tender at his instance within the said period of three months.

Following the clause, the executive engineer forfeited the earnest deposit. M/s Krishnaveni Constructions contend that an offer can be withdrawn till it is accepted. Further, an associated agreement not to withdraw an offer has to be supported by consideration, which is absent in the above case. Thus, the executive engineer should refund the earnest deposit with interest. The Andhra Pradesh High Court ruled:

… an offer made containing a promise not to revoke it and keep it open does not prevent the offerer from revoking the offer, for normally such a promise is unsupported by any consideration. But, if a promise to keep the offer open is supported by consideration, the offerer is bound by the promise and cannot revoke the offer: It is on this principle that a condition in the tender that the tender cannot be withdrawn before it is accepted is invalid and does not prevent a tenderer to withdraw his bid before its acceptance.

On facts stated above, it is crystal clear that the tenderer, that is to say, the petitioner-firm was bound by its offer till the orders of the Government accepting or rejecting its offer was communicated to it within three months therefrom as per the relevant clause of the tender in question. But, there is no material on record to infer that the promise to keep the offer open till the stipulated period was supported by any consideration and, therefore, the aforementioned condition appears to be invalid and the clause of forfeiture is unenforceable.

The Darsi Panchayat Raj was perhaps aware of the requirement of consideration for forfeiting the earnest deposit. It was towards this that it had mentioned the activities of the engineers as 'consideration'. While the concept of consideration has become technical, it is not illusory. By merely using the word 'consideration', an agreement does not get invested with consideration. The court noted it to be 'no consideration in the eyes of law.'

Sharad Trading Co. v. *State of Madhya Pradesh*[6] is one of the few cases of tender with the government where consideration could be found for agreement not to revoke tender. In this case, Sharad Trading Co. was awarded the contract to collect *tendu* leaves from forests for the year 1972. The contract had provision for renewal for three years, a year at a time. There was a provision for forfeiture for withdrawing the application for renewal. Sharad Trading Co. made an application for renewal. It, however, withdrew it before a decision could be taken. The government forfeited the security deposit. The legality of forfeiture of security deposit was contested. The court ruled that the forfeiture was binding as it was a part of the original contract, supported by consideration. The only case on forfeiture of earnest money deposit on which the Supreme Court has given a decision is *National Highway Authority of India* v. *M/s Ganga Enterprises.*[7]

Court Case: National Highway Authority of India v. M/s Ganga Enterprises

We had taken up this case in an earlier chapter. Ganga Enterprises withdrew its tender after it was opened. Following the withdrawal, the National Highway Authority of India forfeited the tender deposit. The Delhi High Court held that the offer was withdrawn before it was accepted and thus no completed contract had come into existence. The High Court ruled that the agreement against revocation was not binding as it was not supported by

consideration. Thus, the forfeiture was illegal. The Supreme Court disagreed with the position of the high court. The Supreme Court was of the following opinion:

The Indian contract Act merely provides that a person can withdraw his offer before its acceptance. But withdrawal of an offer, before it is accepted, is a completely different aspect from forfeiture of earnest/security money which has been given for a particular purpose. A person may have a right to withdraw his offer but if he has made his offer on a condition that some earnest money will be forfeited for not entering into contract or if some act is not performed, then even though he may have a right to withdraw his offer, he has no right to claim that earnest/security be returned to him. Forfeiture of such earnest/security, in no way, affects any statutory right under the Indian Contract Act. Such earnest/security is given and taken to ensure that a contract comes into existence. It would be an anomalous situation that a person who, by his own conduct, precludes the coming into existence of the contract is then given advantage or benefit of his own wrong by not allowing forfeiture. It must be remembered that, particularly in government contracts, such a term is always included in order to ensure that only a genuine party makes a bid. If such a term was not there even a person who does not have the capacity or a person who has no intention of entering into the contract will make a bid. The whole purpose of such a clause i.e. to see that only genuine bids are received would be lost if forfeiture was not permitted.

The right of the party to forfeit an earnest money deposit comes from an agreement between the parties. To be enforceable, the agreement must be supported by consideration. Thus, there must be a binding agreement for forfeiture. The judgment, however, justifies forfeiture on other grounds. Future judgments may elaborate and further develop the law on forfeiture of deposit on withdrawal of tender.

To conclude, an offer can be revoked till it is accepted. However, the parties can reach an agreement that the offeror will not revoke the

---

[6] *Sharad Trading Co.* v. *State of Madhya Pradesh*, AIR 1980 Madhya Pradesh 91.

[7] *National Highway Authority of India* v. *M/s Ganga Enterprises*, AIR 2003 SC 3823.

offer. An agreement not to revoke the offer is a widely followed business practice. The offeror is made to pay an amount at the time of making the offer that can be forefeited if the offer were withdrawn. As the offeror is bound not to revoke, this is a detriment to him. This becomes the consideration for the other party. For the agreement to be enforceable there must be consideration for the offeror also. This can be either as a benefit flowing to the offeror or a detriment on the other party. Often, this is missing, making the agreement unenforceable. And if there is no enforceable agreement between the parties, there is no basis for forfeiture.

13

Consideration and Third Party

The simple principle that every agreement must be supported by consideration permeates the entire field of contract law. Suppose a person gets into two different contracts with two persons to perform the same duty. Is the second agreement supported by consideration? What if the same two parties had got into two contracts where one person was to perform the same duty in the second contract? In this case, is the second agreement supported with valid consideration? An arrangement by mutual consent between the parties to change the terms of a contract is an agreement. This agreement to be enforceable must also be supported by consideration for both the parties. The changes in terms of a contract by consent take forms of remission, alteration or novation. We will be examining these topics in this chapter. Section 1 of the chapter has unanswered cases on the above themes. Applying the principles of the consideration to the cases will help us develop an approach to the topics. In the subsequent sections, we will take our discovery forward with review of court cases.

CASES FOR ANALYSIS

Case: Duty to Third Party

B and C are two neighbouring manufacturing units, receiving water from a common pump. B got in a contract with a mechanic to repair the pump, which had led to disruption of the water supply. The mechanic had diagnosed the problem and had committed to fix the problem by 5.00 PM in the evening. C was aware of the contract between the mechanic and B but arranges a separate contract with the mechanic to do the same job for Rs 2,000. How many parties are there? How many contracts are formed? Identify the considerations for the parties in the contract(s). Is the agreement between C and the mechanic enforceable? Why would C get into a contract of this nature?

Case: Buyer, Principal, and Agent

'Agency' is a special kind of a contractual relationship, in which an agent acts on behalf of his principal to bind him in contractual relationships with third parties. M is a cloth manufacturer and A his agent in a city. A created a contract between M and a buyer B for the sale of a specific quantity of fabric. A apprehended that B would breach the contract. A offered B Rs 50,000 for taking the delivery of fabric from M as contracted. B accepted the offer. The contract between M and B was successfully performed. Thereafter, A refused to pay Rs 50,000 to B. What could be the reasons/benefit for A to get in the contract with B? A claims that B was already under an obligation to receive the fabric and pay for it. B claims payment of Rs 50,000.

Case: Duty Imposed by Law

The law in India requires that no person will sell any packaged commodity to any one at a price higher than the retail sale price declared on the package. It is in the interest of the manufacturers that the dealers maintain the price line, as a high price reduces the sales and its margins. To ensure this, a manufacturer got into a contract with its dealers to the effect that they would not sell the products at a price exceeding the maximum retail sale price. In return, the manufacturer would give them 0.5 per cent of the sale value of the goods. The manufacturer had introduced the scheme when the prices of the commodities were highly volatile. However, at the end of the year, the obligations of the manufacturer became very substantial, and it refused to pay the amount to the dealers. According to the manufacturer, the agreement did not have consideration as the act was required to be done by the law. In other words, can a person claim an act required to be performed by law to be the consideration for a contract? How would the state respond to such contracts? Do such contracts strengthen or weaken the authority of the state?

Case: Pre-existing Duty to the Same Person

X does not perform his duty according to the terms of contract with Y. Y can claim damages for this breach of contract. Y may also get the right to terminate the contract. We will explore termination and damages in subsequent chapters. X and Y can also modify the terms of the contract with mutual consent. This is an agreement to change the terms of an existing contract. The agreement to change the contract would be enforceable only if it is supported by consideration for both the parties. As we know, consideration for a party can be a benefit to him or detriment to the other. Changes in contracts can take three forms. First, the parties can mutually agree to terminate the contract before the parties have fully performed their parts. A termination with mutual consent is called 'remission'. Second, the parties can alter the terms of the contract. This is called 'alteration'. Third, the parties can replace an existing contract with another one. This is called 'novation'. Let us find the consideration for the parties in the following modification of contract and identify whether it is remission, alteration, or novation.

A hotel group, Heritage Ltd, formed a contract with a contractor C, to get 20 work stations, according to their specified design, to be made for its executives. The contract was signed on the 2nd of the month. The work was to be completed by the 30th of the month. Heritage was to pay Rs 30 lakh for the job. Consider the following different situations based on the above contract. For each situation, identify the consideration for the parties and decide whether there is an enforceable agreement.

Situation 1: On the second day, after the contract had been signed, Heritage requested the contractor to not go ahead with the contract. The contractor agreed to it.

Situation 2: The contractor completed the work on the 20th of the month. Heritage was yet to pay the contractor. The parties mutually agreed to terminate the contract.

Situation 3: On the fourth day, Heritage paid Rs 3 lakh to the contractor. On the afternoon of the eighth day, Heritage asked the contractor not to go ahead with the contract. The contractor responded that it was fine with him. He would keep the Rs 3 lakh given to him.

Situation 4: On the eighth day, Heritage asked the contractor to complete the work by the 15th of the month, instead of 30th. The contractor agreed to it.

Situation 5: On the third day, Heritage asked the contractor to complete the work by the 15th of the month, instead of by the 30th as agreed earlier, and Heritage would pay an additional Rs 20,000 for it. The contractor agreed to it.

Situation 6: On the 20th day, the contractor told the Heritage that it was financially unfeasible for him to complete the work for Rs 30 lakh. Heritage agreed to pay Rs 35 lakh instead.

Situation 7: On the afternoon of the second day, the parties decided that, instead of the workstation, the contractor would make 30 pieces of furniture for furnishing the hotel rooms according to a design given by Heritage. The furniture would be completed in three months. Heritage would pay a total of Rs 40 lakh to the contractor.

Court Case: Extra Charge
A builder B was building a set of offices. He had sub-contracted the wood work to a party C. Midway, C expressed his inability to complete the work for Rs 15 lakh as material costs had gone up. C pleaded that he would incur

a loss. B and C reached an agreement that C would do the work and B would pay him Rs 20 lakh. B agreed to it as a delay in the project would have led to damages to be paid to the owner. After the project was completed, B refused to pay the additional amount. The parties are in dispute.

Court Case: Missing Nephew
Let us revisit the case *Lalman Shukla* v. *Gauri Dutt*.[1] Gauri Dutt gave money for railway fare and other expenses to his *munim* Lalman to go to Haridwar to find his missing nephew. Later, Gauri Dutt announced a reward of Rs 501 to anyone who could locate his missing nephew. Lalman found the boy and claimed the reward, but Gauri Dutt gave him only Rs 20. Lalman filed a suit for recovery of Rs 501.

Duty to a Third Party
We took up the case where C gets in a contract with a mechanic to do the same work he was to do under a contract with B. There are two distinct agreements with different parties. B has got into an agreement as he sees a benefit in it. This could be speedy restoration of water supply or to be doubly sure that the pump is repaired. As the contract meets the requirements of consideration, it is an enforceable contract. An old case on the theme is *Shadwell* v. *Shadwell*.[2] The modern expression is in *New Zealand Shipping Company Limited.* v. *A.M. Satterthwaite & Company Limited*[3] and *Pao* v. *Lau*.[4] In *The New Zealand*

[1] *Lalman Shukla* v. *Gauri Dutt*, (1913) 11 ALJ 489.
[2] *Shadwell* v. *Shadwell*, (1860) CB(NS) 159.
[3] *The New Zealand Shipping Company Limited* v. *A.M. Satterthwaite & Company Limited*, (1975) AC 154 (PC).
[4] *Pao On and Others* v. *Lau Yiu and Another*, (1980) AC 614.

Shipping Company Limited. v. A.M. Satterthwaite & Company Limited the court formulated the law: 'An agreement to do an act which the promisor is under an existing obligation to a third party to do, may quite well amount to valid consideration and does so in the present case.' An interesting case demonstrating application of the principle in a business context is Gopal Company Ltd., Bhopal v. Hazarilla Company.

Court Case: Gopal Company Ltd, Bhopal v. Hazarilla Company

Bhopal Textiles Limited is a manufacturer of textiles.[5] Gopal and Company Limited is one of their selling agents. 'Agency' is a special kind of contractual relationship. In this, an agent acts on behalf of a principal to bind the principal in a contractual relationship with third parties. On 9 May 1948, a partnership firm, Hazarilal Company, entered in a contract with Bhopal Textiles Limited to buy 2101 bales of cloth. The contract was made through the agent Gopal Company Ltd. After the contract was made, there were several correspondences between the mill and the buyer. Since the making of the contract, the prices had fallen, and as a result, the buyer was hesitant in going ahead with the contract. The buyer took delivery of 623 bales in May. The mill brought to the notice of the buyer that under Clause 6 of the contract, the mill could resell the remaining goods and collect the difference in price from the buyer. The buyer then asked the mill for a rebate as he was suffering a loss due to the fall in the price of cloth.

The agent, realising that the buyer was close to breaching the contract, stepped in. The agent offered the buyer Rs 25,000 to

[5] Gopal Company Limited, Bhopal v. Hazarilla Company, AIR 1963 Madhya Pradesh 37.

receive the remaining goods and perform the contract with the mill. The buyer accepted the offer. After the buyer had performed his obligations to the mill, the agent refused to give him the promised Rs 25,000. Hazarilal Company moved the court to claim the money. The contention of the agent was that there was no consideration for their promise to pay Rs 25,000 to Hazarilal Company. The buyer was already under an obligation to buy the goods from the mill. Buying the goods could not be a consideration for the agent. The Madhya Pradesh High Court ruled:

It is true that the plaintiff [buyer] was under a contract with the Mills to lift the bales and in agreeing to do what he was already bound to do under the contract, he did not impose upon himself, any fresh obligation. The question of a promise to perform an existing duty under a contract arises in two contexts. It may be between the same parties, for example an express promise by A to B, to do something which B can already call on him to do. In such a case, there is no fresh advantage to B, nor any detriment to A. Such a promise cannot therefore, be a good consideration. The question may arise in another context, namely, a promise is made in consideration of doing or promising to do something which a subsisting contract with a third person has already bound him to do.

…

The well-known leading cases on this point are Shadwell v. Shadwell [1860] 142 ER 62 and Scotson v. Pegg [1861] 158 ER 121. Smith and Thomas [A Casebook on Contract, second edition], have given a brief report of these cases on pages 175 and 178 respectively and have added a third case, Abbot v. Doane, (1895) 163 Mass 433 from the Supreme Judicial Court of Massachusetts. In the first case, A had written to his nephew B, promising to pay an annuity if he married X. B was already engaged to X. The question was whether the promise of A could support a binding contract. The majority of the judges held that the promise was capable of supporting a binding contract.… In the second case, the defendant's promise was to unload a cargo of coal at a certain rate in consideration of the plaintiff delivering the coal to him, which the plaintiff was already bound to do under a prior contract with the shippers of the coal from whom the defendant had bought it. Wide B, observed as follows in deciding the case for the plaintiff:

> 'But if a person chooses to promise to pay a sum of money in order to induce another to perform that which he has already contracted with a third person to do, I confess I cannot see why such a promise should not be binding. Here, the defendant, who was a stranger to the original contract, induced the plaintiffs to part with the cargo, which they might not otherwise have been willing to do, and the delivery of it to the defendant was a benefit to him. I accede to the proposition that if a person contracts with another to do a certain thing, he cannot make the performance of it a consideration for a new promise to the same individual. But there is no authority for the proposition that where there has been a promise to one person to do a certain thing, it is not possible to make a valid promise to another to do the same thing.'

From the third case, we need only quote a passage from the decision of Allan J:

> 'It seems to us better to hold, as a general rule, that if A has refused or hesitated to perform an agreement with B, and is requested to do so by C, who will derive a benefit from such performance, and who promises to pay him a certain sum therefore, and A thereupon undertakes to do it, the performance by A of his agreement in consequence of such request and promise by C, is a good consideration to support C's promise.'

From these decisions, it appears that the second agreement brings into existence, a new contract between different parties and therefore, a promise to do a thing which the promisee is already bound to do under a contract with a third party, can be good consideration to support a contract.

Pao On v. *Lau Yiu*, a case from the privy council, is another case on the subject.

Court Case: Pao On and Others v. Lau Yiu and Another

The Pao family owned share capital of a private company ('Shing On') incorporated in Hong Kong.[6] Mr Lau and family were the majority shareholders in a public investment company called Fu Chip in Hong Kong. The main asset of the private company Shing On was a building. The Paos wished to realize the value of the building by selling the shares of Shing On. Fu Chip agreed to acquire shares of Shing On. On 27th February 1973, two written agreements were entered. The first was a contract for the sale of shares by the Paos to the company Fu Chip. There would have been no problems if the Paos were to be paid in cash for the sale of their shares. Fu Chip was to pay by allotting shares of Fu Chip. In the contract, the market value of a $1 share of Fu Chip was deemed to be $2.50. On this basis, the Paos were allotted 4.2 million ordinary shares of $1 each in Fu Chip.

There were further concerns for the contracting parties. The Paos would have come to own a large number of shares of Fu Chip. If they were to put up the shares for sale in the market, over-supply would depress their market value. This would be detrimental to the Laos, the majority share holders in Fu Chip. To protect against this, the contract provided that the Paos would not, before the end of April 1974, sell or transfer 2.5 million of the 4.2 million shares to be allotted to them. The Paos, however, realized that by giving an undertaking to postpone sale of the Fu Chip shares, they exposed themselves to the risk that the price of the shares might fall below $2.50 during this period. The main beneficiaries of this protection were the Laus. The Paos thus sought from the Laus a guarantee against a fall in the price of the shares. On the same day, that is, 27 February, a subsidiary agreement was entered where the Laus agreed to buy back from the Paos on or before

---

[6] *Pao On and Others* v. *Lau Yiu and Another*, (1980) AC 614.

30 April 1974, 2.5 million of the allotted Fu Chip shares at the price of $2.50 a share. The effect of the two agreements was significant for the parties. As the judgment noted:

The commercial effect of these two agreements was remarkable. Lau had got very much the better bargain, as he himself recognized. No cash was required of him or Fu Chip on completion. If Fu Chip shares fell below $2.50 on 30th April 1974, the Paos would, however, be protected by the obligation on Lau to buy back 60% of the shares at $2.50 a share. They secured, therefore, their 'guarantee' against a fall in the share price. But if the price on that date was higher, the Paos still remained bound to sell back the shares at $2.50. The Paos had elected shares as their price for the issued capital of Shing On because shares could go up in value whereas cash could not, and they expected, as everyone else (including the Laus) did in February 1973, that share values would rise. Yet by the form of guarantee against a fall in the value of the shares which they accepted they deprived themselves, so far as 60% of their holding was concerned, of the very advantage which by taking their price in shares they hoped to gain, and without receiving any other benefit for having to wait a year before they could realise cash on 60% of their price. It is not surprising either that Lau thought he had the better of the bargain or that Mrs Pao became indignant when she appreciated what she and her family had given away by the subsidiary agreement. She and her husband, therefore, made up their minds that they would not complete the main agreement unless they could substitute a guarantee by way of indemnity for the subsidiary agreement.

The Paos indicated to the Laus and Fu Chip that they would not complete the main agreement with Fu Chip unless the subsidiary agreement was cancelled and replaced with a true guarantee by way of an indemnity, guaranteeing the price of 2.5 million of the allotted shares at $2.50 a share. An 'indemnity' is a special form of contract agreeing to cover up the losses. Fu Chip knew that they were in a strong legal position. They could claim specific performance of the main contract.

However, they were anxious to complete the transaction without recourse to litigation. Fu Chip had recently gone public. Litigation would have impaired public confidence. Thus, Laus agreed to cancel the subsidiary agreement and replace it with an indemnity. On 4 May 1973, the Laus signed a guarantee that the price of the 2.5 million of the allotted shares would not be less than $2.50 a share on the marketing day immediately following 30 April 1974, and that they would indemnify the Paos if the shares fell below that price.

Between 4 May and 30 April 1974, share prices slumped and by 30th April Fu Chip shares had fallen to 36 cents a share. The Laus did not fulfil their promise of indemnity under the guarantee of 4 May 1973. One of the contentions was that there was no consideration for the indemnity. In other words, the Paos already were under a contract not to sell the shares for a specified period by the main contract with Fu Chip. The same duty could not be a consideration with other parties, the Laus. Scarman, J noted:

… the consideration for the promise of indemnity … was primarily the promise given by the Paos to the Laus, to perform their contract with Fu Chip, which included the undertaking not to sell 60% of the shares allotted to them before 30th April 1974. Thus the real consideration for the indemnity was the promise to perform, or the performance of, the Paos' pre-existing contractual obligations to Fu Chip. This promise was perfectly consistent with the consideration stated in the guarantee. Indeed, it reinforces it by imposing on the Paos an obligation now owed to the Laus to do what, at Lau's request, they had agreed with Fu Chip to do.

Their Lordships do not doubt that a promise to perform, or the performance of, a pre-existing contractual obligation to a third party can be valid consideration. In *New Zealand Shipping Co Ltd* v. *A M Satterthwaite & Co Ltd* the rule and the reason for the rule were stated as follows:

An agreement to do an act which the promisor is under an existing obligation to a third party to

do, may quite well amount to valid consideration:
... the promisee obtains the benefit of a direct
obligation ...

Unless, therefore, the guarantee was void as having
been made for an illegal consideration or voidable
on the ground of economic duress, the extrinsic
evidence establishes that it was supported by valid
consideration.

The case presents an interesting situation—
while some of the contracting parties as
incorporated bodies were distinct in the eyes
of the law, the parties were otherwise related
in their interests. Thus, the second contract
was deliberately entered to enforce the first
one. The first contract was not to sell the
shares before a specified date. The second
contract was an indemnity for not selling the
same shares.

In all the cases, the parties getting in the
second contract have been aware of the first
contract. What if a party to the contract did
not know of the pre-existing contract? There
is no decided court case on this. It is unlikely
for this contract to be enforceable. The non-
disclosure of information may amount to
misrepresentation. It can also be the case of
a contract formed under mistake. In both the
cases, the contract becomes voidable. It can
be set aside on the insistence of the innocent
party. We will take this up in a later part of
the book.

Duty Imposed by Law

Can the duty imposed by law be a consideration for a contract? Law and its requirements
come before contracts. The law has to be
followed first. How can a duty required by
the law be a subject matter of voluntary bargaining and contract? Further, for the state
and law to recognize such contracts would
be detracting from its power and authority.
It makes a mockery of the law by suggesting
that following the law is a matter of individual

volition and contracting. It would amount to
recognizing that the governing mechanism
is weak and private initiatives are needed to
see to it that the law is fulfilled. For all these
reasons, performance of a duty imposed by
the law cannot be consideration for a contract. The landmark case on this is *Collins* v.
Godefroy.[7] An attorney was required by the
court to give evidence. An interested party
formed a contract with him to pay him for
the loss of time. The court ruled:

... if it be a duty imposed by law upon a party ... to
attend from time to time to give evidence, then
a promise to give him any remuneration for loss
of time incurred in such attendance is a promise
without consideration. We think that such a duty is
imposed by law ... we are all of opinion that a party
cannot maintain an action for compensation for loss
of time in attending a trial as a witness ...

Let us consider the following hypothetical
case. Most people find it difficult to compute
income tax and fill in the form for submission
to the department. To facilitate this, the state
gives training to educated unemployed youth,
and appoints them as 'resource persons' to
help people confused by their income tax
forms. They are paid by the government on
the basis of the number of applications completed. A resource person gets in a contract
with a tax payee to prepare the form, and
also to submit it to the department. How is
this different from the previous case? What
is the consideration for the tax payee? Is the
contract enforceable?

In this case, we note that the consideration for the tax payer is more than the duty
imposed by law. The additional responsibility
of submitting the form, logically, constitutes
valid consideration. We need to note an additional factor in this case. In most cases, the

[7] *Collins* v. *Godefroy*, (1831) 1 B & Ad 950.

government employees are prohibited from taking any other employment or getting into any contract. As a result, in most cases, such contracts would be contrary to law and thus, void. The resource person, in this case, however, is not a regular employee. Thus, he is free to engage in other kinds of employment. Taking this route, British courts have held valid contracts that have further obligations than the duty imposed by law. The landmark cases on this are *Ward* v. *Byham*[8] and *Williams* v. *Williams*[9]. Both the cases were family affairs and agreement for maintenance. Lord Denning was on the panel in both the cases. In *Ward* v. *Byham*, he expressed his predilection for the direction the law should take: 'I have always thought that a promise to perform an existing duty, or the performance of it, should be regarded as good consideration, because it is a benefit to the person to whom it is given.' Thus, the duty imposed by the law cannot be the consideration for a contract. However, an additional obligation can be a valid consideration.

PRE-EXISTING DUTY TO THE SAME PERSON

Having examined the cases, we will have reached the conclusion that a duty owed by a party to a contract cannot be the consideration for another contract between the same two parties. For example, a carpenter had contracted to make chairs for Rs 20,000 for a customer. Midway, he asks for Rs 25,000 instead. The customer agrees to give him the money. In the first agreement, the consideration for the carpenter is cash, and for the customer, the undertaking of the carpenter to make the furniture. The carpenter is already under a duty to make the furniture for Rs 20,000. In the subsequent agreement, the

customer gets additional Rs 5,000 but there is no consideration for the customer. Thus, the agreement is not enforceable. The classical case on this is *Stilk* v. *Myrick*.[10]

Court Case: Stilk v. Myrick

This case is from the early 1800s. Stilk, a seaman, agreed to sail from London to the Baltic sea and back at the rate of £5 per month.[11] When the vessel arrived at an intermediate port, two seamen deserted. The captain of the ship failed to find sailors to replace the deserters. The captain agreed with the rest of the crew that if they worked the ship back to London, he would divide between them the pay that would have been due to the two deserters. On their arrival at London, this extra pay was refused. Stilk brought up the case to recover the extra wages. The contention in the case was that the promise of the captain to pay extra wages lacked consideration. The seaman was already under a duty to work the ship to its return journey to London. Lord Ellenborough ruled:

… the agreement is void for want of consideration. There was no consideration for the ulterior pay promised to the mariners who remained with the ship. Before they sailed from London they had undertaken to do all they could under the emergencies of the voyage. They had sold all their services till the voyage should be completed. If they had been at liberty to quit the vessel at Cronstadt, the case would have been quite different or if the captain had capriciously discharged the two men who were wanting, the others might not have been compellable to take the whole duty upon themselves, and their agreeing to do so might have been a sufficient consideration for the promise of an advance of wages. But the desertion of a part of the crew is to be considered an emergency of the voyage as much as their death and those who remain are bound by

---

[8] *Ward* v. *Byham*, (1956) 2 All ER 318.
[9] *Williams* v. *Williams*, (1957) 1 All ER 305.
[10] *Stilk* v. *Myrick*, (1809) 2 Camp 317.
[11] Ibid.

the terms of their original contract to exert themselves to the utmost to bring the ship in safety to her destined port.

The judgment considered several situations to assert that it was the same duty. As suggested by it, if the crew were at liberty to quit the vessel at the intermediate port, the original contract would have come to an end. The seaman would have been paid for part of the journey. The promise of the captain at the intermediate port would have created a new agreement. It was understood by the crew at the time of making of the contract that in the case of death of a sailor or desertion, additional work would fall on them. Being at high sea, there would be no possibility of finding substitutes. A case from India courts on pre-existing duty between the same parties is *Lalman Shukla* v. *Gauri Dutt*.

Case: Lalman Shukla v. Gauri Dutt
The case has been taken up earlier as the *Missing Nephew case*. The court decided:[12]

In the present case, the claim cannot be regarded as one on the basis of a contract. The plaintiff was in the service of the defendant. As such servant, he was sent to search for the missing boy. It is true that it was not within the ordinary scope of his duties as a *munim,* to search for a missing relative of his master, but when he had agreed to go to Haridwar in search of the boy, he had undertaken that particular duty. Being under that obligation, which he had incurred before the reward in question was offered, he cannot, in my opinion, claim the reward. There was already a subsisting obligation and, therefore, the performance of the act cannot be regarded as a consideration for the defendant's promise.

Lalman had undertaken to look for the missing boy under the contract of employment. Finding the missing boy could not a valid

consideration for the unilateral offer for finding the missing boy.

Court Case: Ramachandra Chintaman v. Kalu Raju
Ramachandra Chintaman was a lawyer for Kalu Raju, representing him in certain litigation.[13] The full fee for the lawyer and certain earnest money was paid by Kalu Raju. Later, Kalu Raju entered in an agreement with the lawyer, promising to pay Rs 61 as a reward if he won the matter or negotiated an amicable settlement. Appropriately, the agreement was called *inam chithi*. The matter got settled in favour of Kalu Raju but he refused to pay the reward to the lawyer. The lawyer made a claim for the reward. The court ruled:

We are of opinion that the agreement was executed without consideration, and thus, being a *nudum pactum,* the suit founded upon it is unsustainable. The plaintiff [lawyer], having accepted a *vakalatnama* from the defendant [Kalu Raju], upwards of two months previously to the execution of the agreement, was already bound to render his best services as a pleader to him and had, as appears from the agreement, accepted that vakalatnama upon the terms of receiving his usual fee as a pleader. There was no fresh consideration proceeding from the plaintiff [lawyer] when he obtained the inam chithi. He could not be more firmly bound by it to render to the defendants [Kalu Raju], his professional services, than he already was by the acceptance of the vakalatnama. It may be noted, too, that the agreement, appropriately enough, describes itself as an inam chithi. Not, indeed, that this is of any importance, inasmuch as, even if this were not so, it would be sufficiently manifest to the ordinary fee and earnest money mentioned in the agreement, was utterly without consideration.

To conclude, a pre-existing duty of a person can be a consideration for another contract with a third party. However, a pre-existing

[12] *Lalman Shukla* v. *Gauri Dutt*, (1913) 11 ALJ 489.

[13] *Ramachandra Chintaman* v. *Kalu Raju*, (1878) ILR 2 Bom 362.

duty cannot be a consideration for another agreement between the same parties. The implication of this is that an agreement to change the terms of an existing contract may not be binding if the second agreement is not supported by new consideration. In this case, the parties will continue to be bound by the earlier contract. We will explore this subject further in the part on discharge of contracts.

14

Promissory Estoppel

The promissory estoppel is an innovation of the British courts, where in some situations a person may be bound to his promise even if there is no formal agreement or consideration for the agreement. Let us examine the topic with the following cases.

Case: Donation

X made a promise to a voluntary organization to give a donation of Rs 50,000 to build a school for children of poor families. X told the voluntary organization that they could go ahead with the construction of the school building with their funds for the time being. When the building was half done, X refused to pay the money. In this case, there is only a gratuitous promise by X. In the British law, there is no consideration in the agreement as X does not get anything in return. X is not bound to give the money.

Case: Maintenance

Sigma Limited has an annual maintenance contract for maintaining the computers of Newell Limited. The contract could be renewed by mutual consent. The renewal of the contract was done by the parties by signing a standard form contract, designed by Sigma Limited. Sigma Limited had worked with Newell Limited for 6 years. A month before the contract was to expire, Newell Limited wrote to Sigma Limited, informing them that they would be renewing the contract and, further, they would have a hundred more computers to maintain. Thus, Sigma Limited should get ready with additional manpower to manage double the number of computers. In preparation, Sigma Limited employed three more computer engineers. Two weeks later, Newell Limited informed Sigma Limited that they would not be signing the annual maintenance contract with them.

Newell Limited was not bound to renew the contract. Till the standard contract document was signed, there was no agreement between the parties. The letter from Newell Limited was only a promise to renew the contract. A promise on its own is not binding.

In both the cases, the one who made the promise is not bound by it as either no agreement is formed between the parties, or if an agreement is formed, it does not have any consideration. However, there is injustice here. Relying on the promise, another person has suffered a detriment or loss. The courts felt that strict application of the legal right was resulting in harsh and unfair results. The courts decided to give remedy by suspending the application of the legal right in appropriate cases. The principle where legal right could be suspended in some situations came to be called equity. Often, a person was barred from enforcing his legal right—this came to be expressed with the term estoppel, that is, to prevent, bar, or obstruct.

In the above cases, the estoppel developed by the courts was to prevent the party from going back on his promise. This came to be called promissory estoppel. Following promissory estoppel, X will be bound by his promise to pay Rs 50,000 even if there is no consideration. In the second case, Newell Limited is bound by the promise even if no agreement is reached between the parties as yet.

PRINCIPLES OF PROMISSORY ESTOPPEL

As estoppel detracts from legal rights of persons, there are limitations on its availability and scope. The case which developed and consolidated promissory estoppel is *Central London Property Trust, Ltd* v. *High Trees House, Ltd.*

Court Case: *Central London Property Trust, Limited* v. *High Trees House, Limited*

Central London Property Trust, Ltd was the owner of a block of flats.[1] It leased the flats to another company, High Trees House, Ltd, for a term of 99 years from 29 September 1937, at a rent of £2,500 a year. The two companies were closely linked. Central London Property Trust, Ltd held all the shares of the High Trees House, Ltd. The companies were also linked through their directors and secretaries. High Trees House, Ltd. was to rent out the flats to others.

[1] *Central London Property Trust, Limited* v. *High Trees House, Limited*, (1947) KB 130.

Then the Second World War began. Due to the absence of people from London due to the war, only one-third of the flats got occupied. With war conditions prevailing, it was plain to those who ran these companies that the rent payable under the lease could not be paid out of the profits. In those circumstances, following discussions, Central London Property Trust, Ltd wrote to High Trees House, Ltd on 3 January 1940: 'We confirm the arrangement made between us by which the ground rent should be reduced as from the commencement of the lease to £1,250 per annum.' At the meeting of Central London Property Trust, Ltd in April 1940, the it was resolved that the tenants would be charged ground rent from 1 March 1939, at the reduced rate of £1,250 a year in place of the £2,500 a year provided in the lease. The court made it clear that it was a temporary arrangement to deal with the exceptional circumstances of the war. The premises came to be fully occupied in 1945. Meanwhile, Central London Property Trust, Ltd. went into liquidation. The receiver claimed arrears of rent at the rate of £2,500, while the tenant claimed that the rent in perpetuity had been reduced to £1,250. Alternately, the rent was to be restored to its original value, £2,500, only on full occupancy, that is, 1945. Lord Denning, thus, decided the case:

If I consider this matter without regard to recent developments in the law there is no doubt that the whole claim must succeed. This is a lease under seal, and at common law, it could not be varied by parol or by writing, but only by deed; but equity has stepped in, and the courts may now give effect to a variation in writing. That equitable doctrine could hardly apply, however, in this case because this variation might be said to be without consideration.

…

There has been a series of decisions over the last fifty years which, although said to be cases of estoppel, are not really such. They are cases of promises which were intended to create legal relations and which, in the knowledge of the person making the promise, were going to be acted on by the party to whom the promise was made, and have in fact been so acted on. In such cases the courts have said these promises must be honoured. ... Although said by the learned judges who decided them to be cases of estoppel, all these cases are not estoppel in the strict sense. They are cases of promises which were intended to be binding, which the parties making them knew would be acted on and which the parties to whom they were made did act on. In each case the court held the promise to be binding on the party making it, even though under the old common law it might be said to be difficult to find any consideration for it. The courts have not gone so far as to give a cause of action in damages for breach of such promises, but they have refused to allow the party making them to act inconsistently with them. It is in that sense, and in that sense only, that such a promise gives rise to an estoppel. The cases are a natural result of the fusion of law and equity; for the cases ... show that a party will not be allowed in equity to go back on such a promise. The time has now come for the validity of such a promise to be recognised. The logical consequence, no doubt, is that a promise to accept a smaller sum in discharge of a larger sum, if acted on, is binding, notwithstanding the absence of consideration, and if the fusion of law and equity leads to that result, so much the better. At this time of day it is not helpful to try to draw a distinction between law and equity. They have been joined together now for over seventy years, and the problems have to be approached in a combined sense. ...

I am satisfied that such a promise is binding in law, and the only question is the scope of the promise in the present case. I am satisfied on the evidence that the promise was that the ground rent should be reduced to £ 1,250 a year as a temporary expedient, while the block of flats was not fully or substantially fully let owing to the conditions prevailing. That means that this reduction of rent applied up to the end of 1944.

Promise: Clear and Definite

Let us consider a variation of the cases we took up at the beginning of the chapter. X instead told the voluntary organization that he 'might consider giving Rs 50,000'. Or Newell Ltd wrote to Sigma Limited saying that it was likely that they would renew the contract. It stands to reason that the promise should be clear, definite, and unequivocal. This is insisted on in formation of contracts. The standard of it should be even higher for invoking promissory estoppel as a legal right is being suspended. The case on the theme is *Woodhouse* v. *Nigerian Produce Limited*.

Court Case: Woodhouse Ac Israel Cocoa Limited Sa and Another v. Nigerian Produce Marketing Company Limited

In this case before the House of Lords, it was not clear between the parties in a contract of sale whether the reference to the 'Currency of account' was to the Nigerian pound or the British pound (pound sterling).[2] As both the currencies were equivalent, ordinarily, it would not have mattered. However, devaluation of the Nigerian pound made a difference. The party claimed promissory estoppel. The court ruled:

Counsel for the appellants was asked whether he knew of any case in which an ambiguous statement had ever formed the basis of a purely promissory estoppel, as contended for here ... He candidly replied that he did not. I do not find this surprising, since it would really be an astonishing thing if, in the case of a genuine misunderstanding as to the meaning of an offer, the offeree could obtain by means of the doctrine of promissory estoppel something that he must fail to obtain under the conventional law of contract.

Reliance on Promise

Let us consider variations of the cases we had taken up in the beginning of the chapter.

---

[2] *Woodhouse Ac Israel Cocoa Limited Sa and Another* v. *Nigerian Produce Marketing Company Limited*, (1972) AC 741.

- X promised Rs 50,000 to the voluntary organization, but the organization had decided to go ahead with the construction of the building nevertheless.
- Sigma Limited has a large turnover of the employees and it frequently hires employees. It had advertised for the position of three computer engineers even before it received the letter from Newell Limited.

In the above variations, a promise was made, but the other person did not rely on the promise. Let us do another variation of the cases.

- X promised Rs 50, 000 to the voluntary organization. The organization started the construction. X backed out but other donors came forward.
- Sigma Limited, given the promise of an assignment from Newell Limited, hired three employees. Sigma Limited backed out and the three employees also left as they got a better job elsewhere.

In the above variations, there is reliance on the promise, but no injustice to the party relying on the promise. Let us take a different case.

Omega Limited hired 50 computers from Equipment Hire Limited for five years. In the second year of the contract, the prices of the computers came down drastically. Omega Limited brought this to the notice of Equipment Hire Limited. Computers were available in the market for hire at 50 per cent of the rental contracted by Omega Limited. Equipment Hire Limited wrote to Omega Limited that they would charge only 75 per cent of the rental for the remaining three years. At the end of the contract period, however, Equipment Hire Limited demanded the full rental for the computers. A dispute arose between the parties.

The promise of Equipment Hire Limited is not supported by consideration, and thus not binding. Further, Omega Limited had in any case contracted to pay a certain amount. There is no harm or detriment to Omega Limited; the promise was to benefit Omega Limited. Nevertheless, it is unfair and unjust for Omega Limited. The courts do not go by detriment or benefit but whether there is inequity.

We have thus developed two propositions for a party to avail promissory estoppel: First, the person must reply to the promise, and there should be inequity in allowing the person to back out from the promise. The case on this is *Socit Italo-Belge pour le Commerce et l'Industrie Sa* v. *Palm and Vegetable Oils (Malaysia) Sdn Bhd The Post Chaser.*[3] The promise can be express or implied. This is of no consequence. This is brought out by the judgment of Lord Denning in *Crabb* v. *Arun District Council.*[4] Estoppel has the limited purpose of preventing a person from enforcing his legal right as it would lead to inequity. It cannot create a new right for the other party.[5]

PROMISSORY ESTOPPEL: INDIAN COURT
Promissory estoppel has been adopted and settled by the Indian courts, as exemplified in the following two cases.

Court Case: Delhi Cloth and General Mills Limited v. Union of India
Delhi Cloth and General Mills Limited (DCM) intended to set up a fertilizer factory at Kota in Rajasthan.[6] The district then was

[3] *Socit Italo-Belge pour le Commerce et l'Industrie Sa* v. *Palm and Vegetable Oils (Malaysia) Sdn Bhd The Post Chaser*, (1982) (1) All ER 19.

[4] *Crabb* v. *Arun District Council*, Court of Appeal, (1975) 3 All ER 865.

[5] *Combe* v. *Combe*, (1951) 2 KB 215.

[6] *Delhi Cloth and General Mills Limited* v. *Union of India*, AIR 1987 SC 2414.

said to be an industrially backward area. The main raw material was Naphtha, which was to be transported from the Koyali Refinery of the Indian Oil Corporation, Baroda. The mode of transportation was by rail. The railway has different classifications of freight and freight charges. Before the actual setting up of the factory, DCM sent a letter to the Railway Board, asking for a concessional freight rate for the carriage of Naphtha under Classification 62.5-B. This would have meant a reduction of about 43 per cent in the normal tariff. In the letter, DCM pointed out that if such concessional rate was not fixed, the company would be put in a disadvantageous position compared to the other factories located at ports or near the refineries. The Railway Board, thus, responded to the request:

I am directed to state that the Railway Board agree to quote a special rate equal to class 85-B (Special) CC : K for transport of Naptha in train loads from Bombay or Koyali to Kota, for manufacture of fertilizers. The proposed special rate will apply at owner's risk.

Since the special rate is being quoted ahead of the actual setting up of the factory the rate may need to be reviewed when the traffic actually begins to move. The Railway may accordingly be approached before the traffic actually starts moving.

When the factory was almost ready for operation, DCM wrote to the Railway Board for the rate under classification 62.5-B. The Railway Board, as its letter suggests, was not convinced that the DCM was at a disadvantage due to its location in Kota. Declining the request of DCM, the Railway Board responded:

… if on the basis of facts and figures your cost of production (date to be furnished for at least one complete year) vis-à-vis the sale price of fertilizers, it can be established that production of fertilizers at Kota uneconomical, until freight concession on the movement of Naptha from Bajuva/Trombay to Kota is granted, the Railway Board would be prepared to reconsider the question.

DCM moved the Railway Tribunal, the adjudicating body on freight disputes. DCM claimed promissory estoppel. The tribunal was of the view that the assurance of the Railway Board was not mainly responsible for the setting up of the Fertilizer Factory at Kota. Further, the tribunal on evidence before it saw that the freight movement at normal rate was viable. In other words, there was no loss or damage to DCM. It noted:

… the complainant has suffered no material injury by virtue of the withdrawal of the concessional rate and the charging of the normal rate. It is well settled that the principle of estoppel cannot be applied unless the person pleading estoppel can show that he has been prejudiced by the conduct of the party on whose assurance he has acted.

The case came in appeal before the Supreme Court. The Supreme Court was forthright in pointing out the wrong conception of the tribunal on promissory estoppel. For prommisory estoppel to apply, no loss or damage need be caused to the person. The Supreme Court ruled:

Here the Railways Rates Tribunal apparently appears to have gone off the track. The doctrine of promissory estoppel has not been correctly understood by the tribunal. It is true, that in the formative period, it was generally said that the doctrine of promissory estoppel cannot be invoked by the promisee unless he has suffered 'detriment' or 'prejudice'. It was often said simply, that the party asserting the estoppel must have been induced to act to his detriment. But this has now been explained in so many decisions all over. All that is now required is that the party asserting the estoppel must have acted upon the assurance given to him. Must have relied upon the representation made to him. It means, the party has changed or altered the position by relying on the assurance or the representation. The alteration of position by the party is the only indispensable requirement of the doctrine. It is not necessary to prove further any damage, detriment or prejudice to the party asserting the estoppel. The Court, however, would compel the opposite party to adhere to the representation acted upon or abstained from acting. The entire doctrine proceeds on the premise that it is reliance based and nothing more.

This principle would be clear if we study the cases in which the doctrine has been applied ever since it was burst out into sudden blaze in 1946. Lord Denning in *Central London Properties Ltd.* v. *High Trees House Ltd.*, 1947 KB 130, sitting as a trial Judge, asserted: 'A promise intended to be binding, intended to be acted upon, and in fact acted upon is binding....'

The history of the High Trees principle is too well known to bear repetition. It will be enough to make the following points. The promisor is bound because he led the promisee to commit himself to change the position. If the promisee has acted upon the promise, the promisor is precluded from receding his promise. No further detriment to the promisee upon his temporal interests need be established. This position has been made clear by Lord Denning himself in his article 'Recent Developments in the Doctrine of Consideration', *Moderm Law Review*, Vol. 15 at p. 5.

'A man should keep his word. All the more so when the promise is not a bare promise but is made with the intention that the other party should act upon it. Just a contract is different from tort and from estoppel, so also in the sphere now under discussion promises may give rise to a different equity from other conduct. The difference may lie in the necessity of showing detriment where one party deliberately promises to waive, modify or discharge his strict legal rights, intending the other party to act on the faith of promise, and the other party actually does act on it, then it is contrary, not only to equity but also to good faith, to allow the promisor to go back on his promise. It should not be necessary for the other party to show that he acted to his detriment in reliance on the promise. It should be sufficient that he acted on it.'

... Bhagwati, J. (as he then was) in *Motilal Padampat Sugar Mills Co. Ltd.* v. *State of U.P.* (AIR 1979 SC 621 at p. 651). The learned Judge then said:

'We do not think that in order to invoke the doctrine of promissory estoppel it is, necessary for the promisee to show that he suffered detriment as a result of acting in reliance on the promise. But we may make it clear that if by detriment we mean injustice to the promisee which could result if the promisor were to recede from his promise then detriment would certainly come in as a necessary ingredient. The detriment in such a case is not some prejudice suffered by the promisee by acting on the promise, but the prejudice which would be caused to the promisee, if the promisor were allowed to go back on the promise.'

The concept of detriment as we now understand is whether it appears unjust, unreasonable or inequitable that the promisor should be allowed to resile from his assurance or representation, having regard to what the promisee has done or refrained from doing in reliance on the assurance or representation.

It is, however, quite fundamental that the doctrine of promissory estoppel cannot be used to compel the public bodies or the government to carry out the representation or promise which is contrary to law or which is outside their authority or power. Secondly, the estoppel stems from equitable doctrine. It, therefore, requires that he who seeks equity must do equity. The doctrine, therefore, cannot also be invoked if it is found to be inequitable or unjust in its enforcement.

We may also state that for the purpose of invoking the doctrine, it is not necessary for the company to show that the assurance ... was mainly responsible for establishing the factory at Kota. There may be several representations to one party from different authorities in regard to different matters. Or, there may be several representations from the same party in regard to different matters. As in the instant case, there was one representation by the Rajasthan Government to supply power to the company at concessional rate. There was another representation from the same government to exempt the company from payment of tax for certain period. There may be other representations from the same or some other authorities. If those representations have been relied upon by the company, the Court would compel those parties to adhere to their respective representations. It is immaterial whether each of the representations was wholly responsible or partly responsible for locating the factory at Kota. It is sufficient if the company was induced to act on that representation.

The last and final aspect of the matter to which attention should be drawn is that for the purpose of finding whether an estoppel arises in favour of the person acting on the representations, it is necessary to look into the whole of the representation made.

It is also necessary to state that the representation must be clear and unambiguous and not tentative or uncertain. In this context we may usefully refer to the following passage from Halsbury's Laws of England, (Halsbury's Laws of England 4th Edn. Vol. 16 p. 1071 para 1595):

'1595. Representation must be unambiguous—To found an estoppel a representation must be clear and unambiguous, not necessarily susceptible of only one interpretation, but such as will reasonably be understood by the person to whom it is made in the sense contended for and for this purpose the whole of the representation must be looked at. This is merely an application of the old maxim applicable to all estoppels that they 'must be certain to every intent...'

The question now is whether the assurance given by the Railway Board in the letter was clear and unqualified. But unfortunately, it is not so. It was subject to review to be undertaken when the company starts moving the raw material.

...

What does this letter mean? The first part of the letter offering the concessional rate ... has been completely watered down in the second part of the letter. It has been expressly stated that the rate may need be reviewed when the traffic actually begins to move. The company was put to notice that it has to again approach the Railway Administration. The Railway authorities now state that they have reviewed the whole matter and found no justification to offer a concessional freight rate for Naptha, since fertilizers are deliberately given a low classification in the tariff. From the tenor of [the letter] the Railways are entitled to state so and it does not amount to resiling from the earlier assurance. No question of estoppel arises in favour of appellant out of the representation made in [the letter].

We, therefore, agree with the conclusion of the Tribunal but not for all the reasons stated.

Court Case: Amrit Banaspati Co. Limited v. State of Punjab

The State Government of Punjab announced its 'New Policy' declaring incentive and concessions for the setting up of industries. One of the incentives was the refund of sales tax to those persons who set up selective large-scale industries in specified areas.[7] Acting on the representation, an industrialist met the Chief Minister personally and had several meetings with officials of the government. The refund of sales tax was one of the promises made that was not realized. The Supreme Court noted that taxation was a sovereign power of the state and it could not be promised away. Denying remedy, the court noted:

But Promissory Estoppel being an extension of principle of equity, the basic purpose of which is to promote justice founded on fairness and relieve a promisee of any injustice perpetrated due to promisor's going back on its promise, is incapable of being enforced in a court of law if the promise which furnishes the cause of action or the agreement, express or implied, giving rise to binding contract is statutorily prohibited or is against public policy.

In summary, in this chapter, we examined promissory estoppel, which is a creation of the courts on the principles of equity. Equity is suspension of the rights of a person if the enforcement would lead to unfairness and injustice. An agreement is enforceable only if there is an agreement between the parties backed up by consideration. The courts may dispense this requirement in appropriate cases under promissory estoppel. The promise can be express or implied but it must be clear and definite. The courts apply it if it appears unjust or unreasonable that the promisor should be allowed to disregard the promise, in consideration of what the other party has done or refrained from doing in reliance on the promise.

[7] *Amrit Banaspati Co. Limited* v. *State of Punjab*, AIR 1992 SC 1075.

15

Intention to Create Legal Relations

Suppose an agreement was supported by consideration, but one of the parties claimed that it was never their intention to create a legally binding relationship. Thus, on the one hand, according to the principles of contract law, a contract is formed and binding. On the other hand, it was a part of the agreement itself that the agreement would not be binding. The courts have had to think through this contradiction. Let us explore the issue with the following case.

Intention of the Parties

Case: Award
The Foundation for Advancement of Education announced to a college that it would give an award of Rs 25,000 to all the students who secure more than 90 per cent marks in the board examination. Ajeet secured 92 per cent marks but the Foundation refused to give the money to him as they had run out of funds. Does Ajeet have a legal claim? The relationship between Ajeet and the Foundation has all the constituents of a contract. The Foundation has made a unilateral offer and Ajeet has accepted it. The consideration for Ajeet is Rs 25,000, and for the Foundation it is performance of the condition of getting more than 90 per cent marks. It is an enforceable contract.

What if Ajeet's father had put up a promise to give his son Rs 10,000 on securing more than 90% marks but refused to fulfil it. Like the case of the Foundation, it has an offer, acceptance and consideration for both the parties. Despite this, we would be reluctant to enforce the contract. The father made a promise but never contemplated that he could be taken to a court of law to fulfil it. The father was committed enough to make the promise but never intended to go that far. In other words, it was implied by the parties that they were not creating legal relations.

The point was first brought out before a court in *Balfour* v. *Balfour*. The case was between a husband and wife, where the husband was in Ceylon and the wife in England. The wife was claiming money the husband had promised for her support. Two judges ruled that there was no consideration in the agreement. Atkin, however, noted that in all family relations, for example, husband and wife, there will always be an undertaking by both the parties, for example, to maintain the household expenses and take care of children. Thus, technically, these contracts have considerations for both sides. His ground for rejecting the claim was elsewhere: 'Nevertheless they are not contracts, and they are not contracts because the parties did not intend that they should be attended by legal consequences. It would be the worst possible example to hold that agreements such as this resulted in legal obligations which could be enforced in the courts.'

The argument that contracts are about agreements and that the contract should not be enforceable if the parties, expressly or impliedly, do not intend to bind themselves in a legal sense was taken up in subsequent cases. Interestingly, the first case was in a business context: *Rose and Frank Company v. J R Crompton Limited.*[1] The manufacturer and distributors drew up a document setting on several restraints on buying, selling, and territories for operations. The last clause of the document provided: '… it will be carried through by each of the three parties with mutual loyalty and friendly co-operation. This is hereinafter referred to as the "honourable pledge" clause.' A dispute arose between the parties and the contention was raised that the parties did not intend to create legal relations. Scrutton, LJ, at the Court of Appeal, stated:

Now it is quite possible for parties to come to an agreement by accepting a proposal with the result that the agreement concluded does not give rise to legal relations. The reason of this is that the parties do not intend that their agreement shall give rise to legal relations. This intention may be implied from the subject matter of the agreement, but it may also be expressed by the parties. In social and family relations such an intention is readily implied, while in business matters the opposite result would ordinarily follow. But I can see no reason why, even in business matters, the parties should not intend to rely on each other's good faith and honour, and to exclude all idea of settling disputes by any outside intervention, with the accompanying necessity of expressing themselves so precisely that outsiders may have no difficulty in understanding what they mean. If they clearly express such an intention I can see no reason in public policy why effect should not be given to their intention.

The assumption in the case of business relations is that the parties intended to create legal relations. However, the parties can exclude this by specifically providing for it. The assumption where the parties are tied in familial or social relations is that the parties did not intend to create legal relations. However, these assumptions are also to be examined in their specific details. In *Jones v. Padavatton*,[2] the mother had provided for her daughter's stay and study in London. The court ruled that the parties did not intend to create legal relations. However, in *Merritt v. Merritt*,[3] where spouses were separating, the court decided that the arrangement they had entered for the subsequent payment of the mortgage of the house was binding. In *Albert v. Motor Insurers' Bureau*,[4] a car owner provided transport to his co-workers for many years with definite expectations of contribution to the journey. The court ruled that it was like running a taxi service.

The Indian Contract Act says nothing about the intention to create legal relations. This is not surprising, as the founding case on this, *Balfour v. Balfour*, came decades after the making of the act. The foundation of the concept is in the intention of the parties, express and implied communication between the parties, and the formation of agreement. Thus, it is applicable in India. In the

---

[1] *Rose and Frank Company* v. *J R Crompton Limited*, Court of Appeal, (1923) 2 KB 261.

[2] *Jones* v. *Padavatton*, (1969) 2 All ER 616.
[3] *Merritt* v. *Merritt*, (1970) 2 All ER 760.
[4] *Albert* v. *Motor Insurers' Bureau*, (1972) AC 301.

following case, the Supreme Court recognized the principle but did not give benefit to the party making the claim.

Court Case: Commissioner of Wealth Tax, Bhopal v. Abdul Hussain Mulla Muhammad Ali

Abdul Hussain Mulla Mohammad Ali advanced a loan of Rs 4 lakhs to Faizullabhai Mandlawala, Sidhpur. Both of them were partners of a firm called Rising Sun Flour and Oil Mills at Ujjain.[5] The borrower employed the sum as part of his capital in the firm. Wealth tax, as the name suggests, was a tax on the wealth of the person. A loan does not lower the wealth of a person because the loaned money would be returned. The tax payer raised the contention that the parties did not intend to create legal relations, thus, there was no obligation to pay back the debt or for him to enforce it. The Supreme Court fully endorsed the British judgments that a valid contract may be set aside on the grounds that the parties did not intend to create legal relations. However, it did not recognize this case as qualifying. It noted:

The contention has, no doubt, its possibilities. But where, as here, the tax implications of large financial obligations are sought to be put an end to, the burden is heavy on the assessee to establish that what would otherwise be the incidents of the transaction were excluded from contemplation by the parties. Here, one partner has lent a large sum to the other to be utilised as capital in the partnership venture. The transaction is in the context of a commercial venture. The presumption is that legal obligations are intended.

CONSIDERATION

The courts have insisted on the concept of consideration as it distinguished business relationship among traders from social relationships. Business relationships were exchanges of benefit and detriment as opposed to social and familial relationships where a person benefited another. A social relationship was about co-operation and mutual help. Social relationships were for society to shape, while business relations were for the law and courts to resolve. It was for the contracting parties to settle on the bargain. Thus, the courts insisted on consideration but not its adequacy. This development made the requirement of consideration a technical requirement. Capitalism, founded on exchange, has recreated the economic and social order. As exchange became dominant, even social and familial relationships started fitting the description of an exchange, and technically, meet the description of consideration. The concept of consideration was not able to contain the context. The concept of 'intention to create legal relations' was an intervention to recapture and fortify the distinction between business and family relationships.

As we have noted, the concept of consideration became a mere technical requirement a long time back. Scholars have long argued for its abolition. In other words, consideration should not be a requirement for an agreement to be enforceable. The thirteenth report of the Law Commission, devoted to the subject of contract, noted: 'We have devoted anxious thought to the modern attitude towards the doctrine of consideration and to the desirability of its abolition or, at any rate modification. This doctrine was borrowed from English common law.'[6] Concepts are outdone by the changing context. With the passage of time, these may retain only a notional significance or at worst become a hindrance.

[5] *Commissioner of Wealth Tax, Bhopal v. Abdul Hussain Mulla Muhammad Ali*, AIR 1988 SC 1417.

[6] Law Commission of India (1958), Contract Act, 1872, 13th Report, New Delhi.

However, concepts can neither be introduced nor expunged at will. With the passage of time, concepts become foundational as subsequent events are built on them. And foundations cannot be undone without destabilizing the entire structure. The Law Commission noted:

Notwithstanding the…views of eminent jurists, however, we are unable to recommend an abolition of the doctrine. It has become so firmly rooted in our concept of contract, that a wholesale rejection of the doctrine would have the result of overturning the very structure on which our law of contract is based and would require a complete and thorough overhaul of the law.

Not surprisingly, the doctrine of consideration remains contested. A contemporary commentator has noted: '…the doctrine of consideration is a doctrine that is under attack. It does not appear to fit with the demands of commercial practice and it is difficult to explain its existence and content in theoretical terms.'[7] Although foundational ideas cannot be ousted, they can be interpreted and re-interpreted to harmonize them with the changing context. Lord Steyn, thus, records the process:

I have had no radical proposals for the wholesale review of the doctrine of consideration. I am not persuaded that it is necessary. And great legal changes should only be embarked on when they are truly necessary. First, there are a few cases where even in modern times courts have decided that contractual claims must fail for want of consideration. On the other hand, on careful examination it will usually be found that such claims could have been decided on other grounds, e.g., the absence of an invitation to create legal relations or the fact that the transaction was induced by duress. Once a serious intention to enter into legal relations and concluded agreement

is demonstrated in a commercial context there is virtually a presumption of consideration which will almost invariably prevail without a detailed search for some technical consideration. On balance it seems to me that in modern practice the restrictive influence of consideration has markedly receded in importance. Secondly, it seems to me that in recent times the courts have shown a readiness to hold that the rigidity of the doctrine of consideration must yield to practical justice and the needs of modern commerce.[8]

Thus, despite its reduction to being a mere technical requirement, consideration will continue to remain a necessary requirement for formation of a contract. The concept of consideration has an important bearing in relation to the welfare measures provided by the state. The welfare state provides all kinds of services and benefits to the subject. In this, the state sees itself as a benefactor to the subjects and not legally bound and answerable to the subjects. For example, the state provides free medical service. As the patient has not paid for the service, there is no enforceable contract between the parties. The subject does not have a remedy to claim damages for a deficient service. In *Indian Medical Association* v. *V.P. Shantha* it was argued that there was a consideration involved in this relationship. After all, it is the people who pay taxes that run government establishments. This is to be treated as consideration for the service. The Supreme Court, thus, recorded the argument:

A contention has also been raised that even in the government hospitals/health centres/dispensaries where services are rendered free of charge to all the patients the provisions of the Act shall apply because the expenses of running the said hospitals are met by appropriation from the Consolidated Fund which is

---

[7] Ewan Mckendrick (2008), *Contract Law: Text, Cases and Material*, 3rd edition, (Oxford: Oxford University Press), p. 252.

[8] Lord Steyn (1997), Contract Law: Fulfiling the Reasonable Expectations of Honest Men, (1997) 113 LQR., quoted in Ewan Mckendrick (2008), *Contract Law*, p. 253.

raised from the taxes paid by the tax payers. We do not agree.

The essential characteristics of a tax are that (i) it is imposed under statutory power without the taxpayer's consent and the payment is enforced by law; (ii) it is an imposition made for public purpose without reference to any special benefit to be conferred on the payer of the tax and (iii) it is part of the common burden, the quantum of imposition upon the tax payer depends generally upon his capacity to pay.... The tax paid by the person availing the service at a government hospital cannot be treated as a consideration or charge for the service rendered at the said hospital and such service though rendered free of charge does not cease to be so because the person availing the service happens to be a tax payer.[9]

This is a consistent position. Contractual relationships are consensual and one-to-one, where a party offers and another accepts. It would be stretching it too far to say that taxes are consideration. The concept of consideration remains a foundational concept. However, its significance is eroded by enactments and court judgments.

[9] *Indian Medical Association* v. *V.P. Shantha*, AIR 1996 SC 550.

Part 3

SETTING THE CONTRACT ASIDE

A contract that appears valid may yet not be enforced due to certain factors associated with the nature of the contract or its formation. The non-enforcement of such contracts takes two forms: the contract is either 'void' or 'voidable'. In the case of a void, the parties thought they had a contract but no enforceable contract was ever formed. If there is a conflict between following the directions of the law and contractual rights and obligations, the law would be privileged. Thus, contracts tainted with illegality are void. This is covered in Chapter 20. In the evolution of the common law, the courts recognized that certain kinds of contracts were not desirable for individuals or society as a whole. The courts came to declare these contracts as void. These include wager agreements, contracts restraining a person from seeking remedy from a court, contracts in restrain of marriage, contracts in restraining a person from following his trade and profession, and wager agreements. Chapter 21 covers the subject. A contract where both parties are mistaken about the subject matter of the contract cannot be enforced as there has been no meeting of minds. Such contracts are also void. This is covered in Chapter 22. A minor, due to his lack of experience and knowledge, is not capable of binding himself into contractual obligations. Thus, contracts formed with a minor are void. Similarly, a contract formed with a person of unsound mind is void. The inability to get in a contract is covered in Chapter 19.

In contrast to void contracts are voidable contracts. A voidable contract can be completely set aside on the insistence of one of the parties to the contract, the suffering party. In other words, the contract can be made a void contract. However, if the suffering party does not elect this option, the contract can be enforced like a valid contract. A contract formed through *coercion, undue influence, misrepresentation, or fraud is a voidable contract. As the consent of a party to the contract has not been freely secured, these contracted are treated under the head of 'free consent'. This is covered in Chapters 17 and 18.*

16

Coercion and Undue Influence

X makes Y sign a contract document selling shares at gun point. A customer buys a food processor because the retailer had claimed that the product was made in France, though it was actually made in Taiwan. A patient signed a contract to pay a large sum of money to a doctor for immediate surgery, which was actually unnecessary. In all the cases, the offer was accepted, leading to formation of an agreement. We can even say there was a meeting of minds. However, the consent of the person has been manipulated. If it were not for the coercion, misrepresentation, or undue influence, the person may not have consented to the agreement. Should the innocent party be given the benefit of setting aside the contract? It would be unjust if he were not allowed to set aside the contract. Consider the reverse case where the innocent party wants the contract to be performed while the other party wants it to be set aside. If the innocent party wishes to go ahead with the contract, the other party should be held to be bound to the contract. Thus, such contracts are not a nullity, but can be set aside at the option of the innocent party. For this reason, these contracts are called voidable. This is distinct from a void contract, where one is never formed. A voidable contract is one that can be turned into nullity, hence the name.

The Indian Contract Act gives expression to these principles under a chapter titled 'free consent'. Section 13 provides:

13. Consent defined—Two or more persons are said to consent when they agree upon the same thing in the same sense.

The definition is expressing consent as a meeting of minds. Section 14 defines free consent:

14. Free consent defined—Consent is said to be free when it is not caused by—

(1) coercion, as defined in section 15, or

(2) undue influence, as defined in section 16, or

(3) fraud, as defined in section 17, or

(4) misrepresentation, as defined in section 18, or

(5) mistake, subject to the provisions of sections 20, 21 and 22.

Consent is said to be so caused when it would not have been given but for the existence of such coercion, undue influence, fraud, misrepresentation or mistake.

If consent has been caused by coercion, undue influence, fraud, misrepresentation or mistake, it is not free consent. The innocent party has the right under Section 19 and 19A to set aside the contract. The sections read:

19. Voidability of agreements without free consent—When consent to an agreement is caused by coercion fraud or misrepresentation, the agreement is a contract voidable at the option of the party whose consent was so caused.

19A. Power to set aside contract induced by undue influence—When consent to an agreement is caused by undue influence, the agreement is a contract voidable at the option of the by party whose consent was so caused.

Having developed an overall framework, let us detail the scope and implications of coercion, undue influence, misrepresentation, and fraud. In this chapter, we will take up coercion and undue influence.

COERCION

From coercion, we generally mean to illegally force or compel another person. Let us note the scope of coercion as defined in Section 15.

15. Coercion defined—'Coercion' is the committing, or threatening to commit, any act forbidden by the Indian Penal Code (45 of 1860), or the unlawful detaining, or threatening to detain, any property, to the prejudice of any person whatever, with the intention of causing any person to enter into an agreement.

Explanation—It is immaterial whether the Indian Penal Code (45 of 1860) is or is not in force in the place where the coercion is employed.

The Indian Penal Code is a dossier of offences against body and property. Let us explore the application of the section by deciding whether the following constitute coercion.

1. X beat up Y and made him sign a contract.
2. X told Y that if he did not agree to give him a loan, he would burgle his house.
3. X told Y that if he did not agree to give him a loan, he would have his house burgled.
4. X told Y that if he did not agree to give him a loan, he would burgle his son's house.
5. X told Y that if he did not agree to give him a loan, he would have his son's house burgled.
6. X told Y that if he did not agree to give him a loan, he would infect his computer with a virus.
7. A warehouse refused to let a client collect his goods unless the owner agreed to sell 50 per cent of the goods to him at the prevailing market price.

In (1), the person has committed the offence of beating up a person. In (2), (3), (4), and (5), X has threatened to burgle, which is an offence under the Indian Penal Code. Thus, all the acts qualify as coercion under Section 15. Infecting a computer is an offence under the Information Technology Act, but is not covered under the IPC. Obviously, when the IPC was enacted, there were no computers. Thus, (6) may not be coercion under Section 15. In (7), the warehouse has unlawfully detained the property and thus, this is coercion under Section 15. In some cases, the offence is caused to the person with whom agreement is to be made. In other cases, the offence is caused to others. Is this relevant? The section has two parts. It first requires checking if a forbidden act or its threat has been caused to 'any person'. If yes, was this to cause 'any person' to enter in a contract? Thus, the person who is made to get into a contract must not himself be the victim. For one reason or the other, it is coercion if the offending act was the reason for getting into the agreement. Let us further develop our understanding of the section with court judgments.

Court Case: *Askari Mirza* v. *Bibi Jai Kishori Alias Iqbal Rani*

Bibi Jai Kishori gave a loan to Askari Mirza.[1] Later, she claimed to have discovered that Askari Mirza had lied to her to secure the loan. She threatened to file criminal case against him. Kishori and Mirza entered an agreement for her to get the money immediately. Askari Mirza claimed that the agreement was secured by coercion constituting the threat of filing criminal charges. The court thus had to decide whether a threat of filing criminal charges was coercion within Section 15. The Privy Council, referring to the definition in Section 15 noted:

To threaten a criminal prosecution is not per se an act forbidden by the Indian Penal Code. Such an act could only be one forbidden by the Indian Penal Code if it amounted to a threat to file a false charge. And so a plaintiff, who sets up a plea of coercion based upon a threat of this nature, has to establish three things, namely, that a threat was uttered; that it was a threat to commit an act forbidden by the Indian Penal Code; and the threat was uttered with the intention of causing the plaintiff to enter into the agreement complained of.

Only filing of a false charge or threatening to file a false charge is an offence under the IPC. The threat of filing a charge for an offence that a person has indeed committed is not forbidden by the IPC. Consistent with this, the court noted: 'Of course, if the charge of cheating was a true one, there is an end to the plaintiff's case, for a threat to bring such a charge would not be an act forbidden by the Indian Penal Code.'

Court Case: *Chikkam Ammiraju* v. *Chikkam Seshamma*

A person threatened to commit suicide and got his wife to execute a document transferring property to his brother.[2] The question before the court was whether threat of committing suicide constituted coercion under Section 15. The circumstances of the case are exceptional. However, it sheds light on the scope of Section 15. Let us note the relevant provision in the IPC on suicide. Section 306 makes abetment of suicide an offence. This does not apply to the case. Section 309 provides:

Attempt to commit suicide—Whoever attempts to commit suicide and does any act towards the commission of such offence, shall be punished with simple imprisonment for a term which may extend to one year or with fine, or with both.

While attempting to commit suicide is an offence, committing suicide is not an offence. It is not an offence as the offender is no longer there to be punished. The husband had threatened to commit suicide and not threatened to 'attempt to commit suicide'. If he had attempted to commit suicide, he would have done an act forbidden by Section 309. This would have constituted coercion under Section 15. The judges were divided in their opinion. The majority view was delivered by Seshagiri Aiyar, J:

I have come to the conclusion that the facts do bring the case within section 15, Contract Act.... A man who commits suicide goes unpunished because the law cannot reach him, and not because the offence is not forbidden. The Code makes a person who abets the committing of suicide punishable. It also reaches a man who attempts to commit suicide. Although therefore there is no provision in the Penal Code

---

[1] *Askari Mirza* v. *Bibi Jai Kishori Alias Iqbal Rani*, (1912) 16 IC 344.

[2] *Chikkam Ammiraju* v. *Chikkam Seshamma*, AIR 1918 Mad 414.

which forbids in terms the commission of suicide, there can be no doubt that the intention of the legislature is to forbid such an act. The term 'any act forbidden by the Indian Penal Code' is wider than the term 'Punishable by the Penal Code'. Simply because a man escapes punishment it does not follow that the act is not forbidden by the Penal Code. For example, a lunatic or a minor may not be punished. This does not show that their criminal acts are not forbidden by the Penal Code. On the same analogy, a man who commits suicide escapes punishment because by committing the act, he is out of the reach of the law. Where the abetment of it and the attempt to do it are both made punishable by the Penal Code, I am prepared to hold that the act itself is one forbidden by the Penal Code.

An act becomes coercion only if it is to the 'prejudice of any person'. Ordinarily, it is the victim of the act. In this case, the victim was the same person. He was threatening to hurt himself. Thus, it was argued before the court that the threat to commit suicide did not meet the requirement of prejudice under Section 15. The court ruled:

I agree ... that mere sentimental prejudice is not what the law contemplates. Some legal injury must flow in order that the man may be said to have been prejudiced. Accepting this test, I am unable to hold that the wife to whom the threat was addressed by a husband that he would commit suicide in case she does not execute a document, is not prejudicially affected by such a threat. In my opinion, the possibility of the husband dying leaving the wife and the child uncared for is sufficient in the eye of the law to furnish the ground of prejudice.

The minority view was of Oilfield, J. He noted:

The question is whether a threat to commit suicide is a threat to commit an act forbidden by the Penal Code within the meaning of section 15, Contract Act; and it is conceded that it is not forbidden either directly or in the sense that a penalty is provided for it. It, therefore, can be regarded as forbidden only by implication. It is accordingly in place to consider whether section 15 can be construed by implication or should be read strictly.

The judge was of the view that the term 'attempt' must be interpreted in its legal sense and not as to 'endeavour' and the provision should be interpreted strictly. He concluded:

It is argued that a threat to commit suicide is indistinguishable from one to attempt to do so and that such an attempt is forbidden by section 309, IPC which penalises it. The answer is that threats of these two descriptions are distinguishable ... a threat to attempt to commit suicide is not only different from one to commit suicide, but is, like other threats to commit an attempt, a contradiction in terms. For an attempt in the legal sense can be recognised as such only after the criminal's intention has been frustrated, not when it is expressed; that is, when the threat is made.

Thus, the judge distinguished between suicide and attempting suicide. As committing suicide was not punishable, threat of suicide could not lead to coercion within Section 15. This appears more convincing, but was the minority view.

Court Case: Andhra Sugars Limited v. State of AP

Under the Andhra Pradesh Sugarcane (Regulation of Supply and Purchase) Act, 1961, and the rules framed under it, the cane grower in the factory zone is free to make or not to make an offer of sale of cane to the occupier of the factory.[3] But if he makes an offer, the occupier of the factory is bound to accept it. It was claimed that the agreement was caused by coercion. The Supreme Court ruled:

The consent of the occupier of the factory to the agreement is not caused by coercion, undue influence, fraud, misrepresentation or mistake. His consent is free as defined in Section 14 of the Indian Contract Act though he is obliged by law to enter into the agreement. The compulsion of law is not coercion as defined in Sec. 15 of the Act. In spite of the compul-

---

[3] *Andhra Sugars Limited* v. *State of AP*, AIR 1968 SC 599.

sion, the agreement is neither void nor voidable. In the eye of the law, the agreement is freely made.

The Supreme Court took the position that it would be a case of coercion only if the contract was entered in by committing or threatening to commit an offence under the Indian Penal Code. The imposition of the law is not coercion within Section 15. The position was reiterated in *S.S. Sakhar Karkhana Limited v. C.I.T., Kolhapur*. Under the co-operative laws, the sugar co-operatives of Maharashtra compulsorily took deposits from its farmer members. The Supreme Court noted on the agreement between the co-operatives and its members:

... the mere fact that the contract has to be entered into in conformity with and subject to restrictions imposed by law does not per se impinge on the consensual element in the contract. 'Compulsion of law is not coercion' and despite such compulsion, 'in the eye of law, the agreement is freely made', as pointed out in Andhra Sugars Ltd. v. State of A.P.

In common law, the equivalent of coercion is duress. Duress earlier only covered threat to injure the person. As common law is an evolving field, duress has come to include duress of good and economic duress. Thus, the concept of duress has become similar to coercion.

Undue Influence

Note the difference between the following two contracts. Contrast a situation in which a retailer persuaded a curious customer to buy a product with the case where a doctor prevailed on a patient to undergo an immediate surgery, or a lawyer persuaded a client to sell some disputed property to him for a cheap price. In every contract, parties would have different capabilities to influence each other. This is normal and cannot be considered undue influence. However, some relationships are asymmetric, and by their very nature allow a person to exercise undue influence over another. The focus of undue influence under Section 16 is on these asymmetric relationships. Section 16 provides:

16. **Undue influence defined**—(1) A contract is said to be induced by 'undue influence' where the relations subsisting between the parties are such that one of the parties is in a position to dominate the will of the other and uses that position to obtain an unfair advantage over the other.

(2) In particular and without prejudice to the generality of the foregoing principle, a person is deemed to be in a position to dominate the will of another—

(a) where he holds a real or apparent authority over the other or where he stands in a fiduciary relation to the other; or

(b) where he makes a contract with a person whose mental capacity is temporarily or permanently affected by reason of age, illness, or mental or bodily distress.

(3) Where a person who is in a position to dominate the will of another, enters into a contract with him, and the transaction appears, on the face of it or on the evidence adduced, to be unconscionable, the burden of proving that such contract was not induced by undue influence shall lie upon the person in a position to dominate the will of the other.

Nothing in this sub-section shall affect the provisions of section 111 of the Indian Evidence Act, 1872 (1 of 1872).

Let us map the entire section. Section 16(1) states the general principle that a relationship where one party can 'dominate the will' of the other is a requisite for undue influence. Section 16(2)(a) presumes a relationship of domination where a person holds a real or apparent authority over the other. Examples of real authority can be that of a law enforcement officer over the subject, a master over a servant, or a judge over a litigant. Apparent authority, as distinguished from real authority, is where, objectively, the person does not have authority but an appearance of authority is created, for example, when a person pretends to be a law enforcement officer.

Section 16(2)(a) also presumes a relationship of domination where a party is in a fiduciary relationship. The term 'fiduciary relationship' comes from the law on trusts. In a relationship of trust, an owner transfers the property to a trustee. The trustee undertakes to manage the property and give its benefit to certain beneficiaries named by the owner. A trustee does not have any personal interest in the property and does not profit from the ownership. His interest is the benefit of the beneficiaries. A trustee is in a fiduciary relationship to the beneficiary. The term has been extended to mean, in general, a relationship of trust and confidence. Some relationships are intrinsically fiduciary in nature, for example, the relationship between solicitor and client, trustee and beneficiary, spiritual adviser and devotee, medical attendant and patient, and parent and child. A parent would be in a fiduciary relationship to a minor, but not necessary to a grown-up child. A child may be in a fiduciary relationship to old parents.

There can also be an overlap between fiduciary relationship and authority. Parents have authority over children and are also in a fiduciary relationship with them. In either case, it is deemed that the person has the power to dominate the will of the other. Section 16(2)(b) does not need elaboration. Let us distinguish Section 16(1) from 16(2). Once it is established that any of the conditions set in Section 16(2) is met, it would be presumed that the person is in a position to dominate the will of another. However, there may be cases other than those covered by Section 16(2) where a person has come to acquire the power to dominate the will of another. Take the case where a person is indebted to another person and is not able to repay the debt. The creditor is not in a fiduciary relationship, nor does he have any authority over him. Yet, he may be in a position to dominate the will of the debtor to get into an unfair contract. This will depend on the nature of the debt and the dependence of the debtor on the creditor. This would be covered under Section 16(1). It would also have to be established that the person had come to be in a position to dominate the will of another.

Applying either Section 16(1) or Section 16(2), we have to first establish that a person was in a position to dominate the will of the other. If this is established, it has to be ascertained that the position was used to obtain an unfair advantage. On this, Section 16(3) will apply. Unconscionable transaction means grossly unfair transaction. In the case of unfair bargain, Section 16(3) puts the onus on the person who was in a position to dominate the will of the other to establish that there was no undue influence. Section 16(3) will apply only when the person is in a position to dominate the will of the other. On whom would the onus lie for establishing that there was a relationship for one to dominate the will of the other? It would lie on the person trying to set aside the contract, or every contract could be stalled by making the other person establish that he was not in a position to dominate the will of the other.

The usual cases on undue influence, under the common law as well as in India, have arisen where a senile person, under the influence of a close relative or caregiver has given away all or a significant part of his property to that person. A recent common law case is *Hammond* v. *Osborn*.[4] Other examples are religious organizations or leaders to whom a follower gives away his property. For example, in *Mannu Singh* v. *Umadat Pandey*,[5] an

[4] *Hammond* v. *Osborn*, (2002) EWCA Civ 885.
[5] *Mannu Singh* v. *Umadat Pandey*, (1890) 12 All 523.

old person gifted all his property to a guru to benefit his soul in the next world. In *Philip Lukka* v. *Franciscan Association*,[6] an invalid devotee gifted his property to Franciscan Association, after a priest named Father Franscis promised him that the Association would look after him and his mother.

All such cases are either outright gifts or a notional consideration moving from the recipient. As the gifts are duly executed, that is, recorded in writing and registered, these are binding contracts. Thus, there is rarely a doubt that the consideration between the parties is not incommensurate. The issue the courts have had to settle is the person on whom the onus lies for setting aside the contract and the procedure by which the different requirements under Section 16 would be assessed. Let us examine and understand this through the following cases.

Court Case: *Raghunath Prasad* v. *Sarju Prasad*

A property was mortgaged and a loan taken at the rate of 24 per cent.[7] On the failure to pay the annual interest, the interest was to be added to the principal to calculate the interest. In eleven years, the loan amount had escalated eleven times. The court had no doubt that the interest rate was very high. It was argued before the court that the contract was unconscionable and it should be rescinded or rectified. The Privy Council noted the sequence for giving the benefit of Section 16 to a party.

Their Lordships think it desirable to make clear their views upon, in particular, Sub-S. 3 of S. 16 of the Contract Act…By this subsection three matters

---

[6] *Philip Lukka* v. *Franciscan Association*, AIR 1987 Ker 204.

[7] *Raghunath Prasad* v. *Sarju Prasad*, AIR 1924 (PC) 60.

---

are dealt with. In the first place the relations between the parties to each other must be such that one is in a position to dominate the will of the other. Once that position is substantiated the second stage has been reached, viz., the issue whether the contract has been induced by undue influence. Upon the determination of this issue a third point emerges, which is that of the ONUS PROBANDI. The burden of proving that the contract was not induced by undue influence is to lie upon the person who was in a position to dominate the will of the other.

Error is almost sure to arise if the order of these propositions be changed. The unconscionableness of the bargain is not the first thing to be considered. The first thing to be considered is the relations of these parties. Were they such as to put one in a position to dominate the will of the other?

While the unfairness of a bargain is always striking, it is not this to be noted first. The court has to establish, first, that one party was in a position to dominate the will of the other; second, that the position of power and domination was used, and third, the result of the use of power is an unfair transaction. Only at this stage does the onus fall on the person to prove that the contract was not induced by undue influence. In the case above, the courts below had not explored the relationship between the parties. The judgment was given on the basis of the terms of the mortgage itself. The Privy Council was of the view that merely because a person takes a loan on an exorbitant term, it does not establish anything about the nature of the relationship between the parties. The Privy Council ruled:

In these circumstances, even though the bargain had been unconscionable (and it has the appearance of being so) a remedy under the Indian Contract Act does not come into view until the initial fact of a position to dominate the will has been established. Once that fact is established, then the unconscionable nature of the bargain and the burden of proof on the issue of undue influence come into operation. In the present case, for the reasons stated the stages are not reached.

The Supreme Court in *Ladli Prashad Jaiswal v. Karnal Distillery Co. Limited* specified on whom the onus lies at different stages of the proceedings:

A transaction may be vitiated on account of undue influence where the relations between the parties are such that one of them is in a position to dominate the will of the other and he uses his position to obtain an unfair advantage over the other. It is manifest that both the conditions have ordinarily to be established by the person seeking to avoid the transaction: he has to prove that the other party to a transaction was in a position to dominate his will ...[8]

This can be established either by presumption under Subsection (2) or by leading evidence under Subsection (1). Once this has been established by the person seeking to set aside the contract, he has to establish that the contract 'on the face of it or on the evidence adduced, appears to be unconscionable.' Only on this, under Subsection (3), 'the burden of proving that the transaction was not induced by undue influence' would lie upon the person in a position to dominate the will of the other. The requirement on the party seeking to set aside the contract to establish only 'on the face of it' of the unfairness of the bargain is consistent. A greater requirement would negate Subsection (3). The Supreme Court concluded:

... sub-sec. (3) has manifestly a limited application: the presumption will only arise if it is established by evidence that the party who had obtained the benefit of a transaction was in a position to dominate the will of the other and that the transaction is shown to be unconscionable. If either of these two conditions is not fulfilled the presumption of undue influence will not arise and burden will not shift.

Court Case: *Subhas Chandra Das Mushib* v. *Ganga Prosad Das Mushib*

A person had gifted a significant part of his property to his grand-son.[9] Other family members sought to set aside the gift on the grounds that it was caused by undue influence. The Supreme Court noted that on fiduciary relations, 'Generally speaking the relation of solicitor and client, trustee and *cestui que* trust, spiritual adviser and devotee, medical attendant and patient, parent and child are those in which such a presumption arises.' These are relationships that are intrinsically fiduciary; other relationships may be fiduciary, depending on the facts. Merely because the parties are related does not make the relationship a fiduciary one. It would need to be established that the specific relationship was fiduciary. As it was not established before the courts below, the court did not presume the relationship to be one of domination. The court re-iterated the sequence for claiming the benefit of Section 16:

We may now proceed to consider what are the essential ingredients of undue influence and how a plaintiff who seeks relief on this ground should proceed to prove his case and when the defendant is called upon to show that the contract or gift was not induced by undue influence. The instant case is one of gift but it is well settled that the law as to undue influence is the same in the case of a gift *inter vivos* as in the case of a contract.

Under S. 16 (1) of the Indian Contract Act a contract is said to be induced by undue influence where the relations subsisting between the parties are such that one of the parties is in a position to dominate the will of the other and uses that position to obtain an unfair advantage over the other. This shows that the court trying a case of undue influence must consider two things to start with, namely, (1) are the relations between the donor and the donee such that the donee is in a position to dominate the will of the donor and

---

[8] *Ladli Prashad Jaiswal v. Karnal Distillery Co. Limited*, AIR 1963 SC 1279.

[9] *Subhas Chandra Das Mushib* v. *Ganga Prosad Das Mushib*, AIR 1967 SC 878.

(2) has the donee used that position to obtain an unfair advantage over the donor?

Sub-section (2) of the section is illustrative as to when a person is to be considered to be in a position to dominate the will of another. These are *inter alia* (a) where the donee holds a real or apparent authority over the donor or where he stands in a fiduciary relation to the donor or (b) where he makes a contract with a person whose mental capacity is temporarily or permanently affected by reason of age, illness, or mental or bodily distress.

Sub-section (3) of the Section throws the burden of proving that a contract was not induced by undue influence on the person benefiting by it when two factors are found against him, namely that he is in a position to dominate the will of another and the transaction appears on the face of it or on the evidence adduced to be unconscionable.

In *M. Rangasamy* v. *Rengammal*[10], a Supreme Court case, a women gifted her landed property to her daughters, through a deed which was executed. The deed was challenged by other family members as caused by undue influence. The Supreme Court, relying on *Subhas Chandra Das Mushib* v. *Ganga Prosad Das Mushib*, noted:

It was further said that merely because the parties were nearly related to each other or merely because the donor was old or of weak character, no presumption of undue influence can arise.... The High Court presumed the undue influence merely on account of near relationship. The presumption made by the High Court on the basis of relationship was not warranted by law. The whole approach of the High Court was wrong and it cannot be sustained.[11]

Court Case: Krishna Mohan Kul v. Pratima Maity

A 106-year-old person executed a deed gifting landed property to a near relative.[12] The old man was illiterate and in poor physical and mental health. Other members of the family challenged the deed. On the facts of the case, the party was in a fiduciary relationship. Section 16(3) ends with the exception that 'Nothing in this sub-section shall affect the provisions of section 111 of the Indian Evidence Act.' The Section reads:

111. Proof of good faith in transactions where one party is in relation of active confidence—Where there is a question as to the good faith of a transaction between parties, one of whom stands to the other in a position of active confidence, the burden of proving the good faith of the transaction is on the party who is in a position of active confidence.

Illustrations

(a) The good faith of a sale by a client to an attorney is in question in a suit brought by the client. The burden of proving the good faith of the transaction is on the attorney.

(b) The good faith of a sale by a son just come of age to a father is in question is a suit brought by the son. The burden of proving the good faith of the transaction is on the father.

The Supreme Court ruled that the party in whom the confidence is reposed has to establish that the transaction is fair. The court noted:

When fraud, misrepresentation or undue influence is alleged by a party in a suit, normally, the burden is on him to prove such fraud, undue influence or misrepresentation. But, when a person is in a fiduciary relationship with another and the latter is in a position of active confidence the burden of proving the absence of fraud, misrepresentation or undue influence is upon the person, in the dominating position; he has to prove that there was fair play in the transaction and that the apparent is the real, in other words, that the transaction is genuine and bona fide. In such a case the burden of proving the good faith of the transaction is thrown upon the dominant party, that is to say, the party who is in a position of active confidence. A person standing in a fiduciary relation to another has a duty to protect the interest given to his care and the Court watches

---

[10] Ibid.

[11] Ibid.

[12] *Krishna Mohan Kul* v. *Pratima Maity*, AIR 2003 SC 4351.

with zealously all transactions between such persons so that the protector may not use his influence or the confidence to his advantage. When the party complaining shows such relation, the law presumes everything against the transaction and the onus is cast upon the person holding the position of confidence or trust to show that the transaction is perfectly fair and reasonable, that no advantage has been taken of his position.

...

This principle has been engrained in Section 111 of the Indian Evidence Act, 1872 (in short the 'Evidence Act'). The rule here laid down is in accordance with a principle long acknowledged and administered in Courts of Equity in England and America. This principle is that he who bargains in a matter of advantage with a person who places a confidence in him is bound to show that a proper and reasonable use has been made of that confidence. The transaction is not necessarily void *ipso facto*, nor is it necessary or those who impeach it to establish that there has been fraud or imposition, but the burden of establishing its perfect fairness, adequacy and equity is cast upon the person in whom the confidence has been reposed. The rule applies equally to all persons standing in confidential relations with each other. Agents, trustees, executors, administrators, auctioneers, and others have been held to fall within the rule. The Section requires that the party on whom the burden of proof is laid should have been in a position of active confidence.... Where an active, confidential, or fiduciary relation exists between the parties, there the burden of proof is on the donee or those claiming through him. It has further been laid down that where a person gains a great advantage over another by a voluntary instrument, the burden of proof is thrown upon the person receiving the benefit and he is under the necessity of showing that the transaction is fair and honest.

As the judgment brings out, it is enough for the party seeking to set aside the contract to establish that the relationship between the parties is fiduciary or of confidence. The party is not required to establish that the power to dominate was indeed used to get into an unfair transaction.

The burden will shift on the other person to establish that the transaction is genuine and bona fide.

As contract law in the UK is not codified, it continues to be common law, and the courts are adapting the principles to the changing times. A leading case on undue influence in the House of Lords' judgment on *Royal Bank of Scotland* v. *Etridge (No. 2)*.[13] The case was a clubbing together of eight appeals. As the court noted: 'Each case arises out of a transaction in which a wife charged her interest in her home in favour of a bank as security for her husband's indebtedness or the indebtedness of a company through which he carried on business. The wife later asserted she signed the charge under the undue influence of her husband.' The case shows that with the changing times, a newer context has been arising for claiming undue influence. In common law, there was a presumed undue influence if the parties were in a fiduciary relationship and the transaction was 'manifestly disadvantageous'. The court reduced the requirement of disadvantage from 'manifestly disadvantageous' to 'calls for explanation'. While the requirement of 'manifestly disadvantageous' was adequate for commercial transactions, it was too narrow for non-commercial cases. Which transactions would 'call for explanation'? This will depend on the details of the transaction. Anything other than ordinary would tend to get 'calls for explanation'. The court, however, noted that a couple's income is ordinarily pooled and the wife benefits from the profit from her husband's business. Thus, standing a guarantee to the spouse's business does not ordinarily call for an explanation. Of course, this is only a presumption. The other

---

[13] *Royal Bank of Scotland* v. *Etridge*, (*No. 2*), (2001) 3 WLR 1021.

party can rebut the presumption and establish that there was no undue influence.

To conclude, a contract where the consent of the party is secured through coercion or undue influence is void. The meaning of the term 'coercion' is confined to committing or threatening to commit any offence forbidden by the Indian Penal Code. In addition, unlawful restraining of property is also coercion. In exploring the application of undue influence, we have to judge whether the nature of the

relationship between the parties is fiduciary or of confidence. In this case, the person has to establish that there has been no misuse of the fiduciary relationship, and the transaction is genuine and bona fide. In other relationships, the party seeking to set aside the contract has to first establish that the parties were in a position for one to dominate the will of the other. After this, the party will need to establish that the position of power and domination was used to secure an unfair transaction.

17

Misrepresentation and Fraud

The founding principle of contract is a simple one: Agreement is what the parties have settled on through a communicative process between them. As every agreement has to be reduced to making the offer and its acceptance, another way of expressing this is to settle on what was offered and what was the communication surrounding the offer.

Let us take an illustration. In a consumer electronics store, a customer is shown a laptop with a label bearing the description: processor speed: 2.4 GHz; RAM: 2 Gb; two hard disks, 40 Gb each. On inquiry, the store informed the customer that the manufacturing company had opened a service centre in the town just a month back. The customer bought the laptop.

On running the machine, he realized that the total RAM was only 1 Gb. The representation by the company was a term of the contract. The seller is in breach of the contract. However, if the customer discovered that the company had no service centre in the town, this would not be a breach of the term. The representation was not a term of the offer; it was only a piece of information surrounding the offer. It was relevant in inducing the customer in buying the laptop, but was not a term of the contract. 'Representation' is another word for expression and communication. Some representation can be significant in inducing the other party to get into a contract. If it were not for the representation, the party would not have entered into the contract. When the representation is incorrect, it becomes a 'misrepresentation'. A deliberate misrepresentation is a fraud. The remedy available for a person against misrepresentation and fraud is to set the contract aside. In some cases, a term of a contract can also qualify as a misrepresentation. However, as the remedy for a breach of a term is better, there is no gain in treating it like a misrepresentation.

In this chapter, we will explore the subject of misrepresentation and fraud. In the first section of the chapter, we will develop an outline of the different aspects of misrepresentation and fraud. A statement of a fact can be true or false. Can an opinion also be true or false for it to be a fraud or misrepresentation? We will explore this in Section 2 of the chapter. Silence is no representation. Thus, ordinarily, it cannot lead to misrepresentation. There are exceptions to this principle.

We will explore this in Section 3 of the book. Section 4 will explore the rights and remedies available to a person who has entered into a contract due to misrepresentation.

EXPRESS AND IMPLIED REPRESENTATION

Deep had short-listed four brands of food processors with the intention to buy one. The storekeeper showed him one and said, 'This is the bestselling brand in India. I sell ten of these machines everyday and nobody has ever come back to me with a complaint.' Deep bought the food processor but was not happy with the purchase. The food processor worked fine and was indeed of the bestselling brand in India. However, another brand was as good and Rs 2,000 cheaper. In this case, there is no misrepresentation as the statements made by the shopkeeper are correct. Deep has no remedy. Consider a variation of the case. After buying the food processor, Deep learns that the brand is not the bestselling brand. The shopkeeper has made a misrepresentation to Deep, and he would qualify for a remedy. What if the shopkeeper had put up a sign next to a food processor that said, 'Bestselling brand of food processor.' Communication between the negotiating parties can be secured through written words, spoken words, visuals, or actions and gestures. The emphasis is on the communication being secured and not on how it is accomplished. Thus, representation and misrepresentation can be done through any modality.

Silence

A customer was in a store with his family, looking to buy a food processor. The shopkeeper overheard their conversation. Judging by the brand name of a food processor, the family were under an impression that it was made in France. The shopkeeper knew that the manufacturer was an Indian company, and had only given the product a French-sounding brand name. The family realized this only after they bought the product. The customer now wants to set aside the contract on the grounds of misrepresentation. The customer claims that the shopkeeper misled him by his silence. Was the shopkeeper duty-bound to speak? 'Ordinarily', silence communicates nothing, and thus cannot be a misrepresentation. This principle will admit exceptions, for as we know, silence can sometimes communicate more effectively than actual expression. We will deal with this in detail later.

Reliance on Misrepresentation

Let us consider again the case of Deep, who was looking to buy a food processor. The storekeeper said, 'This is the bestselling brand in India.' He bought the food processor, but the storekeeper's claim was incorrect. Deep worked for a consumer research company, and he knew that that particular brand was only third bestselling brand. However, he wanted to buy a compact food processor that would not occupy much space, and so he settled for that particular make. In this case, while the shop has made a statement that is incorrect, it did not induce the other party to enter into the contract. This is not a case of misrepresentation, giving Deep a right to set aside the contract. In this case, by getting into the specific details, we could assess whether the incorrect statement induced Deep to get into the agreement. Another way of looking at it is to ask whether an ordinary and reasonable person would be induced into the contract. To summarize, the following are the constituents of misrepresentation.

1. A person makes a false statement to another.
2. A statement could be made in express terms or by conduct.

3. Silence ordinarily does not lead to misrepresentation. There are exceptions to this principle.

4. The statement should induce the party to enter into the contract.

5. The person entering into the contract must rely on the communication.

Common law distinguished innocent misrepresentation from intentional misrepresentation. The term for intentional misrepresentation is fraud, and this has been used in the India Contract Act. We associate the term 'fraud' with deception leading to a criminal act. The term is also used to refer to someone who has committed it; for example, 'X is a fraud.' The use of the term in law is to do with the nature of exchange between two persons. It is an act of deliberate deception towards securing something by taking unfair advantage of another. It is deception in order to gain by another's loss. It will take a shape depending on the context in which it is practiced. It can become a criminal act. For example, A pretends to be B and makes C part with his goods. This is criminal misappropriation by fraudulent means. Interestingly, in criminal law, there is no crime called fraud. Persons commit crime by using fraudulent means, as opposed to outright force and coercion. In public law, fraud includes supplying false information to public authorities to secure a licence or some advantage. Thus, fraud on its own only means deliberate deception.

In a commercial context, fraud relates to the formation of contracts where a person induces another to get into a contract by intentional deception. In other words, fraud is misrepresentation that is done deliberately and intentionally. Common law, in the course of the evolution of contract law, made a distinction between misrepresentation and fraudulent misrepresentation. It also used the term 'innocent misrepresentation' for 'misrepresentation'. In the Indian Contract Act, 'fraudulent misrepresentation' was classified as 'fraud'. For common law, the distinction was important. In both cases the contract could be set aside. The party doing so could claim damages for fraudulent misrepresentation. However, damages could not be claimed for simple 'misrepresentation'. The enactment of the Misrepresentation Act, 1968 in the UK changed this. At the time of its drafting, the India Contract Act took away the distinction between misrepresentation and fraud in claiming of damages. However, the distinct terms continued to be used. We can now note the expression given to misrepresentation and fraud in the Indian Contract Act under Sections 17 and 18:

17. **Fraud defined**—'Fraud' means and includes any of the following acts committed by a party to a contract, or with his connivance, or by his agent, with intent to deceive another party thereto or his agent, or to induce him to enter into the contract:—

(1) the suggestion, as a fact, of that which is not true, by one who does not believe it to be true;

(2) the active concealment of a fact by one having knowledge or belief of the fact;

(3) a promise made without any intention of performing it;

(4) any other act fitted to deceive;

(5) any such act or omission as the law specially declares to be fraudulent.

Explanation—Mere silence as to facts likely to affect the willingness of a person to enter into a contract is not fraud, unless the circumstances of the case are such that with regard to them, it is the duty of the person keeping silence to speak, or unless his silence is, in itself, equivalent to speech.

18. **Misrepresentation defined**—'Misrepresentation' means and includes—(1) the positive assertion, in a manner not warranted by the information of the person making it, of that which is not true, though he believes it to be true;

(2) any breach of duty which, without an intent to deceive, gains an advantage to the person committing it, or any one claiming under him, by misleading

another to his prejudice or to the prejudice of any one claiming under him;

(3) causing, however innocently, a party to an agreement to make a mistake as to the substance of the thing which is the subject of the agreement.

The above distinction had emerged from several cases over a long period of time in addressing basic questions about the nature of truth, belief, intent, and communication. In *Derry* v. *Peek*,[1] the House of Lords summarized the gist of the previous cases.

I think the authorities establish the following propositions: First, in order to sustain an action of deceit, there must be proof of fraud, and nothing short of that will suffice. Secondly, fraud is proved when it is shown that a false representation has been made (1) knowingly, or (2) without belief in its truth, or (3) recklessly, careless whether it be true or false. Although I have treated the second and third as distinct cases, I think the third is but an instance of the second, for one who makes a statement under such circumstances can have no real belief in the truth of what he states. To prevent a false statement being fraudulent, there must, I think, always be an honest belief in its truth. And this probably covers the whole ground, for one who knowingly alleges that which is false, has obviously no such honest belief. Thirdly, if fraud be proved, the motive of the person guilty of it is immaterial. It matters not that there was no intention to cheat or injure the person to whom the statement was made.

As mentioned earlier, the distinction between fraud and misrepresentation was important in common law, there was remedy only for fraud.

Only a statement representing a fact can be true or false. In this context, can an opinion be a misrepresentation? We shall explore this issue in the next section.

FACT AND OPINION

An investment manager was trying to convince a customer to invest in a particular mutual fund. He said, 'The fund has declared 32 per cent dividend this year.' However, the manager had gotten the different funds mixed up. The fund he was speaking of was actually 20 per cent. The manager has stated a fact and the wrongness of it can be verified. This is a case of misrepresentation. Take an alternate situation where the manager knew that the declared dividend for the fund was 20 per cent, but, realising that the customer would not verify this, told him that the declared dividend was 32 per cent. As in this misrepresentation the manager 'does not believe it to be true', this is fraud. Could misrepresentation include an opinion? Consider the case where an investment manager tells a customer, 'This fund is going to do very well.' This later proved incorrect. Would the statement be considered misrepresentation? The fund had not done well in the past and there was no cogent reason for the fund manager's opinion. Could this be fraud? The following cases explore whether there can be fraud and misrepresentation in relation to opinions.

Court Case: Smith v. Land and House Property Corporation

Smith advertised for sale by auction a property described as 'now held by a very desirable tenant, Mr Frederick Fleck, for an unexpired term of twenty-eight years, at a rent of oe400 per annum.'[2] The particulars of the advertisement stated: '… the whole property is let to Mr Frederick Fleck (a most desirable tenant), at a rental of oe400 per annum (clear of rates, taxes, insurance, &c.), for an unexpired term of 27½ years, thus offering a first-class investment.'

Land and House Property Corporation was one of the bidders. The property could

---

[1] *Derry* v. *Peek*, (1889) LR 14 App Cas 337.

[2] *Smith* v. *Land and House Property Corporation*, (1884) 28 ChD 7.

not be auctioned as the reserve price was not reached. After the auction, the Land and House Property Corporation made an offer to purchase the property and an agreement was signed on the same day for purchase. Fleck was not a 'most desirable tenant' as claimed in the advertisement. In the two years of his occupancy, he had been unable to pay the rent. He had paid a part of it only under the threat of legal proceedings. Rent was already in arrears at the time of the sale. Fleck, in fact, was insolvent, and shortly afterwards filed his petition for liquidation, which was initiated in September. Following this, Land and House Property Corporation refused to complete the contract. Smith brought an action for specific performance of the contract. Land and House Property Corporation made a counter-claim for the return of the deposit, cancellation of the contract, and compensation on the grounds of misrepresentation. Bowen, LJ ruled:

In considering whether there was a misrepresentation, I will first deal with the argument that the particulars only contain a statement of opinion about the tenant. It is material to observe that it is often fallaciously assumed that a statement of opinion cannot involve the statement of a fact. In a case where the facts are equally well known to both parties, what one of them says to the other is frequently nothing but an expression of opinion. The statement of such opinion is in a sense a statement of a fact, about the condition of the man's own mind, but only of an irrelevant fact, for it is of no consequence what the opinion is. But if the facts are not equally known to both sides, then a statement of opinion by the one who knows the facts best involves very often a statement of a material fact, for he impliedly states that he knows facts which justify his opinion. Now a landlord knows the relations between himself and his tenant, other persons either do not know them at all or do not know them equally well, and if the landlord says that he considers that the relations between himself and his tenant are satisfactory, he really avers that the facts peculiarly within his knowledge are such as to render

that opinion reasonable. Now are the statements here statements which involve such a representation of material facts? They are statements on a subject as to which prima facie the vendors know everything and the purchasers nothing. The vendors state that the property is let to a most desirable tenant, what does that mean? I agree that it is not a guarantee that the tenant will go on paying his rent, but it is to my mind a guarantee of a different sort, and amounts at least to an assertion that nothing has occurred in the relations between the landlords and the tenant which can be considered to make the tenant an unsatisfactory one. That is an assertion of a specific fact.

Court Case: Bisset v. Wilkinson

This case came before the Privy Council from New Zealand. Bisset bought land in 1907 and after reclamation and improvement, had it subdivided in 1911 for sale. He sold some blocks and two for sheep-farming. One block was called 'Homestead' and the other 'Hogan's'. Homestead measured 2,400 acres and Hogan's 348 acres. In 1919 he sought to sell both the blocks. The intending buyers were Wilkinson and a partner, who were buying the blocks for sheep-farming. Wilkinson had no experience of farming. His partner had been in charge of sheep on an extensive sheep-farm carried on by his father. The partner carefully inspected the blocks of land and accompanied and advised Wilkinson in his negotiation with Bisset. A written agreement was reached between the parties in May 1919 for the sale of Homestead and Hogan's. According to the terms of the contract, a part of the purchase price was paid on signing of the contract. The balance amount was to be paid in May 1924.

The buyers took possession of the land but had difficulty in sheep farming profitably. They decided to use the land for dairy farming instead. Wilkinson's partner withdrew from the partnership. Wilkinson did not make the interest payment and asked for an extension.

Bisset brought an action for recovering the interest payment and for Wilkinson to rescind the contract. The rescission of the contract was sought on the grounds of misrepresentation. Wilkinson claimed that Bisset: '... represented and warranted that the land which was the subject of the agreement had a carrying capacity of two thousand sheep if only one team were employed in the agricultural work of the said land.' Bisset admitted: 'I told them that if the place was worked as I was working it, with a good six-horse team, my idea was that it would carry two thousand sheep. That was my idea and still is my idea.... I do not dispute that they bought it believing it would carry the two thousand sheep.' Lord Merivale delivered the following judgment:

In an action for rescission ... when misrepresentation is the alleged ground of relief of the party who repudiates the contract, it is, of course, essential to ascertain whether that which is relied upon is a representation of a specific fact, or a statement of opinion, since an erroneous opinion stated by the party affirming the contract, though it may have been relied upon and have induced the contract on the part of the party who seeks rescission, gives no title to relief unless fraud is established. The application of this rule, however, is not always easy, as is illustrated in a good many reported cases, as well as in this. A representation of fact may be inherent in a statement of opinion and, at any rate, the existence of the opinion in the person stating it is a question of fact.

...

In the present case ... the material facts of the transaction, the knowledge of the parties respectively, and their relative positions, the words of representation used, and the actual condition of the subject-matter spoken of, are relevant to the two inquiries necessary to be made: what was the meaning of the representation? Was it true?

In ascertaining what meaning was conveyed to the minds of the now respondents by the appellant's statement as to the two thousand sheep, the most material fact to be remembered is that, as both parties were aware, the appellant had not and, so far as appears, no other person had at any time carried on sheep-farming upon the unit of land in question. That land as a distinct holding had never constituted a sheep-farm. The two blocks comprised in it differed substantially in character. Hogan's block was described by one of the respondents' witnesses as 'better land.' 'It might carry,' he said, 'one sheep or perhaps two or even three sheep to the acre.' He estimated the carrying capacity of the land generally as little more than half a sheep to the acre. And Hogan's land had been allowed to deteriorate during several years before the respondents purchased.

The judge with approval quoted the following from the judgment of the court below:

In ordinary circumstances, any statement made by an owner who has been occupying his own farm as to its carrying capacity would be regarded as a statement of fact.... This, however, is not such a case. The defendants knew all about Hogan's block and knew also what sheep the farm was carrying when they inspected it. In these circumstances ... the defendants were not justified in regarding anything said by the plaintiff as to the carrying capacity as being anything more than an expression of his opinion on the subject.'

The two cases, *Smith* v. *Land and House Property Corporation*[3] and *Bisset* v. *Wilkinson*[4] show that, ordinarily, 'opinion' cannot be true or false, like a statement of fact. However, if the party expressing the opinion possesses a greater knowledge about the subject, facts, information, or skill, their opinion would be received as a statement of fact. In the *Bisset case*, the seller had owned land for nine years, during which he had sold parcels of land. His own history of raising sheep was nondescript. However, one of the buyers, the partner, had managed a sheep-farm and would be expected to have considerable knowledge. Thus, the opinion of the seller in relation to the capacity of land was not taken to be a misrepresentation. In contrast, in *Smith* v. *Land and House*

[3] Ibid.
[4] *Bisset* v. *Wilkinson*, (1927) AC 177 (PC).

Property Corporation, the advertiser had the knowledge of the conduct of the tenant that the buyer of the property did not possess.

Another case where the issue of opinion and fact has been explored is *ESSO Petroleum Co. Limited* v. *Mardon*.[5] ESSO set up a petrol pump in a British town and made a forecast of sales. The city planning authorities did not allow ESSO to have an entrance opening to the main road. ESSO did not take this into account and continued to represent the original estimate to Mr Mardon, who finally took the pump on rent. The business failed miserably. Citing *Bisset* v. *Wilkinson*, ESSO claimed that much the way the statement by the farmer that an area of land 'would carry 2,000 sheep' was only an expression of opinion, the forecast of sale of 200,000 gallons was an expression of opinion and not a statement of fact. Lord Denning differed on the application of the Bisset case to the present case: 'It is very different from the New Zealand case where the land had never been used as a sheep farm and both parties were equally able to form an opinion as to its carrying capacity.' Lord Denning summarised the law and concluded:

...if a man, who has or professes to have special knowledge or skill, makes a representation by virtue thereof to another—be it advice, information or opinion—with the intention of inducing him to enter into a contract with him, he is under a duty to use reasonable care to see that the representation is correct, and that the advice, information or opinion is reliable. If he negligently gives unsound advice or misleading information or expresses an erroneous opinion, and thereby induces the other side to enter into a contract with him, he is liable in damages.

...

... it was a forecast made by a party—Esso—who had special knowledge and skill. It was the yardstick

(the e.a.c.) by which they measured the worth of a filling station. They knew the facts. They knew the traffic in the town. They knew the throughput of comparable stations. They had much experience and expertise at their disposal. They were in a much better position than Mr. Mardon to make a forecast.... It is just as if Esso said to Mr. Mardon: 'Our forecast of throughput is 200,000 gallons. You can rely upon it as being a sound forecast of what the service station should do. The rent is calculated on that footing.'

Applying this principle, it is plain that Esso professed to have—and did in fact have—special knowledge or skill in estimating the throughput of a filling station. They made the representation—they forecast a throughput of 200,000 gallons—intending to induce Mr. Mardon to enter into a tenancy on the faith of it. They made it negligently. It was a 'fatal error.' And thereby induced Mr. Mardon to enter into a contract of tenancy that was disastrous to him. For this misrepresentation they are liable in damages.

Thus, as the case law has developed, opinion can also be representation in the context of asymmetry between the skill and knowledge of the parties. One can go a step ahead and suggest that in the context of increasing specialization, more often than not, there will be asymmetry in skill and knowledge of the parties, making 'opinion' a candidate for misrepresentation. Of course, if the person intentionally gives wrong information, it would be a fraud.

DUTY OF DISCLOSER

Contracts are voluntarily formed. Parties are free to set their terms through offer and acceptance. Neither is under an obligation to make an offer or representations associated with the offer. It is for the contracting parties to explore and negotiate before getting into an agreement. In other words, holding back information that would have led the party to reject the contract cannot be a misrepresentation. The Indian Contract Act

---

[5] *ESSO Petroleum Co. Limited* v. *Mardon*, (1976) QB 801.

illustrates this with the followings under Section 17:

(a) A sells, by auction, to B, a horse which A knows to be unsound. A says nothing to B about the horse's unsoundness. This is not fraud in A.

(d) A and B, being traders, enter upon a contract. A has private information of a change in prices which would affect B's willingness to proceed with the contract. A is not bound to inform B.

'Silence' has to be used not in the literal sense of being quiet but not making any communication. A person can make a representation in writing, orally or by implication. Silence means not making any communication through any of the means. Let us explore the general principle further with *Peek* v. *Gurney*.[6]

Court Case: *Peek* v. *Gurney*

Overend and Gurney was a partnership that ran a very successful business for many years.[7] However, the partnership had lately become insolvent. The partners decided to salvage the situation by forming a company. The intention was to get subscribers to inject capital in the company, which would buy the insolvent partnership. If the subscribers were told this, obviously, nobody would have subscribed to the company. The matter was, thus, presented in the prospectus:

The company is formed for the purpose of carrying into effect an arrangement which has been made for the purchase from Messrs Overend, Gurney and Co of their long-established business as bill-brokers and money dealers, and of the premises in which the business is conducted, the consideration for the goodwill being 500,000 pounds, one half being paid in cash, and the remainder in shares of the company, with 15 pounds per share credited thereon, terms which, in the opinion of the directors, cannot

[6] *Peek* v. *Gurney*, (1861–1873) All ER Rep 116.
[7] Ibid.

fail to ensure a highly remunerative return to the shareholders.

This was followed by the statement: 'The vendors guaranteeing the company against any loss on the assets and liabilities transferred.' A subscriber claimed that not divulging the insolvency of the partnership was misrepresentation inducing him to subscribe to the capital of the company. The court observed:

The case must be examined with reference to the charge which is made against the respondents of having concealed material facts, by which the appellant alleges that he was deceived and drawn in to the purchase of his shares in the company.... The concealment in the present case was of the all-important fact of the true state of the affairs of the old firm, which, if they had been disclosed, the wildest speculator would have turned away from a proposal to build a company on such a foundation. That there was a moral obligation upon the respondents not to put forward a scheme which depended for its success upon keeping the public in ignorance of what ought in fairness to have been made known to them, no one can doubt. ... The question, however, is not as to the moral obligation of the respondents, but whether their intentional concealment, from whatever motive, of a fact so material that if it had been made known no company could have been formed renders them liable to an action for damages...

I am not aware of any case in which an action at law has been maintained against a person for an alleged deceit, charging merely his concealment of a material fact which he was morally but not legally bound to disclose.

The court noted the statement in the prospectus 'the vendors guaranteeing the company against any loss on the assets and liabilities transferred' and explored:

What would be understood by any person reading these representations? Unquestionably that the old firm was a sufficiently flourishing concern for the goodwill of the business to be worth half a million, and that the proposed company, being guaranteed against any lose on the assets and liabilities transferred, the terms agreed upon for the transfer of the business could not fail to ensure a highly remunerative return to the purchasers. At this time the old firm was insolvent to the extent of 3,000,000 pounds, and the goodwill of the business was really not worth one farthing.

… mere concealment will not be sufficient to give a right of action to a person who, if the real facts had been known to him, would never have entered into a contract, but that there must be something actively done to deceive him and draw him in to deal with the person withholding the truth from him, it appears to me that this additional element exists in the present case. The concealment of the insolvent state of the old firm of Overend and Gurney was absolutely essential towards the formation of the limited company, and the respondents not merely were silent as to this important fact, but actively represented that the firm was in such a flourishing condition that the goodwill of the business was worth half a million. It is said that the prospectus is true as far as it goes, but half a truth will sometimes amount to a real falsehood, and I go farther and say, that to my mind it contains a positive misrepresentation.

The provisions in Section 17 on silence and active concealment are drawn from the case.

Active Concealment and Half-Truth

A party can induce another to get in a contract by stating positive aspects. Concealing the negatives has the opposite effect. If a party knew of great negatives, he would not get into the contract. Silence is no representation. However, a communication made to conceal information is not silence but representation. Silence cannot constitute 'active concealment'. Active concealment will always have communication from the party that conceals information. In *Peek* v. *Gurney*, it was a statement conveying that the partnership was in a good financial health. The principle is expressed in Section 17(2).

A vendor says to a buyer, 'Turning to the shortcomings in the house, the traffic from the highway leads to noise.' The vendor did not disclose that the area gets waterlogged,

making access to the house difficult. The vendor was under no obligation to bring out the shortcomings in the house. However, having broached the question of 'shortcomings' in the house, not disclosing all shortcomings, that is, speaking half-truths, amounts to misrepresentation. In *Gluckstein* v. *Barnes*,[8] Lord Macnaghten said, 'And everybody knows that sometimes half a truth is no better than a downright falsehood.' Lord Cairns expressed it in *Peek* v. *Gurney*: 'Partial and fragmentary statement of fact, as that the withholding of that which is not stated makes that which is stated absolutely false.' It was, thus, expressed in *Arkwright* v. *Newbold*:[9]

Supposing you state a thing partially, you may make as false a statement as much as if you misstated it altogether. Every word may be true, but if you leave out something which qualifies it you may make a false statement. For instance, if pretending to set out the report of a surveyor, you set out two passages in his report, and leave out a third passage which qualifies them, that is an actual misstatement.

The half truths in *The King* v. *Kylsant (Lord)*[10] was, thus, summarized by the court:

The falsehood in this case consisted in putting before intending investors, as material on which they could exercise their judgment as to the position of the company, figures which apparently disclosed the existing position, but in fact hid it. In other words, the prospectus implied that the company was in a sound financial position and that the prudent investor could safely invest his money in its debentures. This inference would be drawn particularly from the statement that dividends had been regularly paid over a term of years, although times had been bad—a statement which was utterly misleading when the fact that those dividends had been paid, not out of current earnings, but out of funds which had been earned during the abnormal period of the war, was omitted.

[8] *Gluckstein* v. *Barnes*, (1900) AC 240.
[9] *Arkwright* v. *Newbold*, (1881) ChD 301.
[10] *The King* v. *Kylsant (Lord)*, (1932) 1 KB 442.

The court ruled this to be a case of intentional misrepresentation.

Duty to Speak

A person may be under a duty to 'speak'. Being silent when he should have spoken is misleading the other party. In this case, silence becomes speech. This is an exception to the general principle that silence cannot be misrepresentation. Of course, silence and speech here are used not in the literal sense, but refer to the totality of means of communication. The law may impose the duty on a person to disclose information. For example, the companies law requires the prospectus for raising capital from the public to disclose numerous details. The prospectus runs into hundreds of pages. Missing out any of the requirements would be a misrepresentation. A person may voluntarily assume this duty. Take the communication where A says to B, 'As most of the goods are fine, just point out the one's which are not fine.' B says, 'Fine. We will follow this process.' B has voluntarily taken the duty to disclose the defective goods. Silence in relation to a defective good would be a misrepresentation.

Consider an illustration for Section 17: B says to A, 'If you do not deny it, I shall assume that the horse is sound.' A says nothing. Here, A's silence is equivalent to speech. But there is a problem with this illustration. In the first part, B is proposing a communicative arrangement to A. This may or may not be acceptable to A. A's silence to the proposal cannot be taken to be consent. Thus, A has not assumed a duty to speak. The illustration should have been thus worded: B says to A, 'If you do not deny it, I shall assume that the horse is sound.' A says, 'Fine.' B says to A, 'The horse is sound.' Here, A's silence is equivalent to speech.

There are some kinds of contracts whose entire foundation is good faith between the parties. This is a small group of contracts called contracts of *uberrimae fidei*. Two examples of this are trust and insurance. In a fiduciary relationship, the parties are in a relationship of trust, confidence, and dependence. This imposes upon the party in whom confidence is reposed a duty to make relevant disclosures. Section 17 features an illustration where A is prospecting to sell a horse to B and the horse is unsound: 'B is A's daughter and has just come of age. Here, the relation between the parties would make it A's duty to tell B if the horse is unsound.'

In an insurance contract, the relevant information is known only to the applicant. It is impossible for the insurer to get the details on its own. The entire business of insurance depends on this vital information for working out the risk. Thus, mercantile custom came to require the applicant to disclose all information that would be relevant to the insurer for making a decision on a contract of insurance. This was assimilated in the law. Lord Mansfield in *Carter* v. *Boehm* noted:

Insurance is a contract upon speculation. The special facts, upon which the contingent chance is to be computed, lie most commonly in the knowledge of the insured only: the under-writer trusts to his representation, and proceeds upon confidence that he does not keep back any circumstance in his knowledge, to mislead the under-writer into a belief that the circumstance does not exist...[11]

A case from the Supreme Court on life insurance is *Mithoolal Nayak* v. *Life Insurance Corporation of India*.[12] Mahajan Deolal had been unwell and was treated by doctors. The

[11] *Carter* v. *Boehm*, (1766) 3 Burr 1905.
[12] *Mithoolal Nayak* v. *Life Insurance Corporation of India*, AIR 1962 SC 814.

application form for life insurance had the following question: 'Have you within the past five years consulted any medical man for any ailment, not necessarily confining you to your house? If so, give details and state names and addresses of medical men consulted.' Deolal answered, 'No'. Another question in the application was whether the applicant suffered from shortness of breath, anaemia, or asthma. Deolal had answered this too in the negative though he was being treated for this. The insurance company accepted the application and issued him a policy. Deolal passed away and the policy amount was claimed. The insurance company claimed that concealing the information was fraud and the contract should be set aside. The Supreme Court concurred. The concealment of illness attracted Section 17(2). Deolal obviously knew that he had been to a doctor. The court ruled: 'Judged by the standard laid down in S. 17, Mahajan Deolal was clearly guilty of a fraudulent suppression of material facts when he made his statements,… statements which he must have known were deliberately false.' It was a clear case of fraud and the court did not have to emphasize on the requirement of good faith.

The subsequent cases from the Supreme Court relying on *Mithoolal Nayak* v. *Life Insurance Corporation of India* have emphasized the stringent requirement of good faith. In *Life Insurance Corporation of India* v. *Smt. G. M. Channabasamma*,[13] the Supreme Court noted:

It is well settled that a contract of insurance is contract uberrima fides and there must be complete good faith on the part of the assured. The assured is thus under a solemn obligation to make full disclosure of material facts which may be relevant for the insurer to take into account while deciding whether the proposal should be accepted or not. While making a disclosure of the relevant facts, the duty of the insured to state them correctly cannot be diluted.

In *Life Insurance Corporation of India* v. *Asha Goel*,[14] the Supreme Court stated that the requirement of disclosure is not only at the stage of formation of the contract but also its performance. It noted:

The contracts of insurance including the contract of life assurance are contracts uberrima fides and every fact of material must be disclosed, otherwise, there is good ground for rescission of the contract. The duty to disclose material facts continues right up to the conclusion of the contract and also implies any material alteration in the character of the risk which may take place between the proposal and is acceptance. If there are any misstatements or suppression of material facts, the policy can be called in question. For determination of the question whether there has been suppression of any material facts it may be necessary to also examine whether the suppression relates to a fact which is in the exclusive knowledge of the person intending to take the policy and it could not be ascertained by reasonable enquiry by a prudent person.

Disclosure of Changes

A person makes a representation that is correct. Subsequently, before the parties get into a contract, the representation has ceased to be correct. The person who made the representation knows this, but the other party does not. Will the silence amount to misrepresentation? The question was explored in *With* v. *O'Flanagan*.[15] The court ruled that the party owed a duty to the other to bring the change of situation to notice. The court noted: '…the duty rests upon the party who has made the representation not to leave the other party under an error when the representation has become falsified by a

---

[13] *Life Insurance Corporation of India* v. *Smt. G.M. Channabasamma*, AIR 1991 SC 392.

[14] *Life Insurance Corporation of India* v. *Asha Goel*, AIR 2001 SC 549.

[15] *With* v. *O'Flanagan*, (1936) 1 All ER 727.

change of circumstances.' The basis for this was not only in the case law but 'the plainest principles of equity.' Thus, silence in the context of having made a representation may become a misrepresentation. The court in *HIH Casualty and General Insurance Limited* v. *The Chase Manhattan Bank* has summarized the position in relation to silence and misrepresentation:[16]

The general rule is that mere non-disclosure does not constitute misrepresentation, and that in the absence of a duty to speak there can be no liability in fraud, however dishonest the silence. However, in certain circumstances a combination of silence together with a positive representation may itself create a misrepresentation. Such a situation may be called partial non-disclosure, and such cases may be explained as either instances of actual misrepresentation or as cases where a duty to speak arises because of matters already stated.

RESCISSION AND DAMAGES

The innocent party, on discovering the fraud or misrepresentation, can set aside the contract. He can do this, obviously, only if he had relied on the misrepresentation or fraud for getting in the contract. The innocent party, if he wishes, can also continue with the contract. This is the reason such contracts are called voidable contracts. These are not immediately non-existent by default, but can be made non-existent on the insistence of the innocent party. Section 19 expresses these principles:

19. **Voidability of agreements without free consent**—When consent to an agreement is caused by coercion, fraud or misrepresentation, the agreement is a contract voidable at the option of the party whose consent was so caused.

[16] *HIH Casualty and General Insurance Limited* v. *The Chase Manhattan Bank*, (2001) 2 Lloyd's Rep 483.

A party to a contract, whose consent was caused by fraud or misrepresentation, may, if he thinks fit, insist that the contract shall be performed, and that he shall be put in the position in which he would have been if the representations made had been true.

Exception—If such consent was caused by misrepresentation or by silence, fraudulent within the meaning of section 17, the contract, nevertheless, is not voidable, if the party whose consent was so caused had the means of discovering the truth with ordinary diligence.

Explanation—A fraud or misrepresentation which did not cause the consent to a contract of the party on whom such fraud was practised, or to whom such misrepresentation was made, does not render a contract voidable.

The explanation produces the principle that the contract can be rescinded only if it caused the party to get into the contract. How does one decide in a given case whether the contract was caused by misrepresentation or fraud? One answer is to ask whether a reasonable person would have been induced by the misrepresentation. The exception in the section expresses this idea. Further, in the case of misrepresentation, both parties are innocent. The exception balances out the responsibilities of the two parties. The party making the representation must pay for not being careful and diligent in ensuring that the representation was correct. It balances this by requiring the other party not to get into a contract with eyes closed. The party should show ordinary diligence in discovering the truth.

Let us first develop a broad understanding of the options, processes, and remedies for the parties. We will follow this up with a review of cases. X bought a laptop from a retailer S for Rs 50,000 on Monday. X was to pay the price on Thursday. On Wednesday, X discovered that the shop had made a misrepresentation. X decided to continue with the contract. When did the ownership pass to X? On Monday. X must meet the terms of the contract and pay the money on Thursday. Consider the alternative situation: X communicated his decision to set aside the contract to S on Wednesday. The parties decide to proceed as if the contract was never made. X must return the laptop to S. S should compensate X for any loss caused to him. It is not that there never was a contract between the parties. It is that the innocent party has a choice to continue with the contract or insist that he be put in a position as if no contract was ever made.

Once the innocent party discovers the misrepresentation, he has a choice to continue with the contract or rescind it. A contract is formed through a communicative process between the parties, creating rights and obligations for them. The innocent party must communicate to the other party that the contract was being rescinded. As contracts can be formed through express and implied communication, the communication for rescission could also be expressly implied. Once the communication of rescission is secured, the parties need not perform their duties any further under the contract. Instead, they should work to put themselves in a situation as if the contract was not made, and compensate the innocent party for the damages suffered by him. Section 66 expresses the communicative process for rescission of a contract:

66. Mode of communicating or revoking rescission of voidable contract—The rescission of a voidable contract may be communicated or revoked in the same manner, and subject to the same rules, as apply to the communication or revocation of a proposal.

Section 64 provides that on the effect of rescission. It reads:

64. Consequences of rescission of voidable contract—When a person at whose option a contract is voidable rescinds it, the other party thereto need not perform any promise therein contained in which

he is promisor. The party rescinding a voidable contract shall, if he have received any benefit thereunder from another party to such contract, restore such benefit, so far as may be, to the person from whom it was received.

A contract is rescinded the moment the innocent party secures the communication of rescission to the other party. The contract comes to an end and the parties need not perform the terms of the contract any further. The law gives the option to the innocent party to put himself in a situation as if he never suffered the misrepresentation or fraud by getting into the contract. However, if we set the clock back, we must also account for all that was transacted till the contract lasted. We would now ask how this could be justice if the innocent party has had to restore the benefits. He is first misled to get into the contract and then has to suffer the inconvenience of unwinding back as if no contract had ever been made.

Section 75 provides for compensation to the innocent party. It reads:

75. Part rightfully rescinding contract entitled to compensation—A person who rightfully rescinds a contract is entitled to compensation for any damage which he has sustained through the non-fulfilment of the contract.

The principle for giving remedy under the contract law is to compensate the party for losses caused by the other. The damages are compensation, not a penalty. It is a basic principle of law that no person should enrich himself by depriving another of their property or right. The combination of Sections 64 and 75 ensure compensation, but no unjust enrichment. We will be examining both unjust enrichment and damages in detail in later parts of the book. Let us explore the above themes with a review of court judgments.

In *Clough* v. *London and North Western Railway Co.*[17] it was noted: 'It is, however, quite true that no man can at once treat the contract as avoided by him, so as to resume the property which he parted with under it, and at the same time keep the money or other advantages which he has obtained under it.' Lord Blackburn noted the principle of restitution in *Erlanger and Others* v. *New Sombrero Phosphate Co*[18]:

It is, I think, clear on principles of general justice, that as a condition to a rescission there must be a restitutio in integrum. The parties must be put in status quo. It is a doctrine which has often been acted upon both at law and in equity. It would be obviously unjust that a person who has been in possession of property under the contract which he seeks to repudiate should be allowed to throw that back on the other party's hands without accounting for any benefit he may have derived from the use of the property, which, though not destroyed, has been in the interval deteriorated, and without making any compensation for that deterioration.

The benefit parties to a contract have drawn from each other would depend on the nature of the contract. In the case above, it was the benefit from working of a mine. Consistent with this, the Patna High Court has noted:[19]

Even if the petitioner had not set up the plea, it is clear that a court, before making an order for rescission of the contract … must make an order that the opposite party should restore the benefit they had received under the contract. For the principle is that there must be 'restitutio in integrum' as a condition of rescission of the contract. It is obvious that for a relief of this description the defendant-petitioner cannot be asked to bring a separate suit.

Thus, the courts insist on restitution of benefits before rescission of a voidable contract.

Communication of Rescission

The innocent party acquires an option to continue with the contract or rescind it. In *Clough* v. *London and North Western Railway Co.*[20] the court noted on the communicative process:

We think that so long as he has made no election he retains the right to determine it either way, subject to this, that if in the interval whilst he is deliberating, an innocent third party has acquired an interest in the property … And lapse of time without rescinding will furnish evidence that he has determined to affirm the contract; and when the lapse of time is great, it probably would in practice be treated as conclusive evidence to show that he has so determined.

The most quoted passage on the modality of communication for rescission of a contract is by Lord Blackburn in *Scarf* v. *Jardine*[21]. Blackburn said: 'Where there is a right to elect the party is not bound to elect at once; he may wait and think which way he will exercise his election'. However, the innocent person must make up his mind and communicate the decision to the other. Communicating the choice is called election. The election is complete when the decision is:

communicated … to the other side in such a way as to lead the opposite party to believe that he has made that choice, he has completed his election and can go no further; and whether he intended it or not, if he has done an unequivocal act … the fact of his having done that unequivocal act to the knowledge of the persons concerned is an election.

Thus, in the case of a dispute whether the party decided to continue or rescind, one would look for an unequivocal act from the

[17] *Clough* v. *London and North Western Railway Co.*, (1871) LR 7 Ex 26.

[18] *Erlanger and Others* v. *New Sombrero Phosphate Co.*, (1874–1880) All ER Rep 271.

[19] *Pramada Prasad Mukherjee* v. *Sagarmal Agarwalla*, AIR 1954 Pat 439.

[20] *Clough* v. *London and North Western Railway Co.*, (1871) LR 7 Ex 26.

[21] *Scarf* v. *Jardine*, (1862) 7 App Cas 345.

innocent party. *Car and Universal Finance Co., Limited* v. *Caldwell*[22] provides a good overview of the theme.

Court Case: Car and Universal Finance Co., Ltd v. Caldwell

Caldwell sold his car to Norris and accepted a cheque as down payment. When he presented the cheque to the bank the next morning, it was dishonoured. Caldwell learnt from the bank that the account holder had done the same to another seller the previous week. Norris had disappeared with the car. Caldwell went to the police to inform them of the fraud perpetrated on him. The police showed him a photograph and Caldwell recognized it to be the person. The police informed him that a warrant was out for his arrest in the name of Rowley. Caldwell also asked the Automobile Association to trace the car and restore it to him. The swindler had sold the car within two or three days of its acquisition, and the buyer had also already sold it. A bona fide third party acquires a good title under a subsisting voidable contract. The person in the possession of the car claimed to be the owner as Caldwell had not rescinded the contract. Caldwell claimed that informing the police of his intention of car being restored to him was an election to rescind the contract. Thus, the swindler made the sale after the contract was rescinded. Lord Upjohn summarized the principle on election:

Where one party to a contract has an option unilaterally to rescind or disaffirm it by reason of the fraud or misrepresentation of the other party, he must elect to do so within a reasonable time and cannot do so after he has done anything to affirm the contract with knowledge of the facts giving rise to the option to rescind. In principle and on authority he must in my judgment in the ordinary course communicate his intention to rescind to the other party. This must be so because the other party is entitled to treat the contractual nexus as continuing until he is made aware of the intention of the other to exercise his option to rescind. So the intention must be communicated and an uncommunicated intention, for example by speaking to a third party or making a private note, will be ineffective.

The court noted the 'exceptional contractual circumstances' in cases like this where the offender disappears to evade any communication being made to him. The court noted that the offender only needs to be evasive enough to deprive the other party of his right to rescind the contract. The court thus ruled that if the party can 'establish clearly and unequivocally that he terminates the contract and is no longer to be bound by it', the contract should be taken to be rescinded. The communication of Caldwell to the Police and Automobile Associate of his request for the car to be restored to him was taken to be the election to rescind the contract.

Suppose one party communicates his election of rescission of a contract and the other party challenges it before a court. The court holds rescission valid. When did the rescission become effective, when the court gave its judgment or when the party communicated its decision to rescind? Section 64 is clear on this. The rescission becomes effective the moment the election of rescission is communicated to the other party. It is not for the other party to accept or reject it. The other party approach the court and claim that the rescission was unlawful. If the court accepts it, it would be an unlawful termination of the contract by the party who elected rescission. The other party would claim damages. Atkinson in *Abram Steamship Company, Limited* v. *Westville Shipping Company, Limited* noted:

---

[22] *Car and Universal Finance Co., Limited.* v. *Caldwell*, (1965) 1 QB 525.

Where one party to a contract expresses by word or act in an unequivocal manner that by reason of fraud or essential error of a material kind inducing him to enter into the contract he has resolved to rescind it, and refuses to be bound by it, the expression of his election, if justified by the facts, terminates the contract, puts the parties in *status quo ante* and restores things, as between them, to the position in which they stood before the contract was entered into … but if the other party to the contract questions the right of the first to rescind, thus obliging the latter to bring an action at law to enforce the right he has secured for himself by his election, and the latter gets a verdict, it is an entire mistake to suppose that it is this verdict which by itself terminates the contract and restores the antecedent status. The verdict is merely the judicial determination of the fact that the expression by the plaintiff of his election to rescind was justified, was effective, and put an end to the contract.[23]

Loss of Right to Rescission

The right to rescind can be lost in some circumstances. The innocent party has the right to elect to continue with the contract or rescind it. Once he elects to continue with the contract, the right to rescind is lost for ever. The election can happen through express communication or impliedly, through the conduct of the parties.

Court Case: Long v. Lloyd

A transport contractor put an advertisement in a newspaper for the sale of a truck.[24] The truck was describes as in 'exceptional condition'. On the phone, again, the seller described the truck as 'in first-class condition.' The buyer took a trial run with the seller and the seller said that the truck was capable of 40 miles per hour and it could do 11 miles to a gallon. During the trial run, some defects were revealed, but the seller

assured the buyer that 'there was nothing wrong with the vehicle about which he had not told him.'

The buyer was also a transport contractor. He took the truck to pick up a consignment. On the way, the dynamo stopped functioning. The buyer also noticed a broken oil seal and a crack in a wheel. Further, the truck gave him only 5 miles to a gallon. The buyer complained of these defects to the seller the same day. The seller denied knowledge of this and said that the truck was fine when it left him. The seller, however, agreed to pay half the cost of replacing the dynamo, which the buyer accepted. The buyer took the truck on another work two days later. The truck broke down on its journey. The buyer wrote to the seller accusing him of wilful and deliberate misrepresentation. The letter stated: 'Under these circumstances I ask for the return of my money, and the vehicle will be returned to you by about Tuesday.' The seller contested the rescission of the contract. The court noted that after the first trip, the seller got to know of the misrepresentation but accepted the offer of the seller for paying half the cost of replacement of the dynamo. The court concluded:

We find this difficult to reconcile with the continuance of any right of rescission which the plaintiff might have had down to that time.

But the matter does not rest there. On the following day the plaintiff, knowing all that he did about the condition and performance of the lorry, dispatched it, driven by his brother, on a business trip to Middlesbrough. That step, at all events, appears to us to have amounted, in all the circumstances of the case, to a final acceptance of the lorry by the plaintiff for better or for worse, and to have conclusively extinguished any right of rescission remaining to the plaintiff after completion of the sale.

As a voidable contract can also be continued as a valid one, we have to take it as subsisting

[23] *Abram Steamship Company, Limited* v. *Westville Shipping Company, Limited*, (1923) AC 773.
[24] *Long* v. *Lloyd*, (1958) 1 WLR 753.

till it is rescinded. And as the contract is subsisting, a bona fide right created in another person should be valid. As a result, a contracting party can create valid rights in a bona fide third party till the contract is rescinded. An example, as we saw in the Caldwell case, is the buyer of contested goods selling them before the communication of rescission is made to him. In this case, it is not possible for the parties to be restored to their pre-contract position. Thus, the contract cannot be set aside. The innocent party can only claim damages. This has been important in the series of cases reviewed in an earlier chapter on mistaken identity. A swindler assumes a false name and acquires property from a seller on credit. He immediately sells it further and disappears. The two innocent parties are left disputing whether there was a valid contract between the ownership and the swindler or not. If there was a contract, it is voidable due to the misrepresentation of identity. However, it cannot be rescinded if the swindler has already sold the goods to a *bona fide* buyer. In *Cundy* v. *Lindsay*,[25] Lord Cairns stated the principle:

If it turns out that the chattel has been stolen by the person who has professed to sell it, the purchaser will not obtain a title. If it turns out that the chattel has come into the hands of the person who professed to sell it, by a de facto contract, that is to say, a contract which has purported to pass the property to him from the owner of the property, there the purchaser will obtain a good title, even although afterwards it should appear that there were circumstances connected with that contract which would enable the original owner of the goods to reduce it, and to set it aside, because these circumstances so enabling the original owner of the goods, or of the chattel, to reduce the contract and to set it aside, will not be allowed to interfere with a title for valuable consideration obtained by some third party during the interval while the contract remained unreduced.

A delay in rescission can happen in two different situations. The innocent party, after discovering the misrepresentation, might not have rescinded the contract for a long period. In *Clough* v. *London and North Western Railway Co.*,[26] the court noted the general principle that a delay amounted to election to affirm the contract: 'Lapse of time without rescinding will furnish evidence that he has determined to affirm the contract; and when the lapse of time is great, it probably would in practice be treated as conclusive evidence to show that he has so determined.' The second situation is where the innocent party discovers the misrepresentation after a long time. The case on this is *Leaf* v. *International Galleries*.[27]

Court Case: *Leaf* v. *International Galleries*

A buyer bought a painting that had represented as a painting by the famous John Constable. The painting was of the Salisbury Cathedral. The terms of the contract described the painting as 'original oil painting Salisbury Cathedral by J. Constable, £85.' The buyer hung the painting in his house. Five years later, he took it to an auction house to have it sold. At this stage, it was discovered that the painting was not a Constable. The buyer took it back to the sellers and told them he wanted his money back. This was a breach of the contract in not delivering the contracted good. It was also a case of innocent misrepresentation. If the seller had not represented the painting to be done by Constable, the buyer would not have bought it. The buyer had relied on the misrepresentation. The buyer could have claimed damages under breach of the terms of the contract, but instead went to the court

[25] *Cundy* v. *Lindsay*, (1878) 3 App Cas 459.

[26] *Clough* v. *London and North Western Railway Co.*, (1871) LR 7 Ex 26.
[27] *Leaf* v. *International Galleries*, (1950) 2 KB 86.

to rescind the contract on the grounds of misrepresentation. Jenkins for the Court of Appeal noted:

Clearly if, before he had taken delivery of the picture, he had obtained other advice and come to the conclusion that the picture was not a Constable, it would have been open to him to rescind. It may be that if, having taken delivery of the picture on the faith of the representation, he, within a reasonable time, took other advice and satisfied himself that it was not a Constable, he might have been able to make good his claim to rescission notwithstanding the delivery…in my judgment, contracts such as this cannot be kept open and subject to the possibility of rescission indefinitely…the buyer [should] either…verify, or, as the case may be, disprove, the representation within a reasonable time or else to stand or fall by the representation. If he is allowed to wait five, ten, or twenty years and then re-open the bargain, there can be no finality.

This was a case of innocent misrepresentation. The court may have taken a different position if it were caused by fraud. A question associated with delay is the capacity of the parties to restore benefits derived from the contract. The earlier position of the court was that if the parties were not in a position to return the goods transacted, the right of rescission was lost.[28] For example, a person who buys a bottle of water and consumes it is not in a position to return it. The court set up the principle: 'A party can never repudiate a contract after, by his own act, it has become out of his power to restore the parties to their original condition.'[29] A flexible approach was to allow rescission but prevent unjust enrichment by the innocent party accounting for the profits and benefits.[30] The courts have not recognized it as a right of the innocent party

to claim rescission and pay money equivalent to the benefits. They take a decision on the best practical course depending in a given case.

REVIEW OF INDIAN CASES

We will close the chapter with a review of cases from the Supreme Court of India. *Delhi Development Authority* v. *Skipper Construction Co. (P) Limited* [31] is an illustration of Section 17(3). Under this, a promise made without any intention of performing it is a fraud. A builder had made three times the number of bookings than were actually available. The Supreme Court construed it to be a fraud under Section 17(3). The Supreme Court noted[32]:

In our view, builders are not in law supposed to enter into agreements with more number of buyers than there are flats, unless each of the buyers in excess of the number of available units of accommodation is put on notice that his purchase will depend upon the availability of units of accommodation. Accepting booking from excess number of buyers without adequate notice to them about the contingent nature of their contracts cannot be said to be fair dealing.

Under Section 64, the party rescinding the contract has to restore the benefits derived. The Patna High Court has noted:[33]

Even if the petitioner had not set up the plea, it is clear that a court, before making an order for rescission of the contract … must make an order that the opposite party should restore the benefit they had received under the contract. For the principle is that there must be 'restitutio in integrum' as a condition of rescission of the contract. It is obvious that for a relief of this description the defendant-petitioner cannot be asked to bring a separate suit.

[28] *Clarke* v. *Dickson*, (1858) EB & E 148.
[29] Ibid.
[30] *Erlanger and Others* v. *New Sombrero Phosphate Co*, (1874–1880) All ER Rep 271.
[31] *Delhi Development Authority* v. *Skipper Construction Co. (P) Limited*, AIR 2000 SC 573.
[32] Ibid.
[33] *Pramada Prasad Mukherjee* v. *Sagarmal Agarwalla*, AIR 1954 Pat 439.

Thus, the courts insist on restitution of benefits before rescission of a voidable contract. However, the courts do not restore the benefits if the contract is caused by fraud. In *Mithoolal Nayak* v. *Life Insurance Corporation of India*,[34] the applicant had furnished the information that he had not been treated by a doctor although he had indeed. The Supreme Court ruled it to be a fraud. The insurance company sought to rescind the contract. The contention of the opposing party was that under Section 64, the company should restore the benefits; it should return the premium collected. The Supreme Court ruled against it:

… one of the terms of the policy was that all moneys that had been paid in consequence of the policy would belong to the company if the policy was vitiated by reason of a fraudulent suppression of material facts by the insured. … where the contract is bad on the ground of fraud, the party who has been guilty of fraud or a person who claims under him cannot ask for a refund of the money paid. It is a well-established principle that courts will not entertain an action for money had and received, where, in order to succeed, the plaintiff has to prove his own fraud. …

It is a general principle of justice that no person should enrich himself at the expense of the other. The restitution is to give effect to this. However, the courts do not aid the parties who have committed an intentional wrong.

Ningawwa v. *Byrappa Shiddappa Hireknrabar*[35] is a landmark case from the Supreme Court involving all aspects of free consent, undue influence, misrepresentation, and fraud. We will end the chapter with a review of the case. Before this, however, let us note that the remedy for the party to a contract

caused by undue influence is similar to the one for misrepresentation and fraud. Section 19A provides:

19A. Power to set aside contract induced by undue influence—When consent to an agreement is caused by undue influence, the agreement is a contract voidable at the option of the by party whose consent was so caused.

Any such contract may be set aside either absolutely or, if the party who was entitled to avoid it has received any benefit thereunder, upon such terms and conditions as to the Court may seem just.

The addition the Section makes gives powers to the court to set aside the contract absolutely or partially. Under Section 19, the innocent party can either rescind the contract or continue with it. There is no provision for partial rescission or continuation of the contract.

Court Case: Ningawwa v. Byrappa Shiddappa Hireknrabar

Ningawwa, a young, illiterate women, inherited from her father two plots of land, Nos 91 and 92 of Lingadahalli village.[36] She also became the owner of Plot Nos 407/1 and 409/1 of Tadavalga village. Her husband, Shiddappa was the original owner of the two plots in Tadavalga village. The plots were mortgaged and later redeemed by funds supplied by Ningawwa. Thus, the re-conveyance of the two plots was taken in the name of the Ningawwa.

Shiddappa persuaded Ningawwa to execute a gift deed to him in respect of plots 407/1 and 409/1 of Tadavalga village. She was taken to Bijapur by her husband on 16 January 1938, the gift deed was prepared, and she signed it. The document was registered on 18 January 1938 at Indi. Shiddappa died in the end of December, 1949. He had married a second time in the year 1941, and after his

[34] *Mithoolal Nayak* v. *Life Insurance Corporation of India*, AIR 1962 SC 814.

[35] *Ningawwa* v. *Byrappa Shiddappa Hireknrabar*, AIR 1968 SC 956.

[36] Ibid.

death, the relatives of the second wife began to assert their rights on Plot Nos 91 and 92 of Lingadahalli village. Ningawwa grew suspicious and made enquiries from the *karnam* (land record official) of the village. She found that the gift deed she had executed also included Plot Nos 91 and 92 of Lingadahalli village. The two additional plots were entered without her knowledge. Following this discovery, Ningawwa moved the court for possession of all the four plots of land. This was contested by Shiddappa's second wife and her three children.

The trial court came to the conclusion that Shiddappa obtained the gift of the property by the exercise of undue influence over Ningawwa. Further, he had represented to her that it related only to Plot Nos 407/1 and 409/1 of Tadavalga village and he had fraudulently included in the document Plot Nos 91 and 92 of Lingadahalli village. The trial court gave a decree in favour of Ningawwa with regard to Plot Nos 91 and 92 of Lingadahalli village. The trial court, however, dismissed the suit in respect of Plot Nos 407/1 and 409/1 on the ground that the suit was barred under Article 91 of the Limitation Act. The Limitation Act stipulates a time period within which suits have to be filled. The case moved in appeal to the Mysore High Court. The High Court also held that the suit was barred by limitation as it was not filed within three years of the execution of the deed. As regards Plot Nos 91 and 92 of Lingadahalli village, the High Court held that the alleged fraud had not been established by Ningawwa. The case came in appeal to the Supreme Court. The Supreme Court ruled:

At the time of the gift deed, the appellant [Ningawwa] was a young woman of about 24 years of age. She was illiterate and ignorant and all her affairs were being managed by her husband who stood in a position of active confidence towards her. The trial court found

that the appellant's husband was in a position to dominate her will. The document of gift also appears to be grossly undervalued at Rs 1,500 while actually the value of the property was about Rs 40,000 at the relevant date. The trial court has found that plots Nos 91 and 92 of Lingadahalli village were the most valuable and fertile lands owned by the appellant [Ningawwa] before the execution of the gift deed. It is the admitted position that not only the appellant and her husband but her husband's two brothers and their families lived on the income of the two plots. There appears to be no reason whatever for the appellant to agree to transfer the valuable lands of plot Nos 91 and 92 of Lingadahalli village inherited by her from her father to her husband.

...

On behalf of the respondents (second wife) Mr. Naunit Lal, however, stressed the argument that the trial court was wrong in holding that the gift deed was void on account of the perpetration of fraud. It was submitted that it was only a voidable transaction and the suit for setting aside the gift deed would be governed by Article 95 of the Indian Limitation Act. In our opinion, the proposition contended for by Mr. Naunit Lal must be accepted as correct. It is well established that a contract or other transaction induced or tainted by fraud is not void, but only voidable at the option of the party defrauded. Until it is avoided the transaction is valid, so that third parties without notice of the fraud may in the meantime acquire rights and interests in the matter which they may enforce against the party defrauded.

'The fact that the contract has been induced by fraud does not make the contract void or prevent the property from passing, but merely gives the party defrauded a right on discovering the fraud to elect whether he shall continue to treat the contract as binding or disaffirm the contract and resume the property. If it can be shown that "the party defrauded" has at any time after knowledge of the fraud either by express words or by unequivocal acts affirmed the contract, "his" election is determined for ever. The party defrauded may keep the question open so long as he does nothing to affirm the contract.' *Clough* v. *L and N.W. Ry.*, (1871) LR 7 Ex 26 at p. 34.

The legal position will be different if there is a fraudulent misrepresentation not merely as to the contents of the document but as to its character.

The authorities make a clear distinction between fraudulent misrepresentation as to the character of the document and fraudulent misrepresentation as to the contents thereof. With reference to the former, it has been held that the transaction is void, while in the case of the latter, it is merely voidable. In *Foster* v. *Mackinon*, (1869) 4 C. P. 704 the action was by the endorsee of a bill of exchange. The defendant pleaded that he endorsed the bill on a fraudulent representation by the acceptor that he was signing a guarantee. In holding that such a plea was admissible, the court observed:

> 'It (signature) is invalid not merely on the ground of fraud, where fraud exists, but on the ground that the mind of the signer did not accompany the signature; in other words, that he never intended to sign, and therefore in contemplation of law never did sign, the contract to which his name is appended ... The defendant never intended to sign that contract or any such contract. He never intended to put his name to any instrument that then was or thereafter might become negotiable. He was deceived, not merely as to the legal effect, but as to the 'actual contents' of the instrument.'

We have earlier examined the situation above, where a person puts a signature, without any fault of his, could not have a real understanding of the nature of the document. This was available due to 'defective education, illness or innate capacity'. The term for this is *non est factum*. This provision is rarely applied. Ningawwa knew she was signing a gift document. Thus, it was not available to her.

It is not the contention of the appellant [Ningawwa] in the present case that there was any fraudulent misrepresentation as to the character of the gift deed but Shiddappa fraudulently included in the gift deed plots 91 and 92 of Lingadahalli village without her knowledge. We are accordingly of the opinion that the transaction of gift was voidable and not void and the suit must be brought within the time prescribed under Article 95 of the Limitation Act.

...

It was contended on behalf of the respondents that the *terminus a quo* for the limitation was the date of the execution of the gift deed and the claim of the appellant (Ningawwa) was therefore barred as the suit was filed more than three years after that date. We are unable to accept this argument as correct. Article 95 prescribes a period of limitation of three years from the time when the fraud becomes known to the party wronged.

In the present case, the appellant stated that she did not come to know of the fraud committed by her husband in respect of plots 91 and 92 of Lingadahalli village till his death. The trial court has discussed the evidence on this point and reached the conclusion that the case of the appellant is true.

The appellant lived with her husband on affectionate terms till the time of his death. Till then she had no reason to suspect that any fraud had been committed on her in respect of the two plots in Lingadahalli village. ... The suit was instituted by the appellant [Ningawwa] within a few days after she came to know of the fraud. We are therefore of the opinion that the suit was brought within time prescribed under Art. 95 of the Indian Limitation Act so far as plots 91 and 92 of Lingadahalli village are concerned.

As regards plot Nos 407/1 and 409/1 of Tadavalga village the trial court has found that the husband of the appellant was in a position of active confidence towards her at the time of the gift deed and that he was in a position to dominate her will and the transaction of gift was on the face of it unconscionable. Section 16 (3) of the Indian Contract Act says that where a person who is in a position to dominate the will of another enters into a transaction with him which appears, on the face of it, or on the evidence adduced, to be unconscionable, the burden of proving that such transaction was not induced by undue influence, shall lie upon the person in a position to dominate the will of another. Section 111 of the Indian Evidence Act also states:

> 'Where there is a question as to the good faith of a transaction between parties, one of whom stands to the other in a position of active confidence, the burden of proving the good faith of the transaction is on the party who is in a position of active confidence.'

The trial court found that the respondents had not adduced sufficient evidence to rebut the presumption under these statutory provisions and reached the finding that the gift deed was obtained by the appellant's [Ningawwa's] husband by undue influence as alleged by her. The finding of the trial court has been affirmed by the high court. But both the trial court and the high court refused to grant relief to the appellant on the ground that the suit was barred under Art. 91 of the Limitation Act so far as plot Nos 407/1 and 409/1 were concerned. On behalf of the appellant it was contended that the lower courts were wrong in taking this view. We are, however, unable to accept this argument as correct. Article 91 of the Indian Limitation Act provides that a suit to set aside an instrument not otherwise provided for (and no other provision of the Act applies to the circumstances of the case) shall be subject to a three years' limitation which begins to run when the facts entitling the plaintiff to have the instrument cancelled or set aside are known to him. In the present case, the trial court has found upon examination of the evidence, that at the very time of the execution of the gift deed, the appellant [Ningawwa] knew that her husband prevailed upon her to convey survey plot Nos 407/1 and 409/1 of Tadavalga village to him by undue influence.... In view of this finding of the trial court it is manifest that the suit of the appellant is barred under Art 91 of the Limitation Act so far as plot Nos 407/1 and 409/1 of Tadavalga village are concerned. On behalf of the appellant Mr. K.R. Chaudhuri presented the argument that the appellant continued to be under the undue influence of her husband till the date of his death and the three years' period under Art. 91 should therefore be taken to run not when the appellant had knowledge of the true nature of the gift deed but from the date when she escaped the influence of her husband by whose will she was dominated. It is not possible to accept this argument in view of the express language of Art. 91 of the Limitation Act which provides that the three years' period runs from the date when the plaintiff came to know the facts entitling her to have the instrument cancelled or set aside.

...

For the reasons expressed we hold that this appeal must be allowed and the appellant must be granted a decree that the gift deed is not binding on her so far as plot Nos 91 and 92 of Lingadahalli village are concerned and she is further entitled to recover possession of the said two plots from the defendant-respondents with mesne profits.

Thus, the same gift deed is a subject of two different provisions. The inclusion of plots 91 and 92 of Lingadahalli village was fraudulent, and thus voidable. The period of limitation for taking up a claim was three years from the time she got to know of it. In respect of plot Nos 407/1 and 409/1 of Tadavalga village, she knew she was signing a gift deed. However, the gift was secured under the undue influence of the husband. Thus, this was also voidable. However, the period of limitation of three years for setting aside the contract started when the influence was exerted and the deed signed. Ningawwa had signed the gift deed on 16 January 1938. She should have gone to the court to set aside the gift on the grounds of undue influence by January 1941. But she got to know of the foul play only after her husband died in 1949. By that time, the access to the court had got barred by limitation.

To summarize, a representation that is false is misrepresentation. A misrepresentation deliberately done is fraud. A contract induced by misrepresentation or fraud is a voidable contract. Representing what is not a fact is certainly misrepresentation. However, opinion can also be representation in the context of asymmetry between the skill and knowledge of the parties. Ordinarily, silence is not misrepresentation. However, in speaking half-truths, silence can be misrepresentation. There are some kinds of contracts whose entire foundation is good faith between the parties. This is a small group of contracts called contracts of *uberrimae fidei*. Two examples of this are trusts and insurance, where the parties are under an obligation to make disclosures. A voidable contract will continue to operate till the innocent party communicates his election of setting aside the contract. In this case, the parties restore benefits derived from each other and the innocent party is compensated for damages suffered.

18

Capacity to Contract

In writing the Indian Contract Act, the intention was to codify common law. However, once the law was written down, the text could assume its own meaning, different from common law. The provisions in the Indian Contract Act, on the capacity of a minor to contract, as read by the courts, created a departure from common law. The departure was confirmed by the Privy Council in *Mohiri Bibee* v. *Dharmodardas Ghose*[1] in holding the contracts with minors void *ab initio*. Following the case, there could not be restitution of unfair advantages gained by a minor misrepresenting himself to be a major (a person of full legal age). This was rectified by the provisions in the re-enacted Specific Relief Act, 1963. As a result, the law in India has come to be different from common law. Thus, we will not study the subject as deriving from common law, but with reference to the general principles and provisions in the act. Further, the current law on restoration of gains by a minor is as provided in the Specific Relief Act, 1963. The preceding cases, based on earlier provisions, are of no contemporary relevance. Reference to them would hinder rather than aid understanding. The same is true of the common law judgments.

PROVISIONS IN THE INDIAN CONTRACT ACT

A shopkeeper left his shop for ten minutes with only his twelve-year-old son at the counter. The boy got in an agreement with a customer to sell a book costing Rs 500 for Rs 100. The shopkeeper returned and insisted on receiving Rs 500. The customer insists that an agreement had already been formed. The basic elements of an offer and acceptance, leading to an agreement between the boy and the customer, may be present. However, a minor is not mature enough to fully understand the world around him like the meaning or the consequences of getting into an agreement. Thus, a minor needs the protection of the law from being entangled in contractual obligations. Section 11 of the Contract Act provides this protection:

11. Who are competent to contract—Every person is competent to contract who is of the age of majority according to the law to which he is subject, and who is of sound mind, and is not disqualified from contracting by any law to which he is subject.

---

[1] *Mohori Bibi* v. *Dharmodas Ghose*, (1903) 30 IA 114.

The section applies not only to minors but also to persons of unsound mind. We will refer only to minors but should bear in mind the general application of the section. To look at it another way, a minor is not competent to contract. The law has fixed the age at which a person becomes a major at 18 years under the Majority Act, 1875. Thus, on turning eighteen, a person becomes capable of getting into a contract. How does a minor then become a consumer of goods and services? A father buys a plane ticket for his minor daughter to visit her grandmother. In this, the contracting parties are the airlines and the father. The minor daughter is a beneficiary. In several contracts, including education, transportation, and health care, a minor is a beneficiary of a contract entered into by a major. However, we see minors freely availing goods and services on their own account in relation to shopping, transportation, food, and entertainment. How is it that a minor is contracting when he does not have the capacity to contract? The section does not prohibit persons from getting into a relationship of exchange with minors. It only states that a minor is not competent to contract, and thus the court would not recognize it.

Although minors need to be protected, at the same time, minors cannot be isolated from the society. They need to socialize, gain experience, and be educated to become a major. Thus, goods and services will necessarily be provided to them. If there were no protection for the persons providing the goods and services, nobody would interact with them. Thus, the law also protects persons who benefit a minor. It has been a basic principle of law that no person should enrich himself at the expense of others. It became a principle of common law to restore the benefits arising from 'unjust enrichment'. The principles also came to be called the 'principle of restitution'.

Law today has several branches. Most of these branches were developed in the twentieth century. Earlier, there were only limited branches, like contracts, trusts, and equity. At that time, the closest the principle of restitution came to was the contract. Thus, it was accommodated within contract law. The principles were codified under a separate chapter in the Indian Contract Act, which we will deal with later. In relation to the minors, the following could be applicable. Section 64 provides:

64. Consequences of rescission of voidable contract—When a person at whose option a contract is voidable rescinds it.… The party rescinding a voidable contract shall, if he have received any benefit thereunder from another party to such contract, restore such benefit, so far as may be, to the person from whom it was received.

We explored the section in the previous chapter while studying misrepresentation, fraud, and undue influence. A party rescinding a contract has to restore benefits to the other party. As we would notice, Section 11 only mentions that the minors do not have the capacity to contract. It does not explicitly mention whether the contract is void or voidable. If we take the contract with a minor to be voidable, the minor would be able to set aside the contract. However, the minor must restore the benefits received from the other party. Another section of general relevance is Section 65:

65. Obligation of person who has received advantage under void agreement, or contract that becomes void—When an agreement is discovered to be void, or when a contract becomes void, any person who has received any advantage under such agreement or contract is bound to restore it, or to make compensation for it to the person from whom he received it.

A valid contract can subsequently become void due to changes in law prohibiting the contract or making it illegal. Another reason can be change in circumstances that make it impossible to perform the contract. If we take a contract with a minor to be void, under Section 65, both the parties must restore benefits derived from each other. Section 68 specifically deals with minors. It reads:

68. Claim for necessaries supplied to person incapable of contracting, or on his account—If a person, incapable of entering into a contract, or any one whom he is legally bound to support, is supplied by another person with necessaries suited to his condition in life, the person who has furnished such supplies is entitled to be reimbursed from the property of such incapable person.

Section 68 is not dealing with claims arising from an agreement. It covers everyone who helps a minor by supplying goods and services necessary for him.

Contract with Minor: Void *Ab Intio*

The meaning of Section 11 appears clear. As a minor is not capable of entering into a contract, no one can ever form a contract with him. In common law, in conjunction with statutory law, some contracts with minors were void while others were voidable. After the enactment of the Indian Contract Act, some judges in India maintained that a contract with a minor was voidable, as the act was codifying the common law. Other judges vigorously protested as the meaning of the Section 11 was clear in declaring the contract void. The debate before the courts as to whether a contract with a minor in India was void or voidable was not an academic point made to achieve conceptual neatness. It crucially related to the application of Section 64. The decision of the Privy Council in *Mohiri*

Bibee v. *Dharmodardas Ghose*[2] established that the contract with a minor was void. It also settled the application of Sections 64, 65, and 68 to a contract with a minor.

In *Mohiri Bibee* v. *Dharmodardas Ghose*, a minor mortgaged houses to a moneylender for a loan of Rs 20,000 at 12 per cent interest. The mortgage was executed and the moneylender paid him the first instalment, Rs 10,500. Two months later, the mother, as the guardian of the minor, approached the court, claiming that, as the son was underage, the mortgage was void and inoperative. The courts in India took the contract to be voidable and declared the mortgage inoperative, but they did not give any relief to the moneylender. The claim of the moneylender was that under Section 64, the loan amount should be restored to them. The Privy Council ruled that Section 64 did not apply as a contract with a minor is not voidable but void. The Privy Council insisted that the judges should go by the 'true construction of the Contract Act' as opposed to imputing meaning from common law. Referring to Sections 10 and 11, the Privy Council noted:

Looking at these sections their Lordships are satisfied that the Act makes it essential that all contracting parties should be 'competent to contract', and expressly provides that a person who by reason of infancy is incompetent to contract cannot make a contract within the meaning of the Act. This is clearly borne out by later sections in the Act. Section 68 provides that 'If a person incapable of entering into a contract … is supplied by another person with necessaries suited to his condition in life, the person who has furnished such supplies is entitled to be reimbursed from the property of such incapable person'. It is beyond question that an infant falls within the class of persons here referred to as incapable of entering into a contract; and it is clear from the Act that

---

[2] Ibid.

he is not to be liable even for necessaries, and that no demand in respect thereof is enforceable against him by law, though a statutory claim is created against his property.... The question whether a contract is void or voidable presupposes the existence of a contract within the meaning of the Act, and cannot arise in the case of an infant. Their Lordships are therefore of opinion that in the present case there is not any such voidable contract as is dealt with in section 64.

Thus, according to the Privy Council, there can never be a contract with a minor. To the extent one would call an exchange with a minor a contract, it would be void *ab initio*, that is, there never was a contract. As his contract was not voidable, the moneylender claimed the benefit of restoration under Section 65, which provides for restoration of benefits when a contract is discovered to be void by the parties. The court ruled that Section 65 also did not apply to a contract with a minor. It noted: '... this section, like Section 64, starts from the basis of there being an agreement or contract between competent parties; and has no application to a case in which there never was, and never could have been, any contract.'

Thus, according to the Privy Council, a contract was beyond the category of void and voidable. It was void *ab initio*; void 'from the beginning'. Following this, Sections 64 and 65 did not apply. A party contracting with a minor cannot claim restitution of benefits under the sections. The court found support for its view in Section 68. If the restitution was to be done under Section 64 or 65, the lawmaker would not have included Section 68. It has been included because a contract with a minor is a distinct category beyond void and voidable contract.

Thus, a person dealing with a minor can find protection only in Section 68. This can take two shapes. To illustrate, a person pays the fee for his nephew, a minor, as time limit for paying the fee is nearly over. Under Section 68, the person is entitled to recover the money from the property of the minor. A bookstore sells school textbooks to a child on credit. The child refuses to pay the money. Despite the appearance of an agreement, in law, as there can be no contract with a minor, there is no contract between the parties. Thus, the communication between the child and the shopkeeper is irrelevant. The shopkeeper has provided a necessity and he has to be paid. The payment is not of the agreed amount, but a reimbursement of the expenses.

In *Mohiri Bibee* v. *Dharmodardas Ghose*, another enactment, the Specific Relief Act, 1877, could have helped the moneylender recover the money. The British courts had developed specific relief under the field of equity. In certain contexts, the ends of justice required remedy for the aggrieved. The courts had developed the context and principles for the remedy. The Specific Relief Act, 1877, was a codification of common law. Section 41 of the Specific Relief Act, 1877, provided:

41. **Power to require party for whom instrument is cancelled to make compensation**—On adjudging the cancellation of an instrument, the court may require the party to whom such relief is granted to make any compensation to the other which justice may require.

In this case, potentially, the section applied as the court, on the insistence of the minor, had cancelled the mortgage deed. The court could ask him to compensate the other party. In this case, the party was a moneylender who had entered into the contract with full knowledge of the infancy of the borrower. The Privy Council did not consider it a case that required the money to be returned. It noted:

These sections no doubt do give a discretion to the court, but the court of first instance and subsequently the appellate court, in the exercise of such discretion, came to the conclusion that under the circumstances of this case justice did not require them to order the return by the respondent of money advanced to him with full knowledge of his infancy, and their Lordships see no reason for interfering with the discretion so exercised.

Thus, a party getting into an exchange with a minor could only seek reimbursement for supplying necessities under Section 68 or compensation under Section 41 of the Specific Relief Act, 1877.

IMPLICATION OF VOID CONTRACT

Several implications apply when a contract with a minor is void. Imagine a situation in which an airline sells air tickets to minors. The minors have paid the money and received the tickets. The airline can get a better fare from last-minute bookings. It informs the minors that there never was a contract and returns their money to them. The minors are now stranded.

A seventeen-year old person buys a laptop and takes it home. Two days later, he takes the laptop back to the seller for the installation of software. In this while, the prices of laptops have gone up by 15 per cent. The seller returns the money and keeps the laptop on the ground that a contract with a minor is void *ab initio*.

The position has logical force, but as such, a minor would never manage to secure an exchange with anyone. The courts have found a way out of this in favour of the minors. The Bombay High Court in *the Great American Insurance* v. *Madanlal* noted:

The provisions of the law which make a contract by a minor not binding were no doubt intended to be for the benefit of the minor, and courts in this country, when faced with a contract which has been carried out by or on behalf of the minor, the performance of which by the other party is then resisted on the ground of minority, have struggled hard to avoid holding the contract wholly void to the detriment of the minor.[3]

Two decades later, Desai, J in *Vijayakumar Motilal* v. *Newzealand Insurance Co. Ltd*[4] explained the developments:

The proposition laid down by their Lordships of the Privy Council being in general terms would have led to startling results if very strictly applied. For in that case instead of guarding the interest of minors over whom the law throws its aegis of protection, it would have done incalculable harm to their rights and caused much hardship. Pushed to a logical conclusion the Privy Council decision would have made it impossible for a minor to get benefit under or enforce any contract entered into by him when the consideration had been wholly received by the other contracting party. But no such difficult position has arisen, since the courts in India have, as a rule, in effect, confined the application of the Privy Council ruling only to cases where a minor is charged with obligations and the other contracting party seeks to enforce those obligations against the minor.

Thus, if a contract is executed and a party approaches the court against a minor to have it set aside, the court would not set aside the contract. Similarly, if a minor has rendered his consideration, on the behest of the opposing party, the court would not set aside the contract on the grounds of minority.

Estoppel

A minor could misuse the benefit given to him by fraudulently representing himself as a major to get in a contract. After receiving benefits, he could claim to be a minor and set aside the contract. It is a principle of equity that one who intentionally causes another person to believe a thing should not be allowed to deny the truth of it. The principle

---

[3] *The Great American Insurance* v. *Madanlal*, (1935) 37 BOMLR 461.

[4] *Vijayakumar Motilal* v. *Newzealand Insurance Co. Limited*, AIR 1954 Bom 347.

is stipulated in Section 115 of the Evidence Act:

115. **Estoppel**—When one person has, by his declaration, act or omission, intentionally caused or permitted another person to believe a thing to be true and to act upon such belief, neither he nor his representative shall be allowed, in any suit or proceeding between himself and such person or his representative, to deny the truth of that thing.

In the context of minors, the question was, if a minor claims to be a major to induce the other party to get into a contract, should he be allowed to later claim that he was a minor? In *Sadiq Ali Khan* v. *Jai Kishori*,[5] the Privy Council held that as a contract with a minor is a nullity in Indian law, it is 'incapable of founding a plea of estoppel'. That is, as there can never be a contract with a minor, allowing estoppel would go against the law. Thus, estoppel, even if a minor has acted fraudulently, cannot be allowed. John Beaumont, CJ in *Gadigeppa Bhimappa Meti* v. *Balangowda Bhimangowda*[6] elaborated the reason for it. The substantive law is that a contract with a minor is void. If the procedural law allowed estoppel, the courts would end up enforcing a contract with a minor, something the law has prohibited. Thus, procedural law cannot overrule the substantive law. The judge noted: 'Section 11 of the Indian Contract Act being a matter of substantive law, it must prevail over Section 115 of the Indian Evidence Act; which is merely a matter of procedure.' The judge further noted:

I am not quite sure myself, however, that there is any real conflict between the two sections. Section 115 of the Indian Evidence Act … only provides that

in certain circumstances and as between the parties no evidence of certain things shall be allowed to be given. But where the evidence to be excluded goes to show that the court has no jurisdiction to make the order which it is asked to make, it seems to me that the court must, for its own protection, look at the evidence. It is not really looking at the evidence for the purpose of defeating one party, it is looking at the evidence for the purpose of seeing that its own process is not abused.

Thus, where a minor represents fraudulently or otherwise that he is a major and induces another to enter into a contract, the minor is not barred from claiming the benefit of being a minor However, as the court in *Sadiq Ali Khan* v. *Jai Kishori*[7] emphasized, the onus of establishing minority is 'heavy' and lies on the person claiming it.

Ratification on Turning Major

Let us explore the following four exchanges with a minor M.

1. A seller enters in a contract to sell a music player to a minor. The minor pays the money and receives the music player. The seller moves the court to get the contract declared void.

2. A seller enters into a contract to sell a music player to a minor. The minor pays the money and receives the music player. The minor moves the court to get the contract declared void.

3. A seller enters into a contract to sell a music player to a minor. After the agreement, the seller realizes that the buyer is a minor. He is reluctant to go ahead with the performance of the contract. Three weeks later, the minor becomes a major and tells the seller that he had turned major and they can go ahead with the contract.

[5] *Sadiq Ali Khan* v. *Jai Kishori*, AIR 1928 Privy Council 152.
[6] *Gadigeppa Bhimappa Meti* v. *Balangowda Bhimangowda*, AIR 1931 Bom 561.

[7] *Sadiq Ali Khan* v. *Jai Kishori*, AIR 1928 Privy Council 152.

4.   A seller enters into a contract to sell a music player to a minor. The seller delivers the music system. The minor sells the music system and refuses to pay the price on the grounds of being a minor. A month later, he becomes a major, and promises to pay the due sum.

If the parties have made the exchange and the minor has no objection, the courts do not interfere with the transaction. However, even if the transaction is made, on the insistence of the minor, the contract would be declared to be void and restoration of benefits could take place. This answers Cases 1 and 2. In Case 3, the first contract was void. However, the parties have entered another contract when the minor became a major. The consideration for the parties is the same, but it is a different contract. The newly turned major put up the offer, which the seller could have rejected. As the seller has accepted, a new binding contract was formed between the parties. In Case 4, the party, on becoming a major, has undertaken to perform his part of the contract. Does this undertaking make the contract made with the minor binding?

The promise on becoming a major leads to the formation of the second agreement. In this agreement, the promise of the major is the consideration for the other party. The question is: Is the performance already done by the other party under the void contract a valid consideration to support the second agreement? The answer could come from two provisions in the Indian Contract Act. The past act of the other party could qualify as consideration under Section 2(d). It reads:

Section 2 (d) When, at the desire of the promisor, the promisee ... has done or abstained from doing ... something, such act or abstinence or promise is called a consideration for the promise:

Alternately, Section 25(2) makes exceptions to the requirement of consideration. If the past act qualified under the subsection, the agreement would be binding, even if there is no consideration. It reads:

25. (2) it is a promise to compensate, wholly or in part, a person who has already voluntarily done something for the promisor ...

We will explore the theme by reviewing the case before the Allahabad High Court, *Suraj Narain Dube* v *Sukhu Aheer*.[8] In the case, Suraj Narain lent a sum of money to Sukhu Ahir, who then was a minor. Four years later, Sukhu ahir had become a major. He gave a simple money bond to Suraj Narain, promising to pay the principal and the accumulated interest. The parties later contested the validity of the bond. Sulaiman, CJ presented one line of reasoning:

Under Section 11 a minor is not competent to contract. He is disqualified from contracting. He can, therefore, neither make a valid proposal, nor make a valid acceptance ... He cannot, therefore, for the purposes of the Act be strictly called a promisor ... Nor can, therefore, anything done by the promisee be strictly called a consideration at the desire of a promisor as contemplated by Cl (d). It may, therefore, be urged that an agreement by a minor cannot be strictly described as being one for "consideration" as defined in the Act. It is not, however necessary to decide this point.

Thus, as a contract with a minor is void *ab initio*, the exchange can never be a consideration for the minor. However, this point was not decided, as Section 2(d) was clearly inapplicable. The judge noted: 'No doubt under Section 2 a past consideration may be a good consideration, but that past consideration must be an existing one and a valid one.' Past consideration applies in the cases where

[8] *Suraj Narain Dube* v. *Sukhu Aheer*, AIR 1928 All 440.

a person does something at the request of another person, who then makes a promise for the act just performed. For example, at the request of X, Y finds his wallet and X promises him Rs 50 for it. If Y agrees to find X's wallet for Rs 50 and finds it, he has performed the contract. It is not an act without a promise. Past consideration applies where the act is done 'at the desire' of the person but without promise by him. The promise will come later. Thus, Section 2(d) has no application. Turning to the application of Section 25(2), the judge noted:

Section 25, Sub-clause (2) applies when there is a promise to compensate wholly or in part a person who has already voluntarily done something for the promisor. The word 'compensate' has been used advisedly and does not connote the same idea as repayment of a loan. The word 'voluntarily' also indicates to my mind that something has been done without any promise of compensation. It may or may not have been done out of one's own accord without any request of the other person, but there should not be any understanding between the parties that compensation would be given for the act in future.

Section 25(2) does not apply to benefits passed to a minor under a void contract as it was not 'voluntarily' done but as a part of an agreement already formed. Thus, when a minor attains majority and makes a promise in relation to a contract made during his minority, we have to examine whether there is a consideration for the minor or not. The past act on its own is not a consideration. However, if there is an additional consideration, the result may be very different. For example, a minor bought goods but did not pay for it. On attaining majority, he borrowed a sum of money from the seller and executed a bond for paying a total of both the sums. In this case, the consideration for the minor was the loan. As a result, the second agreement was binding. Of course, the major was returning a much larger sum than he had borrowed. But the consideration between the parties does not need to be commensurate.

Minor and Agency

A contract of agency is a special form of contract involving three parties. A principal appoints an agent. By the authority of the principal, the agent interacts with the third party and contractually binds the third party and the principal. For example, a stockbroker, acting as the agent of the shareholder, binds him with the buyer to sell the shares. What if the principal is a minor? A minor M, employs an agent A, who in turn creates a contractual relationship between M and C. As a minor is not capable of getting in a contract, the contract between M and C is void. Thus, a minor cannot employ an agent to form a contract. The Indian Contract Act has a separate chapter on principal agent relationship. Consistent with our conclusion, it provides:

183. Who may employ agent—Any person who is of the age of majority according to the law to which he is subject, and who is of sound mind, may employ an agent.

Only a person who is a major can employ an agent. P employs a minor, M, as his agent. M creates a contractual relationship between P and C. As a contract with a minor is void, the contract of agency between P and A is void. If a person appoints a minor as an agent, the minor cannot be responsible to the agent. However, is the contract between P and C, created through the minor agent, valid? One possible answer is that as P and C are competent to enter into the contract, it is valid. Alternatively, one could argue that as the agent was minor, the entire arrangement is struck with the nullity of a void contract. A rejoinder to this is that if P has risked appointing a minor as his agent, P alone should bear the responsibility for it. The Indian Contract Act takes this view. Section 184 reads:

184. Who may be an agent—As between the principal and third persons any person may become an agent, but no person who is not of the age of majority and of sound mind can become an agent, so as to be responsible to his principal according to the provisions in that behalf herein contained.

A minor agent is not responsible to his principle. However, the minor can create a valid contract between the principal and third parties.

RESTITUTION OF BENEFITS

Following the decision of the Privy Council in the *Mohiri Bib* v. *Dharmodas Ghose case*, the High Courts developed contrary positions on the application of Section 41, Specific Relief Act, 1877. The cases had a similar theme. A minor fraudulently represents himself as a major and gets in a contract. The minor receives benefits but does not meet his promise. He then seeks to get the benefit of being a minor. The high courts were in agreement that under Section 41, if the plaintiff seeks to set aside a transaction on the grounds of his minority, he should restore the benefits. The high courts differed sharply in the cases where the minor was a defendant before a court. Suppose a minor enters into a contract to sell a property and receives the consideration, but fails to deliver the property, the buyer moves the court for the enforcement of the contract. The defendant, the minor, claims that the contract is inoperative and retains the benefits. The Law Commission noted the positions of the high courts:

According to the Lahore High Court, the equitable principle underlying the section should be equally applicable *to* the plaintiff and the defendant, and that, accordingly, when a minor enters into a contract on a false representation as to his age, and in a suit on the contract refuses to perform it on the ground of his minority, he must restore the proprietary or pecuniary benefit derived by him from the contract whether he is the plaintiff or the defendant in the suit.

In other words, according to the Lahore High Court, the minor defendant should be bound not only to restore the property, if any, but also the monetary consideration obtained under the contract.

In contrast, the Allahabad High Court was prepared to accept the restoration of specific property but not to the extent of repayment of the pecuniary benefit. To illustrate, X, a minor, buys a cycle on credit for Rs 1,200 but later refuses to pay, claiming the contract to be void. According to the Allahabad High Court, the cycle should be restored to the seller. Consider the variation where X has sold the cycle and no longer has it. In this case, the position of the Allahabad High Court was that X should not be made to pay the value of the cycle as this 'would be tantamount to enforcing the minor's pecuniary liability under the contract which is void'. The position of the Lahore High Court was that X should be made to pay the value of the cycle. According to the Lahore High Court, this was not performance of the contract but its negation. The transaction being void, parties were only being reverted to the condition in which they were before the contract was made. Enforcement of the contract would have lead to not only restoration but also paying of damages. The Law Commission fully supported the position of the Lahore High Court. It noted:

We have already recommended the acceptance of the *doctrine* of unjust enrichment. According to that doctrine, the obligation to restore an unjust benefit should not depend upon the mere accident of a person coming before the court as a plaintiff or defendant. We also agree with the view that restoration of *status* quo *ante* would not amount to the enforcement of the void contract against the defendant. The principle applicable to, a minor will also apply to the case of a person of unsound mind.

We recommend, therefore, that a sub-section should be included in the new provision suggested by us to the effect that when a defendant successfully resists a suit on the ground that the contract is void, owing to his incapacity at the time of the contract, he must restore any benefit, whether proprietary or monetary, which he has actually received under the contract. But no question of liability to make any compensation would arise in such a case.

The Law Commission, consistent with the above position, was in disagreement with the interpretation of the Privy Council in *Mohiri Bibee* v. *Dharmodardas Ghose* on Section 65 of the Indian Contract Act. According to the Law Commission, a contract with a minor was void and Section 65 applied to it. It recommended amending the section to make it applicable to contracts with minors. The Contract Act has not been amended. However, the Specific Relief Act was re-enacted in 1963. The Parliament, in substance, reproduced the subsection drafted by the Law Commission on the restoration of benefits by the minors. The new section reads:

33. **Power to require benefit to be restored or compensation to be made when instrument is cancelled or is successfully resisted as being void or voidable**—(1) On adjudging the cancellation of an instrument, the court may require the party to whom such relief is granted, to restore, so far as may be any benefit which he may have received from the other party and to make any compensation to him which justice may require.

(2) Where a defendant successfully resists any suit on the ground—

(a) that the instrument sough to be enforced against him in the suit is voidable, the court may, if the defendant has received any benefit under the instrument from the other party, require him to restore, so far as may be, such benefit to that party or to make compensation for it;

(b) that the agreement sought to be enforced against him in the suit is void by reason of his not having been competent to contract under section 11 of the Indian Contract Act, 1872, (9 of 1872) the court may, if the defendant has received any benefit under the agreement from the other party, require him to restore, so far as may be, such benefit to that party, to the extent to which he or his estate has benefited thereby.

Thus, the new provision sets aside the discussion following the Privy Council judgment and gives powers to the court to restore benefits derived by a minor, particularly in the cases where the minor has misrepresented himself to be a major.

Reimbursement for Necessities

The only remedy for a party dealing with a minor under the Indian Contract Act where the contract is set aside is under Section 68. The section reads:

68. **Claim for necessaries supplied to person incapable of contracting, or on his account**—If a person, incapable of entering into a contract, or any one whom he is legally bound to support, is supplied by another person with necessaries suited to his condition in life, the person who has furnished such supplies is entitled to be reimbursed from the property of such incapable person.

The section applies not only to a minor but anyone incapable of contracting, for example, a mentally ill person. The section applies when a person supplies with as well as without an agreement. As the contract with a minor is void, even if the supplies have been made under an agreement, the agreement is of no relevance. In fact, the section applies only when there is no valid contract between the parties. Further, the reimbursement is not of the 'price' under the contract but 'reimbursement'. The provision derives from common law, where a contract in which a person supplies necessities to a minor is binding on the minor. Thus, in each case, the important point was whether the goods or services supplied were necessary for the minor. The courts have, for a very early time, considered the necessities of a minor in a broader sense. Barone Parke in *Peters* v. *Fleming*[9] noted:

… from the earliest time down to the present, the word 'necessaries' is not confined in its strict sense to such articles as were necessary to support life, but extended to articles fit to maintain the particular person in the state, degree and station in life in which he is and therefore we must not take the word 'necessaries' in its unqualified sense but with the qualification as above pointed out.

We will review two common law cases to develop the meaning of necessities of a minor.

Court Case: Nash v. Inman

Inman joined Trinity College, Cambridge, as an undergraduate.[10] Nash was a tailor who supplied him, within eight months, with thirteen waistcoats and a variety of other things of that kind. The cash price for the goods sold came to over £120. The tailor remained unpaid, and thus moved the court. Before the trial court, it was established that Inman was a minor. The trial judge ruled that the goods supplied were not necessities. The case came in appeal before the Court of Appeal. The court noted:

I think that the modern rule as regards liability for necessaries may be stated as being that an infant may contract for the supply of articles suitable for his support in his station in life if he has not already a sufficient supply. In order to render an infant's contract an enforceable contract it must satisfy two requisites—viz, that it shall be for goods suitable for his support in his station in life, and that, in

addition to this characteristic, he has not already got a sufficient supply of these necessaries.

The court recognized that a waistcoat might be a necessity. However, a supply of thirteen waistcoats was not.

Court Case: Roberts v. Gray

John Roberts was the reigning billiards champion, and Joseph George Gray, a minor but very capable upcoming billiard player.[11] He had acquired a reputation for himself, but not comparable to that of Roberts. An agreement was made between John Roberts, Joseph George Gray, and his father. According to the court, John Roberts in effect said:

I will make a tour of the world with you; you shall play with me and I will play with you; you will learn a great deal from playing in my company; I will pay all the travelling expenses and all the hotel bills and everything of that kind at first-class hotels, and for first-class steamers, and so on. I will pay not only your expenses, but also the expenses of your father, and at the end of the tour the money, including the valuable presents of jewellery which it is expected will be received, shall be pooled and divided between us.

The two players developed a dispute over the billiard balls to be used and Gray repudiated the contract. Roberts came to the court claiming damages for the breach of contract. A contract for necessaries entered into by a minor is binding on him. The dispute in this case was whether a contract to play billiard was a necessity. Cozens-Hardy MR noted:

… that an infant's contract for necessaries is binding; and … that doctrine also applied not merely to bread and cheese and clothes, but to education and instruction. … education must not be taken in its narrow technical sense as merely meaning education to enable a man by the work of his hands thereafter to maintain himself as an artisan, but it had a much wider meaning. It applies to education and

---

[9] *Peters* v. *Fleming*, (1840) 6 M. & W. 42.
[10] *Nash* v. *Inman*, (1908–1910) All ER Rep 317.

[11] *Roberts* v. *Gray*, (1911–1913) All ER Rep 870.

instruction in the social state in which the infant is, and in which he may expect to find himself when he becomes an adult.

If, therefore, this is a contract falling within a class to which the doctrine of necessaries applies, and if, taken as a whole, it is for the infant's benefit, I see no foundation whatever for the argument that the infant is not liable for damages in the event of his repudiating or declining to perform the contract entered into.

Is it possible to doubt that playing billiards in company with a noted player like John Roberts was instruction, and must be instruction of the most valuable kind for an infant billiardist who desired to make playing billiards the occupation of his life? ... the terms of the contract were reasonable; that the probabilities of large profits from the engagement being duly carried out by the infant were so great that it was practically certain a large sum of money would be obtained by the infant in addition to the instruction which he would obtain; and that the instruction would be for his benefit during the remainder of his life.

A relatively modern case from an Indian court is *Kunwarlal* v. *Surajmal*.[12] In 1952, a minor had rented a house in a town Sujaplur, in Madhya Pradesh, for Rs 15 a month to live in it and carry on his studies. After living in the house for several months, the minor claimed the contract was void and refused to pay the rent. The landlord moved the court to recover the rent under Section 68. The Madhya Pradesh High Court noted:

In view of the provisions of Sec. 68 of the Contract Act, the claim of Rs. 15/- can be treated as a claim for the supply of necessities to a person incapable of contracting. It cannot be denied that the house given to the minor for the purpose of living and continuing his studies was for a necessity, suited to the conditions of minor's life.

MINOR, GUARDIAN, AND PROPERTY

A woman leaves a house to her minor grandson in her will. The ownership of the house

[12] *Kunwarlal* v. *Surajmal*, AIR 1963 MP 58.

passes to the minor. A minor is not capable of contracting, but he can own property. A minor can acquire property through inheritance and gifts. A minor needs guidance and support to become major. This can be to receive education, health service, and other benefits. Further, as a minor is not capable of looking after his property, he needs a major to manage it for him. The responsibility for all this falls on the guardian of the minor. Of course, it is the parents who are the natural guardians of their children, the father more than the mother in a patriarchal social context. The question of guardianship, and rights and obligations of guardians, was a matter of personal law. In India, as the courts were set up along with the British Raj, the courts administered the personal law. Over a period of time, the courts settled on the principles for different religions. The Guardians and Wards Act, 1890, was enacted for the provisions for the court to appoint guardians and provide on the general duties of guardians.

The Guardians and Wards Act, 1890

The Guardians and Wards Act, 1890, charges the guardian with several duties in relation to the ward. Section 4 defines a guardian to be 'a person having the care of the person of a minor or of his property or of both his person and property'. Section 20 states the guardian to be in a fiduciary relationship to the ward. Section 24 imposes duties in relation to the person of the minor. It reads:

24. Duties of guardian of the person—A guardian of the person of a ward is charged with the custody of the ward and must look to his support, health and education, and such other matters as the law to which the ward is subject requires.

The 'law to which the ward is subject' refers to the personal law of the ward. A guardian is entrusted with the management of the property of the minor. Section 27 imposes duties on the guardian for the management of the property. It reads:

27. Duties of guardian of property—A guardian of the property of a ward is bound to deal therewith as carefully as a man of ordinary prudence would deal with it, if it were his own and subject to the provisions of this Chapter, he may do all acts which are reasonable and proper for the realization, protection or benefit of the property.

As we have established earlier, a minor cannot contract himself or through an agent. However, legislation makes it possible for the guardian to enter into a relationship on behalf of a minor. We will explore it with two cases *The Great American Insurance* v. *Madanlal*[13] and *Raj Rani* v. *Prem Adib*.[14]

Court Case: Great American Insurance v. Madanlal

In *Great American Insurance* v. *Madanlal*,[15] the business of a minor was being managed by a guardian, who was his brother-in-law. A contract of fire insurance was taken over certain bales of cotton, and the insurance amount was paid. The bales were destroyed in a fire. The insurance company raised the contention that as the insurer was a minor, the contract was void, and the minor could not come before the court to seek enforcement of the contract. The court noted:

If the contention of the defendants is right, it means that property of minors cannot be insured. A great many joint family businesses descend upon minors, and such businesses are in practice managed by some adult member of the family in the name of the minor, and if that member of the family cannot effect an insurance on behalf of the minor, the position is an extremely serious one.

Every minor has a guardian and under Section 27 of the Guardians and Wards Act, 1890, the Guardian is bound to take care of the property. The court noted:

Under Section 27 of the Act, the guardian of the property of the ward is bound to deal with it as carefully as a man of ordinary prudence would deal with it if it were his own ... he may do all acts which are reasonable and proper for the realisation, protection or benefit of the property. It is, in my opinion, clear that Goverdhandas [brother-in-law of the minor] had authority to insure the minor's property against fire, and having insured that property, it is, I think, also clear that the minor, being a person for whose benefit the contract was made, and out of whose estate presumably the premium was paid ... the minor would be entitled to sue on the contract. That being so, I think the appeal fails.

Thus, a guardian acts on behalf of a minor and can create interests for others in the property of the minor.

Court Case: Raj Rani v. Prem Adib

Prem Abid entered into an agreement with Dhiraj Singh Muramal to employ his daughter, Raj Rani, as an artist in his concern, Prem Adib Pictures.[16] The employment was for a period of one year on a monthly salary. As the daughter was a minor, Dhiraj Singh Muramal entered into the agreement on behalf of and for the benefit of Raj Rani. The contract was signed by both father and daughter. Raj Rani reported for work and participated in rehearsals. But a month later, Prem Abid gave the role to another artist. Raj Rani continued to report for work but was left idle. In the third month, according to Raj Rani, Prem Abid falsely alleged breach of agreement by Raj Rani and terminated the contract. Prem Abid refused to pay the salary due for three months.

---

[13] *The Great American Insurance* v. *Madanlal*, (1935) 37 BOM LR 461.

[14] *Raj Rani* v. *Prem Adib*, (1949) 51 BOM LR 256.

[15] *The Great American Insurance* v. *Madanlal*, (1935) 37 BOM LR 461.

[16] *Raj Rani* v. *Prem Adib*, (1949) 51 BOM LR 256.

Raj Rani approached the court seeking remedy under the contract. A minor can neither get in a contract herself nor through an agent. Thus, if there was any binding contract, it must be between the father and Prem Abid. In the arrangement, no benefit moves from the father to Prem Abid. The only promise was of the daughter to provide the employment. As the daughter could not enter into the contract, her part of the consideration was invalid. The court thus ruled that the agreement between the father and Prem Abid was not supported by consideration, and there was no enforceable contract between the parties.

The court, however, proceeded to note that the legislature had made enactments to bind parties in obligations with minors and guardians. A potentially relevant act was the Apprentices Act, 1850. Under the act, an agreement reached with the guardian for a minor to 'learn trades, crafts and employments, by which, when they come to full age, they may gain a livelihood' was binding. The act provided a detailed form for the parties to sign to form an agreement. In the present case, the nature of employment was not covered under the act. The court lamented:

The contract of apprenticeship entered into by the guardian is protected by the Apprentices Act (XIX of 1850) provided the case falls within the terms of that Act, but no such exception is made in the case of contracts of service. I realize that as a result of this judgment minors may lose the benefit of contracts of service which have been considered so beneficial to them as to be put in the category of necessaries. I am, however, not concerned with the policy of the Legislature under which all contracts of minors were made void and therefore unenforceable by or against the minor.

If it were a contract where the minor had already given her consideration, the court would have made the contract binding on the other party. In the case of employment, the consideration from the employee had not yet been given. The court held that the contract was not binding. The question of compensation for the three months of work did not come up before the court as it was a separate question and the parties settled it.

Hindu Minority and Guardianship Act, 1956

The Guardians and Wards Act, 1890 is the general law on the powers and duties of guardians. This works in conjunction with the personal law of the minor. Of the personal laws, the Hindu law has been codified and modified by the Hindu Minority and Guardianship Act, 1956. Under the Act, first the father is the natural guardian of a minor, and 'after' him the mother. The other possible guardians can be 'a guardian appointed by the will of the minor's father or mother' and 'a guardian appointed or declared by a court'. Section 8 provides on the powers of natural guardian.

8. **Powers of natural guardian**—(1) The natural guardian of a Hindu minor has power, subject to the provisions of this section, to do all acts which are necessary or reasonable and proper for the benefit of the minor or for the realization, protection or benefit of the minor's estate; but the guardian can in no case bind the minor by a personal covenant.

(2) The natural guardian shall not, without the previous permission of the court,—

(a) mortgage or charge, or transfer by sale, gift, exchange or otherwise, any part of the immovable property of the minor; or

(b) lease any part of such property for a term exceeding five years or for a term extending more than one year beyond the date on which the minor will attain majority.

(3) Any disposal of immovable property by a natural guardian, in contravention of sub-section (1) or sub-section (2), is voidable at the instance of the minor or any person claiming under him.

(4) No court shall grant permission to the natural guardian to do any of the acts mentioned in sub-section (2) except in case of necessity or for an evident advantage to the minor....

The section gives the power to the guardian to prudently manage the property of the minor for the benefit of the minor. The Guardians and Wards Act, 1890, stipulates the guardian to be in a fiduciary relationship with the minor. Thus, the guardian has to prudently manage the property of the minor. In addition, the section further safeguards the immovable property of the minor by requiring the prior permission of the court for sale, mortgage, gift, or exchange of the property. In addition, a lease longer than five years also requires prior permission of the court. Subsection 8(3) gives the minor the power to set aside the contract. The minor can exercise this option only on becoming a major. The Limitations Act prescribes a ward a period of three years from attaining majority for setting aside the contract. Section 11 bars a *de facto* guardian from dealing with a minor's property. It reads:

11. *De facto* **guardian not to deal with minor's property**—After the commencement of this Act, no person shall be entitled to dispose of, or deal with, the property of a Hindu minor merely on the ground of his or her being the *de facto* guardian of the minor.

Let us look at some court judgments.

Court Case: Manik Chand v. Ramchandra
Two minors entered into an agreement through their mother and guardian to purchase a house for a specified amount.[17] The purchasers paid an earnest deposit, about 10 per cent of the purchase value. The balance was to be paid at the time of the registration

[17] *Manik Chand* v. *Ramchandra*, AIR 1981 SC 519.

of the sale deed. The seller did not carry out his part of the agreement. Following this, the buyers moved the court for specific performance of the contract. The high court ruled that as the contract was entered on behalf of the minors, a decree for specific performance could not be granted for want of mutuality. The case came in appeal before the Supreme Court. The Supreme Court noted:

A minor has no legal competence to enter into a contract or authorise someone else on his behalf to enter into a contract. But under the Hindu law the natural guardian is empowered to enter into a contract on behalf of the minors and the contract would be binding and enforceable if the contract is for the benefit of the minor.

The court set aside a discussion of the past court judgment as the Hindu Minority Act, 1956, had codified the principles. It noted:

It is unnecessary to go into this question any further as after the passing of Hindu Minority Act, 1956, the guardian of a Hindu Minor has power to do all acts which are necessary or reasonable and proper for the benefit of the minor or for realisation protection or benefit of the minor's estate. This provision makes it clear that the guardian is entitled to act so as to bind the minor if it is necessary or reasonable and proper for the benefit of the minor. The power thus conferred by the section is in no way more restricted than that was recognised under the Hindu Law. It is not disputed in this case that the contract entered into by the guardian is for the benefit of the minor. It appears quite strange that the respondent should plead that the transaction is not for the benefit of the minor when the minor is convinced it is in his benefit and that it is worth pursing the litigation up to this Court. It is common knowledge that the prices of immovable property have been on the rise and there can be no doubt that the transaction is for the benefit of the minor.

The seller contended that Section 8 prohibits the guardian from binding the minor by his personal covenant. The term 'covenant' stands for a written signed document between two parties to do certain things. In other words, the allegation of the seller was that as the mother had entered into the agreement, it was a personal covenant to pay. The court found this argument to be only an attempt to avoid 'insurmountable difficulties'. It clarified on the nature of personal covenant and guardianship:

We are unable to accept this contention for it cannot be said that the guardian by the contract was binding the minor by his personal covenant. As it is within the competence of the guardian, the contract is entered into effect on behalf of the minor and the liability to pay the money is the liability of the minor ... We are unable to accept the plea that in a contract for purchase of property, the guardian would be binding the minor by his personal covenant. In the result we find that the contract entered into by the guardian on behalf of the minors is enforceable.

In *Vishwambhar* v. *Laxminarayana*,[18] the mother as the guardian of a minor daughter sold her landed property without court's permission.[19] After attaining majority, the daughter moved the court to set aside the contract. The court ruled that the alienation of the property was voidable. However, under the Limitation Act, the person has to file a suit within three years of attaining majority. As the daughter had done so after three years, the sale could not be set aside.

Court Case: Amirtham Kudumbah v. Sarnam Kudumban

The father of a minor sold the minor's landed property without the prior permission of the court.[20] The buyer sold the property to Amirtham. On becoming a major, the

---

[18] *Vishwambhar* v. *Laxminarayana*, AIR 2001 SC 2607.
[19] Ibid.
[20] *Amirtham Kudumbah* v. *Sarnam Kudumban*, AIR 1991 SC 1256.

ex-minor sold the same property to Sarman. Sarnam filed a suit within three years of the seller becoming a major for setting aside the sale made by the father and restoring the property to him. The question before the court was on the right of Sarnam to come to the court. The Supreme Court, referring to Section 8(3), noted:

The property was transferred by him without obtaining the previous permission of the court and the transfer was not for the benefit of the minor. Such a sale by the minor's father who is his natural guardian is, unlike in the case of transfer by a *de facto* guardian (section 11), not a void sale, but only a voidable sale. Such a sale until set aside is sufficiently effective to pass title, but being a voidable sale, what the buyer has obtained is a defensible title which is liable to be set aside at the instance of the person entitled to impeach it.... The effect of this subsection, is that any disposal of immovable property by a natural guardian otherwise than for the benefit of the minor or without obtaining the previous permission of the Court is voidable.

Under Section 8(3), the voidability is at 'the instance of the minor or any person claiming under him'. The court interpreted it thus:

A person entitled to avoid such a sale is either the minor or any person claiming under him. This means that either the minor, or his legal representative in the event of his death, or his successor-in-interest claiming under him by reason of transfer *inter vivos*, must bring action within the period prescribed for such a suit, i.e. three years from the date on which the minor died or attained majority, as the case may be. In the present case, the suit was brought, as found by the courts below, within three years after the minor attained majority.

As the minor had transferred the property to Sarnam, the right to set aside the contract had passed to him.

Transfer of Properties Act

The Transfer of Properties Act, 1882 is a general law that deals with transfer of immovable property and creation of interest in immovable property. A transfer of property can happen through sale or gift. The general question is, can the property of a minor be transferred? Can a minor receive property under the act? Let us analyse some of the sections. Section 7 provides that every person who is competent to contract can transfer property. Thus, a minor cannot transfer property himself. As we have explored earlier, a guardian can transfer property with the permission of the court. However, in the Transfer of Properties Act, there is no corresponding requirement for receiving property. Section 6 only lists certain kinds of interests in property that cannot be transferred. Let us examine transfer to a minor through a gift with the following case.

Court Case: K. Balakrishnan v. K. Kamalam

The case involves a family consisting of Devyani, her husband, and two children, a son named Balakrishnan and daughter named Kamalam.[21] Devyani inherited property from her grandparents. In 1945, she executed a gift deed by which she gifted one-eighth of a specified land property to the son and another one-eighth to the daughter. The son was sixteen years old at that time, and the daughter, four. Years later, in 1970, she executed a cancellation deed whereby she cancelled the gift deed. Two days later, she executed a will bequeathing the same property to her daughter Kamalam. Devyani died in 1982. The brother and sister disputed the cancellation of the gift deed, by which the brother was being dispossessed of the property. The ground for cancelling the gift deed was that the son was sixteen years of age in 1945. Being a minor, he was not capable of

---

[21] *K. Balakrishnan* v. *K. Kamalam*, AIR 2004 SC 1257.

owning or holding property. The following Sections of the Act apply to the case.

122. 'Gift' defined: 'Gift' is the transfer of certain existing movable or immovable property made voluntarily and without consideration, by one person, called the donor, to another, called the donor, and accepted by or on behalf of the donee.

127. Onerous gifts:...A donee not competent to contract and accepting property burdened by any obligation is not bound by his acceptance. But if, after becoming competent to contract and being aware of the obligation, he retains the property given, he becomes so bound.

126. When gift may be suspended or revoked: The donor and donee may agree that on the happening of any specified event which does not depend on the will of the donor a gift shall be suspended or revoked.

...

Save as aforesaid, a gift cannot be revoked.

The Supreme Court ruled:

A minor is not competent to enter into a contract.... A minor suffers disability from entering into a contract but he is thereby not incapable of receiving property. The Transfer of Property Act does not prohibit transfer of property to a minor.

Section 127 throws light on the question of validity of transfer of property by gift to a minor. It recognises minor's capacity to accept the gift without intervention of a guardian, if it is possible, or through him.... S. 127... clearly indicates that a minor donee, who can be said to be in law incompetent to contract under S. 11 of the Contract Act is, however, competent to accept a non-onerous gift. Acceptance of an onerous gift, however, cannot bind the minor. If he accepts the gift during his minority of a property burdened with obligation and on attaining majority does not repudiate but retains it, he would be bound by the obligation attached to it.

...

The position in law, thus, under the Transfer of Property Act read with the Indian Contract Act is that 'the acquisition of property being generally beneficial, a child can take property in any manner whatsoever either under intestacy or by Will or by purchase or gift or other assurance *inter vivos*, except where it is clearly to his prejudice to do so. A gift *inter vivos* to a child cannot be revoked. There is a presumption in favour of the validity of a gift of a parent or a grandparent to a child, if it is complete. When a gift is made to a child, generally there is presumption of its acceptance because express acceptance in his case is not possible and only an implied acceptance can be excepted.'

Section 122 (quoted above...) covers the case of a minor donee being a person under legal disability. The section, therefore, employs the expression 'accepted by or on behalf of donee.'... As we have seen above, S. 127 clearly indicates competence of a minor donee to accept the gift, he is capable of so doing. Such acceptance of a gift can be made by himself or on his behalf by someone else.

Reverting to the facts of this case the mother who is one of the guardians of the donee, was herself the donor and the minor was in her custody living with her in the same house. The minor's father, who is the natural guardian under S. 6 of the Hindu Minority and Guardianship Act, was also present and living with the minor in the same house jointly with other members of the family. The parties belong to an educated Kerala family. As is apparent from the record, the donee was 16 years of age at the time of making of gift and as stated in the witness-box, he understood and had knowledge that her mother had gifted the property to him and his younger sister. According to him after the execution of the gift deed, the document written in Malayalam was brought to the house which was read by the donee and he handed it over to his father.

...

Where a gift is made in favour of a child of the donor, who is the guardian of the child, the acceptance of gift can be presumed to have been made by him or on his behalf without any overt act signifying acceptance by the minor. In the instant case, mother who is the natural guardian gifted the property to her minor son in the year 1945. The donee was an educated lad of 16 years of age, capable of understanding and living jointly with the donor. Knowledge of the execution of the gift would have been derived in normal circumstances, by the minor, being beneficiary, sooner or later after its execution. Knowledge of gift deed to both the parents as natural guardians and the donee is sufficient to indicate acceptance of gift by the minor himself or on his behalf by the parents. The gift deed was revoked by the mother much after its execution... By that time, the donee had become

major and he never repudiated the gift.... mother—the donor was herself the natural guardian of the minor donee. The father was also a guardian and had knowledge of the gift. He also did not repudiate the gift on behalf of the donee. The donee himself was of 16 years of age and could understand the nature of beneficial interest conferred on him. He also had knowledge of the gift deed and on attaining majority did not repudiate it. These are all circumstances which reasonably give rise to an inference, if not of express but implied acceptance of the gift. Where a gift is made by parent to a child, there is a presumption of acceptance of the gift by the donee. This presumption of acceptance is founded on human nature. 'A man may be fairly presumed to assent to that to which he in all probability would assent if the opportunity of doing so were given to him.' (See Halsbury's Laws of England, 4th Edition 20 paragraph 48).

...

As seen above, in the case of a minor donee receiving a gift from her parents, no express acceptance can be expected and is possible, and acceptance can be implied even by mere silence or such conduct of the minor donee and his other natural guardian as not to indicate any disapproval or repudiation of it... Consequently, conclusion has to follow that the gift having been duly accepted in law and thus being complete, it was irrevocable under S. 126 of the Transfer of Property Act. Section 126 prohibits revocation of a validly executed gift except in circumstances mentioned therein. The gift was executed in 1945. It remained in force for about 25 years during which time the donee had attained majority and had not repudiated the same. It was, therefore, not competent for the donor to have cancelled the gift and executed a Will in relation to the property.

On his own, a minor cannot transfer property but he can receive property. This can be through inheritance, gift and even a purchase. As a gift is beneficial to a person, there is presumption of its acceptance. The acceptance can be construed impliedly in the person having knowledge of the gift.

To conclude the chapter, in India, a contract with a minor is void *ab initio*. However, the guardian of a minor has duties and the power to bind a minor in contractual obligations. The law puts the guardian in a fiduciary relationship with the ward. The law also regulates alienation of immovable property owned by a minor. To the extent a minor gets in a contractual relationship on his own, if the minor has paid the consideration, the courts do not set aside the contract on the insistence of the other party. The courts reason that the law is to protect minors and not penalize them. In other cases, such as where a minor comes to set aside a contract or the minor has misrepresented to get in a contract, the courts set aside the contract. The courts have the powers under the Specific Relief Act, 1963 to restore the benefits derived by both parties. In addition, Section 68 of the Indian Contract Act makes provisions to reimburse any person who provides necessities to a minor. The provision is applicable to a person who provides for a minor without an agreement. It is also available in the case where parties have entered into an agreement and the minor has received a benefit. The necessities of a minor are construed in broad terms.

Part 4

VOID CONTRACT

The state and law take precedence over contracts. Contracts are rights and obligations created by private arrangement and these cannot transgress the prohibitions of the law. Thus, a contract should not be in violation of the law or opposed to the law. The law does not recognize a contract that violates it, and therefore, does not enforce the rights and obligations that the parties have assumed. Such contracts are called void contracts. Illegality is one basis for a contract being void, and we shall examine it in Chapter 19. In the evolution of contract law, the courts recognized that some kinds of contracts were not desirable for individuals or society as a whole. They declared such contracts as void. These included contracts restraining a party from legal proceedings, contracts in restraint of marriage, wager agreements, contracts opposed to public policy, contracts restraining a person from pursuing his trade and profession, and contracts tainted with immorality. We will examine these in Chapter 20. When both the parties to a contract are mistaken about an essential aspect of the contract, there is no meeting of minds. These contracts are also taken as void contracts. This will be discussed in Chapter 21.

19

Contracts and Illegality

Law would certainly have objections to enforcing rights and obligations arising from a contract tainted with illegality. However, there can be a range of degree to which a contract can be embroiled in illegality. At one extreme, the object of the contract can be to violate a law. At the other, there may be a minor infringement in the course of performance of a contract. A line must be drawn in between to hold a contract void on the grounds of illegality. Let us introduced ourselves to the subject through the following illustration.

Abhay and Mahim entered into a contract where Abhay would pay Mahim Rs 50,000 to beat up and intimidate Jeet. Mahim did his part, but Abhay only paid him Rs 10,000 and refuses to pay the balance. Should the contract between the parties be enforced? The prohibitions of the state come before individual freedom and contracts. The very purpose of the state is to regulate society by specifying what individuals can do and what they must not do. The state enforces this by commanding obedience and penalizing the violators. In the first place, the parties should not have performed an illegal act. Having done so, how can they come before the courts and ask for justice? The state would certainly not respect the interests of the parties to such contracts. Thus, contracts that detract from the law should not be enforced. Illegality can vitiate a contract in several different ways. In this case, the object of the contract was to perform an act prohibited by the law. Thus, the object of the contract was itself illegal. Let us take up the following two contracts to examine other ways in which illegality can taint a contract.

A shop selling mobile phones tells a customer that there are two kinds of phones, wholly legitimate ones, costing Rs 1,500, and stolen phones, available for as little as Rs 400. The customer insisted on buying only a legitimate phone. Another customer overheard the conversation and asked the shopkeeper for a stolen phone. The object of both contracts is the sale of a mobile phone. The object, on its own, is not illegal. However, the consideration in the second case, where the customer buys a stolen mobile phone, is tainted with illegality. The consideration being illegal, the contract is tainted with illegality. The court would not enforce it. The courts have thus stated, 'It is an established principle, that the court will not lend its aid in order to enforce a contract entered into with a view of carrying into effect anything which is prohibited by law.'[1]

LAW AND CONTRACTS

Section 23 of the Indian Contract Act thus expresses the common law principles:

23. What considerations and objects are lawful and what not—The consideration or object of an agreement is lawful, unless—

it is forbidden by law; or

is of such a nature that, if permitted, it would defeat the provisions of any law; or

is fraudulent; or

involves or implies injury to the person or property of another; or

the court regards it as immoral, or opposed to public policy.

In each of these cases, the consideration or object of an agreement said to be unlawful. Every agreement of which the object or consideration is unlawful is void.

The section declares a contract tainted with illegality or immorality void. It also declares a contract opposed to public policy void. We will take up the issue of public policy in a separate chapter. In this chapter we shall explore contracts tainted with illegality. Another way of expressing the provision is: First, a contract whose object or consideration is 'forbidden by law' is void. Second, a contract, on the face of it, may be fine. However, if allowed, it may result in defeating the law. Such contracts are also void. The second category is only an expression of the first. A contract contrary to law should not be enforced whether the contract violates the law directly or indirectly. Law refers to the existing law created by acts, rules, notifications, orders, and ordinances. The principle is simple and clear. However, its application becomes nuanced, and at times

ambiguous and confusing. Let us map the field with the following landmark common law cases.

Court Case: Re an Arbitration Between Mahmoud and Ispahani

Ispahani entered into a contract with Mahmoud to buy 150 tons of linseed oil from him.[2] The prevailing law, Seeds, Oils, and Pats Order, 1919, required every person buying or selling food products, including edible oil, to get a license from the government. Clause 3 of the order, read with the schedule, provided that 'a person shall not ... buy or sell or offer or attempt to buy or otherwise deal in' rapeseed oil without a licence issued by the food controller. The violation of the order was a punishable offence. Mahmoud had a licence required by the order. During the negotiations between the parties, he enquired whether Ispahani had a licence under the order to buy the linseed oil. Ispahani informed him that he had applied for one. In a subsequent meeting a few weeks later, Ispahani informed the seller Mahmoud that he had acquired his license. Mammoud had no reasons to doubt him, and the parties reached a written agreement for the sale contract. The fact was, however, that Ispahani did not have a license.

Mahmoud tendered delivery of the first instalment of the linseed oil, but the buyer refused it, stating that he had not made a binding contract. Mahmoud gave notice to him to the effect that he intended to sell the linseed oil to another party and recover the difference between the sale prices as damages. When Mahmoud had followed through with this, the buyer contended that the contract was illegal as no licence had been issued to him. Thus, the contract was void, and as a

[1] Le Blanc, J, in *Langton* v. *Hughes*, (1813) 1 M. & S. 593.

[2] *Re an Arbitration between Mahmoud and Ispahani*, (1921) All ER Rep 217.

result, damages could not be charged from him. Scrutton, LJ, for the Court of Appeal, noted:

I should like to say at once that we are not dealing here with the commercial or business merits of the seller or of the buyer. If we were, there is obviously a great deal to be said for the commercial and business merits of the seller, and nothing whatever for those of the buyer. We are simply dealing with the legal position of the parties.... The seller, who had a licence to sell, sold linseed oil to the buyer, who had no licence to purchase. It is clear that an offence under the order was committed; an act prohibited by the order had been done.... If so, the court is bound not to render assistance in enforcing an illegal contract.

As I understand, two reasons are given why the court should enforce this contract. First of all, it is said that the court will not listen to a person who says: 'Protect me from my own illegality.' In my view, the court is bound, once it knows that the contract is illegal, itself to take the objection and to refuse to enforce the contract, whether its knowledge comes from the statement of the party who was guilty of the illegality, or whether its knowledge comes from outside sources. The court does not sit to enforce illegal contracts ... it is for the protection of the public that the court refuses to enforce such a contract.

The other point is that, where a contract can be performed either lawfully or unlawfully, and the defendant without the knowledge of the plaintiff elects to perform it unlawfully, he cannot plead its illegality. That, in my view, does not apply to a case where the contract sought to be enforced is altogether prohibited, and in this case to contract with a person who had no licence was altogether prohibited. It was not that the seller might lawfully contract with the buyer and chance his getting the licence before the seller delivered the goods. The contract was absolutely prohibited; and, in my view, if an act is prohibited by statute for the public benefit, the court must enforce the prohibition, even though the person breaking the law relies upon his own illegality.

Illegality in relation to a contract can arise in three different ways. If the formation of a contract or object of a contract is forbidden by law, the contract is a nullity and the courts cannot enforce it. This is irrespective of whether the parties intended it or not. The only thing that has to be assessed is whether the contract is in violation of the law. The larger interest of maintaining the sanctity of law takes precedence over the claims of the parties. In this case, as Bankes, LJ said in his judgment, 'however shabby it may appear to be … the court will not lend its aid to the enforcement of the contract.' In this case, the seller was innocent and misrepresented to. Nevertheless, as the contract was forbidden by the order, it was void.

In some cases, a contract is not in violation of the law, but a party performs it in unlawful manner. For example, a contract for the sale of an electric bulb for a specified price is perfectly valid. However, the law requires that every electric appliance that is manufactured or sold should bear the certification of quality. Suppose that a seller supplies bulbs that are not quality certified. The seller has violated the law, and the consideration rendered to the buyer is in violation of the law. As the buyer is innocent, the court should aid him in adequate performance of the contract. However, consider a variation of the case. A buyer and seller get in an agreement to deal in bulbs that are not quality certified. A contract for the sale of bulbs on its own is illegal. However, this particular contract is to perform an act that is forbidden by law. In this case, we need to investigate the intention of the parties at the time of entering into the contract. The argument was put up in the case that the infirmity came up at the time of performance of the contract. The buyer could have and should have got a licence before goods were delivered. The court was clear that the point had no application to the case. It was a contract whose formation was forbidden by the law. The following case is on the theme of illegality in performance of a contract.

Court Case: Anderson v. Daniel

The law required the seller of fertilizers to give a written invoice to the buyer declaring the chemical percentage of nitrogen, phosphate, and potash.[3] The law imposed a penalty on the erring vendor. As fertilizer, one vendor delivered some sweepings from the hold of the ships that carried nitrate of soda, sulphate of ammonia, potash or superphosphates as cargo. In the process of unloading such ships, many bags and casks burst, and some of the contents fall into the hold. From time to time, the holds are cleaned out and the sweepings are sold for manure.

The vendor did not give the buyer an invoice, and the buyer did not pay for the goods. The seller moved the court to get the due amount. The buyer contended before the court that as the invoice was not supplied, the sale was illegal and the buyer could not recover the price. Atkin, LJ, for the Court of Appeal noted:

The question of illegality in a contract generally arises in connection with its formation, but it may also arise, as it does here, in connection with its performance. In the former case, where the parties have agreed to something which is prohibited by Act of Parliament, it is indisputable that the contract is unenforceable by either party. And I think that it is equally unenforceable by the offending party where the illegality arises from the fact that the mode of performance adopted by the party performing it is in violation of some statute, even though the contract as agreed upon between the parties was capable of being performed in a perfectly legal manner. If a man contracts to supply bricks, which when delivered are found not to be of the statutory dimensions, or a printer employed to print a book delivers it without his name being affixed to it as required by the statute in that behalf, the party so supplying the bricks or printing the book is not entitled to any remuneration for his services, which are ex hypothesi illegal

and ought not to have been rendered in the form in which they were rendered. That is, I think, the principle which has been laid down in the cases.

The principles above are clear. However, courts have confronted ambiguities in applying them in a certain class of cases. The law may not prohibit an act in express terms, but, it may be inferred from penalties or other provisions. This calls for interpreting the statute itself. It may be contentious as to what should be inferred from a penalty. Further, a contract may perform an act forbidden by law. However, the violation of the law may not constitute the entire contract. The violation may be a small part of the contract. Alternatively, what has been violated may itself be a small detail in a field of law. For example, suppose the buyer and seller agree on a sale contract for goods worth Rs 20 lakh. The environmental pollution clearance certificate for the truck has lapsed. As the goods have to be moved urgently, the parties have agreed to employ the truck as a part of the contract. Should the contract be declared void on the insistence of one of the parties? If the seller had employed the truck without the knowledge of the buyer, could the buyer have refused to pay on the grounds of illegality in performance of the contract? Our answer would be no. Let us explore these aspects with the following case.

Court Case: St John Shipping Corporation v. Joseph Rank Limited

The British Parliament had enacted the Merchant Shipping (Safety and Load Line Conventions) Act, 1932, which made it an offence to load a ship to the extent that her load line was submerged.[4] This was to prevent ships from overloading. The penalty for

[3] *Anderson* v. *Daniel, Court of Appeal,* (1924) 1 KB 138.

[4] *St John Shipping Corporation* v. *Joseph Rank Limited,* 1956 (3) All ER 683.

violation of the law was a fine. The court was to impose a fine on the basis of the earning capacity of the ship. However, the fine could not exceed £100 for every inch by which the load line was submerged. In 1932, £100 must have been the upper limit of the earning capacity per inch of overloading. Since then, the nature of cargo and freight changed, but the law was not revised. This led to an anomaly. A shipowner would gladly overload and pay the fine; he would still be in profit. This was the problem the exporter and importer were trying to address.

A seller shipped ten thousand tons of grain from Mobile, Alabama, USA, to Birkenhead, UK, with St John Shipping Corporation. The UK buyer was Joseph Rank Limited. The ship was overloaded, and the master of the ship was prosecuted. The ship was fined the maximum amount, that is, £1,200. By overloading, the ship had earned £2,295. Joseph Rank Limited, in association with the person sending the consignment, decided to inflict an additional punishment. They withheld £2000 from St John Shipping Corporation. The shipping company sued for recovery of the money. The contention was that the performance of the contract was done by committing an illegality. This prevents them from enforcing the contract at all. Devlin noted:

There are two general principles. The first is that a contract which is entered into with the object of committing an illegal act is unenforceable. The application of this principle depends upon proof of the intent, at the time the contract was made, to break the law ... The second principle is that the court will not enforce a contract which is expressly or impliedly prohibited by statute. If the contract is of this class it does not matter what the intent of the parties is; if the statute prohibits the contract, it is unenforceable whether the parties meant to break the law or not.

An example of the first principle is a ship owner who enters into a contract with the master of the ship to overload the ship and share the profit. The object of the contract is to perform an illegal act. An example of the second principle is when parties get in a sale contract without a license when the law requires every sale to be done with a license. Joseph Rank Limited was relying on the principle enunciated by Atkin in *Anderson* v. *Daniel* that illegality in performance vitiates the contract for the party violating the law. The judge continued:

The principle enunciated by Atkin ... is an offshoot of the second principle that a prohibited contract will not be enforced. If the prohibited contract is an express one, it falls directly within the principle. It must likewise fall within it if the contract is implied. ... The same reasoning must be applied to a contract which, though legal in form, is performed unlawfully. ... But whether it is the terms of the contract or the performance of it that is called in question, the test is just the same: is the contract, as made or as performed, a contract that is prohibited by the statute?

Thus, any illegality conducted in the course of performance of a contract would not make it bad. We have to look at the whole contract as it was performed and ask whether it was the sort of contract that was prohibited by the statute. The question can be answered only by looking at the statute and exploring the contracts it aims to prohibit. The judge noted:

The fundamental question is whether the statute means to prohibit the contract. The statute is to be construed in the ordinary way; one must have regard to all relevant considerations and no single consideration, however important, is conclusive.

Two questions are involved. The first—and the one which hitherto has usually settled the matter—is: does the statute mean to prohibit contracts at all? But if this be answered in the affirmative, then one must ask: does this contract belong to the class which the statute intends to prohibit? For example, a person is forbidden by statute from using an unlicensed vehicle on the highway. If one asks oneself whether there is in such an enactment an implied prohibition of all contracts for the use of unlicensed vehicles, the answer may well be that there is, and that contracts of hire would be unenforceable. But if one asks oneself whether there is an implied prohibition of contracts for the carriage of goods by unlicensed vehicles or for the repairing of unlicensed vehicles or for the garaging of unlicensed vehicles, the answer may well be different. The answer may be that collateral contracts of this sort are not within the ambit of the statute.

This relates to the concern we had raised earlier on a contract and the extent of violation of the law. Not every violation of the law makes a contract void. The answer is to examine the statute and settle on the kind of contracts it prohibits, then turn to the contract and judge whether it falls in the category. It is evident that the Merchant Shipping (Safety and Load Line Conventions) Act, 1932, was enacted to regulate the safety of ships, not contract of carriage. The judge further noted: 'In my judgment, contracts for the carriage of goods are not within the ambit of this statute at all. A court should not hold that any contract or class of contracts is prohibited by statute unless there is a clear implication, or "necessary inference," ... that the statute so intended.' The judge was in favour of a cautious approach in constructing the scope of a statute. He noted:

... unless you get a clear implication of that sort, I think that a court ought to be very slow to hold that a statute intends to interfere with the rights and remedies given by the ordinary law of contract. Caution in this respect is, I think, especially necessary in these times when so much of commercial life is governed by regulations of one sort or another, which may easily be broken without wicked intent. Persons who deliberately set out to break the law cannot expect to be aided in a court of justice, but it is a different matter when the law is unwittingly broken. To nullify a bargain in such circumstances frequently means that in a case—perhaps of such triviality that no authority would have felt it worth while to prosecute—a seller, because he cannot enforce his civil rights, may forfeit

a sum vastly in excess of any penalty that a criminal court would impose; and the sum forfeited will not go into the public purse but into the pockets of someone who is lucky enough to pick up the windfall or astute enough to have contrived to get it. It is questionable how far this contributes to public morality...

The courts have faced two conflicting principles. One, not to aid a contract tainted with illegality, and two, the injustice in nullifying a contract for any and every violation of law. The approach of the British courts has been thus described by Bingham, LJ in *Saunders* v. *Edwards*:

Where issues of illegality are raised, the courts have (as it seems to me) to steer a middle course between two unacceptable positions. On the one hand it is unacceptable that any court of law should aid or lend its authority to a party seeking to pursue or enforce an object or agreement which the law prohibits. On the other hand, it is unacceptable that the court should, on the first indication of unlawfulness affecting any aspect of a transaction, draw up its skirts and refuse all assistance to the plaintiff, no matter how serious his loss or how disproportionate his loss to the unlawfulness of his conduct. ... But I think that on the whole the courts have tended to adopt a pragmatic approach to these problems, seeking where possible to see that genuine wrongs are righted so long as the court does not thereby promote or countenance a nefarious object or bargain which it is bound to condemn.[5]

Let us move to review the cases from Indian courts.

REVIEW OF COURT JUDGMENT

Court Case: Brij Mohan Parihar v. M.P. State Road Transport Corporation

The Madhya Pradesh Road Transport Corporation (Corporation) had obtained permits under the Motor Vehicles Act, 1939, to ply

---

[5] *Saunders* v. *Edwards*, 1987 (2) All ER 651.

buses on different routes.[6] The case relates to its permit for the Gwalior to Chinor via Dabra route, which was valid for a period of five years, ending on 23 December 1982. The Corporation had appointed Brij Mohan Parihar to ply his bus on the route as their nominee. The duration of the appointment was coterminous with the validity of the permit. The Corporation applied for the renewal of the permit. Till a decision was reached, it was issued a temporary permit. As a result, the Corporation allowed Mr Parihar to ply his bus on a monthly basis during that period. Under the agreement, Mr Parihar was liable to pay to the Corporation a nomination fees or supervision charges and additional taxes. On 12 August 1984, the Corporation invited tenders from private operators for running buses as nominees of the Corporation. Mr Parihar was aggrieved by the advertisement as this would take away his business. The Supreme Court appraised the contract between Mr. Parihar and the Corporation, and referring to the provisions of the Motor Vehicles Act, noted:

The provisions of the Act and in particular, Sections 42 and 59 clearly debar all holders of permits, including the Corporation, from indulging in such unauthorised trafficking in permits. The agreement entered into by the petitioner with the Corporation is clearly contrary to the Act and cannot, therefore, be enforced.... It follows that the advertisement issued by the Corporation is equally ineffective.... If the Corporation cannot run its vehicle under a permit issued to it, it must surrender it so that the Regional Transport Authority may grant the permit to some other deserving applicant or it must transfer it to somebody else with the permission of the Regional Transport Authority granted under Section 59 of the Act. It cannot, however, allow the permit to be used by somebody else to run his vehicle either for consideration or without consideration.... It is hoped that the Corporation will desist from entering into such agreements with third parties, which are wholly illegal and from continuing to allow them to run their vehicles as its nominees.

Court Case: M.G. Brothers Lorry Service v. M/s. Prasad Textiles

M/s Prasad Textiles sent a consignment with a transport company M/s M.G. Brothers Lorry Service.[7] Clause 15 of the Way Bill, the receipt for sending the goods containing the terms of the contract, provided: 'No suit shall lie against the firm in respect of any consignment without a claim made in writing in that behalf and preferred within thirty days from the date of booking or from the date of arrival at the destination by the party concerned.' The lorry service failed to deliver the consignment as the goods were destroyed in a cyclone. M/s Prasad Textiles did not move its claim within the specified period. Section 10 of the Carriers Act, 1865, however, provides as follows:

No suit shall be instituted against a common carrier for the loss of, or injury to goods entrusted to him for carriage, unless notice in writing of the loss or injury has been given to him before the institution of the suit and within six months of the time when the loss or injury first came to the knowledge of the plaintiff.

The Supreme Court noted on the conflict between the terms of the contract and Section 10 of the Carriers Act:

... it appears to us that Condition 15 of the Way Bill was designed to avoid the liability contemplated under Section 10 of the Carriers Act, 1865 ... Condition 15 only intended to defeat or by-pass the provisions of Section 10 of the Carriers Act.... if Condition 15 be permitted then it will defeat the provisions of Section 10 of the Carriers Act ... In that view of the matter, we are of the opinion that Condition 15 must be held to be void in view of Section 23 of the Indian

[6] *Brij Mohan Parihar* v. *M.P. State Road Transport Corporation*, AIR 1987 SC 29.

[7] *M.G. Brothers Lorry Service* v. *M/s Prasad Textiles*, AIR 1984 SC 15.

Contract Act because its object was to defeat the provisions of Section 10 of the Carriers Act.

Court Case: *Biharilal Jaiswal Etc* v. *Commissioner of Income Tax*

Biharilal Jaiswal obtained a licence for retail sale of country spirit for twenty-two shops from the Madhya Pradesh Excise Department.[8] The licence was effective for the period commencing on 1 April 1968 and ending on 31 March 1969. The grant of licence was governed by the Madhya Pradesh Excise Act and the rules framed under it. Biharilal Jaiswal entered into a partnership with ten other people to conduct the business. The Income Tax Act, under Section 184 and 185, made provision for partnerships to get themselves registered with the income tax authorities for the purposes of taxation. This was beneficial for people computing their taxable income. The income Tax Officer rejected the application for registration on the ground that the partnership was illegal, as it was formed in violation of Clause (VI) of the General Licence Conditions Prescribed by the Madhya Pradesh Excise Rules, and thus it could not be registered under the Income Tax Act. Clause (VI) of the General Licence Conditions prescribed by the Excise Rules read:

VI. Transfer or Sublease of Licence: No privilege of supply or sale shall be sold, transferred or sub-leased, nor shall a holder of any such privilege enter into a partnership for the working of such privilege in any way or manner without the written permission of the Collector, which shall be endorsed on the licence. A partner, sub-lessee, transferee shall be bound by all the conditions of the licence, but the original licencee also shall continue to be responsible to the State Government for the due payment of the licence fees and proper working of the shop, except that in the case of

---

[8] *Biharilal Jaiswal Etc* v. *Commissioner of Income Tax*, (1996) 1 SCC 443.

a transfer his responsibility shall cease as soon as the transfer is endorsed on the licence.

The Supreme Court ruled:

… any agreement whereunder the licence is transferred, sub-let or a partnership is entered into with respect to the privilege/business under the said licence, contrary to the prohibition contained in the relevant excise enactment, is an agreement prohibited by law. The object of such an agreement must be held to be of such a nature that if permitted it would defeat the provisions of the excise law within the meaning of Section 23 of the Contract Act. Such an agreement is declared by Section 23 to be unlawful and void.

The Contract Act deals with the rights and obligations of the contracting parties. The partnership was void under Section 23 as the formation of partnership for the licensed business was prohibited. The relevance of a contract being void is not only for the contracting parties. As a contract is the foundation on which all business relationships are built, it can have varied relevance. The question in this case was: Could the void partnership be treated as a genuine one for the purposes of registration under Section 185(1) of the Income Tax Act? The Supreme Court ruled:

When the law prohibits the entering into a particular partnership agreement, there can be in law no partnership agreement of that nature. The question of such an agreement being genuine cannot, therefore, arise. … where there is a specific prohibition as in the case before us, any partnership entered into would be unlawful and void agreement within the meaning of Section 23 and no other law, whether State or Central, can recognize such an agreement. … One arm of law cannot be utilised to defeat the other arm of law. Doing so would be opposed to public policy and bring the law into ridicule. … It would probably have been a different matter if the Income Tax Act had specifically provided that registration can be granted notwithstanding that the partnership is violative of any other law—but it does not say so.

We may clarify that our holding does not mean that such an illegal partnership cannot be taxed. It is certainly bound to be taxed either as an unregistered partnership firm or as an association of persons. The only question considered herein is its right to claim registration under the Income Tax Act.

Court Case: Mannalal Khetan v. Kedar Nath Khetan

The case involves several individuals, companies, and partnerships, all involving different branches of Khetan family.[9] The members of the Khetan family owned shares in the companies and ran a partnership business. There were large income-tax arrears and other tax liabilities outstanding against the firms and individual partners. There is a provision for 'attaching' the property of a person for non-payment of taxes. This is to prevent the person from selling the property and denying the state their taxes. The first step for the state is to attach (that is, take possession of) some or all of the property of the person. If the person pays the taxes, the attachment of the property can be abandoned. If not, with appropriate sanction, the attached property is auctioned to recover the taxes. Once the due taxes are realized, the attachment of the remainder of the property can be abandoned.

Towards this, the shares held by the members of the Khetan family in the private companies were attached. The companies in which shares were held were informed as much. The members of the Khetan family entered into an agreement to exchange their shares in different companies to settle their disputes. Within company law, there is a prescribed procedure by which shares of a company are transferred and registered in the records of the company. Section 108 of the Companies Act prescribes:

[9] *Mannalal Khetan* v. *Kedar Nath Khetan*, AIR 1977 SC 536.

… a company shall not register a transfer of shares … unless a proper instrument of transfer duly stamped and executed by or on behalf of the transferor and by or on behalf of the transferee … has been delivered to the company along with the certificate relating to the shares or debentures … or if no such certificate is in existence along with the letter of allotment of the shares.

The board of directors of the company passed a resolution transferring the shares. This was done without following the above procedure. The members of the Khetan family, disadvantaged by this action of the company, contested the enforcement of the agreement form by the members for transfer of the shares. The dispute came before the Supreme Court. The case involved questions on company law, the provisions on transfer of shares, and contracts and illegality. At times, a law clearly prohibits certain activities. At other times, the requirement of the law and its scope may be contentious. The first question in this case was: Did company law prohibit the board from transferring the shares? Only if the answer to this question were yes would the agreement among the members to transfer the shares be a violation of the law. The Supreme Court explored both questions with reference to Section 108 of the Companies Act. It noted:

The words 'shall not register', are mandatory in character. The mandatory character is strengthened by the negative form of the language. The prohibition against transfer without complying with the provisions of the Act is emphasised by the negative language. … Negative words are clearly prohibitory and are ordinarily used as a legislative device to make a statutory provision imperative.

…

Where a contract, express or implied, is expressly or by implication forbidden by statute, no court will lend its assistance to give it effect. A contract is void if prohibited by a statute under a penalty, even without express declaration that the contract is void, because such a penalty implies a prohibition. The penalty may be imposed with intent merely to deter persons from entering into the contract or for the purposes of revenue or that the contract shall not be entered into so as to be valid at law. A distinction is sometimes made between contracts entered into with the object of committing an illegal act and contracts expressly or impliedly prohibited by statute. The distinction is that in the former class one has only to look and see what acts the statute prohibits; it does not matter whether or not it prohibits a contract; if a contract is made to do a prohibited act, that contract will be unenforceable. In the latter class, one has to consider what act the statute prohibits, but what contracts it prohibits. One is not concerned at all with the intent of the parties, if the parties enter into a prohibited contract, that contract is unenforceable.

It is well established that a contract which involves in its fulfilment the doing of an act prohibited by statute is void. The legal maxim a *pactis privatorum publico juri non derogatur* means that private agreements cannot alter the general law. Where a contract, express or implied, is expressly or by implication forbidden by statute, no court can lend its assistance to give it effect. What is done in contravention of the provisions of an Act of the Legislature cannot be made the subject of an action.

If anything is against law though it is not prohibited in the statute but only a penalty is annexed the agreement is void. In every case where a statute inflicts a penalty for doing an act, though the act be not prohibited, yet the thing is unlawful, because it is not intended that a statute would inflict a penalty for a lawful act.

Penalties are imposed by statute for two distinct purposes (1) for the protection of the public against fraud, or for some other object of public policy; (2) for the purpose of securing certain sources of revenue either to the State or to certain public bodies. If it is clear that a penalty is imposed by statute for the purpose of preventing something from being done on some ground of public policy, the thing prohibited, if done, will be treated as void, even though the penalty if imposed is not enforceable.

The provisions contained in Section 108 of the Act are for the reasons indicated earlier mandatory.... Therefore, the company by registering the transfer of shares was obviously permitting the transfer and such action on the part of the company being in violation of the prohibition is contrary to law.... When the receiver held the scripts and the transfer forms it was not open to the persons in whose names the shares originally stood to exercise rights of ownership in respect thereof or to transfer their ownership to anyone else.

From the judgment we can identify the following ways in which a contract can be void: (1) A statute declares a class of contracts to be void. (2) A statute prohibits formation of certain kinds of agreements. (3) A statute prescribes a penalty for entering in certain kinds of contracts. (4) A contract can be fulfilled only by doing what the law has prohibited. In this case, the dispute was on the contract between two parties to transfer the shares of a company. As the shares were attached, the contract could not have been performed without violating the prohibitions contained in Section 108 of the Company Law. Thus, the contract between the members of the Khetan family to transfer the shares was void.

Court Case: Nanakram v. Kundalrai

This case relates to a lease of a building premises that was executed in a manner inconsistent with the Central Provinces and Berar Letting of Houses and Rent Control Order, 1949.[10] Clause 22(1) of the Order required the landlord, within seven days of becoming aware that his house will become available for occupation, to intimate the deputy commissioner of the vacancy. The occupation of the house was to be done under Clause 23. This clause anticipated two situations. If the landlord indicates that he needs the house for his own occupation, and if the deputy commissioner was satisfied of the genuineness of the landlord's need, he would permit him to occupy the house. Alternatively, if the landlord had indicated his intention to

---

[10] *Nanakram* v. *Kundalrai*, AIR 1986 SC 1194.

rent the premises, it was in the powers of the deputy commissioner to direct the landlord to take a tenant assigned by him. The allotment of tenancy was to be done from a class of persons including government officers and evicted persons. Clause 23(3) provided that if the deputy commissioner did not pass any order within fifteen days of the receipt of the intimation by the landlord under Clause 22, the landlord would be free to rent it to any person.

Kundalraj owned a building that he rented to Nanakram from 1 October 1968 without following the procedure, prescribed in Clause 22, of notifying the Deputy Commissioner of the vacancy and giving him the discretion of appointing a tenant. Nanakram used the premises to run a shop. On 19 January 1980, Kundalraj petitioned the Controller for permission to terminate the lease of Nanakram on the ground that he wanted the premises for his son, who wanted to start a business. The contention was that as the tenancy was created in violation of Clause 22 and 23, it was void and there was no valid relationship of landlord and tenant. The Supreme Court ruled:

The landlord is prohibited by Cl. 22(1) from occupying the house or granting a lease except in accordance with Cl. 23. There is a prohibition under Cl. 22(2) on any other person seeking to occupy the house, except again in accordance with Cl. 23. In Cl. 23 it is the Deputy Commissioner who will order the landlord to let the vacant house to a person indicated by him, a person who falls in one of the categories specified in the clause or, if he is satisfied, he may permit the landlord himself to occupy the house..... Nowhere does the Rent Control Order mandate that the Deputy Commissioner must eject a person who has entered into possession of a house in violation of Cl. 22. If upon a view of the circumstances prevailing then, the Deputy Commissioner takes no action in the matter, there is no reason why the lease between the landlord and the tenant, although inconsistent

with Cl. 22, should not be binding as between the parties thereto. It is not a void transaction. There is nothing in the Rent Control Order declaring it to be so. Now if the lease is not void then it is not open to either party to avoid the lease on the ground that it is inconsistent with Cl. 22. The parties would be bound, as between them, to observe the conditions of the lease, and it cannot be assailed by either party in a proceeding between them.

In a following case, *Nutan Kumar* v. *2nd Additional District Judge*[11] the Allahabad High Court was not convinced with the judgment and differed with it. In appeal, the Supreme Court reversed the judgment of the Allahabad High Court. The question was, why should a contract that violates a tenancy law not be void? The Supreme Court, upholding its judgment in *Nanakram* v. *Kundalrai*, thus summarized it:

In the case of Nanakram v. Kundalrai ... the question was whether a lease in violation of statutory provisions was void. It was held that in the absence of any mandatory provision obliging eviction in case of contravention of the provisions of the Act the lease would not be void and the parties would be bound, as between themselves, to observe the conditions of lease. It was held that neither of them could assail the lease in a proceeding between themselves.

In other words, if eviction were a penalty, it would have implied that a contract without following the order was void. The court in this case brought out that not every violation of a law would lead to a contract being declared void. The scope and object of the tenancy law was to regulate the conduct of the landlord and not the contract between the landlord and the tenant. Thus, the contract was not forbidden by the law.

[11] *Nutan Kumar* v. *2nd Aditional District Judge*, AIR 2002 SC 3456.

Court Case: B.O.I. Finance Limited v. Custodian

Some banks used to enter into contracts with different brokers for the purchase and sale of certain securities that were not listed on any stock exchange.[12] The transaction consisted of two inter-connected legs. The first, or the ready leg, consisted of the sale of securities at a specified price. The securities were sold and their price realized. The second or forward leg consisted of a sale-back of the same securities to the banks at a latter date, at a price determined on the first date. The government issued a notification under the Securities Contracts (Regulation) Act, prohibiting such forward contracts. It expressly permitted sale of securities by spot delivery, or the first leg of the transaction. The dispute in the case was about whether the entire agreement would become void or the two transactions could be severed. To appraise the case, we would need to understand Section 57 of the Contract Act. It provides:

57. Reciprocal promise to do things legal, and also other things illegal—Where persons reciprocally promise, firstly, to do certain things which are legal, and, secondly, under specified circumstances, to do certain other things which are illegal, the first set of promises is a contract, but the second is a void agreement.

The Supreme Court ruled:

Section 57 applies to cases where two sets of promises are distinct. When the void part of an agreement can be properly separated from the latter does not become invalid. The ready-forward transaction consists of two parts. In the ready leg, there is a purchase or sale of securities at a stated price, which is executed on payment of consideration for the spot delivery of the security certificates together with transfer forms. The full and absolute ownership of the title in securities vests in the purchaser, the entire property in the

---

[12] *B.O.I. Finance Limited* v. *Custodian*, AIR 1997 SC 1952.

security passing immediately upon such delivery and payment. The seller is divested of all the rights, title and interests in the said securities. The forward leg is to be performed at a later date on the stated price being paid. The securities are to be delivered back when the title in interest therein would pass to the original seller. It is clear that such a ready-forward transaction consists of a set of reciprocal promises. The first set of promises was fully executed, but the second set remained executory. Section 57 of the Contract Act would thus be attracted to the present case, the effect of which would be that the first set of promises would constitute a binding contract but the second or the forward leg would be void and unenforceable. Neither the object, nor the consideration of the ready leg is illegal, unlawful or prohibited under Section 23 of the Contract Act. The forward leg is neither the consideration nor the object for entering into the ready leg. At best, it may be that the forward leg provided the parties with the motive for entering into the contract, but that would not affect the severability of the forward leg, which alone is declared illegal under the Securities Control Regulation Act.

…

… It is only the future sale or the re-sale of the securities at a later date which the notification did not permit. This later part of the agreement could not have been entered into and is clearly severable and cannot affect the transfer of the title which had already taken place at the time of the execution of the ready leg.

The definition of 'lawful' in Section 23 provides two further grounds; either the consideration or object of an agreement is fraudulent, or it 'involves or implies injury to the person or property of another'. This was to hold contracts which were undesirable but yet not in violation of any law void. Since then, there has been a proliferation of legislative activity. It is hard to find an act that is fraudulent and yet not prohibited by some law or the other. Similarly, every form of injury to a person or property is prohibited by some law or the other. Thus, the provision does not find much application.

To conclude, a contract may interface with illegality in many ways. A law may prohibit certain kinds of contracts. The prohibition may be provided in express terms or could be inferred from penalty and other terms. Such contracts are void and unenforceable. A contract may not directly violate a law, but if permitted, would defeat the provisions of a law. Such contracts are also void. A contract where the parties had agreed to violate a law is void. However, illegality committed by a party in performing a contract without the knowledge or concurrence of the other party does not make the contract void. In judging whether a law forbids a contract, one has to construct the entire statute in ascertaining the class of contracts that are forbidden.

20

Void Contracts

Contract law was created as principles by common law courts. The courts recognized that some kinds of contracts were not desirable for individuals or society as a whole. The courts declared such contracts as void. These included contracts restraining a party from legal proceeding, contracts in restrain of marriage, wager agreements, contracts opposed to public policy, contracts restraining a person from pursuing his trade and profession, and contracts tainted with immorality. We will explore this subject in this chapter.

IMMORALITY

Like illegality, the object or the consideration of a contract can be immoral. In both cases, the contract becomes 'tainted with immorality', and is void. It is the courts that judge whether a particular act is immoral or not. Understandably, the standards by which we judge an act vary with times. In *Gherulal Parakh* v. *Mahadeodas Maiya*, the Supreme Court stated that the meaning of morality is confined to sexual morality.[1] It noted:

[1] *Gherulal Parakh* v. *Mahadeodas Maiya*, AIR 1959 SC 781.

The word 'immoral' is a very comprehensive word. Ordinarily it takes in every aspect of personal conduct deviating from the standard norms of life. It may also be said that what is repugnant to good conscience is immoral. Its varying content depends upon time, place and the stage of civilization of a particular society. In short, no universal standard can be laid down and any law based on such fluid concept defeats its own purpose.

The Supreme Court, however, noted that the application of immorality in Section 23 is in a limited sense of sexual immorality. It noted:

The case law both in England and India confines the operation of the doctrine to sexual immorality. To cite only some instances: settlements in consideration of concubinage, contracts of sale or hire of things to be used in a brothel or by a prostitute for purposes incidental to her profession, agreements to pay money for future illicit cohabitation, promises in regard to marriage for consideration, or contracts facilitating divorce are all held to be void on the ground that the object is immoral.

In this context, we can review the following a leading case on the theme.

Court Case: Pearce v. Brooks

Brooks, a prostitute, hired a decorative brougham (a kind of horse-drawn carriage) from Pearce, a coachbuilder, as a part of her display to attract men.[2] Brooks returned the brougham in a damaged condition and also failed to pay the instalments on the hire of the brougham. Pearce brought an action to recover the due amount and money for damage done to the brougham. Pearce knew that Brooks was a prostitute and that the brougham would be used in the course of her 'calling'. Pollock CB observed:

I have always considered it as settled law, that any person who contributes to the performance of an illegal act by supplying a thing with the knowledge that it is going to be used for that purpose, cannot recover the price of the thing so supplied. ... Nor can any distinction be made between an illegal and an immoral purpose; the rule which is applicable to the matter is, *Ex turpi causâ non oritur actio*, (No action can be based on a disreputable cause.) and whether it is an immoral or an illegal purpose in which the plaintiff has participated, it comes equally within the terms of that maxim, and the effect is the same; no cause of action can arise out of either the one or the other... If, therefore, this article was furnished to the defendant for the purpose of enabling her to make a display favourable to her immoral purposes, the plaintiffs can derive no cause of action from the bargain.

Thus, a contract whose consideration or object is immoral is void. The courts, however, construe immorality to include only sexual immorality.

RESTRAIN OF LEGAL PROCEEDINGS

It is the duty of the State and courts to give justice. A party taking away the right of an individual to go to a court is usurping the powers and role of the state. It is understandable that a contract of this nature should not be enforced. Section 28 expresses the principle:

28. **Agreements in restraint of legal proceedings void**—Every agreement, by which any party thereto is restricted absolutely from enforcing his rights

under or in respect of any contract, by the usual legal proceedings in the ordinary tribunals, or which limits the time within which he may thus enforce his rights, is void to that extent.

The section, however, exempts arbitration proceedings. 'Arbitration' is a means by which contracting parties agree to submit their disputes to some other person(s) rather than to a court. This is mutually beneficial to the parties. Court proceedings can be expensive and time-consuming. The interest of the contracting parties, however, is often to get on with their agreement by quickly resolving any dispute. Further, as court proceedings are open, they make the terms of the dealings of the parties public. Neither of the contracting parties may want to make their terms public. To safeguard the interests of the contracting parties, arbitration has long been subject to legislative supervision.

A restraint in a contract can take three forms: A party may have taken an obligation to not go to any court at all to seek remedy. Clearly, this is a violation of the section. In *Bharat Sanchar Nigam Limited* v. *Motorola India Private Limited*,[3] the terms of the tender provided that the quantum of liquidated damages 'assessed and levied by the purchaser shall be final and not challengeable by the supplier' in arbitration or to any court. The Supreme Court found it 'clearly in restraint of legal proceedings under section 28 of the Indian Contracts Act'.

The second form a restraint takes is in limiting the court a person could go to. Earlier in the book, we explored the basis on which the jurisdiction of a court in relation to contracts is decided under the Civil Procedure Code. Several courts may have concurrent jurisdiction. This can include the place where

---

[2] *Pearce* v. *Brooks*, (1866) LR 1 Ex 213.

[3] *Bharat Sanchar Nigam Limited* v. *Motorola India Private Limited*, AIR 2009 SC 357.

the contract was made and contract is to be performed. In *Hakam Singh* v. *M/s. Gammon (India) Limited*,[4] the Supreme Court ruled:

It is not open to the parties by agreement to confer by their agreement jurisdiction on a court which it does not possess under the Code. But where two courts or more have under the Code of Civil Procedure jurisdiction to try a suit or proceeding an agreement between the parties that the dispute between them shall be tried in one of such courts is not contrary to public policy. Such an agreement does not contravene S. 28 of the Contract Act.

Thus, the parties could not vest a court with jurisdiction when it did not have one under the code. But an agreement to limit jurisdiction among the competent courts is not in violation of Section 28.

The third form of limiting jurisdiction of courts is to reduce the time limit for approaching a court. The Limitation Act provides a time period within which a civil suit must be filed. A contract that lowers the time period violates Section 28. In *Muni Lal* v. *Oriental Fire and General Insurance Company Limited*, [5] the Supreme Court noted:

Section 28 of the Contract Act prohibits prescription of shorter limitation than the one prescribed in the Limitation Act. An agreement which provides that a suit should be brought for the breach of any terms of the agreement within a time shorter than the period of limitation prescribed law is void to that extent. The reason being that such an agreement is absolutely to restrict the parties from enforcing their rights after the expiration of the stipulated period, although it may be within the period of general limitation.

However, there were reservations about the application of the principle in insurance contracts that worded the limitation in a particular manner. The amendment of the section in 1997 has made it clear that all clauses that reduce the normal period of limitation are void.

MARRIAGE AND FAMILY LIFE

X enters into a contract with Y, where Y would divorce her husband and C would pay her Rs 5 lakh in consideration. Y divorced her husband, but X is in breach for not paying the consideration. The case is brought before the court. Marriage and raising a family have been important pillars of human society in all cultures. Thus, contracts undermining the institution of marriage were held as void by common law. In the Indian Contract Act, it manifests in two forms. Contracts to interfere in marital relations are void. An example of this is a contract to get a divorce so as to marry another person. In addition, Section 26 provides:

26. **Agreement in restraint of marriage void**—Every agreement in restraint of the marriage of any person, other than a minor, is void.

The restraint on marriage can be of several kinds, it can be not to marry at all, not to marry for a fixed period, or to marry only a particular person or a class of persons. Such contracts are void. In *Rao Rani* v. *Gulab Rani*,[6] two women claimed to be married to the deceased. The dispute was on succeeding to the landed property of the person. The two women reached an agreement, where both their names were entered as the joint owners of the property in the revenue records. In the event that either of the widows remarried, she would forfeit her interest in the property. The entire property would vest in the other women. One of the women did remarry, and a dispute arose about the validity of the

---

[4] *Hakam Singh* v. *M/s Gammon (India) Limited*, AIR 1971 SC 740.

[5] *Muni Lal* v. *Oriental Fire and General Insurance Company Limited*, AIR 1996 SC 642.

[6] *Rao Rani* v. *Gulab Rani*, (1942) ILR All 810.

contract. The court ruled that it was not a void contract as there was no 'restraint' on marriage. It only provided that if a woman elected to marry, she would be deprived of her rights.

WAGER AGREEMENTS

Section 30 of the India Contract Act makes wager agreements void. It provides:

30. Agreements by way of wager void—Agreements by way of wager are void; and no suit shall be brought for recovering anything alleged to be won on any wager, or entrusted to any person to abide the result of any game or other uncertain event on which any wager is made.

Exception in favour of certain prizes for horse-racing....

The only exception the section makes is to winnings from horse racing. We know that 'wager' refers to the amount of money risked in betting and gambling. Let us explore the scope of the term by identifying the wagers agreements in the following:

1. A and B agree that A would pay B Rs 10 lakh if it rains on Monday in city X.
2. A and B agree that A would give his car to B if it rains on Monday in city X.
3. A and B agree that A would give Rs 5,000 to B if P, a famous cricketer, hits a six in a cricket match.
4. A company has announced that it would give Rs 50,000 to a famous cricketer P if he hits at least one six in a match.
5. A and B agree that A will pay B Rs 10 lakh if it rains on Monday in city X. B is organizing a cricket match and A is an insurance company.

All of these contracts have an element of chance or contingency. However, only situations 1, 2 and 3 are wager agreements. The parties do not have a real interest in the event other than winning or losing the money or the promised good. Situation 4 is a unilateral contract. In situation 5, the parties have a real interest in the event. It is not merely for winning or losing money. We know this as a contract of insurance. Thus, wager agreements are where the parties contract to transact consideration on the happening of an uncertain event without any real interest in the event itself. The Queen's bench in the Carbolic Smoke Ball case explored the scope of a wager agreement:

It is not easy to define with precision what amounts to a wagering contract, nor the narrow line of demarcation which separates a wagering from an ordinary contract; but, according to my view, a wagering contract is one by which two persons, professing to hold opposite views touching the issue of a future uncertain event, mutually agree that, dependent upon the determination of that event, one shall win from the other, and that other shall pay or hand over to him, a sum of money or other stake; neither of the contracting parties having any other interest in that contract than the sum or stake he will so win or lose, there being no other real consideration for the making of such contract by either of the parties. It is essential to a wagering contract that each party may under it either win or lose, whether he will win or lose being dependent on the issue of the event, and, therefore, remaining uncertain until that issue is known. If either of the parties may win but cannot lose, or may lose but cannot win, it is not a wagering contract.

The section does not declare wager agreements to be illegal. This is done by the penal laws. Every wager is not necessarily illegal. If it is illegal, of course, the contract would be void on the grounds of illegality. The section provides that even if a wager agreement is legal, a court cannot take up the case and grant remedy. The following Supreme Court case explores wager in relation to Sections 23 and 30.

Court Case: *Gherulal Parakh* v. *Mahadeodas Maiya*

Gherulal Parakh and Mahadeodas Maiya entered into a partnership to make wagering contracts.[7] The arrangement was that Maiya would agree to buy a certain quantity of goods at a certain price on a future date from some parties based in Hapur. The parties never intended to buy or sell the goods. The difference between the reigning market price for the pre-appointed date and the speculated price was the gain from the wager. It was agreed between the partners that the wager contracts would be made in the name of Mahadeodas Maiya on behalf of the firm and that the profit and loss resulting from the transactions would be borne by them in equal shares. The net result of all these transactions was a loss. As the contracts were in the name of Mahadeodas Maiya, he had to pay the Hapur merchants the entire amount due to them. Gherulal Parakh denied his liability to bear his share of the loss. Maiya filed a suit claiming the equal share of Gherulal Parakh in bearing the loss. The contention of Gherulal was that the object of forming the partnership was the wager. Wagers fall under Section 23 as forbidden by law, immoral, and opposed to public policy. Thus, the partnership was not enforceable. The Supreme Court examined the application of Section 23 to an agreement made for a wager.

Re (i)—forbidden by law

Under S. 30 of the Indian Contract Act, agreements by way of wager are void ... the argument proceeds, such a transaction, being void under the said section, is also forbidden by law within the meaning of S. 23 of the Contract Act. The question, shortly stated, is whether what is void can be equated with what is forbidden by law. This argument is not a new one, but has been raised in England as well as in India and

[7] *Gherulal Parakh* v. *Mahadeodas Maiya*, AIR 1959 SC 781.

has uniformly been rejected. ... Sir William Anson in his book 'On Law of Contracts' succinctly states the legal position thus, at page 205:

'... the law may either actually forbid an agreement to be made, or it may merely say that if it is made the courts will not enforce it. In the former case it is illegal, in the latter only void; but inasmuch as illegal contracts are also void, though void contracts are not necessarily illegal, the distinction is for most purposes not important, and even judges seem sometimes to treat the two terms as inter-changeable.'

... (under) S. 30 of the Indian Contract Act ... though a wager is void and unenforceable, it is not forbidden by law and therefore the object of a collateral agreement is not unlawful under S. 23 of the Contract Act; and partnership being an agreement within the meaning of S. 23 of the Indian Contract Act, it is not unlawful, though its object is to carry on wagering transactions. We, therefore, hold that in the present case the partnership is not unlawful within the meaning of S. 23(a) of the Contract Act.

Re (ii)—Public Policy

Public policy or the policy of the law is an illusive concept; it has been described as 'untrustworthy guide', 'variable quality', 'uncertain one' 'unruly horse', etc; the primary duty of a Court of Law is to enforce a promise which the parties have made and to uphold the sanctity of contracts which form the basis of society, but in certain cases, the court may relieve them of their duty on a rule founded on what is called the public policy; for want of better words Lord Atkin describes that something done contrary to public policy is a harmful thing, but the doctrine is extended not only to harmful cases but also to harmful tendencies; this doctrine of public policy is only a branch of common law, and, just like any other branch of common law, it is governed by precedents; the principles have been crystallized under different heads and though it is permissible for courts to expound and apply them to different situations, it should only be invoked in clear and incontestable cases of harm to the public; though the heads are not closed and though theoretically it may be permissible to evolve a new head under exceptional circumstances of a changing world, it is advisable in the interest of stability of society not to make any attempt to discover new heads in these days.

This leads us to the question whether in England or in India a definite principle of public policy has been evolved or recognized invalidating wagers. So far as England is concerned... there has never been such a rule of public policy in that country.... The legal position is the same in India.

Re. Point 3—Immorality

The word 'immoral' is a very comprehensive word. Ordinarily it takes in every aspect of personal conduct deviating from the standard norms of life. It may also be said that what is repugnant to good conscience is immoral. Its varying content depends upon time, place and the stage of civilization of a particular society. In short, no universal standard can be laid down and any law based on such fluid concept defeats its own purpose. The provisions of S. 23 of the Contract Act indicate the legislative intention to give it a restricted meaning. Its juxtaposition with an equally illusive concept, public policy, indicates that it is used in a restricted sense; otherwise there would be overlapping of the two concepts. In its wide sense what is immoral may be against public policy, for public policy covers political, social and economic ground of objection. Decided cases and authoritative text-books writers, therefore, confined it, with every justification, only to sexual immorality. The other limitation imposed on the word by the statute, namely, 'courts consider immoral', brings out the idea that it is also a branch of the common law like the doctrine of public policy, and, therefore, should be confined to the principles recognised and settled by courts. Precedents confine the said concept only to sexual immorality and no case has been brought to our notice where it has been applied to any head other than sexual immorality. In the circumstances, we cannot evolve a new head so as to bring in wagers within its fold.

...

For the foregoing reasons we must hold that the suit partnership was not unlawful within the meaning of S. 23 of the Indian Contract Act.

A wager agreement may be illegal, but nevertheless it would be a void agreement. The implication appears to be that any entity organizing a lottery can refuse to pay the prize money. This is what happened in *Subhash*

Kumar Manwani v. *State of MP*.[8] The lottery was held after obtaining licence under the relevant law and was perfectly legitimate. The high court, however, refused to give remedy to the unpaid winner. It noted:

The principle and purpose behind Section 30 of the Contract Act to treat an agreement by way of wager as void is that the law discourages people to enter into games of chance and make earning by trying their luck instead of spending their time, energy and labour for more fruitful and useful work for themselves, their family and the society.... it is clear that the nature of the agreement for payment of a prize won on a lottery ticket continues to be in the nature of a wager to which the provisions of Section 30 of the Contract Act would be applicable irrespective of the fact that in order to check, reduce or control the evil of such gambling both Centre and the State have been permitted legislative powers in the Constitution.

AGREEMENTS OPPOSED TO PUBLIC POLICY

Section 23 declares a contract opposed to public policy void. This is surprising. Policy is different from law. The state declares the direction it wishes to pursue. We know this as policy. A policy becomes binding on the subjects only when it manifests itself as the law. In this context, it is surprising that the courts have been given the nebulous power to declare a contract void on the grounds of it being opposed to public policy. It was, thus, commented in 1853 by Justice Parke on 'public policy': 'It is the province of the statesman, and not the lawyer, to discuss, and the legislature to determine what is best for the public good, and to provide for it by proper enactments. It is the province of the judge to expound the law only'[9]

[8] *Subhash Kumar Manwani* v. *State of MP*, AIR 2000 MP 109.
[9] *Egerton* v. *Brownlow (Earl)*, (1853) 4 HL Cas 1.

This can be explained by putting contract law in its historical perspective. In our contemporary context, the division between the legislature and the judiciary is sharp and well-defined. Also, we live in times where every aspect of our life is legislated. It was not always like this. In the past, the judges were only the extensions of the King. It was natural for them to act on behalf of the King, and prohibit what he would not have approved of. The modern state took over from the King and the common law formulated the principle of the holding contracts that were opposed to public policy void.

In dealing with the wide powers given to them, the judges came up with different heads for themes that attracted the principle on public policy. Two of them, agreements in restraint of marriage and agreements in restraint of trade, became prominent and principles in their own rights. These are codified as Sections 26 and 27 in the Indian Contract Act. The other heads of public policy have been trading with the enemy, trafficking in public office, interference with administration of justice, and unfair or unreasonable dealings.

Over the years, there has been a proliferation of laws, legislating on all aspects of economic and social life. One would have expected what was opposed to public policy to have been subsumed as illegality in Section 23. Despite the legislation, with the changes in society, numerous contexts emerge requiring the courts to apply the principle of public policy. The relationship between the state, law, and society is interactive and dynamic. If some issues are settled by the law, newer ones emerge for the state and courts to formulate policy on. The courts have been uncomfortable all along with the wide and unregulated power under the head of public policy. Since its inception, the category has

been described with terms like 'untrustworthy guide', 'variable quality', 'uncertain one', and 'unruly horse'. Despite this, for the reasons stated above, the rule finds application. Let us review the following landmark case on the theme.

Court Case: Central Inland Water Transport Corporation Ltd v. Brojo Nath Ganguly

Several service contracts have a clause stating that the employee can terminate the service by serving a notice for a fixed period, say three months.[10] Similarly, the employer can terminate the service of the employee simply by serving a notice of three months. The employer does not need to give any reason for the termination. Brojo Nath Ganguly was an employee of the Central Inland Water Corporation Limited, whose services were terminated by a three-month notice from the Corporation. The case came before the Supreme Court, challenging the constitutional validity of the termination. In addition to the Corporation being the 'State', within the meaning of the provisions on Fundamental Rights, the arrangement could also be seen as one of a service contract between two parties. It was contended that excessive and arbitrary powers in the hands of the employer to terminate services of an employee without assigning any reason was coercive and opposed to public policy. The Supreme Court ruled:

The Contract Act does not define the expression 'public policy' or 'opposed to public policy'. From the very nature of things, the expressions 'public policy', 'opposed to public policy', or 'contrary to public policy' are incapable of precise definition. Public policy, however, is not the policy of a particular government. It connotes some matter which

---

[10] *Central Inland Water Transport Corporation Limited* v. *Brojo Nath Ganguly*, AIR 1986 SC 1571.

concerns the public good and the public interest. The concept of what is for the public good or in the public interest or what would be injurious or harmful to the public good or the public interest has varied from time to time. As new concepts take the place of old, transactions which were once considered against public policy are now being upheld by the courts and similarly where there has been a well-recognized head of public, policy—the courts have not shirked from extending it to new transactions and changed circumstances and have at times not even flinched from inventing a new head of public policy. There are two schools of thought—'the narrow view' school and 'the broad view' school. According to the former, courts cannot create new heads of public policy whereas the latter countenances judicial law-making in this area. The adherents of 'the narrow view' school would not invalidate a contract on the ground of public policy unless that particular ground had been well established by authorities. Hardly ever has the voice of the timorous spoken more clearly and loudly than in these words of *Lord Davey in Janson v. Driefontein Consolidated Mines, Limited* (1902) AC 484, 500, 'Public policy is always an unsafe and treacherous ground for legal decision.' That was in the year 1902. Seventy-eight years' earlier, Burrough, J., in *Richardson* v. *Mellish* (1824) 2 Bing 229, 252 SC 130 ER 294, 303, and (1824-34) All ER Reprint 258, 266. described public policy as 'a very unruly horse, and when once you get astride it you never know where it will carry you.' The Master of the Rolls, Lord Denning, however, was not a man to shy away from unmanageable horses and in words which conjure up before our eyes the picture of the young Alexander the Great Taming Bucephalus, he said in *Enderby Town Football Club Ltd.* v. *Football Association Ltd.*, (1971) Ch 591, 606, 'With a good man in the saddle, the unruly horse can be kept in control. It can jump over obstacles.' Had the timorous always held 'the field, not only the doctrine of public policy but even the Common Law or the principles of Equity would never have evolved. Sir William Holdsworth in his 'History of English Law', Volume III, page 55, has said:

'In fact, a body of law like the common law, which has grown up gradually with the growth of the nation, necessarily acquires some fixed principles, and if it is to maintain these principles it must be able, on the ground of public policy or some other like ground, to suppress practices which, under ever new disguises, seek to weaken or negative them.'

It is thus clear that the principles governing public policy must be and are capable, on proper occasion, of expansion or modification. Practices which were considered perfectly normal at one time have today become obnoxious and oppressive to public conscience. If there is no head of public policy which covers a case, then the court must in consonance with public conscience and in keeping with public good and public interest declare such practice to be opposed to public policy. Above all, in deciding any case which may not be covered by authority our courts have before them the beacon light of the Preamble to the Constitution. Lacking precedent, the court can always be guided by that light and the principles underlying the Fundamental Rights and the Directive Principles enshrined in our Constitution.

The normal rule of Common Law has been that a party who seeks to enforce an agreement which is opposed to public policy will be non-suited. The case of *A. Schroeder Music Publishing Co. Ltd.* v. *Macaulay* (1974 1 WLR 1308), however, establishes that where a contract is vitiated as being contrary to public policy, the party adversely affected by it can sue to have it declared void. The case may be different where the purpose of the contract is illegal or immoral. In *Kedar Nath Motani* v. *Prahlad Rai* (1960) 1 SCR 861 : (AIR 1960 SC 213) reversing the high court and restoring the decree passed by the trial court declaring the appellants' title to the lands in suit and directing the respondents who were the appellants' benamidars to restore possession, this court, after discussing the English and Indian law on the subject, said (at page 873) (of SCR): (at pp. 218–19 of AIR):

'The correct position in law, in our opinion, is that what one has to see is whether the illegality goes so much to the root of the matter that the plaintiff cannot bring his action without relying upon the illegal transaction into which he had entered. If the illegality be trivial or venial, as stated by Williston and the plaintiff is not required to rest his case upon that illegality, then public policy demands that the defendant should not be allowed to take advantage of the position. A strict view, of course, must be taken of the plaintiff's conduct, and he should not be allowed to circumvent the illegality by resorting to some subterfuge or by misstating the facts. It however, the matter is clear and the illegality is not required to be pleaded or proved as part of the cause of action and the plaintiff recanted before the illegal purpose was achieved, then, unless it be of such a gross nature as to outrage the conscience of the court, the plea of the defendant should not prevail.'

The types of contracts to which the principle formulated by us above applies are not contracts which are tainted with illegality but are contracts which contain terms which are so unfair and unreasonable that they shock the conscience of the court. They are opposed to public policy and require to be adjudged void.

...

We will now test the validity of R. 9(i) by applying to it the principle formulated above.... Rule 9(i) confers upon the Corporation the power to terminate the service of a permanent employee by giving him three months' notice in writing or in lieu thereof to pay him the equivalent of three months' basic pay and dearness allowance.... It confers absolute and arbitrary power upon the Corporation.... There are no guidelines whatever laid down to indicate in what circumstances the power given by Rule 9(i) is to be exercised by the Corporation. No opportunity whatever of a hearing is at all to be afforded to the permanent employee whose service is being terminated in the exercise of this power.... Rule 9(i) thus confers an absolute, arbitrary and unguided power upon the Corporation. It violates one of the two great rules of natural justice—the audi alteram partem rule. It is not only in cases to which Art. 14 applies that the rules of natural justice come into play.

...

A clause such as Rule 9(i) in a contract of employment affecting large sections of the public is harmful and injurious to the public interest for it tends to create a sense of insecurity in the minds of those to whom it applies and consequently it is against public good. Such a clause, therefore, is opposed to public policy and being opposed to public policy, it is void under section 23 of the Indian Contract Act.

...

It was also submitted on behalf of the Appellants that Rule 9(i) was supported by mutuality inasmuch as it conferred an equal right upon both the parties, for under it just as the employer could terminate the employee's service by giving him three months' notice or by paying him three months' basic pay and dearness allowance in lieu thereof, the employee could leave the service by giving three months' notice and when he failed to give such notice, the Corporation could deduct an equivalent amount from whatever may be payable to him. It is true that there is mutuality in clause 9(i)—the same mutuality as in a contract between the lion and the lamb that both will be free to roam about in the jungle and each will be at liberty to devour the other. When one considers the unequal position of the Corporation and its employees, the argument of mutuality becomes laughable.

...

In the result, both these appeals fail and are dismissed but the order passed by the Calcutta High Court is modified by substituting for the declaration given by it a declaration that clause (i) of Rule 9 of the 'Service, Discipline and Appeal Rules 1979' of the Central Inland Water Transport Corporation Limited is void under S. 23 of the Contract Act, 1872, as being opposed to public policy and is also ultra vires Art. 14 of the Constitution to the extent that it confers upon the Corporation the right to terminate the employment of a permanent employee by giving him three months notice in writing or by paying him the equivalent of three months basic pay and dearness allowance in lieu of such notice.

State, law, and public policy are interactive spheres. A contract in violation of a law is void. In addition, going beyond the existing law, a contract opposed to public policy can be declared void by the courts. Trafficking in public office, interference with administration of justice, and unfair or unreasonable dealings are some of the grounds on which the courts declare a contract to be opposed to public policy, and thus void.

RESTRAINT ON TRADE

Agreements in 'restraint of trade' are void. Section 27 provides:

Section 27. Agreement in restraint of trade void— Every agreement by which any one is restrained from exercising a lawful profession, trade or business of any kind, is to that extent void.

Exception 1—One who sells the good-will of a business may agree with the buyer to refrain from carrying on a similar business, within specified local limits; so long as the buyer, or any person deriving title to the good-will from him, carries on a like business therein, provided that such limits appear to the court reasonable, regard being had to the nature of the business.

The wording of the provision appears harsh and sweeping. Binding and restraining others is the very essence of contracts. Thus, every contract would become void under of Section 27. The genesis of the provision, in common law, is in the general sense of justice and equity that a person should not be deprived of his occupation, trade, or profession. These are the very means by which a person comes to have an existence in a physical and social sense. To begin with, the common law courts took all agreements in restraint of trade to be bad. As trade, commerce, and business practices changed, the courts formulated that reasonable restraint need not be declared void. Thus, the common law courts ask two questions: First, is there a restrain on trade? Second, is the restrain reasonable? The Indian Contract Act has worded it absolutely in only the first sense. The courts, however, recognize that impositions on the contracting parties can be to both foster and restrain trade. A leading case on the theme is *Gujarat Bottling Co. Limited, M/s v. Coca Cola Company.*

Case: Gujarat Bottling Co. Ltd, M/s. v. Coca Cola Company

The case is a corporate tussle between Coca Cola and Pepsi. Coca Cola got in a franchise agreement for bottling and distributing its products with a company, Gujarat Bottling Company Ltd (GBC).[11] During the subsistence

[11] *Gujarat Bottling Co. Ltd., M/s. v. Coca Cola Company*, AIR 1995 SC 2372.

of the agreement, the shareholdings of GBC changed and it came in the hands of Pepsi. GBC could not bottle and market for Pepsi as its franchise agreement, signed in 1993, had several clauses putting restrictions on it. Clause 20 and 23 gave the powers to Coca Cola to terminate the agreement without notice. Clause 21 provided for either party terminating the agreement by giving a one-year notice. Clause 14 contained, in the words of the Supreme Court, '...a negative covenant by GBC not to manufacture, bottle, sell, deal or otherwise be concerned with the products, beverages of any other brands or trade marks/ trade names during the subsistence of the agreement including the period of one year's notice as contemplated in paragraph 21.'

GBC contended that the clause was in restraint of trade and, thus, void. The Supreme Court noted:

We do not propose to go into the question whether reasonableness of restraint is outside the purview of Section 27 of the Contract Act and for the purpose of the present case we will proceed on the basis that an enquiry into reasonableness of the restraint is not envisaged by Section 27. On that view instead of being required to consider two questions as in England, the courts in India have only to consider the question whether the contract is or is not in restraint of trade. It is, therefore, necessary to examine whether the negative stipulation contained in paragraph 14 of the 1993 Agreement can be regarded as in restraint of trade. This involves the question, what is meant by a contract in restraint of trade?

The Supreme Court turned to the ESSO case, a landmark judgment on restraint on trade, and inferred that a stipulation in a contract can be for advancement of trade and should not be regarded as being in restraint of trade. The judgment in the ESSO Petroleum case had summarized its position:

Somewhere there must be a line between those contracts which are in restraint of trade and whose reasonableness can, therefore, be considered by the courts and those contracts which merely regulate the normal commercial relations between the parties and are, therefore, free from doctrine.

...

The doctrine does not apply to ordinary commercial contracts for the regulation and promotion of trade during the existence of the contract, provided that any prevention of work outside the contract, viewed as a whole, is directed towards the absorption of the parties' services and not their sterilisation. Sole agencies are normal and necessary incident of commerce and those who desire the benefits of a sole agency must deny themselves the opportunities of other agencies.

...

It is not to be supposed, or encouraged, that a bare allegation that a contract limits a trader's freedom of action exposes a party suing on it to the burden of jurisdiction. There will always be certain general categories of contracts as to which it can be said, with some degree of certainty, that the doctrine does or does not apply to them. Positively, there are likely to be certain sensitive areas as to which the law will require in every case the test of reasonableness to be passed: such an area has long been and still is that of contracts between employer and employees as regards the period after the employment has ceased. Negatively, and it is this that concerns us here, there will be types of contract as to which the law should be prepared to say with some confidence that they do not enter into the field of restrain of trade at all.

...

How, then can such contracts be defined or at least identified? No exhaustive test can be stated (probably no precise non-exhaustive test. But the development of the law does seem to show that Judges have been able to dispense from the necessity of jurisdiction under a public policy test) of reasonableness such contracts or provisions of contracts as, under contemporary conditions, may be found to have passed into the accepted and normal currency of commercial or contractual or conveyancing relations.

The Supreme Court concluded:

There is a growing trend to regulate distribution of goods and services through franchise agreements providing for grant of franchise by the franchiser on certain terms and conditions to the franchisee. Such agreements often incorporate a condition that the franchisee shall not deal with competing goods. Such a condition restricting the right of the franchisee to deal with competing goods is for facilitating the distribution of the goods of the franchiser and it cannot be regarded as in restraint of trade.

...the 1993 Agreement is an agreement for grant of franchise by Coca Cola to GBC to manufacture, bottle, sell and distribute the various beverages for which the trade marks were acquired by Coca Cola. 1993 Agreement is thus a commercial agreement whereunder both the parties have undertaken obligations for promoting the trade in beverages for their mutual benefit. The purpose underlying paragraph 14 of the said agreement is to promote the trade and the negative stipulation under challenge seeks to achieve the said purpose by requiring GBC to wholeheartedly apply to promoting the sale of the products of Coca Cola. In that context, it is also relevant to mention that the said negative stipulation operates only during the period the agreement is in operation because of the express use of the words 'during the subsistence of this agreement the period of one year as contemplated in paragraph 21,' in paragraph 14. Except in cases where the contract is wholly one sided, normally the doctrine of restraint of trade is not attracted in cases where the restriction is to operate during the period the contract is subsisting and it applies in respect of a restriction which operates after the termination of the contract.

Every contract necessarily restrains the parties by binding them with obligations to each other. The restraints are beneficial and productive. Without rights and obligations there would be complete anarchy. The restraints give certainty to the parties. However, excessive and unreasonable restraint can completely suppress the other person and is not desirable in the larger social interest. The common law courts came up with the principle that a person should not be deprived of his occupation, trade, or profession. These are the very means by which a person comes to have an existence in the physical and social sense. Thus, the concept 'restraint of trade' originally dealt with the trade, occupation and profession of individuals. As corporate bodies came into being, the principles were extended to them. As a result, the provision is of great significance to the individuals as well as commercial organizations.

The provision finds application in relation to stipulations in employment contracts prohibiting employees from taking up employment with competitors. In this, on the one hand, the employees' right to seek appropriate employment should not be constrained. On the other hand, the employer should not suffer a loss by passing on trade secrets and other information to the competitors. The restraints during the terms of employment have usually been held not to be void and not against Section 27 of the Contract Act.[12] However, the courts do not favour restraint after the termination of the contract. The Supreme Court in *Superintendence Company of India (P) Limited* v. *Krishna Murgai*[13] noted:

A contract in restraint of trade is one by which a party restricts his future liberty to carry on his trade, business or profession in such manner and with

such persons as he chooses. A contract of this class is prima facie void, but it becomes binding upon proof that the restriction is justifiable in the circumstances as being reasonable from the point of view of the parties themselves and also to the community.

In summary, common law courts declared certain kinds of contracts void. The reason for each was different. The court could not be a part of something clearly immoral. Wager was never looked upon as legitimate or socially desirable. The institution of marriage has always been held too sacrosanct for it to be tampered with. Every person needs a trade or occupation, and a contract cannot deny a person this very basis for survival. In the past century, the states have vigorously legislated to govern all aspects of economic and social life. Thus, such contracts can also fall under the head of illegality. However, our ever-changing social life produces newer issues, continually making the categories relevant.

[12] *Niranjan Shankar Golikari* v. *Century Spinning and Manufacturing Co., Limited*, AIR 1967 SC 1098.
[13] *Superintendence Company of India (P) Limited* v. *Krishna Murgai*, AIR 1980 SC 1717.

21

Mutual Mistake

In an earlier chapter, we looked at contracts formed by mistaken identity. We saw the case where one party was mistaken about the identity of the other. In fact, this mistake was induced by one of the parties. This was a case of unilateral mistake, where only one party is mistaken about a substantive aspect of the contract. 'Snapping up' is another form of unilateral contract where the acceptor knows that the offeror is mistaken about the price or some other significant aspect of the contract, and rushes to accept the offer and bind the offeror to the terms. In some contracts, both the parties are mistaken about a significant aspect of the contract. Both the parties may even be mistaken about the same thing. This is called common mistake. If the parties are mistaken in different ways on the same aspect, it is called mutual mistake. When both the parties are mistaken, there is no meeting of minds, the very basis for formation of an agreement. Thus, these agreements are taken to be void.

Sections 20, 21 and 22 provide as follows:

20. Agreement void where both parties are under mistake as to matter of fact—Where both the parties to an agreement are under a mistake as to a matter of fact essential to the agreement, the agreement is void.

Explanation—An erroneous opinion as to the value of the thing which forms the subject-matter of the agreement is not to be deemed a mistake as to a matter of fact.

21. Effect of mistakes as to law—A contract is not voidable because it was caused by a mistake as to any law in force in India; but a mistake as to a law not in force in India has the same effect as a mistake of fact.

22. Contract caused by mistake of one party as to matter of fact—A contract is not voidable merely because it was caused by one of the parties to it being under a mistake as to a matter of fact.

The mistake should be a matter of fact 'essential' to the contract. In other words, it should be fundamental and go to the roots of the contract as opposed to being peripheral. Whether a mistake is 'essential' to the contract will depend on the nature of the mistake. The mistake can be as to the existence of the subject matter. In *Couturier* v. *Hastie*,[1] a buyer sold a cargo of corn to a sub-buyer. At the time of the sale, without the knowledge of the buyer, the master of the ship had sold the corn at a port as it was in danger of perishing. Thus, at the time of the contract both the parties were mistaken about the very existence of

[1] *Couturier* v. *Hastie*, (1852) 8 Exch 40.

the good. Another example is the sale of life insurance on a person, who had died unbeknownst to both parties. *Strickland v. Turner*.[2] A common mistake on the existence of the subject matter can also be in relation to the rights over the subject matter. In *Cooper v. Phibbs*,[3] a person A agreed to take a lease of a fishery from B, though, contrary to the belief of both parties at the time, A was a tenant for life of the fishery and B appears to have had no title at all. In *Bell v. Lever Brothers Limited*[4] Lord Atkin thus described the mistake in relation to the subject matter:

... the agreement of A and B for the purchase of a specific article is void if in fact the article had perished before the date of sale. In this case, though the parties in fact were agreed about the subject-matter, yet a consent to transfer or take delivery of something not existent is deemed useless, the consent is nullified. As codified in the Sale of Goods Act, 1893, the contract is expressed to be void if the seller was in ignorance of the destruction of the specific chattel. ... Corresponding to mistake as to the existence of the subject-matter is mistake as to title in cases where unknown to the parties the buyer is already the owner of that which the seller purports to sell him. The parties intended to effectuate a transfer of ownership; such a transfer is impossible ...

Another kind of mistake can be on the quality of the subject matter. An example is *Kennedy v. Panama, New Zealand and Australian Royal Mail Co.*,[5] where a person applied for shares in a company on the faith of a prospectus, which stated falsely but innocently that the company had a binding contract with the government of New Zealand for the carriage of mails. On discovering the true facts the subscriber brought an action for the recovery of the sums that he had paid on calls. The company claimed mutual mistake. In this contract on the sale of shares, the contention was not on the existence of the shares but its quality. Dealing with this category, Atkin in Bell noted:

Mistake as to quality of the thing contracted for raises more difficult questions. In such a case a mistake will not affect assent unless it is the mistake of both parties and is as to the existence of some quality which makes the thing without the quality essentially different from the thing as it was believed to be. Of course it may appear that the parties contracted that the article should possess the quality which one or other or both mistakenly believed it to possess. But in such a case there is a contract and the inquiry is a different one, being whether the contract as to quality amounts to a condition or a warranty, a different branch of the law. ... In these cases I am inclined to think that the true analysis is that there is a contract, but that the one party is not able to supply the very thing, whether goods or services, that the other party contracted to take, and, therefore, the contract is unenforceable by the one if executory, while, if executed, the other can recover back money paid on the ground of failure of the consideration.

Thus, the mistake is far less likely to be fundamental in the cases where the mistake is in relation to the quality of the subject matter. A Court of Appeal case, *Great Peace Shipping Limited v. Tsavliris Salvage (International) Limited*,[6] has created a new foundation for mistake by linking it with impossibility of performance of a contract. We will look at impossibility of performance later. The court formulated:

it suggests that the following elements must be present if common mistake is to avoid a contract: (i) there must be a common assumption as to the existence of a state of affairs; (ii) there must be no warranty by either party that that state of affairs

---

[2] *Strickland v. Turner*, (1852) 7 Exch 208.

[3] *Cooper v. Phibbs*, (1867) LR 2 HL 149.

[4] *Bell v. Lever Brothers Limited*, (1932) AC 161.

[5] *Kennedy v. Panama, New Zealand and Australian Royal Mail Co.*, (1867) LR 2 QB 580.

[6] *Great Peace Shipping Limited v. Tsavliris Salvage (International) Limited*, (2003) QB 679.

exists; (iii) the non-existence of the state of affairs must not be attributable to the fault of either party; (iv) the non-existence of the state of affairs must render performance of the contract impossible; (v) the state of affairs may be the existence, or a vital attribute, of the consideration to be provided or circumstances which must subsist if performance of the contractual adventure is to be possible.

As the requirement for declaring a contract void on grounds of mistake is stringent and exceptional, as the court noted 'cases where contracts have been found to be void in consequence of common mistake are few and far between.' The following cases from the Supreme Court will help us examine the issue further.

Court Case: Tarsem Singh v. Sukhminder Singh

Tarsem Singh owned agricultural land and intended to sell some of it.[7] Sukhminder Singh was a potential buyer. They negotiated to buy a specific measure of land at a certain rate. Sukhminder Singh paid an earnest deposit of Rs 77,000. He was to pay the balance amount before the sub-registrar of Patiala and get the sale deed before 15 November 1988. It was agreed between the parties that if Sukhminder Singh failed to pay the balance amount of sale consideration, the earnest money would be forfeited by Tarsem Singh. Sukhminder Singh claimed breach of contract in that he was ready and willing to pay the money, but Tarsem Singh was not wiling to execute the sale deed. Sukhminder Singh claimed specific performance of the contract.

Each region of the country has had different local measurements of land. The plurality of terms has further increased with metric

[7] *Tarsem Singh* v. *Sukhminder Singh*, AIR 1998 SC 1400.

system measurements like acre and hectare. The two prevalent local measures in the state were *bigha* and *kanal*. The Additional District Judge found that the parties did not have a consensus on either the total measure of the land to be sold, or the rate and the total consideration.

Tarsem Singh intended to sell in terms of *kanal*s and Sukhminder Singh intended to purchase it in terms of *bigha*s. Tarsem Singh thought he was selling 48 kanals 11 marlas at the rate of Rs 24,000 per acre. Sukhminder Singh thought he was buying 48 *bigha*s 11 *marla*s. From one measure, the price was Rs 1,56,150, and from another, Rs 2,35,750. Referring to Section 20, the Supreme Court noted:

This Section provides that an agreement would be void if both the parties to the agreement were under a mistake as to a matter of fact essential to the agreement. The mistake has to be mutual and in order that the agreement be treated as void, both the parties must be shown to be suffering from mistake of fact. Unilateral mistake is outside the scope of this Section. ... The other requirement is that the mistake, apart from being mutual, should be in respect of a matter which is essential to the agreement.

'Bigha' and 'Kanal' are different units of measurement. In the Northen part of the country, the land is measured in some states either in terms of 'bighas' or in terms of 'kanals'. Both convey different impressions regarding area of the land. ... Therefore, the dispute was not with regard to the unit of measurement only. Since these units relate to the area of the land, it was really a dispute with regard to the area of the land which was the subject-matter of agreement for sale, or, to put it differently, how much area of the land was agreed to be sold, was in dispute between the parties and it was with regard to the area of the land that the parties were suffering from a mutual mistake. The area of the land was as much essential to the agreement as the price which, incidentally, was to be calculated on the basis of the area. The contention of the learned counsel that the 'mistake' with which the parties were suffering, did not relate to a matter essential to the agreement cannot be accepted.

Court Case: Kalyanpur Lime Works Limited v. State of Bihar

The State of Bihar had leased the Murli Hills to the Kuchwar Lime and Stone Co. Limited for twenty years for the purpose of quarrying limestone.[8] The lease contained a prohibition against assignment of the leasehold rights without the permission of the Government. The liquidators of the company assigned the leasehold interest of the company to one Subodh Gopal Bose for Rs 35,000 by an unregistered deed dated 30 September 1933. For breach of the contract, under the contract, the government forfeited the lease and re-took possession of the Hills. Following this, the government gave the lease to the Kalyanpur Lime Works Limited (Lime Co.) on the same terms. The Lime Co. obtained possession on 15 April 1934 and started quarrying operations on 15 May 1934.

On 24 September 1934, Kuchwar Co. sued the Secretary of State for India for declaration that the leases in their favour had not been validly forfeited and for an injunction restraining him from granting leases to anyone else and for damage. The case went to the Privy Council. Kuchwar Co. suceeded in its legal proceedings. As a result, Lime Co. had to vacate the quarries. This happened in April 1936. Possession was restored to Kuchwar Co. The lease expired on March 1948 and the State of Bihar regained possession. Lime Co. repeatedly asked the State of Bihar to execute the leases agreed upon between the parties, and to get the leases registered. The State of Bihar refused, and instead gave the lease to another company, Dalmia Jain and Co. Limited. Lime Co. moved the court for specific performance of contract. One of the contentions raised by the State of Bihar was that the contract was void and unenforceable under Section 20 of the Contract Act because both parties were under a mistake of fact as regards the title of the government to the subject matter of the proposed leases. The Supreme Court ruled:

… it is difficult to see how the agreement can be challenged under Section 20 of the Contract Act as being vitiated by reason of a mistake as to a matter of fact essential to the agreement. Neither party was under any mistake of that: both parties knew that Kuchwar Co. had assigned its interest to Bose and that the assignment having been made without the consent of the lessor, its interest was liable to be forfeited. The Government Pleader advised to government that it had the right to forfeit, the leases and to grant a fresh leases to the Lime Co. The Lime Co. accepted the position and proceeded on the assumption that the government possessed the right to forfeit the leases and then to grant them to the Lime Co. It is not easy to discover any mistake of fact on the part of either of the parties.

…

The mistake, if any, was with regard to the effect of the law of registration the validity of the assignment deed. At the most, such mistake would be a mistake of law and under Section 21 of the Indian Contract Act the contract would not be void on that ground.

To conclude, when both the parties to a contract are mistaken about a fact essential to the contract, the contract is void. The parties may be under the same mistake or their mistake may be different, putting them at cross purposes. A contract where both the parties are mistaken about a significant aspect is void.

[8] *Kalyanpur Lime Works Limited* v. *State of Bihar*, AIR 1954 SC 165.

Part 5

DISCHARGE AND PERFORMANCE

Contract law, like any other law, has to be divided into sub-themes to facilitate its study. As the parts are organically related, every division and classification is arbitrary. With this general caution, we can note that some parts of contract law are classified as discharge. Once a contract is formed, the parties come to have rights and obligations to one another. The rights and obligations come to an end once the contract is performed. Thus, the parties are freed from further obligations. However, this is not the only way in which the parties can get freed of the obligations. The term for being freed of contractual obligations is called discharge. It is an important concern for the parties, whether they have obligations or not. This has made discharge a classificatory category subsuming diverse contexts and situations in which a party's obligations come to an end. A party to a contract gets a discharge in the following situations.

A contingent contract is the one where the rights and obligations of a party develop only on the occurrence of a contingency. An insurance contract is an example of a contingent contract. In other words, if the contingency does not happen, the party would be discharged from contractual obligations. This is the sense in which it is included under the head of discharge. However, a contingent contract is an important form of contract with numerous applications. We will take this up in Chapter 23.

It may become impossible to perform a contract due to changes in the context subsequent to the formation of the contract. One form of this is a change in the law that makes the contract illegal. Obviously, the contract can no longer be enforced. The contract was not void when it was made, but became void when it became illegal. A subsequent impossibility makes a contract void, and the parties are discharged of their obligations. We will take this up in Chapter 24.

Parties to a contract can extinguish their rights and obligations under the contract by mutual consent. This is by an agreement to change the terms of an existing contract. In this, while the parties may develop new rights and obligations, they may be discharged of the obligations under the original contract. We will take this up in Chapter 25.

Parties are discharged of their obligations when they perform their respective obligations. The provisions on performance are on the processes by which parties successfully perform their obligations. This includes the time and place of performance and performance of contracts where parties take joint liability. While performance leads to discharge, the provisions are important in themselves to the performance. Thus, this part has been given the heading discharge and performance. We will take up the subject in Chapter 26.

On the breach of a contractual obligation, the other party may get the right to elect to terminate the contract. On termination, the parties are discharged of their contractual obligations. The aggrieved party claims damages. Termination leads to discharge; however, the theme has integral linkages with damages and compensation. Thus, the topic of breach will be taken up with damages, and compensation will also be dealt with in a later chapter.

22

Contingent Contract

A contingent contract, as the name suggests, is a concluded contract; however, there is a contingency in the unfolding of the contract. The rights and obligations of the parties would develop on the happening or not happening of a contingency. We will explore the nature of a contingent contract by identifying the consideration for the parties, and difference from a wager agreement. Let us explore this through the following illustrations.

1. A contracts to pay B Rs two lakh, if B's house is burnt. B pays him Rs 5,000 per year in consideration. This is a contract of insurance.

2. A agrees to pay B Rs 2 crore if B's ship sinks. B pays A Rs 5 lakh for the facility. In this case B's ship is being insured.

3. B is organizing a cricket match. A agrees to pay B Rs 20 lakh if it rains heavily on Monday, leading to cancellation of the match. B pays A Rs 50,000 for the service. This is a contract of insurance.

4. The sponsors of a city cricket team had an agreement with the owners of the city team that they would pay Rs 5 lakh as bonus to the owners of the city team for every win.

These contracts are subject to an uncertain event happening or not happening. Such contracts are called contingent contracts. Contrast it with the case where A offers a reward of Rs 10,000 to B if B finds his missing son. The communication from A is only a unilateral offer. If B finds the missing son, it would constitute the consideration as well as acceptance of the offer so as to bring a contract into existence. Once the son has been found, there is no longer a contingency. Thus, there is no contingency after the contract is made. In contrast, in the case of a contingent contract, the contract is already formed. However, its performance can be demanded only if the event happens. Thus, if A agrees to pay B if B's ship sinks, there is already a contract between A and B. But B can demand the money only if the ship sinks. In other words, in a contingent contract, the contingency is collateral to the contract. Contrast the following two contracts.

Agreement 1: A and B got into an agreement that A would give Rs 500 to B if C, an international cricketer, scores a century in the match on Monday. If he does not score a century, B will give A Rs 200.

Agreement 2: C is an international cricketer and Swan Limited is a cricket bat manufacturing company. Under a contract, C is to put the logo of Swan Limited on his bat for the final match of the tournament. If C scores 50 or more runs in the match, Swan Limited will pay him Rs 2 lakh.

Both the contracts have contingencies. The first, however, is a wager agreement while the second one is not. The distinction is important because wager agreements are not enforceable. The first is a wager agreement because A and B have no real interest in C scoring a century. The event is relevant only for deciding the winner. In the second contract, the parties have a real interest in the event itself. Swan Limited is advertising itself, and C's score is of interest to the promotion of the company.

Provisions in the Indian Contract Act

Usually, contracts insuring life, property, or profit are contingent contracts. Section 31 of the Indian Contract Act defines a contingent contract thus:

31. Contingent contract defined—A 'contingent contract' is a contract to do or not to do something, if some event, collateral to such contract, does or does not happen.

A contingent contract is a concluded contract. Like any other contract, it supported by consideration for both the parties. For example, A contracts to pay B Rs 2 lakh if B's house is burnt down. B pays him Rs 5,000 per year in consideration. This is a contract of fire insurance. The consideration for A is Rs 5,000 and for B, the obligation of A to pay in the event of destruction by fire. In a contingent contract, the obligation for a party arises on the happening or not happening of an uncertain

event. Most insurance contracts are contingent contracts.[1] The term 'collateral' makes the event connected with the contract; for example, an insured building being destroyed in a fire. In the absence of this, the contract will become a wager. A contract to pay a sum of money on the expiry of a certain time is not a contingent contract, as the provided time is bound to expire. Similarly, a contract to pay a sum of money on the death of a person is not a contingent contract, as the event is bound to happen one day. However, a contract to pay a sum if a person dies within one year is a contingent contract, as the death of the person within one year is an uncertain event. This is how a contract of life insurance is also a contingent contract. The Supreme Court in *Chandulal Harjivandas* v. *Commissioner of Income-tax*, Gujarat noted: 'Life insurance in a broader sense comprises any contract in which one party agrees to pay a given sum upon happening of a particular event contingent upon the duration of human life, in consideration of the immediate payment of a smaller sum or certain equivalent periodical payments by another party.'[2] Let us explore contingent contracts further with the following cases.

Court Case: Ramzan v. Hussaini

The contract of sale was with respect to a house that was under a mortgage.[3] Ramzan entered in a contract to sell the house to Hussaini on the following terms:

This house is under mortgage with Jethmal Bastimal for Rs. 1000/-. When you will get this house, the

[1] *Commissioner of Excess Profits Tax, West Bengal* v. *Ruby General Insurance Co. Limited*, AIR 1957 SC 669.

[2] *Chandulal Harjivandas* v. *Commissioner of Income-tax, Gujarat*, AIR 1967 SC 816.

[3] *Ramzan* v. *Hussaini*, AIR 1990 SC 529.

description of which is given below, redeemed from M/s. Jeth Mal Bastimal and take the papers of the registry in your possession, on that day I will have the sale deed of the said house, written executed and registered in your favour.

Hussaini filed a suit claiming specific performance of the contract fourteen years after redeeming the mortgage. The seller contended that the suit was barred by limitation, the period being three years under the Limitation Act. The High Court ruled that, as no date was prescribed in the contract for the seller to perform his part, the date of performance became open-ended. As a result, the suit by Hussaini was not barred by limitation. The Supreme Court found the agreement 'a typical illustration of a contingent contract within the meaning of S. 31 of the Indian Contract Act, 1872.' The contingent event was Hussaini redeeming the mortgage. The seller became liable to execute the sale deed on that date. The court ruled that the 'period of limitation thus started running on that date.' As a result, the suit by Hussaini was barred by limitation.

Court Case: Harbakhsh Singh v. *Ram Rattan*
Sukhdev Singh was half-owner of a land property that was under dispute with the other owner(s).[4] He sold his half to Ram Rattan for a consideration of Rs 48,500 and received Rs 10,000 as earnest money. Under the contract, he was to apply to the court to partition his share in the property and execute it in favour of Ram Rattan. The terms of the agreement provided as follows:

The parties shall be bound to get the sale deed executed and completed after one month of the final decision by a court of competent jurisdiction of the suit for partition of the property and that the first party [Sukhdev Singh] shall be bound to inform the

4 *Harbakhsh Singh* v. *Ram Rattan*, AIR 1988 P & H 60.

second party [Ram Rattan] about it. In case it takes more than a year for the decision of the partition proceedings, then the first party would be liable to pay on the earnest money of Rs. 10,000/- interest at the rate of 3 per cent per annum to the second party which would be payable monthly and would be adjusted against rent. ... If the second party commits a breach of the agreement, the earnest money shall stand forfeited and if the first party commits breach, then the second party would be entitled to get the sale deed registered through court by specific performance of the agreement.

Sukhdev Singh filed a suit for the partition of the property, but it was dismissed by the court. Following this, Sukhdev Singh tried to get out of the contract. He argued that the sale was a contingent contract, contingent on the partition of the property being done by a court. As the court has not partitioned the property, the contract could not be enforced. The high court did not accept this. The high court noted:

...it is evident that the contract of sale was not contingent and it was only the execution of the sale deed which was postponed to a future date. There is a clear difference between a contract under which a present obligation is created but the performance is postponed to a future date and a contract under which there is no present obligation at all and the obligation arises by reason of some condition being complied with or some contingency occurring. In the present case, the vendor had agreed to sell his half a share in the property in dispute, but the sale deed was agreed to be executed after a month of the partition of the property and separation of his share. To get the property partitioned and his share separated was an obligation undertaken by the vendor for the benefit of the vendee. It was not a condition precedent without the happening of which no obligation to transfer the share could arise. If the vendor failed to get his share separated, the vendee could get the same done after the completion of the sale through court, which right had been given to him under the contract. If the sale was of a specified portion, then the situation might have been different. The sale here being of the unspecified share, it could not be said that the contract was a contingent one and the plaintiff was not entitled to enforce it without the share of the vendor having been separated.

Thus, the court's position was that the sale had already taken place. It was not contingent on partition. Only the execution of the sale deed and its registration was fixed for a later period.

Section 32 deals with the time of enforcement of a contingent contract. It reads:

32. **Enforcement of contracts contingent on an event happening**—Contingent contracts to do or not to do anything if an uncertain future event happens cannot be enforced by law unless and until that event has happened.

If the event becomes impossible, such contracts become void.

The meaning of the section is evident. Under a contingent contract, till the uncertain event happens, the obligation of the other party does not arise and it cannot be enforced. For example, in a concluded contract of fire insurance of a building, the person taking the insurance is bound to pay the premium within the stipulated time. However, the insurance company will be under an obligation to pay the insured amount only if and when the building is destroyed in fire. In a contract of ship insurance, the claim will arise only when the ship sinks. The section carries the following illustrations:

(a) A makes a contract with B to buy B's horse if A survives C. This contract cannot be enforced by law unless and until C dies in A's lifetime.

(b) A makes a contract with B to sell a horse to B at a specified price, if C, to whom the horse has been offered, refuses to buy him. The contract cannot be enforced by law unless and until C refuses to buy the horse.

Further, if the happening of the event becomes impossible, the contract would become void. The section illustrates it thus:

(c) A contracts to pay B a sum of money when B marries C. C dies without being married to B. The contract becomes void.

We will further examine contingent contracts with the following review of cases.

Court Case: Commissioner of Wealth Tax, Mysore v. Vijayaba

A person died leaving behind considerable moveable and immoveable properties.[5] He had not bequeathed the property by will, and as a result, the property was to devolve on his two sons according to the personal law, but the brothers had a dispute. The younger brother contemplated legal proceedings against his elder brother, but their mother intervened. She did not want litigation as it would have brought disrepute to the family. She sent a letter to the younger son saying:

Your father had expressed in the presence of many people that he will give you rupees fifty lakhs. To keep up his words and promise and also that I should get peace of mind I am writing to you that if your brother Vikramsinghji Maharaja of Gondal does not give you the full amount, then you must get the balance of amount from me. That is my sincere desire. I will also press Vikram that he should give you the amount of Rupees fifty lakhs.

The elder brother paid only Rs 20 lakh. The mother met the obligations to the younger son. The nature of the agreement between the mother and son, where she agreed to pay if the elder brother failed to pay, became important from the point of view of taxation. If it was a valid contract, the amount given to the son was debt owed, and thus deductible from wealth for the purposes of wealth tax calculation. If not, the mother must pay tax on the wealth given to the son. The

[5] *Commissioner of Wealth Tax, Mysore* v. *Vijayaba*, AIR 1979 SC 982.

Supreme Court concurred with the following contention:

her letter…was a contingent contract within the meaning of S. 31 of the Contract Act…under Sec. 32 such a contract becomes enforceable by law when the future event contemplated in the contingent contract has happened.… it was a contingent liability the contingency did happen and the assessee became liable to pay the amount as a debt…

Court Case: Harnandrai Fulchand v. Pragdas Budhsen

A seller agreed to sell bales of cotton that were to be manufactured by a mill.[6] The contract stipulated the quantity to be 864 bales and the price, and mentioned: 'The said goods are to be taken delivery of as and when the same may be received from the Mills. Delivery is to be caused to be given in full by the 31st December in the year 1918.' The mill failed to supply the goods. One of the grounds on which the seller disclaimed an obligation to supply the goods was that the contract was a contingent contract. The performance was contingent on the mill supplying the goods. Lord Summner for the Privy Council noted:

The agreement is simple and of a common type, and the whole question in dispute is whether it is an absolute contract to deliver the whole of the goods mentioned or whether the sellers are relieved from their obligation to deliver a part of them in the events which happened. … It was … suggested that the words 'as and when same may be received from the Mills' should be construed, as if they were 'If and when the same may be received from the Mills.' This is to convert words, which fix the quantities and times for deliveries by instalments into a condition precedent to the obligation to deliver at all, and virtually makes a new contract.

The high court, in interpreting the terms, asked what a reasonable businessman would have bound himself to. Lord Summer pointed out this to be a mistake. He contrasted it with the correct view:

To interpret a business bargain expressed in the language of commerce, it is no doubt important to appreciate the methods and the point of view of business men, but this is merely a prudent way of qualifying the mind to construe their words, and so to determine their meaning, and is a very different thing from postulating that reasonable men would have been likely to agree to one kind of liability and not to another, and from thus concluding that, whatever the words of the contract say, that kind of liability and that alone, is the obligation of the contract. As a matter of fact there is nothing surprising in a merchant's binding himself to procure certain goods at all events. It is a matter of price and of market expectations. No doubt it is a speculation, but many dealings even in cotton goods are of that character.

The Privy Council ruled that it was not a contingent contract. The case found application in the following Supreme Court case.

Court Case: Ganga Saran v. Firm Ram Charan Ram Gopal

A seller entered into a contract to supply cotton bales of a particular specification.[7] The seller was to receive the goods from Victoria Mills. The contract provided: 'We shall continue sending goods as soon as they are prepared to you upto … (17-11-47). We shall go on supplying goods to you of the Victoria Mills as soon as they are supplied to us by the said Mill.' The seller failed to supply the goods and claimed that the contract was a contingent one. The obligation to supply arose only on receiving the goods from the mill. The Supreme Court differed. It noted:

The agreement does not seem to us to convey the meaning that the delivery of the goods was made

6 *Harnandrai Fulchand* v. *Pragdas Budhsen*, AIR 1923 PC 54.

7 *Ganga Saran* v. *Firm Ram Charan Ram Gopal*, AIR 1952 SC 9.

contingent on their being supplied to the respondent-firm by the Victoria Mills. We find it difficult to hold that the parties ever contemplated the possibility of the goods not being supplied at all. The words 'prepared by the Mill' are only a description of the goods to be supplied, and the expressions 'as soon as they are prepared' and 'as soon as they are supplied to us by the said Mill' simply indicate the process of delivery. It should be remembered that what we have to construe is a commercial agreement entered into in a somewhat common form, and, to use the words of Lord Sumner in the case to which reference has been made, 'there is nothing surprising in a merchant's binding himself to procure certain goods at all events, it being a matter of price and of market expectations.' Since the true construction of an agreement must depend upon the import of the words used and not upon what the parties choose to say afterwards, it is unnecessary to refer to what the parties have said about it.

Thus, the obligation of the seller to supply the goods was not contingent on the mill supplying him the goods.

Section 33 provides the rule that if the contracted contingency is of an event not happening, till it becomes impossible for the event not to happen, one cannot be sure. It reads:

33. Enforcement of contracts contingent on an event not happening—Contingent contracts to do or not to do anything if an uncertain future event does not happen can be enforced when the happening of that event becomes impossible, and not before.

It has the following illustration:

A agrees to pay B a sum of money if a certain ship does not return. The ship is sunk. The contract can be enforced when the ship sinks.

Section 34 provides for when the contingency is dependent on the actions of a person. It reads:

34. When event on which contract is contingent to be deemed impossible, if it is the future conduct of a living person—If the future event on which a contract is contingent is the way in which a person will act at an unspecified time, the event shall be considered to become impossible when such person does anything which renders it impossible that he should so act within any definite time, or otherwise than under further contingencies.

Illustration
A agrees to pay B a sum of money if B marries C. C marries D .The marriage of B to C must now be considered impossible, although it is possible that D may die and that C may afterwards marry B.

A contingent contract may specify a time limit for the happening of an event. The section provides that the contract becomes void if the event does not happen on the expiry of the time limit. Section 35 reads:

35. When contracts become void which are contingent on happening of specified event within fixed time—Contingent contracts to do or not to do anything if a specified uncertain event happens within a fixed time become void if, at the expiration of the time fixed, such event has not happened, or if, before the time fixed, such event becomes impossible.

When contracts may be enforced which are contingent on specified event not happening within fixed time—Contingent contracts to do or not to do anything if a specified uncertain event does not happen within a fixed time may be enforced by law when the time fixed has expired and such event has not happened or, before the time fixed has expired, if it becomes certain that such event will not happen.

Illustrations
(a) A promises to pay B a sum of money if a certain ship returns within a year. The contract may be enforced if the ship returns within the year, and becomes void if the ship is burnt within the year.
(b) A promises to pay B a sum of money if a certain ship does not return within a year .The contract may be enforced if the ship does not return within the year, or is burnt within the year.

Consider the following illustration. In a sale contract, the goods were to be delivered by the seller to the premises of the buyer on Monday. The contract provided that if, due to floods, the access to the premises of the buyer were blocked such that a lorry could not manoeuvre, the contract will stand terminated. The seller must return the advance taken from the buyer and the seller will be under no obligation to supply the goods. This is a sale contract where the consideration for the parties is the ownership in goods and the price. The buyer is under an obligation to pay, and the seller, to deliver goods. However, a contingent event can change the rights and obligations of the parties. Thus, this is also a contingent contract where the rights and obligations depend on the happening of an event. It is opposite of an insurance contract, where rights developed on the event. In this case, the existing rights get extinguished on the happening of the event. The following are other examples of this kind of a contract.

1. The contract included: 'We undertake to supply the goods by 15 April. However, if the goods are not supplied to us by the mill, we would be under no obligation to supply the good.'

2. The contract provided: 'If we fail to obtain the requisite licence from the government, we will be under no obligation to supply the contracted goods.'

3. The contract read: 'We will be under no obligation to set up the pandal if it rains heavily.'

In contrast, consider a contract where a buyer is to supply the goods to the premises of the buyer on Monday. However, that day, the truck of the seller could not enter the buyers premises as the road leading to the premises was flooded. The contract did not mention anything about flooding of the road. This is not a contingent contract. The seller has taken an unconditional obligation to supply the goods on Monday. The seller will claim that he could not perform the contract due to impossibility. In the next chapter, we will take up the theme of impossibility.

23

Impossibility and Frustration

A valid contract becomes void if it subsequently becomes illegal or its performance becomes impossible due to change in subsequent events. The impossibility could be due to flood, fire, natural disaster, epidemics, strike, riot, civil war, etc. The contract is said to be frustrated. The issue is the most theorized field in contract law. It has accumulated a lot of deadwood, particularly in the cross-referencing between India law and common law. The Indian courts had extensively referred to the common law judgments on impossibility, not to follow them but to bring out that these were different from the provisions in the Indian Contract Act, 1872. Interestingly, the new position formulated by the common law is the same as in the India Contract Act. Thus, Indian law and common law have converged, making the prior case law irrelevant. We need to ignore prior material and focus on grasping the current legal position.

EVOLUTION OF THE CONCEPT OF IMPOSSIBILITY

The founding position was that parties must meet their obligations without excuse. This was expressed in *Paradine* v. *Jane*, a case dating back to 1647. Take the case where a horse contracted to be sold dies. Could it be insisted that the horse be sold even if it no longer existed? The answer of common law in such cases was no. This led to the exception that if the subject matter of the contract itself was destroyed, the parties should be excused from performance. This idea was systematized, elaborated, and deployed in *Taylor* v. *Caldwell*.[1] In this case, a hall that was rented for a musical performance was destroyed in a fire. In *Krell* v. *Henry*,[2] it was taken further. In *Taylor* v. *Caldwell*, the dominant context was destruction of property at the centre of the contract. In *Krell* v. *Henry*, it was extended to an event at the centre of the contract. In this case, a person had let a room for viewing the coronation procession of the king. The king fell ill and the procession was cancelled. The exception came to be widely applied in the cases of ships unable to deliver their consignment due to war.

The courts had to accommodate the exceptions in the theory that contracts were about meetings of minds. The direction that was attempted was that the parties had agreed on

[1] *Taylor* v. *Caldwell*, (1863) 122 ER 309.
[2] *Krell* v. *Henry*, (1903) 2 KB 740.

the exceptions impliedly. There are logical problems with the position. If a party implied that events would become impossible and entered into a contract nevertheless, he meant the contract to be enforced. If impossibility were implied, the parties may have had a different understanding of it. Over decades of accumulated cases, the exceptions could no longer be neatly and coherently accommodated in the prevailing theory of contracts being about meeting of minds. Thus, as mentioned before, frustration is the most theorized field in contract law. The puzzle generated volumes of leading cases on the subject. In *Davis Contractors, Limited* v. *Fareham Urban District Council*,[3] the courts finally abandoned the accommodation of frustration in implied terms. The new justification was simply that it was unfair to demand that a person to perform an impossible act, and thus the courts could not enforce the rule of absolute obligations. In *Ocean Tramp Tankers Corporation* v. *V/O Sovfracht*, Lord Denning, thus, explained the development of the law on frustration:

This means that, once again, we have had to consider the authorities on this vexed topic of frustration. But I think that the position is now reasonably clear. It is simply this: If it should happen, in the course of carrying out a contract, that a fundamentally different situation arises for which the parties made no provision—so much so that it would not be just in the new situation to hold them bound to its terms—then the contract is at an end. It was originally said that the doctrine of frustration was based on an implied term. In short, that the parties, if they had foreseen the new situation, would have said to one another: 'If that happens, of course, it is all over between us'. But the theory of an implied term has now been discarded by everyone, or nearly everyone, for the simple reason that it does not represent the truth. The parties would not have said: 'It is all over between us'. They would have differed about what was to happen. Each

would have sought to insert reservations or qualifications of one kind or another.

...

We are thus left with the simple test that a situation must arise which renders performance of the contract 'a thing radically different from that which was undertaken by the contract': see *Davis Contractors, Ltd.* v. *Fareham U.D.C.*, per LORD RADCLIFFE. To see if the doctrine applies, you have first to construe the contract and see whether the parties have themselves provided for the situation that has arisen. If they have provided for it, the contract must govern. There is no frustration. If they have not provided for it, then you have to compare the new situation with the old situation for which they did provide. Then you must see how different it is. The fact that it has become more onerous or more expensive for one party than he thought is not sufficient to bring about a frustration. It must be more than merely more onerous or more expensive. It must be positively unjust to hold the parties bound. It is often difficult to draw the line. But it must be done, and it is for the courts to do it as a matter of law.[4]

The Indian Contract Act was written down in 1872. By that time, *Taylor* v. *Caldwell* case was decided, introducing the doctrine of frustration on the grounds of impossibility. The principle that a contract which had become opposed to the law could not be enforced had always existed. The two formed the basis for the following formulation of the principle in the Indian Contract Act. Section 56 provides:

56. **Agreement to do impossible act**—An agreement to do an act impossible in itself is void.

Contract to do act afterwards becoming impossible or unlawful—A contract to do an act which, after the contract is made, becomes impossible, or, by reason of some event which the promisor could not prevent, unlawful, becomes void when the act becomes impossible or unlawful.

The section provides for three situations. An agreement to do an impossible act is void.

---

[3] *Davis Contractors, Limited* v. *Fareham Urban District Council*, (1956) AC 696.

[4] *Ocean Tramp Tankers Corporation* v. *V/O Sovfracht.*, (1964) 1 All ER 161.

This is initial impossibility. It applies to the cases where the act was impossible at the time of making of the agreement. The second situation relates to a contract that was lawful when made. However, a subsequent change in the law or events makes it unlawful to perform the contract. It is clear that there can be no excuse for violating the law. The laws made by the state take precedence over contractual obligations. Thus, the law declares the contract to be void when it becomes unlawful.

The third situation is after a contract is made, the changes in the situation make it impossible to perform the contract. This provision codified the common law principle. The difference, however, was this: Once the principle became a statutory provision, the Indian courts did not have to introduce the conceptual basis for the law. In contrast, the common law courts, based on the system of precedence, could not escape from justifying the principle. Finally, *Davis Contractors, Limited* v. *Fareham Urban District Council in 1954* created new grounds and *Ocean Tramp Tankers Corporation* v. *V/O Sovfracht* further strengthened the position. The Indian courts had all along insisted that Section 56 has provided a positive law, and thus the Indian courts, unlike the British courts, need not go into intention of the parties. As the Supreme Court noted in *Naihati Jute Mills Limited* v. *Khyaliram Jagannath*:[5]

The necessity of evolving one or the other theory was due to the common law rule that courts have no power to absolve a party to the contract from his obligation. On the one hand, they were anxious to preserve intact the sanctity of contract while on the other the courts could not shut their eyes to the harshness of the situation in cases where performance became impossible by causes which could not

have been foreseen and which beyond the control of parties. Such a difficulty has, however, not to be faced by the courts in this country ... so far as the courts in this country are concerned they must look primarily to the law as embodied in Sections 32 and 56 of the Contract Act.

In fact, the common-law cases displayed a wide array of approaches and conflicting theories. In no small measure, this made the Indian courts confine themselves to the statutory provisions. The Supreme Court, referring to the common-law cases, concluded:

These differences in the way of formulating legal theories really do not concern us so long as we have a statutory provision in the India Contract Act. In deciding cases in India, the only doctrine that we have to go by is that of supervening impossibility or illegality as laid down in Section 56 of the Contract Act taking the word 'impossible' in its practical and not literal sense. It must be borne in mind, however, that Section 56 lays down a rule of positive law and does not leave the matter to be determined according to the intention of the parties.

In a subsequent case, the Supreme Court was to reiterate the position:

In English law ... the question of frustration of contract has been treated by courts as a question of construction depending upon the true intention of the parties. In contrast, the statutory provisions contained in S. 56 of the Indian Contract Act lay down a positive rule of law and English authorities cannot therefore be of direct assistance, though they have persuasive value in showing how English courts have approached and decided cases under similar circumstances.

In fact, the cases cited in the judgments need not even have persuasive value, as the Davis and subsequent cases have displaced those cases. The British position after the Davis case has also become the same as that of the Indian law. However, there has been no case relating to the matter from an Indian court assimilating the new position of the British courts. The judgment was just about referred to as the

---

[5] *Naihati Jute Mills Limited* v. *Khyaliram Jagannath*, AIR 1968 SC 522.

emergent view in the last landmark case on frustration from the Supreme Court, *Naihati Jute Mills Limited* v. *Khyaliram Jagannath*. Thus, we must shed the entire comparative explorations in the cases and only cull the applicable law in India from these cases.

DEVELOPMENT OF THE LAW IN INDIA

Section 56 declares that a contract to perform an act becomes void if the law subsequently makes the act or the contract unlawful or it becomes impossible to perform the contract. The following two cases explore the issue.

Court Case: Satyabrata Ghose v. Mugneeram Bangur and Co.

Mugneeram Bangur and Co. was the owner of a large tract of land situated in the vicinity of the Dhakuria Lakes within Greater Calcutta.[6] The company started a scheme for development of this land for residential purposes, which was described as Lake Colony Scheme No. 1. The company divided the entire area into a large number of plots for sale. The business model of the company was to enter into agreements with different purchasers for sale of the plots of land and accept only a small portion of the consideration money from them by way of earnest at the time of the agreement. The company undertook to construct the roads and drains necessary to make the lands suitable for building and residential purposes. Once this work was completed, the purchaser would be called upon to complete the conveyance by payment of the balance of the consideration money.

The Second World War began, and in November–December 1941, all the land under the scheme was requisitioned for military

purposes for the war effort. As no one knew how long the government would occupy the land, the company gave two options to the buyer. One, treat the contract as cancelled and collect your earnest deposit. Two, take the conveyance of the plot by paying the full consideration. In this case, the company undertook to construct the roads and drains, as circumstances would permit, after the termination of the war. If a buyer elected for neither of the two options, the agreement would be deemed to be cancelled and the earnest deposit forfeited.

In January 1946, after the war was over, a person filed a suit that the contract between the parties was subsisting and he could get a conveyance executed and registered on payment of the consideration money mentioned in the agreement. The main contention of the company was that the contract of sale stood discharged by frustration as requisition of the land by the government made its performance impossible. The Supreme Court, referring to Section 56, noted:

The first paragraph of the Section ... speaks of something which is impossible inherently or by its very nature, and no one can obviously be directed to perform such an act. The second paragraph enunciates the law relating to discharge of contract by reason of supervening impossibility or illegality of the act agreed to be done. The wording of this paragraph is quite general ... This much is clear that the word 'impossible' has not been used here in the sense of physical or literal impossibility. The performance of an act may not be literally impossible but it may be impracticable and useless from the point of view of the object and purpose which the parties had in view; and if an untoward event or change of circumstances totally upsets the very foundation upon which the parties rested their bargain, it can very well be said that the promisor finds it impossible to do the act which he promised to do. ... It must be borne in mind, however, that Section 56 lays down a rule of positive law and does not leave the matter to be determined according to the intention of the parties. ...

---

[6] *Satyabrata Ghose* v. *Mugneeram Bangur and Co.*, AIR 1954 SC 44.

...the question of construction may manifest itself in two totally different ways. In one class of cases the question may simply be, as to what the parties themselves had actually intended; and whether or not there was a condition in the contract itself, express or implied, which operated, according to the agreement of the parties themselves, to release them from their obligations; this would be a question of construction pure and simple and the ordinary rules of construction would have to be applied to find out what the real intention of the parties was.

According to Indian Contract Act, a promise may be express or implied vide Section 9. In cases, therefore, where the court gathers as a matter of construction that the contract itself contained impliedly or expressly a term, according to which it would stand discharged on the happening of certain circumstances, the dissolution of the contract would take place under the terms of the contract itself and such cases would be outside the purview of Section 56 altogether...they would be dealt with under Section 32 of the Indian Contract Act which deals with contingent contracts or similar other provisions contained in the Act.

In the large majority of cases however the doctrine of frustration is applied not on the ground that the parties themselves agreed to an implied term which operated to release them from the performance of the contract. The relief is given by the court on the ground of subsequent impossibility when it finds that the whole purpose or basis of a contract was frustrated by the intrusion or occurrence of an unexpected event or change of circumstances which was beyond what was contemplated by the parties at the time when they entered into the agreement. Here there is no question of finding out an implied term agreed to by the parties embodying a provision for discharge, because the parties did not think about the matter at all nor could possibly have any intention regarding it.

When such an event or change of circumstance occurs which is so fundamental as to be regarded by law as striking at the root of the contract as a whole, it is the court which can pronounce the contract to be frustrated and at an end. The court undoubtedly has to examine the contract and the circumstances under which it was made. The belief, knowledge and intention of the parties are evidence, but evidence only on which the court has to form its own conclusion whether the changed circumstances destroyed altogether the basis of the adventure and its underlying object...

It is well settled and not disputed before us that if and when there is frustration the dissolution of the contract occurs automatically. It does not depend, as does rescission of a contract on the ground of repudiation or breach, or on the choice or election of either party. It depends on the effect of what has actually happened on the possibility of performing the contract...What happens generally in such cases and has happened here is that one party claims that the contract has been frustrated while the other party denies it. The issue has got to be decided by the court 'ex post facto', on the actual circumstances of the case....

One can readily see the resonance in the position taken by the Supreme Court and the formulation by Lord Denning in *Ocean Tramp Tankers Corporation* v. *V/O Sovfracht*, which followed. The situation when the contract is made and the change in the event are to be contrasted to see whether the change is fundamental. The court found several facts that made it rule that there was no impossibility: First, the contract did not provide any time frame within which the company was to take up and complete the work of developing the roads and drainage. The first requisition order was passed fifteen months after the contract was made. During this time, the company had done no work. Second, the war was already on, when the parties entered into the contract. Third, requisition orders for taking temporary possession of lands for war purposes were normal events during this period. Fourth, due to the war efforts, there was scarcity of building material. It was left entirely to the convenience of the company to complete the work. The Supreme Court ruled:

The company, it must be admitted, had not commenced the development work when the requisition order was passed in November 1941. There was no question, therefore, of any work or service being interrupted for an indefinite period of time. Undoubtedly the commencement of the work was delayed but was the delay going to be so great and of such a character that it would totally upset the basis of the bargain and commercial object which the parties had in view? The requisition orders, it must be remembered, were, by their very nature, of a temporary character and the requisitioning authority could, in law, occupy the position of a licence in regard to the requisitioned property. The order might continue during the whole period of the war and even for some time after that or it could have been withdrawn before the war terminated... we do not think that the order of requisition affected the fundamental basis upon which the agreement rested or struck at the root of the adventure.

Court Case: Naihati Jute Mills Limited v. Khyaliram Jagannath

Naihati Jute Mills Limited agreed to purchase two thousand bales of jute from Khyaliram Jagannath.[7] The contract was in the standard form prescribed by the Indian Jute Mills Association. It provided that shipment or rail despatch was to be made between August and November, 1958. As the import of Pakistan jute required an import licence, the contract provided:

Buyers to provide the sellers with the letters of authority and sellers to open letters of credit. If buyers fail to provide the sellers with import licence within November 1958 then the period of shipment would be up to December, 1958 and the price mentioned in the contract would be increased by 50 NP. If buyers fail to provide licence by December 1958 then the contract would be settled at the market price prevailing on January 2, 1959 for goods of January and February 1959 shipment.

Thus, the buyer was to get an import license and give it to the seller to import the goods. The term above contemplated the contingency

⁷ Naihati Jute Mills Limited v. Khyaliram Jagannath, AIR 1968 SC 522.

of the buyer not getting an import licence. One of the printed terms provided:

Buyers shall not however be held responsible for delay in delivering letters of authority or opening letters of credit where such delay is directly or indirectly caused by or due to act of God, war, mobilisation, de-mobilisation, breaking off trade relations between governments, requisition by or interference from government or force majeure. In any of the aforesaid circumstances whereby buyers are prevented from delivering letters of authority or opening letters of credit within one month from the date of the contract, there may be a further extension of time (the delivery period to be extended accordingly) by mutual agreement between the buyers and the sellers otherwise the contract shall be deemed to be cancelled and sellers shall have no claim whatsoever against the buyers.

On 8 August 1958, Naihati Jute Mills Limited applied to the Jute Commissioner Calcutta, for an import licence. On 19 August 1958, the Administrative Officer refused to certify the licence on the ground that the mill had sufficient stock to keep their factory going for some more months. On 26 August 1958, the Licensing Authority refused to issue the licence. On 29 November 1958, the mill requested the Jute Commissioner to certify the issue of a licence stating that by that time their stock had been considerably reduced. On 11 December 1958, the Jute Commissioner refused to issue the licence and asked the mill to meet their requirements from the purchase of Indian jute. Khyaliram Jagannath claimed damages from the mill on the ground that the mill had failed to furnish the licence provided by the contract. The seller claimed the contract had provided for this contingency. The mill disclaimed any liability under the contract on the grounds of impossibility. The Supreme Court ruled:

... so far as the courts in this country are concerned they must look primarily to the law as embodied in Sections 32 and 56 of the Contract Act. In

Satyabrata Ghose v. *Mugneeram* (AIR 1954 SC 44) also. Mukherjea, J. (as he then was) stated that Section 56 laid down a rule of positive law and did not leave the matter to be determined according to the intention of the parties.

Since under the Contract Act a promise may be express or implied in cases where the court gathers as a matter of construction that the contract itself contains impliedly or expressly a term according to which it would stand discharged on the happening of certain circumstances the dissolution of the contract would take place under the terms of the contract itself and such cases would be outside the purview of Section 56... they would be dealt with under Section 32.
...

The Court can grant relief on the ground of subsequent impossibility when it finds that the whole purpose or the basis of the contract was frustrated by the intrusion or occurrence of an unexpected event or change of circumstances which was not contemplated by the parties at the date of the contract. There would in such a case be no question of finding out an implied term agreed to by the parties embodying a provision for discharge because the parties did not think about the matter at all nor could possibly have any intention regarding it. When such an event or change of circumstances which is so fundamental as to be regarded by law as striking at the root of the contract as a whole occurs it is the court which can pronounce the contract to be frustrated and at an end. This is really a positive rule enacted in Section 56 which governs such situations.

The court noted that the parties had provided for the contingency of the buyer not getting the licence. The court noted the second clause (the force majeure clause) quoted above on delay. However, it noted that the licence was refused because of a personal disqualification and not by 'any change in the government's policy which could not be foreseen by the parties.' Thus, the contingency provided by the parties was binding under Section 32.

APPLICATION OF SECTION 56

In this section, we will review the application of the principles by the courts in India.

Subsequent Illegality

Performance of a contract can become unlawful due to a change in the law subsequent to the contract. The first case we take up is the judgment of the Supreme Court in *Boothalinga Agencies* v. *V.T.C. Poriaswami Nadar*. Boothalinga Agencies was in the business of manufacture and sale of coffee powder.[8] It was, for this purpose, importing chicory under actual user's licence issued by the government. On 26 November 1955, it entered in a contract to sell a specific consignment on its way to Madras on a ship to a buyer. On 7 December 1955, the Central Government promulgated the Imports (Control) Order which made it illegal to violate the conditions of the licence. A condition of the licence was that the goods would not be sold but only used as raw material in the factory. The goods arrived at Madras on 13 December 1955 and were cleared by the agency on 20 December 1955. As the market price of Chicory rose in this while, Boothalinga Agencies did not give the delivery to Nadar. They claimed the bar imposed by the order. The Supreme Court ruled: 'In consequence, even though the contract was enforceable on 26 November 1955 when it was entered into, the performance of the contract became impossible or unlawful after 7 December 1955, and so the contract became void under Section 56 of the Indian Contract Act after the coming into force of the Imports (Control) Order, 1955.'

In *Rozan Mian* v. *Tahera Begum*, Tahera entered into a contract with Rozan to sell just the structure without the land.[9] This was possible under the Calcutta Thika Tenancy Act, 1949. As the agreement was not carried out,

---

[8] *Boothalinga Agencies* v. *V.T.C. Poriaswami Nadar*, AIR 1969 SC 110.

[9] *Rozan Mian* v. *Tahera Begum*, AIR 2007 SC 2883.

Rozan moved the court for specific perform-ance of the contract. While the dispute was pending before the court, the Calcutta Thika Tenancy (Acquisition and Regulation) Act, 1981, was promulgated. The act vested all lands and interests of the landlords vested with the government. It prohibited transfer of *thika* tenancy. An agreement transfer-ring *thika* tenancy was declared void. The Supreme Court ruled that subsequent legis-lation had made the agreement between the parties void.

Subsequent Events

The followings are some of the cases on the application of Section 56 on the claims of a subsequent event frustrating the contract.

Court Case: Alluri Narayana Murthy Raju v. Dist Collector, Visakhapatnam

The district collector of Visakhapatnam awarded a tender for quarrying of sand in village Maddi from the river Gostani to Alluri Narayana Murthy Raju.[10] The period of contract for quarrying was two years. The villagers of Maddi prevented him from carry-ing on quarry operations on the ground that it would lead to depletion of ground water, affecting the irrigation channels. The preven-tion continued despite police complaint, court injunction, and police protection. Alluri said that the contract was frustrated, and claimed the refund of the contract money already paid to the administration. The court iden-tified Section 32 and 56 as the two relevant provisions. As neither party had pleaded that there was a term in the contract on the hap-pening of the event, Section 32 did not apply. The Andhra Pradesh High Court ruled that Section 56 applied to the case. It noted:

...the conclusion is inevitable that on account of the events that have taken place subsequent to entering into the contract, which were beyond the contem-plation and control of the parties to the contract, performance of contract has become impossible. Therefore, the second limb of Section 56 is squarely attracted to this case and thus the doctrine of frus-tration envisaged by the said provision applies in all fours to the contract...

Court Case: Markapur Municipality v. Dodda Ramireddi

The municipalities are charged with the responsibility of keeping the streets clean.[11] Towards this, Markapur Municipality em-ployed labour to collect pig dung from the streets. The Municipality came up with a more efficient way of dealing with its duty. It auctioned the right to collect the dung from the streets for a fixed period of time. The auc-tioneer, however, was obstructed by the pig owners, who collected it themselves as they followed their pigs. The court examined the legal nature of the transaction:

The pigs do not admittedly belong to the municipality. It is not disputed that the owners who follow the pigs have got the right to collect the dung for themselves. It is of course open to the municipality to prevent the movement of pigs within the municipal area. The only right of the municipality is to collect the dung which was abandoned on the roads as part of its duty to clean the public streets by removing the rubbish. After the municipality collects the dung as rubbish, it becomes the owner thereof entitled to dispose of the same by sale to third parties. But at the stage when the dung is being deposited by the pigs, there is no right in the municipality to collect the same and hence the municipality is not competent to transfer any such right in favour of an intending purchaser.

Thus, the goods that were subject matter of the contract never came into existence. The court ruled:

---

[10] *Alluri Narayana Murthy Raju* v. *Dist Collector, Visakhapatnam*, AIR 2008 AP 264.

[11] *Markapur Municipality* v. *Dodda Ramireddi*, AIR 1972 AP 299.

The contract therefore became impossible of performance as the goods never came into existence. The contract between the parties rested upon the fundamental condition that the dung becomes available to the purchaser and when the said event did not happen due to no fault of either party to the bargain, there is a clear case of frustration of the contract.

Court Case: Punj Sons Private Limited v. Union of India

Punj Sons Private Limited, New Delhi, entered into a contract with the Union of India for the supply of a large number of milk containers of twenty-litre capacity.[12] The containers were to be coated with 'hot dip tin coating'. This was done by using tin ingots. In the regulatory context of the 1960s and 1970s, tin ingots could be obtained only by obtaining a release order from the Mines and Minerals Trading Corporation (MMTC), a state body. Both the parties knew that tin ingot was essential for the manufacture, and it could be procured only with the release order of the MMTC. However, it was not a part of the contract that the Union of India would arrange the release order for the tin ingot. After the parties entered in the contract, the Union of India made inter-departmental communication for the release order for the tin ingots, but the MMTC did not issue the order. The Delhi High Court noted:

There is thus no manner of doubt that the contract became impossible of performance because of the non-availability of one of the essential items that is tin ingots, which was essential for the manufacture and supply of the contracted store. The learned counsel for the Union of India contended that there was no condition or stipulation in the agreement regarding the supply of tin ingots by the claimant and the objector was bound under the contract to supply the contracted store within the stipulated period. I do not

agree in this contention. The parties very well knew at the time of entering into the contract that tin ingots was required for 'hot dip tin coating' of the cans. It is clear from the record that tin ingots was a canalised item and it could not be procured from the open market without a release order. In the circumstances, the condition of the supply of tin ingots can be implied from the nature of the contract.

In the judgment above, if it was an implied term of the contract for the Union of India to get the release order, it was in breach of the contract. The contract could not then be frustrated. When the parties entered the contract, it was known to them that the tin ingot could not be acquired without the release order. There is no subsequent event that made it more difficult than when the contract was made.

Price Escalation

Business parties claim frustration on the grounds of changes in the market conditions and imposition of taxes, making it onerous for them to perform a contract. The following two cases are on this theme.

Court Case: Alopi Parshad and Sons, Limited, M/s. v. Union of India

The contract for purchasing *ghee* required by army personnel expressly stipulated payment of charges at a specified rate.[13] The sellers claimed additional expenditure incurred on account of the abnormal rise in prices due to the start of the Second World War. The Supreme Court ruled:

Performance of the contract had not become impossible or unlawful; the contract was in fact performed...and they have received remuneration expressly stipulated to be paid therein. The Indian Contract Act does not enable a party to a contract

---

[12] *Punj Sons Private Limited* v. *Union of India*, AIR 1986 Del 158.

[13] *Alopi Parshad and Sons, Limited, M/s* v. *Union of India*, AIR 1960 SC 588.

to ignore the express covenants thereof, and to claim payment of consideration for performance of the contract at rates different from the stipulated rates, on some vague plea of equity.

The parties to an executory contract are often faced, in the course of carrying it out, with a turn of events which they did not at all anticipate—a wholly abnormal rise or fall in prices, a sudden depreciation of currency, an unexpected obstacle to execution, or the like Yet this does not in itself affect the bargain they have made. If, on the other hand, a consideration of the terms of the contract, in the light of the circumstances existing when it was made, shows that they never agreed to be bound in fundamentally different situation which has now unexpectedly emerged, the contract ceases to bind at the point-not because the court in its discretion thinks it just and reasonable to qualify the terms of the contract, but because on its true construction it does not apply in that situation.

...

There is no general liberty reserved to the courts to absolve a party from liability to perform his part of the contract, merely because on account of an uncontemplated turn of events, the performance of the contract may become onerous. That is the law both in India and in England...

Frustration applies to a contract that is not yet performed. This is called an executory contract. It cannot apply to contracts that are already performed. In this case, the goods were already supplied. There could be no basis for paying more than the stipulated amount in the contract.

Court Case: Easun Engineering Co. Limited v. Fertilisers and Chemicals Travancore Limited

Fertilisers and Chemicals Travancore Ltd. (FEDO) entered into contract with EASUN for the supply and installation of eighteen power transformers.[14] The terms of the agreement were finalized on 7 March 1973. The contract did not have a price escalation clause. EASUN was to deliver the transformers at the project site for a fixed cost. The delivery was to commence on 19 October 1973 and completed by 19 February 1974. The erection and commissioning of the transformers was to be completed by 19 June 1974. EASUN could deliver only six of the 18 transformers. These were also delayed. The six transformers were delivered during the period between 14 June 1974 and 17 March 1975. The time of delivery was of essence to the contract. The contract provided that if EASUN failed to conform to fabrication schedule, FEDO could terminate the contract and reassign to other suppliers. FEDO terminated the contract and claimed damages. The claim of EASUN was that the price of transformer oil had risen by 400 per cent due to the war and increased taxation. Thus, it had become impossible for it to perform the contract. The Supreme Court, following the decision in *Alopi Parshad* v. *Union of India*, found 400 per cent increase abnormal, leading to a 'fundamentally different situation'. The increase in the words of the decision in *Satyabrata* v. *Mugneeram* had 'totally upsets the very foundation upon which parties rested their bargain'. Thus, the court ruled that the section applied to the case.

Executory Contracts

A contract that is already performed is an executed contract, and a contract that is yet to be performed is an executory contract. A contract cannot be impossible to perform if it has been performed. Thus, impossibility applies to only executory contracts. The following two cases are on lease of land. An interest in land, including a lease beyond certain duration, has to be registered with the registrar.

[14] *Easun Engineering Co. Limited*, v. *Fertilisers and Chemicals Travancore Limited*, AIR 1991 Mad 158.

Court Case: Raja Dhruv Dev Chand v. Raja Harmohinder Singh

This was a case of a lease of land that was executed.[15] Following the partition of the country, the person could not enjoy the benefits of the lease. Thus, a claim of frustration was made. The Supreme Court noted: 'There is a clear distinction between a completed conveyance and an executory contract, and events which discharge a contract do not invalidate a concluded transfer. ... By its express terms S. 56 of the Contract Act does not apply to cases in which there is a completed transfer.' In other words, the agreement to lease had become a lease as the parties had moved ahead and made the transfer of the property. However, a lease agreement will also provide for the parties to enjoy the fruits of it over the period of the lease. There also may be rights and obligations during the period of the lease. Do we take the lease contract as executed or executory? The court concluded: 'Authorities in the courts in India have generally taken the view that S. 56 of the Contract Act is not applicable when the rights and obligations of the parties arise under a transfer of property under a lease.'

In *Amir Chand* v. *Chuni Lal*, the reason that Section 56 did not apply to an executed lease was explained:

The rights of the parties after a lease was granted rest not in contract. Though under S.4 of the Transfer of Property Act, the chapters and sections of the said Act relating to contracts are to be taken as part of the Contract Act yet that does not mean that the provisions of Contract Act are to be read into the Transfer of Property Act.

Once a lease is executed, it is governed by the Transfer of Properties Act. Section 56 of the Contract Act cannot be imported into the Transfer of Property Act.

Court Case: Sushila Devi v. Hari Singh

The parties entered in an agreement to lease a plot of land for three years.[16] The lease deed was to be registered within fifteen days of the acceptance of the offer. Due to the partition of the country, neither could the lessee get access to the plot, nor could the agreement be executed. The Supreme Court ruled:

Once a valid lease comes into existence the agreement to lease disappears and its place is taken by the lease. It becomes a completed conveyance under which the lessee gets an interest in the property. There is a clear distinction between a completed conveyance and an executory contract. Events which discharge a contract do not invalidate a concluded transfer (see *Raja Dhruv Dev Chand* v. *Harmohinder Singh*, (AIR 1968 SC. 1024). ... But in this case, there was no lease. There was only an agreement to lease.... For one reason or the other, the contemplated lease deed was neither executed nor registered. Therefore we have before us only an agreement to lease and not a lease. Such an agreement comes within the scope of S.56 of the Contract Act.

...

From the facts found in this case it is clear that the plaintiffs sought to take on lease the properties in question with a view to enjoy those properties either by personally cultivating them or by sub-leasing them to others. That object became impossible because of the supervening events. Further the terms of the agreement between the parties relating to taking possession of the properties also became impossible of performance.

Force Majeure Clause

The development in relation to frustration of contracts made the contracting parties mindful in stipulating terms that could prevent frustration of the contract. The modality was to make express provisions on all things

---

[15] *Raja Dhruv Dev Chand* v. *Raja Harmohinder Singh*, AIR 1968 SC 1024.

[16] *Sushila Devi* v. *Hari Singh*, AIR 1971 SC 1756.

which could frustrate a contract, like war, floods, earth quake, and other natural calamities.Once an express provision was made, the express provision would apply. The strategy, on the face of it, gave the liberty to an interested party to demand performance even in the event of war, earthquake, natural calamities or other radical changes in the context. All that was needed was to make a stipulation to this effect. However, to require a person to do something impossible or near impossible, even if expressly agreed, would be struck down by the courts as void.

Thus, contracts provide express terms on events that can make performance impossible. However, these do not insist on performance at all costs. Balancing is done to require performance when impossible conditions cease and normalcy returns. The clause on impossibility in standard terms of contract is called *force majeure*. In the absence of this clause, the parties would have been excused the moment the impossibility arose. The stipulation makes it possible for the party to extend the performance of the contract as well as retain the option of terminating the contract. A *force majeure* clause lists the events that could cause impossibility, for example, (1) war/hostilities, (2) riot or civil commotion, (3) earthquake, flood, tempest, lightning or other natural disasters, and (4) restrictions imposed by the government or other statutory bodies that prevents or delays the execution of the contract. In its second leg, it provides that, first, the contract cannot be cancelled, but only extended to the extent of the occurrence of the event, and second, the party who has put up the terms retains the option of cancelling the project in the event of the delay lasting over a specified time.

Section 65 provides for restitution of the benefits obtained by the parties if a contract is frustrated. A contract can become void for several reasons. Frustration is only one among them. The section is a general one, providing for restitution in all contracts that become void. We will take up restoration of benefits in another chapter.

To summarize, a contract to do an impossible act is void. A change in law can make the performance of a valid contract illegal. The contract becomes void when the illegality arises. Performance of a contract can become impossible due to the subsequent change in events. If the parties have anticipated and provided for the occurrence of the event, it would be a contingent contract under Section 32. If the parties have not provided for it, the courts would assess the severity of the changed context under Section 56. It has to be assessed whether the change of circumstances is fundamental and strikes at the root of the contract itself. If the answer is yes, the contract is frustrated. The change or event need not be confined to a physical event. Further, impossibility is not to be taken in a literal sense. It includes a performance that is impractical or useless from the point of view of the object of the contract the parties had when they formed that contract. However, a contract that is already performed cannot be frustrated under the section.

24

Manner of Performance

Performance of a contractual obligation discharges the parties of their obligations. It also raises questions in relation to the person who should perform the contract, the time and place of performance, reciprocal promises, and the discharge when parties take joint liabilities. We will examine these in the chapter. Let us begin with the following illustration. Under a contract, A was to deliver a table of certain dimensions to B. B was delivered the table. The table matched with the description. In this context, consider the following situations.

1. The table was delivered not by A but C. obviously, C and A had an arrangement between them.
2. The agreed date for the delivery of table was 20 June. A delivered the table on 21 June.
3. The table was to be delivered at B's farm house. A delivered the table at B's city house.

In the above cases, the parties have a problem with the manner of performance of the contract. We could list some of these as follows: Who should perform the contract? When should the contract be performed? Where should the contract be performed?

How should the contract be performed? The Indian Contract Act, following common law, provides for these aspects. We will explore the provisions and the case law on these different issues.

WHO SHOULD PERFORM THE CONTRACT?

Let us think through the following cases and formulate principles on who should perform a contract.

Case 1. Under a contract, an interior designer was to design a retail showroom. The contract specifically mentioned that the designer herself would design and execute the project. The designer instead subcontracted it to another party. The customer was delivered a very elegantly and tastefully done retail store. Despite this, the customer has raised objections to the manner of performance of the contract.

Case 2. A painter was commissioned to paint a portrait. The painter sent his assistant instead. The customer refused to let the assistant to execute the work. The painter is claiming breach of contract by the customer.

Case 3. A painter was commissioned to do a portrait painting. The painter sent his assistant instead. After a conversation with the assistance, the customer realised that the assistant was very talented. He led the assistant do the portrait.

Case 4. Under a contract, a carpenter was to deliver a teak table of certain dimensions. The buyer was delivered a table of the specified dimensions. The buyer, however, realised that the carpenter had gotten the job done by another party. The customer refused to take delivery of the table.

In Case 1, the interior designer should design and execute the contract herself as it is agreed between the parties. In Case 2, it is apparent that one approaches a painter for the specific skill of the painter. It is impliedly agreed between the parties that the painter himself should do the painting. Case 3 is similar to Case 2. It is impliedly agreed that the painter himself should do the painting. However, if the customer accepts performance from the assistant, he later cannot claim that the painter ought to have performed the contract. In Case 4, there is no express term for the carpenter himself to make the table. The contract is only for the delivery of a table of certain dimensions made with teak wood. Thus, we derive the following the principles:

1. A contract must be performed by the party alone if the contract expressly provides performance by the party.
2. A contract must be performed by the party alone if it is implied that the party must perform the contract.
3. If a party accepts performance from another person, he cannot later object that the performance should have been by the party himself.
4. In other cases, apparently, there is no obligation for the party to perform the contract himself.

The Indian Contract Act expresses the principles in Sections 40 and 41. The Sections read:

40. Person by whom promise is to be performed—If it appears from the nature of the case that it was the intention of the parties to any contract that any promise contained in it should be performed by the promisor himself, such promise must be performed by the promisor. In other cases, the promisor or his representatives may employ a competent person to perform it.

Illustrations
(a) A promises to pay B a sum of money. A may perform this promise, either by personally paying the money to B or by causing it to be paid to B by another; and, if A dies before the time appointed for payment, his representatives must perform the promise, or employ some proper person to do so.
(b) A promises to paint a picture for B. A must perform this promise personally.

41. Effect of accepting performance from third person—When a promisee accepts performance of the promise from a third person, he cannot afterwards enforce it against the promisor.

In some contracts, two or more persons may have jointly promised the performance of a contract. In others, a person may have promised the performance to two or more persons jointly. The following sections provide on these:

42. Devolution of joint liabilities—When two or more persons have made a joint promise, then, unless a contrary intention appears by the contract, all such persons, during their joint lives, and, after the death of any of them, his representative jointly with the survivor or survivors, and, after the death of the last survivor, the representatives of all jointly, must fulfil the promise.

43. Any one of joint promisors may be compelled to perform—When two or more persons make a joint promise, the promisee may, in the absence of express agreement to the contrary, compel any one or more of such joint promisors to perform the whole of the promise.

Each promisor may compel contribution—Each of two or more joint promisors may compel every other joint promisor to contribute equally with himself to the performance of the promise, unless a contrary intention appears from the contract.

Sharing of loss by default in contribution—If any one of two or more joint promisors makes default in such contribution, the remaining joint promisors must bear the loss arising from such default in equal shares.

Explanation—Nothing in this section shall prevent a surety from recovering from his principal, payments made by the surety on behalf of the principal, or entitle the principal to recover anything from the surety on account of payments made by the principal.

Illustrations

(a) A, B and C jointly promise to pay D 3,000 rupees. D may compel either A or B or C to pay him 3,000 rupees.

(b) A, B and C jointly promise to pay D the sum of 3,000 rupees. C is compelled to pay the whole. A is insolvent, but his assets are sufficient to pay one-half of his debts. C is entitled to receive 500 rupees from A's estate, and 1,250 rupees from B.

(c) A, B and C are under a joint promise to pay D 3,000 rupees. C is unable to pay anything, and A is compelled to pay the whole. A is entitled to receive 1,500 rupees from B.

(d) A, B and C are under a joint promise to pay D 3,000 rupees, A and B being only sureties for C. C fails to pay. A and B are compelled to pay the whole sum. They are entitled to recover it from C.

In *Rama Shankar Singh* v. *Shyamlata Devi*,[1] A and B were joint lessees of a land. The lease had indicated the contribution of each of them in the annual rent; however, the lease was a joint one. The Supreme Court ruled that the lessees were jointly and severally liable. A decree obtained against one of the parties to a joint contract was not adequate. The Madras High Court, on Section 42, has noted:

Section 43 of the Indian Contract Act makes the liability on all contracts joint and several, and enables the promisee to sue one or more of the several joint promisors as he chooses, and excludes the right of

any of them to be sued along with his co-promisors. A decree obtained against some only of the joint promisors and remaining unsatisfied, is no bar to a second suit on the contract against the other joint contractors … so long as the liability of the defendants remains undischarged.[2]

Section 44 provides on the effect of release of one of the joint promisors. It reads:

44. Effect of release of one joint promisor—Where two or more persons have made a joint promise, a release of one of such joint promisors by the promisee does not discharge the other joint promisor or joint promisors; neither does it free the joint promisors so released from responsibility to the other joint promisor or joint promisors.

Court Case: Devilal v. Himat Ram

Himat Ram and Narottam Swaroop had taken a joint contract to construct the Udaipur Town Hall.[3] They were joined by other parties. Devilal was a subcontractor to this joint venture, and came to be in dispute with them. In the course of a suit against them, Himat Ram died and his legal representatives were not brought on record. Thus, the claim against Himat Ram abated. On the liability of the remaining parties, the Rajasthan High Court noted:

… the plaintiff has claimed a money decree against all the defendants jointly and severally for the amount which may be found due to the plaintiff … that each of several joint promisors is liable to the promisee, and the abatement of appeal against one of them does not result in abatement of the appeal as a whole.

It may be pointed out that under Section 44 of the Indian Contract Act where two or more persons have made a joint promise, a release of one of such joint promisors by the promisee does not discharge the other joint promisor or joint promisors; nor does it free the joint promisor so released from the

[1] *Rama Shankar Singh* v. *Shyamlata Devi*, AIR 1970 SC 716.

[2] *T. Radhakrishna* v. *K.V. Muthukrishnan*, AIR 1970 Mad 337.

[3] *Devilal* v. *Himat Ram*, AIR 1973 Raj 39.

responsibility to the other joint promisor or joint promisors. In view of this provision the release of one of joint promisors does not discharge the other joint promisors. Consequently, in the present case there is no impediment in the way of the appellant proceeding against the remaining respondents even though Himat Ram has died and his legal representatives have not been brought on the record.

Section 45 provides on devolution of rights when there are multiple parties.

45. Devolution of joint rights—When a person has made a promise to two or more persons jointly, then, unless a contrary intention appears from the contract, the right to claim performance rests, as between him and them, with them during their joint lives, and, after the death of any of them, with the representative of such deceased person jointly with the survivor or survivors, and, after the death of the last survivor, with the representatives of all jointly.

Illustration
A, in consideration of 5,000 rupees, lent to him by B and C, promises B and C jointly to repay them that sum with interest on a day specified. B dies .The right to claim performance rests with B's representative jointly with C during C's life, and after the death of C with the representatives of B and C jointly.

Time and Place of Performance

The provisions on time of performance in the Indian Contract are commonsensical. Section 47 provided:

47. Time and place for performance of promise, where time is specified and no application to be made—When promise is to be performed on a certain day, and the promisor has undertaken to perform it without application by the promisee, the promisor may perform it at any time during the usual hours of business on such day and at the place at which the promise ought to be performed.

Illustration
A promises to deliver goods at B's warehouse on first January. On that day A brings the goods to B's warehouse, but after the usual hour for closing it, and they are not received. A has not performed his promise.

The contracting parties must do what is agreed between them. The section merely applies the principle to time and place of performance of contract. In some contracts, the time of performance is specified. However, the other party is required to confirm it or indicate the place of performance. In other words, prior to performance, the other party has to make some communication. This is the meaning of the expression 'without application by the promisee' in the section. Section 48 deals with the cases where the time of performance is fixed; however, the other party has to make the communication. It reads:

48. Application for performance on certain day to be at proper time and place—When a promise is to be performed on a certain day, and the promisor has not undertaken to perform it without application by the promisee, it is the duty of the promisee to apply for performance at a proper place and within the usual hours of business.

Explanation—The question 'what is a proper time and place' is, in each particular case, a question of fact.

Section 49 is a corollary of Sections 47 and 48:

49. Place for performance of promise, where no application to be made and no place fixed for performance—When a promise is to be performed without application by the promisee, and no place is fixed for the performance of it, it is the duty of the promisor to apply to the promisee to appoint a reasonable place for the performance of the promise, and to perform it at such place.

Illustration
A undertakes to deliver a thousand maunds of jute to B on a fixed day. A must apply to B to appoint a reasonable place for the purpose of receiving it, and must deliver it to him at such place.

These three sections were for contracts where the time of perform was provided. Section 46 is for the contracts where the time of performance is not fixed. Understandably, the performance has to be in a reasonable time. It reads:

46. Time for performance of promise, where no application is to be made and no time is specified—Where, by the contract, a promisor is to perform his promise without application by the promisee, and no time for performance is specified, the engagement must be performed within a reasonable time.

Explanation—The question 'what is a reasonable time' is, in each particular case, a question of fact.

Sections 47, 48 and 49 provide for the time and place of performance of contract. We can revisit the sections to summarize the law on place of performance of contract. The parties may have provided, in express or implied terms, for the place of performance of the contract. The performance must be at the place. A contract may not have mentioned the place of performance. If the contract is 'without application', the party who has to perform should ask for the place of performance. Alternately, if the contract is 'with application', the other party should specify the place where the contract is to be performed.

Time of Essence

Under a contract, a retail store was to deliver and install a washing machine to a domestic user on Monday. The store called the customer on Monday evening and informed him that their technicians were tied up at another site. The store promised to deliver and install the machine on Tuesday. Is the store in breach on contract? As the store has not met the contracted time of delivery of the machine, the store is in breach of contract. For every breach by a party, the other party gains the right to claim damages. The customer can claim damages for the breach. Can the customer, however, terminate the contract for the breach? We learnt earlier that for every breach a contract cannot be terminated. A

contract can be terminated only for a breach of a condition. Is the time of performance a condition of the contract in the above case? It is not. In this kind of a consumer contract, ordinarily, parties do not intend it to be essential to the contract. There are contracts, however, where the time of performance is central and vital to the contract. Section 55 is an application of the principle that a contract can be terminated only for a breach of a condition in relation to time of performance. The section uses the alternate expressions 'essential' and 'essence' for condition. It reads:

55. Effect of failure to perform at fixed time, in contract in which time is essential—When a party to a contract promises to do a certain thing at or before a specified time, or certain things at or before specified times, and fails to do any such thing at or before the specified time, the contract, or so much of it as has not been performed, becomes voidable at the option of the promisee, if the intention of the parties was that time should be of the essence of the contract.

Effect of such failure when time is not essential—If it was not the intention of the parties that time should be of the essence of the contract, the contract does not become voidable by the failure to do such thing at or before the specified time; but the promisee is entitled to compensation from the promisor for any loss occasioned to him by such failure.

Effect of acceptance of performance at time other than that agreed upon—If, in case of a contract voidable on account of the promisor's failure to perform his promise at the time agreed, the promisee accepts performance of such promise at any time other than that agreed, the promisee cannot claim compensation for any loss occasioned by the non-performance of the promise at the time agreed, unless, at the time of such acceptance he gives notice to the promisor of his intention to do so.

The first paragraph provides that a contract can be set aside by the aggrieved party if time was of 'essence' to the contract. The second paragraph provides that a contract cannot be set aside if time was not of essence to the contract. The third paragraph provides that, having accepted delayed perform, the party cannot claim damages unless he brought his intention to claim damages at the time of accepting the delayed performance.

Why is time not of essence in every contract? In other words, why does the law not instead provide that unless the intention of the parties appears otherwise, time is of essence to every contract? In the contemporary context, there is a general expectation of punctuality. A party may feel that, having provided the time of performance for a contract, there is no excuse for delay. In the past, however, means of transport and communication were limited. Several factors, including inclement weather and unfavourable wind, could delay the movement of goods and persons. Thus, parties came to assume that there could be delays.

Section 55 states that time is not of essence unless the parties specifically mention it. The parties can express their intention in express terms or impliedly. Written contract documents often contain the statement: 'Time of essence to the contract.' The courts have formulated presumptions when parties have not provided on it in express terms. In commercial contracts, it is assumed that time is of essence. The Supreme Court in *China Cotton Exporters, M/s* v. *Beharilal Ramcharan Cotton Mills Limited* noted: 'Remembering, as we must, that in commercial contracts, time is ordinarily of the essence of the contract...'[4] Time is not of essence in the sale of immovable property. In *Chand Rani* v. *Kamal Rani*, the Supreme Court summarized the principle:[5]

It is a well-accepted principle that in the case of sale of immovable property, time is never regarded as the essence of the contract. In fact, there is a presumption against time being the essence of the contract. This principle is not in any way different from that obtainable in England. Under the law of equity which governs the rights of the parties in the case of specific performance of contract to sell real estate, law looks not at the letter but at the substance of the agreement. It has to be ascertained whether under the terms of the contract the parties named a specific time within which completion was to take place, really and in substance it was intended that it should be completed within a reasonable time. An intention to make time the essence of the contract must be expressed in unequivocal language.

However, time is considered to be of essence in a contract for renewal of lease. In *Caltex (India) Limited* v. *Bhagwan Devi Marodia*, the Supreme Court noted:[6]

At common law stipulations as to time in a contract giving an option for renewal of a lease of land were considered to be of the essence of the contract even if they were not expressed to be so and were construed as conditions precedent.... The reason is that a renewal of a lease is a privilege and if the tenant wishes to claim the privilege he must do so strictly within the time limited for the purpose.

RECIPROCAL PROMISES

In every contract, both parties have to perform their respective parts. The respective performance is the consideration of the parties. For example, in a sale contract, one party has to deliver goods and the other has to pay. Some contracts may have a series of performances by both parties, for example, party A delivering goods to party B every month. In some contracts, the respective performances may be linked to each other. For example, A will give wheat and packing material to B, and B will make wheat flour,

---

[4] *China Cotton Exporters, M/s* v. *Beharilal Ramcharan Cotton Mills Limited*, AIR 1961 SC 1295.

[5] *Chand Rani* v. *Kamal Rani*, AIR 1993 SC 1742.

[6] *Caltex (India) Limited* v. *Bhagwan Devi Marodia*, AIR 1969 SC 405.

pack it, and give it to A. A gives the wheat but not the packing material. B cannot perform his task unless A performs his. Thus, in some contracts, performance by one party may be dependent on the performance by the other. The dependence may be due to the very nature of the contract or the parties may have provided for it. The following sections are on performance and reciprocal performance.

50. Performance in manner or at time prescribed or sanctioned by promisee—The performance of any promise may be made in any manner, or at any time which the promisee prescribes or sanctions.

Illustrations

(a) B owes A 2,000 rupees. A desires B to pay the amount to A's account with C, a banker. B, who also banks with C, orders the amount to be transferred from his account to A's credit, and this is done by C. Afterwards, and before A knows of the transfer, C fails. There has been a good payment by B.

(b) A and B are mutually indebted. A and B settle an account by setting off one item against another, and B pays A the balance found to be due from him upon such settlement. This amounts to a payment by A and B, respectively, of the sums which they owed to each other.

(c) A owes B 2,000 rupees. B accepts some of A's goods in reduction of the debt. The delivery of goods operates as a part payment.

(d) A desires B, who owes him Rs.100, to send him a note for Rs.100 by post. The debt is discharged as soon as B puts into the post a letter containing the note duly addressed to A.

51. Promisor not bound to perform, unless reciprocal promisee ready and willing to perform—When a contract consists of reciprocal promises to be simultaneously performed, no promisor need perform his promise unless the promisee is ready and willing to perform his reciprocal promise.

Illustrations

(a) A and B contract that A shall deliver goods to B to be paid for by B on delivery.

A need not deliver the goods, unless B is ready and willing to pay for the goods on delivery.

B need not pay for the goods, unless A is ready and willing to deliver them on payment.

(b) A and B contract that A shall deliver goods to D at a price to be paid by instalments, the first instalment to be paid on delivery.

A need not deliver, unless B is ready and willing to pay the first instalment on delivery.

B need not that pay the first instalment, unless A is ready and willing to deliver the goods on payment of the first instalment.

52. Order of performance of reciprocal promise—Where the order in which reciprocal promises are to be performed is expressly fixed by the contract, they shall be performed in that order; and, where the order is not expressly fixed by the contract, they shall be performed in that order which the nature of the transaction requires.

Illustrations

(a) A and B contract that A shall build a house for B at a fixed price. A's promise to build the house must be performed before B's promise to pay for it.

(b) A and B contract that A shall make over his stock-in-trade to B at a fixed price, and B promises to give security for the payment of the money. A's promise need not be performed until the security is given, for the nature of the transaction requires that A should have security before he delivers up his stock.

53. Liability of party preventing event on which the contract is to take effect—When a contract contains reciprocal promises, and one party to the contract prevents the other from performing his promise, the contract becomes voidable at the option of the party so prevented; and he is entitled to compensation from the other party for any loss which he may sustain in consequence of the non-performance of the contract.

Illustration

A and B contract that B shall execute certain work for A for a thousand rupees. B is ready and willing to execute the work accordingly, but A prevents him from doing so. The contract is voidable at the option of B; and, if he elects to rescind it, he is entitled to recover from A compensation for any loss which he has incurred by its non-performance.

54. Effect of default as to that promise which should be first performed, in contract consisting of reciprocal promises—When a contract consists of reciprocal promises, such that one of them cannot be performed, or that its performance cannot be claimed till the other has been performed, and the promisor of the promise last mentioned fails to perform it, such promisor cannot claim the performance of the reciprocal promise, and must make compensation to the other party to the contract for any loss which such other party may sustain by the non-performance of the contract.

Illustrations

(a) A hires B's ship to take in and convey, from Calcutta to the Mauritius, a cargo to be provided by A, B receiving a certain freight for its conveyance. A does not provide any cargo for the ship. A cannot claim the performance of B's promise, and must make compensation to B for the loss which B sustains by the non-performance of the contract.

(b) A contracts with B to execute certain builder's work for a fixed price, B supplying the scaffolding and timber necessary for the work. B refuses to furnish any scaffolding or timber, and the work cannot be executed. A need not execute the work, and B is bound to make compensation to A for any loss caused to him by the non-performance of the contract.

(c) A contracts with B to deliver to him, at a specified price, certain merchandise on board a ship which cannot arrive for a month, and B engages to pay for the merchandise within a week from the date of the contract. B does not pay within the week. A's promise to deliver need not be performed, and B must make compensation.

(d) A promises B to sell him one hundred bales of merchandise, to be delivered next day, and B promises A to pay for them within a month. A does not deliver according to his promise. B's promise to pay need not be performed, and A must make compensation.

Court Case: Nathulal v. Phoolchand

Nathulal owned a ginning factory constructed on a plot of agricultural land. The land was entered in the revenue records in the name of his brother, Chittarmal.[7] On 26 February 1951, Nathulal agreed to sell the land and the ginning factory for Rs 43,011 to Phoolchand. He received a part payment Rs 22,011,

and put Phoolchand in possession of the property. The terms of the agreement were in writing. Under the terms of the agreement, Nathulal had undertaken to get the name of his brother Chittarmal removed from the revenue records. Following this, Phoolchand was to pay the balance on or before 7 May 1951. Phoolchand was willing to do so. However, the land continued to be in the name of Chittarmal till 6 October, 1952. As Phoolchand did not pay the money by the appointed date, Nathulal terminated the contract. The dispute in the case was whether the termination was justified. The Supreme Court ruled:

If, therefore, under the terms of the contract the obligations of the parties have to be performed in a certain sequence, one of the parties to the contract cannot require compliance with the obligations by the other party without in the first instance performing his own part of the contract which in the sequence of obligations is performable by him earlier. In view of the arrangement made by Phoolchand it was clear that he had at all relevant times made necessary arrangements for paying the amount due, but so long as Nathulal did not carry out his part of the contract, Phoolchand could not be called upon to pay the balance of the price. It must therefore be held that Phoolchand was at all relevant times willing to carry out his part of the contract.

Thus, Phoolchand was not in breach of the contract. The parties had to perform their parts in a sequence. Unless Nathulal performed his part, Phoolchand could not be called upon to pay.

Court Case: National Insurance Company Limited v. Seema Malhotra

Mr Yash Pal Malhotra entered into an insurance contract on 21 December 1993 with the National Insurance Company Limited by insuring a Maruti car for a sum

[7] *Nathulal* v. *Phoolchand*, AIR 1970 SC 546.

of Rs 1,50,000.[8] On the same day, he gave a cheque for Rs 4,492 towards the first instalment of the premium and the insurance company issued a cover note as contemplated in section 149 of the Motor Vehicles Act. The car met with an accident on 31 December 1993. Mr Malhotra died and the car was badly damaged. In the meanwhile, the cheque had gone for clearance. Mr Malhotra's bank intimated the insurance company that the cheque was dishonoured as there were no funds in his account. Following this, on 20 January 1994, the insurance company send an intimation to Mr Malhotra's address. It read, 'Notwithstanding anything contained to the contrary, it is hereby agreed and declared that your cheque has been dishonoured by the bank. So we are cancelling the above said policy with immediate effect. The company is not at risk.'

Mr Malhotra's widow and children filed a claim for the loss of the vehicle. The insurance company refused this. The case was taken to the State Consumer Protection Commission. The Commission, thus, decided:

… it is a settled law that the insurer even if it had issued a cover note is entitled to cancel the policy if it fails to cash the cheque for premium. The concept of contract in essence envisages a proposal, acceptance and passing of consideration. In the absence of any consideration there can be no contract and that is all what is recognised by section 64VB of the Insurance Act, 1938. The insurer was justified in repudiating the contract and it has done it in time and soon after the cheque bounced. In this view of the matter there is no need for us to go to any other point that may arise in this case.

Mrs Malhotra moved the High Court of Jammu and Kashmir. The High Court took a different view. It noted:

[8] *National Insurance Company Limited* v. *Seema Malhotra*, AIR 2001 SC 1197.

While ordering the cancellation of the policy in question, respondent insurance company instead of cancelling the same due to dishonour of cheque for the premium from the date it was issued i.e., December 21, 1993, chose to cancel it 'with immediate effect'. This clearly indicates that till the issuance of this communication respondent insurance company itself treated the policy as subsisting. Besides this, it had not chosen to treat the same as cancelled from the date of issue. In the face of this position, this case need not detain us any further and for this reason the argument addressed on behalf of the insurance company based on section 64VB of the Insurance Act, 1938, also does not hold good. There was nothing which prevented the insurance company to have informed the appellants that the policy stood cancelled from the date of its issuance, and as such it is not liable for the payment of any compensation.

Section 64VB of the Insurance Act, 1938, provided that 'in the case of risks for which premium can be ascertained in advance, the risk may be assumed not earlier than the date on which the premium has been paid in cash or by cheque to the insurer.' The case went in appeal to the Supreme Court. The Supreme Court noted on the insurance business:

The essence of the insurance business is the coverage of risk by undertaking to indemnify the insured against loss or damage. They agree to pay the damages arising out of any accident by taking a chance that no accident might happen. The motivation of the insurance business is that the premium would turn to be the profit of the business in case no damage occurs. Such business of the insurance company can be carried on only with the premium paid by the insured persons on the insurance policy. The only profit, if at all the insurance company makes, of the insurance business is the premium paid when no accident or damage occurs. But to ask the insurance company to bear the entire loss of damages of somebody else without the company receiving a pie towards premium is contrary to the principles of equity, though the insurance companies are made liable to third parties on account of statutory compulsions due to the initial agreement, entered into between the insured and the company concerned.

The Supreme Court ruled as follows:

Sections 51, 52 and 54 of the Indian Contract Act, can profitably be referred to for the purpose of deciding the point. They are subsumed under the sub-title 'Performance of reciprocal promises' in the said Act. Section 51 deals with a contract concerning reciprocal promises to be simultaneously performed and in such a contract the promisor is absolved from performing his promise unless the promisee is ready or willing to perform his part of the promise. Section 52 says that where the order in which reciprocal promises are to be performed has not been expressly provided in the contract such promise shall be performed in that order which the nature of the transaction warrants. Illustration (b) given to section 52 highlights the utility of the provisions. That illustration is as follows: A and B contract that A shall make over his stock-in-trade to B at a fixed price, and B promises to give security for the payment of the money. A's promise need not be performed until the security is given, for the nature of the transaction requires that A should have security before he delivers up his stock.

Section 54 of the Contract Act is to be read in that background. It is extracted below:

'When a contract consists of reciprocal promises, such that one of them cannot be performed, or that its performance cannot be claimed till the other has been performed, and the promiser of the promise last mentioned fails to perform it, such promiser cannot claim the performance of the reciprocal promise, and must make compensation to the other party to the contract for any loss which such other party may sustain by the non-performance of the contract.'

In a contract of insurance when an insurer gives a cheque towards payment of premium or part of the premium, such a contract consists of reciprocal promises. The drawer of the cheque promises the insurer that the cheque, on presentation, would yield the amount in cash. It cannot be forgotten that a cheque is a bill of exchange drawn on a specified banker. A bill of exchange is an instrument in writing containing an unconditional order directing a certain person to pay a certain sum of money to a certain person. It involves a promise that such money would be paid.

Thus, when the insured fails to pay the premium promised, or when the cheque issued by him towards the premium is returned dishonoured by the bank concerned the insurer need not perform his part of the promise. The corollary is that the insured cannot claim performance from the insurer in such a situation.

Under Section 25 of the Contract Act an agreement made without consideration is void. Section 65 of the Contract Act says that when a contract becomes void any person who has received any advantage under such contract is bound to restore it to the person from whom he received it. So, even if the insurer has disbursed the amount covered by the policy to the insured before the cheque was returned dishonoured, the insurer is entitled to get the money back.

However, if the insured makes up the premium even after the cheque was dishonoured but before the date of accident it would be a different case as payment of consideration can be treated as paid in the order in which the nature of transaction required it. As such an event did not happen in this case the insurance company is legally justified in refusing to pay the amount claimed by the respondents.

In the light of the above legal position we uphold the contention of the appellant insurance company. We, therefore, allow this appeal and set aside the impugned judgment of the Division Bench of the High Court. The order passed by the State Consumer Commission will stand restored.

In this chapter, we have explored the several facets of performance of a contract. This included the person who should perform the contract, the time and place of performance of the contract, and reciprocal promises. Performance of a contractual obligation discharges the parties of their obligations. In the next chapter, we will explore discharge of contractual obligations by mutual consent.

25

Discharge by Mutual Consent

Much in the way parties voluntarily create contractual obligations, they can free themselves of the obligations by mutual consent. This can take three forms. First, the parties enter into an agreement to bring an existing contract between them to an end. This is called remission. The parties stand discharged of their contractual obligations under the contract. Second, the parties by agreement can change the terms of an existing contract. This is called alteration. In this case, while the parties are discharged of some of the contractual obligations, they take up new obligations. Third, the parties by agreement replace an existing contract with another one. This is called novation. In this case, the parties are completely discharged of the contractual obligations from the first contract. However, they take up new obligations under the second contract. Thus, in all the three forms, the parties reach an agreement changing an existing contract. This agreement to be binding must also be supported by consideration for both parties. We took up this aspect in the discussion on consideration. Thus, the parties will be discharged of their original obligations only if the subsequent agreement provides for it and

is supported by consideration. Let us study this with the following illustrations.

Remission, Alteration, and Novation

X and Y have a contract whereby X will buy fabric and make a dress for Y, and Y will pay him Rs 4,000. X and Y mutually agree not to go ahead with the agreement. This is called remission. The consideration for the parties for the second agreement, that is, the agreement not to go ahead with the earlier contract, is the discharge from their respective obligations, that is, for one to make the dress and the other to pay. If Y has already paid Rs 3,000, there is still consideration for the both the parties. X need not make the dress and Y need not pay the remaining Rs 1,000. If Y, however, has already paid Rs 4,000, there is no consideration for Y in a remission. Similarly, if X has already delivered the dress there is no consideration for X in the remission. Such agreements cannot be enforced. Section 62 of the Contract Act embodies this principle. It states:

62. **Effect of novation, rescission, and alteration of contract**—If the parties to a contract agree to substitute a new contract for it, or to rescind or alter it, the original contract need not be performed.

The courts have confirmed that Section 62 requires agreement, and consideration for it to be enforceable.[1] In *Unikol Bottlers Limited, M/s* v. *M/s Dhillon Kool Drinks*, the Delhi High Court explored the requirement of consideration in the case of termination of an agreement by mutual consent.

> Section 62 of the Contract Act recognises the right of the parties to agree to put an end to a contract. The mutual agreement to put an end to existing rights and obligations of the parties under a contract is … termination of a contract simpliciter. Salmond has beautifully put this in the following words:—'the vinculum juris of contractual obligation may be severed and destroyed by mutual consent just as it was constituted thereby'.
>
> If at all consideration is needed it can be found inasmuch as both the parties agree to give up their respective rights and benefits under the original agreement as also they release each other from mutual burdens and obligations under the agreement. The discharge of one party from its obligation to perform further is a sufficient consideration for discharge of the other party from further performing its obligations under the contract. Therefore, I do not find any substance in this ground of attack on the Supplemental Agreement.[2]

Thus, whether there is still something left for both the parties to do is decisive in holding the second agreement binding. Abandonment of the remaining duties is the respective consideration for the parties. Where one party has fully performed its part, there would be no consideration for that party. For this reason, the judgments use the words 'executory' and 'executed', in relation to the consideration.

X and Y change the terms of the contract for dress-making. Instead of cotton, the dress is to be made with silk fabric. As a term of a contract is changed, this is alteration of

the contract. The agreement is not enforceable as there is no consideration for the dressmaker. If a customer were to pay him Rs 4,050 instead of Rs 4,000, the additional Rs 50 would become consideration for the dressmaker. Similarly, an agreement for delay in delivery of the dress is not enforceable as there is no consideration for the customer. The extension of time is a consideration for the dressmaker, but there is no consideration for the customer. If the agreement stipulates that the customer will pay Rs 2,950 instead of Rs 3,000, the rebate of Rs 50 would be the consideration for the customer.

Novation of Terms of Contract

Zed Limited had a contract to buy thirty computers from a vendor for Rs 3 lakh. The vendor delivered fifteen computers. The parties reworked the contract where the vendor would not supply the remaining computers but would install antivirus software in 300 computers belonging to Zed Limited. In this case, an existing contract is replaced by another one. This is called novation. In this case, both the parties have consideration.

There are two facets to remission, alteration, or novation of contracts. It is not possible for the parties to contemplate each and every aspect of a contract, or each contingency that may arise in relation to it. The parties often change the terms for their mutual benefit, and should have the flexibility to do so. On the other hand, a party that has partly performed the contract can hold the threat of withdrawing from the contract, forcing the other party to agree to change the terms of the contract. The common law courts have developed the law in this context of contrary demands.

The common law courts used the term 'accord and satisfaction' to judge the validity of the new agreement. 'Accord' is another term for agreement. Thus, the courts

---

[1] *Union of India* v. *Kishorilal Gupta and Bros*, AIR 1959 SC 1362.

[2] *Unikol Bottlers Limited* v. *M/s Dhillon Kool Drinks*, AIR 1995 Del 25.

determined whether there was an agreement for alteration or novation. 'Satisfaction' represented mutual benefit to the parties. This was the consideration for the agreement. Scrutton, LJ in *British Russian Gazette and Trade Outlook Ltd.* v. *Associated Newspapers, Limited*, thus, described the concept of 'accord and satisfaction':[3]

Accord and satisfaction is the purchase of a release from an obligation whether arising under contract ... by means of any valuable consideration, not being the actual performance of the obligation itself. The accord is the agreement by which the obligation is discharged. The satisfaction is the consideration which makes the agreement operative.

Thus, an agreement to alter a contract must have 'satisfaction', that is, consideration, to be operative. Let us explore novation and the scope of Section 62 with *Union of India* v. *Kishorilal Gupta and Bros*.

Court Case: Union of India v. Kishorilal Gupta and Bros

A firm of contractors of the name of Kishorilal Gupta and Brothers entered into three contracts with the British Government in 1943 and 1944 to manufacture and supply certain military stores with raw material supplied by the government.[4] Before the contracts could be concluded, disputes arose between the parties. The government cancelled the contracts. The contractor claimed damages, and the government, the value of the unused raw material. The parties mutually settled their claims for the three contracts. In each settlement, the contractor was to pay a certain sum to the government. The settlements were done at different points of time.

As the settlement for the third contract was the last one between the same parties, it also assimilated the claims in the previous one. In other words, the claims were reduced in one document. The document provided for monthly payments and required the contractor to hypothecate some of its properties. The contractor failed to do this.

Each of the three original contracts contained an arbitration clause, and government moved to appoint arbitrators. The third and final settlement had provided: 'The contracts stand finally concluded in terms of the settlement and no party will have further or other claim against the other.' The contention of the contractor was that the mutual agreement between the parties had extinguished the original contracts. It was claimed that as the new contract did not have an arbitration clause, the dispute could not be taken to arbitration. The Supreme Court ruled: 'One of the modes by which a contract can be discharged is by the same process which created it i.e., by mutual agreement; the parties to the original contract may enter into a new contract in substitution of the old one.' The new contract can have different effects on the original contract. Let us explore the court's reasoning with simple illustrations.

X has given raw material to Y to manufacture goods and supply. A dispute arises between the parties. The parties settle on Monday that X will keep the raw material and pay Rs 2 lakh to Y by Friday in full and final settlement. The original contract is fully discharged by the second one. Even if X does not pay the due amount by Friday, the original contract will not get revived. Consider an alternate second agreement where the parties provided that the claims under the original contract would stand discharged subject to X paying Rs 2 lakh to Y by Friday. In this case, the first contract will be extinguished only on

---

[3] *British Russian Gazette and Trade Outlook Limited* v. *Associated Newspapers, Limited*, (1933) 2 KB 616.

[4] *Union of India* v. *Kishorilal Gupta and Bros*, AIR 1959 SC 1362.

successful performance of the second contract. The Supreme Court drew on the above point from the Privy Council in *Payana Reena Saminathan* v. *Pana Lana Palaniappa*, 1914 AC 618 and Scrutton, LJ in *British Russian Gazette and Trade Outlook Limited* v. *Associated Newspapers, Limited*, 1933–2 KB 616 and noted:

… a contract may be discharged by the parties thereto by a substituted agreement and thereafter the original cause of action arising under the earlier contract is discharged and the parties are governed only by the terms of the substituted contract. The ascertainment of the intention of the parties is essentially a question of fact to be decided on the facts and circumstances of each case.

The third and final agreement in the case had provided: 'The contracts stand finally concluded in terms of the settlement and no party will have any further or other claim against the other.' Thus, the court ruled: 'The parties in express terms agreed that the earlier contract stood finally determined and that no party would have any claim thereunder against the other.' The following case further explores the theme of rescission and consideration.

Court Case: Compagnie Noga D'importation Et D'exportation Sa v. Abach

X and Y enter into a written agreement.[5] Subsequently, X and Y enter into another written agreement where, in the same document, the parties rescind the previous contract, and enter in another one where the same duty is to be performed by X, but the duties of Y are changed. The contention is on the construction of the arrangement and decision whether the last agreement has consideration or not. One party relied on *Stilk* v. *Myrick*,

[5] *Compagnie Noga D'importation Et D'exportation Sa* v. *Abach*, (2003) 2 All ER(Comm) 915.

claiming that a promise to perform an existing contractual obligation does not constitute good consideration for a new agreement. The two contracts were the same. The opposing party contended: '… the principle in *Stilk* v. *Myrick* has no application where the earlier agreement has been contractually rescinded. In such a case consideration was supplied by the mutual release of the executory promises under the earlier agreement as well as the provision of fresh consideration in the later agreement.' The counter-contention of the first party was:

… one must look at the substance and not the form. The substance is that the … obligations remained the same under both agreements. … If this had been done by varying the earlier agreement there would have been no consideration for the variation. It should not matter that it was done by rescission and replacement. He accepted however that there would be consideration if there was a real interval between the two. But here, as the rescission and replacement took place simultaneously or within a fictional *scintilla temporis*, it could not and should not provide consideration.

Scintilla temporis means tiny bit of time. Thus, the contention was that as one reads the document, the rescission would come first and creation of the second contract later. However, the events are separated by only a tiny bit of time and it is ludicrous to claim that they are separated. It should be assumed that the rescission and replacement took place simultaneously. The Court of Appeal ruled:

The essential difference between rescission and variation for present purposes is that a contract comes to an end when it is rescinded but continues if it is varied. If the rescinded agreement is replaced by a new agreement containing the same obligations, it is not the old agreement which compels the performance of those obligations but the new agreement. It follows that the principle in *Stilk* v. *Myrick* has no application to this situation because it is premised on the continuation of the obligations in the old agreement. Mr Flint (counsel) accepted this analysis in a case where there was an interval between the rescission and replacement, but I do not see that there can be any difference in principle between the two situations.

...

The problem with his submission is that it assumes that the obligations under the old agreement continue whereas the parties have expressly agreed to tear that agreement up. That is not appealing to the substance of the transaction, as Mr Flint submits, but creating a fiction which the parties have expressly disavowed. It is not necessary in my judgment to create a *scintilla temporis* for there to be a rescission and replacement. It can be achieved concurrently by the same document in the way it was done in this case. That is what the parties in this case intended.

As we noted in *Union of India* v. *Kishorilal*, in an agreement of novation, it depends on the agreement between the parties whether the original contracts is discharged on the making of the agreement or performance of the agreement. The following is another case relating to the issue.

Court Case: Lata Construction v. Dr Rameshchandra Ramniklal Shah

M/s Lata Construction is a builder.[6] It was building a housing complex named Madhusudanin Vile Parle, Mumbai. Builders start selling specific flats even before the construction starts. Dr Rameshchandra Ramniklal Shah entered into an agreement with M/s Lata Construction on 27 January 1987 to buy a specific flat in the building. On signing of the contract, Mr. Shah paid the builder Rs 3,70, 000. Thereafter, Dr Shah paid a total of Rs 2,00,000 as and when demanded by Lata Construction. Dr Shah was based in Libya. By June 1988, when he returned from Libya, the construction of the building was complete.

6   *Lata Construction* v. *Dr Rameshchandra Ramniklal Shah*, AIR 2000 SC 380.

Dr Shah requested Lata Construction to receive the balance payment and deliver possession of the flat. Lata Construction refused to do this on the plea that the building was still under construction and the electricity, plumbing, tiling, and fencing was in progress. They, however, assured Dr Shah that as and when the building would be completed in all respects, they would accept the balance amount and deliver possession.

In April 1990, when Dr Shah returned from Libya on a short visit to India and visited the building, he found that the flat was locked and outside the main door of the flat a name plate bearing 'Indira Joshi' had been put up. Obviously, the builder had sold the flat to another person. Finally, in January 1991, Lata Construction expressed their inability to give possession of the flat to Dr Shah. Dr Shah entered into a fresh agreement with Lata Construction on 23 February 1991, where Lata Construction would pay Dr Shah a sum of Rs 9,51,000 in three instalments in lieu of the flat on or before 30 May 1991. The schedule for payment was Rs 3,00,000 by 20 March 1991; Rs 3,00,000 by 20 April 1991; and Rs 3,51,000 by 30 May 1991.

Lata Construction did not honour the commitment. Following this, Dr Shah approached the National Consumer Commission. The Commission directed Lata Construction to pay a sum of Rs 9,51,000, with interest at the rate of 18 per cent per annum with effect from 23 February 1991 till the date of payment. Another sum of Rs 1,00,000 was allowed as compensation for pain and suffering undergone by Dr Shah. The Commission also allowed a sum of Rs 10,000 to Dr Shah as costs of the proceedings. Lata Construction challenged the decision of the National Commission before the Supreme Court. One of the arguments of Lata Construction was that the second agreement replaced the first agreement. As the second agreement was only to pay a debt, and not to provide a service, the dispute could not be taken to the consumer forum. A consumer can approach a court for a 'defect' in goods sold or 'deficiency' in service provided. The Supreme Court ruled:

One of the essential requirements of 'Novation'; as contemplated by Section 62, is that there should be complete substitution of a new contract in place of the old. It is in that situation that the original contract need not be performed. Substitution of a new contract in place of the old contract which would have the effect of rescinding or completely altering the terms of the original contract, has to be by agreement between the parties. A substituted contract should rescind or alter or extinguish the previous contract. But if the terms of the two contracts are inconsistent and they cannot stand together, the subsequent contract cannot be said to be in substitution of the earlier contract.

In the instant case, the rights under the original contract were not given up as it was specifically provided in the subsequent contract that the rights under the old contract shall stand extinguished only on payment of the entire amount of Rs 9,51,000/-. Since the amount was not paid by the appellants as stipulated by the subsequent contract, the rights under the original contract were still available to the respondents and he could legally claim enforcement of those rights. Obviously, under the original contract, the appellants were under an obligation to provide a flat to the respondents. This right would come to an end only when the appellants had, in pursuance of the subsequent contract, paid the entire amount of Rs 9,51,000/- to the respondents. Since they had not done so, the respondents could legally invoke the provisions of the earlier contract and claim before the Commission that there was 'deficiency in service' on the part of the appellants.

Whether an agreement is only altering the terms of an existing contract or replacing the original one with a new one is extremely significant. If it is only altering, the original contract will subsist except the changes. If it is being replaced, as we saw in the *Union of India* v. *Kishorilal* case, the entire contract will

cease to have effect. The Bombay High Court in *Andheri Bridge View Co-operative Housing Society Limited* v. *Krishnakant Anandrao Deo*,[7] has explored the difference:

Now, even if the parties have referred to an agreement as being not a new one but an old one with certain modifications, that would carry no weight if the law on the point is something contrary to what is understood by the parties. For example, we know that when there is a change in the constitution of a firm then the firm is a new partnership notwithstanding the fact that the parties may refer to it as the old partnership with a changed constitution. So also I would say that where there are material or substantial changes which go to the root of the agreement then this has to be regarded in law as a new agreement. What would be the position if the parties agree to sell property A and at a later stage they agree that not property A but property B should be sold? Clearly this would be a new agreement notwithstanding the fact that all other terms regarding rate for payment etc. may also be similar. So also payment of price or the rate of payment is a material part of the agreement for sale. Both the subject-matter and the rate of payment are material parts of any agreement for sale and change in either of these terms brings about a new agreement.

Thus, the court declared that the substance of the contract, and not its form, were to be regarded in deciding whether it was an alteration of a contract or replacement by a new contract.

Novation of Parties
Novation can also apply when new parties are brought to the contract. The key word in section 62 is 'parties to the contract agree'. Section 62, thus, illustrates this:

(a) A owes money to B under a contract. It is agreed between A, B and C that B shall thenceforth accept C as his debtor, instead of A. The old debt to B is

[7] *Andheri Bridge View Co-operative Housing Society Limited* v. *Krishnakant Anandrao Deo*, AIR 1991 Bom 129.

at an end, and a new debt from C to B has been contracted.

(c) A owes B 1,000 rupees under a contract. B owes C 1,000 rupees. B orders A to credit C with 1,000 rupees in his books, but C does not assent to the arrangement. B still owes C 1,000 rupees, and no new contract has been entered into.

The following case is on the theme of novation of parties.

Court Case: Godan Namboothiripad v. Kerala Financial Corporation

The Kerala Financial Corporation sanctioned a loan to Gopinatha Menon for purchase of a transport vehicle.[8] The loan was to be repaid in instalments. Gopinatha Menon defaulted in paying the instalments. In consequence of this default, the vehicle was seized by the Corporation. Godan wrote to the Corporation requesting them to release the vehicle, and undertook to pay the balance amount due to them. The Corporation acquiesced to the request. Subsequently, Godan Namboothiripad also defaulted in paying the instalment. A dispute arose on the liabilities of the parties. The Supreme Court ruled:

Thus the Corporation as well as Gopinatha Menon who were parties to the old contract agreed for a new contract with the appellant...in respect of the loan amount and accordingly the Corporation agreed to release the vehicle in favour of the appellant. We, therefore find...that there was novation of contract whereby the original debtor Gopinatha Menon ceased to be a debtor and the appellant undertook the liability as the principal debtor to pay the outstanding dues.

Thus, novation can create a new contract between the same parties or, by consent of the parties, replace parties to the contract.

[8] *Godan Namboothiripad* v. *Kerala Financial Corporation*, AIR 1998 Ker 31.

Agreement Altering Payment of Debt

A person can owe money to another for many reasons. It could be a loan, sale price, damages, fine, or earnest deposit. The money would be payable by a certain time and at a mentioned place. An agreement to change the terms of a debt can be binding only if it is supported by consideration for both the parties. A person who agrees to get less than due does not seem to benefit from the agreement. Should such contracts be enforced? Will the agreement discharge the person of his earlier liabilities? We will develop a perspective on it by looking at the following cases.

Case: Part-paid Seller

S sold goods to B for Rs 30, 000. After receiving the goods, B told S that he could not afford to pay Rs 30,000. The parties settled that S would receive Rs 25,000 instead of Rs 30,000. After S received Rs 25,000, he demanded the remaining Rs 5,000. Was there an agreement to receive a lesser sum than was due? What is the consideration for the parties in the second agreement? Is the agreement enforceable? Does it matter how B came to owe the money to S for the second agreement between them?

Case: Part-payment of Debt

B owes C, Rs 1 lakh payable on or by 15th of the month in Mumbai. Consider the enforceability of the following agreements between the parties as full and final settlement of the debt:

- Payment of Rs 80, 000 on 15th of the month in Mumbai.
- Payment of Rs 1 lakh on 20th of the month in Mumbai.
- Payment of Rs 1 lakh on 15th of the month in Delhi.
- Payment of Rs 80, 000 on 10th of the month in Mumbai.

A creditor agrees to receive less than the due amount, at the time and place originally agreed on. The consideration for the debtor is the benefit of paying the lesser amount. However, there is no benefit to the creditor. In practice, it is advantageous for the creditor to take what he gets from a debtor who is otherwise unable or unwilling to pay. However, the creditor has the right to receive the full amount. Thus, there can be 'accord', but never any 'satisfaction' for a creditor in receiving a lesser sum than what is due. Thus, an agreement to receive a lesser amount than what was owed can never be supported by consideration. As a result, such contracts cannot be enforced. The classic case on the theme is *Pinnel's* case.

Court Case: Pinnel's Case

The case dates back to 1602. X owed money to Y.[9] Under an agreement, X was required to pay 8 pounds 10s on 11 November 1600. On Y's request, X paid Y 5 pounds 2s 2d on 1 October 1600. Y accepted it as full satisfaction of the debt. Y later went to the court, claiming the balance amount. In deciding the case, Sir Edward Coke formulated the following doctrine:

… that payment of a lesser sum on the day in satisfaction of a greater cannot be any satisfaction for the whole, because it appears to the judges that by no possibility a lesser sum can be a satisfaction to the plaintiff for a greater sum; but the gift of a horse, a hawk, or a robe, etc, in satisfaction is good, for it shall be intended that a horse, hawk, or robe might be more beneficial to the plaintiff than the money in respect of some circumstance, or otherwise the plaintiff would not have accepted of it in satisfaction. But when the whole sum is due, by no intendment the acceptance of a parcel can be a satisfaction to the plaintiff; but in the case at Bar it was resolved that the payment and acceptance of parcel before the day in satisfaction of

the whole would be a good satisfaction in regard of circumstance of time; for peradventure parcel of it before the day would be more beneficial to him than the whole at the day, and the value of the satisfaction is not material; so if I am bound in 20 pounds to pay you 10 pounds at Westminster, and you request me to pay 5 pounds at the day at York, and you will accept it in full satisfaction for the whole 10 pounds, it is a good satisfaction for the whole, for the expenses to pay it at York is sufficient satisfaction.

The meaning of the passage is clear. It is interesting to note the distinction the court made between cash and goods. In today's context, cash means goods and goods mean cash. This near equivalence is a result of the commodification of the economy. This happened with the development of trade and commerce. It was not always like this, and the distinction was relevant. Again, in today's context, the place of payment is not significant as banks can arrange to pay anywhere for a small charge. But in the 1600s, the place of payment was an important factor for the parties. A modern case on the theme is the House of Lords case, *Foakes* v. *Beer*.[10] It was an agreement to accept less than what was due. The court noted:

As to accord and satisfaction … there could be no complete satisfaction so long as any future instalment remained payable.… The question, therefore, is nakedly raised by this appeal whether your Lordships are now prepared, not only to overrule as contrary to law the doctrine stated … in Pinnel's Case … but to treat a prospective agreement … for satisfaction of a debt … less than the whole debt, as binding in law …

The answer of the court was 'no'. The court, however, was ambivalent about the answer. If the position protected the creditor from the debtor securing unfair advantage, often, debtor and creditor find such arrangements

---

[9] *Pinnel's Case*, (1602) 5 Co Rep 117a.

[10] *Foakes* v. *Beer*, (1881–1885) All ER Rep 106.

mutually beneficial. In *Foakes* v. *Beer*, Lord Blackburn asserted:

… all men of business, whether merchants or tradesmen, do every day recognise and act on the ground that prompt payment of a part of their demand may be more beneficial to them than it would be to insist on their rights and enforce payment of the whole. Even where the debtor is perfectly solvent, and sure to pay at last, this often is so. Where the credit of the debtor is doubtful it must be more so.

The House of Lords could not exceed the weight of authority of the previous cases. Since then, with the advancement of trade and commerce, the claim to recognize an agreement to pay less than due has become weightier. The courts, thus, have attempted to weaken the authority of previous cases by qualifying them. However, they have not managed to break away from their authority of. This has led to ambivalences in the position of the law. In *D & C Builders Limited* v. *Rees*[11] the Court of Appeal applied *Foakes* v. *Beer* and reasserted: '… payment of a lesser sum than the amount of a debt due cannot be a satisfaction of the debt, unless there is some benefit to the creditor added so that there is an accord and satisfaction.'

In *Williams* v. *Roffrey Bros and Nicholls (Contractors) Limited*,[12] a sub-contractor, for genuine reasons, midway claimed inability to complete some carpentry work. The contractor agreed to pay more for the same work as he would have incurred penalty if the completion of the housing project were delayed. The court diluted the concept of consideration by recognizing that if the party 'obtains

in practice a benefit, or obviates a disbenefit', it would lead to satisfaction of the party.

In re Selectmove,[13] before the Court of Appeal, also involved an agreement to pay less than due. The debtor relied on the decision in *Williams* v. *Roffey Bros. & Nicholls (Contractors) Limited.* for the proposition that a promise to perform an existing obligation can amount to good consideration provided that there are 'practical benefits' to the promisee. The court noted:

I see the force of the argument, but the difficulty that I feel with it is that if the principle of the Williams case is to be extended to an obligation to make payment, it would in effect leave the principle in *Foakes* v. *Beer* without any application. When a creditor and a debtor who are at arm's length reach agreement on the payment of the debt by instalments to accommodate the debtor, the creditor will no doubt always see a practical benefit to himself in so doing.… But that was a matter expressly considered in *Foakes* v. *Beer* yet held not to constitute good consideration in law. *Foakes* v. *Beer* was not even referred to in the Williams case, and it is in my judgment impossible, consistently with the doctrine of precedent, for this court to extend the principle of the Williams case to any circumstances governed by the principle of *Foakes* v. *Beer*. If that extension is to be made, it must be by the House of Lords or, perhaps even more appropriately, by Parliament after consideration by the Law Commission.

Williams v. *Roffrey* was different from the other cases as it was about paying more for the same job. This could be treated as equivalent to a person getting more than due. Following this, it could be argued that much the way an agreement to get less than due is not supported by consideration, so is an agreement to get more than due. Through this route, the case could be used to challenge the decision in the Pinnel's case. The court

---

[11] *D & C Builders Limited* v. *Rees*, (1965) 3 All ER 837.

[12] *Williams* v. *Roffrey Bros and Nicholls (Contractors) Limited*, (1991) 1 QB 1.

[13] *In re Selectmove*, (1995) 1 WLR 474.

did not allow this. It did not agree to see a contractual term for payment of money as a debt. This was partly out of the concern in not upsetting the House of Lord's decision in the Pinnel's case.

AGREEMENT ON PAYMENT OF DEBT: INDIAN LAW

With the expansion of trade and commerce, the contradictions experienced by the British courts have become acute. The contradiction has long been evident, even before the Indian Contract Act was made. The makers of the Indian Contract Act reconciled this contradiction by dispensing with the requirement of consideration where the parties agree to settle a debt for a lesser amount. Section 63 of the India Contract Act provides:

63. Promise may dispense with or remit performance of promise—Every promisee may dispense with or remit, wholly or in part, the performance of the promise made to him, or may extend the time for such performance, or may accept instead of it any satisfaction which he thinks fit.

Illustrations

(a) A promises to paint a picture for B. B afterwards forbids him to do so. A is no longer bound to perform the promise.

(b) A owes B 5,000 rupees. A pays to B, and B accepts, in satisfaction of the whole debt, 2,000 rupees paid at the time and place at which the 5,000 rupees were payable. The whole debt is discharged.

(c) A owes B 5,000 rupees. C pays to B 1,000 rupees, and B accepts them, in satisfaction of his claim on A. This payment is a discharge of the whole claim.

(d) A owes B, under a contract, a sum of money, the amount of which has not been ascertained. A, without ascertaining the amount, gives to B, and B, in satisfaction thereof, accepts, the sum of 2,000 rupees. This is a discharge of the whole debt, whatever may be its amount.

(e) A owes B 2,000 rupees, and is also indebted to other creditors. A makes an arrangement with his creditors, including B, to pay them a composition of eight annas in the rupee upon their respective demands. Payment to B of 1,000 rupees is a discharge of B's demand.

The Privy Council in *Chunna Mal-Ram Nath Firm* v. *Mool Chand-Ram Bhagat Firm*,[14] settled the contrary interpretations by the high courts that under the section both agreement and consideration is needed. It noted: 'The language of the section does not refer to any such agreement and ought not to be enlarged by any implication of English doctrines.' The Supreme Court in *Citi Bank N.A.* v. *Standard Chartered Bank*[15] emphasized the difference between Sections 62 and 63. Novation, rescission, or alteration of a contract under Section 62 of the Indian Contract Act can only be done with the agreement of both the parties to the contract. However, under Section 63, a promisee can act unilaterally. Let us look at Section 63 using the first illustration. A under a contract is to paint a picture for B for a price. B proposes to A that he not go ahead with the contract. A accepts it. This is remission of the contract with mutual consent under Section 62. B tells A that he need not do the painting. B cannot later claim breach of contract by A. In fact, A will have the right to claim damages for the breach of contract. As the section is under the chapter on discharge of agreements, it provides for different situations in which the parties can be discharged from their obligations. The section, by its wording and illustrations, is providing for a contract where a person accepts a lesser amount than due. Let us look at the implications of the section with the cases from the Indian courts.

---

[14] *Chunna Mal-Ram Nath Firm* v. *Mool Chand-Ram Bhagat Firm*, AIR 1928 PC 99.

[15] *Citi Bank N.A.* v. *Standard Chartered Bank*, AIR 2003 SC 4630.

Court Case: Lala Kapurchand Godha v.
Mir Nawab Himayatalikhan Azamjah

In 1931, the Prince of Berar bought jewellery on credit.[16] He acknowledged the purchase and the due thus: 'I promise...to pay to you...the said sum of rupees thirteen lacs twenty thousand seven hundred and fifty only together with simple interest thereon @10% per annum.' The owed amount escalated from Rs 13,20,750 in 1931 to Rs 27,79,000 in 1948. The Nizam of Hyderabad acknowledged the debt in 1949. In 1949, Hyderabad came under military occupation. A committee was set up on 8 February 1949 by the military governor, known as the Princes Debts Settlement Committee. The committee was set up to scrutinize all debts of the Prince of Berar and his younger brother. The committee considered the claim of the jewellers. The committee recommended that the jeweller should be paid a sum of Rs 20 lakh in full satisfaction of their claim. In settling the claim, the committee also made a reduction of 10 per cent for all the suppliers of goods to the two princes because the committee was of the opinion that in most of the cases the suppliers had inflated the prices. The committee also thought that the reasonable rate of interest would be 6 per cent in the case of creditors who had to wait for a number of years for payment of their dues.

The jewellers were not agreeable to this. They were first given Rs 11,25,000. Towards receiving the second and final instalment, the jewellers raised the following receipt in February, 1950:

Received from the Controller General of Accounts and Audit, Hyderabad Government, the sum of Rs 8,75,000/- (Rupees eight lacs and seventy five

[16] *Lala Kapurchand Godha v. Mir Nawab Himayatalikhan Azamjah*, AIR 1963 SC 250.

thousand only) in full and final payment of the balance of rupees twenty lacs allowed by the government in respect of my claim under the pronote dated 15th February 1948 passed by the Prince of Berar in my favour, reserving however my right to recover the balance amount due under the said pronote from the Prince of Berar.

The relevant authorities refused to make payment on the terms of the receipt where the jewellers had reserved their right to recover the balance amount due from the Princes of Berar. The funds for settling the claims were limited. The committee had to settle all claims within this budget. Kapurchand, the jeweller entitled to claim the money, testified before the court:

I was told that unless I signed the receipt for full payment, no cheque would be issued to me. Thereupon I endorsed the receipt for full payment.... I protested and said that as I was asked to endorse full payment, I was doing so despite the fact that I was not receiving full payment. Thereafter I signed the receipt as well as the vouchers and handed over the documents to the Accountant-General.

The Supreme Court reviewed the evidence and concluded that there was no coercion on Kapurchand for signing the document. However, he had realised that he would not get anything if he did not sign. Kapurchand discharged all dues and recorded 'received payment in full.' On 14 August 1950 the jewellers served a notice on the Prince of Berar to make payment of the balance of Rs 9,99,940 with interest of 10 per cent. As the money was not paid, a suit was instituted on 5 February 1951 in the High Court of Bombay for recovery of the amount. The case came before the Supreme Court to decide whether there was accord and satisfaction. The Supreme Court ruled:

The legal position is clear enough.... It seems to us that this case is completely covered by S. 63 and illustration (C) thereof. The appellants having accepted payment in full satisfaction of their claim are not now entitled to sue the respondent for the balance. A reference may also be made in this connection to S. 41 of the Contract Act under which when a promisee accepts performance of the promise from a third person, he cannot afterwards enforce it against the promiser. There is some English authority to the effect that discharge of a contract by a third person is effectual only if authorised or ratified by the debtor. In India, however, the words of S. 41 of the Contract Act leave no room for doubt, and when the appellants have accepted performance of the promise from a third person, they cannot afterwards enforce it against the promisor, namely, the respondent.

When a statute clearly covers a case, it is hardly necessary to refer to decisions. ... With the niceties of English law in the matter of accord and satisfaction we are not concerned. The position in the present case is that the appellants must have known that they could receive the second instalment and retain the first instalment by accepting the condition on which the sum of Rs 20 lacs was offered to them, namely, that they must record a full satisfaction of their claim. They accepted the money on the condition on which it was offered and it is not now open to them to say, either in fact or in law, that they accepted the money but not the condition.

Section 41 provides:

41. Effect of accepting performance from third person—When a promisee accepts performance of the promise from a third person, he cannot afterwards enforce it against the promisor.

As the performance of the debt was accepted from the government, it could not be raised against the princes. The question then was whether the performance was complete. The Supreme Court has emphasized acceptance of a lesser amount is binding. Another case on the theme is from the Calcutta High Court, *M/s Saraswat Trading Agency* v. *Union of India*.

Court Case: M/s Saraswat Trading Agency v. Union of India

In a contract involving the railways, the parties brought a dispute to an arbitrator.[17] The arbitrator gave award in terms of payments to be made by the railways to the contractor, M/s Saraswat Trading Agency. The railway officers were of the view that the award was on the higher side. They tried to negotiate with the contractor to accept a lesser amount. The contractor, however, was not agreeable to it. The only concession the contractor was willing to make was to give a rebate of 2 per cent if the full payment was made by 26 October 1993. The parties negotiated further and the contractor agreed to accept Rs 17,07,973 in full and final settlement. The total due amount was Rs 26,00,000. The railways prepared a pay order for Rs 17,07,973 but did not hand it over to the contractor. Instead, a cheque for Rs 16,56,734 drawn on the Reserve Bank of India was given to the contractor on 13 October 1993. The cheque was encashed by the contractor. The contractor gave the following receipt to the railways:

RECEIVED from South Eastern Railway vide cheque No. 055237 dated 13-10-1993 on the Reserve Bank of India, Calcutta, for Rs 16,56,734/- against item 1(II) of the Award dated 25-8-1993 published by the Sole Arbitrator Shri H.K. Padhee CFIM-II/GRC in connection with Goods and parcels handing work at Itwards and group of Stations continued up to 2-8 1991.

The railways attempted to explain the deduction towards income tax and other cess. However, this was certainly not a part of the negotiations between the parties. Having realised the cheque, the contractor moved

[17] *M/s Saraswat Trading Agency* v. *Union of India*, 2002 AIR Cal 51.

the court for enforcement of the award of the arbitrator, nullifying the negotiation and settlement reached between the parties. The case came before the Calcutta High Court. The court explored the legal status of the parties to accept a lesser amount than the due amount. The court ruled:

If there was an accord and satisfaction, then, that is an end of the matter and the appeal must fail.

The law of accord and satisfaction is that a person entitled to the performance of a promise might accept, instead of the original promise, something different; this different thing is agreed upon by an accord reached between the promisor and the promisee.

Thus accord is a name given to a special agreement which has as its foundation another earlier agreement. Sometimes, however, the foundation is a debt, otherwise arisen than on an agreement.

Satisfaction is the performance of the different promise as per the new agreement of accord and its acceptance by the promisee.

If for example, a person has promised to deliver a long red pencil, the promisee might agree after the contract, to take a short blue pencil instead, and in that event the delivery of a short blue pencil and its acceptance will be a discharge of both the original contract and the new contract of accord. The process of accord or satisfaction is permitted both in England and in India. There is, however, at least one important difference in the law of the two countries in this regard, and that is this, that in England the accord to take a lesser sum for a larger sum is not valid, but in India it is. This particular difference has, as its beginning, a famous dictum of Lord Coke made at the time of James I, that a promisee can take a horse or a hawk or a gown instead of the promisee, but not a lesser sum. The proposition has stuck in England and even in the comparatively recent case of *D and C Builders* v. *Rees* reported at (1965) 3 All ER 837, this principle can be seen in its operation.

In our country, however, we are not concerned with these niceties of the English law of accord and satisfaction, as the Supreme Court pointed out in the case of the Prince of Berar, reported at AIR 1963 SC 250. The law in our country in this regard is to be found mainly codified in S. 63 of the Indian Contract Act, 1872.

Clearly the English people thought that the law in their country in this regard was archaic and unsatisfactory. But they could do nothing about it in their own country where the legal system is very conservative. But in India they had a free hand. So, the law was changed by enacting S. 63.

...

The Supreme Court has clarified [Prince of Berar's case] that accord and satisfaction is basically a question of fact in each case. The Court has to find out whether the lesser sum or the different performance has been accepted by the promisee in full satisfaction or not.

Before we give our decision on this main point we wish to make it clear, once for all, that the mere encashment of a cheque for a smaller sum given by the debtor to the creditor is not, standing alone, a sufficient proof of accord and satisfaction. The authority in this regard is the case of *Day* v. *McLea* reported at (1889) 22 QBD 610. It has been relied upon D and C Builders (1965 (3) All ER 837) (above) and in the Indian Courts also, including in the Prince of Berar's case (AIR 1963 SC 250). Were it otherwise, and were we to hold otherwise, we would be putting in the hands of all debtors a weapon of legal trickery. As a standard practice every debtor would send to the creditor a lesser sum by way of a cheque with appropriate covering documents taking the chance that the cheque might be encashed. If encashed the debtor can then get away without paying the balance sum. The law cannot permit this. Therefore, mere payment and acceptance of a lesser sum without the accord that it will be in extinction of the balance liability, will not be a full satisfaction of the debt.

We are convinced here on the facts of the case that the appellant had agreed to take Rs 17,07,973/-, if paid within 14-10-1993, as full satisfaction of all claims on the award, the aggregate amount under which was nearly Rs 26,00,000/-.

Thus, the accord between the parties was there, for taking the lesser sum for the larger one. However, when the stage of satisfaction came, i.e. the payment of the lesser sum agreed to be taken for the larger one, the respondent (railways) fortunately or unfortunately slipped up. They did not pay Rs 17,07,973/-, but they paid instead the sum of Rs 16,56,734/-.

The cheque for the said sum of Rs 16,56,734/- was no doubt encashed. But that, as we have said, is not determinative of the matter. ... We find that instead of paying Rs 17,07,973/- within 14-10-1993 for the purpose of discharging the larger debt under the award of nearly Rs 26,00,000/-, railways paid instead a sum of Rs 16,56,734/- for achieving the same result. Was this enough?

In deciding this issue, we have to look upon the award as if it had already crystallized into a debt … parties looked upon the award as a document giving rise to a liability and requiring its satisfaction. Both the parties thought that if things were allowed to rest where those were, if the railway authorities did not seek to challenge the award by handing over their papers to their legal department, the awarded sum would have to be paid. That is why they negotiated in the above manner indicated.

We are of the opinion that the payment of Rs 16,56,734/- was not the same as the stipulated payment of Rs 17,07,973/-. Although the time was adhered to i.e. the money was paid within 14-10-1993, yet the sum agreed in the accord was not paid. The balance sum of Rs 50,000/- and odd, although a small amount comparatively speaking, can never be paid now in accordance with the accord because the time for payment has irretrievably gone by.

The case has used the word 'satisfaction' in two senses, one as in 'accord and satisfaction', the second as actually being paid the lesser sum of money. We need to distinguish between the two of them. As we learnt in the *Union of India* v. *Kishorilal* case,[18] in the phrase 'accord and satisfaction', the satisfaction is not about receiving the money. It is the consideration for the agreement changing the original contract. As the Section 63 has dispensed with the requirement of consideration, the expression 'accord and satisfaction', drawn from common law source, has become irrelevant. It only needs 'accord', not consideration. Thus, ideally, use of 'accord and satisfaction', in relation to Section 63 should be discontinued. A part of the confusion comes from the illustrations to the section using 'satisfaction' for discharge of the debt.

In this context, whether the party has accepted the lesser amount as a discharge of the debt is a crucial concern. In several cases, particularly involving government tenders and contractors, the contractors receive a lesser amount but mention 'received under protest' or other qualifying words.[19] Such qualifiers do not amount to dispensing within Section 63 and thus, the party retains the right to claim the balance amount. Section 63 also provides for the case where a party extends the time for performance under a contract, as in the following case.

Court Case: Keshavlal Lallubhai Patel v. Lalbhai Trikumlal Mills Limited

We reviewed the case in an earlier chapter. Due to the Quit India Movement, the manufacturer-seller extended the time for delivery till normalcy returned. The Supreme Court noted:

The true legal position in regard to the extension of time for the performance of a contract is quite clear under S. 63 of the Indian Contract Act. Every promisee, as the section provides, may extend time for the performance of the contract. The question as to how extension of time may be agreed upon by the parties has been the subject-matter of some argument at the Bar in the present appeal. There can be, no doubt, we think, that both the buyer and the seller must agree to extend time for the delivery of goods. It would not be open to the promisee by his unilateral act to extend the time for performance of his own accord for his own benefit.

To conclude, remission is discharge of contractual obligations by mutual consent. Changing the terms of a contract by mutual agreement is called alteration. An agreement to change the terms of a contract itself has to be supported by consideration for both the

---

[18] *Union of India* v. *Kishorilal Gupta and Bros,* AIR 1959 SC 1362.

[19] See *Union of India* v. *Navilakha,* AIR 1997 Bom 209; and *Mohammad Usman* v. *Union of India,* AIR 1982 Raj 100.

parties to be enforceable. Novation is replacement of one contract by another. A novation can replace a contract between the same parties or change the parties to the contract. In novation, as a previous contract has to be extinguished, one has to examine the terms of the new contract. The new contract can extinguish the old one on its formation or on successful performance of the new contract. The difference between the two can be very significant for the parties. An agreement to accept less than due does not have consideration for the creditor. Thus, the agreement should not be enforceable. The British courts have followed the principle for a very long time. At the same time, in practice, parties accept less than due because they find value in it. The British courts recognize this and would prefer to accommodate it. However, the courts are bound by the authority of the past cases and are unable to reverse it. As India was not bound by the past British cases, the reversal was effected in the Indian Contract Act. Under the Act, an agreement to accept less than due in the final settlement is binding on the parties.

Part 6

RESTITUTION, BREACH, AND DAMAGES

Contracts create rights and obligations to the parties. Parties must do what they have undertaken. If not, contracts themselves would be meaningless. Thus, on every breach of a contract, the suffering party has a right to claim damages. The principle for award of damages is to put the parties in the position they would have been if the contract had been performed. As contract law emerged with the commercial practices of the traders, a monetary equivalent was introduced as compensation for the loss. Only in some cases, do the courts insist on specific performance of the contractual obligations. As determining adequate compensation was complex, the contracting parties themselves specified an amount to be paid in the case of breach. This came to be called liquidated damages. The courts do not award any amount that is listed as liquidated damages. We will take up these aspects on damages in Chapters 29–33.

For every breach of a term of a contract, the suffering party has a right to damages. However, if the breach is of the very essence of the contract, the party has the additional right of terminating the contract. On the communication of termination, the parties stand discharged of their contractual obligations. Following the principle, contracts also specify the terms that would be taken as essential to the contract. A party to a contract may intimate in advance his intention of being in breach of a term of a contract. This is called anticipatory breach. If the other party accepts the anticipatory breach, the contract comes to an end. The parties are discharged of their contractual obligations and the second party will claim damages for the breach. The theme of breach and termination is taken up in Chapters 27 and 28.

It has been an old principle that no one should enrich himself at the expense of others. The remedy for the party who was deprived of his right was restitution. The principle found application in the cases where the parties exchanged benefits in the hope of getting in a contract but no contract materialized. This could be for several different reasons. The negotiations between the party could fail. The contract formed between the parties could turn out to be void. A party could exercise the right to set aside a voidable contract. Due to this proximity, the principles of restitution were included in the Contract Act as a separate chapter. Also, as the branches of law then were limited, the Contract Act was the closest where the principles could be codified. The principles find varied application, including restitution in void and voidable contracts. This is taken up in the following chapter.

26

Restitution and Quasi-Contracts

In a void contract, parties exchange benefits to realise only later that there were no binding contractual terms for the exchange. The same happens in the case where a voidable contract is set aside; the exchange is without the support of contractual terms. In some cases, parties may exchange goods and benefits in the hope of getting in a contract that does not materialize. An example is life insurance companies collecting an advance premium along with the offer document itself. Should a person be allowed to keep what he gets? *Nul ne doit senrichir aux depens des autres*, that is, 'No one ought to enrich himself at the expense of others', is an old principle. It will be familiar to every culture.

In the course of the development of common law, it came to be known as the 'principle of restitution'. Law has several branches today. Most of them were developed in the twentieth century. Earlier, there were only limited branches, like contracts, trust, and equity. At that time, the closest the principle of restitution came to was the contract. As in a contract, there was movement of benefit between the parties. Thus, it was accommodated within contract law as quasi-contract. That is, it is not a contract, but may appear like one. Later, common law

developed it as a separate field. The development of the field was thus summarized in *Fibrosa* v. *Fairbairn* by Lord Wright:

… any civilised system of law is bound to provide remedies for cases of what has been called unjust enrichment or unjust benefit, that is, to prevent a man from retaining the money of, or some benefit derived from, another which it is against conscience that he should keep. Such remedies in English Law are generically different from remedies in contract or in tort, and are now recognised to fall within a third category of the common law, which has been called quasi-contract or restitution.[1]

The principle was written down in the Indian Contract Act under a chapter titled 'Quasi-Contract'. The chapter is spread from Section 68 to 72. Before examining the provisions, let us look at the following illustrations. Should the doctrine of restoring benefit apply in these cases?

Illustration 1. A and B are friends. A let his friend use his car for 3 days. When B returned the car, A demanded Rs 3,000 for the rental for the car.

Illustration 2. A grocer home-delivered to its customer. The customer had placed the order on the phone and the store home

---

[1] *Fibrosa* v. *Fairbairn*, (1943) AC 32.

delivered it. The customer would settle the bills at end of the month. A new delivery boy, by mistake, delivered goods to a wrong address. The recipient consumed the goods and refused to pay for it, claiming that it was the store that had made the mistake by doing wrong delivery.

Illustration 3. A customer was to pay Rs 70 to a store for his purchase. He tendered a hundred rupee note. The attendant, inadvertently, took the note to be a five hundred rupee note. He gave the customer Rs 430. The customer collected the cash and his shopping. Minutes later, the attendant realized his mistake. He is demanding the money from the customer.

Illustration 4. A bank, by mistake, credited an account with Rs 50,000. The account holder took it as a windfall and spent the money. The bank is demanding the money from the customer.

In illustration 1, A and B are friends. It is understood between the parties that the use of the car is free. In the case of a gift, there is enrichment for one at the cost of the other. However, there is no restitution as this is what was intended. In other illustrations, where a person comes to get goods, money, or services, whether by mistake or otherwise, and benefits from it, he should compensate the owner for the benefit. Consistent with this, Section 70 provides:

Where a person lawfully does anything for another person, or delivers anything to him, not intending to do so gratuitously, and such other person enjoys the benefit thereof, the latter is bound to make compensation to the former in respect of, or to restore, the thing so done or delivered.

The Supreme Court explored the application of this section in *State of WB* v. *M/s B.K. Mondal and Sons.*

Section 70· Restoration of Benefits

Court Case: State of WB v. M/s B.K. Mondal and Sons

Mondal and Sons got into a contract to put up temporary storage godowns in Arambagh in the District of Hooghly, for use by the Civil Supplies Department of the State of Bengal.[2] They completed the contract and were paid for it. While they were doing the work, they were requested by the sub-divisional officer of Arambagh to submit an estimate for the construction of a *kutcha* road, guard room, office, kitchen, and room for clerks at Arambagh for the Department of Civil Supplies. The additional deputy director of civil supplies visited Arambagh and instructed them to proceed with the construction in accordance with the estimates submitted by them. Similarly, more work was taken up and completed on a letter written by the sub-divisional officer. The administration failed to pay the bills submitted by Mondal and Sons. There must have been some internal problem within the administration in getting the money released. Mondal and Sons filed a suit for recovery of the pending amount. Section 175(3) provides that all contracts made by the government must be in writing and executed in the name of the governor. The State of West Bengal contended that as no contract was executed, there never was any contract for the claim to arise. The courts had held the mandatory nature of the requirement. The Supreme Court recognized it:

In our opinion, there can be no doubt that failure to comply with the mandatory provisions of the said Section makes the contracts invalid. ... There can be no doubt that in enacting the provisions of S. 175(3)

[2] *State of WB* v. *M/s B.K. Mondal and Sons*, AIR 1962 SC 779.

the Parliament intended that the state should not be burdened with liability based on unauthorised contracts and the plain object of the provision, therefore, is to save the state from spurious claims made on the strength of such unauthorised contracts. Thus the provision is made in the public interest and so there can be no difficulty in holding that the word 'shall' used in making the provision is intended to make the provision itself obligatory and not directory.

Failing the claim of a contract between the parties, the claim of Mondal and Sons was that under Section 70, it was entitled to receive the payment of the pending bills. The Supreme Court explored the meaning, scope, and application of Section 70. It noted:

It is plain that three conditions must be satisfied before this Section can be invoked. The first condition is that a person should lawfully do something for another person or deliver something to him. The second condition is that in doing the said thing or delivering the said thing he must not intend to act gratuitously; and the third is that the other person for whom something is done or to whom something is delivered must enjoy the benefit thereof. When these conditions are satisfied S. 70 imposes upon the latter person the liability to make compensation to the former in respect of, or to restore, the thing so done or delivered. In appreciating the scope and effect of the provisions of this Section it would be useful to illustrate how this Section would operate. If a person delivers something to another it would be open to the latter person to refuse to accept the thing or to return it; in that case S. 70 would not come into operation. Similarly, if a person does something for another it would be open to the latter person not to accept what has been done by the former; in that case again S. 70 would not apply. In other words, the person said to be made liable under S. 70 always has the option not to accept the thing or to return it. It is only where he voluntarily accepts the thing or enjoys the work done that the liability under S. 70 arises.

...

S. 70 requires that a person should lawfully do something or lawfully deliver something to another. The word 'lawfully' is not a surplusage and must be treated as an essential part of the requirement of S. 70. What then does the word 'lawfully' in S. 70 denote? ... the thing delivered or done must not be delivered or done fraudulently or dishonestly nor must it be delivered or done gratuitously. Section 70 is not intended to entertain claims for compensation made by persons who officiously interfere with the affairs of another or who impose on others services not desired by them. Section 70 deals with cases where a person does a thing for another not intending to act gratuitously and the other enjoys it. It is thus clear that when a thing is delivered or done by one person it must be open to the other person to reject it. Therefore, the acceptance and enjoyment of the thing delivered or done which is the basis for the claim for compensation under S. 70 must be voluntary. It would thus be noticed that this requirement affords sufficient and effective safeguard against spurious claims based on unauthorised acts.

Section 70 occurs in Chapter V which deals with certain relations resembling those created by contract. In other words, this chapter does not deal with the rights or liabilities accruing from the contract. It deals with the rights and liabilities accruing from relations which resemble those created by contract.... Therefore, in cases falling under S. 70 the person doing something for another or delivering something to another cannot sue for the specific performance of the contract nor ask for damages for the breach of the contract for the simple reason that there is no contract between him and the other person for whom he does something or to whom he delivers something. All that Section 70 provides is that if the goods delivered are accepted or the work done is voluntarily enjoyed then the liability to pay compensation for the enjoyment of the said goods or the acceptance of the said work arises. Thus, where a claim for compensation is made by one person against another under S. 70, it is not on the basis of any subsisting contract between the parties, it is on the basis of the fact that something was done by the party for another and the said work so done has been voluntarily accepted by the other party. That broadly stated is the effect of the conditions prescribed by S. 70.

The State Government contended that applying Section 70 would amount to virtually permitting the circumvention of the mandatory provisions of S. 175(3). The Supreme

Court, however, was clear that S. 175(3) had no relevance to the case. Section 175(3) did not recognize contracts unless these were duly executed, while Section 70 applied only if there was no valid contract. In this case, Section 70 applied to the case as there was no valid agreement between the parties. The court ruled:

… it was open to the appellant (State of WB) to refuse to accept the said warehouse, and to have the benefit of it. It could have called upon the respondent (B.K. Mondal and Sons) to demolish the said warehouse and take away the materials used by it in constructing it; but, if the appellant (State of WB) accepted the said warehouse' and used it and enjoyed its benefit then different considerations come into play and S. 70 can be invoked.

…

In this connection it may be relevant, to consider illustration (a) to S. 70. The said illustration shows that if A a tradesman leaves goods at B's house by mistake, and B treats the goods as his own he is bound to pay A for them. Now, if we assume that B stands for the State Government, can it be said that A was contravening the provisions of S. 175(3) when by mistake he left the goods at the house of B? The answer to this question is obviously in the negative. Therefore, if goods are delivered by A to the State Government by mistake and the State Government accepts the goods and enjoys them a claim for compensation can be made by A against the State Government, and in entertaining the said claim the court could not be upholding the contravention of S. 175(3) at all either directly or indirectly. Once it is realised that the cause of action for a claim for compensation under S. 70 is based not upon the delivery of the goods or the doing of any work as such but upon the acceptance and enjoyment of the said goods or the said work it would not be difficult to hold that S. 70 does not treat as valid the contravention of S. 175(3) of the Act. That being so, the principal argument urged by Mr. Sen [Counsel for State of WB] that the respondents [Mondal and Sons] construction of S. 70 nullifies the effect of S. 175(3) of the Act cannot be accepted.

The case cogently discusses all aspects of the application of Section 70. It comes out clearly that Section 70 will apply only when the goods or services are given without a contract. If a contract is present, the compensation will come as a part of the contract. The other requirement is that provision of the goods or services must not be gratuitous and must be lawful. In this context, it is interesting to discuss the judgment given by Sarkar, J, who was in agreement but brought out additional facts. Mondal and Sons knew, as the court noted, '… right from the beginning, that the officers who were requesting the plaintiff to proceed with the work, had no authority to enter into a binding contract with the plaintiff and that they were awaiting sanction from higher officials which they hoped to get.' The judge was settled that there was no agreement between the Government and Mondal and Sons. In this context, he noted:

Now, if the work was done at the request of the officers of the Government who had no authority to make the request for the Government and the respondent was aware of this, it would follow that the work had been done at the request made by the officers in their personal capacity. In such a case it seems to us that if the request resulted in a contract between the officers and the respondent under which the officers were personally bound to pay the respondent reasonable remuneration for the work…

The judge, however, concluded that Mondal and Sons and the officers never intended to get into a personal contract. Thus, the conclusion of the judge was that there was no contract between the parties, paving the way for the application of Section 70.

Court Case: Mulamchand v. State of MP

Section 175 (3) of the Government of India Act, 1935 required that all government contracts to be in writing and executed in the name of the governor-general. Article 299 of the Constitution of India adopted the provision. It requires all government contracts to be in writing and executed in the name of the president or governor, as the case may be. Mulamchand paid Rs 10,000 for collection of forest produce from government forests.[3] However, the contract was not executed under Article 299. He collected forest produce for some time, before a dispute arose between the parties on his right to collect forest produce. The Supreme explored application of Section 70.

... the provisions of Section 175 (3) of the Government of India Act and the corresponding provisions of Article 299 (1) of the Constitution have not been enacted for the sake of mere form but they have been enacted for safeguarding the Government against unauthorised contracts. The provisions are embodied in Section 175 (3) of the Government of India Act and Article 299 (1) of the Constitution on the ground of public policy—on the ground of protection of general public—and these formalities cannot be waived or dispensed with.... But if money is deposited and goods are supplied or if services are rendered in terms of the void contract, the provisions of Section 70 of the Indian Contract Act may be applicable. In other words if the conditions imposed by Section 70 of the Indian Contract Act are satisfied then the provisions of that section can be invoked by the aggrieved party to the void contract.... The important point to notice is that in a case falling under Section 70 the person doing something for another or delivering something to another cannot sue for the specific performance of the contract, nor ask for damages for the breach of the contract, for the simple reason that there is no contract between him and the other person for whom he does something or to whom he delivers something. So where a claim for compensation is made by one person against another under Section 70 it is not on the basis of any subsisting contract between the parties but on a different kind of obligation. The juristic basis of the obligation in such a case is not founded upon any contract or tort but upon a third category of law, namely, quasi-contract or restitution.

In *Modi Sugar Mills Limited, M/s* v. *Union of India*,[4] under a contract, the Union of India supplied wheat flour for manufacturing biscuits in containers. The containers were not a part of the contract. Modi Sugar Mills Limited retained the containers. The Supreme Court ruled it that Section 70 applied in relation to the containers and the Union of India be paid the price for the containers.

SECTION 72: MISTAKEN DELIVERY

Section 72 provides as follows:

72. **Liability of person to whom money is paid or thing delivered by mistake or under coercion**—A person to whom money has been paid, or anything delivered, by mistake or under coercion, must repay or return it.

The general scope of the section is apparent. The application of the section has been in the field of taxation. At times, the government levies a tax without authority. In other cases, a person may mistakenly pay more tax than was due. Cases have arisen around whether the government is bound to return the surplus amount. For example, in *Mahabir Kishore* v. *State of MP*,[5] despite an order of the high court declaring a levy to be invalid, the State of Madhya Pradesh continued to levy it. The other two leading cases on the theme are *Mafatlal Industries Limited* v. *Union of India* and *Sahakari Khand Udyog Mandal Limited* v. *Commissioner of Central Excise and Custom*.[6] The courts have ruled that the section applies to everyone, including the government. We will put together the basis for the law from the three cases. In *Mahabir*

---

[3] *Mulamchand* v. *State of M.P.*, AIR 1968 SC 1218.

[4] *Modi Sugar Mills Limited, M/s* v. *Union of India*, AIR 1984 SC 1248.

[5] *Mahabir Kishore* v. *State of MP*, AIR 1990 SC 313.

[6] *Sahakari Khand Udyog Mandal Limited* v. *Commissioner of Central Excise and Custom*, AIR 2005 SC 1897.

Kishore v. *State of MP*, the Supreme Court recounted the common law principle of unjust enrichment:

No one ought to enrich himself at the expense of others. … The doctrine of 'unjust enrichment' is that in certain situation it would be 'unjust' to allow the defendant to retain a benefit at the plaintiff's expense. … The principle of unjust enrichment requires: first, that the defendant has been 'enriched' by the receipt of a 'benefit'; secondly, that this enrichment is 'at the expense of the plaintiff'; and thirdly; that the retention of the enrichment be unjust. This justifies restitution. Enrichment may take the form of direct advantage to the recipient's wealth such as by the receipt of money or indirect one for instance where inevitable expense has been saved.

Section 72 of the Indian Contract Act deals with liability of person to whom money is paid or thing delivered, by mistake or under coercion. … Our law having been codified, we have to apply the law. … There is no doubt that the instant suit is for refund of money paid by mistake and refusal to refund may result in unjust enrichment depending on the facts and circumstances of the case.

Thus, the court recognized undue taxation by the government as unjust enrichment. In the other two cases, the companies had passed the tax burden to the consumers. The question arose whether restitution from the government to the companies should be allowed. The Supreme Court did not allow this. It noted:

The person claiming restitution should have suffered a 'loss or injury'. In my opinion, in cases where the assessee or the person claiming refund has passed on the incidence of tax to a third person, how can it be said that he has suffered a loss or injury? How is it possible to say that he has got ownership or title to the amount claimed, which he has already recouped from a third party? So, the very basic requirement for a claim of restitution under Section 72 of the Contract Act is that the person claiming restitution should plead and prove a loss or injury to him; in other words, he has not passed on the liability. If it is not so done, the action for restitution or refund, should fail. … the person claiming restitution, should plead and prove that 'he has not passed on' the liability to another. That is the nature of 'accounting' in cases falling under Section 72 of the Contract Act.[7]

SECTION 64: RESTITUTION IN VOIDABLE CONTRACTS

The chapter has specific provisions for restitution in void and voidable contracts. We are familiar with them. Section 64 provides that when a person sets aside a voidable contract, he has to restore the benefits derived. The section reads:

64. Consequences of rescission of voidable contract—When a person at whose option a contract is voidable rescinds it, the other party thereto need not perform any promise therein contained in which he is promisor. The party rescinding a voidable contract shall, if he has received any benefit thereunder from another party to such contract, restore such benefit, so far as may be, to the person from whom it was received.

A voidable contract gives the innocent party the option to either continue with the contract or set it aside. If the innocent party decides to set aside the contract, effect is to be given as if the parties never got into the contract. The innocent party should not have a complaint if he were treated as if the contract never got made. To put the parties in the position, the innocent party must restore the benefits, and compensated for any loss suffered by the other party. The courts insist on restitution before rescinding a contract. However, in the case of contracts caused by fraud, the courts do not aid the fraudulent party. There are further grounds for a party to set aside a contract besides fraud, misrepresentation, and undue influence. Section 39 provides:

---

[7] *Mafatlal Industries Limited* v. *Union of India*, (1997) 5 SCC 539.

39. When a party to a contract has refused to perform, or disabled himself from performing, his promise in its entirety, the promise may put an end to the contract, unless he has signified, by words or conduct, his acquiescence in its continuance.

There was uncertainty whether 'put an end to a contract', a phrase used by the English judges, meant the same as 'voidable' in the Indian Contract Act. If it did, Section 64 would apply to it. The Privy Council in *Muralidhar* v. *International Film Co.*[8] constructed several provisions in the act to conclude that Section 64 applied to a contract set aside under Section 39.

Court Case: Muralidhar v. International Film Co.

Muralidhar Chatterjee entered carried on business from Calcutta as a distributor of films.[9] He entered into a contract with International Film Co., an importer of films. The arrangement was that the company would import and give Chatterjee a new print of films. Chatterjee in turn will give it to the exhibitors. After the use of the print was over, it was to be handed back to the company. Chatterjee was to first pay a sum of Rs 1,750 towards the cost of each print. The company was to supply the print within four to five weeks of the money being paid. The exact price of the print was worked out at the time of delivery, including the cost of the print, freight, and duty paid. The revenue received by Chatterjee from the exhibitors was to be shared between the parties. Initially, Chatterjee was to retain 62.5 per cent of the revenue and give the rest to the company. Once Chatterjee had recovered half the price paid for a film, the parties were to share the revenue equally.

---

[8] *Muralidhar* v. *International Film Co.*, AIR 1943 PC 34.
[9] Ibid.

Chatterjee paid a total sum of Rs 4,000 for two films. One film was delivered but he could not successfully get it exhibited. The company asked for the print back to try and get it exhibited elsewhere. Chatterjee wrote to the company complaining of delay on their part and breach of contract. He declined to work with the company any more and claimed refund of Rs 4,000 already paid and Rs 5,000 in damages. The company denied that it was in breach of the contract. In the subsequent communications, both parties maintained their positions. Finally, the company communicated to Chatterjee due to his breach the company was terminating the contract and would claim damages from him. Chatterjee moved the court claiming damages.

The court ruled that the company was not in breach for Chatterjee to terminate the contract. Accepting this, Chatterjee raised a new contention: Even if the company had terminated the contract for his breach, he was entitled to a refund of the money paid under Section 64. The court accepted this and ruled in favour of Chatterjee. The Privy Council took 'strong objection to the informality' with which the new point was allowed. The due procedure for amending the pleadings was not followed. The company should have been given an opportunity to claim damages and set it off against the claim of Chatterjee. As a result, the question that came before the Privy Council was: When a party has 'put an end to' a contract under S. 39, is he liable to restore any benefit received by him under the contract from another party under Section 64? This was an 'important question of commercial law' for the Privy Council. The judgment first listed several provisions it was going to refer to. The relevant provisions are:

2. In this Act the following words and expressions are used in the following senses, unless a contrary

intention appears from the context: ... (g) An agreement not enforceable by law is said to be void; (h) An agreement enforceable by law is a contract; (i) An agreement which is enforceable by law at the option of one or more of the parties thereto, but not at the option of the other or others, is a voidable contract; (j) A contract which ceases to be enforceable by law becomes void when it ceases to be enforceable.

39. When a party to a contract has refused to perform, or disabled himself from performing, his promise in its entirety, the promise may put an end to the contract, unless he has signified, by words or conduct, his acquiescence in its continuance.

llustration

(a) A, a singer, enters into a contract with B, the manager of a theatre, to sing at his theatre two nights in every week during the next two months, and B engages to pay her 100 rupees for each night's performance. On the sixth night A willfully absents herself from the theatre. B is at liberty to put an end to the contract.

53. When a contract contains reciprocal promises, and one party to the contract prevents the other from performing his promise, the contract becomes voidable at the option of the party so prevented; and he is entitled to compensation from the other party for any loss which he may sustain in consequence of the non-performance of the contract.·

Illustration

A and B contract that B shall execute certain work for A for a thousand rupees. B is ready and willing to execute the work accordingly, but A prevents him from doing so. The contract is voidable at the option of B; and, if he elects to rescind it, he is entitled to recover from A compensation for any loss which he has incurred by its non-performance.

55. When a party to a contract promises to do a certain thing at or before a specified time, or certain things at or before specified times, and fails to do any such thing at or before the specified time, the contract, or so much of it as has not been performed, becomes voidable at the option of the promisee, if the intention of the parties was that time should be of the essence of the contract.

...

64. When a person at whose option a contract is voidable rescinds it, the other party thereto need not perform any promise therein contained in which he

is promisor. The party rescinding a voidable contract shall, if he has received any benefit thereunder from another party to such contract, restore such benefit, so far as may be, to the person from whom it was received.

65. When an agreement is discovered to be void or when a contract becomes void, any person who has received any advantage under such agreement or contract is bound to restore it, or to make compensation for it, to the person from whom he received it.

Illustration

(c) A, a singer, contracts with B, the manager of a theatre, to sing at his theatre for two nights in every week during the next two months, and B engages to pay her 100 rupees for each night's performance. On the sixth night, A wilfully absents herself from the theatre, and B, in consequence, rescinds the contract. B must pay A for the five nights on which she had sung.

66. The rescission of a voidable contract may be communicated or revoked in the same manner, and subject to the same rules, as apply to the communication or revocation of a proposal.

75. A person who rightly rescinds a contract is entitled to compensation for any damage which he has sustained through the non-fulfilment of the contract.

Illustration

A, a singer, contracts with B, the manager of a theatre, to sing at his theatre for two nights in every week during the next two months, and B engages to pay her 100 rupees for each night's performance. On the sixth night, A wilfully absents herself from the theatre, and B in consequence rescinds the contract. B is entitled to claim compensation for the damage which he has sustained through the non-fulfilment of the contract.

The Privy Council noted:

The language employed by the Act presents certain problems of construction. When one party to a contract has refused to perform his obligation thereunder so as to give rise to a right in the other party to put an end to the contract, is the latter a person at whose option the contract is voidable, and if he does put an end to the contract, does he rescind a voidable contract? When he has so rescinded, has the contract become void? Or is the language of S. 64 as to a person at whose option a contract is voidable restricted to cases where fraud, undue influence, mistake or other element vitiates the original consensus so that the party who has an option to refuse to be bound by the contract must either accept it as a whole or take no advantage from it whatsoever, treating it as void *ab initio*? Or are Ss. 64 and 65 restricted to cases to which the terms 'void' or 'voidable' have been expressly applied by the Act? In a case within S. 39 the party who rightly 'puts an end to' or 'rescinds' (S. 75) the contract is entitled to damages for the defaulting party's breach. In this sense the contract has not ceased to be 'enforceable by law.' On the other hand, neither party is any longer bound to perform his promise…

Though the Indian Act is to be interpreted according to the meaning of the words used in it, … S. 39 and S. 64 cannot be read together as a matter of course if they do not appear by the mere force of their own language to link up. The question must therefore be whether there is elsewhere in the Act sufficient to show that the contract which may be 'put an end to' is 'voidable'? To this question their Lordships think the answer must be yes. The presence of illust. (c) to S. 65 cannot be made consistent with any other view. The effect of S. 39 is explained by the example there given of a singer who wilfully absents herself from the theatre. The same example serves also under S. 65 as illust. (c) and under S. 75. It is a prominent feature of this portion of the Act. The right of one party upon refusal by the other to perform the contract is described indifferently by the Act as a right to 'put an end to' or 'rescind' it; and illust. (c) plainly imports that this right is either that of 'a person at whose option the contract is voidable' (S. 64) or is such that by the exercise of it the contract 'becomes void' (S. 65). Of these two propositions it is to be observed that they are not mutually exclusive, whether or not each involves the other. It has been suggested that the illustrations given under S. 65 are intended to refer to Ss. 64 and 65 taken together, or at least that illust. (c) is to be read as referable to S. 64. Another view is that the sections overlap. It is difficult to suppose that the singer's contract has become 'void' under S. 65 without being 'voidable' under S. 64. But no view which can be taken upon these matters can provide an escape from the conclusion that a liability to make restitution attaches to the party putting an end to a contract under S. 39. Nor can the illustration be ignored or brushed aside because it is not part of the body of the section.

On the breach of a contract, the other party may acquire a right to bring the contract to an end. This, in effect, makes the contract voidable under Section 64 at that point. If the party elects, the contract ends. The Privy Council did not resolve that on election, under Section 65, the contract became void. It noted the problem in declaring the contract to have become void. The conclusion was that restitution had to be done under Section 64. The Privy Council found support in its construction in the other provisions:

Further, under S. 53, if one party prevents the other from performing his promise, 'the contract becomes voidable at the option of the party so prevented,' and the latter may 'elect to rescind it:' this section, like S. 75, expressly confers a right to recover damages. Again, under S. 55, where time is of the essence and one party has made default 'the contract, or so much of it as has not been performed, becomes voidable at the option of the promisee': the last paragraph of the section deals with the right to damages. And S. 66 describes how 'the rescission of a voidable contract' may be communicated. From these sections it must be conceded that, as language is used in this Act, the right to treat a contract as voidable and to rescind it may be accompanied by a right to recover damages for the wrongful act which grounds the right of rescission.

The Privy Council noted the difficulties in harmonizing all the definitions and provisions. A voidable contract caused by misrepresentation and the like is rolled back and made void. There is no question of the terms of the contract applying as the contract has been made void. Under the definition, a void contract is not enforceable by law. However, in a contract set aside under Section 39, the contract does not fully become void as the party retains the right to damages under the contract. Similarly, there were difficulties in relating Section 65 to its illustration (c).

In the case of a contract 'becoming void', the illustration failed to illustrate the section. Instead, it illustrated the provision contained in Section 64.

The Privy Council noted on these difficulties:

Their Lordships prefer to confine themselves to a reason which is apparent on the face of the Act—that the right to recover damages has been dealt with by the draftsman as a right expressly conferred by the statute in cases where the contract has been rendered 'voidable' by the wrongful act of a party thereto and has been 'rescinded' by the other party accordingly. The right to damages presents no insuperable objection to the application of S. 64 to cases of rescission under S. 39, and S. 64 applies in their Lordships' judgment to the present case. Their Lordships are not concerned to make the Act agree in its results with the English law.

Thus, the harmonization was that even if the contract is taken to be void by the application of some provisions, express provisions on damages vest in the party the right to damages. The Privy Council concluded the principle:

It is at least certain that if the party who rightfully rescinds a contract can recover damages from the party in default and is afforded proper facilities of set-off, the Indian legislature may well have thought that his just claims have been met. The fact that a party to a contract is in default affords good reason why he should pay damages, but further exaction is not justified by his default. Where a payment has been made under a contract which has—for whatever reason—become void the duty of restitution would seem to emerge. A cross claim for damages stands upon an independent footing, though it arises out of the same contract and can be set off.

The company accepting the restitution claimed that Rs 4,000 was not the benefit to it as it was meant for the cost of the print, freight, and duty. The benefit would have come to it from the revenue sharing. The Privy Council disagreed with the view. It noted:

He was paying the money to the defendants in part discharge of the consideration due or to become due to them from him under the contract now rescinded. It was a benefit or advantage, and it was received under the contract. Sections 64 and 65 do not refer by the words 'benefit' and 'advantage' to any question of 'profit' or 'clear profit', nor does it matter what the party receiving the money may have done with it. To say that it has been spent for the purposes of the contract is wholly immaterial in such a case as the present. It means only that it has been spent to enable the party receiving it to perform his part of the contract—in other words, for his own purposes.

The implication of this then would be that the innocent party has to immediately return all the money it has received from the party in breach. This is the reason the Privy Council was unhappy that the application of Section 64 was taken up informally. If due process were followed, the innocent party would have brought its claim of damages and the two would have been set off. The Privy Council explained the way the process should work:

If on the footing that all sums received have to be returned, the defendants can show that after paying for the positive print, the shipping charges and so forth they have made a loss owing to the refusal of the plaintiff to carry out the contract, then these charges will be reflected in their claim for damages. If, on the other hand, the defendants have been so fortunate as to get another person to take the plaintiff's place on terms equally remunerative to them, these payments will not even mean that the defendants have suffered more than nominal damages. On general principles they may set off such damage as they have sustained, but the Act requires that they give back whatever they received under the contract.

Following this, the Privy Council ruled that the sum of Rs 4,000 was to be restored to Murlidhar. However, the high court should give time to the company to make claim for damages and set it off against the amount.

SECTION 65: RESTITUTION IN VOID CONTRACTS

Section 65 provides for restoration of benefits in a void contract. It reads:

65. Obligation of person who has received advantage under void agreement, or contract that becomes void—When an agreement is discovered to be void, or when a contract becomes void, any person who has received any advantage under such agreement or contract is bound to restore it, or to make compensation for it to the person from whom he received it.

The section applies to a 'contract which becomes void'. In other words, the contract was a valid one when made but it subsequently becomes void. We have already noted the difficult in constructing that a contract set aside under Section 39 'becomes void' under Section 65. In this case, as restitution is allowed under Section 64, the question becomes superfluous. A valid contract becomes void due to subsequent impossibility. The section illustrates it with the following example:

A contracts to sing for B at a concert for 1,000 rupees, which are paid in advance. A is too ill to sing. A is not bound to make compensation to B for the loss of the profits which B would have made if A had been able to sing, but must refund to B the 1,000 rupees paid in advance.

In *Alluri Narayana Murthy Raju* v. *Dist Collector, Visakhapatnam*,[10] reviewed in Chapter 23, the auctioneer could not extract sand from the riverbed as he was prevented by the villagers. The high court awarded a full refund of the auction amount. However, the auctioneer was not given any interest. The high court took the view that the contract was set aside on the grounds of frustration only on its decision. Thus, the sum became payable only on its decision and not before.

In the following case, the court decided on the scope of restitution.

Court Case: State of Rajasthan v. Associated Stone Industries (Kotah) Limited[11]

The Ruler of the erstwhile State of Kotah entered into an agreement with the Associated Stone Industries (Kotah) Limited, granting monopoly rights to the company to quarry *Kacha* stone from certain tracts of land. The State of Kotah ultimately became a part of the State of Rajasthan and the Union of India. On 1 April 1950, the Finance Act extended the Indian Income-tax Act, 1922, to Rajasthan. As a result, income tax became leviable in the territory that formed part of the erstwhile State of Kotah. As the contract was in lieu of payment of income tax, it became void on 1 April 1950. The company continued its operations. The State of Rajasthan served notice to it on 2 June 1952, cancelling the agreement. A dispute came before the court to decide on the restoration of benefits by the company since the contract became void. The high court took the annual royalty as the basis to calculate the amount. The case came before the Supreme Court in appeal. The State Government contended that under Section 65, the net profit earned by the company was the advantage it received and should be restored to the government. The Supreme Court ruled:

It is difficult to agree with this submission. It is not as if all that the company did was to excavate stone. The company in order to market the excavated stone had to carry on various other activities besides extracting stone from the quarries, such as, polishing, plastering, flooring painting, cementing, etc. It is not as if the company was investing funds separately for each one of the activities carried on by it. A huge establishment had to be maintained and the net profits could

---

[10] *Alluri Narayana Murthy Raju* v. *Dist Collector, Visakhapatnam*, AIR 2008 AP 264.

[11] *State of Rajasthan* v. *Associated Stone Industries (Kotah) Limited*, AIR 1985 SC 466.

only be arrived at after the final product was sold and the accounts were taken of all the activities.

...

We do not have the slightest doubt that net profits realised by the company as a result of all its various business activities can never be the measure of the compensation to be awarded under S. 65 of the Contract Act. It is not as if S. 65 of the Contract Act works in one direction only. If one party to the contract is asked to disgorge the advantage received by him under a void contract so too the other party to the void contract may ask him to restore the advantage received by him.... As a result of the contract being void, the state could at the most recover from the contractor the value of the rough stone excavated from the quarries. But then it would have to make good to the company the expenditure incurred by the company in the quarrying operations and extraction of the rough stone. It is for that reason that the Court instead of involving the parties and itself in impossible and speculative calculations adopted the basis of royalty as the measure of compensation. Royalty, as is well-known, is, in the case of a lease of a mine, the payment reserved by the grantor proportionate to the amount of the demised mineral worked within a certain period. In a case like the present where the grantor is the state and the lease is for excavation of stone, the measure of the compensation payable to the grantor should be the reasonable royalty which the state would have otherwise received from the grantee. Had the grantee not paid a pie under the contract on the ground that the contract was void, he would in our opinion be liable to pay reasonable royalty for the excavated stone. In addition, he would also be liable to pay compensation for the exclusive rights grant to him. That was how the high court proceeded with the matter and we see nothing wrong with the approach of the high court, which in the circumstances of the case was perhaps the only reasonable way of solving the problem.

Agreement Discovered to be Void

Another basis for the application of the section is 'when an agreement is discovered to be void'. On the fact of it, it applies when, objectively, an agreement is void but the parties are unaware of it, only realizing it to be void subsequently. The courts, as we will see,

have emphasized on the employment of the word 'agreement' in the phrase 'agreement is discovered to be void'. Within the definitions in the Contract Act, a contract is an agreement enforceable by law. An agreement not enforceable by law is void. Thus, this part of Section 65 refers to contracts that were void from inception. The Privy Council in *Harnath Kaur* v. *Indeer Bahadur Singh*[12] observed:

The section deals with (a) agreements and (b) contracts. The distinction between them is apparent by Section 2; by clause (e) every promise and every set of promises forming the consideration for each other is an agreement, and by clause (h) an agreement enforceable by law is a contract. Section 65, therefore, deals with (a) agreements enforceable by law and (b) with agreements not so enforceable. By clause (g) an agreement not enforceable by law is said to be void. An agreement, therefore, discovered to be void is one discovered to be not enforceable by law, and, on the language of the section would include an agreement that, was void in that sense from its inception as distinct from a contract that becomes void.

A contract is void at the time of its making on two grounds, mutual mistake and illegality. Both the parties to a contract could be mistaken about an essential aspect of it, forming a void agreement. Only later would they discover the agreement to be void. The following case is based on mutual mistake.

Court Case: Tarsem Singh v. Sukhminder Singh

We have seen this case in an earlier chapter. Tarsem Singh sold land to Sukhminder Singh.[13] There was a breach of contract. In the course of seeking remedy before the trial court, it was revealed that both the parties were mistaken about the system of measure

---

[12] *Harnath Kaur* v. *Indeer Bahadur Singh*, AIR 1922 PC 403.

[13] *Tarsem Singh* v. *Sukhminder Singh*, AIR 1998 SC 1400.

they were going to follow for the extent of land and amount of money. The contract, thus, was void due to a mistake since its inception. The seller claimed to retain the earnest money given to him by the buyer. The Supreme Court examined the application of Section 65:

Since ... the agreement in question was void from its inception as the parties suffered from mutual mistake with regard to the area and price of the plots of land agreed to be sold, the forfeiture clause would, for that reason, be also void and, therefore, the petitioner could not legally forfeit the amount and seek the enforcement of forfeiture clause.

...

This section, which is based on equitable doctrine, provides for the restitution of any benefit received under a void agreement or contract and, therefore, mandates that any 'person' which obviously would include a party to the agreement, who has received any advantage under an agreement which is discovered to be void or under a contract which becomes void, has to restore such advantage or to pay compensation for it, to the person from whom he received that advantage or benefit. ...

One of the essential elements which go to constitute a free consent is that a thing is understood in the same sense by a party as is understood by the other party. It may often be that the parties may realise, after having entered into the agreement or after having signed the contract, that one of the matters which was essential to the agreement, was not understood by them in the same sense and that both of them were carrying totally different impressions of that matter at the time of entering into the agreement or executing the document. Such realisation would have the effect of invalidating the agreement under Section 20 of the Act. On such realisation, it can be legitimately said that the agreement was 'discovered to be void'. The words 'discovered to be void', therefore, comprehend a situation in which the parties were suffering from a mistake of fact from the very beginning but had not realised, at the time of entering into the agreement or signing of the document, that they were suffering from any such mistake and had, therefore, acted bona fide on such agreement. The agreement in such a case would be void from its inception, though discovered to be so at a much later stage.

Another reason for a contract being void from the beginning is illegality.

Restitution in Contracts Void Due to Illegality

Let us first become familiar with some common law principles in relation to restitution of illegal contracts. These principles are applied by Indian courts. The general legal principle is that the courts will not assist the wrongdoers. The maxim is *ex turpi causa non oritur action* (no action can be based a diesreputable cause). Going by this, the courts would not give restitution in any case involving illegality. A firm application of the principle could lead to injustice or favouring the wrongdoer. Thus, three exceptions to the principle have been carved.

The first exception is that restitution may be allowed where the parties are not equally guilty. The expression for this is 'not *in pari delicto*'. This applies to the cases where one party is ignorant and unaware of the illegality in the contract. This can happen in the cases where a person aware of the illegality may fraudulently misrepresent it as legal and valid to the other person. The principle makes restitution possible for the innocent party.

The second exception is to award restitution if the contract is not substantially performed. Lord Denning thus explained it in *Kiriri Cotton Co. Limited* v. *Ranchhoddas Keshavji Dewani*:[14]

In accordance with this principle, so long as the illegal transaction has not been fully executed and carried out, the courts have in many cases shown themselves ready to entertain a suit for recovery of the money paid or property transferred. These were cases in which it appeared to the court that, even though the transaction was illegal, nevertheless it was better to allow the plaintiff to resile from it

[14] *Kiriri Cotton Co. Limited* v. *Ranchhoddas Keshavji Dewani*, (1960) AC 192.

before it was completed, and to award restitution to him rather than to allow the defendant to remain in possession of his illegal gains. ... But so soon as the illegal transaction has been fully executed and carried out the courts will not entertain a suit for recovery ... unless it appears that the parties were not in *pari delicto*.

Thus, the exception may apply even if the parties are aware of the nature of the transaction. Further, if the parties are not in *pari delicto*, restitution will happen even if the contract is performed. The third exception is that if the claimant can establish a right to the money or property without relying on the unenforceable agreement. We can now explore the application of Section 65 to contracts void due to illegality.

Court Case: Kuju Collieries Limited v. Jharkhand Mines Limited

The parties entered into a mining lease contract that was prohibited and declared void by Bihar Mineral Concession Rules of 1949.[15] The parties were aware that the lease was illegal. As the lessee could not get the possession over the land, he moved the court for restitution of Rs 80,000 paid by it. The case came before the Supreme Court in appeal. The court delivered the following judgment:

We are of the view that Section 65 of the Contract Act cannot help the plaintiff on the facts and circumstances of this case. ... The section makes a distinction between an agreement and a contract. According to Section 2 of the Contract Act an agreement which is enforceable by law is a contract and an agreement which is not enforceable by law is said to be void. Therefore, when the earlier part of the section speaks of an agreement being discovered to be void it means that the agreement is not enforceable and it, therefore, not a contract. It means that it was void. It may be that the parties or one of the parties to

the agreement may not have, when they entered into the agreement, known that the agreement was in law not enforceable. They might have come to know later that the agreement was not enforceable. The second part of the section refers to a contract becoming void. That refers to a case where an agreement which was originally enforceable and was, therefore, a contract, becomes void due to subsequent happenings. In both these cases any person who has received any advantage under such agreement or contract is bound to restore such advantage, or to make compensation for it to the person from whom he received it. But where even at the time when the agreement is entered into both the parties knew that it was not lawful and, therefore, void, there was no contract but only an agreement ... Therefore, Section 65 of the Contract Act did not apply.

An agreement where the parties are aware of the illegality in the contract are taken to know that the contract is void. Obviously, they cannot 'discover' what they already know. Thus, Section 65 does not apply to the agreement. However, would the section apply if the parties were not aware of the illegality but discovered it subsequently? The above case approved the view taken by the Andhra Pradesh High Court in *Budhulal* v. *Deccan Banking Co. Limited*.[16] The High Court had noted:

There may be cases where parties enter into an agreement honestly thinking that it is a perfectly legal agreement and where one of them sues the other or wants the other to act on it, it is then that he may discover it to be void. There is nothing specific in Section 65 Indian Contract Act ... to make it inapplicable to such cases. A person who, however, gives money for an unlawful purpose knowing it to be so, or in such circumstances that, knowledge of illegality or unlawfulness can as a finding of fact be imputed to him, the agreement under which the payment is made cannot on his part be said to be discovered to be void.

---

[15] *Kuju Collieries Limited* v. *Jharkhand Mines Limited*, AIR 1974 SC 1892.

[16] *Budhulal* v. *Deccan Banking Co. Limited*, AIR 1955 Hyd 69.

The High Court added that the courts in no case assist a person who comes with unclean hands. The Supreme Court with approval added that the courts do not assist when both the parties are at fault, *pari delicto*. The Supreme Court also approved the following passage in *Sivaramakrishnaiah* v. *Narhari Rao*[17] on the application of Section 65:

This cannot be taken advantage of by parties who knew from the beginning the illegality thereof. It only applies to a case where one of the parties enters into an agreement under the belief that it was a legal agreement. i.e. without the knowledge that the agreement is forbidden by law or opposed to public policy and as such illegal. The effect of Section 65 is that, in such a situation, it enables a person not in *pari delicto* to claim restoration since it is not based on an illegal contract but dissociated from it. That is permissible by reason of the section because the action is not founded on dealings which are contaminated by illegality. The party is only seeking to be restored to the status ante. Section 65 also does not recognise the distinction between a contract being illegal by reason of its being opposed to public policy or morality or a contract void for other reasons. Even agreements, the performance of which is attended with penal consequences, are not outside the scope of Section 65. At the same time, courts will not render assistance to persons who induce innocent parties to enter into contracts of that nature by playing fraud on them to retain the benefit which they obtained by their wrong.

Following these decisions of the high courts and their approval by the Supreme Court, the Orissa High Court in *Fakir Chand Seth* v. *Dambarudhar Bania*[18] ruled restitution for a lender who did not know the agreement to be against the law. A person entered in an agreement and advanced money to procure paddy. The Orissa Rice and Paddy Control Order, 1965, regulated procurement of paddy, and the person was not authorized to procure it. However, he did not know this. It was contended that the knowledge of law should be imputed to a party, because ignorance of a statutory provision cannot be set up as a defence. The Orissa High Court ruled against it as opposed to the judgment of the Supreme Court in *Kuju Collieries* v. *Jharkhand Mines Limited*, AIR 1974 SC 1892. It noted:

The learned court held that the knowledge of illegality of the transaction must be imputed to the parties for which the court should not render any assistance to the plaintiff for realisation of the loan advanced by the plaintiff. We are not prepared to accept the said decision as laying the correct law as it is not consistent with the view expressed by the Supreme Court…

In other words, if it were to be deemed that the parties knew the law, there would never be any contract where the parties subsequently discover the contract to be void. If this were the case, the Supreme Court would not have elaborated the point. Thus, it is possible to have restitution in the case where the plaintiff subsequently discovers the illegality.

Contract with Minor and Restitution

As seen in Chapter 18, the Privy Council in *Mohiri Bibee* v. *Dharmodas Ghose*[19] noted, 'The question whether a contract is void or voidable presupposes the existence of a contract within the meaning of the Act, and cannot arise in the case of an infant.' Thus, according to the Privy Council, Section 64 and 65 had no application to a contract with a minor. Section 68 provides for restitution in the case of dealings with a minor or a party incapable of contracting. It reads:

68. Claim for necessaries supplied to person incapable of contracting, or on his account—If

---

[17] *Sivaramakrishnaiah* v. *Narhari Rao*, AIR 1960 AP 186.

[18] *Fakir Chand Seth* v. *Dambarudhar Bania*, AIR 1987 Ori 50.

[19] *Mohori Bibi* v. *Dharmodas Ghose*, (1903) 30 IA 114.

a person, incapable of entering into a contract, or any one whom he is legally bound to support, is supplied by another person with necessaries suited to his condition in life, the person who has furnished such supplies is entitled to be reimbursed from the property of such incapable person.

Thus, in dealings with a minor or a person incapable of contracting, no contract is made. The section only provides for restitution for supplying towards the upkeep of the person. The inclusion of the provision was one of the reasons for the Privy Council to rule the not application of Section 64 and 65.

To summarize, no person should enrich himself at the expense of others. There should be restitution to restore the benefits derived. The principles on restitution were written down as a part of the Indian Contract Act. The provisions apply when there is no contract between the parties. If there is a subsisting contract between the parties, the terms of the contract apply. The provisions cover a range of situations where parties may need to restore benefits. Section 64 and 65 are specific to the cases where the parties have attempted to get in a contractual relationship. Section 64 makes provisions for restitution when a voidable contract is set aside by a party. Section 65 applies when a subsequent impossibility makes a contract void. It also applies to contracts where the parties subsequently discover that the contract made by them was void. Section 68 makes provisions for reimbursement to anyone who supplies necessities to minors. Section 70 applies when a person draws a benefit from a good or service of another and the benefit was not intended as a gift. Section 72 applies where money or goods are given to another by mistake or under coercion. The section finds wide application in the state in the imposition and collection of taxes.

27

Breach and Termination

On every breach of a term of a contract, the suffering party has a right to damages. However, if the breach is of the very essence of the contract, the party has the additional right to terminate the contract. A party to a contract may intimate in advance his intention of being in breach of an essential term of the contract. This is called anticipatory breach. If the other party accepts the anticipatory breach, the contract comes to an end. The right of the party to elect to terminate the contract is provided in Section 39 of the Indian Contract Act. We have already looked at the section. It reads:

39. **Effect of refusal of party to perform promise wholly**—When a party to a contract has refused to perform, or disabled himself from performing, his promise in its entirety, the promisee may put an end to the contract, unless he has signified, by words or conduct, his acquiescence in its continuance.

The courts from the beginning took the section to be expressing settled common law principles. Richard Garth, CJ in *Schiller* v. *Sooltan Chand* noted: 'That section, as I understand it, only means to enact what was the law in England, and the law here, before the Act was passed,—meaning that where a party to a contract refuses altogether to perform,

or is disabled from performing, his part of it, the other side has a right to rescind it.'[1] Following this, the courts did not scrutinize the text of the section to note differences with the common law. Instead, they followed the developments in common law as the guide for the elaboration of the principle. In *Rash Behary Shaha* v. *Nrittya Gopal Nundy*, the Calcutta High Court, referring to the British cases, noted: 'These cases were determined after the passing of the Indian Contract Act, but the views of the learned Judges are useful guides in determining what amounts to a "refusal" in cases of the present class.'[2] As a result of this convergence, the common law cases, as opposed to literal interpretation of the text of the section, have served as the basis for the court judgment. The only intensive reading of the section was in *Muralidhar* v. *International Film Co.*,[3] to conclude that 'put an end to the contract' has the effect of making the contract voidable for the purposes of restitution. Thus, we will study breach and

[1] *Schiller* v. *Sooltan Chand*, (1879) ILR 4 Cal 252.
[2] *Rash Behary Shaha* v. *Nrittya Gopal Nundy*, (1906) ILR 33 Cal 477.
[3] *Muralidhar* v. *International Film Co.*, AIR 1943 PC 34.

anticipatory breach by studying the current common law position and its application by the Indian courts. We will take up breaches in this chapter and anticipatory breaches in the next. Let us begin with the following illustration.

Case: Breach of Contract

Food Mart Limited, a retail store in a city, entered into an annual service contract with ACon Limited, for the maintenance of its thirty air-conditioners. The terms of the contract were as follows:

1. Food Mart Limited will pay 25 per cent of the consideration on signing of the contract, 40 per cent at the end of the third month of the signing of the contract, and the remaining 35 per cent at the end of the sixth month of the signing of the contract.
2. ACon Limited will service the 30 air-conditioners every month.

The parties signed the contract on 1 April. At the time of signing the contract, Food Mart Limited gave a cheque for 25 per cent of the consideration. ACon Limited provided their service for the months of April and May. However, they failed to provide their service in the month of June. When a party does not meet the terms of a contract, it is said to be in breach of that term of the contract.

Food Mart Limited does not want to continue with ACon Limited as they find them unreliable. They apprehend that the service will continue to be erratic. Their point of view is that it is better to find another party than suffer the existing one. Can they end the contract? In other words, can Food Mart Limited free themselves from the obligation of paying the two remaining instalments and ACon Limited from doing the monthly maintenance? Of course, ACon Limited will have to pay damages for breaching the contract. The answer should be yes. Once a party to a contract has breached a term, the innocent party should be allowed to free himself. Contracts are voluntarily formed. Breach by a party is indicative of a disinterest to continue. The other party should be free to make alternate arrangements.

Let us consider an alternate situation. Food Mart Limited has had its air-conditioners maintained by ACon Limited for the past eight years. This was the first time that they experienced a problem. This situation occurred because several of the employees of ACon Limited fell ill at the same time. Food Mart Limited got their air conditioners serviced in the month of June by another party. However, they want to continue with ACon Limited. Should Food Mart Limited be allowed to continue with the rest of the contract? The answer is yes.

In simple contracts, parties have a limited number of rights and liabilities. For example, while buying consumer goods, the buyer pays and gets the goods. If the buyer does not pay, the seller does not deliver the goods. However, in most business contracts, there are usually several rights and obligations on the parties, which have to be performed at different times. In such a situation, not having the option of continuing with the contract even after some lapses would be detrimental to both the parties. Most contracts would never get completed as there would always be some breach or the other.

CONDITION AND WARRANTY

Thus, when a party to a contract breaches a term, the innocent party has an option to either bring the contract to an end or continue with it. In this, however, we encounter another problem. A contract has several terms. Some of the terms would be of great significance. Other terms would only be supportive. For example, in the above contract, one of the terms was that ACon Limited would bring its own mopping cloth for cleaning the air conditioner. However, the technician of ACon, who came in the month of June, forgot to bring the mopping cloth, and asked Food Mart to supply it. The technician thus serviced the air conditioners with a mopping cloth supplied by Food Mart. This is also a breach of the contract. Should Food Mart be allowed to terminate the contract for this breach?

In the beginning, business practices were simple—a seller delivered and the buyer paid. Breach of a term meant breach of the contract. As business practices evolved, however, contracts came to have several terms. Not all the terms of a contract were equally important. The courts began to check whether a term 'went to the root of the contract'. Another notion that gained popularity was whether the breach affected the contract in its 'entirety'. On further deliberation, the courts developed a distinction between the core part of a contract and its subsidiary part. The innocent party could terminate the contract only for a breach of the core part. For the breach of a subsidiary part, he could not terminate the contract, but could only claim damages. The core part came to be called 'condition', and the subsidiary part came to be called 'warranty'.

ACon's failure to do the maintenance in the month of June is a breach of a condition of the contract. The very purpose of the contract is defeated by ACon's not doing the servicing. However, the technician's not bringing the mopping cloth is only a breach of a warranty. Food Mart can deduct the price of the mopping cloth supplied as compensation for the breach, but cannot terminate the contract. The concept of condition and warranty was developed by the common law in relation to

contracts. The idea found codification in the Sale of Goods Act, 1893 of UK. Section 12 of the Indian Sale of Goods Act, 1930, puts it as follows:

12. Condition and warranty—(1) A stipulation in a contract of sale with reference to goods which are the subject thereof may be a condition or a warranty.

(2) A condition is a stipulation essential to the main purpose of the contract, the breach of which gives rise to a right to treat the contract as repudiated.

(3) A warranty is a stipulation collateral to the main purpose of the contract, the breach of which gives rise to a claim for damages but not to a right to reject the goods and treat the contract as repudiated.

(4) Whether a stipulation in a contract of sale is a condition or a warranty depends in each case on the construction of the contract. A stipulation may be a condition, though called a warranty in the contract.

Thus, the central purpose of the concept of condition and warranty is to give the contracting parties the rights to terminate the contract. The concept was explained in *Wallis, Son and Wells* v. *Pratt*.[4]

A party to a contract who has performed or is ready and willing to perform his obligations under that contract is entitled to the performance by the other contracting party of all the obligations which rest upon him. But from a very early period of our law it has been recognised that such obligations are not all of equal importance. There are some which go so directly to the essence of the contract, and are so essential to its very nature, that their non-performance may fairly be considered by the other party as a substantial failure to perform the contract at all. On the other hand, there are other obligations which, though they must be performed, are not so vital that a failure to perform them goes to the substance of the contract. Both clauses are equally obligations under the contract, and the breach of any one of them entitles the other party to damages. But in the case of the former class he has the alternative of treating the contract as being completely broken

---

[4] *Wallis, Son and Wells* v. *Pratt and Haynes*, (1911–1913) All ER Rep 989.

by the non-performance, and (if he takes proper steps) be can refuse to perform any of the obligations resting upon himself and sue the other party for a total failure to perform the contract. Although the decisions are fairly consistent in recognising this distinction between the two classes of obligations under a contract, there has not been a similar consistency in the nomenclature applied to them. I do not, however, propose to discuss this matter, because later usage has consecrated the term 'condition' to describe an obligation if the former class, and 'warranty' to describe an obligation of the latter class. I do not think that the choice of terms is happy especially so far as regards the word 'condition,' for it is a word which is used in many other connections, and has considerable variety of meaning. But its use with regard to the obligations under a contract is well known and recognised, and no confusion need arise if proper regard be had to the context.

This usage has been followed in the codification of the law of the contract of sale in the Sale of Goods Act. … It will be seen, therefore, that a condition and a warranty are alike obligations under a contract, a breach of which entitles the other contracting party to damages. But in the case of a breach of a condition he has the option of another and higher remedy— namely, that of treating the contract as repudiated. But, as I have said, he must act promptly if he desires to avail himself of this higher remedy…

The term 'condition' is used to convey different meanings. In a contract document, the term can be used in its legal sense. Common usage of the term, however, indicates contingency, in the sense of 'subject to'. The term can find use in contract documents in this sense too; for example, 'delivery of goods is on the condition of cheque being realized.' Further, contract documents have come to use 'condition' in a loose sense as 'terms and conditions'. The technical meaning of the term 'condition' and warranty is as we have discussed above.

As business practices further developed, courts found even the classification of the terms in condition and warranty inadequate. In *Hong Kong Fir Shipping Company* v.

Kawasaki Kisen Kaisha Limited,[5] it was a term for keeping the ship seaworthy. The centrality of seaworthiness in a shipping contract cannot be doubted. A ship, however, can cease to be seaworthy due to a hole in its hull or trivial things like a light bulb not working. Both of them could not be of equal significance. The court, thus, introduced a third term, called an 'intermediate' term. The intermediate term on its own was neither a condition nor a warranty. The consequence of significance of the breach would decide whether the party could terminate the contract or not. Thus, 'seaworthiness' could be an intermediate term. A hole in the hull would make it a condition, and an insignificant thing, a warranty. Following the case, the courts have added intermediate terms as an additional category.

BREACH AND TERMINATION

Let us become familiar with some of the terms associated with the above process. When a party is not able to meet any of its terms, it is said that the term is 'breached'. Breach of a 'condition', or that of a term going to the root of the contract, gives the right to the innocent party to terminate the contract. Such a breach is called a 'repudiatory breach'. When one party commits a 'repudiatory breach' of the contract, the innocent party gets the option to either terminate the contract or continue with it. In this situation, what should the party who has breached do? Should he assume that the contract is over and do nothing further, or should he carry on with the contract till the innocent party communicates his decision of terminating the contract? The parties had come together to co-operate and exchange goods and services. If termination could be assumed, there would be no option available

[5] *Hong Kong Fir Shipping Company* v. *Kawasaki Kisen Kaisha Limited*, (1962) 2 QB 26.

to the innocent party. Further, a contract would get terminated even if the parties involved would have preferred to continue with it. For these reasons, the innocent party has the right of terminating the contract, but he must communicate the decision to terminate to the party in breach. The choice of the innocent party is called 'election' and the decision to terminate is called 'assent'. Once the innocent party terminates the contract, both the parties are discharged from their future responsibilities under the contract. Till then, both the parties are bound by the contract. The term 'repudiation' some times is used to refer to a repudiatory breach. Other times, it is used as the election to terminate the contract.

It is important to be clear about the concepts and the terms. In various judgments, the courts have used a term to mean different things. At other times, different incidences and concepts are represented by the same term. The result has been a proliferation of terms. This can lead to confusion and ambiguity in the concepts themselves. Let us examine the principles we have formulated on repudiation with a review of court judgments. *Heyman* v. *Darwin* is a landmark case on repudiation of contract.

Court Case: Heyman and Another v. Darwins Limited

Darwins Limited was a manufacturer of steel in Sheffield.[6] It entered in an agreement with Heyman to be their sole selling agents in a wide area of territories, including Australia, New Zealand, and India. Heyman was to sell the products in the name of Darwins Limited. The manufacturer sent the goods from England at a declared price to the agent. The agent

was free to negotiate a higher price from the buyer. The difference was the commission of the agent. The duration of the agreement was to be for a minimum of three years, starting from 1 April 1938. Darwins Limited received communication from dissatisfied customers making monetary claims for the supplied steel, which they said was of unsatisfactory quality. The contention of Darwins Limited was that their product was fine but the agent was selling steel for purposes for which it was not suitable. Thus, Darwins Limited wrote from Sheffield on 18 July 1939: '…under our contract with you these claims are your responsibility and we therefore cannot make any further remittances to you until we are satisfied that no such claims will be made, or alternatively that any that have been made have been settled.'

Heyman protested, 'I do not know by what right you pretend to hold any of our money as guarantee against possible claims.' Heyman reported obtaining further orders in Australasia. The manufacturer, however, responded: '…we can only accept further orders on the strict understanding that from the amounts due to you a certain percentage must be retained to build up a reserve for the reasons already stated.' On 8 September, Heyman replied that this seemed to them to be a breach of contract by the manufacturer, and they refused to give any such understanding. On 7 November, the manufacturer wrote to express its dissatisfaction at the way in which the agreement was working out, and added: '…in the circumstances we would either suggest cancelling this agreement altogether or entering into negotiations with the view to drawing up another arrangement which would have to be such that satisfaction would be assured for all parties concerned.'

On 21 December 1939, the solicitors of Heyman wrote to the manufacturer, referring

[6] *Heyman and Another* v. *Darwins Limited,* (1942) AC 356.

to the previous communication, and asserting that letters show that the manufacturer had 'repudiated and/or evinced an intention not to perform' the agreement. The agent claimed damages for repudiation. An associated question was whether the case would be taken up in arbitration. Viscount Simon LC ruled:

The first head of claim … appears to be advanced on the view that an agreement is automatically terminated if one party 'repudiates' it. That is not so. As Scrutton LJ said in *Golding* v *London & Edinburgh Insurance Co Ltd.*: 'I have never been able to understand what effect repudiation by one party has unless the other accepts it.' If one party so acts or so expresses himself, as to show that he does not mean to accept and discharge the obligations of a contract any further, the other party has an option as to the attitude he may take up. He may, notwithstanding the so-called repudiation, insist on holding his co-contractor to the bargain and continue to tender due performance on his part. In that event, the co-contractor has the opportunity of withdrawing from his false position, and, even if he does not, may escape ultimate liability because of some supervening event not due to his own fault which excuses or puts an end to further performance…. Alternatively, the other party may rescind the contract, or (as it is sometimes expressed) 'accept the repudiation, ' by so acting as to make plain that, in view of the wrongful action of the party who has repudiated, he claims to treat the contract as at an end, in which case he can sue at once for damages. In the Hirji Mulji case, Lord Sumner said:

> 'Recission (except by mutual consent or by a competent court) is the right of one party, arising upon conduct by the other, by which he intimates his intention to abide by the contract no longer. It is a right to treat the contract as at an end if he chooses, and to claim damages for its total breach, but it is a right in his option…'

However, repudiation by one party standing alone does not terminate the contract. It takes two to end it, by repudiation, on the one side, and acceptance of the repudiation, on the other.

The following is a much quoted extract from the judgment of Lord Porter in the case:

To say that the contract is rescinded or has come to an end or has ceased to exist may in individual cases convey the truth with sufficient accuracy, but the fuller expression that the injured party is thereby absolved from future performance of his obligations under the contract is a more exact description of the position. Strictly speaking, to say that, upon acceptance of the renunciation of a contract, the contract is rescinded is incorrect. In such a case the injured party may accept the renunciation as a breach going to the root of the whole of the consideration. By that acceptance he is discharged from further performance and may bring an action for damages, but the contract itself is not rescinded.

The case establishes that repudiation on its own does not bring a contract to an end. The innocent party has to accept the repudiation by bringing it to the notice of the breaching party. The case also uses the term 'rescinded'. The terms 'rescission' and 'rescinded' have been associated with the setting aside of a contract on the grounds of misrepresentation. The terms were extended and used in other contexts to mean the setting aside of a contract. Setting aside of contracts in the two cases is very different. In the case of misrepresentation, the setting aside of a contract has retrospective effect. It is as if the contract was never got made. Everything done under the contract is reversed. In the case of termination of contract by repudiation, rights and obligations are valid as long as the contract lasts. The termination only discharges the parties of future liabilities. To prevent the confusion that could arise from the use of the same word in different contexts, the term *rescinded ab initio* (meaning rescinded from the beginning) came to be used in the case of misrepresentation. In this context of the likely confusion that could arise from the use of the term, the general consensus is that the terms rescission and rescinded should only be used in relation to setting aside of contracts on the grounds of misrepresentation. In the case of repudiation, termination would be an adequate expression. The concern about the terms and their meanings is not excessive and unwarranted, as the courts have struggled with the terms and their meaning. In *Photo Production Limited* v. *Securicor Transport Limited*, Lord Wilberforce, for the House of Lords, with reference to the above quoted passage of Lord Porter In *Heyman* v. *Darwins Limited* noted:

A vast number of expressions are used to describe situations where a breach has been committed by one party of such a character as to entitle the other party to refuse further performance: discharge, rescission, termination, the contract is at an end, or dead, or displaced; clauses cannot survive, or simply go. I have come to think that some of these difficulties can be avoided; in particular the use of 'rescission', even if distinguished from rescission *ab initio*, as an equivalent for discharge, though justifiable in some contexts may lead to confusion in others. To plead for complete uniformity may be to cry for the moon.[7]

The House of Lords was referring to the confusion the use of the terms had led to in the judgments from the courts. The court recommended use of the words 'discharge' or 'termination' to describe the ending of a contract due to repudiation. The word discharge is used as the parties are discharged from their future obligations.

Provisions in the Indian Contract Act

Section 39 of the Indian Contract Act provides on breach and termination.

39. Effect of refusal of party to perform promise wholly—When a party to a contract has refused to perform, or disabled himself from performing, his promise in its entirety, the promisee may put an end

to the contract, unless he has signified, by words or conduct, his acquiescence in its continuance.

The relevance of 'in its entirety' is that the breach should undermine the contract as a whole. In other words, the breach should be of a condition of the contract. The two illustrations to the section are as follows:

(a) A, a singer, enters into a contract with B, the manager of a theatre, to sing at his theatre two nights in every week during the next two months, and B engages to pay her 100 rupees for each night's performance. On the sixth night A wilfully absents herself from the theatre. B is at liberty to put an end to the contract.

(b) A, a singer, enters into a contract with B, the manager of a theatre, to sing at his theatre two nights in every week during the next two months, and B engages to pay her at the rate of 100 rupees for each night. On the sixth night A wilfully absents herself. With the assent of B, A sings on the seventh night. B has signified his acquiescence in the continuance of the contract, and cannot now put an end to it, but is entitled to compensation for the damage sustained by him through A's failure to sing on the sixth night.

The second illustration brings out the principle that the contract does not come to an end when it is breached. The second party has a right to elect to terminate. As B has allowed her to continue to perform, by conduct, he has elected not to terminate the contract. Both the illustrations, as the second is only an extension of the first, have an ambiguity. Did absence on the sixth night set aside the contract in its 'entirety'? Each performance was a separate event. The events could be severed. A subsequent absence could not take away the performance already done on the previous nights. And as the second illustration shows, the singer continued the performances. The first illustration, by giving the right to B to terminate the contract, brings out that a contract can be terminated for any breach. Richard Garth, CJ in *Schiller*

[7] *Photo Production Limited* v. *Securicor Transport Limited*, (1980) 1 All ER 556.

v. *Sooltan Chand*, referring to the contention by the parties, noted:

It has been urged upon us by the appellants' counsel that the default of the singer was only a partial refusal to perform her contract; and that the plaintiffs in this case were equally guilty of a partial refusal to perform theirs.… That illustration is perhaps not a happy one; because it may lead, as I think it has led in this instance, to misapprehension.

This, perhaps, was another reason the courts went by the common law principles than the text of the section. Further, as *Muralidhar* v. *International Film Co.* constructed the section, on breach of an essential term to the contract, the contract becomes voidable and gives the right to rescind the contract to the innocent party. Section 66 would govern the communication of the election to terminate the contract. It reads:

66. Mode of communicating or revoking rescission of voidable contract—The rescission of a voidable contract may be communicated or revoked in the same manner, and subject to the same rules, as apply to the communication or revocation of a proposal.

Thus, the communication of the election to terminate the contract can be express or implied.

Intention and Repudiation

A is the seller and B, the buyer. A breaches a condition of the contract but did not intend to do this. It happened despite his best attempts. A is willing to continue with the contract. B is also keen to continue. The parties can find a way out. Consider the alternative situation, where B sees it as a good excuse to get out of the contract. Can B terminate the contract? In other words, must A intend to terminate the contract, so as to give the right to B to assent to the termination? Or, will the breach of a condition automatically create the right for the innocent party, irrespective

of the intention of the breaching party? Let us explore this issue with the case *Union Eagle Limited* v. *Golden Achievement Limited*.

Court Case: Union Eagle Limited v. Golden Achievement Limited

Union Eagle Limited entered into a written agreement on 1 August 1991, to buy a flat on Hong Kong Island from Golden Achievement Limited for \$HK 42m.[8] In accordance with the contract, the purchaser paid a deposit of \$HK 420,000 to the solicitors of the vendor. Completion of the sale was to take place on or before 5.00 p.m. on 30 September 1991 by transfer of the money. Time was of essence to the agreement. Clause 12 provided:

If the Purchaser shall fail to comply with any of the terms and conditions of this Agreement, the deposit money and any part payment of purchase price so paid shall be absolutely forfeited as and for liquidated damages (and not a penalty) to the Vendor and who may (without being obliged to tender an Assignment to the Purchaser) rescind this Agreement and either retain the Property the subject of this Agreement or any part or parts thereof or resell the same…

The purchase price could be tendered only at 5.10 p.m., as the person carrying the cheque got held up in traffic. The vendor communicated his decision to terminate the contract and did not accept the payment. The contention of the purchaser was that a trivial non-performance on his part should not result in the termination of the contract. The case came before the Privy Council. The contention of the purchaser was that the failure to perform in time was a repudiatory breach. However, the decision to terminate the contract vests in the other party. Till the other party communicates its decision to terminate, the contract subsists. Thus, at 5.11 p.m., the contract

---

[8] *Union Eagle Limited* v. *Golden Achievement Limited*, (1997) 2 All ER 215.

was alive for the benefit of both parties. At 5.10 p.m. the purchaser was still entitled to complete the contract. Instead, refusal by the vendor to accept the cheque was a repudiatory breach by the vendor. The Privy Council ruled:

It is true that until there has been acceptance of a repudiatory breach, the contract remains in existence and the party in breach may tender performance. Thus a party whose conduct has amounted to an anticipatory breach may, before it has been accepted as such, repent and perform the contract according to its terms. But he is not entitled unilaterally to tender performance according to some other terms. Once 5.00 pm had passed, performance of the contract by the purchaser was no longer possible. The vendor could be required to accept late performance only on the grounds of some form of waiver or estoppel.

It is clear that the buyer intended to continue with the contract. There was a repudiatory breach, but no intention to discontinue the contract. We can understand the resolution of this in either of the two ways. One, the intention of the breaching party is immaterial. Once there is a repudiatory breach, the innocent party gets the right to terminate the contract. Alternately, the intention of the breaching party is not to be inferred from statements of the breaching party but from the act of meeting the terms of the contract. Once there is a repudiatory breach, it can be inferred that the party intends to terminate the contract.

Court Case: State of Kerala v. Cochin Chemical Refineries Limited

Cochin Chemicals and Refineries Limited got into an agreement with the State of Travancore-Cochin for what in essence was a sale agreement where the price was paid in advance.[9] The State of Travancore-Cochin

gave a loan of Rs 2.5 lakh. The company was to mortgage its property for the loan. The repayment of the loan was to be done by supplying ground-nut cake. The company was to supply 600 tons of the cake each month for five months, from November 1950 to March 1951. The price of the goods was to be fixed by the government. It was to be the rate at which the State of Travancore-Cochin could procure the cake from other sources in those months. The accounts were to be tallied and closed after 31 March 1951. The company was to pay the deficit loan amount, if any. The company did not receive the loan amount. It arranged for the supply of goods and, from time to time, wrote letters to the appropriate officers of the state, asking them to give instructions about the depots where the supplies were to be made.

However, no instructions for supply were given to the company. The company moved the court, claiming damages of Rs 3,600 for failure to advance the loan amount of Rs 2,50,000, and Rs 1,68,600 in damages for breach of the contract to purchase 3,000 tons of groundnut cake. The trial court decreed the suit for Rs 3,600 being damages for failure to advance the loan, and for Rs 1,23,000 being damages for breach of contract to purchase groundnut cake. In appeal, the State Government only challenged the award of damages for not taking the delivery of the goods. The contention of the government was that the obligation to take delivery of the goods was contingent on the government advancing Rs 2,50,000. As the government did not give the money, there was no question of it receiving the goods. The high court did not agree with the contention. The case came before the Supreme Court in appeal. The Supreme Court recognized that the two transactions of loan, mortgage, and sale were inter-related, forming a composite

---

[9] *State of Kerala* v. *Cochin Chemical Refineries Limited*, AIR 1968 SC 1361.

contract. The court summarized the common law principle:

Breach of contract by one party does not automatically terminate the obligation under the contract. The injured party has the option either to treat the contract as still in existence, or to regard himself as discharged. If he accepts the discharge of the contract by the other party, the contract is at an end. If he does not accept the discharge, he may insist on performance.

On the failure of the government to advance the loan, the company did not elect to terminate the contract. Thus, there was a subsisting contract between the parties. The government was in breach the second time in not accepting the supply of the goods.

Court Case: V. Ganesan v. State Bank of India

The All India Central Bank Employees' Federation is a trade union of officers and other staff of the nationalized banks.[10] Following a call from the Federation, the staff of the banks staged a thirty-minute demonstration during working hours on three days in the month of November 1977. The management of the banks deducted three days' worth of salary from the employees who had participated in the demonstration. The Federation came before the court, challenging the decision. The contention of the bank was:

...that the contract of employment was indivisible. The petitioners [staff] were bound to work for the whole of the month for which the salary had been agreed to be paid. The working hours for the staff had been fixed ... If the petitioners refused to perform the work for the required number of hours as fixed ... the banks would be then within their competence to deduct the salary for a day despite the fact that the petitioners were allowed to work for rest of the day.

[10] V. Ganesan v. State Bank of India, (1981) (1) LLJ 64.

The contention of the staff was:

... when the petitioners [staff] committed breach of the contract by not turning up for work for certain hours during the three days, it would have been open to the banks to accept the breach and to terminate the contract of employment. On the other hand, by not terminating the contract but by allowing the petitioners to work after their abstention from duty, the banks must be deemed to have acquiesced the breach of the contract said to have been committed by the petitioners [staff] and they cannot, therefore, refuse to pay the salary for the period of the day for which they had worked.

The high court relied on classic common law judgments and on *Kerala* v. *C.C. Refineries* to note that the employees were in the breach of the contract and the banks had the option of terminating the contract. However, the banks elected to continue with the contract. It noted:

... an innocent party to the contract is not bound to treat the contract as discharged. He may, at his option elect either to treat the contract as a continuing contract, or to say that the breach by the other party has discharged his liability. If he chooses the former course, he can still sue for damages for any loss sustained as a result of the breach. But the contract, with all its terms and conditions, remains alive for the benefit of the wrongdoer as well as of himself. Each party is entitled to hold the other to his bargain and to continue to tender due performance on his part. But if the innocent party continues to press for performance, or accepts performance, by the other party after becoming aware of the breach, he will be held to have affirmed the contract.

...

I am ... of the view that by permitting the petitioners to perform their work for the rest of the day and by accepting such performance, the banks must be deemed to have acquiesced in the breach committed by the petitioners.... It will, therefore, be idle on the part of the respondents to contend that they were not bound to pay for the period for which the petitioners had worked.... The petitioners, therefore, by working for the remaining part of the day had earned the salary for the day. This the banks are not entitled to withhold.

To conclude, the breach of a contract can be of a term that is the very essence of the contract. In this case, the innocent party gets the right to terminate the contract. The party can elect to terminate the contract or continue with it. The contract subsists till the party elects and communicates his decision to terminate the contract. The communication of election to terminate the contract can be express or implied.

28

Anticipatory Breach

In the preceding chapter, we looked at the breach of a term of a contract, as when a party to the term of a contract failed to perform that term when the time for performance arrived. At other times, a party to a contract may intimate to the other party in advance that he will not be able to perform his duty under the contract. There is no breach as yet, only an indication of one. This is called anticipatory breach. The other party can accept the breach or insist on performance of the contract. Anticipatory breach is also covered by Section 39. Let us begin our exploration of the theme of anticipatory breach with the following case. A buyer entered into a contract with a seller on the following terms:

1. The buyer will pay Rs 1 lakh to the seller, the price of the air-conditioner, on the 15th of the month.
2. The seller will deliver to the buyer an air-conditioner of a particular make, with a capacity of 3 tons, between the 20th and 25th of the month.

The seller later informed the buyer on the 10th of the month that he would not be able to deliver the air conditioner as the manufacturer is unable to supply it. The buyer wrote back to the seller, saying that, according to the contract, the seller was under an obligation to supply the goods by the 25th. The buyer would not like negotiate this. Can the buyer take this position? Yes. The parties are bound by the terms of the contract. The buyer need not discuss any deviation from these terms. In this case, the contract subsists and the parties must perform their respective obligations. Let us consider a different response from the buyer. The buyer realizes that it would be best to make alternate arrangements and not rely on the seller. The buyer can write back to the seller saying that he accepts the buyer's statement that he will not be delivering the air conditioner. Of course, the seller would have to pay damages for not meeting the terms of the contract.

In 'anticipatory breach', a party anticipates a breach and communicates to the other party that he will be breaching the contract. Of course, the intended breach must be of a condition, that is, it must be a repudiatory breach, for the innocent party to get the right to terminate the contract. On receiving such communication, the innocent party develops a right to exercise the option of either terminating the contract or continuing with it. If the contract is terminated, the rights and liabilities of both the parties come to an end. If not, the parties continue to be bound by the terms of the contract. Let us review the cases on the subject.

ELECTION TO ACCEPT ANTICIPATORY BREACH

Court Case: Frost v. Knight

Knight promised to marry Frost on the death of his father.[1] However, before the father died, he announced that he would not marry Frost and broke off the engagement. Frost sued for breach of contract. The dispute was whether she could claim damages till the contract was actually breached. The breach of contract would have happened only on the death of Knight's father. Sir Alexander Cockburn, CJ summarized the law:

The law with reference to a contract to be performed at a future time where the party bound to performance announced prior to the time his intention not to perform it … may be thus stated. The promisee, if he pleases, may treat the notice of intention as inoperative, and await the time when the contract is to be executed, and then hold the other party responsible for all the consequences of non-performance, but in that case he keeps the contract alive for the benefit of the other party as well as his own; he remains subject to all his own obligations under it, and enables the other party not only to complete the contract if so advised, notwithstanding his previous renunciation of it, but also to take advantage of any supervening circumstance which would justify him in declining to complete it. On the other hand the promisee may, if he thinks fit, treat the repudiation of the other party as a wrongful putting an end to the contract, and may at once bring his action on the breach of it; in which action he will be entitled to such damages as would have arisen from the non-performance of the contract at the prescribed time, subject, however, to abatement

in respect of any circumstances which may have afforded him the means of mitigating his loss.
…

It is true … that there can be no actual breach of a contract by reason of non-performance so long as the time for performance has not yet arrived. On the other hand, however, there is … a breach of a contract when the promisor repudiates it, and declares he will no longer be bound by it. The promisee has an inchoate right to the performance of the bargain, which becomes complete when the time for performance has arrived. In the meantime he has a right to have the contract kept open as a subsisting and effective contract. Its unimpaired and unimpeached efficacy may be essential to his interests. His right acquired under it may be dealt with by him in various ways for his benefit and advantage. Of all such advantage the repudiation of the contract by the other party and the announcement that it never will be fulfilled must of course deprive him. It is, therefore, quite right to hold that such an announcement amounts to a violation of the contract in omnibus, and that upon it the promisee if so minded may at once treat it as a breach of the entire contract, and bring his action accordingly.

As mentioned earlier, the case uses the word 'repudiate' as a declaration that the person would not be meeting the obligations under the contract. The case makes reference to mitigation of loss. Once a contract is breached, whether through repudiation or otherwise, the innocent party becomes entitled to claim damages. The innocent party, however, must act reasonably and not only take care of its own interest but also reduce the overall loss. The other party has to pay damages, but it should not be undue. Thus, the innocent party is charged with the responsibility of 'mitigation of losses'.

Court Case: White and Carter (Councils) Limited v. Mcgregor

The main business of White and Carter (Councils) Limited is supplying litter

[1] *Frost* v. *Knight*, (1861–1873) All ER Rep 221.

receptacles to town councils in urban areas throughout Great Britain.[2] They are paid not by the councils but by advertisers who enter into agreements with them in accordance with a standard form of contract. They are allowed to attach plates carrying advertisements to these receptacles. The company makes its profit from the payments made to it by the advertisers. Mcgregor runs a garage and was one of the advertisers. The parties successfully performed a contract for three years. The contract was renewed for another three years. The new contract started from the day on which the previous one ended. The payment that had to be made was 2s per week per plate, together with 5s per annum per plate, both payable annually in advance. The first payment became due seven days after the first display.

The very day on which the contract was renewed, Mcgregor wrote to White and Carter (Councils) Limited, cancelling the contract. White and Carter (Councils) Limited did not accept it and displayed their advertisement. The first payment was due seven days after the first display. Mcgregor refused to pay the due sum. Clause 8 of the contract provided: 'In the event of an instalment... remaining unpaid for a period of four weeks... the whole amount due for the 156 weeks or such part of the said 156 weeks as the Advertiser shall not yet have paid shall immediately become due and payable.'

Following the clause, White and Carter (Councils) Limited sued for the contract amount for the period of three years. Mcgregor refused the claim, saying that he had repudiated the contract before anything had been done under it. Following the repudiation, White and Carter (Councils) Limited

² *White and Carter (Councils) Limited* v. *Mcgregor*, (1962) AC 413.

could not carry out the contract and sue for the contract price. The only remedy for them was the damages, as the contract stood terminated the very day it was made. Thus, the payment clause, including Clause 8, never unfolded. The case came before the House of Lords. The court found it 'unfortunate' that Mcgergor 'have saddled themselves with an unwanted contract'. The principle of law was clear. The court formulated the principle:

The general rule cannot be in doubt.... If one party to a contract repudiates it in the sense of making it clear to the other party that he refuses or will refuse to carry out his part of the contract, the other party, the innocent party, has an option. He may accept that repudiation and sue for damages for breach of contract whether or not the time for performance has come; or he may if he chooses disregard or refuse to accept it and then the contract remains in full effect.

...

It is settled as a fundamental rule of the law of contract that repudiation by one of the parties to a contract does not itself discharge it.... It follows that, if, as here, there was no acceptance, the contract remains alive for the benefit of both parties and the party who has repudiated can change his mind but it does not follow that the party at the receiving end of the proffered repudiation is bound to accept it before the time for performance and is left to his remedy in damages for breach.

Thus, on the basis of the application of the principle, White and Carter (Councils) Limited was justified in not accepting the anticipatory breach of Mcgregor. There was discomfort with the outcome. The court developed a hypothetical case:

A company might engage an expert to go abroad and prepare an elaborate report and then repudiate the contract before anything was done. To allow such an expert then to waste thousands of pounds in preparing the report cannot be right if a much smaller sum of damages would give him full compensation for his loss. It would merely enable the expert to extort a settlement giving him far more than reasonable compensation.

The remedy for this could only be in equity. The court formulated the general principle:

The other ground would be that there is some general equitable principle or element of public policy which requires this limitation of the contractual rights of the innocent party. It may well be that, if it can be shown that a person has no legitimate interest, financial or otherwise, in performing the contract rather than claiming damages, he ought not to be allowed to saddle the other party with an additional burden with no benefit to himself.

The court was divided in its decision. The majority view was that in the facts of the case, the contractual rights could not be suspended on the grounds of equity. In the words of Lord Hodson:

It is trite that equity will not rewrite an improvident contract where there is no disability on either side. There is no duty laid upon a party to a subsisting contract to vary it at the behest of the other party so as to deprive himself of the benefit given to him by the contract. To hold otherwise would be to introduce a novel equitable doctrine that a party was not to be held to his contract unless the court in a given instance thought it reasonable so to do. In this case it would make an action for debt a claim for a discretionary remedy. This would introduce an uncertainty into the field of contract which appears to be unsupported by authority...

Court Case: Cochin Port S.C.S. Association v. Harrisons and Crosfield Limited

Ivan D'Souza was employed as a clerk in the Steamer Department of Harrisons & Crosfield Limited since 1954.[3] His duty was to supply provisions and to meet the claims of the staff and crew when ships arrived at the Cochin Port. For this purpose, he was entrusted with the company's funds. The practice followed was that he would meet the necessary expenses and furnish bills and

[3] *Cochin Port S.C.S. Association* v. *Harrisons and Crosfield Limited*, 1982 (2) LLJ 141.

accounts to the company. On 7 December 1973, D'Souza sent a telegram to the management, resigning from its service. This was followed by a letter of the same date, which contained the following 'postscript': 'I would be sending you various bills for respective ships which please debit to the concerned people and adjust where required in the event there are outstandings. This would be done in the course of a month.'

The management made attempts to ascertain his reasons for resigning from the job. After discussions, D'Souza agreed to continue in service. He was, however, irregular in attendance from February 1974 onwards. On 11 May 1974, he forwarded another letter to the management, through an advocate, reading as follows:

In continuation of my telegram and letter dated 7-12-73 tendering my resignation, I hereby reaffirm the same, and submit that I resign the clerk's job of your concern forthwith, to better my prospects. As I have not yet received your reply accepting my resignation, kindly treat this letter of mine as final, and that I would be no more in your services. My legitimate dues may be paid to me at your earliest convenience.

The management replied on 29 May 1974 that an amount in excess of Rs 69,000 was found to be due from him. Before considering his request, the matter had to be settled. D'Souza wrote back on 12 June 1974, denying the alleged liability. On 31 July 1974, the company wrote to the police, complaining that D'Souza had misappropriated over Rs 69,000. The parties took the dispute on the question of termination of service to the Central Government Industrial Tribunal at Madras. Before the tribunal, D'Souza contended that as his resignation was not accepted by the company, he should be reinstated in the job. The case came in appeal before the high court. The high court ruled:

When one person offers employment to another, and that other agrees to work on certain terms, the relationship between the two is contractual and the agreement itself is called a contract of service. In services under the government some corporations' rules and regulations define the rights and obligations of the parties; and where service conditions are thus mostly governed by law, elements of contract fade out of the picture and statute becomes the symbol of the relationship. In private employment also, statutes, rules, standing orders, settlements and awards may regulated the mutual obligations and rights to some extent. But in areas not covered by law, what operates is still the contract of service, i.e., the express or implied terms of the agreement. When it is said that an employee is inefficient, dishonest, disobedient or habitually late, and when he is found guilty of one or other of these charges, the legal principle behind it is that in every contract of employment, there is an implied warranty that the employee will be competent for the work, that he will take due care of the employer's property, that he is bound to obey lawful and reasonable orders, that he would report for work punctually, and that breach of these warranties entitles the employer to terminate the contract of employment by the method of what is known as dismissal for 'misconduct'. What is the remuneration payable for the work done, how many hours a week the employee should work, whether he can claim wages for periods of absence, whether he is entitled to sickness benefits and such other questions are normally matters of contract, sometimes express, sometimes implied. In the matter of variation, frustration, rescission and termination, as also in matters relating to validity or voilability of a contract of employment, the general principles of the law of contract are applicable. It is trite law for example, that no party to a contract can vary its terms unilaterally. Under the pristine law of master and servant, a master's right is only to hire and fire, and he cannot 'suspend' a servant from work and deny wages for the period. If the master does so, he is unilaterally varying the contract and will be bound to pay full wages during such period, unless the matter is governed by an express agreement to the contrary or by statutory rules and regulations. Frustration occurs when the performance of contract becomes impossible. Section 56 of the Contract Act provides that a contract to do an act which becomes impossible of performances after

making, either by reason of an event which the promisor could not prevent or because of operation of law becomes void. Thus where a factory is gutted by fire, or work is stopped in mines for reasons beyond the control of the employer, the contract of employment may become void. A contract may be determined by operation of law also; and where a partnership employing a number of persons is dissolved, their employment is supposed to come to an end. Rescission takes place when both parties to a contract agree to put an end to it as if it had never been made. A 'discharge' of the contract takes place when what is required of both parties has been performed, as for example, when a person is employed for a particular work and that is completed. Where a contract specifies that it can be terminated by notice on either side, for a specific period, it comes to an end when notice is so given by one and the period expires. Resignation, with which we are here concerned, is only one of the many methods by which one of the parties to a contract of employment attempts to terminate it, and the question is whether the contract stands discharged or determined where the man resigns but the employer does not accept it.

[The court cited from *White and Carter* v. *McGregor* and of *Kerala* v. *C.C. Refineries* and stated the principle]

The general principle thus seems to be that a mere declaration by one party that he is unwilling to perform his part of the contract is not sufficient to extinguish the contract: the other party can still say if he is not willing to assent to the declaration, that the contract remains intact and that he will hold the declarant to its terms.

…

The Tribunal was, therefore, in error in holding that D'Souza's resignation had effectively put an end to his service the moment he had sent in his resignation letter; and without anything more, it could not also have taken the view that the resignation 'must be deemed to have been accepted by the management'. When D'Souza informed the management by the letter of 11th May, 1974 that 'I would be no more in your service' he only disclosed an intention to be no longer bound by the contract of service. That did not sever the relationship or dissolve the vinculum juries, that only furnished a right to the management to terminate the contract of service on the ground that he was in breach thereof.

But the above conclusion does not fully answer the real question in this case. Admittedly, the management had neither accepted the employee's resignation nor terminated the contract by dismissing him from service; but does it follow that he should be deemed to have been in service all the while? To answer this question, I think, one has again to fall back on the principles of contract. Ordinarily, every contract is prima facie permanent and irrevocable; but some contracts, by their very nature, are considered to be terminable, contracts involving trust and confidence, personal relationship between the parties and mutual satisfaction with their conduct, such as contractors of partnership and contracts of employment, belong to this latter class. Where a person employs another, it is an implied term of the contract that the employer could get himself discharged from the obligation undertaken by him by giving notice to the employee. The employee has also a similar right, again implied, to give reasonable notice and quit. If a master terminates the service of a servant without reasonable notice, the latter can claim damages; and if a servant quits employment without notice, the master can also make a like claim against the servant. The quantum of damages will be assessed by taking into account the loss sustained by one party because of the breach committed by the other. The law does not impose an obligation on the employer to employ the servant for ever, nor does it require the employee to serve for ever. In this sense an employee is entitled to tell his employer that he intends to quit, say at the expiry of one month from the date on which the intention is communicated. That is resignation. If there is an agreement between the parties that the contract is terminable by one month's notice, the employer can do nothing except to wait for the period and watch the employee walking out. If on the other hand, the employee gives a week's notice and walks out, the employer can bring an action against him on the ground that the contract survives and that the refusal of the employee to perform it entitles him to damages. He cannot, however, insist that the employee should work for the remaining three weeks, because a contract of employment cannot be specifically enforced. The employer cannot also bring an action after months of waiting and hold the employer liable for losses sustained during the whole of the period; the Court will certainly tell him that after a period of notice reasonably fixed by law, he

was bound to employ another and carry on. Therefore, in the case of a resignation which remains unaccepted, the employee cannot be deemed to be in service for months or years together; after the lapse or a reasonable period of notice, the contract would be deemed to have come to an end.

...

By resigning, therefore, what a servant does is only to mention a date from which he wants to be relieved of his obligation. The date may be too early, and may leave the employer without sufficient notice; yet, there is no reason to think that the bond will survive the expiry of a date which will amount to sufficient or reasonable notice, on the facts and circumstances of the case.

The petitioner's case that D'Souza should be deemed to have continued in service for all times notwithstanding his resignation, cannot, therefore, be accepted. He should be deemed to have left service, though not from the date of resigning as the Tribunal seems to have thought, yet from some date coinciding within the expiry of what could be considered as reasonable notice. On his own showing, D'Souza had resigned on 7-12-73 and was not willing to return to work, till at least September, 1974. As this period of nine months is longer than any period of 'reasonable notice' a court could think of, it must be held that by the time D'Souza started having second thoughts, the contract of employment had come to and end and there was no question of reinstating him on the basis that he was still in service.

Court Case: Grandhi Subramanayam v. Vissamsetti Visweswara Rao

After examining the product, Grandhi Subramanayam entered into an agreement with Vissamsetti Visweswara Rao to purchase two rolling machines for a sum of Rs 53,000.[4] Under the contract, the buyer paid Rs 20,000. The machine was to be delivered by the seller on the payment of the balance amount of Rs 33,000. A month after signing the contract, Grandhi wrote to the seller that he

[4] *Grandhi Subramanayam* v. *Vissamsetti Visweswara Rao*, AIR 2002 AP 71.

apprehended that inferior and worn-out machines might be delivered to him in place of the machines that had been agreed to earlier. He, therefore, asked for a refund of Rs 20,000. The seller replied, disputing the allegations and expressing his willingness to deliver the machines against the payment of the balance of the purchase price of Rs 33,000. He further contended that the contract could not be unilaterally cancelled by Grandhi. Grandhi filed a suit for a refund of Rs 20,000, the amount he had paid to the seller, with interest. The case came in appeal before the high court. The high court referred to the Judgment of Lord Diplock in *R.V. Ward Limited* v. *Bignall*:

Rescission of a contract discharges both parties from any further liability to perform their respective primary obligations under the contract, that is to say, to do thereafter, those things which by their contract they had stipulated that they would do. Where rescission occurs as a result of one party's exercising his right to treat a breach by the other party of a stipulation in the contract as a repudiation of the contract, this gives rise to a secondary obligation of the party in breach to compensate the other party for the loss occasioned to him as a consequence of the rescission, and this secondary obligation is enforceable in an action for damages; but until there is rescission by acceptance of the repudiation, the liability of both parties to perform their primary obligations under the contract continues. Thus, under a contract for the sale of goods which has not been rescinded, the seller remains liable to transfer the property in the goods to the buyer and to deliver possession of them to him until he has discharged these obligations by performing them, and the buyer remains correspondingly liable to pay for the goods and to accept possession of them.

The election by a party not in default, to exercise his right of rescission by treating the contract as repudiated may be evinced by words or by conduct. Any act which puts it out of his power to perform thereafter, his primary obligations under the contract, if it is an act which he is entitled to do without notice to the party in default, must amount to an election to rescind the contract. If it is an act which he is not

entitled to do, it will amount to a wrongful repudiation of the contract on his part, which the other party can in turn, elect to treat as rescinding the contract.[5]

The high court applied the principle to the case:

Therefore, having regard to the finding of fact arrived at by the learned trial court as affirmed by the learned single judge, there cannot be any doubt whatsoever that the plaintiff cannot claim refund of the amount as the defendant had all along been ready and willing to perform his part of contract. He has not either expressly or by necessary implication accepted the repudiation on the part of the plaintiff.

In other words, the seller had not elected to terminate the contract. Under the terms of the contract, the buyer had no choice other than paying the money and receiving the goods.

INTIMATION OF ASSENT

We have seen earlier that when a party to a contract breaches a term going to the root of the contract, the innocent party gets the right to elect to terminate the contract. However, the innocent party should communicate his decision to terminate the contract to the party in breach. Section 66 of the Indian Contract Act provides that the communication can be express or implied. Is becoming passive an adequate communication of termination? The following is an interesting case on the theme.

Court Case: Vitol Sa v. Norelf Limited, The Santa Clara

On 11 February 1991, Norelf Limited of Bermuda entered into a contract to sell to Vitol SA of Geneva a cargo of propane.[6] The

---

[5] *R.V. Ward Limited* v. *Bignall* (1967) 2 All ER 449.

[6] *Vitol Sa* v. *Norelf Limited, The Santa Clara*, (1996) AC 800.

cargo was to be loaded on the vessel *Santa Clara* at Houston. The contract provided 1–7 March as the dates when the vessel was to arrive, berth, and leave Houston. The contract provided the following on the passing of the ownership of the goods: 'Title, beneficial ownership and risk of loss shall pass from seller to buyer when the product reaches the flange connecting the shore line with the vessel line at the loading port.... The price quoted includes the cost of carriage.' After loading the cargo on the Santa Clara, the sellers (Norelf) was to promptly tender the bill of lading to the buyers (Vitol). Vitol was to make the payment through electronic transfer within 30 days of the date on which the bill of lading was drawn. It was expressly agreed that English law would be the governing law. The agreement contained a provision that arbitration would take place in London.

The market for propane was very volatile. There was a sharp fall in its price after the making of the contract. The buyer would have had to incur large losses if the transaction were to proceed as planned. Conversely, the seller would have had to incur large losses if the transaction were to collapse. The Santa Clara was loading the cargo at the Houston terminal on 8 March 1991. The buyers (Vitol) sent a telex to the sellers on 8 March:

It was a condition of the contract that delivery would be effected 1–7 March 1991.... We are advised that the vessel is not likely to complete loading now until sometime on 9 March—well outside the agreed contractual period. In view of the breach of this condition, we must reject the cargo and repudiate the contract. We do however, reserve our position to claim damages in these circumstances.

On Monday, 11 March, the telex sent by the buyer came to the notice of the sellers. In the meantime, on Saturday, 9 March, the vessel had been loaded and proceeded to its destination. The buyer was confident that, following the breach of the condition of the schedule for loading, the seller had breached the term. The buyer only had to intimate its decision to bring the contract to an end. In other words, the seller had breached a condition of the contract and the buyer had elected to terminate the contract. The seller did not make any further communication with the buyer. The seller began trying to resell their cargo from Tuesday, 12 March onwards, and they succeeded in doing so by Friday, 15 March, at a price of $170 per tonne. The price at which Vitol had agreed to buy was $ 400 per tonne.

The first communication of the seller, in response to the telex of Vitol, came six months later, on 9 August 1991. The solicitors of Norelf claimed approximately $1 million on the basis of the difference between the contract price of propane and the price achieved by Norelf on resale. The claim was referred to arbitration. The arbitrator brought out that the delay did not go to the root of the contract so as to give Vitol the right to terminate the contract. Thus, the telex of 8 August instead became an anticipatory breach. Norelf became the innocent party.

The innocent party has the right to choose between terminating the contract or continuing with it. However, it must elect between the two and communicate its response to the other party. Norelf had done nothing to either perform the contract or communicate that it was terminating the contract. It was supposed to send the bill of lading to Vitol, which it had not. The bone of contention in the case was whether the innocent party could remain inactive. The arbitrator noted the following in its award:

...the rejection telexes constituted an anticipatory breach of the contract by Vitol. Unless that breach was accepted by Norelf, it was of no effect...the breach could have been remedied by withdrawal of the rejection contained in the telexes at any time before it was accepted. However, the breach was never remedied and, in my opinion, the tenor of the rejection telexes was such that the failure of Norelf to take any further step to perform the contract, which was apparent to Vitol, constituted sufficient communication of acceptance.

The question of law that the courts had to decide was, whether an innocent party can ever demonstrate its acceptance of repudiation simply by failing to perform its own contractual obligations. At the Queen's Bench Division, Phillips, J noted[7]:

It depends upon the circumstances. Failure to progress an arbitration is a good example of inertia that is likely to be equivocal. But in other types of contractual relationship where the parties are bound to perform specific acts in relation to one another, a failure to perform an act which a party is obliged to perform if the contract remains alive may be very significant. It is not difficult to envisage circumstances in which if such conduct follows a renunciation, the obvious inference will be that the innocent party is responding to the repudiation by treating the contract as at an end. I do not have to decide whether the failure on the part of [the sellers] to tender to [the buyers] a bill of lading, or any of the subsequent unspecified failures to perform the contract which were apparent to [the buyers], gave clear indication to [the buyers] that, in view of [the buyers'] wrongful action, [the sellers] were treating the contract as at an end. That is a question of fact for the arbitrator. What I have to decide is whether, as a matter of law, mere failure to perform contractual obligations can ever constitute acceptance of an anticipatory repudiation by the other party. In my judgment, for the reasons that I have given, it can.

The case came before the House of Lords. The extracts from its judgment are as follows:

…the principles governing an anticipatory breach of a contract and the acceptance of the breach by an aggrieved party…I would accept as established law

the following propositions: (1) Where a party has repudiated a contract the aggrieved party has an election to accept the repudiation or to affirm the contract: (2) An act of acceptance of a repudiation requires no particular form: a communication does not have to be couched in the language of acceptance. It is sufficient that the communication or conduct clearly and unequivocally conveys to the repudiating party that that aggrieved party is treating the contract as at an end. (3) It is rightly conceded by counsel for the buyers that the aggrieved party need not personally, or by an agent, notify the repudiating party of his election to treat the contract as at an end. It is sufficient that the fact of the election comes to the repudiating party's attention, for example notification by an unauthorised broker or other intermediary may be sufficient.

The arbitrator did not put forward any heterodox general theory of the law of repudiation. On the contrary, he expressly stated that unless the repudiation was accepted by the sellers and the acceptance was communicated to the buyers the election was of no effect. It is plain that the arbitrator directed himself correctly in accordance with the governing general principle. The criticism of the arbitrator's reasoning centres on his conclusion that 'the failure of [the sellers] to take any further step to perform the contract which was apparent to [the buyers] constituted sufficient communication of acceptance'. By that statement the arbitrator was simply recording a finding that the buyers knew that the sellers were treating the contract as at an end. That interpretation is reinforced by the paragraph in his award read as a whole. The only question is whether the relevant holding of the arbitrator was wrong in law.

It is now possible to turn directly to the first issue posed, namely whether non-performance of an obligation is ever as a matter of law capable of constituting an act of acceptance. On this aspect I found the judgment of Phillips J entirely convincing. One cannot generalise on the point. It all depends on the particular contractual relationship and the particular circumstances of the case. But, like Phillips J, I am satisfied that a failure to perform may sometimes signify to a repudiating party an election by the aggrieved party to treat the contract as at an end. Postulate the case where an employer at the end of a day tells a contractor that he, the employer, is repudiating the

[7] *Vitol Sa* v. *Norelf Limited, The Santa Clara,* (1994) 4 All ER 109.

contract and that the contractor need not return the next day. The contractor does not return the next day or at all. It seems to me that the contractor's failure to return may, in the absence of any other explanation, convey a decision to treat the contract as at an end. Another example may be an overseas sale providing for shipment on a named ship in a given month. The seller is obliged to obtain an export licence. The buyer repudiates the contract before loading starts. To the knowledge of the buyer the seller does not apply for an export licence with the result that the transaction cannot proceed. In such circumstances it may well be that an ordinary businessman, circumstanced as the parties were, would conclude that the seller was treating the contract as at an end. Taking the present case as illustrative, it is important to bear in mind that the tender of a bill of lading is the pre-condition to payment of the price. Why should an arbitrator not be able to infer that when, in the days and weeks following loading and the sailing of the vessel, the seller failed to tender a bill of lading to the buyer, he clearly conveyed to a trader that he was treating the contract as at an end?

TERMINATION CLAUSE IN CONTRACTS

Contracts are voluntarily formed. The parties are free to stipulate on every aspect of the contract, including those on breach and termination. So long as the clause does not give rise to illegality, the courts would enforce it. The general law on breach of contract and anticipatory breach is enforced only when the contract is silent on it. Contracts can provide on the implications of breach and termination through two means. A contract can expressly provide the 'conditions' of the contract. As a result, even if the consequence of the breach of the term is not of much significance, it would still be a repudiatory breach of the contract. Another means is to expressly provide the terms for the breach for which the innocent party can terminate the contract. A term on termination could read as follows:

Termination for Default: The purchaser...may terminate this contract in whole or in part

(a) if the Supplier fails to deliver any or all of the goods within the period(s) specified in the contract...

(b) if the supplier fails to perform any other obligation(s) under the contract.

By expressly providing the terms, the breach of any term creates the right in the buyer to terminate the contract. All standard contracts now have provisions on termination of contracts. Of course, cases do appear before the courts for the interpretation of terms. The stronger party, by making the stipulations, can terminate even for a breach that is in substance insignificant. The courts cannot ignore express provisions in the contracts. However, the courts interpret the terms stringently. The following case is on termination clause.

Court Case: Lombard North Central Plc v. Laurence Arthur Butterworth

Butterworth is a finance company.[8] Lombard North is an accountancy firm. Lombard purchased a particular model of computer, and then entered into an agreement of hiring with Butterworth. Butterworth agreed to lease the computer to Lombard for a period of five years. There was to be an initial payment of £584.05 and nineteen subsequent instalments of the same amount, payable at intervals of three months. Clause 2(a) of the contract stipulated that punctual payment was of essence to the contract. Under Clause 5, Butterworth could terminate the contract if an instalment was not paid in time. Clause 6 entitled Butterworth, in the event of termination, to recover all arrears and what remained of nineteen instalments. Lombard failed to pay the instalments punctually. Butterworth terminated the contract and initiated proceedings for recovery of the arrears and

[8] *Lombard North Central Plc v. Laurence Arthur Butterworth*, (1987) QB 527.

remaining instalments. Lombard contested paying of the subsequent instalments. Justice Mustill noted.

... Does the provision in clause 2(a) of the agreement that time for payment of the instalments was of the essence have the effect of making the defendant's late payment of the outstanding instalments a repudiatory breach? ... The reason why I am impelled to hold that the plaintiffs' contentions are well-founded can most conveniently be set out in a series of propositions.

1. Where a breach goes to the root of the contract, the injured party may elect to put an end to the contract. Thereupon both sides are relieved from those obligations which remain unperformed.

2. If he does so elect, the injured party is entitled to compensation for (a) any breaches which occurred before the contract was terminated, and (b) the loss of his opportunity to receive performance of the promisor's outstanding obligations.

3. Certain categories of obligation, often called conditions, have the property that any breach of them is treated as going to the root of the contract. Upon the occurrence of any breach of condition, the injured party can elect to terminate and claim damages, whatever the gravity of the breach.

4. It is possible by express provision in the contract to make a term a condition, even if it would not be so in the absence of such a provision.

5. A stipulation that time is of the essence, in relation to a particular contractual term, denotes that timely performance is a condition of the contract. The consequence is that delay in performance is treated as going to the root of the contract, without regard to the magnitude of the breach.

6. It follows that where a promisor fails to give timely performance of an obligation in respect of which time is expressly stated to be of the essence, the injured party may elect to terminate and recover damages in respect of the promisor's outstanding obligations, without regard to the magnitude of the breach.
...

These bare propositions call for comment. The first three are uncontroversial. The fourth was not, I believe, challenged before us, but I would in any event regard it as indisputable. That there exists a category of term, in respect of which any breach whether large or small entitles the promisee to treat himself as discharged, has never been doubted in modern times, and the fact that a term may be assigned to this category by express agreement has been taken for granted for at least a century.

The fifth proposition is a matter of terminology, and has been more taken for granted than discussed. That making time of the essence is the same as making timely performance a condition ... The sixth proposition is a combination of the first five. There appears to be no direct authority for it, and it is right to say that most of the cases on the significance of time being of the essence have been concerned with the right of the injured party to be discharged, rather than the principles upon which his damages are to be computed. Nevertheless, it is axiomatic that a person who establishes a breach of condition can terminate and claim damages for loss of the bargain, and I know of no authority which suggests that the position is any different where late performance is made into a breach of condition by a stipulation that time is of the essence.

To conclude, a party to a contract may intimate in advance that he would not be performing an essential term of the contract. This is called anticipatory breach. The innocent party can elect to accept the anticipatory breach or reject it. The communication of election can be in express or implied. Acceptance of anticipatory breach discharges the parties of further contractual obligations. The innocent party will claim damages for the breach of contract. If the anticipatory breach is not accepted, the contract would continue uninterrupted. All contracts now have a termination clause, detailing the grounds for termination of the contract.

29

Remoteness of Damage

There is a breach of contract when a party fails to meet its obligation under the contract. Every breach of a term of a contract entitles the innocent party to claim compensation. In the case of a breach of a warranty (a subsidiary aspect), the innocent party can only claim damages and not terminate the contract. In the case of a breach of a condition, the innocent party has a choice to either continue with the contract or terminate it. In either case, the innocent party will have a right to compensation for the breach. In this chapter, we will explore the principles for awarding damages. Every breach has consequences. The farther we go, the greater the liability of the breaching party. In this chapter, we will also explore the basis for limiting the consequences of breach.

PRINCIPLES FOR DAMAGES

Let us explore the principles underlying award of damages with the following case.

Case: Breach of Contract

Under a sale contract, Vivek was to supply fifty pendrives (Remington, 1Gb) to Ashish on Thursday for Rs 50,000. Ashish was buying these to gift them to his associates and customers during a meeting on Thursday. On Thursday, Vivek informed Ashish that he would not be able to supply the contracted goods. As Ashish needed them for the function that evening, he contacted three other suppliers and got the pendrives of the same description supplied within hours by the seller who had offered the most competitive price. Ashish had to pay him Rs 55,000. As Vivek had breached the contract, how should he be made to compensate Ashish?

One approach towards achieving justice could be to insist that the parties do what they had undertaken to do. In other words, Vivek should be compelled to supply the pendrives. This would be unfair and harsh on Vivek. There could be many reasons due to which Vivek had not been able to do his part. For example, he could be buying the pendrives from a manufacturer who was unable to supply them to him.

Parties come together in a contract for an equal exchange. Therefore, a monetary equivalent is usually adequate compensation for a breach. As a principle, it is best not to make the parties do what they had undertaken to do under the contract. When the party is specifically required by the court to perform the contract, this remedy is called 'specific performance' of contract. The courts award 'specific performance' only in rare cases. In most cases, a monetary compensation is awarded. Contract law emerged to deal with disputes among traders. The traders are usually interested only in the monetary value of things. Thus, a money equivalent is often adequate remedy.

As such, how should Vivek be made to compensate Ashish? If Vivek pays Rs 5,000 to Ashish as compensation, it would be as good as the contract being performed. What if Ashish got the pendrives on Thursday for Rs 52,000. A compensation of Rs 2,000 would put the parties in the same situation where they would have been had the contract not been breached. And what if Ashish got the pen drives for Rs 40,000? Ashish is better off for the contract being breached. Ashish demands, however, that he should be paid Rs 5,000 by Vivek as penalty for having breached the contract. Should a penalty be awarded?

To answer this question, let us consider the case where the contract between the parties had stated specifically that, in addition to the actual damages, Vivek would pay Rs 5,000 if he breached the contract. Should the penalty be enforced? It is the right of the state to demand a desired conduct from its subjects at the threat of punishment and penalty. Imposing a penalty is the sole prerogative of the state. Individuals imposing penalties on each other would amount to usurping the power of the state. This cannot be allowed. Thus, in a contract, parties only have the right to be compensated for damages. They do not have the right to impose penalty on the other party or benefit from the breach. We can, thus, summarize the broad principles on compensation as follows:

1. Specific performance is awarded only in transactions dealing with immovable property.
2. In most cases, a monetary equivalent is provided to compensate the innocent party for the breach of the contract.
3. Compensation is not a penalty. It is only aimed at putting the parties in the position they would have been in if the contract had been performed and not breached.

As has been noted in *Ruxley Electronics and Construction Limited* v. *Forsyth*:

Damages for breach of contract must reflect, as accurately as the circumstances allow, the loss which the claimant has sustained because he did not get what he bargained for. There is no question of punishing the contract breaker. Given this basic principle, the court, in assessing the measure of the claimant's loss, has ultimately to determine a question of fact …Since the law relating to damages for breach of contract has developed almost exclusively in a commercial context, these criteria normally proceed on the assumption that each contracting party's interest in the bargain was purely commercial and that the loss resulting from a breach of contract is measurable in purely economic terms.[1]

REMOTENESS OF DAMAGE
The following case will bring out the principle of remoteness of damage.

Case: Consequences of Breach
Sudip had contracted to transport computer components from Mumbai to Bangalore for Prakash for a consideration of Rs 2 lakh. Later, Sudip was offered a more lucrative deal, and so he refused to transport Prakash's goods. Prakash gets Akash to do the work for him. However, it costs him Rs 2.25 lakh. Prakash is certainly entitled to receive compensation

---

[1] *Ruxley Electronics and Construction Limited* v. *Forsyth*, (1996) AC 344.

from Sudip. Prakash first claims Rs 25,000, the additional amount he had to pay to get the goods transported.

The consignment was being transported for a commissioned project. Prakash was on the verge of getting another project from the same company. The delay, however, has led to the company decrying Prakash as unreliable. Consequently, the project is awarded to someone else. Prakash is claiming Rs 15 lakh as damages for the loss of business. Several other projects from others would have come to him if he had been awarded this project. Prakash is claiming Rs 20 lakh for this loss of business opportunity.

Any event would lead to several consequences. It is, thus, not surprising that Prakash can extend the ripples of Sudip's failure to transport the goods to several other subsequent events and expand his claim for damages. The question, however, is, where does one stop? A contract is a law made by the parties themselves. Do we have to go by what has actually been agreed to among the parties? What could they have been planning? What had been their shared horizons within which the contract had been made? If the parties had already contemplated a breach and had specified the damages payable for such a breach, the specified amount would be payable. Determination of the boundaries to which the consequences of a breach of contract can extend is an important concern. We can summarize this as follows:

1. If the parties have provided on the consequences of breach in the contract itself, by mentioning the consequences or the amount, the stipulation would apply. For example, a courier company may provide that it is not responsible for any losses caused due to late delivery of a consignment.

2. If the contract has not provided for the consequences of a breach, the only thing we can go with is what had impliedly been agreed between the parties,

Several of these themes are inter-related. Let us begin our exploration with remoteness of damages. Cases in which the parties have not stipulated the damages are governed by the principle settled in 1854 in the case *Hadley* v. *Baxendale*.[2]

Court Case: Hadley v. Baxendale

Hadley operated a flourmill at Gloucester that was driven by a steam engine. A crankshaft of the engine broke, and the mill had to be shut down. The engineers who had made the steam engine were based at Greenwich. It became necessary to send the shaft to them to serve as a pattern for making a new one. It was sent with the carriers, Pickford & Co., represented by Baxendale. The carriers promised to deliver the shaft at Greenwich the next day and collected two pounds for the job. However, the delivery got delayed by one week because the carriers sent it by canal rather than by rail. As a result, the new shaft was delivered late. The mill had to stay closed in the meanwhile. Hadley claimed £300 as loss of profit for five days.

The court's criterion for awarding damages was to find out what the exact intents, purposes and awareness of the parties were. The judge noted that the only communication that had taken place between the parties at the time of the contract was that 'the article to be carried was the broken shaft of a mill and that the plaintiffs [Hadley] were the millers of that mill.' The actual situation had not explicitly been planned by or known to the parties

[2] *Hadley* v. *Baxendale*, (1843–1860) All ER Rep 461.

since Hadley had not told Baxendale about the circumstances under which the shaft was being sent and the carrier had not explicitly agreed to the terms of being responsible for the closure of the mill on account of any delays. There had been no special arrangement of this kind.

In the absence of any explicit communication, we have to infer from the parties' actions. The court reasoned that the carriers had no way of knowing that Hadley would lose profits if the shipment was delayed. For all they knew, the mill had a spare shaft that they would put into service. Also, the mill could have been shut down for reasons other than the broken shaft. One can, of course, imagine any sequence of events. People ordinarily anticipate things that usually happen. As the court put it: 'But it is obvious that, in the great multitude of cases of millers sending off broken shafts to third persons by a carrier under ordinary circumstances, such consequences would not, in all probability, have occurred…' The court, thus, inferred: 'It follows, therefore, that the loss of profits here cannot reasonably be considered such a consequence of the breach of contract as could have been fairly and reasonably contemplated by both the parties when they made this contract.'

Another way of expressing the same principle is: 'Where two parties have made a contract which one of them has broken, the damages which the other party ought to receive in respect of such breach of contract should be such as may fairly and reasonably be considered either arising naturally, i.e., according to the usual course of things, from such breach of contract itself.' The court was, thus, stating that towards exploring the intents and plans of the parties, we should first look for any explicit or special arrangements made. If there is no special arrangement, we

should look at the practices as these happen 'naturally' in a 'majority of the cases'. The principle formulated in this case has been applied to all cases on compensation since. The summary above should help us grasp the following judgment of Alderson B:

We think the proper rule in such a case as the present is this. Where two parties have made a contract which one of them has broken the damages which the other party ought to receive in respect of such breach of contract should be such as may fairly and reasonably be considered as either arising naturally, ie, according to the usual course of things, from such breach of contract itself, or such as may reasonably be supposed to have been in the contemplation of both parties at the time they made the contract as the probable result of the breach of it. If special circumstances under which the contract was actually made were communicated by the plaintiffs to the defendants, and thus known to both parties, the damages resulting from the breach of such a contract which they would reasonably contemplate would be the amount of injury which would ordinarily follow from a breach of contract under the special circumstances so known and communicated. But, on the other hand, if these special circumstances were wholly unknown to the party breaking the contract, he, at the most, could only be supposed to have had in his contemplation the amount of injury which would arise generally, and in the real multitude of cases not affected by any special circumstances, from such a breach of contract. For, had the special circumstances been known, the parties might have specially provided for the breach of contract by special terms as to the damages in that case; and of this advantage it would be very unjust to deprive them.

The above principles are those by which we think the jury ought to be guided in estimating the damages arising out of any breach of contract. It is said that other cases, such as breaches of contract in the non-payment of money, or in the not making a good title to land, are to be treated as exceptions from this, and as governed by a conventional rule. But as, in such cases, both parties must be supposed to be cognisant of that well-known rule, these cases may, we think, be more properly classed under the rule above enunciated as to cases under known special circumstances, because there both parties may reasonably be presumed to contemplate the estimation of the amount of damages according to the conventional rule. In the present case, if we are to apply the principles above laid down, we find that the only circumstances here communicated by the plaintiffs to the defendants at the time the contract was made were that the article to be carried was the broken shaft of a mill and that the plaintiffs were the millers of that mill. But how do these circumstances show reasonably that the profits of the mill must be stopped by an unreasonable delay in the delivery of the broken shaft by the carrier to the third person? Suppose the plaintiffs had another shaft in their possession put up or putting up at the time, and that they only wished to send back the broken shaft to the engineer who made it; it is clear that this would be quite consistent with the above circumstances, and yet the unreasonable delay in the delivery would have no effect upon the intermediate profits of the mill. Or, again, suppose that, at the time of the delivery to the carrier, the machinery of the mill had been in other respects defective, then, also, the same results would follow. Here it is true that the shaft was actually sent back to serve as a model for a new one, that the want of a new one was the only cause of the stoppage of the mill, and that the loss of profit really arose from not sending down the new shaft in proper time, and that this arose from the delay in delivering the broken one to serve as a model. But it is obvious that, in the great multitude of cases of millers sending off broken shafts to third persons by a carrier under ordinary circumstances, such consequences would not, in all probability, have occurred, and these special circumstances were here never communicated by the plaintiffs to the defendants.

It follows, therefore, that the loss of profits here cannot reasonably be considered such a consequence of the breach of contract as could have been fairly and reasonably contemplated by both the parties when they made this contract. For such loss would neither have flowed naturally from the breach of this contract in the great multitude of such cases occurring under ordinary circumstances, nor were the special circumstances, which, perhaps, would have made it a reasonable and natural consequence of such breach of contract, communicated to or known by the defendants. The judge ought, therefore, to have told the jury that, upon the facts then before

them, they ought not to take the loss of profits into consideration at all in estimating the damages. There must, therefore, be a new trial in this case.

REMOTENESS IN INDIAN CONTRACT ACT

The Indian Contract Act adopted the principle formulated in the *Hadley* v. *Baxendale* case. Section 73 of the Indian Contract Act provides:

73. **Compensation for loss or damage caused by breach of contract**—When a contract has been broken, the party who suffers by such breach is entitled to receive, from the party who has broken the contract, compensation for any loss or damage caused to him thereby, which naturally arose in the usual course of things from such breach, or which the parties knew, when they made the contract, to be likely to result from the breach of it.

Such compensation is not to be given for any remote and indirect loss or damage sustained by reason of the breach.

Compensation for failure to discharge obligation resembling those created by contract—When an obligation resembling those created by contract has been incurred and has not been discharged, any person injured by the failure to discharge it is entitled to receive the same compensation from the party in default, as if such person had contracted to discharge it and had broken his contract.

Explanation—In estimating the loss or damage arising from a breach of contract, the means which existed of remedying the inconvenience caused by the non-performance of the contract must be taken into account.

The principles of *Hadley* v. *Baxendale* are in the first two paragraphs. The principle has two parts in limiting consequences of breach. First, if the parties have in express terms or impliedly provided for the consequences, these should be followed. We imply from the conduct of the specific parties and their negotiations and dealings. The law cannot throw up its hands in despair if the parties do not provide for themselves. A boundary for the consequences has to be drawn somewhere.

The law imputes to the contract in the way such contracts usually happen in practices. Thus, the second option is to take the contract and its breach to be as it usually happens in general practice. The Supreme Court, referring to the common law principles and Section 73 noted:

Although the Contract Act makes separate provisions for the consequences in each case, the rule laid down as to measure of damages is the same, namely, the party in breach must make compensation in respect of the direct consequences flowing from the breach and not in respect of loss or damage indirectly or remotely caused, which is also the rule in English common law. The rule is based on the broad principle ... that the party who has suffered the loss should be placed in the same position, as far as compensation in money can do it, as if the party in breach had performed his contract or fulfilled his duty.[3]

We can explore the remoteness of breach by exploring the illustrations to the section. The illustrations are based on cases that were settled before the enactment of the act. Illustration (a) provides:

(a) A contracts to sell and deliver 50 maunds of saltpetre to B, at a certain price to be paid on delivery. A breaks his promise. B is entitled to receive from A, by way of compensation, the sum, if any, by which the contract price falls short of the price for which B might have obtained 50 maunds of saltpetre of like quality at the time when the saltpetre ought to have been delivered.

The illustration is of the measure of damages. The general principle is to put the party in the position they would be in if the contract were performed. On the breach, B would have bought the goods from another source. If the price were higher, the difference would be his loss, which A should pay. In addition, the innocent party would incur additionally costs in looking for an alternative. We will explore

[3] *Pannalal Jankidas v. Mohanlal*, AIR 1951 SC 144.

the principle for measure of damage in detail in the next chapter. In this chapter, we will explore the remoteness of damage. Towards this, we will group the illustrations in two categories, flowing from Section 73, 'Usual Course' and 'Agreed between the Parties'.

Usual Course
The following are the illustrations to the principle that if not shared between the parties, one has to go by the way things are usually done and understood.

(n) A contracts to pay a sum of money to B on a day specified. A does not pay the money on that day; B, in consequence of not receiving the money on that day, is unable to pay his debts, and is totally ruined. A is not liable to make good to B anything except the principal sum he contracted to pay, together with interest up to the day of payment.

(p) A contracts to sell and deliver 500 bales of cotton to B on a fixed day. A knows nothing of B's mode of conducting his business. A breaks his promise, and B, having no cotton, is obliged to close his mill. A is not responsible to B for the loss caused to B by the closing of the mill.

(q) A contracts to sell and deliver to B, on the first of January, certain cloth which B intends to manufacture into caps of a particular kind, for which there is no demand, except at that season. The cloth is not delivered till after the appointed time, and too late to be used that year in making caps. B is entitled to receive from A, by way of compensation, the difference between the contract price of the cloth and its market price at the time of delivery, but not the profits which he expected to obtain by making caps, nor the expenses which he has been put to in making preparation for the manufacture.

(r) A, a ship-owner, contracts with B to convey him from Calcutta to Sydney in A's ship, sailing on the first of January, and B pays to A, by way of deposit, one-half of his passage-money .The ship does not sail on the first of January, and B, after being in consequence detained in Calcutta for some time and thereby put to some expense, proceeds to Sydney in another vessel, and, in consequence, arriving too late in Sydney, loses a sum of money. A is liable to repay to B his deposit with interest, and the expense to which he is put by his detention in Calcutta, and the excess, if any, of the passage-money paid for the second ship over that agreed upon for the first, but not the sum of money which B lost by arriving in Sydney too late.

Shared between the Parties

The following are the illustrations to the principle that the parties are bound by the consequences they have contemplated.

(e) A, the owner of a boat, contracts with B to take a cargo of jute to Mirzapur, for sale at that place, starting on a specified day. The boat, owing to some avoidable cause, does not start at the time appointed, whereby the arrival of the cargo at Mirzapur is delayed beyond the time when it would have arrived if the boat had sailed according to the contract. After that date, and before the arrival of the cargo, the price of jute falls. The measure of the compensation payable to B by A is the difference between the price which B could have obtained for the cargo at Mirzapur at the time when it would have arrived if forwarded in due course, and its market price at the time when it actually arrived.

(i) A delivers to B, a common carrier, a machine, to be conveyed, without delay, to A's mill informing B that his mill is stopped for want of the machine. B unreasonably delays the delivery of the machine, and A, in consequence, loses a profitable contract with the government. A is entitled to receive from B, by way of compensation, the average amount of profit which would have been made by the working of the mill during the time that delivery of it was delayed, but not the loss sustained through the loss of the government contract.

(k) A contracts with B to make and deliver to B, by a fixed day, for a specified price, a certain piece of machinery. A does not deliver the piece of machinery at the time specified, and in consequence of this, B is obliged to procure another at a higher price than that which he was to have paid to A, and is prevented from performing a contract which B had made with a third person at the time of his contract with A (but which had not been then communicated to A), and is compelled to make compensation for breach of that contract. A must pay to B, by way of compensation, the difference between the contract price of the piece of machinery and the sum paid by B for another, but not the sum paid by B to the third person by way of compensation.

(l) A, a builder, contracts to erect and finish a house by the first of January in order that B may give possession of it at that time to C, to whom B has contracted to let it. A is informed of the contract between B and C. A builds the house so badly that, before the first of January, it falls down and has to be re-built by B, who, in consequence, loses the rent which he was to have received from C, and is obliged to make compensation to C for the breach of his contract. A must make compensation to B for the cost of rebuilding the house for the rent lost, and for the compensation made to C.

In the Illustration (e), the owner of the boat knows that the jute is being taken to Mirzapur for sale. It is understood between the parties that delay could cause losses to B. In Illustration (j), A and B have shared that the consequences of the delay in the carriage of the machine would be in the mill remaining idle. A mill is run to make a profit. A normal implication of the mill remaining closed is loss of profit to the mill owner. Loss of a contract due to a mill being closed for a few days is not the usual result. Thus, the damages do not extend to the loss of the contract. Illustration (k) is also on the same principle. In a normal sale contract, the buyer may or may not have obligations to one or more third party. Further, a seller may or may not take responsibility for the obligation of the buyer to third parties. In Illustration (l), the parties have shared the consequences of breach in the loss of tenancy.

The Supreme Court has recognized that Section 73 codifies the judgment in *Hadley* v. *Baxendale*. In *Pannalal Jankidas* v. *Mohanlal* it noted:

The rule stated by Alderson B has consistently been accepted as correct; the only difficulty has been in applying it. The distinction drawn is between damages arising naturally (which means in the normal course of things) and cases where there were special and extraordinary circumstances beyond the reasonable provision of the parties. The distinction between these types is usually described in English Law as that between general and special damages; the latter are such that if they are not communicated it would not be fair or reasonable to hold the defendant responsible for losses which he could not be taken to contemplate as likely to result from his breach of contract.

An application of the principle is in *Union of India* v. *Hari Mohan Ghosh*.[4] Hari Mohan booked a consignment of artificial silk readymade garments. The consignment was lost. He claimed the value of the goods as well as loss of profit. The Gauhati High Court disallowed loss of profit. It noted:

The loss of profit is not loss or damages which naturally arose in the usual course of things from the breach. In a case of non-delivery of goods such loss would be just the value of goods and the like but not damages due to the loss of profits. The plaintiff could be entitled to damages due to loss of business if he had made known to the Railway when the goods were booked that such loss was likely to result from the breach of it.

In *State* v. *K. Bhaskaran*,[5] the Kerala High Court has attempted to unify the two principles in Section 73 on remoteness of damages. The government awarded a work contract but unlawfully terminated it. The question was on the award of damages. The High Court noted:

The defendant is liable only for 'natural and proximate consequences of a breach or those consequences which were in the parties' contemplation at the time of contract.' The above quoted phrases are words of art and usually represent two ways of expressing a single requirement. Proximate and natural consequences are those that flow directly or closely from the breach in the usual and normal course of events—those which a 'reasonable man' or a person of ordinary prudence would when the

bargain is made foresee, as expectable results of later breach. The phrase 'in the parties' contemplation' normally means in the reasonable contemplation of the defendant. Thus understood, it has got only the same meaning as the companion phrase 'natural and proximate'. Brevity and clarity are better served by abandoning these traditional phrases of legal art and using 'instead the gist of their meaning. We propose the following statement of the rule. The defendant is liable only for reasonably foreseeable losses—those that a normally prudent person, standing in his place possessing his information when contracting would have had reason to foresee as probable consequences of future breach.

It may not be easy to abandon the traditional phrases or join the two principles in a master one. In one, we have to assess the communication, express and implied, between the parties from the vantage of a reasonable person. In the second, we have to completely ignore the communication between the parties and draw out the reasonable expectation of the parties in that class of contract. The problem before the courts has not been the formulation of the principle or their meaning but applying 'this criterion in a case of prospective profits and consequential losses.' The court ruled:

The claim of the plaintiff in this case is that, the breach of the contract by the government deprived him of reasonably expected profits.... The measure of damage no doubt is the amount of profit lost to the contractor by the breach. This is a measure of compensation for the loss which arose in the usual course of things. This can be stated as the loss which the parties knew when they made the contract, as likely to result from the breach of it. When the plaintiff entered into the contract, he agreed to complete the work for the stated amount reckoning a sum for his profit also.

In *Victoria Laundry (Windsor), Limited* v. *Newman Industries, Limited*[6] the court deviated from the principles set in *Hadley* v.

---

[4] *Union of India* v. *Hari Mohan Ghosh*, AIR 1990 Gau 14.

[5] *State* v. *K. Bhaskaran*, AIR 1985 Ker 49.

[6] *Victoria Laundry (Windsor), Limited* v. *Newman Industries, Limited*, (1949) 2 KB 528.

Baxendale. However, this was only a short deviation as the principles were restored as the ruling principles in the *Heron case*.[7] In Indian law, as we have noted above, the original principle is codified in the Indian Contract Act. The cases on remoteness of damage have abated as all commercial contracts have a clause stating: 'Neither party shall be liable to the other party for indirect or consequential losses.'

To conclude, for every breach of contract, the innocent party has the right to damages from the party in breach. The consequences of a breach are limited by what the parties have expressly or impliedly provided, or the way the class of contract is normally conducted. Specific performance is awarded only in transactions dealing with immovable property. In most cases, a monetary equivalent is provided to compensate the innocent party to put him in the position he would be if the contract were performed. A party is only compensated for the loss and not allowed to impose a penalty or to make a gain from the breach.

[7] The Heron II, (1969) 1 AC 388.

30

Measure of Damages

There are two aspects to damages for breach of a contract. The first is how far we should take the consequences of the breach, which we have already discussed. The second aspect, having settled on the first, is the principles by which the damages should be measured. The principle for award of damages is to give the innocent party a sum of money that will put him in the position in which he would have been but for the breach. This is called 'performance interest'. In some cases, however, performance interest is not an indication of the losses, or it is not possible to assess the losses. In these cases, the courts may decide to put the parties in the position they would have been in if no contract had been made. This is called expectation interest. Performance interest is the most common way of awarding damages. We will be exploring both principles in this chapter. Let us begin with the following illustration.

X contracted to sell shares of a company to Y for Rs 50,000. Later, Y refused to take the shares and pay for it. X found another buyer for Rs 48,000. How do we compensate the parties? If Y paid X Rs 2,000, it would be as good as Y having performed the contract. A small overhead may also be given for the expenses for finding another buyer. The principle we are following is to put the parties in the position they would be, by monetary compensation, if the contract is performed. The principle has been summarized and expressed best by Parke B, in a 1848 case, *Robinson* v. *Harman*: 'The rule of the common law is, that where a party sustains a loss by reason of a breach of contract, he is, so far as money can do it, to be placed in the same situation with respect to damages, as if the contract had been performed.'[1] Every case exploring compensation and damages begins with this quote. Lord Bridge of Harwich has thus given expression to the principle in a contemporary court judgment:[2]

Damages for breach of contract must reflect, as accurately as the circumstances allow, the loss which the claimant has sustained because he did not get what he bargained for. There is no question of punishing the contract breaker. Given this basic principle, the court, in assessing the measure of the claimant's loss has ultimately to determine a question of fact ... Since the law relating to damages for breach of contract has developed almost exclusively in a commercial

---

[1] *Robinson* v. *Harman* (1848) 1 Exch 850.
[2] *Ruxley Electronics and Construction Limited* v. *Forsyth*, (1996) AC 344.

context, these criteria normally proceed on the assumption that each contracting party's interest in the bargain was purely commercial and that the loss resulting from a breach of contract is measurable in purely economic terms.

PERFORMANCE INTEREST

Let us explore and decide the damages that should be awarded to the innocent party in following cases, which are illustrations to Section 73.

(b) A hires B's ship to go to Bombay, and there take on board, on the first of January, a cargo which A is to provide and to bring it to Calcutta, the freight to be paid when earned. B's ship does not go to Bombay, but A has opportunities of procuring suitable conveyance for the cargo upon terms as advantageous as those on which he had chartered the ship. A avails himself of those opportunities, but is put to trouble and expense in doing so.

…

(g) A contracts to let his ship to B for a year, from the first of January, for a certain price. Freights rise, and, on the first of January, the hire obtainable for the ship is higher than the contract price. A breaks his promise. He must pay to B, by way of compensation, a sum equal to the difference between the contract price and the price for which B could hire a similar ship for a year on and from the first of January.

(l) A, a builder, contracts to erect and finish a house by the first of January in order that B may give possession of it at that time to C, to whom B has contracted to let it. A is informed of the contract between B and C. A builds the house so badly that, before the first of January, it falls down and has to be re-built by B, who, in consequence, loses the rent which he was to have received from C, and is obliged to make compensation to C for the breach of his contract.

…

(r) A, a ship-owner, contracts with B to convey him from Calcutta to Sydney in A's ship, sailing on the first of January, and B pays to A, by way of deposit, one-half of his passage-money. The ship does not sail on the first of January, and B, after being in consequence detained in Calcutta for some time and thereby put to some expense, proceeds to Sydney in another vessel, and, in consequence, arriving too late in Sydney, loses a sum of money.

In Illustration (b), A can only receive the expenses incurred for arranging the alternate carriage. In Illustration (g), A 'must pay to B, by way of compensation, a sum equal to the difference between the contract price and the price for which B could hire a similar ship for a year on and from the first of January.' The Illustration does not mention the expenses for finding the alternate carriage. If there were expenses, following Illustration (b), these expenses would also be payable. In Illustration (l), if the contract had been performed, B would not have incurred the cost of rebuilding the house. Thus, A should reimburse him the cost of rebuilding the house. It was expressly understood by the parties that A had contracted to rent the house to C. The consequences of breach reached to the contract between B and C. Thus, A should pay to B the rent B lost and the compensation he had to pay to C.

In Illustration (r), in the usual course of things, in the case of a breach of carriage, the passenger would have to buy another ticket and suffer miscellaneous expenses in the while. However, as a result of the delay in reaching Sydney, he would incur losses is remote to the contract which is for carriage.

Thus, 'A is liable to repay to B his deposit with interest, and the expense to which he is put by his detention in Calcutta, and the excess, if any, of the passage-money paid for the second ship over that agreed upon for the first.' These disputes do not arise anymore as most contracts have a clause limiting the liabilities are stipulating an amount to be paid in the case of breach. The terms become binding on the parties. For example, if a passenger with a confirmed ticket is denied boarding, international airlines undertake to put up passengers in a hotel for a limited number of days and put him free of additional cost in the next available flight.

Business Contract

A businessperson enters into a contract to earn a profit. Thus, in a contract where a party is a businessperson, in the usual course of things, parties understand that there would be a loss of profit if the contract is breached. Thus, if the contract does not provide on the consequences of breach, the loss of profit is awarded as damages. The theme can be divided in to further parts. In a sale contract, there is a reference to the sale price. This makes quantification of the loss relatively easy. The courts have formulated specific principles in relation to this. In other business contracts the assessment would be on the general principles. Let us first look at non-sale contracts by deciding the damages that should be awarded to the innocent party in the following cases, which are illustrations to Section 73:

(i) A delivers to B, a common carrier, a machine, to be conveyed, without delay, to A's mill informing B that his mill is stopped for want of the machine. B unreasonably delays the delivery of the machine. ...

  (p) A contracts to sell and deliver 500 bales of cotton to B on a fixed day. A knows nothing of B's mode of conducting his business. A breaks his promise, and B, having no cotton, is obliged to close his mill. A is not responsible to B for the loss caused to B by the closing of the mill.

In Illustration (i), the parties know that the mill will be idle if the contract is breached. As a result of this, the loss to the party will be of profit. In the second case, it is not shared between the parties the B has a mill and it would be closed if the delivery were delayed. Thus, if a breach ends a business contract, the courts take the loss to be the loss of profit. In *State* v. *K. Bhaskaran*,[3] where the government wrongfully terminated a work contract, the Kerala High Court stated the principle:

The measure of damage no doubt is the amount of profit lost to the contractor by the breach. This is a measure of compensation for the loss which arose in the usual course of things. This can be stated as the loss which the parties knew when they made the contract, as likely to result from the breach of it. When the plaintiff entered into the contract, he agreed to complete the work for the stated amount reckoning a sum for his profit also.

Let us explore further with the following cases.

Court Case: A.T. Brij Paul Singh, M/s v. State of Gujarat

M/s Brij Paul Singh was awarded a contract to provide a concrete surface to a stretch of road in Gujarat.[4] The contract amount was Rs 16,59,900. After the execution of project had commenced, the State Government illegally terminated the contract. The contractor moved the court claiming loss of profit. The Supreme Court ruled:

... there shall be a reasonable expectation of profit is implicit in a works contract and its loss has to be compensated by a way of damages if the other party to the contract is guilty of breach of contract cannot be gainsaid. ... Now if it is well-established that the respondent was guilty of breach of contract inasmuch as the rescission of contract by the respondent is held to be unjustified, and the plaintiff-contractor had executed a part of the works contract, the contractor would be entitled to damages by way of loss of profit. ... What must be the measure of profit and what proof should be tendered to sustain the claim are different matters. But the claim under this head is certainly admissible.

The high court for a similar road work on another stretch of the same road had accepted 15 per cent as the rate of profit. Following this, the Supreme Court accepted 15 per cent as reasonable rate.

[3] *State* v. *K. Bhaskaran*, AIR 1985 Ker 49.

[4] *A.T. Brij Paul Singh, M/s* v. *State of Gujarat*, AIR 1984 SC 1703.

Court Case: Dwarka Das v. State of MP

Dwarka Das was awarded a contract through a tender to construct a boy's hostel in Ujjain.[5] The total value of the contract was Rs 2 lakh. The superintending engineer was alleged to have obstructed the progress of the work. As a result, the work could not be completed within the time schedule. Following this, the State of Madhya Pradesh terminated the contract. Dwarka Das moved the court, claiming that this was breach of contract by the State of Madhya Pradesh. Dwarka Das claimed loss of profit at the rate of 10 per cent of the value of the project, amounting to Rs 20,000, as damages for breach of contract. The trial court allowed it. However, the high court disallowed it. The Supreme Court explained the concept of loss of profit being a basis for claiming damages. The court ruled:

This court in A. T. Brij Pal Singh v. State of Gujarat (AIR 1984 SC 1703), while interpreting the provisions of Section 73 of the Contract Act, has held that damages can be claimed by a contractor where the government is proved to have committed breach by improperly rescinding the contract and for estimating the amount of damages court should make a broad evaluation instead of going into minute details. It was specifically held that where in the works contract, the party entrusting the work committed breach of contract, the contractor is entitled to claim the damages for loss of profit which he expected to earn by undertaking the works contract.... In the instant case however the trial court had granted only 10% of the contract price, which we feel was reasonable and permissible...

In a work contract or service contract, a party enters the contract to earn profit. Thus, the courts award loss of profit as damages. It is not easy for the courts to assess the expected profit. The courts, thus, settle on a reasonable percentage of the contract value. A sale contract does not pose this difficulty.

[5] *Dwarka Das* v. *State of MP*, AIR 1999 SC 1031.

Sale Contract

In a sale contract too a business person enters into the contract to earn profit. The profit or loss, however, reflects in the market prices. The courts need not estimate the loss as a percentage of the sale price. The loss can be more accurately quantified with reference to the market prices. The courts, thus, have come up with the basis for awarding damages with reference to the market prices. Let us examine and decide the damages that should be awarded to the innocent party in following sale contract, which are illustrations to Section 73.

Illustration (a) reads: 'A contracts to sell and deliver 50 maunds of saltpetre to B, at a certain price to be paid on delivery. A breaks his promise.' The buyer would have to buy the goods from another source. If a higher price is paid, this is the loss to the buyer. The illustration gives the following solution: 'B is entitled to receive from A, by way of compensation, the sum, if any, by which the contract price falls short of the price for which B might have obtained 50 maunds of saltpetre of like quality at the time when the saltpetre ought to have been delivered.'

Illustration (o) reads: 'A contracts to deliver 50 maunds of saltpetre to B on the first of January, at a certain price. B afterwards, before the first of January, contracts to sell the saltpetre to C at a price higher than the market price of the first of January.' As a result, A had no saltpetre to deliver to B on first January. How should the damages payable by A to B be calculated? The contracts of A with B and C are different. A was in breach of the contract with B when he does not deliver it on 1 January. As a result, B will buy on 1 January from another source. The damages payable by A will be the difference in the market price on 1 January and the contract price. The illustration gives the following solution:

'In estimating the compensation payable by A to B, the market price of the first of January, and not the profit which would have arisen to B from the sale to C, is to be taken into account.' If A informs B in advance that he would not be able to supply the goods on 1 January, this would be anticipatory breach. The principles for damages in the case of anticipatory breach are nuanced. We will take it up later.

Illustration (d) reads: 'A contracts to buy B's ship for 60,000 rupees, but breaks his promise.' In this case, the buyer is in breach. The seller, on the breach, would find another buyer. If the sale price is lower, the difference with the contract price would be his loss. The illustration gives the following: 'A must pay to B, by way of compensation, the excess, if any, of the contract price over the price which B can obtain for the ship at the time of the breach of promise.'

Illustration (h) reads: 'A contracts to supply B with a certain quantity of iron at a fixed price, being a higher price than that for which A could procure and deliver the iron. B wrongfully refuses to receive the iron.' In this illustration, the seller is buying and making a resale. The profit of the seller is the difference between his sale and purchase price. The illustration gives the answer: 'B must pay to A, by way of compensation, the difference between the contract price of the iron and the sum for which A could have obtained and delivered it.'

Let us further examine loss of profit in a sale contract with the following case.

Court Case: Re Vic Mill Limited

A supplier got an order to make a machine of a particular specification.[6] The purchaser repudiated the order. The supplier got an-

other order for somewhat similar machinery. To mitigate his losses, the supplier made necessary alterations in the machinery and sold to the second purchaser. The first purchaser claimed that the measure of damages was merely the cost of the conversion of the machinery for the second purchaser and his slight loss on the re-sale, whereas the supplier claimed that the measure of his damages was the loss of his profit. Hamilton, LJ ruled:

That was a reasonable mode of mitigating the damages, but it by no means follows that the damages are confined to the cost, a trivial one, of adapting the machines to the needs of the second customer, and the loss on re-sale to him, which was only £23, making £28 in all. The fallacy of that is in supposing that the second customer was a substituted customer, that had all gone well, the makers would not have had both customers, both orders, and both profits. In fact, what they did, acting reasonably, and I think very likely more than reasonably in the interests of the Vic Mill was to content themselves with earning the profit on the second contract at the cost of adapting the machines, which has been taken at £5; but they are still losers of the profit which they would have made on the Vic Mill contract, because they could, if they had been minded, have performed both the contracts, and have made the profit on both the contracts but for the breach by the Vic Mill Company of their contract.

Thus, loss of profit was the basis for the award of damages.

Court Case: W L Thompson Limited v. R Robinson (Gunmakers) Limited

R Robinson Limited signed an order form to buy a Standard Vanguard from motor car dealers and agents W L Thompson Limited.[7] The manufacturer of the car was George Thompson Limited. Robinson Limited breached the contract by refusing to take

---

[6] *Re Vic Mill Limited*, (1913) 1 Ch 473.

[7] *W L Thompson Limited* v. *R Robinson (Gunmakers) Limited*, (1955) 1 All ER 154.

the delivery. Thompson Limited, to mitigate damages, immediately rescinded its contract with the manufacturer for the supply of the car. The manufacturer had already supplied the car to the dealer. It took back the car and sold it to another purchaser without charging any damages from the dealer. This was to maintain amicable business relations.

Thompson Limited claimed that if the buyer had performed the contract, it would have earned a profit of £61. The profit was calculated on the basis of margins given by the manufacturers to the dealers, which was standard. The prices at which the dealers could sell the car was fixed by the manufacturer. The dealers' profit on the transaction was also fixed: £61 in the case of a Standard Vanguard. The argument of the dealer was that had there been a performance and not a breach, he would have got the profit of £61. As he has lost a sale, he should be awarded £61 in damages. The argument of Robinson Limited was that there was no loss to the dealer as he could have sold the car to another customer, or, as it had happened in this case, get the supplier to release the dealer from liability. In either case, there is no loss to the dealer. And thus, the loss or damages should be nominal. Upjohn, J noted:

… it would seem to me on the facts to be quite plain that the plaintiffs loss in this case is the loss of their bargain. They have sold one Vanguard less than they otherwise would. The plaintiffs, as the defendants must have known, are in business as dealers in motor cars and make their profit in buying and selling motor cars, and what they have lost is their profit on the sale of this Vanguard. … True the motor car in question was not sold to another purchaser, but the plaintiffs did what was reasonable, they got out of their bargain with George Thompson Ltd but they sold one less Vanguard, and lost their profit on that transaction.

However, while the above would be true following the general principles, the sale of

goods has provided for damages where a seller refuses to accept the goods. Section 50(3) provides:

(1) Where the buyer wrongfully neglects or refuses to accept and pay for the goods, the seller may maintain an action against him for damages for non-acceptance.

(2) The measure of damages is the estimated loss directly and naturally resulting, in the ordinary course of events, from the buyers breach of contract.

(3) Where there is an available market for the goods in question the measure of damages is prima facie to be ascertained by the difference between the contract price and the market or current price at the time or times when the goods ought to have been accepted, or, if no time was fixed for acceptance, then at the time of the refusal to accept.

The case explored the working of the provision. The judge interpreted the 'available market' to mean:

… an available market merely means that the situation in the particular trade in the particular area was such that the particular goods could freely be sold, and that there was a demand sufficient to absorb readily all the goods that were thrust on it, so that if a purchaser defaulted the goods in question could readily be disposed of … in March, 1954, there was not a demand in the East Riding which could readily absorb all the Vanguard motor cars available for sale. If a purchaser defaulted, that sale was lost and there was no means of readily disposing of the Vanguard contracted to be sold, so that there was not, even on the extended definition, an available market.

The judge further noted:

But there is this further consideration: even if I accepted the defendants broad argument that one must now look at the market as being the whole conspectus of trade, organisation and marketing, I have to remember that s 50(3) provides only a prima facie rule, and, if on investigation of the facts, one finds that it is unjust to apply that rule, in the light of the general principles mentioned above it is not to be applied. In this case, as I said in the earlier part of my judgment, it seems to me plain almost beyond argument that, in fact, the loss to the plaintiffs is 61. Accordingly, however one interprets s 50(3), it seems to me on the facts that I have to consider one reaches the same result.

Why should the demand and supply make any difference to a bargain being lost and the loss of profit not being awarded? The argument was explained in clearer terms in a later case *Charter* v. *Sullivan*, also involving a car dealer and a buyer:[8]

The plaintiff, however, is a motor car dealer whose trade for the present purpose can be described as consisting in the purchase of recurrent supplies of cars of the relevant description from the manufacturers, and selling the cars so obtained, or as many of them as he can, at the fixed retail price. He thus receives, on each sale that he is able to effect, the predetermined profit allowed by the fixed retail price, and it is obviously in his interest to sell as many cars as he can obtain from the manufacturers. The number of sales that he can effect, and consequently the amount of profit which he makes, will be governed, according to the state of trade, either by the number of cars that he is able to obtain from the manufacturers, or by the number of purchasers whom he is able to find. In the former case demand exceeds supply, so that the default of one purchaser involves him in no loss, for he sells the same number of cars as he would have sold if that purchaser had not defaulted. In the latter case supply exceeds demand, so that the default of one purchaser may be said to have lost him one sale.

Ordinarily, the difference between the buying and selling price indicates the loss of profit in a sale contract. In the exceptional cases, where the demand far exceeds the supply, the breach may not lead to any loss to the vendor. In this case, the court may allow only nominal damages.

Court Case: Murlidhar Chiranjilal v. Harishchandra Dwarkadas

Both Chiranjilal and Dwarkadas were traders based in Kanpur.[9] They entered into a

contract for the sale of canvas at a specified rate per yard. The delivery was to be made through a railway receipt for Calcutta. That is, the goods were to be put on the train and a receipt obtained, entitling the holder to collect the goods in Calcutta. The cost of transport from Kanpur to Calcutta and the labour charges were to be borne by Dwarkadas. It was agreed that the railway receipt would be for the date 5 August 1947. Chiranjilal, however, failed to deliver the railway receipt and informed Dwarkadas on 8 August 1947 that booking from Kanpur to Calcutta was closed. Thus, he had not been able to deliver the goods. Dwarkadas moved the court to recover damages. He proved that the rate of canvas on or about the date of the breach was significantly higher in Calcutta and claimed the difference as damages.

Chiranjilal contended that the relevant price for calculating damages should be the price prevalent in the Kanpur market. Dwarkadas should have bought similar canvas from the Kanpur market and sent it to Calcutta. And then, if he had suffered damages due to a higher price, he would have been eligible to those damages. Dwarkadas argued that it was not necessary for him to worry about the prices in the Kanpur market. According to him, the contract clearly stated that the goods were to be transported to and sold in Calcutta and, therefore, it was the price in Calcutta that should be taken into account while arriving at the measure of damages, for the parties knew when they made the contract that the goods were to be sold in Calcutta. The Supreme Court laid down the principle as follows:

The two principles on which damages in such cases are calculated are well-settled. The first is that, as far as possible, he who has proved a breach of a bargain to supply what he contracted to get is to be placed, as far as money can do it, in as good a situation as if

---

[8] *Charter* v. *Sullivan*, (1957) 1 All ER 809.
[9] *Murlidhar Chiranjilal* v. *Messrs Harishchandra Dwarkadas*, AIR 1962 SC 366.

the contract had been performed; but this principle is qualified by a second, which imposes on a plaintiff the duly of taking all reasonable steps to mitigate the loss consequent on the breach, and debars him from claiming any part of the damage which is due to is neglect to take such steps. These two principles also follow from the law as laid down in S. 73 read with the explanation thereof. If therefore the contract was to be performed at Kanpur it was the respondent's duty to buy the goods in Kanpur and rail them to Calcutta on the date of the breach and if it suffered any damage thereby because of the rise in price on the date of the breach as compared to the contract price, it would be entitled to be re-imbursed for the loss. Even if the respondent did not actually buy them in the market at Kanpur on the date of breach it would be entitled to damages on proof of the rate for similar canvas prevalent in Kanpur on the date of breach, if that rate was above the contracted rate resulting in loss to it.

...

But the learned counsel for the respondent relies on that part of S. 73 which says that damages may be measured by what the parties knew when they made the contract to be likely to result from the breach of it. It is contended that the contract clearly showed that the goods were to be transported to and sold in Calcutta and therefore it was the price in Calcutta which would have to be taken into account in arriving at the measure of damages for the parties knew when they made the contract that the goods were to be sold in Calcutta.... Now there is no dispute that the buyer had purchased canvas in this case for re-sale; but we cannot infer from the mere fact that the goods were to be booked for Calcutta that the seller knew that the goods were for re-sale in Calcutta only. As a matter of fact it cannot be denied that it was open to the buyer in this case to sell the railway receipt as soon as it was received in Kanpur and there can be no inference from the mere fact that the goods were to be sent to Calcutta that they were meant only for sale in Calcutta, it was open to the buyer to sell them anywhere it liked. Therefore this is not a case where it can be said that the parties knew when they made the contract that the goods were meant for sale in Calcutta alone and thus the difference between the price in Calcutta at the date of the breach and the contract price would be the measure of damages as the likely result from the breach. The contract was for

delivery f.o.r. Kanpur and was an ordinary contract in which it was open to the buyer to sell the goods where it liked.

This is a simple case of purchase of goods for re-sale anywhere and therefore the measure of damages has to be calculated as they would naturally arise in the usual course of things from such breach. That means that the respondent had to prove the market rate at Kanpur on the date of breach for similar goods and that would fix the amount of damages, in case that rate had gone above the contract rate on the date of breach.... As the respondent had failed to prove the rate for similar canvas in Kanpur on the date of breach it is not entitled to any damages in the circumstances.

Court Case: Union of India v. M/s Commercial Metal Corpn

Union of India entered into a contract with the Commercial Metal Corporation to purchase 200 metric tonnes of leaded bronze ingots.[10] The Corporation supplied 163.020 metric tonnes. The Corporation wrote a letter to the Union of India dated 7 November 1973 that there was an exorbitant increase in the price of basic raw material. As a result, it was not possible for them to supply the remaining goods at the contract price of Rs 12.37 per kg. They asked the government to increase the price to Rs 19.45 per kg. The Union of India did not agree to the price increase but extended the time for delivery. The Union of India finally cancelled the contract on 15 February 1975. The shortfall in supply was 36.980 metric tonnes. The Union of India claimed damages for the short supply at the rate of Rs 7.08 per kg, the increase indicated by the Corporation. The main claim of the Corporation against the demand was that the Union of India had made no purchase. Thus, it has not suffered any loss. The Delhi High Court disagreed. It noted:

[10] *Union of India* v. *M/s Commercial Metal Corpn*, AIR 1982 Del 267.

I cannot accept the broad contention that unless the purchaser repurchases the equivalent goods in the market after the date of the breach he cannot claim damages against the seller. In case of non-delivery by the seller the measure of damages is the difference between the market price and the contract price. The market price on the date following the breach is the yardstick by which the buyer's claim for damages is evaluated and quantified. The market value is taken because it is presumed to be the true value of the goods to the purchaser. If he does not get his goods he should receive by way of damages enough to enable him to buy identical goods in the open market.

…

The rule that measures the buyer's damages by the difference between the contract price and the market price at the time and place of delivery is so well entrenched in the law that no one has questioned it since its formulation in 1854 by Alderson. B. in the Court of Exchequer in *Hadley* v. *Baxendale*…This 'breach-date rule' does not require him actually to go into the market and buy the substitute goods before he can succeed in his action for damages.… No one has said that the buyer in a case of non-delivery by the seller must go into the market and buy like goods in order to claim damages. This has never been the law. The decisive element is the date of breach and the market price prevailing on that date. But not the fact that the buyer actually went into the market and got similar goods and suffered loss thereby. The law does not penalise the buyer's inaction. Even if the buyer does not go into the market he is entitled to damages all the same if he can show that the market had risen on the date of the breach.

…

The object of an award of damages for breach of contract is to place the plaintiff, so far as money can do it, in the same situation, with respect to damages, as if the contract had been performed. He is thus enabled to recover damages in respect of the loss of gains of which he has been deprived by the breach. He is entitled to sue for the loss of his bargain, that is to say, for the loss of the particular benefit which he expected to receive by the contract which has been broken. This is the benefit which the buyer expects from the promised performance. With the amount of money, that is, the difference between the contract price and the market price the buyer should therefore be in the same financial position as he would have

been if the seller had performed his contractual obligation to deliver the goods. In other words, the plaintiff is entitled to compensation for the loss of his bargain, so that his expectations arising out of or created by the contract are protected. This protection of expectations is the distinguishing mark of an action for damages for breach of contract.

Thus, in a sale contract, the difference in the contract price and the prevailing market price when the goods were to be delivered and where the goods were to be delivered is taken as the loss. In some cases, it may not be possible to work out the performance interest of the parties. In such cases, another measure, 'reliance interest', may suffice.

RELIANCE INTEREST

Let us explore the topic of reliance interest with the following case.

Case: Musical Performance

A company contracted with a music group for a musical performance on the day of its foundation. The function was for the benefit of the employees and their families. The company spent Rs 40,000 on hiring lights and a sound system for the show. Hours before the show, the music group informed them that it would not be able to perform. The employees were informed that there would be no music show. The employees were disappointed, but as they are not the contracting party, we can leave them aside. The company had not taken up the contract to make a profit. Nor could the artists be substituted by others, especially at the last minute. The company's claims are for the losses it has suffered, Rs 40,000, due to the breach of the contract. This is the best way of doing justice to the company, but it is different from performance interest. In this case, the parties have gone in the reverse to be in a situation as if the contract had not been made. That is, if the contract had not been made, lights and equipment would not have been hired. This is called 'reliance interest' in contract in awarding damages and compensation.

Thus, 'performance interest' and 'reliance interest' are contrasting ideas of awarding damages. It is academic writers who conceived the two terms. The courts, instead of being divided by the two contrasting concepts, assess the loss on a case-to-case basis and follow the best means of compensating the injured party.

Court Case: Anglia Television Limited v. Reed

The facts of the case in the words of Lord Denning are:

Anglia Television Ltd were minded in 1968 to make a film of a play for television entitled 'The Man in the Wood'. It portrayed an American married to an English woman. The American has an adventure in an English wood. The film was to last for 90 minutes. Anglia Television made many arrangements in advance. They arranged for a place where the play was to be filmed. They employed a director, a designer and a stage manager, and so forth. They involved themselves in much expense. All this was done before they got the leading man. They required a strong actor capable of holding the play together. He was to be on the scene the whole time. Anglia Television eventually found the man. He was Mr Robert Reed, an American who has a very high reputation as an actor. He was very suitable for this part. By telephone conversation on 30 August 1968 it was agreed by Mr Reed through his agent that he would come to England and be available between 9 September and 11 October 1968 to rehearse and play in this film. He was to get a performance fee of £1,050, living expenses of £100 a week, his first class fares to and from the United States, and so forth. It was all subject to the permit of the Ministry of Labour for him to come here. That was duly given on 2 September 1968. So the contract was concluded. But unfortunately there was some muddle with the bookings. It appears that Mr Reed's agent had already booked him in America for some other play. So on 3 September

1968 the agent said that Mr Reed would not come to England to perform in this play. He repudiated his contract. Anglia Television tried hard to find a substitute but could not do so. So on 11 September they accepted his repudiation. They abandoned the proposed film. They gave notice to the people whom they had engaged and so forth.[11]

Lord Denning stated the issues and ruled:

Anglia Television then sued Mr Reed for damages. He did not dispute his liability, but a question arose as to the damages. Anglia Television do not claim their profit. They cannot say what their profit would have been on this contract if Mr Reed had come here and performed it. So, instead of claim for loss of profits, they claim for the wasted expenditure. They had incurred the director's fees, the designer's fees, the stage manager's and assistant manager's fees, and so on. It comes in all to £2,750. Anglia Television say that all that money was wasted because Mr Reed did not perform his contract.

Mr Reed's advisers take a point of law. They submit that Anglia Television cannot recover for expenditure incurred before the contract was concluded with Mr Reed. They can only recover the expenditure after the contract was concluded. They say that the expenditure after the contract was only £854.65, and that is all that Anglia Television can recover.

...

It seems to me that a plaintiff in such a case as this had an election: he can either claim for his loss of profit; or for his wasted expenditure. But he must elect between them. He cannot claim both. If he has not suffered any loss of profits—or if he cannot prove what his profits would have been—he can claim in the alternative the expenditure which has been thrown away, that is, wasted, by reason of the breach. If the plaintiff claims the wasted expenditure, he is not limited to the expenditure incurred after the contract was concluded. He can claim also the expenditure incurred before the contract, provided that it was such as would reasonably be in the contemplation of the parties as likely to be wasted if the contract was broken. Applying that principle here, it is plain that, when Mr Reed entered into this contract, he must

[11] *Anglia Television Limited* v. *Reed*, (1971) 3 All ER 690.

have known perfectly well that much expenditure had already been incurred on director's fees and the like. He must have contemplated—or, at any rate, it is reasonably to be imputed to him—that if he broke his contract, all that expenditure would be wasted, whether or not it was incurred before or after the contract. He must pay damages for all the expenditure so wasted and thrown away.

Court Case: C. & P. Haulage (a firm) v. Middleton

Mr Middleton was an automobile engineer and repairman.[12] He worked in a garage he had set up at his own home. The local authority objected to this use of domestic property and they served him a notice to desist from running a garage from his home. C. & P. Haulage was a partnership firm which carried on the business of plant hire. Mr Middleton had done work for them and they had hired machinery to him. One of the partners agreed to let Mr Middleton use a yard they were using only for storage. The firm was using the area. The parties entered into an agreement. It contained terms that emanated from the firm. It read:

Before offering you the use of our yard at Winton Approach we would like you to agree to the following: 1) The use of the yard to be reviewed every six months. 2) We require spare keys to any locks which you may wish to fix on outer doors. 3) We require to know whom besides yourself will be working in the yard. 4) We would not accept any liability for any injury or accident while on our premises. 5) Any fixtures you put in are left. 6) The rates and electricity to be paid by you via C. & P. The bills will be seen by you.

Mr Middleton moved in and began using the premises. He had to do a considerable amount of work to make the premises suitable for his purpose. A wall had to be built enclosing the premises, locks had to be fitted,

[12] C. & P. Haulage (a firm) v. Middleton, (1983) 3 All ER 94.

and electricity had to be laid on. The licence to use the premises was to be renewed every six months. Six months went by and the firm gave no notice to Mr Middleton to move out. Thus, the occupancy for the next six month began. In October, a senior partner of the firm had some difficulty in getting oil from a drum which had been moved without his permission. He became very angry, and told Mr Middleton to get out. The locks were changed. Mr Middleton managed to get his essential equipment out of the premises. He went back to his own garage and told the council about his predicament. The council was very sympathetic. They gave him permission to use his premises for one year.

Mr Middleton claimed £1,767.51 in damages. This covered labour and material used in building the wall, laying on the electricity, and moving a telephone. Mr Middleton, under the contract, could not have removed the fixtures. However, he could make a claim for his losses. A relevant context of the contract was that the firm could have terminated the contract on 15 December 1979, on the completion of the second round of occupancy. Mr Middleton was made to vacate the premises on 5 October 1979. Thus, the damages were for the deprivation of occupation of the premises for ten weeks. Ackerman, referring to the trial court judgment noted:

The learned judge concluded that since in those ten weeks Mr Middleton had been able to return to his own garage and pay no rent, he had suffered no damage, and he accordingly gave judgment against Mr Middleton.... The learned judge approached the case essentially on this basis, that the accepted principle in relation to the assessment of damages for breach of contract was to put the plaintiff in the same position, as far as one could, as he would have been in if the contract had been performed; and in order to evaluate whether if the contract had been performed what was the nature, if any, of the damage that he should be entitled to claim, one had to look at the consequences of the breach of contract.

The consequences of this breach of contract were that so far from Mr Middleton suffering any damage as a result of being excluded from the premises ten weeks earlier than would lawfully have been the case, thanks to the tolerance of the planning authorities he had in effect been saved the payment, which was likely to be between £60 and £100 a week, which he would have had to have paid for the use of C. & P. Haulage's premises. He accordingly came to the conclusion that if he was to award the damages claimed, he would be putting Mr Middleton in a better position than would have been the case if the contract had been lawfully determined.

...

That is not the approach which Mr Middleton seeks. He is not claiming for the loss of his bargain, which would involve being put in the position that he would have been in if the contract had been performed. He is not asking to be put in that position. He is asking to be put in the position he would have been in if the contract had never been made at all. If the contract had never been made at all, then he would not have incurred these expenses, and that is the essential approach he adopts in mounting this claim; because if the right approach is that he should be put in the position in which he would have been had the contract been performed, then it follows that he suffered no damage. He lost his entitlement to a further ten weeks of occupation after the 5th October, and during that period he involved himself in no loss of profit because he found other accommodation, and in no increased expense—in fact the contrary—because he returned immediately to his own garage, thereby saving whatever would have been the agreed figure which he would have to have paid C. & P. Haulage.

Ackerman referred to Lord Denning in *Anglia Television Limited* v. *Reed* and noted:

Lord Denning was not contemplating what has been referred to subsequently as the 'bad bargain' case, a case in which a plaintiff has entered into a loss-making contract or, I would include, an otherwise disadvantageous contract. He was considering a case where it would not be possible to establish any loss of profits because the situation could not be prophesied

had the defendant complied with his contractual obligations. Mr Reed in the Anglia Television case had not taken part in the film; the film had never been made. It was therefore quite impossible to assess whether the film, had it been made, would have been a success and would have earned a profit. Therefore Anglia Television were thrown back on limiting their claim to the expense thrown away.

...

It is not the function of the courts where there is a breach of contract knowingly, as this would be the case, to put the plaintiff in a better financial position than if the contract had been properly performed. In this case the plaintiff, if he was right in his claim, would indeed be in a better position because, as I have already indicated, had the contract been lawfully determined as it could have been in the middle of December, there would have been no question of his recovering these expenses.... I do not consider that the plaintiff is entitled in an action for damages for breach of contract to ask to be put in the position in which he would have been if the contract had never been made where it is easy to assess what his position would have been if the contract had been performed.

Accordingly, save in the respect to which I have already made reference, namely that there should be judgment for the appellant for nominal damages of £10, I would dismiss the appeal.[13]

Non-Pecuniary Losses

Breach of contract would certainly lead to inconvenience, pain, and suffering to the other party. However, the courts, as the law evolved, settled on the position that there would be no claims for mental agony, pain, and suffering. There were several reasons for it. First, the court had already given damages for the economic part of the breach. Second, inconvenience, pain and suffering were one degree removed from the core of the contract. Third, it was impossible to assess the pain and suffering experienced by a person

[13] *Anglia Television Limited* v. *Reed*, (1971) 3 All ER 690.

and fix a monetary value to it. Attempting to award damages for suffering would have made the process of law arbitrary. Thus, the law emerged that there would be no award of damages for inconvenience, pain, and suffering. With the development of a consumer society, however, the position of this law, in several cases, appeared to be unjust. The courts have attempted to carve out exceptions to the rule. Let us explore this with the following cases.

Court Case: Ghaziabad Development Authority v. Union of India

The Ghaziabad Development Authority has been constituted under the Uttar Pradesh Urban Planning and Development Act, 1973.[14] The Authority has, from time to time, promoted and advertised several schemes for allotment of developed plots for construction of apartments and/or flats for occupation. Several persons who had subscribed to the schemes approached different forums, complaining of failure or unreasonable delay in the accomplishment of the schemes. Some subscribers also filed complaints before the Monopolies and Restrictive Trade Practices Commission and some raised disputes before the Consumer Disputes Redressal Forum. In some cases, the consumer courts awarded compensation for agony and mental harassment. The case came before the Supreme Court. The Court ruled:

In case of breach of contract, damages may be claimed by one party from the other, who has broken its contractual obligation in some way or the other. The damages may be liquidated or unliquidated. Liquidated damages are such damages as have been agreed upon and fixed by the parties in anticipation of the breach. Unliquidated damages are such

[14] *Ghaziabad Development Authority* v. *Union of India*, AIR 2000 SC 2003.

damages as are required to be assessed. Broadly, the principle underlying assessment of damages is to put the aggrieved party, monetarily, in the same position as far as possible, in which it would have been if the contract would have been performed. Here, the rule as to remoteness of damages comes into play. Such loss may be compensated as the parties could have contemplated at the time of entering into the contract. The party held liable to compensation shall be obliged to compensate for such losses as directly flow from its breach. Chitty on Contracts ... states—

'Normally, no damages in contract will be awarded for injury to the plaintiff's feelings, or for his mental distress, anguish, annoyance, loss of reputation or social discredit caused by the breach of contract; ... The exception is limited to contracts whose purpose is "to provide peace of mind or freedom from distress," ... Damages may also be awarded for nervous shock or an anxiety state (an actual breakdown in health) suffered by the plaintiff, if that was, at the time the contract was made, within the contemplation of the parties as a not unlikely consequence of the breach of contract. Despite these developments, however, the court of appeal has refused to award damages for injured feelings to a wrongfully dismissed employee, and confirmed that damages for anguish and vexation caused by breach of contract cannot be awarded in an ordinary commercial contract.'

The ordinary heads of damages allowable in contracts for sale of land are settled. A vendor who breaks the contract by failing to convey the land to the purchaser is liable to pay damages for the purchaser's loss of bargain by paying the market value of the property at the fixed time for completion less the contract price. The purchaser may claim the loss of profit he intended to make from a particular use of the land if the vendor had actual or imputed knowledge thereof. For delay in performance, the normal nature of damages is the value of the use of the land for the period of delay, viz. usually, its rental value.

In our opinion, compensation for mental agony could not have been awarded as has been done by the MRTP Commission.

The Supreme Court, thus, set aside the award of compensation for mental agony. The courts have worked out an exception to this rule in the case of contracts whose very purpose is to provide comfort and entertainment. *Jarvis v. Swans Tours Limited* is a founding case on this.

Court Case: Jarvis v. Swans Tours Limited

Mr Jarvis, looking for a skiing holiday in Switzerland, read a brochure issued by Swans Tours Limited.[15] Some of the principal attractions mentioned in the brochure were:

HOUSE PARTY CENTRE with special resident host … MRLIALP is a most wonderful little resort on a sunny plateau … Up there you will find yourself in the midst of beautiful alpine scenery, which in winter becomes a wonderland of sun, snow and ice, with a wide variety of fine ski-runs, a skating-rink and an exhilarating toboggan run … No doubt you will be in for a great time, when you book this house-party holiday … Mr. Weibel, the charming owner, speaks English.

The brochure further made promises in relation to food and entertainment. Mr Jarvis booked the Holiday for two weeks and paid £63.45. There was no house party. There were only thirteen guests the first week and none in the second week. Skiing took place some distance away from the hotel. There were only mini-skis, about three feet long. As a result, he could not enjoy skiing as he had wished to. The food and entertainment was equally disappointing. Mr Jarvis moved the court, claiming damages for breach of contract. The country court awarded £31.72. The case came in appeal before the Court of Appeal. Lord Denning, referring to the older judgments, noted:

The courts in those days only allowed the plaintiff to recover damages if he suffered physical inconvenience, such as, having to walk five miles home, as in Hobbs's case; or to live in an overcrowded house: see *Bailey* v. *Bullock*.

[15] *Jarvis* v. *Swans Tours Limited*, (1973) 1 All ER 71.

I think that those limitations are out of date. In a proper case damages for mental distress can be recovered in contract, just as damages for shock can be recovered in tort. One such case is a contract for a holiday, or any other contract to provide entertainment and enjoyment. If the contracting party breaks his contract, damages can be given for the disappointment, the distress, the upset and frustration caused by the breach. I know that it is difficult to assess in terms of money, but it is no more difficult than the assessment which the courts have to make every day in personal injury cases for loss of amenities. Take the present case. Mr Jarvis has only a fortnight's holiday in the year. He books it far ahead, and looks forward to it all that time. He ought to be compensated for the loss of it. … He went to enjoy himself with all the facilities which the defendants said he would have. He is entitled to damages for the lack of those facilities, and for his loss of enjoyment. … I think the damages in this case should be the sum of 125. I would allow the appeal accordingly.

Edmund Davies, LJ noted:

Some of the observations of Mellor J in the 100 year old case of *Hobbs* v. *London & South Western Railway Co* call today for reconsideration. I must not be taken to accept that, under modern conditions and having regard to the developments which have taken place in the law of contract since that decision was given, it is right to say, as the learned judge did:

… for the mere inconvenience, such as annoyance and loss of temper, or vexation, or for being disappointed in a particular thing which you have set your mind upon, without real physical inconvenience resulting, you cannot recover damages. That is purely sentimental, and not a case where the word inconvenience, as I here use it, would apply.

… Mellor, J was dealing with a contract of carriage and the undertaking of the railway company was entirely different from that of the defendants in the present case. These travel agents made clear by their lavishly illustrated brochure with its ecstatic text that what they were contracting to provide was not merely air travel, hotel accommodation and meals of a certain standard. … When a man has paid for and properly expects an invigorating and amusing holiday and, through no fault of his, returns home dejected because his expectations have been largely unfulfilled, in my judgment it would be quite wrong to say that his disappointment must find no reflection in the damages to be awarded.

Court Case: Heywood v. Wellers (a firm)

Sheila Heywood was being molested by an acquaintance who would come to her door steps, call her over the telephone, and send letters.[16] The person threatened her and used abusive language. She approached a Solicitors firm, Weller, who advised her to apply for an injunction restraining the person from molesting her. The firm was negligent and it failed to obtain and maintain the injunction. As a result, Heywood continued to be molested. She moved the court to get damages against the firm for breach of the contract. Apprehending that no solicitor firm would contest her case adequately against another solicitor firm, she represented the case herself. Lord Denning ruled:

Take this instance. If you engage a driver to take you to the station to catch a train for a day trip to the sea, you pay him £2 and then the car breaks down owing to his negligence. So that you miss your holiday. In that case you can recover, not only your £2, but also damages for the disappointment, upset and mental distress which you suffered: see *Jarvis* v. *Swan's Tours Ltd*; *Jackson* v. *Horizon Holidays Limited*.

So here, Mrs Heywood employed the solicitors to take proceedings at law to protect her from molestation by Mr Marrion. They were under a duty by contract to use reasonable care. Owing to their want of care she was molested by this man on three or four occasions. This molestation caused her much mental distress and upset. It must have been in their contemplation that, if they failed in their duty, she might be further molested and suffer much upset and distress. This damage she suffered was within their contemplation within the rule in *Hadley* v. *Baxendale*.

...

It was suggested that, even if Wellers had done their duty and taken the man to court, he might still have molested her. But I do not think they can excuse themselves on that ground. After all, it was not put to the test; and it was their fault it was not put to the test. If they had taken him to court as she wished—and as they ought to have done—it might well have been effective to stop him from molesting her any more. We should assume that it would have been effective to protect her, unless they prove that it would not.

...

So the remaining question is: what damages should be awarded to Mrs Heywood for the molestation she suffered on three or four occasions, and the mental distress and upset she suffered? The judge, unfortunately, did not quantify the damages. In her claim as amended she put them at £150. I would allow her that sum. Some reduction should be made for the fact that, if Wellers had done their duty (and saved her from the molestation), it would have cost her something. I should put that at the figure which Mr Price gave in the beginning, £25.

Court Case: Watts v. Morrow

Mr and Mrs Watts, resident in London, decided to look for a country house for use at weekends and holidays.[17] They both wanted a house which would be, so far as possible, trouble-free and into which they could move without the need for any substantial works of repair. They engaged Mrs Morrow as the surveyor. Mrs Morrow was asked to make a full structural report of the property and to confirm that £177,500 offered was the right price in the current market. Mrs Morrow's report mentioned many defects and made recommendations for repairs. However, the report indicated that the defects could be dealt with as a part of ordinary ongoing maintenance and repair. With the reassurance of the report, Mr and Mrs Watts purchased the property.

---

[16] *Heywood* v. *Wellers* (a firm), (1976) 1 All ER 300.

[17] *Watts* v. *Morrow*, (1991) 1 WLR 1921.

After purchasing the property and taking possession, they asked a builder for quotation for repairs. This is the time they realized the property needed extensive repairs. If Watts had known of this, they would either have not purchased the property or purchased it at a much lower rate. Over the next six months, they spent a considerable amount of time and money in repairing the property. They spent their weekends at the house, not enjoying the comfort of it but supervizing work at the construction site and staying at the construction site with all the associated inconveniences. They claimed damages for diminution of value. In addition, they claimed damages for inconvenience and distress. The trial court had awarded £4,000 for distress and inconvenience. The case came before the Court of Appeal. Lord Justice Bingham summarized and formulated the principle for award of damages for inconvenience:

A contract-breaker is not in general liable for any distress, frustration, anxiety, displeasure, vexation, tension or aggravation which his breach of contract may cause to the innocent party. This rule is not, I think, founded on the assumption that such reactions are not foreseeable, which they surely are or may be, but on considerations of policy.

But the rule is not absolute. Where the very object of a contract is to provide pleasure, relaxation, peace of mind or freedom from molestation, damages will be awarded if the fruit of the contract is not provided or if the contrary result is procured instead. If the law did not cater for this exceptional category of case it would be defective. A contract to survey the condition of a house for a prospective purchaser does not, however, fall within this exceptional category.

In cases not falling within this exceptional category, damages are in my view recoverable for physical inconvenience and discomfort caused by the breach and mental suffering directly related to that inconvenience and discomfort. If those effects are foreseeably suffered during a period when defects are repaired I am prepared to accept that they sound in damages even though the cost of the repairs is not recoverable as such. But I also agree that awards should be restrained, and that the awards in this case far exceeded a reasonable award for the injury shown to have been suffered.

On assessment of the details, the court reduced the damages for inconvenience to £750. In *Farley* v. *Skinner*,[18] the House of Lords reviewed the earlier cases from the Court of Appeal and consolidated the law on award of damages for inconvenience, pain, and suffering.

To conclude, the principle for measure of damage is to put the party in the position he would be if the contract were performed. In business contracts, parties come together to earn a profit. Thus, loss of profit is awarded in the breach of business contract. In a sale contract, the difference between the contract price and the price of the good in the market on the date of performance adequately measures the loss. In other contracts such as work contracts, it is difficult to accurately measure the profit loss for a project that was interrupted. The courts take a percentage of the contract value as a measure of loss. In some cases, it is not possible to measure the performance interest. To put the parties in the position before they made the contract becomes an alternate measure of damages. This is called reliance interest. The general position of the law has been not to award damages for mental distress, anguish, and annoyance. However, where the very object of a contract is to provide pleasure, relaxation, or peace of mind, damages are awarded if the contract is not performed or the contrary result is produced.

---

[18] *Farley* v. *Skinner*, (2001) 4 All ER 801.

31

Liquidated Damages

With every breach of a contract, contracting parties began to realize that while the principle for compensation was clear, it was not easy for the courts to settle on a monetary value while awarding compensation. Contracts are voluntary and based on mutual trust and confidence. It was not conducive to this trust and confidence for the parties to bring in the possibility that they could breach the contract. The two were too contradictory to be parts of the same relationship. However, with experience, traders realized that it was better to contemplate breach and stipulate on the damages, than to leave it for the courts to settle on later. The stipulated damages are called 'liquidated damages'. Further, the innocent party has the right to damages for the losses; however, he must act prudently to minimize them. This is called mitigation of damages. We will look at liquidated damages and mitigation of damages in this chapter.

Contracting parties should be free to stipulate the amount to be paid if a party breached the contract, and the courts should honour the voluntary arrangement. However, left to them, the stronger party would impose a stiff penalty on the weaker party. The object of awarding damages is to put the injured party in the same position he would have been in had the contract been performed. If an aggrieved party were allowed to claim anything more, it would actually amount to a penalty for the other person. Individuals are free to get into contracts for mutual benefit; however, they should not be allowed to impose on others. To penalize individuals and demand compliance is the task of the state. For an individual to penalize another would be intruding in the domain of the state. Effectively, anything in access of the actual damages is a penalty.

Let us consider the following illustration. Sudip had contracted to transport computer components from Mumbai to Bangalore for Prakash for a consideration of Rs 2 lakh. It was agreed that in the case of a breach of contract, Sudip would pay damages worth Rs 50,000. The actual loss came out to be Rs 60,000. Should Prakash be paid Rs 50,000 or Rs 60,000? As the parties have agreed to fix the damages at Rs 50,000 and no more, only Rs 50,000 would be paid. What if the actual loss was only Rs 20,000? The courts have maintained that if the party is still made to pay Rs 50,000, the sum in access of the actual damages, that is, Rs 30,000, would effectively, be a penalty.

The principle entered common law in a specific form. It depended on whether the stipulation in the contract was a penalty clause or liquidated damages. A penalty clause was irrecoverable and liquidated damages could be recovered if they did not exceed a genuine pre-estimate of the loss. Several rules and presumption developed on penalty and liquidated damages. Section 74 in the Indian Contract Act took away the distinction and made it simpler. The court was to award only reasonable compensation for the losses suffered. This could not be in access of the total stipulated amount.

COMPENSATION AND PENALTY

Thus, the principle is that irrespective of the term, that is, 'damage', 'compensation', or 'penalty', all the amounts are added up. It is then concluded that the party in breach had never intended to pay more than this amount. Thus, in no case should that party be made to pay more than this amount. Following this principle, the damages to be paid are calculated. If the actual damages are more than the total amount stipulated, the party pays only the total stipulated amount. If the actual damages are less, only an amount equivalent to the actual damages shall be payable. The argument here is that if the stipulated amount were to be paid in such a situation as well, the difference would effectively become a penalty, and no private person should be allowed to impose a penalty on others. Section 74 of the Indian Contract Act expresses this principle:

74. **Compensation for breach of contract where penalty stipulated for**—When a contract has been broken, if a sum is named in the contract as the amount to be paid in case of such breach, or if the contract contains any other stipulation by way of penalty, the party complaining of the breach is entitled, whether or not actual damage or loss is proved to have been caused thereby, to receive from the party who has broken the contract, reasonable compensation not exceeding the amount so named or, as the case may be, the penalty stipulated for.

Explanation—A stipulation for increased interest from the date of default may be a stipulation by way of penalty.

The Supreme Court has interpreted the above section in several cases. We will examine how the law has developed on the subject.

Court Case: Fateh Chand v. Balkishan Dass

Balkishan Das contracted to sell his rights in land and a building to Fateh Chand.[1] At the time of reaching the agreement, an earnest deposit of Rs 1,000 was made. According to the agreement, Balkishan was to receive Rs 24,000 as the first instalment towards the sale. On receiving this, he was to hand over the possession of the building. Thereafter, within two months, Fateh Chand was to get the sale deed registered. The balance amount of Rs 87,500 would then be paid by Fateh Chand. According to the agreement, if the registration was delayed, the contract was deemed to be cancelled. In this event, Fateh Chand would have to give back possession of the building. Further, the Rs 24, 000 paid by him was to be forfeited.

The seller contended that the entire sum of Rs 25,000 was the earnest deposit and it could be forfeited. The buyer contended that Rs 1,000 alone was the earnest deposit that could be forfeited. The remaining amount was a part of the sale consideration. The stipulation in the agreement that gives the right to forfeit Rs 24,000 to the buyer was a stipulation in the nature of penalty. It can be forfeited only if the seller establishes that he suffered loss as a result of the breach of the contract. We will see later that the courts have

[1] *Fateh Chand* v. *Balkishan Dass*, AIR 1963 SC 1405.

come to treat the earnest deposit as justified if it is reasonable. Any other forfeitures or damages were subject to Section 74. The question in this case was on the forfeiture of Rs 24,000. The Supreme Court ruled:

Section 74 of the Indian Contract Act deals with the measure of damages in two classes of cases (i) where the contract names a sum to be paid in case of breach and (ii) where the contract contains any other stipulation by way of penalty.... The measure of damages in the case of breach of a stipulation by way of penalty is by S. 74 reasonable compensation not exceeding the penalty stipulated for. In assessing damages the court has, subject to the limit of the penalty stipulated, jurisdiction to award such compensation as it deems reasonable having regard to all the circumstances of the case. Jurisdiction of the court to award compensation in case of breach of contract is unqualified except as to the maximum stipulated, but compensation has to be reasonable, and that imposes upon the court duty to award compensation according to settled principles.

The high courts had relied on the phrase 'to be paid in case of such breach' in Section 74 to mean that only the money to be paid by the party was constrained by Section 74 and not the money already paid. The Supreme established that it applied to all sums, whether paid or yet to be paid:

In our judgment the expression 'the contract contains any other stipulation by way of penalty' comprehensively applies to every covenant involving a penalty whether it is for payment on breach of contract of money or delivery of property in future, or for forfeiture of right to money or other property already delivered. Duty not to enforce the penalty clause but only to award reasonable compensation is statutorily imposed upon Courts by S. 74. In all cases, therefore, where there is a stipulation in the nature of penalty for forfeiture of an amount deposited pursuant to the terms of contract which expressly provides for forfeiture, the court has jurisdiction to award such sum only as it considers reasonable, but not exceeding the amount specified in the contact as liable to forfeiture.

As the party had not suffered any loss, no damages were awarded. The forfeited sum had to be returned.

Court Case: Maula Bux v. Union of India

Maula Bux entered into two separate contracts with the Government of India, one for a supply of potatoes and the other for a supply of poultry, at the Military Headquarters, UP Area.[2] He made two 'security deposits' of Rs 10,000 and Rs 8,500 with the Government of India for the two contracts. Clause 8 of the contract provided: 'The officer sanctioning the contract may rescind his contract by notice to me/us in writing: ... (iv) If I/we decline, neglect or delay to comply with any demand or requisition or in any other way fail to perform or observe any condition of the contract.' The contract further provided:

In case of such rescission, my/our security deposit (or such portion thereof as the officer sanctioning the contract shall consider fit or adequate) shall stand forfeited and be absolutely at the disposal of government, without prejudice to any other remedy or action that the government may have to take...

In the case of such rescission, the government shall be entitled to recover from me/us on demand any extra expense the government may be put to in obtaining supplies/services hereby agreed to be supplied, from elsewhere in any manner mentioned in clause 7 (ii) hereof, for the remainder of the period for which this contract was entered into, without prejudice to any other remedy the government may have.

Maula Bux was irregular in meeting the supply schedules. The Government of India terminated the contracts and forfeited the amounts deposited by him. Maula Bux questioned the justification for the forfeiture of the amounts within the Indian Contract Act. The high court took the view that where a sum is deposited

[2] Maula Bux v. Union of India, AIR 1970 SC 1955.

by way of security for due performance of a contract, and where the amount forfeited is not unreasonable, Section 74 of the Contract Act would have no application. The Supreme Court rebutted the view. It reviewed the decision in *Fateh Chand* v. *Balkishan Dass* and reiterated that reasonable amount of earnest deposit did not fall under Section 74: 'Forfeiture of earnest money under a contract for sale of property—movable or immovable—if the amount is reasonable, does not fall within Section 74. That has been decided in several cases.... These cases are easily explained, for forfeiture of a reasonable amount paid as earnest money does not amount to imposing a penalty.' Section 74, however, was to apply to all other forfeiture of money to be paid as damages. The court noted:

But if forfeiture is of the nature of penalty, Section 74 applies. Where under the terms of the contract the party in breach has undertaken to pay a sum of money or to forfeit a sum of money which he has already paid to the party complaining of a breach of contract, the undertaking is of the nature of a penalty.

Counsel for the Union, however, urged that in the present case rupees 10,000 in respect of the potato contract and rupees 8,500 in respect of the poultry contract were genuine pre-estimates of damages which the Union was likely to suffer as a result of breach of contract, and the plaintiff was not entitled to any relief against forfeiture. Reliance in support of this contention was placed upon the expression (used in Section 74 of the Contract Act) 'the party complaining of the breach is entitled, whether or not actual damage or loss is proved to have been caused thereby, to receive from the party who has broken the contract reasonable compensation.' It is true that in every case of breach of contract the person aggrieved by the breach is not required to prove actual loss or damage suffered by him before he can claim a decree and the court is competent to award reasonable compensation in case of breach even if no actual damage is proved to have been suffered in consequence of the breach of contract. But the expression 'whether or not actual damage or loss is proved to have been caused thereby' is intended to cover different classes of contracts which come before the courts. In case of breach of some contracts it may be impossible for the court to assess compensation arising from breach, while in other cases compensation can be calculated in accordance with established rules. Where the court is unable to assess the compensation, the sum named by the parties if it be regarded as a genuine pre-estimate may be taken into consideration as the measure of reasonable compensation, but not if the sum named is in the nature of a penalty. Where loss in terms of money can be determined, the party claiming compensation must prove the loss suffered by him.

As the Union of India had not established losses, it was ordered to refund the forfeited amount with interest. To summarize, the court interpreted Section 74 as follows:

1. The court should assess the actual damages even in the case of contracts where damages are stipulated. Actual damages not exceeding the stipulated amount should be awarded.
2. In some cases, it may not be possible to assess damages. In such cases, if the stipulated sum is a genuine pre-estimate, it should be awarded or taken into consideration for working out a reasonable compensation.

The decision was re-iterated in *Union of India* v. *Rampur Distillery and Chemical Company, Limited*,[3] where the government forfeited the security deposit for breach of contract. The government was allowed to retain only a part of the security deposit. *ONGC* v. *SAW Pipes Limited* was the next major case on the issue.

Court Case: Oil and Natural Gas Corporation Limited v. SAW Pipes Limited

The ONGC is a Public Sector Undertaking.[4] Through a tender, SAW Pipes Limited had

---

[3] *Union of India* v. *Rampur Distillery and Chemical Company, Limited*, 1973 AIR SC 1098.

[4] *Oil and Natural Gas Corporation Limited* v. *SAW Pipes Limited*, AIR 2003 SC 2629.

gotten into a contract with the ONGC to supply equipment for offshore oil exploration and maintenance. The specific materials that were to be supplied were casing pipes of 26- and 30-inch diameters. As per the terms and conditions of the contract, the goods had to be supplied on or before 4 November 1996. According to the agreement, the raw materials were required to be procured from certain reputed and proven manufacturers/suppliers approved by the ONGC. The list of the approved suppliers was provided as a part of the contract.

SAW Pipes Limited, by a letter dated 8 August 1996, placed an order for a supply of steel plates with the Italian suppliers Liva Laminati to make the casing pipes. As timely delivery was of essence, the Italian suppliers were required to ship the material latest by the end of September 1996. However, all over Europe, including Italy, there was a general strike of the steel mill workers in September and October 1996. Thus, SAW, by its letter dated 28 October 1996, communicated to the ONGC that the Italian suppliers were facing labour problems and would be unable to deliver the material as per the schedule. SAW, therefore, requested for an extension of forty-five days for supplying the material. Under the terms of the contract, the supplier was to pay 1 per cent of the contract price for each week of delay. The ONGC extended the time for delivery with a specific statement that liquidated damages would be charged.

The ONGC made deductions for the delay while making payment to SAW pipes for the supply. SAW took the dispute to the Arbitral Tribunal. The Arbitral Tribunal, after considering various decisions of the Supreme Court regarding recovery of liquidated damages, including the Maula Bux case, arrived at the conclusion that it was for the ONGC to establish that they had suffered loss because SAW had not supplied them within the prescribed time limit. The ONGC could not establish the losses.

The delay in the supply of pipes was not the only reason behind the delay in the deployment of the rig on the platform. In other words, even if the pipes had been delivered on time, the project would have been delayed. Thus, the tribunal held that the ONGC had wrongfully withheld the money. The Arbitral Tribunal further held that SAW Pipes was entitled to recover the said amount with interest at the rate of 12 per cent p.a. from 1 April 1997 till the date of the filing of the statement of claim. The ONGC challenged the award of the tribunal. Its contention was that since liquidated damages had been provided in the contract, it was not necessary to establish damages.

The decision of the Supreme Court can be best understood in balancing the dilemma inherent in Section 74 and the principles for award of damages. Following *Maula Bux* v. *Union of India*, in every case, even if damages were stipulated, these had to be assessed. However, if the actual damages were to be established before the courts in all the cases, even if liquidated damages were stipulated, the very purpose of stipulating liquidated damages would be lost. On the other hand, if liquidated damages were to be awarded without establishing the actual damages, it would allow the contracting parties to impose penalties. The Supreme Court in the *ONGC* v. *Saw Pipes Limited* made exceptions to the position in the *Maula Bux* case.

It cannot be disputed that for construction of the contract, it is settled law that the intention of the parties is to be gathered from the words used in the agreement. If words are unambiguous and are used after full understanding of their meaning by experts, it would be difficult to gather their intention different from the language used in the agreement. If upon a reading of the document as a whole, it can fairly be deduced from the words actually used therein that the parties had agreed on a particular term, there is nothing in law which prevents them from setting up that term. Further in construing a contract, the court must look at the words used in the contract unless they are such that one may suspect that they do not convey the intention correctly. If the words are clear, there is very little the court can do about it.

Therefore, when parties have expressly agreed that recovery from the contractor for breach of the contract is pre-estimated genuine liquidated damages and is not by way of penalty duly agreed by the parties, there was no justifiable reason for the arbitral tribunal to arrive at a conclusion that still the purchaser should prove loss suffered by it because of delay in supply of goods.

The Supreme Court gave a new direction to Sections 73 and 74:

...when a contract has been broken, the party who suffers by such breach is entitled to receive compensation for any loss which naturally arises in the usual course of things from such breach. These sections further contemplate that if parties knew when they made the contract that a particular loss is likely to result from such breach, they can agree for payment of such compensation. In such a case, there may not be any necessity of leading evidence for proving damages, unless the court arrives at the conclusion that no loss is likely to occur because of such breach. Further, in case where court arrives at the conclusion that the term contemplating damages is by way of penalty, the court may grant reasonable compensation not exceeding the amount so named in the contract on proof of damages. However, when the terms of the contract are clear and unambiguous then its meaning is to be gathered only from the words used therein. In a case where agreement is executed by experts in the field, it would be difficult to hold that the intention of the parties was different from the language used therein. In such a case, it is for the party who contends that stipulated amount is not reasonable compensation, to prove the same.

The emphasis of the court was on the terms 'experts', 'genuine pre-estimate', and 'unam-

biguous'. Since *Maula Bux* v. *Union of India*, the nature of contracting activities has gone through a sea change. The court recognized that the modern general conditions of contract are drafted by profession bodies. Further, unlike in the past, when the one who printed the contract set unreasonable terms, the terms have come to be fair, balanced, and reasonable. Insisting that the parties establish losses when the losses themselves were genuine pre-estimates and reasonable would not be conducive for the performance of such contracts. The court thus, summarized its discussion thus:

(1) Terms of the contract are required to be taken into consideration before arriving at the conclusion whether the party claiming damages is entitled to the same;

(2) If the terms are clear and unambiguous stipulating the liquidated damages in case of the breach of the contract unless it is held that such estimate of damages/compensation is unreasonable or is by way of penalty, party who has committed the breach is required to pay such compensation and that is what is provided in Section 73 of the Contract Act.

(3) Section 74 is to be read along with Section 73 and, therefore, in every case of breach of contract, the person aggrieved by the breach is not required to prove actual loss or damage suffered by him before he can claim a decree. The court is competent to award reasonable compensation in case of breach even if no actual damage is proved to have been suffered in consequences of the breach of a contract.

(4) Is some contracts, it would be impossible for the court to assess the compensation arising from breach and if the compensation contemplated is not by way of penalty or unreasonable, court can award the same if it is genuine pre-estimate by the parties as the measure of reasonable compensation.

For the reasons stated above, the impugned award directing the appellant to refund the amount deducted for the breach as per contractual terms requires to be set aside and is hereby set aside.

Thus, the courts have had to work within the two boundaries. If the actual damages were to be established before the courts in all cases, even if liquidated damages were stipulated, the very purpose of stipulating liquidated damages would be lost. On the other hand, if liquidated damages were to be awarded without establishing the actual damages, it would allow the contracting parties to impose penalties. The Supreme Court in the *ONGC* v. *Saw Pipes Limited* was making exceptions to the position in *Maula Bux* v. *Union of India*.

FORFEITURE OF EARNEST DEPOSIT

Another aspect of evolution of the law with respect to damages in India has to do with earnest deposit. The courts came to a make a distinction between earnest deposit and liquidated damages. As the following case would bring out, liquidated damages is an estimate of damage if the contract were breached, while earnest deposit is only a small payment at the time of getting in the contract to confirm that the party is 'earnest' about the contract. Earnest deposit is a part of the consideration paid in advance. If the contract were breached, the aggrieved party would have the further right to claim damages. As the earnest deposit is not liquidated damages, as the following case brings out, Section 73 and 74 would not apply to it. However, if there is no loss suffered by a party due to breach of a contract, forfeiture of earnest deposit would also be a penalty. Any kind of forfeiture, irrespective of its name or time of payment, has the potential of being a penalty. Thus, the principle of *Maula Bux* v. *Union of India*, that is, assessing the actual losses to ascertain that the forfeiture is not a penalty should be done. The contending arguments are finally balanced.

Court Case: Hanuman Cotton Mills v. Tata Air Craft Limited

Tata Air Craft Limited advertised in a newspaper for the sale of aero-scrap.[5] Hanuman Cotton Mills responded to the advertisement, expressing its interest in purchasing the scrap. The parties met and settled on the purchase for a total amount of Rs 10,00,000. The General Manager of Tata Air Craft Limited, through a letter dated 18 November 1946 to Hanuman Cotton Mills, confirmed the sale of the entire lot of aero-scrap, and also acknowledged the receipt of Rs 2,50,000. On 22 November 1946, Hanuman Cotton Mills sent a communication where they stated that the transaction had been closed without inspecting the materials, merely on the assurance of Tata Air Craft Limited. Hanuman Cotton Mills further stated that they had since obtained information that the quantity stated to be available was not on the spot, and therefore they would not go ahead with the purchase. They requested Tata Air Craft Limited to treat their letter as cancelling the contract and return the sum of Rs 2,50,000 already paid by them.

Tata Air Craft Limited sent several letters to Hanuman Cotton Mills asking them to pay the balance amount and take delivery of the goods, but Hanuman Cotton Mills refused. Tata Air Craft Limited ultimately forfeited the entire sum of Rs 2,50,000; according to it, was earnest money and cancelled the contract. The standard terms of the contract of Tata Air Craft Limited included the following clauses:

9. Deposits.

The buyer shall deposit with the company 25 per cent of the total value of the stores at the time

[5] *Hanuman Cotton Mills* v. *Tata Air Craft Limited*, AIR 1970 SC 1986.

of placing the order. The deposit shall remain with the company as earnest money and shall be adjusted in the final bills, no interest shall be payable to the buyer by the company on such amounts held as earnest money.

10. Time and method of payment.

(a) The buyer shall, before actual delivery is taken or the stores dispatched under conditions pay the full value of the stores for which his offer has been accepted less the deposit as hereinbefore contained...

(b) If the buyer shall make default in making payment for the stores in accordance with the provisions of this contract the company may without prejudice to its rights under Clause II thereof or other remedies in law forfeit unconditionally the earnest money paid by the buyer and cancel the contract by notice in writing to the buyer and resell the stores at such time and in such manner as the company thinks best and recover from the buyer any loss incurred on such resale. The company shall, in addition be entitled to recover from the buyer any cost of storage, warehousing or removal of the stores from one place to another and any expenses in connection with such a resale or attempted resale thereof. Profit, if any, on resale as aforesaid, shall belong to the company.

Hanuman Cotton Mills conceded that there was a contract between the parties. Its contention, however, was that the forfeiture of Rs 2,50,000 was not justified. The common law courts, following the business practices, had recognized that 'earnest money' or 'deposit' had a specific meaning and significance for the contracting parties. The meaning could be summarized in the following passages from *Farr. Smith and Co. v. Messrs, Limited*:[6]

An earnest must be a tangible thing, in which definition it may be that a deposit is included... That thing must be given at the moment at which the contract is concluded, because it is something given to bind the contract, and, therefore, it must come into existence at the making or conclusion of the contract. The thing given in that way must be given by the contracting party who gives it, as an earnest or token

of good faith, and as a guarantee that he will fulfil his contract, and subject to the terms that if, owing to his default, the contract goes off, it will be forfeited. If on the other hand, the contract is fulfilled, an earnest may still serve a further purpose and operate by way of part payment.

'Earnest'... meant something given for the purpose of binding a contract, something to be used to put pressure on the defaulter if he failed to carry out his part. If the contract went through, the thing given in earnest was returned to the giver, or, if money, was deducted from the price. If the contract went off through the giver's fault, the thing given in earnest was forfeited.

The term 'deposit' also had the same meaning. In *Howe* v. *Smith*, Fry, LJ noted:

'What is the deposit? The deposit, as I understand it ... is a guarantee that the contract shall be performed. If the sale goes on...it goes in part payment of the purchase-money for which it is deposited; but if on the default of the purchaser the contract goes off, that is to say, if he repudiates the contract then...he can have no right to recover the deposit.

Money paid as a deposit must, I conceive, be paid on some terms implied or expressed.... The terms most naturally to be implied appear to me in the case of money paid on the signing of a contract to be that in the event of the contract being performed it shall be brought into account, but if the contract is not performed by the payer it shall remain the property of the payee. It is not merely a part payment, but is then also an earnest to bind the bargain so entered into, and creates by the fear of its forfeiture a motive in the payer to perform the rest of the contract.[7]

Thus, the common law courts had come to distinguish between earnest and deposit. This became distinct from damages, compensation, and penalty. Earnest money did not preclude the party from claiming damages for breach. The Supreme Court, on the reviewing common law cases, including the above quoted cases, expressed the criterion

[6] *Farr. Smith and Co.* v. *Messrs Limited*, (1928) 1 KB 397.

[7] *Howe* v. *Smith*, (1884) 27 Ch D 89.

for deciding whether a sum was earnest or deposit or not:

(1) It must be given at the moment at which the contract is concluded.

(2) It represents a guarantee that the contract will be fulfilled or, in other words, 'earnest' is given to bind the contract.

(3) It is part of the purchase price when the transaction is carried out.

(4) It is forfeited when the transaction falls through by reason of the default or failure of the purchaser.

(5) Unless there is anything to the contrary in the terms of the contract, on default committed by the buyer, the seller is entitled to forfeit the earnest.

Exploring the terms of the contract, the court was clear that Rs 2,50,000 was earnest deposit. It was to be paid at the time of making of the contract. It was to be adjusted as the consideration if the contract was performed. In the case of breach of contract, it was to be forfeited. The forfeiture did not limit the rights of the party to claim damages. Hanuman Cotton Mills raised a very valid point. The money could be forfeited only if there was a breach of the contract. Thus, the party contended that it 'must be treated as the amount to be paid in case of a breach. In the alternative … [it] should be treated as a term containing a stipulation by way of a penalty.' Following *Maula Bux* v. *Union of India*, the court must award only reasonable compensation. The party relied on the following from the case:

Forfeiture of earnest money under a contract for sale of property—moveable or immoveable—if the amount is reasonable, does not fall within S. 74 for the Indian Contract Act. That has been decided in several cases.… These cases are easily explained, for forfeiture of reasonable amount paid as earnest money does not amount to imposing a penalty. But if forfeiture is of the nature of penalty, S. 74 applies. Where under the terms of the contract the party in breach has undertaken to pay a sum of money or to forfeit a sum of money which he has already paid to the party complaining of a breach of contract, the undertaking is of the nature of a penalty.'

However, as the point was not raised before the high court, the Supreme Court was procedure-bound not to take it up. It noted:

It is therefore unnecessary for us to go into the question as to whether the amount deposited … in this case, by way of earnest and forfeited as such, can be considered to be reasonable or not. We express no opinion on the question as to whether the element of unreasonableness can ever be considered regarding the forfeiture of an amount deposited by way of earnest and if so what are the necessary factors to be taken into account in considering the reasonableness or otherwise of the amount deposited by way of earnest.

In this view, it is unnecessary for us to consider the decision of this court in *Maula Bux* v. *Union of India* (AIR 1970 SC 1955) relied on by the appellants.

Both the decisions of the Supreme Court took place in the same year, 1970. The line of reasoning from *Maula Bux* v. *Union of India* did not exist for it to have been contended before the high court. Thus, the interesting point that Section 74 should apply to earnest money was also not resolved. The point has not been raised in the subsequent judgments, and the principle set up by the *Hanuman Cotton Mills* v. *Tata Air Craft Limited*, that the requirement of reasonableness cannot be imposed on earnest deposit, has been approved in subsequent Supreme Court judgments. *Delhi Development Authority* v. *Grihsthapana Co-Operative Group Housing Society Limited* and *H.U.D.A.* v. *Kewal Krishan Goel*, have cemented the principle.[8]

---

[8] *Delhi Development Authority* v. *Grihsthapana Co-Operative Group Housing Society Limited*, 1995 AIR SC 1312; and *H.U.D.A.* v. *Kewal Krishan Goel*, 1996 AIR SC 1981.

MITIGATION OF DAMAGES

While the innocent party has a right to receive damages, he must also mitigate his losses and not further raise the liabilities of the party in breach. This is the principle of mitigation of damages.

Cockburn, CJ in *Frost* v. *Knight*[9] expressed the principle of mitigation as follows: 'In assessing the damages for breach of performance ... take into account whatever the plaintiff has done, or has had the means of doing, and, as a prudent man, ought in reason to have done, whereby his loss has been, or would have been, diminished.' The following passage from the judgment of Viscount Haldane LC in *British Westinghouse Electric & Manufacturing Co Limited* v. *Underground Electric Rys Co of London Limited* is often quoted as a summation of the principle of mitigation:

... there are certain broad principles which are quite well settled. The first is that, as far as possible, he who has proved a breach of a bargain to supply what he contracted to get is to be placed, as far as money can do it, in as good a situation as if the contract had been performed. The fundamental basis is thus compensation for pecuniary loss naturally flowing from the breach; but this first principle is qualified by a second, which imposes on a plaintiff the duty of taking all reasonable steps to mitigate the loss consequent on the breach, and debars him from claiming any part of the damage which is due to his neglect to take such steps.

The following statement of the principle, from the judgment of James, LJ in *Dunkirk Colliery Co.* v. *Lever*[10] is also a leading summary of the principle: 'The person who has broken the contract is not to be exposed to additional cost by reason of the plaintiffs not doing what they ought to have done as reasonable men, and the plaintiffs not being under any obligation to do anything otherwise than in the ordinary course of business'. Let us review cases to understand the principles further.

Court Case: *Payzu, Limited* v. *Saunders*

Saunders was a dealer in silk.[11] She agreed to sell to Payzu Limited a large amount of silk over ten months. The payment for the supplies was to be made on a monthly basis. Payzu Limited failed to make payment for the first delivery. Saunders became suspicious of their intent. She considered this to be a breach of the contract and refused to supply any more installments. By a letter dated 16 January, she offered to deliver goods at the contract price if Payzu Limited paid immediate cash. Payzu Limited refused and tried to get their supplies from the market. Meanwhile, the price of silk had risen, and Payzu Limited could not purchase the silk as it was not adequately available in the market. In the middle of February, Payzu Limited claimed the difference between the reigning price and the price contracted with Saunders as damages.

Saunders claimed that Payzu Limited had breached the contract and she had a right to terminate the contract. The court did not agree with the contention. A contract can be terminated only for the breach of an essential term. On this aspect, the court noted:

It is essential to remember in the present case that by S. 10 of the Sale of Goods Act, 1893, it is provided that unless a different intention appears from the terms of the contract, stipulations as to time of payment are not deemed to be of the essence of a contract of sale, and by S. 31 where there is a sale of goods to be delivered by stated instalments which are to be separately paid for, and the buyer refuses to pay for one or more instalments, 'it is a question in each case depending on the terms of the contract and the circumstances of the case, whether the breach

---

[9] *Frost* v. *Knight*, (1872) LR 7 Ex. 111.

[10] *Dunkirk Colliery Co.* v. *Lever*, (1878) 9 ChD 20.

[11] *Payzu, Limited* v. *Saunders*, (1919) 2 KB 581.

of contract is a repudiation of the whole contract or whether it is a severable breach giving rise to a claim for compensation but not to a right to treat the whole contract as repudiated.' It is to be observed that in the present case the contract did not provide for delivery in any particular number of instalments. The deliveries were to be extended over the period from January to September, and it was contemplated that there would be an unspecified number of deliveries and a corresponding number of payments. ... I entertain no doubt whatever that the plaintiffs' failure to make punctual payment for the November delivery did not amount to a repudiation of the contract, nor did it go to the root of the contract. ...

In fact, the court noted that it was Saunders who had repudiated the contract:

... on the other hand, in my opinion, the defendant's letter of January 16 did in fact and in law amount to an unjustifiable refusal by her to carry out her contractual obligations, for she announced in clear terms that she would thenceforth deliver no further goods to the plaintiffs under the contract unless the plaintiffs paid cash to cover each invoice.

The case instead became that Saunders was in breach of contract and Payzu Limited should be compensated for the losses arising from the breach of the contract. The question then was, what should Payzu Limited have done to mitigate its loss? Should it not have taken up the offer of Saunders to pay cash for the supplies? Relying on the settled principles of mitigation quoted earlier in the chapter, the court noted:

The question, therefore, is what a prudent person ought reasonably to do in order to mitigate his loss arising from a breach of contract ... the plaintiffs in deciding whether to accept the defendant's offer were fully entitled to consider the terms in which the offer was made, its bona fides or otherwise, its relation to their own business methods and financial position, and all the circumstances of the case; and it must be remembered that an acceptance of the offer would not preclude an action for damages for the actual loss sustained. Many illustrations might be given of the extraordinary results which would follow if the plaintiffs were entitled to reject the defendant's offer and incur a substantial measure of loss which would have been avoided by their acceptance of the offer. The plaintiffs were in fact in a position to pay cash for the goods, but instead of accepting the defendant's offer, which was made perfectly bona fide, the plaintiffs permitted themselves to sustain a large measure of loss which as prudent and reasonable people they ought to have avoided.

The case was taken in appeal to the Court of Appeal. Bankes, LJ appoved the decision and noted:

It is plain that the question what is reasonable for a person to do in mitigation of his damages cannot be a question of law but must be one of fact in the circumstances of each particular case. There may be cases where as matter of fact it would be unreasonable to expect a plaintiff to consider any offer made in view of the treatment he has received from the defendant. If he had been rendering personal services and had been dismissed after being accused in presence of others of being a thief, and if after that his employer had offered to take him back into his service, most persons would think he was justified in refusing the offer, and that it would be unreasonable to ask him in this way to mitigate the damages in an action of wrongful dismissal. But that is not to state a principle of law, but a conclusion of fact to be arrived at on a consideration of all the circumstances of the case. ... I think the learned judge came to a proper conclusion on the facts, and that the appeal must be dismissed.

Judgment of Scrutton, LJ noted:

I am of the same opinion. Whether it be more correct to say that a plaintiff must minimize his damages, or to say that he can recover no more than he would have suffered if he had acted reasonably, because any further damages do not reasonably follow from the defendant's breach, the result is the same. ... In certain cases of personal service it may be unreasonable to expect a plaintiff to consider an offer from the other party who has grossly injured him; but in commercial contracts it is generally reasonable to accept an offer from the party in default. However, it is always a question of fact. About the law there is no difficulty.

The appeal was dismissed.

Court Case: *Strutt v. Whitnell*

Strutt was a property developer, whose friends Norman Whitnell and Christine Marjorie Whitnell (husband and wife) purchased a house from him for the price of £4,650 and let it to a tenant.[12] Within a year, structural defects became apparent in the house. Strutt was the property developer but not the builder. As they did not have privity of contract, the Whitnells could not sue the builder. As a friend Strutt arranged to buy back the house so that he could make the claim on the builder. Accordingly, Strutt bought the house back on 3 March 1971.

The contract of re-sale of the house provided that the Whitnells would give vacant possession. Tenancy laws created the right in the tenant to not move from the premises. Whitnells had thought that the tenant would be willing to leave. However, the tenant refused. As a result, the Whitnells were in breach of the contract to Strutt. In a meeting of the parties, Strutt said that he might have to sue them for damages for breach of the term as to vacant possession. On this, Whitnells offered to buy back the house. But at some point of time, their friendship turned sour, and Strutt instead sued the Whitnells for damages amounting to the difference in the value of the house with and without vacant possession.

On the basis of the value of surveyors, the damages were assessed to be £1,900 by the judge. The contention of the Whitnells was that Strutt could have mitigated his damages so as to reduce them from £1,900 to nothing simply by accepting their offer to buy back the house. According to them, there was no

[12] *Strutt* v. *Whitnell and Another*, (1975) 2 All ER 510.

good reason for refusing that offer as he did not want the house to use it himself. It was only a part of his business to buy and sell houses. Mackenna, J noted:

I shall state and consider three different cases.

Case 1: A buyer agrees to buy property having a certain quality and the seller delivers the property without that quality. There is a difference between the market value of the property with the quality and without it. The buyer is clearly entitled to recover the difference between the two values.

Case 2: Suppose, in addition to the facts stated in case 1, that after the sale and after the defect in quality has been discovered, the seller offers to buy back the property at the contract price and the buyer refuses to resell. In that case does the buyer lose his right to recover the difference between the two values? Is he limited to the recovery of nominal damages? I would answer that he is entitled to retain the property and to recover the difference between the values. The seller cannot compel him to forego his right to substantial damages as the price of retaining what has become his own property.

Case 3: Suppose, in addition to the facts stated in case 2, that the seller proves that the buyer had no good reason for refusing to accept his offer to buy back the property. Does that make any difference? I would answer, No. I would say that the buyer is entitled to retain his property without any investigation of his reasons for wishing to do so and that his right to recover the difference between the two values is not contingent on his having acted reasonably in the matter of the seller's offer to repurchase.

Payzu Ltd v. *Saunders* ([1919] 2 KB 581) is distinguishable. In that case the defendant in breach of contract had failed to deliver goods to the plaintiff at the contract price and on the contract conditions, but had offered him goods of the same kind at the same price but on less favourable conditions. If the plaintiff had accepted them he would have suffered only a small loss because of the less favourable conditions, which he could still have recovered by way of damages. But he refused the offer. In those circumstances it was held that he could not recover the difference between the market price and the contract price. He would not have suffered this loss if he had accepted the defendant's offer which it was reasonable for him to do. There was no question in that case of the plaintiff being required to return goods which had already become his property or forfeit his right to substantial damages. That is the difference between *Payzu Ltd* v. *Saunders* and cases 2 and 3.

...

It looks as if the plaintiff has behaved badly towards the defendants, who were his friends, and has merited the description of Shylock which the registrar has given him, and perhaps that additional epithet which would be appropriate to an untruthful witness. If that is so, it is a pity that he must recover substantial damages but this is no ground for deciding his case otherwise than in accordance with the principles of the law of damages which are, I think, well settled in the plaintiff's favour.

Court Case: Bismi Abdullah and Sons, M/s v. Regional Manager, F.C.I., Trivandrum

The tender of Bismi Abdullah and Sons was accepted by the Food Corporation of India for the purchase of rice.[13] The buyer failed to pay the contract amount and collect the stock. The FCI sold the stock four and half months after the breach. By then, the market for rice had crashed. The FCI claimed the difference between the contract price and the price realized by the sale as damages. The Kerala High Court noted:

One of the fundamental principles of law of damages is that the person entitled to claim damages must do all that is within his power to mitigate damage. In case where there is no right to the difference in price on resale available to the seller as per the contract he can claim only the difference between the contract price and the market price on the date of the breach. Where the seller has got such a right the resale must nevertheless be conducted within a reasonable time from the date of breach. The damages must have relation to the market price on the date of breach whether or not the contract empowers the vendor to resell and claim the difference. In other words, the resale can only be taken as a step to enable the party to establish

the market price on the date of the breach. Viewed in this manner the resale must be within a reasonable time from the date of breach so that there may not be much variance in market price between the date of resale and the date of the breach ... more than 4½ months after the date of breach ... by no stretch of imagination, be said to be a reasonable period.

Court Case: M. Lachia Setty and Sons Limited v. Coffee Board, Bangalore

The Coffee Board was a statutory body incorporated under the Coffee Act, 1942.[14] It had a near monopoly in internal and external trade. It collected all coffee grown and auctioned to the traders. In 1952, the prices of coffee soared very high. It took several steps to bring the prices down. M. Lachia Setty and Sons Limited was a trader in coffee. They were awarded a lot in an auction; however, they did not collect it. The Coffee Board re-sold the coffee and collected the difference from the trader. The contention of the trader was that if the Coffee Board had acted quickly, it could have mitigated the loss. The main priority of the Coffee Board, however, was not the mitigation of the loss of individual traders but bringing the prices down. The Supreme Court noted:

At the outset it must be observed that the principle of mitigation of loss does not give any right to the party who is in breach of the contract but it is a concept that has to be borne in mind by the court while awarding damages. The correct statement of law in this behalf is to be found in Halsbury's *Laws of England* (4th Edn.) Vol. 12, para 1193 at page 477 which runs thus :

"1193. Plaintiffs duty to mitigate loss. The plaintiff must take all reasonable steps to mitigate the loss which he has sustained consequent upon the defendant's wrong, and, if he fails to do so, he cannot claim damages for any such loss which he ought reasonably to have avoided".

---

[13] *Bismi Abdullah and Sons, M/s* v. *Regional Manager*, F.C.I., Trivandrum, AIR 1987 Ker 56.

[14] *M. Lachia Setty and Sons Limited* v. *Coffee Board, Bangalore*, AIR 1981 SC 162.

Again, in para 1194 at page 478 the following statement occurs under the heading 'standard of conduct required of the plaintiff:

"The plaintiff is only required to act reasonably, and whether he has done so is a question of fact in the circumstances of each particular case, and not a question of law. He must act not only in his own interests but also in the interests of the defendant and keep down the damages, so far as it is reasonable and proper, by acting reasonably in the matter.... In cases of breach of contract the plaintiff is under no obligation to do anything other than in the ordinary course of business, and where he has been placed in a position of embarrassment the measures which he may be driven to adopt in order to extricate himself ought not to be weighed in nice scales at the instance of the defendant whose breach of contract has occasioned the difficulty....

The plaintiff is under no obligation to destroy his own property, or to injure himself or his commercial reputation, to reduce the damages payable by the defendant. Furthermore, the plaintiff need not take steps which would injure innocent persons"

From the above statement of law it will appear clear that the non-defaulting party is not expected to take steps which would injure innocent persons. If so, then steps taken by him in performance or discharge of his statutory duty also cannot be weighed against him. In substance the question in each case would be one of the reasonableness of action taken by the non-defaulting party.

...

From the above statement of law it will appear clear that the non-defaulting party is not expected to take steps which would injure innocent persons. If so, then steps taken by him in performance or discharge of his statutory duty also cannot be weighed against him. In substance the question in each case would be one of the reasonableness of action taken by the non-defaulting party.

The Supreme Court concluded:

Here the material on record clearly shows that internal coffee prices in the year 1952, particularly from March to October 1952, had soared very high on account of malpractices indulged in by coffee dealers and even the Government of India felt itself very much concerned about it and suggestions had been made by government officials as well as by the members of the Coffee Board to take steps to bring down the coffee prices at reasonable level in the interest of both the trade as well as the consumer and, in fact, several measures, including the step of accepting lower bids in preference to the higher bids, with a view to regulate coffee prices were taken by the Coffee Board pursuant to the government's directive in that behalf. Clearly, these measures were being taken by the Board in discharge of their main function and duty to maintain the coffee prices at proper level in the interest of all concerned, particularly the consumer and were not directed against the defaulting dealers at the concerned pool auction.

To conclude, contracting parties are free to stipulate an amount to be paid in the case of a breach called liquidated damages. The stipulated amount is the maximum a party can be made to pay in the case of a breach. If the actual damages are less, the courts consider the excess amount to be only a penalty and do not award it. However, if the stipulated amount is a genuine pre-estimate of the losses, courts take the amount to be losses and award it as damages. A party breaching a contract should pay money to the innocent party to put him in the position he would be in if the contract had been performed. The principle, however, is qualified in that the innocent party should take reasonable steps to mitigate the losses following the breach. The courts do not award a part of the damage that arises from his own neglect to mitigate his loss.

32

Conclusion

The study of contract law has just begun, and not ended with this book. We started by recognizing that contract law is common-sensical. This gave us a framework for us to begin our journey. However, as we have learnt, common sense can be, at the same time, accessible and profound; changing and invariant; and particular and universal. Law and practices are in a dynamic relationship. Ideas, including ideas on law, come from practices. Contract law emerged as trade and commerce developed. Once in place, practices had to be structured around them. As contract law developed, traders had to follow it. Thus, law shapes practices and practices shape the law. The relationship, however, is not linear or mechanical.

Law emerges in response to the specific context of the time and place but stubbornly persists even when the context has completely changed. An illustration of this is the postal rule. In the early phases of the development of post, an offeror could successfully deny receiving any acceptance even if he had in fact received one. The postal rule was put up to deal with this and provide stability to business, of which the post had become the backbone. The postal rule has persisted. Every

new mode of communication has had to be classified, whether it was post-like or not. Another example is the concept of consideration, which cannot be done away with despite calls for its abolition for a century now.

This brings us to the foundational nature of contract law. Contract law emerged with rising trade and commerce. With the passage of time, trade and commerce developed around it. The foundation of a building cannot be undone without destabilizing the building. Similarly, ideas cannot be withdrawn, even if we know their limitations, as this would destabilize the structures built on them. The modern version of contract law appeared in the late 1800s. Since then, society has undergone a complete transformation. However, as all business relationships have been built on these principles, they cannot be jettisoned for a new set. For example, no matter how elaborate a negotiation for formation of a contract, the contract has to be cast in the formula of offer and acceptance.

Law undergoes a renewal through other processes. The principles remain unchanged, but are applied in a new context. Over a period of time, the meaning of the principle itself may undergo a change. An example is the marginalization of the concept and relevance of consideration. Where this is not adequate, the legislature has endeavoured to harmonize the law with practices. An example is changes in the Specific Relief Act to provide for restitution in an agreement entered in with a minor. Another example is the Consumer Protection Act, breaching the privity of contract rule to vest the rights of consumers in the persons who are not a party to the contract. The codification of the contract law itself, in part, modified common law.

At the time of codification of the contract law, some of the principles that had emerged in the prior decades and centuries were already not conducive to the times then. An example was an agreement to receive less than the debt owed being unenforceable due to lack of consideration. British courts, bound by precedence, could not change the principle. Law makers in India, however, were not bound by common law, and the Indian Contract Act changed the principle. It is interesting to note that the traffic of legal ideas between England and India was not one-way, with ideas brought from England and imposed in India. Ideas were borrowed from common law, but also revised and adapted. Successful ideas from India were taken to other parts of the world.

In interpreting the India Contract Act, the courts recognized the provisions that were intended to be different from the common law. The law in India on these diverged from the common law. Once a law is enacted, the text of the law acquires its own life. On some themes, the courts found the text to be leading to a position different from common law. A notable example of this is an agreement with a minor being void in India as opposed to voidable in the common law. Thus, the law on some aspects of contract law in India diverged from the common law. Interesting, the common law itself has been evolving, creating the possibility for it to converge with the law in India. With these exceptions, the courts in India recognized the India Contract Act to be a codification of common law. The position emerged that unless the common law was in contradiction to the provision in the Indian Contract Act, common law cases before and after the enactment could be a useful guide for contract law in India. This openness in relation to contract law is common to all the commonwealth nations. This has invigorated contract law in India.

Thus, while the contract law derives from commonsense, it has to be understood as an evolving body of principles constituted historically and internationally. The relevance of contract law is, no doubt, important in itself. With an expanding and globalizing economy, there has been a proliferation of contractual activity. This has lead to numerous and varied application of the contract law. But more than this, contract law is the foundation on which business law rests. As trade and commerce developed, the first law to develop was contract law. Alongside and with further development of trade and commerce, business relationships developed as special forms of contract. This included, among others, sale of goods, guarantee, indemnity, agency and partnership. As the activities were contractual, contract law became the foundation and the principles to work with, to develop the law for the activities.

It recognized the relationship to be governed by contract law and took it forward by providing further details for its specific subject matter. In providing the details, in some places it modified and amplified the contract law. As we move on to special forms of contract, our understanding of contract law will be revisited and strengthened.

Case Index

Index